Historical Origins of International Criminal Law: Volume 1

Morten Bergsmo, CHEAH Wui Ling and YI Ping
(editors)

2014
Torkel Opsahl Academic EPublisher
Brussels

ISBN 978-82-93081-11-1

Dedicated to Bonnie Helene Bergsmo

EDITORS' PREFACE

The expansion, successes and failures of international criminal law and justice over the past two decades have been accompanied by more curious and critical questioning about its origins. How did we get to where we are today?

This trilogy *Historical Origins of International Criminal Law: Volumes 1–3* ('HOICL') has been a long time in the making. Since 2009 the editors have discussed the need for such an anthology that would bring researchers working on disparate historical issues together. There was a growing realisation among practitioners and scholars that the key trials and events commonly referred to when telling the story of international criminal law's development were only a few pieces of a bigger puzzle, which may not be as important as originally made out. Our project's timeliness became more evident in light of emerging research conducted on different trials and the ICC Legal Tools Database's increasingly complete collection of historical records on core international crimes that may serve as legal sources.

During our planning of this trilogy and research project, we made efforts to identify and get in touch with researchers from different countries who were already working on historical questions. We also made a point of distributing our call for papers widely, with the hope of being as inclusive and representative as possible in our selection of high quality research. The response to our call for papers was overwhelming, demonstrating the importance of the project and that it should be done at this time. We sought to include multiple perspectives when selecting our authors, including some that we had ourselves not anticipated. We also structured the conference and provided editorial assistance to some non-native English-speaking authors so our project would serve as an opportunity and space for scholarly exchange and continued co-operation across geographical and cultural barriers. Throughout this process we were fortunate to have the support and participation of doyens in the field, but we also made additional efforts to involve early career researchers to build a stronger research community that would grow and span generations.

This is the first volume of the *HOICL* trilogy. Chapters in the first two volumes are arranged in chronological order. The first volume addresses trials and proceedings up to the Nuremberg trials. The second volume studies other trials from the post-Second World War period. The third volume explores more contemporary trials, crimes and legal concepts, as well as thematic lines of inquiry.

A project of this ambition and reach would not be possible without the help we have received from many talented and committed individuals. We would like to thank all authors for their excellent contributions and professionalism. We also thank Assistant Professor ZHANG Binxin (PKU-CILRAP Research Fellow) who played a major role in the final stages of the editing process. Our editorial assistants provided vital help at all stages of the editing and production process: Ryan HONG, XING Yun, CHOONG Xun Ning, Aarshi Tirkey, CHOW Jia Ying, Sangeetha Yogendran, Kristin Xueqin WU and Mark Ortega. We thank Alf Butenschøn Skre for his production expertise. Support was also provided by Tessa Bolton and Nathaniel KHNG. All chapters have been formatted according to the publisher's style guide. An anthology of this scope, with chapter contributors of diverse linguistic backgrounds, would not be possible without our copy-editing and formatting team from Impress Creative and Editorial: Gareth Richards, Jaime HANG, Liani Manta-Khaira and Marco Ferrarese. Their well-rounded expertise and patience were priceless. Finally, we thank the Norwegian Ministry of Foreign Affairs for financial support for this research project of the Centre for International Law Research and Policy.

Morten Bergsmo, CHEAH Wui Ling, YI Ping

PREFACE BY DAVID COHEN

The past few years have seen a renewed interest in historical trials of core international crimes. However, until now, such historical studies have for the most part focused on case studies of individual trials or groups of trials. The Historical Origins of International Criminal Law ('HOICL') research project and anthologies are the first to undertake the study of the historical development of international criminal law in a comprehensive, inclusive and systematic way.

This project's wide scope is reflected in its far-reaching temporal and geographical coverage. As represented in mainstream textbooks, the dominant narrative of international criminal law's history usually begins with the Nuremberg and Tokyo trials at the end of the Second World War, with more focus given to the former than the latter. This conventional narrative then proceeds to examine the establishment and work of the *ad hoc* international criminal tribunals of Yugoslavia and Rwanda, the hybrid tribunals and the International Criminal Court ('ICC'). The HOICL project and anthologies challenge this traditional historical narrative by not limiting themselves to the typical institutional trajectory of Nuremberg/Tokyo – 1990s *ad hoc* tribunals – ICC. Rather, HOICL questions this paradigm and examines a broad range of less explored time periods, geographical regions and institutional settings that demonstrate how communities, states and international organisations have sought to prosecute or deal with core international crimes.

There are many reasons why the time is right for such a project. Due to technological developments and innovative efforts by research institutions, archival sources on these historical trials have been made available and "rediscovered" by scholars. These archival materials are made more easily accessible through Internet tools, such as the ICC Legal Tools Database ('ICC LTD'). The ICC LTD makes available contemporary and historical case law and instruments through its search engine and well-organised user interface. Access is completely free of charge. All users need is an internet connection. Researchers no longer need to secure funds beforehand, and they no longer need to travel extensive distances to public or private archives where such historical records are stored.

Such historical studies have become increasingly relevant as international criminal law enters a normative consolidation stage. The discipline is now leaving behind its frenetic stages of expansion and institution building. As it does so, it becomes ever more important to revisit the discipline's historical origins so as to achieve a better understanding of where we are today and the challenges we will encounter in the future. Appreciating the diverse forms that international criminal law has historically taken contributes to a more critical understanding of our discipline and offers insight into how humanity has sought to address the worst types of atrocities over time.

One of the key achievements of HOICL is the spotlight and attention given to less well-known non-Western cases or personas in international criminal law. Like many other areas of international law, Western actors or institutions continue to predominate in our discussions and research. We read about the role played by the Americans in shaping the direction of post-Second World War trials and of European efforts in the design of the ICC. Much less is known of the thinking and role of non-Western actors involved in or impacted by international criminal justice. Many chapters in the *HOCIL* anthology focus on trials conducted in non-Western societies and their impact, and on the thought and contributions of non-Western actors within the United Nations War Crimes Commission, the Tokyo Trial and other institutional settings. A number of these chapters have been written by young and upcoming scholars from non-Western societies. A more comprehensive and realistic understanding of how non-Western actors and societies perceive international criminal justice is necessary if the discipline is to be truly inclusive.

HOICL authors come from different disciplinary backgrounds. Some are lawyers, others are historians, political scientists or sociologists. They employ a variety of theoretical and disciplinary perspectives and have different types of legal training and professional experience. They have chosen an eclectic and extensive range of research questions, which they have approached using different methodological frameworks. There are quite a few case studies of trials or institutions that take a detail-oriented and meticulous approach, which is useful and necessary when the research topic has yet to be mapped out or comprehensively studied. Some chapters take a comparative approach, juxtaposing different trials against one another to draw out and explain their similarities or differences. Other chapters take a more thematic or conceptual approach to view the justice process through the lenses of show trials, colonialism or political transition. Together, they provide the readers of this volume with a rich resource for exploring the origins of international criminal law, as we understand it today.

FOREWORD BY GEOFFREY ROBERTSON QC

It is a privilege to introduce this important anthology on historical origins of international criminal law, which honours the memory of Judge LI Haopei through the 2014 LI Haopei Seminar. A distinguished diplomat and professor of international law, he lent academic credibility to the International Criminal Tribunal for the former Yugoslavia when, at the age of 87, he became a member of its first bench. His warning in that court's first case, that judges should not stray beyond their competence as lawyers into political jungles where they were likely to get lost, laid down a challenge to his brethren that they must constantly keep in mind. His very presence, in those years, was a comforting signal that whatever China's reluctance to approve humanitarian incursions on state sovereignty, it was nonetheless willing to abide by – and to participate in – the enforcement of a new international criminal law that had been too long absent from the world since it was apparently discovered at Nuremberg.

There is a widespread belief that this all began at the London Conference in 1945, and was created by Robert H. Jackson and Harry S. Truman over the objections of Winston Churchill and the British. There was, indeed, a political deadlock between those two allies: Churchill wanted to give the captured Nazi leaders six hours to say their prayers before putting them in front of a firing squad. Truman famously responded that this course "would not sit easily on the American conscience or be remembered by our children with pride". They had to be given a trial "as dispassionate as the times and horrors we deal with will permit, with a record that will leave our reasons and motives clear". The deadlock was broken by the third ally: Joseph Stalin loved show trials, as long as everyone was shot at the end. From his somewhat bloodthirsty vote, the Nuremberg trials proceeded.

But Nuremberg had been preceded by the remarkable work of the United Nations War Crimes Commission on international law, fashioning centuries-old war crimes law into an instrument for prosecuting and punishing military leaders who had caused untold suffering, especially in Eastern Europe and China. It took up the baton which had been dropped by Woodrow Wilson at Versailles, when he invoked sovereign immunity and refused to allow prosecutions of the Kaiser for aggressively invading

Belgium and instigating unrestricted submarine warfare – a demand for justice made then by the British, under the vengeful slogan "Hang the Kaiser". Article 227 of the Versailles Treaty actually set up an international criminal court – five judges, from Britain, the US, Japan, France and Italy – that never sat. The Kaiser remained unhung and lived happily ever after as a guest of the Dutch government, leaving us with one of history's great hypotheticals: Would Hitler have been given pause had the Kaiser been put on trial? Articles 228 and 229 provided that Germany should try its own war criminals, and "losers' justice" went on display at Leipzig. Of 901 defendants, 888 were acquitted, and the rest were allowed to escape.

These failures to envisage, let alone to find any means to enforce, international criminal justice were compounded by the abject failure to punish the authors of the Armenian massacres. These were the first atrocities to be denounced as a *"crime against humanity"* at an international conference in 1915 – a Grotian moment that came when the draft resolution put forward by Britain and France to condemn "a crime against Christianity" was amended by Russia to read *"a crime against humanity"*. But nemesis never took wing. Britain removed the Young Turks for trial in Malta, but could not work out how international law could punish state officials for obeying their state and killing their own people. They were guilty, Churchill said, of a "crime without a name" and it took international justice 30 years to find that name, with the help of the scholar Raphael Lemkin. It was the name for a crime that goes back to the destruction of Carthage.

At least the Armenian genocide is well known – thanks to Turkey's disgraceful refusal to acknowledge the genocidal truth of Ottoman conduct. In this, Turkey parallels Japan, which whitewashed the bestial treatment of its prisoners of war and its "comfort women", and honours the graves of those responsible for atrocities in the Asia-Pacific. How much is this a consequence of the misbegotten Tokyo trial, which maintained the dishonest pretence that Emperor Hirohito – that worst of war criminals – was totally innocent? As a result of a legally orchestrated lie, this wicked man was kept on his throne – in the 1970s he travelled to Britain to meet the Queen, to Washington to meet Henry Kissinger, and to Los Angeles to meet Mickey Mouse. His impunity led his people to believe that they had every right to whitewash their school textbooks and honour the graves of their criminal commanders, whose guilt was proven but never published because the Allies were so embarrassed at rigging the evidence to exculpate Hirohito that they made no attempt to publicise the reasoning of the Tokyo and other military tribunals, thus helping modern Japan to consign them to oblivion. That is why it is so important that this anthology includes examples of the scholarship which is beginning to illuminate, for example, the record of Australian military tribunals which condemned Japanese commanders who marched prisoners to their death, and the Russian court which tried the scientists of Unit 731 in Manchuria, where experiments took place that were more hideous than Josef Mengele ever envisaged. Unlike Germany, Turkey and Japan have not faced up to their historical demons. It is the task of international law scholarship to reincarnate their commanders, to place them in the dock of history and to assist our understanding of how best to deal with any who emulate their crimes in future.

The cases examined in this anthology show the striving of humankind to find a satisfactory intellectual and practical basis to bring to justice the perpetrators of torture and mass murder, when these crimes are ordered or supported by a sovereign state. We can trace the roots of international criminal justice back to the Roman lawyers who identified *jus gentium* – rules they found to be common to all societies, for which reason they had a specially binding quality. Not because of their intrinsic or self-evident merit, but simply because they were in service in all civilised societies. This did not, of course, take the ancient world very far, and never made a theoretical leap to the idea of universal jurisdiction.

Later, the power of great religions led to some regional enforcement of rules from the Bible and the Qu'ran, with Canon law laid down by the Pope and Sharia law practised through the mosques. The Catholic Inquisition and Muslim apostasy laws crossed state borders. Religion influenced the customs of war: the first war crime was declared by the Lateran Council in 1139, to punish those who used crossbows in wars between Christians. Thereafter, war law developed apace – there were lots of wars in Europe to develop it. Christian soldiers in the fifteenth century were punished for desecrating churches and killing prisoners, while Shakespeare's pedantic Welsh Captain, Fluellen, could, by 1590, point out that killing the boys in the baggage train was "expressly against the law of arms". But although you could always kill a prince on the battlefield, and hold him as a hostage, you were not allowed to put him on trial. Rulers were appointed by God, and had sovereign immunity, a position declared in 1648 by the Treaty of Westphalia. This Treaty was the foundation of international law in Europe, based on the divine right of Kings and the principle of non-intervention in their behaviour, however barbaric towards their own subjects. The best thing about the Treaty of Westphalia was that England was not part of it.

When Charles I was brought to trial in 1649, his first words to his judges were these: "I would know by what power I am called hither – by what lawful authority?" These were the same words, in translation, that Milošević hurled at his international jurists and that Saddam Hussein flung at his local judges. The simple answer – you are called before the power that has supplanted yours – is now inadequate to explain the power that is international criminal law, a power that much depends on moral suasion and on concerns about history repeating itself (*Nunca Mas!*), and which actually draws strength from the increasing doubt about the existence of a vengeful God. We no longer believe in Hell – a place that would be in any event contrary to the Torture Convention – or that murderers will receive justice in the hereafter. International criminal law is fortified by the increasing belief that they either receive it on earth, or not at all.

This anthology's fascinating chapters look at how the aspiration to put tyrants on trial has slowly developed momentum, and which continues in the twenty-first century. It has established a sound juristic and philosophical basis for international justice, and is constructing systems – not yet very effective systems – to provide trials that are reasonably fair, even if at present they are unreasonably long and expensive. But our confidence in the "rightness of international criminal law" – not as "victor's justice", but as utilising victory as an occasion to *do* justice – requires a full understanding of the history of human attempts to punish the authors of barbarism. There is much work still to be done to excavate the historical foundations of international criminal law, and this anthology will be an important spur to that work.

FOREWORD BY IMMI TALLGREN

Searching for the Historical Origins of International Criminal Law

Where to Search and How?

In March 2014 a seminar was convened in Hong Kong to answer the question: What are the main historical origins of international criminal law as a discipline of international law?[1] That the trials of Charles I in 1649, of Japanese soldiers tried for war crimes in Chinese courts from 1945 to 1956, and of eight Finnish leaders for the responsibility of war held under Soviet pressure in Helsinki in 1945–1946, could all figure as topics in the seminar programme suggests that all three have something to contribute to the efforts "to explore and crystallise the sub-discipline of history of international criminal law".[2] The seminar programme was rich and heterogeneous, to a point that a history by a successor of Thomas More of the island named Utopia with its exemplary criminal justice system might not have stood out.[3] Participants were invited to examine what "significant building blocks of contemporary international criminal law"[4] these different histories from various times and spaces constitute.

The expectation of a contribution to be made to international criminal law by the search of its origins was often evoked in the seminar, in different senses. The crucial task of research was seen to consist of bringing to daylight badly known trials, treaty provisions or case law, by translating archives that are cumbersome to access and producing comparative descriptions of judicial practices. One participant, a judge of an international tribunal, expressed the expectation that historical research should have direct practical application: it should facilitate the time-

---

[1] For the concept outline of the seminar, see http://www.fichl.org/fileadmin/fichl/cvs/ 140301-02_HOICL_Seminar_I__concept_and_programme__as_of_140302_.pdf. The author would like to warmly thank the organisers of the Hong Kong seminar on "The Historical Origins of International Criminal Law", the editors of this volume, as well as Antoine Buchet, Sara Kendall, Martti Koskenniemi and Thomas Skouteris for their comments and support.

[2] *Ibid.*

[3] Thomas More, *Utopia*, Penguin, London, 1965 [1516].

[4] See concept statement, *supra* note 1.

consuming technical work of international tribunals that have limited resources. Research and researchers were expected to contribute to the broader goals of international criminal law by serving the next generations of international criminal law judges and confirming the legitimacy of international tribunals. Yet a different kind of expectation was that of unearthing a particular piece of case law or legal opinion from the past in order for it to contribute to the 'discipline' of international criminal law.

To me, these expectations seemed to underline how a search for origins goes far beyond a mechanical effort of filling lacunae, opening hidden cages in a genealogy, or "broaden[ing] the common hinterland to international criminal law".[5] In such a search, are all "origins" discovered seen as healthy roots of a common plant, all equally nourishing? Or does the contribution to the discipline imply a moment of evaluation: some of the past laws, trials or legal opinions are valuable seedlings, others weeds? With such choices involved, the search would seem to implicitly entail advancing some universal conformity of international criminal law, where law and institutional practices would evolve following shared patterns that research contributes to stabilise. What was not addressed in the seminar were the questions on by whom, when, how and why are those patterns conceived, and to what extent is it possible to "construct common ground and transcend the disagreements surrounding"[6] the current international criminal law project, as the organisers courageously aimed to do.

Yet faced with such expectations and challenges, it seems necessary to reflect on exactly these questions and more broadly on the sense of engaging in a "search for origins". Beyond the construction of a new distinct area in the fantasised topography of law, what are disciplinary histories of the "origins" of international criminal law about? In delimiting the specific contours of the area, how to deal with encounters with other disciplines and horizons that are unavoidably part of such an exercise? At its simplest, should one use the epistemology, methodology and disciplinary frame of historical research or legal research, or should a specific hybrid setting for legal history be developed? Is the focus on "law as such" or is it also on its presence or absence in the world as compliance, the latter requiring recourse to interdisciplinary methods in order to investigate social structures as well as individual and collective practices? How to cope with the fact that international criminal law

---

[5] *Ibid.*

[6] *Ibid.*

combines doctrine, institutional practice and scholarship of both international law and criminal law? To what extent should interrogations into the "origins" of international law recognise the relevance of national criminal law and justice systems and their heterogeneous histories as social institutions in different societies? Should such a search also trace how some fragments of national criminal law and institutional models entered the international legal order, while others were left out?

These questions seem to suggest that unambiguously established "epistemologies", "methods" and "disciplinary frames" exist, and that the frontiers between the national and international are clearly drawn. The author would simply need to choose among different options. But surely this is not the case. Approaches to research of history, law, legal history, sociology of law or legal anthropology are heterogeneous, and methodological discussions in each are continuous and controversial.[7] A particular "national" is intertwined, parallel or inseparable with other "nationals" and the "international". Yet this does not liberate a researcher, as a participant in a discourse, from a conscious reflection on these contexts nor from the choice of focus, objectives, frame of argumentation or style. One starting point for a research effort on the origins of international criminal law, then, is to openly render questionable any search for origins.

In historiography, the search for origins as a research mission is passé, for some time. No matter the object of the search – political concepts, legal rules, principles, institutional practices or the ideas underlying them, and individuals and their positions – a search for origins is the safest way to find in the past only what one is looking for today, that is, one's own current concepts and ideas in a more primitive form, pictured on their way of evolution towards the present. To quote Samuel Moyn on human rights histories, "the past is treated as if it were simply the future waiting to happen".[8] Whereas the agency and agenda inherent in any (historical) research can always be seen as limiting, the search for origins is especially limited. There is too much evidence of the risk of such searches turning into fabricating origins for this danger to be

---

[7] It is impossible to "summarise" the rich discussions in different methodologies or philosophies of disciplines here. As one example of their occasional vividness, the critical legal history's takeover of the functionalists and materialists in legal history in North America in the past 30 years can be mentioned; see Robert W. Gordon, "Critical Legal Histories", in *Stanford Law Review*, 1984, vol. 36, nos. 1–2, pp. 57–125; Christopher Tomlins, "After Critical Legal History: Scope, Scale, Structure", in *Annual Review of Law and Social Sciences*, 2012, vol. 8, pp. 31–68.

[8] Samuel Moyn, *The Last Utopia: Human Rights in History*, Harvard University Press, Cambridge, MA, 2010, p. 11.

ignored. Yet behind the red cloth of the term "origins" in historiography today, complex questions remain open. In recent interventions, historians have criticised international legal histories of Gentili, Grotius, Hobbes, Pufendorf or Vattel for trying "to understand the past for what it brought about and not for what it meant to people living in it",[9] being "dogged by debilitating anachronism and 'presentism'".[10] Behind these exchanges figure previous discussions by Quentin Skinner and other scholars referred to as the Cambridge school of intellectual history who have vigorously argued for interpreting classic texts in law, philosophy or politics in their argumentative and social contexts, not as sources of timeless truths or authoritative statements about fundamental concepts.[11] What these critiques often fail to consider, however, is the unavoidable "presentism" in any choice or delimitation of context, and the way in which the researcher's own context influences how the contextual archive is established and organised.[12] The past never exists as neutral boxes of context to be analysed in their own terms, in isolation from the present and its agents. Considering that, to quote Anne Orford, "a legal reading differs from a historical reading, in that it is not concerned with the past

---

[9] Randall Lesaffer, "International Law and its History: The Story of an Unrequited Love", in Matthew Craven, Malgosia Fitzmaurice and Maria Vogiatzi (eds.), *Time, History and International Law*, Martinus Nijhoff, Leiden, 2007, p. 27. See also Ian Hunter, "Global Justice and Regional Metaphysics: On the Critical History of the Law of Nature and Nations", in Shaunnagh Dorsett and Ian Hunter (eds.), *Law and Politics in British Postcolonial Thought: Transpositions of Empire*, Palgrave, New York, 2010, pp. 11–29; Pablo Zapatero, "Legal Imagination Vitoria: The Power of Ideas", in *Journal of the History of International Law*, 2009, vol. 11, no. 2, pp. 221–71.

[10] Ian Hunter, "The Figure of Man and the Territorialisation of Justice in 'Enlightenment' Natural Law: Pufendorf and Vattel", in *Intellectual History Review*, 2013, vol. 23, no. 3, pp. 289–307.

[11] Quentin Skinner, "Meaning and Understanding in the History of Ideas", in *History and Theory*, 1969, vol. 8, no. 1, pp. 3–53. Arguments in broadly similar direction have been defended under *Begriffsgechichte* by German scholars; see Reinhardt Koselleck, "Begriffsgeschichte and Social History", in *Futures Past: On the Semantics of Historical Time*, Columbia University Press, New York, 1979. Contemporary criticisms of Skinner's work brought about a reconsideration of the strict temporal nature of texts or expressed positions in his later work. These later writings are disregarded in recent discussions on history and international legal method, argues Anne Orford, "On International Legal Method", in *London Review of International Law*, 2013, vol. 1, no. 1, pp. 166–97.

[12] On the "place" of historiography that permits and prohibits, see Michel de Certeau, *The Writing of History*, Columbia University Press, New York, 1988, pp. 68–69. On the fallacies of determining a context, see Martti Koskenniemi, "Vitoria and Us: Thoughts on Critical Histories of International Law", in *Rechtsgeschichte – Legal History*, 2014, vol. 22, pp. 119–38.

xiv

as history but with the past as law",[13] research in law and the past of law must allow for "making meaning move across time".[14] Keeping the past separate from the present is then not simple, also considering how in international criminal law, until recently primarily built on customary law or general principles of law, the past is an intimate part of the present law in force.

In international law, methodological discussions on the accounts of the past used to be scarce. Wilhelm Grewe and others with a similar approach saw as their primary objective of study establishing a periodisation and typology of successive international legal orders.[15] For Grewe's realist history, the framework of international law was predetermined by the epochs of the general history of the state system. It is on those general historical foundations that Grewe built his "specialised history of ideas about international law".[16] His method of analysis consisted of efforts to "determine the shape and historical locations" of a "single, cohesive international legal order" in interrelated epochs.[17] Whereas Grewe explicitly stated that his intention was not to write a "complete history of international law", he wanted to provide a foundation for such a project. A number of scholars have taken up questioning that foundation presumptively built by a few European states, such as R.P. Anand, T.O. Elias, Frantz Fanon and, more recently, Tony Anghie, James Tully and Nathaniel Berman. If international law is "a product of the past that conditions the future [...] of all human societies",[18] how that past is understood must be open to critical analysis. Such a focus of research, or at least an outspoken intention in that direction, currently informs politically correct engagements with the histories of international law. The recently published massive *Oxford Handbook of the History of International Law* declares to "depart from the [...] 'well-worn paths' of how the history of international law has been written so far – that is, as a history of rules developed in the

---

13 See Orford, 2013, *supra* note 11, and Anne Orford, "The Past as Law or History? The Relevance of Imperialism for Modern International Law", NYU Institute for International Law and Justice Working Paper 2012/2 (History and Theory of International Law Series), also published in Emmanuelle Jouannet, Hélène Ruiz Fabri and Mark Toufayan (eds.), *Tiers monde: Bilan et perspectives*, Société de législation comparée, Paris, 2013.

14 Orford, 2013, p. 172, see *supra* note 11.

15 Wilhem G. Grewe, *The Epochs of International Law*, De Gruyter, Berlin, 2000.

16 *Ibid.*, p. 30.

17 *Ibid.*, pp. 29–33.

18 Philip Allott, "International Law and the Idea of History", in *Journal of the History of International Law*, 1999, vol. 1, pp. 1–21.

European state system since the 16th century which then spread to other continents and eventually the entire globe".[19] Yet the current efforts of renovation leading to a "global history" offer no easy closures for past unbalances.[20] Another recent focus in international law histories is on conceiving the past of the ideas – understood broadly beyond the legal inventions – and intellectuals that presumably have animated the field. A prominent example is Martti Koskenniemi's *The Gentle Civilizer of Nations*, where the history of international law is studied as interventions of human beings in history by using the language of law.[21] The past 10 to 15 years have witnessed a "historical turn",[22] an important increase of attention to history in international law, albeit not always accompanied by reflections on methodology.[23]

In international criminal law, by contrast, there has been no history boom – yet we might be witnessing a beginning with this project and some recent others[24] – and any specific methodological interrogations on historical research are rare. More attention is directed to the neighbouring but separate questions of "writing history in international criminal trials".[25] Research on international criminal law in general has rapidly

---

[19] Bardo Fassbender and Anne Peters, "Introduction", in Bado Fassbender and Anne Peters (eds.), *Oxford Handbook of the History of International Law*, Oxford University Press, Oxford, 2012, p. 1.

[20] For the limits of the *Oxford Handbook*, see "Book Review Symposium, Bado Fassbender and Anne Peters (eds.), *Oxford Handbook of the History of International Law*", in *The European Journal of International Law*, 2014, vol. 25, no. 1. On "global history" in general, see Laurent Testot (ed.), *Histoire globale: Un nouveau regard sur le monde*, Science humaines, Auxerre, 2008.

[21] Martti Koskenniemi, *The Gentle Civilizer of Nations: The Rise and Fall of International Law 1870–1960*, Cambridge University Press, Cambridge, 2002.

[22] See Koskenniemi, 2014, pp. 119–21, *supra* note 12.

[23] See, however, Craven, Fitzmaurice and Vogiatzi, 2007, *supra* note 9; Randall Lesaffer, "Law between Past and Present", Social Science Research Network, 2008; Andrew Phang, "Which Road to the Past? – Some Reflections on Legal History", in *Singapore Journal of Legal History*, 2013, pp. 1–23; Orford, 2013, see *supra* note 11.

[24] Such as Kevin Jon Heller and Gerry Simpson (eds.), *The Hidden Histories of War Crimes Trials*, Oxford University Press, Oxford, 2013.

[25] Quoting the title of Richard Ashby Wilson, *Writing History in International Criminal Trials*, Cambridge University Press, Cambridge, 2011. On what kind of history does international criminal justice write, see Gerry Simpson, "Linear Law: The History of International Criminal Law", in Christine Schwöbel (ed.), *Critical Approaches to International Criminal Law*, Routledge, 2014. See also Costas Douzinas, "History Trials: Can Law Decide History?", in *Annual Review of Law and Society*, 2012, vol. 8, pp. 273–89; Lawrence Douglas, *The Memory of Judgment: Making Law and History in the Trials of the Holocaust*, Yale University Press, New Haven, 2001; David Luban, "The Legacies of Nuremberg", in *Social Research*, 1987, vol. 54, no. 4, pp. 779–829; Shoshanna Felman,

grown in volume since the early 1990s, following the establishment of the *ad hoc* tribunals for the former Yugoslavia and Rwanda, the International Criminal Court ('ICC') and other international and mixed jurisdictions, accompanied by a wealth of newly drafted legal instruments. The ways in which legal experts, academics, international civil servants, practitioners and NGO activists associating and investing themselves in this field of law account for the past of international criminal law can also be seen to reflect the self-understanding and identity of a rapidly growing new epistemic community. Writing histories of international criminal law participates in the creation of a collective memory of the discipline and its actors, melding together the questions of "how this law came about and what does it mean today" and "who we are". In textbooks and commentaries on international criminal law, the past is represented in a streamlined "light" version, not unlike a potted "Foreign Office International Legal History".[26] What functions or interests do such histories serve? What do they expose, and what do they hide? What are the major styles, plots and tropes? Frequent patterns appear, slightly caricaturised, as follows.

Firstly, accounts of the history of international criminal law tend to take a linear form and, either discretely or openly, they assume a jubilant tone of transhistorical evolution towards the global progress witnessed at present, and the striving for a hopefully even brighter future.[27] The intertwined evolutions of both *jus in bello* and *jus ad bellum* appear as a struggle through times of certain given "precursors" of norms or principles with heterogeneous roots, be they in natural law (first divine and then secularised), in Romano-canonical law or indigenous codes, with variations in what value is assigned to the different "roots".[28] These

---

"Theaters of Justice: Arendt in Jerusalem, the Eichmann Trial, and the Redefinition of Legal Meaning in the Wake of the Holocaust", in *Critical Inquiry*, 2001, vol. 27, pp. 201–38; Martti Koskenniemi, "Between Impunity and Show Trials", in Jochen Frowein and Rüdiger Wolfrum (eds.), *Max Planck Institute Yearbook of United Nations Law*, Martinus Nijhoff, Leiden, 2002, vol. 6, pp. 1–35; Mark Osiel, *Mass Atrocity, Collective Memory and the Law*, Transnational Publishers, New Brunswick, 1997.

26   David Bederman, "Foreign Office International Legal History", in Craven, Fitzmaurice and Vogiatzi, 2007, *supra* note 9, p. 46.

27   The progress narrative is a common and frequently discussed characteristic in international law in general; see Thomas Skouteris, *The Notion of Progress in International Law Discourse*, T.M.C. Asser Press, The Hague, 2010; Nathaniel Berman, "In the Wake of Empire", in *American University International Law Review*, 1999, vol. 14, p. 1515.

28   See, for example, Jean Pictet, *Development and Principles of International Humanitarian Law*, Martinus Nijhoff, Leiden, 1985, p. 6, arguing for recognition of the fact that "the roots of humanitarian law are very much deeper than some European authors with a narrow view of matters have long believed". See also James Turner Johnson, *Just War*

elements are presented as growing stronger on their way through centuries from the scholastics and chivalry codes onwards to Gentili, Grotius and Vattel and so forth, to lead to the milestones of the Lieber Code in 1863 and the first international codification efforts in the late nineteenth and early twentieth centuries, amounting to the institutional developments that allowed for the first moments of exercise of international criminal jurisdiction in the twentieth century.[29] The struggles for law's growing importance and broader geographical reach in the world are characterised by an ethos of defending the ideas of international criminal law as concretisations of more abstract ideas of "rule of law" or "humanity"[30] against politics, state sovereignty – the "bête-noire of the international criminal lawyer"[31] – or hegemony.[32] What exactly that "rule of law" or "humanity" comprises and how these conceptions came about is rarely questioned.

Secondly, the stories of the past of international criminal law frequently emphasise singular events and individuals. Histories of international criminal law tend to deal with the particular and specific

---

Tradition and the Restraint of War: A Moral and Historical Inquiry, Princeton University Press, Princeton, NJ, 1981; Theodor Meron, *War Crimes Law Comes of Age: Essays*, Oxford University Press, Oxford, 1998.

[29] See textbooks, such as Antonio Cassese and Paola Gaeta, *Cassese's International Criminal Law*, 3rd ed., Oxford University Press, Oxford, 2013; Robert Cryer, Håkan Friman, Darryl Robinson and Elizabeth Wilmshurst (eds.), *An Introduction to International Criminal Law and Procedure*, Cambridge University Press, Cambridge, 2010. See also Timothy McCormack, "From Sun Tzu to the Sixth Committee: The Evolution of an International Criminal Law Regime", in Timothy McCormack and Gerry Simpson (eds.), *The Law of War Crimes, National and International Approaches*, Kluwer, The Hague, 1997, p. 31; M. Cherif Bassiouni, "From Versailles to Rwanda in Seventy-Five Years: The Need to Establish an International Criminal Court", in *Harvard Human Rights Law Journal*, 1997, vol. 10, p. 11; Ove Bring, *International Criminal Law in Historical Perspective: Comments and Materials*, Juridiska Faculteten, Stockhom, 2002. On the chivalry codes as the origins of humanitarian law, see Maurice H. Keen, *The Laws of War in the Late Middle Ages*, Routledge, London, 1965; Theodor Meron, *Bloody Constraint: Crimes and Accountability in Shakespeare*, Oxford University Press, New York, 1998.

[30] See Ruti G. Teitel, *Humanity's Law*, Oxford University Press, Oxford, 2012; Antonio Augusto Cancado Trindade, *International Law for Humankind: Towards a New Jus Gentium*, Martinus Nijhoff, Leiden, 2010.

[31] Robert Cryer, "International Criminal Law vs State Sovereignty: Another Round?" in *European Journal of International Law*, 2005, vol. 16, no. 5, p. 980.

[32] See, for example, M. Cherif Bassiouni, "International Criminal Justice in Historical Perspective: The Tension Between States' Interests and the Pursuit of Justice", and Klaus Kress, "The International Criminal Court as a Turning Point", in Antonio Cassese (ed.), *The Oxford Companion to International Criminal Justice*, Oxford University Press, Oxford, 2009, pp. 131–42 and pp. 143–59.

rather than the collective and statistical, and they tend to be concerned with people, cases, trials or institutions, not impersonal circumstances or long-term causalities in the spheres of economics, politics, demography, climate, technology and so on.[33] The focus on events, dramatic turns of history and moments of creation of either law or institutions culminates in the key roles accorded to a few tribunals and trials, until recently most notably in Nuremberg and Tokyo. Events are captured and delimited, frozen out of chaotic temporal continuity and spatial contingency, becoming emblems of evolution that are organised chronologically in the search of a coherent story – descriptive rather than analytical – of an order of international law taking shape. The emphasis on individuals is manifest in the wealth of literature on either famous prosecutors or judges, or, alternatively, infamous accused and convicted. The positive figures tend to be ascribed a broad and decisive beneficial role in these events: they have carried the project of international criminal law ahead. On the other side of the story, the international criminals stand for a limitless capacity for evil, of which they are personally held both responsible and guilty, sometimes by challenging all notions of plausible causality. Victims rarely occupy a significant role in the stories, but they are accorded a function as stereotyped icons of suffering, sometimes reduced to international criminal law's (putative) *raison d'être*. Traces of other essentialisms and archetypes, on race, culture or gender that are more common in popular culture may occasionally find their way into histories of international criminal law.

Thirdly, a barricade is established between international criminal law and its past, as if to neutralise the present. Whereas its genealogical maps would point to a strong influence of either religious ideology and transcendence, be it Christian or other religions setting moral limits to conduct in conflict or condemning violence as such,[34] or of political

---

[33]   In the historiographical discussions, these claims would situate the international criminal law histories as narrative histories, criticised by Braudel, Furet, Le Goff and others from the Annales group; see, for example, Fernand Braudel, *Écrits sur l'histoire*, Paule Braudel (ed.), Arthaud, Paris, 1990. Generally on the Annalistes and the form of narrative, see Hayden White, *The Content of the Form: Narrative Discourse and Historical Representation*, Johns Hopkins University Press, Baltimore, 1987, pp. 31–33, 37–38. On event history versus conceptualising history, see Paul Veyne, *Comment on écrit l'histoire*, Seuil, Paris, 1996. On the "episodic" nature of international law in general, and as its moments of force, see Fleur Johns, Richard Joyce and Sundhya Pahuja (eds.), *Events: The Force of International Law*, Routledge-Cavendish, London, 2011.

[34]   See, for example, Carolyn Evans, "The Double-Edged Sword: Religious Influences on International Humanitarian Law", in *Melbourne Journal of International Law*, 2005, vol. 6, no. 1, pp. 1–32; Michel Veuthey, "International Humanitarian Law and Spirituality", in *Refugee Survey Quarterly*, 2002, vol. 21, no. 3, pp. 45–110.

agendas of transition after wars or other major conflicts, today's international criminal law gets presented at the very end of a linear evolution, grown out of those "origins" and ultimately liberated from them. International criminal law figures as a body of legal rules on international crimes and their punishment that has been adopted in negotiations to become international treaty law, is considered international customary law or general principles and is also incorporated into domestic legislation of most states. As a further advance of historical progress towards a fully-fledged legal order, parts of international criminal law are represented as mirroring and concretising "the constitutional premises of the existing international legal order".[35] These accounts underline not only the aspired essence of international criminal law as secular modern public international law but also its role as a model of the future of international law with institutionalised international enforcement mechanisms, approaching the fulfilment of international law's fantasised national analogy. No longer a mere rhetorical device expressing moral indignation or a biased instrument in the toolbox of the victorious party of an armed conflict, international criminal law stands on its own, entering the world as a technology and practices rationally and neutrally governed, set to grow even stronger and territorially global in the future.

What are the consequences of these tendencies to trace linear progress, to emphasise the sequences of events – Walter Benjamin's "beads of a rosary"[36] – to focus on individuals, and to erect a wall between the past and present? Analysing this calls for other questions, such as the one by E.H. Carr in 1961 – what is history? – and his answer: "History is interpretation".[37] For Carr, historians arbitrarily determine which of the "facts of the past" to turn into "historical facts" according to their biases and agendas.[38] What is international criminal law, in its histories and today? Is it rules, institutions, actors, compliance, objectives, outcomes? Are disciplinary histories most effective in creating knowledge of the past or in giving international criminal law a "temporal depth", constructing it as a quasi-natural epiphany and endowing it with moral and political authenticity, as the writing of the history of modern nations

---

35 Christian Tomuschat, "Obligations Arising for States Without or Against Their Will", in *Recueil des Cours,* vol. 241, 1993, p. 299.

36 Walter Benjamin, "Theses on the Philosophy of History", in Hannah Arendt (ed.), *Illuminations*, Pimlico, London, 1999, pp. 253–64.

37 E.H. Carr, *What is History?* Penguin, London, 1987, p. 23.

38 *Ibid.*, pp. 11–13.

has often done?[39] Efforts of monumental history, as Friedrich Nietzsche called it, to uncritically aggrandise, magnify and celebrate the great events of the discipline of international criminal law and its heroes may at their most extreme lead to the fabrication of a pure point of origin and place it in a linear history.[40] Granting international criminal law the immunity of a grand idea with a transhistorical essence, kept alive as an irresistible flame of progress from generation to generation that occasionally gets oxygen and triumphs, no matter its implantation, is cementing in the past the foundations of the current ideology of international criminal law, using the principal modes of operation characteristic of ideology – legitimation, dissimulation, unification, reification and naturalisation.[41] For example, forcing international criminal law on historical stilts to stand as the neutralised final product of a rationalist and humanist tradition, the ultimate victory of secularisation and legalist positivism, dissimulates the moments when law by its own rules is absent, but must be forced to intervene because its silence is intolerable. Concepts such as *ius cogens*, obligations *erga omnes* or the Martens Clause in the doctrines on sources of law are remembered in those moments of moral agony. Likewise, ritualistic expressions of confidence in international criminal law's technical, instrumental capacity of alleviating human suffering and bringing peace and material justice in the societies concerned reify this leitmotif, silencing questions as to how palpable these benefits are and who refers to them.[42]

The Investigating Committee for the Balkan Wars 1912–1913, established by the Carnegie Endowment for International Peace in 1913, concluded that just one word from the persons in power would have sufficed to stop the wars and all the atrocities committed.[43] The role given to the individual in history serves as a fundamental divide in the

---

[39] Craig Calhoun, *Nationalism*, Open University Press, Buckingham, 1997, p. 5, on the features of the rhetoric of nation.

[40] Friedrich Nietzsche, *The Use and Abuse of History for Life*, Liberal Arts, New York, 1957.

[41] On ideology and its critique, see Susan Marks, *The Riddle of All Constitutions: International Law, Democracy, and the Critique of Ideology*, Oxford University Press, Oxford, 2000. On the modes of operation, see Marks, pp. 18–25.

[42] On the need to "believe" in the benefits of international criminal law, see Immi Tallgren, "Sensibility and Sense of International Criminal Law", in *European Journal of International Law*, 2002, vol. 13, no. 3, p. 561.

[43] See Carnegie Endowment for International Peace, Division of Intercourse and Education, *Report of the International Commission to Inquire into the Causes of and Conduct of the Balkan Wars*, Publication No. 4, pp. 21ff., at 399, Carnegie Endowment, Washington, 1914, reprinted 1993, in *The Other Balkan Wars: A 1913 Carnegie Endowment Inquiry in Retrospect*, Carnegie Endowment for International Peace, Washington, DC.

philosophies of history. Are (some) individual human beings powerful historical agents, turning the course of history at their will and acts? At its extreme, an emphasis on exceptional individuals may lead to the imputation of the problems of the world merely to the evil manipulations or conspiracies of national or international elites and political leaders, who hide their power, the miseries of the world and the fact that they have made other people their servants.[44] In international trials, hiding behind the biggest of leaders may serve as a defence. As Robert Jackson ironically summarised the statements of the Nazi notables in Nuremberg: "These men saw no evil, spoke none, and none was uttered in their presence".[45] From the histories of the great and/or evil men who gave the direction to entire epochs, to history as "the motion of forces, or a machine, in which individuals are merely tossed or digested, or a collective will against which individual men and women are powerless",[46] is the understanding of history also in research on international criminal law marked by a focus on individual "legal truths", neglecting broader "historical truths"? Are the "making" of history of international criminal law and the rendering of international criminal justice vulnerable to the same critique: overly concerned with individual responsibility and, by doing so, either being selective and covertly political in the choice of the accused, and/or omitting to consider broader patterns of responsibility among the social, political or economic actors in a society?[47] Also in writing history, the focus on individuals may affect the understanding of the phenomenon of state criminality, organisational deviation and collective victimisation, obscuring them or evacuating them towards the zones of necessity and legitimacy.

A Demystification of International Criminal Law Histories?

Whatever the concept of history that research on the "historical origins of international criminal law" relies upon, it can be rewarding, albeit challenging, to reach beyond the patterns sketched above towards a

---

[44] Richard Ned Lebow, *The Tragic Vision of Politics, Ethics: Interests and Orders*, Cambridge University Press, Cambridge, 2003.

[45] Robert Jackson, Closing Address, in *Trial of the Major War Criminals Before the International Military Tribunal*, vol. XIX, International Military Tribunal, Nuremberg, 1948, pp. 397–432.

[46] Simpson, 2014, see *supra* note 25.

[47] Gerry Simpson, "International Criminal Justice and the Past", in Gideon Boas, William A. Schabas, Michael P. Scharf (eds.), *International Criminal Justice: Legitimacy and Coherence*, Edward Elgar, Cheltenham, 2012. See also Koskenniemi, 2002, p. 14, *supra* note 25; Tallgren, 2002, *supra* note 43, pp. 594–95.

demystified approach to the past. A demystification of research would require, as a starting point, staying "on guard against the deflecting influence of ideologies and hope", to quote Arthur Nussbaum in the disillusioned period after the Second World War.[48] Now, this is clearly an immensely complex issue, prone to pious intentions and majestic lapses into self-deception. Among the various modes and tropes of representing the past, Roland Barthes argued that those that deliberately accept that despite the efforts of "objective" history, the "real" can never be more than an unformulated signified – and thus call attention to their own process of production – are less ideological and mystifying than others.[49] It matters greatly whether history is understood as found or discovered or, on the contrary, as authored, imagined or invented.

In today's dominant understanding of historiography, histories of the past are always authored, as all stories are, and there is no way for the author to somehow neutrally transmit the past, as if untouched by her subjectivity, no matter how tightly controlled.[50] Precisely because authorship and agendas are an inseparable part of the exercise, they must be constantly questioned. In international law scholarship, active participation in the progressive strengthening and broadening of law and its institutions has traditionally been a condition of meaningful participation in that scholarly community. In international criminal law, can research of the past be pursued free from moral and ethical connotations or agendas?[51] Can it be kept separate from the pioneering efforts or activism in favour of international criminal law and its institutions, seeking to "strengthen and expand the foundations of this relatively young discipline of public international law", or pursuing its "vertical consolidation"?[52] Is it a problem – methodological, ethical, political – if research focuses on ennobling international criminal law or cementing its independence, respectability and perennial stability as a normative regulator of

---

[48]   Arthur Nussbaum, *A Concise History of the Law of Nations*, Macmillan, New York, 1947, pp. 3–4.

[49]   Roland Barthes, "Le discours de l'histoire", in *Social Science Information*, 1967, vol. 6, pp. 63–75.

[50]   See, for example, de Certeau, 1988, *supra* note 12; Keith Jenkins, *Re-Thinking History*, Routledge, London, 1991; Hayden White, *Tropics of Discourse: Essays in Cultural Criticism*, John Hopkins University Press, Baltimore, 1978, pp. 121–34.

[51]   On the identifications and agendas in international criminal law, see Immi Tallgren, "Who Are 'We' in International Criminal Law? On Critics and Membership", in Christine Schwöbel (ed.), *Critical Approaches to International Criminal Law: An Introduction*, Routledge, London, 2014, p. 71.

[52]   The concept outline of the Hong Kong seminar, see *supra* note 1.

international relations, and an object of legislative efforts, adjudication and legal scholarship?

Addressing the choices of method, style, audience and message openly is one way of coping with these dilemmas. A concrete example of a simple choice that matters is the affirmed or disguised subjectivity of commentary texts. [53] Erasing the authorial voice may create an *effet d'histoire*, a "powerful sense that something larger is being conveyed than mere authorial meanings, that the text itself is part of the stream of historical narrative within which it invites the reader: this was written by reality herself". [54] It is necessary to keep an eye on how analytical and normative propositions are at times made in international criminal law commentaries in a manner where "their truth value and normative power emerge from the appeal of the narrative [...] about the way the world came to be as it is". [55]

Demystification is crucial but difficult, considering that international criminal law's core thematic is about prohibiting large-scale atrocities, heinous and devastating acts. How to represent "the horrors that chill the conscience of every individual"? [56] Can or should they be represented and narrated at all? [57] The moral weight and solemnity of violence and suffering tend to inhabit histories of international criminal law, and it is difficult to see why and how this could or should be otherwise. Human sentiments are not a nuisance to be eliminated in and by international law. [58] Behind the layers of rules, professional roles and procedures, international criminal law may appear as if intuitively known

---

[53] For a linguistic analysis of the strategies of self-effacement or omniscience, see Emile Benveniste, *Problems in General Linguistics*, University of Miami Press, Coral Gables, 1971. See also Barthes, 1967, *supra* note 49.

[54] Martti Koskenniemi, "International Law as Therapy: Reading the Health of Nations", in *European Journal of International Law*, 2005, vol. 16, no. 2, p. 333.

[55] *Ibid.*, referring to Hayden White on such uses on historical writing and on the moralising character of history as narrative, in contrast to, for instance, chronology, White, 1987, see *supra* note 33.

[56] Giuseppe Conso, President of the Rome Diplomatic Conference, in M. Cherif Bassiouni (ed.), *The Statute of the International Criminal Court: A Documentary History*, Transnational Publishers, Ardsley, NY, 1998, p. xvii.

[57] See, for example, Saul Friedlander (ed.), *Probing the Limits of Representation: Nazism and the "Final Solution"*, Harvard University Press, Cambridge, MA, 1992. See also Paul Ricoeur, *La mémoire, l'histoire, l'oubli*, Editions du Seuil, Paris, 2000; Martha Minow, *Between Vengeance and Forgiveness: Facing History after Genocide and Mass Violence*, Beacon Press, Boston, 1998.

[58] See Gerry Simpson, "The Sentimental Life of International Law", in *London Review of International Law*, (forthcoming).

to all humans by a sentiment or a shared belief that does not need to be relativised by transnational multiculturalism, contrary to some other disciplines of international law. This may seem to be evidenced by how the elastic accelerations in the development of rules of international criminal law or building up its institutions have tightly followed wars that were seen, each at their time, to represent an "unforeseen re-emergence of barbarism".[59] As Sheldon Glueck wrote in 1944: "The emergence of states with a national policy of deliberate lawlessness and with their invention of 'total war' in the service of a program of world enslavement, compels a realistic modification of inadequate doctrines and principles of law".[60] The path from Solferino to The Hague is traced through a chain of dramatic violence: the world wars, the wars in the former Yugoslavia, genocide in Rwanda, and so forth. That chain may easily seem to point out a truth: when human beings are terribly hurt, other humans come to rescue or at least condemn the violence by the instrument of criminal justice and thereby affirm the inherent common values of the whole species.

Openly questioning such received ideas would be part of a demystifying research on international criminal law. Such an agenda would not be characterised by cynicism or nihilism, nor would it be a desperate capitulation in front of some dark forces of evil inherent in humans, but would rather be pursued in order to gain a more nuanced understanding of the particular histories of international criminal law. This starts with the simple observation that there has been no logic or consistency in how the violent events and strongly felt moral beliefs were channelled into law and institutions in the past. Other acts or periods of devastating violence took place but were not addressed as crimes and put to trial. In the chronological slot from Nuremberg and Tokyo in the 1940s to The Hague in the 1990s, major armed conflicts with massive victimisation of civilians took place, without tangible efforts to assign international criminal responsibility for those responsible: Korea, Algeria, Angola, Vietnam, El Salvador, Nicaragua, the Middle East, Iran, Iraq, Afghanistan, Somalia, and the list goes on. Today, they silently mark the margins of international criminal law, without precedent and without consequence in its evolution. With regard to today's recurrent and

---

[59] As wrote the Frenchman Antoine Pillet about the First World War (on Germans), Antoine Pillet, "La guerre actuelle et le droit des gens", in *Revue générale de droit international public*, 1916, vol. XXIII, p. 471.

[60] Sheldon Glueck, *War Criminals: Their Prosecution and Punishment*, Knopf, New York, 1944, p. 14.

generalised recourse to large-scale violence, only a fraction of which gets addressed as international crimes, the situation does not look different. By identifying some events and acts as criminal, pathological, both international criminal trials and the histories of them may participate in erasing violence, rendering most of the violence either invisible or putatively legitimate.[61]

New Routes: Dissecting and Diverting Histories

What would be valuable in a demystifying search for historical origins of international criminal law? Perhaps the happiest surprise could be the researcher becoming genuinely surprised by her own findings. The research as such would become a process of learning new ways of making intelligible the international legal past, bringing a new sense of proportion to the study of current international legal problems. How may such happy surprises take place? As a first step, it would appear necessary to let go of expectations of a shared starting point and precious heritage, as well as of a common mission to accomplish in the horizon of destiny. A second step would divert the efforts of recovering lost memories and vital roots to multiple, interdisciplinary and hazardous new routes. A third step would be taken towards humbleness, a downscaling in the ambition of figuring out the past.[62] What I picture as demystifying research into the past of international criminal law here does not need to be imagined as a total package of an alternative historiography, as a new grand global explanation. Neither is it about abrupt reversals of histories, as an appeals chamber crushing a previous judgment. Fresh openings and insights into a fragmented past, and into the intellectual and ideological influences of its particular contexts, would suffice to make a promising beginning. They are likely to come about by allowing uncertainties, conflicts or even ambiguities, accepting the research process as interplay between historical records, previous stories of history and the role of the author of a history. In dissecting and diverting histories, research goals may also at times be attained merely by carefully exposing the past (and present) to critical attention. There does not need to be an ambition of solving all the

---

[61] On the argument that war crimes and war itself are structurally indistinguishable, see Elisabeth Dauphinee, "War Crimes and the Ruin of Law", in *Millennium*, 2008, vol. 37, no. 1, pp. 49–67. See also Elaine Scarry, *The Body in Pain: The Making and Unmaking of the World*, Oxford University Press, Oxford, 1985.

[62] See, for example, David Lowethal, *The Past is a Foreign Country*, Cambridge University Press, Cambridge, 1985.

mysteries or filling the gaps. Initiating movement along alternative paths may be valuable as such.

Many contributions in the conference in Hong Kong had the ambition of telling unknown or forgotten stories of events and persons from international criminal law's past. Some aimed specifically at furthering knowledge of national histories, legislation, trials, individual actors or ideas that have not entered the current international criminal law textbook canon and the archives of reference. This is particularly true with regards to the spatial setting of the seminar, Asia, considering the lack of attention to histories reaching beyond the Tokyo Military Tribunal. Trials in Central or Eastern Europe have also been largely unknown or filed under a uniform label of "show trials". The efforts to call attention to these histories are part of a reaction to the historical Eurocentrism of international law and international institutions, today turned into a more geographically dispersed centre and its periphery, yet arguably continuously implicated in patterns of domination and exploitation.[63] A conscious effort of inserting the missing actors – Asians, Africans, semi-peripheral Europeans, stateless peoples deprived of subjecthood in international law, women, economically deprived, and all other marginalised, neglected and forgotten – is an absolutely necessary corrective movement. The same is true for "the application of international law from below",[64] alternative institutional practices in the shadows of the dominant ones. The concepts of counter-memory and counter-narrative developed by Michel Foucault make a useful reference to encourage research in the histories of the dominated, excluded, and subaltern in international criminal law.[65]

Yet the effort of retroactively introducing the absent is a delicate exercise with its own dangers and limits. What exactly is cut and pasted on the surface of dominant narratives, and what functions does the

---

[63] For an analysis of the claim of Eurocentrism, see Martti Koskenniemi, "Histories of International Law: Dealing with Eurocentrism", in *Rechtsgeschichte*, 2011, vol. 19, pp. 152–76. On the continuous inequality and international law, see Anthony Anghie, *Imperialism, Sovereignty and the Making of International Law*, Cambridge University Press, Cambridge, 2003; Sundhuya Pahuja, *Decolonising International Law: Development, Economic Growth and the Politics of Universality*, Cambridge University Press, Cambridge, 2011.

[64] Pacifique Manirakiza, "Customary African Approaches to International Criminal Law", in Jeremy I. Levitt (ed.), *Africa: Mapping New Boundaries in International Law*, Hart, Oxford, 2008.

[65] Michel Foucault, "Nietzsche, Genealogy, History", in Donald F. Bouchard (ed.), *Language, Counter-Memory, Practice: Selected Essays and Interviews*, Cornell University Press, Ithaca, NY, 1977.

exercise serve? How are roles distributed to heroes and villains, to experts and subordinates? Despite an apparently anti-ideological approach, the retouches may risk turning to zooming and assimilation, instrumentalisation and reification of "local histories", as part of the striving for an artificial and retroactive coherence of law and its institutional practice. The propensity to open up the past for those marginalised is not necessarily challenging the most fundamental assumptions that were central to the marginalisation. A demystifying search for origins would therefore be cautious of mechanically filling the empty spaces and silences of the "international criminal justice system". It would also analyse the role of institutional practices of international criminal law as a capricious limelight of history in some conflicts, wars or oppressions, in establishing a hierarchy of importance of violence and suffering, up to obscuring and seemingly legitimising violence that escapes international legal scrutiny. How many perpetrators, victims, witnesses, victimised communities or peoples linger in the grey zone of indifference and oblivion, not catching the interest of an international legal procedure and the subsequent attention of historical research? How to account for victims without a crime, accused without a trial? By aiming "at calming the dead who still haunt the present and at offering them scriptural tombs",[66] is the writing of history seeking remembering or closure, a forgiving for forgetting?

The complexities and challenges of writing histories of the past of international criminal law should not undermine the importance of the efforts. Histories of the origins of international criminal law matter, in many ways, beyond the valuable efforts to stimulate interest in international legal developments. They are elementary in countering the frequent emphasis on the future, as if the currently promised future universalism of international law made less relevant the fact that the claims of a shared long historical provenance remain unsustainable.[67] Exercising the power inherent in creating, reversing or reiterating histories either of particular nations, political, legal or social institutions, epistemic communities, or of "humanity" may also end up in the invention of legal and moral "traditions" that shape and direct an imagined community in its imagined trajectory.[68] In the dialectics of law

---

[66] De Certeau, 1988, p. 2, see *supra* note 12.

[67] See in the context of human rights declarations, Costas Douzinas, *The End of Human Rights*, Hart, 2000, chap. 5. See also Moyn, 2010, *supra* note 8.

[68] Eric Hobsbawm and Terence Ranger (eds.), *The Invention of Tradition*, Cambridge University Press, Cambridge, 1983.

and collective social spaces, law builds its legitimacy and justification on collective memories of it.[69] Histories of international criminal law, built on fragments of particular narratives, archives, accounts of crimes, victimisation, legal procedures and punishments become part of how it is believed that violence should be reacted to, today, whether in the conflicts on the African continent, in Syria, Iraq or Ukraine.

Whether war could ever be outlawed, or whether all war remains within the sovereign imperative,[70] is the iceberg of law, politics and history, of which today's international criminal law is perhaps the most visible tip on the horizon. The recent revision of the ICC Statute to define the crime of aggression – "the supreme international crime" that "contains within itself the accumulated evil of the whole", to quote the International Military Tribunal at Nuremberg[71] – and include it in the ICC's jurisdiction, accentuates the need of a nuanced understanding of the past of international criminal law and its institutional practice. Where the limits of violence as crime and violence as use of force, beneficial if not sacred, are articulated in discourses of criminal justice, the past is increasingly present. It is then not only the spectres of the victims of crimes that "haunt us", as often cherished in rhetorical interventions. It is also the inherited and transmitted ideas and representations of the past engaged in a constant struggle of forgetting and remembering, haunting the political, ideological and cultural spaces where the concept of international criminal law is resorted to today.[72] Histories thus matter also because the construction of memories by international criminal law and the narration of international criminal justice and its actors as the moral backbone of "humanity" may have the tendency of obscuring how the ideas advocated by some powerful nations became the expression of "humanness", followed by cosmopolitan ideology turning that particular kind of "humanity" into the central principle in an imaginary global civil society. The terms and conditions of membership and governance of that society or the

---

[69] See Maurice Halbwachs, *La mémoire collective*, Albin Michel, Paris, 1997, in particular pp. 214–20.

[70] See Carl Schmitt, *Nomos of the Earth in the International Law of the Jus Publicum Europaeum*, Telos Press, New York, 2003, pp. 57–59.

[71] International Military Tribunal, *The United States of America et al. v. Hermann Wilhelm Goering et al.*, Judgment, 1 October 1946, in Office of United States Chief of Counsel, *Nazi Conspiracy and Aggression: Opinion and Judgment*, US Government Printing Office, Washington, DC, 1947, p. 16.

[72] On spectrality, see Jacques Derrida, *Spectres de Marx: l'état de la dette, le travail du deuil et la nouvelle internationale*, Galilée, Paris, 1993; Jacques Derrida and Bernard Stiegler, *Échographies de la télévision: Entretiens filmés*, Galilée, Paris, 1996.

distribution of power, wealth and happiness for the individuals living in it are not independent from the understanding of history.

TABLE OF CONTENTS

PART 2

A Critical Examination of Investigatory and
Prosecuratorial Efforts in the Aftermath of the First World War

PART 3

The Period Between the World Wars and Before Nuremberg and Tokyo

PART 4

Interdisciplinary Analysis of Nuremberg's Record and Legacy

1

Introduction:
Historical Origins of International Criminal Law

CHEAH Wui Ling[*] and CHOONG Xun Ning[**]

1.1. Introduction

International criminal law may be said to comprise "international rules" that declare "certain human behaviour punishable as crimes under international law".[1] These rules aim to protect the "basic values" of the international community as well as the individual, values that are well grounded in the international legal order and are reflected in universal legal instruments such as the United Nations Charter and the 1948 Universal Declaration of Human Rights.[2] The elaboration of these rules in various fora, and their implementation by different national and internationalised bodies, has resulted in an emerging international criminal justice system that is becoming more robust. Nevertheless international criminal law is still relatively young and undeveloped when compared to criminal legal systems at the national level. While we have come a long way, there is still much to be done to operationalise international criminal law in a way that fulfils its promises of accountability and justice.

---

[*] CHEAH Wui Ling is Assistant Professor at the Faculty of Law, National University of Singapore ('NUS'). She is a qualified lawyer, called to the New York Bar, and has a diploma in arbitration from Queen Mary, University of London. She holds LL.B. and LL.M. degrees from NUS, a LL.M. from Harvard University, and a Diploma from the Academy of European Law, European University Institute. She thanks Morten Bergsmo, Gareth Richards, Anna SU and ZHANG Binxin for their invaluable substantive feedback and the entire HOICL editorial team.

[**] CHOONG Xun Ning is currently training to qualify as a solicitor in London. She holds an LL.B. in Law with Transnational Legal Studies from King's College London, and won the Manches Prize for Family Law in 2013. Part of her degree includes a Diploma in Transnational Law from the Center for Transnational Legal Studies where she spent a year in 2011–2012.

[1] Otto Triffterer, "Preliminary Remarks: The Permanent International Criminal Court – Ideal and Reality", in Otto Triffterer (ed.), *Commentary on the Rome Statute of the International Criminal Court: Observers' Notes, Article by Article*, C.H. Beck, Hart and Nomos, Munich, 2008, p. 22.

[2] *Ibid.*

Indeed, as international criminal law passes from the stages of normative expansion and institutional design to that of strengthening institutions and practical implementation, more unforeseen problems and unintended results have come to light. This is to be expected of a rapidly growing field. More patience, knowledge and reflection are required. Some have responded by looking to the past to ask questions of the present.[3] The past may offer us solutions in a number of ways. It may show us that things were not always the way they are today. It may be a source of ideas.[4] Judges and practitioners may be able to mine historical records for legal building blocks and ideas. It may illuminate errors by showing that someone else in a similar situation in the past had chosen to act otherwise.[5] The past can also serve as a negative example and as a warning for the future. History may show us, for example, how the law has been used differently to address mass atrocities. Or we may find similarities with our present that surprise us. These historical events may also answer a host of non-legal questions. They may shed light on how mass atrocities develop and what can be done to stop them. They may also provide us with a window into the past, into how social relations were structured or into how people thought and behaved.[6]

International criminal law has experienced exponential growth since the 1990s. However, there is still much to learn about its origins, and about the historical events, processes and actors that will further our understanding of international criminal law's own history and

---

[3] Taking a more critical perspective, Martti Koskenniemi suggests that such looking to the past may be the result of the "disillusionment" with unfulfilled narratives of international law as some look to the past to understand how we arrived at the present. Martti Koskenniemi, "Histories of International Law: Significance and Problems for a Critical View", in *Temple International and Comparative Law Journal*, 2013, vol. 27, p. 216.

[4] Margaret MacMillan, *The Uses and Abuses of History*, Profile Books, London, 2010, p. 8.

[5] *Ibid.*, p. 22.

[6] Many historians have studied older trials with the aim of reconstructing individual personalities and recovering cultural understandings of the time. See, for example, Carlo Ginzburg, *The Cheese and the Worms: The Cosmos of a Sixteenth-Century Miller*, new ed., Johns Hopkins University Press, Baltimore, 2013; Natalie Zemon Davis, *Fiction in the Archives: Pardon Tales and Their Tellers in Sixteenth-Century France*, Stanford University Press, Stanford, 1987. Others have studied how the criminal law was used to structure social relations. Douglas Hay, "Property Authority and the Criminal Law", in Douglas Hay, Peter Linebaugh, John G. Rule, E.P. Thompson and Cal Winslow (eds.), *Albion's Fatal Tree: Crime and Society in Eighteenth-Century England*, Pantheon Books, New York, 1976, p. 25.

development.[7] What is conventionally articulated about the trajectory of international criminal law history is in reality quite recent in provenance. It usually begins with the Nuremberg and Tokyo Trials after the Second World War. It continues with the establishment of the *ad hoc* International Criminal Tribunal for the former Yugoslavia ('ICTY') and the International Criminal Tribunal for Rwanda in the 1990s. These well-known tribunals are placed alongside the development of hybrid or internationalised courts such as the Timor Leste Serious Crimes Panel, the Special Court for Sierra Leone and the Extraordinary Chambers in the Courts of Cambodia, as well as the rise in domestic prosecutions such as those in Latin America and the International Crimes Tribunal of Bangladesh. And finally, there is some kind of culminating point with the founding of the International Criminal Court ('ICC') in 2002.[8]

But this timeline does not, by any means, tell the whole story. In fact, the origins of international criminal law stretch far beyond the established consensus. For example, in the post-Second World War era hundreds of prosecutions were conducted by the Allied Powers and other national governments throughout Europe and Asia.[9] Despite the large number of trials that took place and the thousands of defendants

---

[7] In this chapter, "international criminal law history" refers to the developmental trajectory of international criminal law while "historical studies" refers to research on past events, processes and actors. The HOICL organisers have interpreted the term "origins" in a broad way, beyond the tracing of starting points or causes so as to avoid what Marc Bloch refers to as the "idol of origins". Marc Bloch, *The Historian's Craft*, Manchester University Press, Manchester, 1992, pp. 24–25.

[8] This conventional narrative of international criminal law history has been criticised by an increasing number of scholars from the critical legal studies tradition. See, for example, Immi Tallgren, "Foreword: Searching for the Historical Origins of International Criminal Law", *HOICL*, vol. 1, 2014, pp. xi–xxx; Sarah Nouwen, "Justifying Justice", in James Crawford and Martti Koskenniemi (eds.), *The Cambridge Companion to International Law*, Cambridge University Press, Cambridge, 2012, p. 328.

[9] For post-war national trials in Asia, the classic reference book by Philip Piccigallo offers a descriptive overview of the various trials. Philip R. Piccigallo, *The Japanese On Trial: Allied War Crimes Operations in the East, 1945–1951*, University of Texas Press, Austin, 2011. There is no such equivalent of trials conducted in Europe, though there are books that deal with groups of trials, such as the subsequent Nuremberg trials conducted by the US. See, for example, Kevin Jon Heller, *The Nuremberg Military Tribunals and the Origins of International Criminal Law*, Oxford University Press, Oxford, 2011; Alexa Stiller and Kim C. Priemel (eds.), *Reassessing the Nuremberg Military Tribunals: Transitional Justice, Trial Narratives, and Historiography*, Berghahn Books, New York, 2012.

prosecuted, we still do not know very much about these post-war trials, though there is now some belated awareness of their existence and even their significance. The international legal community has become cognisant of the fact that the Nuremberg and Tokyo Trials were not the only tribunals organised after the Second World War. In the 1990s, for example, judges at the ICTY drew attention to some post-war national trials by referring to them as evidence of customary international law.[10] The judges' usage of these historical trials underscored how the latter may have an immediate present-day relevance for both practitioners and academics. Curiosity about less well-known historical trials was piqued and research projects were initiated. There have been conferences and publications focusing on these trials and "hidden histories".[11] There has also been more cross-disciplinary exchange between historians, political scientists and lawyers, among others, working in this area.

This *Historical Origins of International Criminal Law* (*'HOICL'*) anthology, published as a trilogy of volumes, has been designed to appeal to practitioners, policy-makers and academics with an interest in international criminal law history. It approaches historical trials and processes from different perspectives, and its contributors comprise judges, government officials, lawyers and researchers from diverse disciplines. Here we first set out the scope and objectives of the *HOICL* anthology and explain their importance. In doing so, we highlight the demand for detailed and empirically based research encouraged by the HOICL project. Second, we give an overview of the innovative research tools available to students of international criminal law history, specifically the ICC Legal Tools Database ('LTD'). We elaborate on how the LTD gives free-of-charge access to an online library containing historical records via the ICC's website. The third part then offers an overview of the different chapters presented in this anthology. This illustrates the broad range of research questions, perspectives and

---

10 Commentators have discussed and criticised judicial deployment of these historical cases as international law sources, arguing that these trials do not have much precedential value because of their lack of reasoned judgments, among others. See David Cohen, "The Historiography of the Historical Foundations of Theories of Responsibility in International Criminal Law", *HOICL*, vol. 1, 2014, pp. 23–83; Marco Sassòli and Laura M. Olson, "The Judgment of the ICTY Appeals Chamber on the Merits in the Tadic Case", in *International Review of the Red Cross*, 2000, vol. 82, p. 733.

11 Kevin Jon Heller and Gerry Simpson (eds.), *The Hidden Histories of War Crimes Trials*, Oxford University Press, Oxford, 2013.

methodologies employed by selected *HOICL* contributors. Finally, we appraise some of the challenges faced in organising the HOICL as a research project and the implementation of its next phase.

1.2. Scope and Objectives of the *HOICL* Anthology

The HOICL project aims for a comprehensive and critical mapping of international criminal law's origins. Two conferences were organised. The first took place in Hong Kong on 1–2 March 2014. Papers presented at this conference and some others specially commissioned are published in Volumes 1 and 2 of the trilogy. The second conference took place in New Delhi on 29–30 November 2014. Papers from that conference are published in Volume 3 of the trilogy.

The majority of today's historical studies in international criminal law focus on trials. The HOICL project expands on this by surveying "trials, treaty provisions, national laws, declarations or other acts of States, and publications [constituting] the significant building blocks of contemporary international criminal law, and why that is so". By bringing together these foundation stones of international criminal law, the HOICL project seeks to "to explore and crystallise a sub-discipline of history of international criminal law" and its "vertical consolidation – an increased awareness and knowledge of the historical and intellectual foundations" (HOICL 1 website).[12] It also intends to ask "critical questions about the substance, process, and institutional roots of international criminal law" (HOICL 2 website).[13]

The HOICL organisers have sought to pursue these objectives in an inclusive and representative way, and to challenge how international criminal law history is usually depicted in Eurocentric and narrow terms by "going beyond the geographical, cultural, and temporal limits set by traditional narratives of international criminal law and justice".[14] Accordingly, the organisers made efforts to include researchers from different countries and diverse legal traditions. They also reached out to researchers from different academic disciplines and schools of thought.

---

[12] For the Hong Kong Conference and project description, see http://www.fichl. org/activities/the-historical-origins-of-international-criminal-law/.

[13] For the New Delhi Conference and project description, see http://www.fichl. org/activities/the-historical-origins-of-international-criminal-law-seminar-2/.

[14] *Ibid.*

By incorporating such a wide range of positions and methodologies, the HOICL project hopes to generate "new knowledge" and broaden international criminal law's "hinterland" beyond the boundaries of what is presently known about its origins.[15]

In addition, the HOICL project aims to promote the importance of methodological rigour in historical international criminal law research. Professional standards distinguish between historical interpretations that are creative or unexpected and those that stretch or distort the evidence. International criminal law histories should be evaluated based on their treatment of evidence and their interpretation, "the twin pillars of historical knowledge".[16] Historical methods call for the testing of evidence to ensure its authenticity and that interpretation should be guided by evidence.[17] While one's interpretative standpoint may influence the selection of evidence and how this evidence is to be understood, this does not mean that all interpretations are possible or that all histories produced are equal. All writers of history acknowledge this and use different "stylistic devices" to indicate how strong or weak their arguments are.[18] The careful researcher recognises when her historical sources are incomplete, states what may be proved, and acknowledges what may only be speculated.

The HOICL project also aspires to build an academic community of excellence composed of practitioners and academics, represented by both established and early career researchers. The organisers hope to encourage constructive debate between practitioners and scholars, and between academic tribes. We believe that this collective aspect of research leads to a qualitative improvement of the research output. The HOICL project is committed to encouraging respectful academic discussion among its contributors from different countries and cultures. Histories are influenced by not only the research questions chosen but also the author's own beliefs, assumptions and context; the author herself

---

[15] Hong Kong Conference and project description, see *supra* note 12.
[16] Michael Stanford, *An Introduction to the Philosophy of History*, Blackwell, Oxford, 1997, p. 62.
[17] Peter Kosso, "Philosophy of Historiography", in Aviezer Tucker (ed.), *A Companion to the Philosophy of History and Historiography*, Blackwell, Oxford, 2010, p. 62.
[18] Richard J. Evans, *In Defence of History*, Granta, London, 2001, p. 108.

is a "social phenomenon".[19] Academic debates should be conducted in a way that respects different scholarly traditions and practices. It is the organisers' intention for the HOICL project to stimulate discussion, co-operation and contention among researchers. This is clear from the range of positions taken by contributors in the *HOICL* anthology. As observed by the eminent historian Sir John Baker, we "never produce final answers" but only help "take the general understanding forward".[20]

Some may argue against the clear objectives adopted by HOICL and for more sceptical or open-ended approaches that avoid "a common mission" and take "multiple, interdisciplinary and hazardous new routes".[21] The organisers believe that for a project with the HOICL's ambition of subject matter and inclusion, it is necessary to have well-defined objectives. Replacing specific research objectives with open-ended ones will not resolve the problem of researcher bias vis-à-vis evidence and interpretation. In history, it has long been recognised that it is impossible for a researcher to approach her sources with no preconceptions or assumptions. Whether we are aware of it or not, we also want to use the past to meet our objectives.[22] Certainty in research objectives and methodological rigour is also particularly important given the little we know about international criminal law's origins. All projects, especially those venturing into undiscovered and expansive spaces, must have a starting point. If the "past is foreign country", a provisional map will be helpful as long as it does not restrict a traveller to its well-worn trails, allows for detours and diversions, and remains open to revision as the journey exposes more fruitful pathways.[23]

1.3. Facilitating International Criminal Law Historical Studies: Access to Sources and Research Tools

The HOICL project and the study of international criminal law history are made possible, in part, due to researchers having enhanced access to

---

[19] E.H. Carr, *What Is History?: The George Macaulay Trevelyan Lectures Delivered in the University of Cambridge*, new ed., Penguin, London, 1990, p. 35.

[20] Sir John Baker, "Reflections on 'Doing' Legal History", in Anthony Musson and Chantal Stebbings (eds.), *Making Legal History: Approaches and Methodologies*, Cambridge University Press, Cambridge, 2012, p. 16.

[21] Tallgren, "Foreword", 2014, pp. xxvi, see *supra* note 8.

[22] Evans, 2001, p. 192, see *supra* note 18.

[23] L.P. Hartley, *The Go-Between*, ed. by Douglas Brooks-Davies, Penguin, London, 2004, p. 1.

historical sources and research tools. Until recently, the archival records of many historical trials could not be easily accessed. Original trial records are housed in public and private archives, but visiting these archives and locating the records within them are challenging. A researcher would have to secure funding for the travel and time needed to conduct such research. These resources are not easily available, especially to researchers from developing countries. It is worth noting that the original records of many historical trials continue to be held in archives located in countries that initiated the trials rather than in countries where the trials actually took place. For example, a researcher from Malaysia undertaking research on war crimes trials conducted by the British in Malaya after the war would have to travel the United Kingdom National Archives in Kew to get access to the original trial records. To overcome these difficulties, a number of research centres have undertaken the copying, collection, collation and organisation of trial records. However, these efforts are usually narrow in compass, which is understandable given the enormous documentation generated by the trials. They focus on trials conducted during a limited time period, by a particular authority or in a specific region. Even when broadly based efforts are undertaken, copies of these records can only be accessed at these research centres which are predominantly located in North America and Europe.

The ICC's Legal Tools Project ('LTP') has irrevocably changed the research landscape. It provides access without any fee to a comprehensive collection of historical records through its Legal Tools Database ('LTD') on the ICC's website.[24] Among the thousands of documents it houses, the LTD contains full transcripts of the Tokyo Trial and legal discussions at the United Nations War Crimes Commission ('UNWCC'). It also contains key legal documents on post-Second World War national trials conducted throughout Europe and Asia. The LTD holds not only historical records but also an up-to-date digitised collection of contemporary international criminal law trials and legal instruments as well as academic commentaries. This accessible and growing online library, which comes equipped with a powerful search engine, has been made possible by the LTP's ongoing collaboration with various research centres and universities around the world.

---

[24] For a list of the centres and entities the ICC LTD works with, see http://www.legal-tools.org/en/work-on-the-tools/table-of-responsibilities/.

The sheer scope of the LTD clearly advances the right to scientific knowledge and enables researchers located anywhere in the world to inspect a thorough range of legal sources as long as they have internet access. [25] Educators, students and interested individuals are able to download primary historical sources directly from the LTD. In addition to facilitating research, the historical records stored in the LTD remain deeply relevant to and may change the direction of contemporary debates. The conflicts addressed by these records may have their genesis in the past but – as demonstrated by delayed prosecutions, civil litigation and victim reparations programmes – their repercussions resonate today.[26]

By increasing the access of researchers to these historical records, the LTD will hopefully facilitate more high-calibre research. Researchers studying such records have already pursued a variety of research questions. Some studies by legal scholars ask how historical materials may be used to address present-day legal questions, a tendency also shared by lawyers analysing domestic historical sources.[27] For example, legal commentators have observed that the UNWCC records may offer valuable evidence of customary international law.[28] Others ask what non-legal lessons may be learnt from historical trials and events. Even when there are no positive lessons, history may teach us what should be avoided. [29] Other researchers aim to determine the "pedigree" of international criminal law in answering the question of how the international criminal law system developed. [30] Researchers have also studied historical trials and processes to answer questions not directly

---

[25] For an assessment of the LTD's services through a human rights perspective, see generally, Alf Butenschøn Skre and Asbjørn Eide, "The Human Right to Benefit from Advances in Science and Promotion of Openly Accessible Publications", in *Nordic Journal of Human Rights*, 2013, vol. 31, no. 3, p. 450.

[26] Nina H.B. Jørgensen and Danny Friedmann, "Enforced Prostitution in International Law through the prism of the Dutch temporary courts martial at Batavia", in *HOICL*, vol. 2, 2014, pp. 331–54.

[27] Anthony Musson and Chantal Stebbings, "Introduction" in Anthony Musson and Chantal Stebbings (eds.), *Making Legal History: Approaches and Methodologies*, Cambridge University Press, Cambridge, 2012, p. 5.

[28] Richard Goldstone, "United Nations War Crimes Commission Symposium", in *Criminal Law Forum*, 2014, vol. 25, p. 12.

[29] Neil Boister and Robert Cryer, *The Tokyo International Military Tribunal: A Reappraisal*, Oxford University Press, Oxford, 2008, p. 2.

[30] Gerry Simpson, "History of Histories", in Heller and Simpson, 2013, p. 5, see *supra* note 11.

related to the law. Some of these studies illuminate how trials forget or sideline victims.[31] Some scholars review historical trials for their "counter-histories", especially when these were previously suppressed by the state.[32] All these efforts expand international criminal law's geographical and temporal origins in a thoughtful way. The HOICL project builds on these endeavours and pursues similarly varied research directions.

1.4. Striving for Diversity: Volumes 1 and 2 of the *HOICL* Trilogy

In keeping with the project's inclusive spirit, chapters in Volumes 1 and 2 of the *HOICL* trilogy present a variety of perspectives. Some have direct repercussions for legal practitioners. David Cohen criticises how contemporary tribunals have used historical cases in ways that do not comply with international law requirements.[33] His rigorous legal analysis casts doubt on how legal practitioners and commentators try to find different ways of using historical sources as precedent. Other authors seek to change the way we understand historical events or actors. Quite a few elaborate on the work and role of non-Western actors with the aim of changing international criminal law's Eurocentric predisposition.[34] Others critically challenge our common perception of certain events or actors. Neil Boister, for example, argues that the Tokyo Trial's popular perception as "victor's justice" cannot stand scrutiny as its truly enduring legacy lies in its judicial dissent and "off-message voices", while Milinda Banerjee reinterprets Judge Radhabinod Pal's well-known dissenting opinion at Tokyo in natural law terms in light of his Indian intellectual background. [35]

Some chapters deal with trials or issues that have yet to be studied in detail. For some historical trials, filling in the gaps may be all that

---

[31] Narrelle Morris, "Justice for 'Asian' Victims: The Australian War Crimes Trials of the Japanese, 1945–51", in Heller and Simpson, see *supra* note 11.

[32] Simpson, 2013, p. 5, see *supra* note 30.

[33] Cohen, 2014, see *supra* note 10.

[34] Anja Bihler, "Late Republican China and the Development of International Criminal Law: China's role in the United Nations War Crimes Commission in London and Chungking", in *HOICL*, vol. 1, 2014, pp. 507–40.

[35] Neil Boister, "The Tokyo Military Tribunal: A Show Trial?" in *HOICL*, vol. 2, 2014, pp. 3–29; Milinda Banerjee, "Does International Criminal Justice Require a Sovereign? Historicising Radhabinod Pal's Tokyo Judgment in Light of his 'Indian' Legal Philosophy", in *HOICL*, vol. 2, 2014, pp. 67–117.

researchers are able to do at this point of the research process. Primary sources have only just been located and even then they are not complete. For example, researchers still do not have access to the complete records of post-Second World War trials in China and there can be more secondary material on these trials.[36] Many researchers are in the initial stages of familiarising themselves with recently located sources to see what questions these sources reveal.[37] Their chapters in the *HOICL* anthology will facilitate the deeper analysis that should be undertaken in the future.

A multicultural perspective is employed by a number of authors in their analysis. Guido Acquaviva explains how commentators have ignored the different linguistic versions of the Nuremberg Judgment and the consequences of this oversight.[38] Through her case study of a post-Second World War trial in Singapore, CHEAH Wui Ling underscores how these trials failed to accommodate its participants' linguistic and cultural differences and how this ultimately undermined their legitimacy. Other authors tackle the darker side of international criminal law.[39] Mark Drumbl notes how the Polish trials were also used to persecute opponents in the post-war political settlement.[40] Immi Tallgren argues that the Finnish trials should be best understood as a form of sacrifice.[41] These authors openly challenge the heroic conceptualisation of war crimes trials. Other chapters point to how historical trials were deployed for various political purposes and, as a result, they problematise the trial as international criminal law's basic structural unit. We expect more of this kind of analysis in the third volume of this anthology, which includes thematic streams such as transitional justice and human rights.

---

[36] Longwan XIANG and Marquise Lee HOULE, "In Search of Justice for China: The Contributions of Judge Hsiang Che-chun to the Prosecution of Japanese War Criminals at the Tokyo Trial", in *HOICL*, vol. 2, 2014, pp. 143–175.

[37] Baker, 2012, p. 7, see *supra* note 20.

[38] Guido Acquaviva, "Doubts about *Nullen Crimen* and Superior Orders: Language Discrepancies in the Nuremberg Judgment and their Significance", in *HOICL*, vol. 1, 2014, pp. 597–622.

[39] CHEAH Wui Ling, "Post-Second World War British Trials in Singapore: Lost in Translation at the Car Nicobar Spy Case", in *HOICL*, vol. 2, 2014, pp. 301–30.

[40] Mark A. Drumbl, "The Supreme National Tribunal of Poland and the History of International Criminal Law", in *HOICL*, vol. 2, 2014, pp. 563–601.

[41] Immi Tallgren, "Martyrs and Scapegoats of the Nation? The Finnish War-Responsibility Trial, 1945–1946", in *HOICL*, vol. 2, 2014, pp. 493–538.

How should such varied chapters be presented in an anthology? To fully represent the diversity of research conducted in line with the HOICL project's objectives it was necessary to organise two conferences and produce three volumes. The editors took care to choose a structure that would avoid reproducing conventional narratives of international criminal law history that have been criticised for being narrow, restricting and incomplete. By organising the chapters chronologically, in Volumes 1 and 2 of the *HOICL* anthology, and by crime and thematically, as mainly done in Volume 3, the editors hope to avoid imposing any preconceived narrative structure. A chronological approach whose reach would be determined by the suggested topics of authors responding to our call for papers is more inclusive, unlike an institution-based timeline that may replicate the traditional international criminal law narrative by spotlighting certain bodies to the exclusion of others.

In doing so we incorporated chapters that reach back before the twentieth century's two world wars such as LIU Daqun's contribution on China's Spring and Autumn period and Geoffrey Robertson's reconstruction of the 1649 trial of Charles I.[42] To avoid replicating the linearity of traditional international criminal law history the organisers brought in chapters that would disrupt its 'flow' or conventional wisdom through their critical questioning of the propaganda function, clumsy implementation or fundamental fairness of specific trials and processes. Chapters underscoring the trials organised by Central and Eastern European and Asian governments, the role of non-Western judges and jurists and the experiences of trial participants introduce multiple voices from the periphery into the landscape of international criminal law history.

1.4.1. An Overview of *HOICL* Chapter Contributions

In Chapter 2, David Cohen traces the use of historical case law by contemporary courts in the development of international criminal law. In particular, he explores how international and domestic courts and tribunals have sought to establish theories of responsibility in the absence of adequate case law. In doing so, Cohen examines in detail the corpus of

---

[42] LIU Daqun, "International Law and International Humanitarian Law in Ancient China", in *HOICL*, vol. 1, pp. 87–113; Geoffrey Robertson QC, "The Tyrannicide Brief", in *HOICL*, vol. 1, 2014, pp. 115–40.

case law and discussions that these tribunals have produced, and concludes that while the work is too inconsistent to be "customary" law, they provide a rich "intellectual resource" for future development of international criminal law.

Part 1 then starts by challenging the commonly accepted beginnings of international criminal law history by looking further back than the Nuremberg and Tokyo Trials. In Chapter 3 LIU Daqun looks to the Spring and Autumn period of Chinese history from 771 to 221 BC, drawing attention to the cultural and political uniqueness of this era and shows the existence of international law and international humanitarian law in "agreements and treaties, regulations and law, customs of usages, and in the works of philosophers and military leaders". In Chapter 4 Geoffrey Robertson analyses the 1649 trial of Charles I in England as the first time a head of state's absolute authority was challenged through prosecution. He stresses how the problem of what to do with a convicted head of state continues today, with similar dilemmas faced by the organisers of the trials of Slobodan Milošević and Saddam Hussein. In Chapter 5 SHI Bei, ZENG Siqi and ZHANG Qi discuss the role played by China in the development of international criminal law after the Second World War through its participation in the UNWCC and the Far Eastern and Pacific Sub-Commission in Chungking ('Sub-Commission'), as well as its role in the drafting of the Universal Declaration of Human Rights. They argue that Chinese contributions reflect the influence of Confucian philosophy.

Part 2 looks at the First World War period and its aftermath, seldom covered in depth by mainstream accounts. In Chapter 6 Jackson N. Maogoto examines the debates that took place at the 1919 Commission on the Responsibilities of the Authors of War and on Enforcement of Penalties on the question of whether or not there should be international trials. He outlines the difference between the Anglo-French position and the US-Japanese position, and analyses how tensions between the Allied Powers undermined prosecutorial efforts. In Chapter 7 Kirsten Sellars links the debates that took place at the 1919 Paris Peace Conference to those surrounding the creation of the Nuremberg Tribunal. She illustrates how arguments used at Nuremberg were in fact not original and emphasises the significance of post-First World War debates that informed later deliberations.

In Chapter 8 Paul Mevis and Jan Reijntjes consider the question of what would have happened if the Allied Tribunal had tried Kaiser

Wilhelm II after the First World War. The authors examine the challenges this trial, if it had taken place, might have encountered. Ultimately, they conclude that even if the Kaiser had been tried before the Allied Tribunal this might not have changed history or prevented the Second World War. In Chapter 9 Joseph Rikhof provides a broad overview of the Istanbul and Leipzig trials that took place after the First World War. By analysing individual trials in detail, he suggests that many common perceptions of them are not entirely accurate and that they deserve more credit than they have usually been given.

The next three chapters take a closer look at the Leipzig trials and the Istanbul trials. In Chapter 10 Wolfgang Form takes us through the Leipzig trials from debates at the Paris Peace Conference to the trials themselves and their outcomes. He indicates that the trials were ineffective and a thorough "farce" in light of the regulations employed, the sentences handed down, the protection of military forces and their obvious function as a form of "masked diplomacy". Matthias Neuner also analyses the Leipzig trials in Chapter 11. He indicates a number of the trials' positive features such as their elaboration of law. Nevertheless, he also shows how time and again the Leipzig trials served as a form of symbolic justice aimed at appeasing the victors of the war. In Chapter 12 Lina Laurinaviciute, Regina M. Paulose and Ronald G. Rogo discuss the Armenian genocide in 1915 and the trials that took place following the war. The authors argue that these trials had a significant role in shaping modern international law and that this fact will become more evident with time.

Part 3 analyses the lead-up to the Nuremberg and Tokyo Trials. In Chapter 13 Anatoly Levshin revisits two common answers to the question of when the crime of aggressive war first came about: at the London Conference on Military Trials or at the Review Conference of the Rome Statute of the ICC in Kampala in 2010. By examining historical records alongside empirical evidence, he argues that the crime of aggressive war was first created in 1945, but only became a fully realised norm in 2010. In Chapter 14 Dan Plesch and Shanti Sattler explore the frequently overlooked work of the UNWCC. They systematically set out the UNWCC's history, structure and member contributions, and make a call for further research into the work of this significant institution.

The next two contributions continue the assessment of the work of the UNWCC through the perspective of specific concepts and actors. In

Chapter 15 Kerstin von Lingen examines the UNWCC debates on crimes against humanity and highlights the role of the Czech representatives Bohuslav Ečer and Egon Schwelb. In Chapter 16 Anja Bihler scrutinises China's participation in the UNWCC in London and the Sub-Commission in Chungking, and focuses in particular on the criticism China faced in relation to the state of its municipal law and its competency in the international legal field. She proposes that appreciating China's contribution to the UNWCC may revise the perception of international criminal law as Eurocentric. In Chapter 17 Kirsten Sellars scrutinises the lively and sometimes contentious debates that took place at the 1945 London Conference in preparation for the International Military Tribunal at Nuremberg, most crucially on whether individuals could be held personally responsible for crimes of war under international law.

The chapters in Part 4 survey the Nuremberg Trial's legacy from multidisciplinary perspectives. In Chapter 18 David S. Koller traces the discursive legacy of the Nuremberg Trials and asks why the Tokyo Trial or other domestic trials have not left a similar impact. In Chapter 19 Guido Acquaviva probes the major language discrepancies between the Russian, French and English versions of the Nuremberg Judgment and suggests that if these three versions were appreciated together, we would have a better grasp of the Judgment itself. Axel Fischer draws on media and literary studies in Chapter 20 to scrutinise the legacy of the American Nuremberg Trial Film Project which undertook a comprehensive film and photographic documentation of the proceedings, intended both for German and international consumption. In doing so, he draws out the long-term effects of the films for legal politics in Germany after the fall of the Berlin Wall.

Following the discussion of the Nuremberg Trials, Part 5 turns attention to the Tokyo Trial and subsequent trials in Japan from different perspectives. In Chapter 21 Neil Boister addresses the criticism of international criminal trials, and particularly the Tokyo Trial, as "show trials". He admits that there is much to substantiate this critique but submits that if the Tokyo Trial were a show trial it was not a successful one. Indeed, its legacy lies largely in the dissent of some judges and the disillusioned voices of other actors which fatally undermine the notion of a true show trial. In Chapter 22 Yuma Totani brings to light two trials conducted after the Tokyo Trial: the Tamura and Toyoda trials. She shows how these trials drew on the Tokyo Trial but also demonstrated contrasting understandings of Japanese culture and criminal law. She proposes that studying these trials deepens our knowledge of the broad range of judicial thinking involved in post-Second World War trials.

The next four chapters evaluate the Tokyo Trial through different national perspectives. In Chapter 23 Milinda Banerjee revisits the controversial judgment of Judge Radhabinod Pal at the Tokyo Trial. Banerjee challenges conventional readings of Pal's judgment and proposes a multifaceted interpretation that situates this judgment in the context of his deep understand of the precepts of Hindu law and of a burgeoning global justice. In Chapter 24 Ann-Sophie Schoepfel-Aboukrat turns our attention to France by examining the French position at both the Tokyo Trial and Saigon Trials. She probes little-used French archival material to determine the French war crimes trials policy, and argues that these trials had the function of redefining post-war nation building within France as well as on the world stage. In Chapter 25 Longwan XIANG and Marquise Lee HOULE document the contributions of the Chinese prosecutor HSIANG Che-chun at the Tokyo Trial. They describe the challenges faced by the Chinese prosecution team and Chinese attitudes towards post-war trials. Lisette Schouten, in Chapter 26, takes a close look at the career of the noted Judge B.V.A. Röling in international law and illustrates how participating in the Tokyo Trial shaped Röling's international law ideas and future efforts to advance them.

The chapters in Part 6 move us to the domestic trials of war criminals in China and countries in Southeast Asia. The first three chapters by LING Yan, Barak Kushner and ZHANG Tianshu address domestic trials of Japanese war criminals in China. In Chapter 27 LING recounts the 1956 trials of Japanese war criminals at the People's Republic of China's Special Military Tribunal. She argues that the prosecutions were generally successful as they reflected existing international criminal law, resulting in the genuine repentance and remorse of all the prosecuted Japanese, which went a long way to normalising post-war Sino–Japanese relations. In Chapter 28 Kushner compares the 1956 trials in China with the 1946–1949 trials organised by the Kuomintang Nationalist government. He situates these trials in the context of China's Civil War and examines Japanese reactions to China's prosecution and how the trials shaped Sino–Japanese relations in the early days of the Cold War. In Chapter 29 ZHANG then carries out a legal analysis of the Chinese trials and the extent to which they complied with and contributed to international criminal law by examining some high-profile cases in Nanjing and Shenyang.

In Chapter 30 CHEAH Wui Ling undertakes a case study of post-Second World War trials in Singapore through the Car Nicobar spy case. She analyses how the trial was plagued by extensive problems of interpretation and emphasises how cultural differences and language barriers can undermine international criminal trials. In Chapter 31 Nina H.B. Jørgensen and Danny Friedmann consider the crime of enforced prostitution committed against so-called "comfort women" during the Second World War and the judgments of the Temporary Courts Martial in Batavia. They draw attention to how this crime still contributes to ongoing tensions between Japan and other countries in the Asia-Pacific region. In Chapter 32 Narrelle Morris traces the dissemination of information on the war crimes prosecutions and investigations of Japanese in Australia. She explores the impact that information restrictions have had on Australian perceptions of war crime prosecutions and argues for more research to be undertaken on Australian war crimes policies that show these trials to be more credible than they have generally been acknowledged to be.

Part 7 moves the exploration of post-Second World War domestic prosecutions to Europe. In Chapter 33 Moritz Vormbaum investigates the German Democratic Republic's large-scale prosecution of crimes committed under National Socialist rule. He notes that though some of the laws enacted were based on international criminal law, the German national courts primarily used these laws for political and propaganda purposes. In Chapter 34 Christian Pöpken then analyses the role of the German Supreme Court in the British Zone of occupation and outlines the institutional and historical factors crucial to the formation of the Court as well as its reasoned judgments that would be referred to by future tribunals such as the ICTY.

In Chapter 35 Ditlev Tamm compares and contrasts the Danish and Norwegian experiences, both having been occupied by Germany during the Second World War. He argues how different occupation experiences subsequently influenced domestic trials and how, more generally, judges struggled to apply international law. In Chapter 36 Immi Tallgren explores the Finnish war-responsibility trials that have not been recognised globally but have had a lasting and substantial impact on Finnish self-definition. She posits the interesting idea that for the accused a trial for war crimes may be a form of "sacrifice", one that can play a role in redefining collective narratives and memories of the past. In Chapter 37 Valentyna Polunina introduces us to the widely dismissed Soviet prosecution of Japanese bacteriological war crimes tribunal in Khabarovsk, why these trials were organised by the Soviet Union and, significantly, why they have generally been dismissed as a contribution to international criminal law.

The next three chapters study the often-overlooked trials undertaken under the auspices of the National Tribunal of Poland ('SNT'). In Chapter 38 Mark A. Drumbl focuses on the trials of Rudolf Höss and Amon Göth. He considers the SNT's effectiveness in demonstrating the extent of Polish suffering during the Second World War and its substantial contributions to international criminal law jurisprudence. In Chapter 39 Patrycja Grzebyk assesses some of the broader accomplishments of the SNT, including the fact that it was arguably the first institution to recognise the biological and cultural dimensions of the crime of genocide and helped to identify theories of responsibility that have shaped modern international law principles such as superior responsibility. In Chapter 40 Marcin Marcinko inspects the *actus reus* of the crime of genocide particularly in the indictments of Greiser, Göth and Höss before the SNT. He argues that the SNT was ahead of its time by showing how many of its judgments correspond with modern perceptions of genocide and how its recognition of genocide had a culturally embedded element.

In Chapter 41 Veronika Bílková undertakes a comparative study of post-Second World War national trials in Czechoslovakia, Yugoslavia and the Soviet Union. She examines differences between these trials and the rather perfunctory consequences they had in the development of international criminal law. In spite of this, she notes the importance of further study of these trials in aiding both the reconciliation process in the region and in providing a benchmark against which the development of international criminal law can be measured. In Chapter 42 Tamás Hoffmann looks at justice as administered by the Hungarian People's Tribunals. He considers the influence of new concepts of the crime of aggression and crimes against humanity on existing Hungarian war crimes law, and their application by the People's Tribunals. In doing so, he challenges the prevailing belief that these People's Tribunals were mere political tools aimed at purging war criminals from Hungarian society. Instead, he suggests that though the People's Tribunals were definitely flawed they did draw on and follow prevailing international criminal law and jurisprudence.

1.5. The Next Phase of HOICL: Challenges Encountered and Moving Forward

Volumes 1 and 2 of the *HOICL* trilogy study a range of international criminal law trials, institutions and actors up to the period after the Second World War. Taken together they provide us with a more comprehensive account of events, actors and processes that may have been obscured by the overwhelming importance afforded to the major trials at Nuremberg and Tokyo or key individuals found in conventional accounts of international criminal law history. More research needs to be undertaken, as underlined by many authors, which builds on the findings presented in this trilogy. This will undoubtedly add further detail and depth to what we already know about these events, processes and actors. We hope that readers will be surprised at the international criminal law topography revealed in the first two volumes of the *HOICL* trilogy. Volume 3 examines the evolution of more contemporary institutions, crimes and legal concepts. Contributors also employ thematic frames of enquiry, such as human rights and transitional justice. We set out below some preliminary observations based on our experiences in the preparation of Volumes 1 and 2 and indicate some possible directions to advance the research project.

1.5.1. Overcoming Language and Research Barriers

The HOICL organisers sought to include diverse voices and perspectives from different countries throughout the HOICL process. Particular attention was given to those who may otherwise be overlooked for linguistic or cultural reasons. In doing so we encountered challenges that signal a deeper problem that results from English being the dominant global language of research. The LTD has already enabled researchers from less wealthy institutions or countries to freely access legal records. However, scholars who have not trained at Anglo-American institutions or who do not have English as their working language may encounter research barriers beyond simple access to legal sources.[43] English has

---

[43]   Koskenniemi, 2013, p. 222, see *supra* note 3.

become the lingua franca of research. That much is clear. Though there are important benefits to having a common working language, linguistic ability risks being mistaken for research capacity. It is not only linguistic difficulties that stand in the way of some scholars but also the inability to employ the rhetorical devices, stylistic flourishes or modes of argument expected by native English-speaking researchers. The difficulties faced by scholars who are non-native English speakers or those from developing countries are supported by empirical research. [44] A researcher's publication success depends on her ability to frame arguments in a way that is commonly accepted by publishers and peer reviewers in the West.[45] Non-native English-speaking researchers find the drafting of the rhetorical parts of a journal article, such as its introduction, particularly difficult.[46] Despite this, many international law journals advise authors to have their articles professionally copy-edited prior to submission, though the cost of expert services is beyond the reach of many scholars from developing countries.

Indeed, to be a successful international law researcher, scholars require many skills not directly related to the quality or persuasiveness of their ideas, such as how to make conference presentations, how to network on the international stage and how to write funding proposals. Not every researcher is able to compete in this manner at the international level. The international law research community needs to pay more attention to these matters given international law's aspirations to inclusivity and representativeness.

---

[44] See, for example, Carmen Pérez-Llantada, Ramón Plo and Gibson R. Ferguson, "'You Don't Say What You Know, Only What You Can': The Perceptions and Practices of Senior Spanish Academics Regarding Research Dissemination in English", in *English for Specific Purposes*, vol. 30, no. 1, 2011, p. 18; Françoise Salager-Meyer, "Scientific Publishing in Developing Countries: Challenges for the Future", in *Journal of English for Academic Purposes*, 2008, vol. 7, p. 121; Theresa Lillis and Mary Jane Curry, "Professional Academic Writing by Multilingual Scholars Interactions with Literacy Brokers in the Production of English-Medium Texts", in *Written Communication*, 2006, vol. 23, p. 3. For a preliminary analysis of the situation in international law, see Freya Baetens and CHEAH Wui Ling, "Being an International Law Lecturer in the 21st Century: Where Tradition Meets Innovation", in *Cambridge Journal of International and Comparative Law*, 2013, vol. 2, pp. 1000–3.

[45] Pérez-Llantada, Plo and Ferguson, 2011, p. 24, see *supra* note 44.

[46] *Ibid.*

1.5.2. Building on the Traditions and Methods of History

The study and analysis of international criminal law's origins is in its early stages. Maintaining close links with and learning from history, as an established and rich academic discipline, will only strengthen its own research agenda. The insights and methodologies of different historical schools – social history, cultural history, intellectual history, global history, post-colonial history, the *longue durée*, and more besides – can all serve as fruitful streams of inspiration and engagement. More importantly, the accumulated knowledge in this diverse historiography serves as a theoretical and critical base for future work on the origins of international criminal law. This is important to ensure that international criminal law historical studies proceed with methodological rigour and produce responsible scholarship. The past has demonstrated the dangers of careless or inaccurate historical work and its abuse. However this will not be a one-way street. Researchers on international criminal law's origins will also contribute theoretical and methodological findings to history which will, in turn, be built upon by historians working on other topics. This is a distinct possibility. The study of international criminal law's origins has already attracted researchers from different disciplinary backgrounds. For example, the chapter contributors in these volumes draw on the theory and methods of various disciplines, such as history, political science, social science and anthropology. Such cross-disciplinary fertilisation will enrich the international criminal law field as well as that of history itself.

The academic exchange and debate made possible by the different disciplinary and cultural backgrounds of contributors to these volumes is exciting but also requires much generosity and humility. Different cultures and academic traditions shape a researcher's work and practices. If we are patient enough to listen and learn from each other, such a rich exchange can shape the field in important ways. It can lead to a more inclusive and shared understanding of how to do historical research. It can also lead to more representative construction and comprehension of international criminal law's origins.[47]

---

[47] Such an approach may be compared to Onuma Yasuaki's proposal of adopting of a "trancivilizational perspective" in the field of human rights, one that encourages a reconceptualisation of substantive norms "from various perspectives of cultures, religions and civilizations". Onuma Yasuaki, *A Transcivilizational Perspective on International Law:*

The writing of history – or rather the *interpretation* of history – has always been contentious. This holds true for the origins of international criminal law. Many scholars were involved in advocating the establishment of the ICC, so it was perhaps inevitable that overly idealistic and sanguine historical narratives of international criminal law's development were advanced. As international criminal law's evident weaknesses and failures become more apparent, and as researchers look to its history to better understand miscarriages of justice, it is only appropriate that international criminal law's earlier narratives are subjected to re-examination and more critical renderings. The organisers hope that the HOICL project, through its findings and community, will stimulate even more curiosity and research undertakings that deepen our appreciation of international criminal law's origins.

Questioning Prevalent Cognitive Frameworks in the Emerging Multi-Polar and Multi-Civilizational World of the Twenty-First Century, Martinus Nijhoff, Leiden, 2010, p. 409.

2

The Historiography of the Historical Foundations of Theories of Responsibility in International Criminal Law

David Cohen[*]

2.1. Introduction

In thinking about historical foundations let us begin by not approaching this issue from the standpoint of a scholar or historian of international criminal law looking back and asking what were the foundations of doctrines like joint criminal enterprise ('JCE') or the responsibility of civilian officials/ superiors. Instead of merely asking whether JCE actually did have a customary law foundation, let us ask why judges in the Second World War era would have thought they needed a doctrine like JCE in the first place. Why, in other words, would the standard panoply of criminal law theories of responsibility not be sufficient? This, we will see, is an issue that created difficulty for the judges of the Second World War era tribunals, who were confronted with the unprecedented task of establishing the criminal responsibility of individuals, for crimes perpetrated by states trying to systematically implement decisions made at the national policy level.

In this respect there are similarities in the standpoint of a judge at the Nuremberg Military Tribunals ('NMT') or, half a century later, a judge at the International Criminal Tribunal for the former Yugoslavia ('ICTY') or Rwanda ('ICTR'). The later judges, however, had a case law legacy to access, albeit a complex, contradictory and only partially accessible one. The Second World War era judges were in many ways making their way through a *terra incognita*. This helps to explain the wide variety of approaches adopted to deal with questions of responsibility, and also explains the equally wide variation in results reached in similar cases.

From the perspective of the Second World War cases, one of the most difficult problems facing judges and prosecutors was how to legally conceptualise the accountability of the multitude of individuals in a myriad of roles that made up what the Justice case judgment [1] characterised as a systematic government-organised programme of criminal activity that produced mass atrocities across an entire continent (in the case of Nazi Germany) or across the entire Asia-Pacific region (in the case of Imperial Japan).[2] As reflected in the composition of accused persons at the International Military Tribunal ('IMT') or in the organisations prosecuted in the Nuremberg Subsequent Proceedings, as Raul Hilberg definitively established,[3] the crimes of the Nazi regime were enabled by the participation and mobilisation of resources of an entire governmental apparatus, economy and society. Defendants below the highest policy levels ranged from bankers, architects, dentists, lawyers and accountants to middle-ranking ministerial officials in various branches of government, military commanders in various positions, public

---

[*] **David Cohen** is Professor of Law at the University of Hawaii, Professor in the Graduate School at UC Berkeley, WSD HANDA Visiting Professor of Human Rights and International Justice at Stanford University, and Distinguished Visiting Fellow at the Hoover Institution at Stanford University. The former Ancker Distinguished Professor for Humanities at UC Berkeley and Professor of Law and Social Thought, University of Chicago, he holds an honorary doctorate, University of Zurich, Faculty of Law. As Director of WSD HANDA Center for Human Rights and International Justice at Stanford University (encompassing the War Crimes Studies Program) and the Asian International Justice Initiative at the East-West Center, he directs human rights, rule of law, and international criminal law training, capacity building, outreach, and trial monitoring projects in Indonesia, Cambodia, Bangladesh, Timor Leste, Sierra Leone, and Rwanda. He has served as Expert Advisor to the Commission on Truth and Friendship of Indonesia and Timor Leste and is currently Advisor to the Human Rights Resource Centre for ASEAN, engaged in research projects on the rule of law, women's and children's rights, and business and human rights in ASEAN. His publications focus on war crimes trials and international criminal law issues from WWII to today. Professor Cohen holds a J.D. degree from the UCLA School of Law and a Ph.D. in classics/ancient history from Cambridge University. Cohen presented the 2014 Li Haopei Lecture on this topic.

[1] Nuremberg Military Tribunal, *United States of America v. Josef Altstoetter, et al.*, Case No. 3, Judgment, December 1947, in *Trials of War Criminals Before the Nuremberg Military Tribunals Under Control Council Law No. 10*, US Government Printing Office, vol. III ('Green Series') ("Justice case") (http://www.legal-tools.org/doc/04cdaf/).

[2] For the sake of convenience, cases such as the Justice case and others of the Nuremberg Subsequent Proceedings will be referred to by these commonly used appellations rather than the formal case name. For example, the High Command case will be referred to as such rather than as *U.S. v. von Leeb et al.* The Table of Cases at the end of this paper provides the full references.

[3] Raul Hilberg, *The Destruction of the European Jews*, 3rd rev. ed., Yale University Press, London, 2003.

---

health officials, judges, private businessmen and individuals who had waded through the blood and gore of mass killings on the Eastern Front.

While judges in some cases, like that of Yamashita, [4] or the Australian trials of high-ranking Japanese generals, were so ill-equipped (as non-lawyers) to deal with these issues that they seem to have failed to even realise their significance, other tribunals were well aware of the dilemmas they faced and the paucity of tools from domestic criminal law that they thought they had at their disposal. This is evidenced by how different tribunals, even within the same organisation, used different metaphors to try to capture the nature of individual responsibility within complex governmental bureaucracies. Were such individuals 'cogs' in a machine and, if so, were the 'cogs' responsible for what the machine did? Was an entire government merely a criminal enterprise and, if so, who below the creators and drivers of that enterprise were responsible for the crimes perpetrated in its name, often under cover of legality?

One tool that was ready to hand was the American doctrine of conspiracy. Although the majority at the Tokyo Trial ('Tokyo') [5] embraced it, it was not embraced by the president of the Tribunal, Sir William Webb. [6] The IMT judges also distanced themselves from its application along with a number of other tribunals such as the Justice case majority (see below). [7] Apart from whatever other difficulties it might pose, the conspiracy doctrine seemed to some to be too crude a tool for capturing responsibility, given the interplay between individuals within the massive bureaucracies, military and security institutions, and other entities that made state-sponsored crimes on such a scale possible.

Another tool provided by the Nuremberg Charter was the notion of membership in a criminal organisation as an independent substantive

---

[4]   US Military Commission, *US v. Yamashita Tomoyuki*, Case No. 21, Judicial Summary, 4 February 1946, US National Archives and and Records Administration (NARA) RG 331, Box 1663–1664 ("Yamashita case") (http://www.legal-tools.org/doc/c574e3/). See also US Supreme Court, *Yamashita v. Styer* (http://www.legal-tools.org/doc/dba2a3/).

[5]   International Military Tribunal for the Far East, *United States of America et al. v. Araki Sadao et al.*, Judgment, 1 November 1948 ("Tokyo Trial") (http://www.legal-tools.org/en/doc/09f24c/).

[6]   *Ibid.* See also W.F. Webb, (unpublished) Judgment, 17 September 1948 in vols. I–III, Webb Papers, Australian War Memorial 92, Series 2, Wallet 1–3.

[7]   Justice case, see *supra* note 1.

offence.[8] Some accused in the NMT proceedings were convicted only on this charge (for example, Altstötter in the Justice case),[9] and many other lower-ranking individuals were convicted on such charges by occupation courts operating in the detention camps set up in the early stages of the Allied occupation of Germany. As we will see, other theories of liability were advanced by prosecutors, sometimes finding acceptance from the judges, and sometimes not. What all of them had in common was the search for an adequate means of establishing the responsibility of individuals in a vast pattern of collective action without resorting to unacceptable methods of vicarious or collective liability.

Nowhere were these issues so clearly confronted as in the Nuremberg Subsequent Proceedings. There are two principal reasons why these cases were the focal point of such issues and why nowhere else were these issues explored in such depth. On one hand, the IMT and the International Military Tribunal for the Far East ('IMTFE') could find a relatively easy solution to the problem of liability. They were dealing, for the most part, with the highest echelons of wartime civilian, military and political leadership. In the case of the IMT they could arrive at the principle that it was not formal position that mattered but rather participation in the inner policy circle around Hitler, where policy was debated and decisions were made, that led to the formulation of the orders and directives that devastated the European continent, from the English Channel to the Urals. In Tokyo, on the other hand, the Majority Judgment[10] embraced the notion of an all-encompassing conspiracy, beginning in the 1920s, to lead Japan down the path to an aggressive war that would start with the conquest of China and lead to domination of what was euphemistically called the Greater East Asia Co-Prosperity Sphere, extending from Burma in the west to Australia in the east. With regards to war crimes, the Tokyo Majority Judgment[11] relied on a notion of what I would call 'cabinet responsibility', which they never clearly articulated and inconsistently applied in their guilty verdicts against all individuals accused.

---

[8] United Nations, *Charter of the International Military Tribunal*, Article 10 ("Nuremberg Charter") (http://www.legal-tools.org/doc/64ffdd/).

[9] Justice case, see *supra* note 1.

[10] Tokyo Trial, see *supra* note 5.

[11] *Ibid.*

Moving from the level of the two International Military Tribunals to the 20 or so national war crimes programmes that tried many thousands of German and Japanese alleged war criminals, for the most part they relied upon military courts of various kinds, largely composed of non-lawyers, that were utterly ill-prepared to deal with the kinds of cases they faced. This was certainly true, for example, of the British, American, Australian, French and Chinese war crimes tribunals, which together conducted more than 3,000 trials resulting in an often chaotic mix of decisions. The greatest failing here, and it is a failing which severely curtails the usefulness of these trials as having any foundational value whatsoever, is that the British, American and Australian tribunals (with miniscule exceptions such as the politically motivated written final decision in the Yamashita case[12]) were forbidden to produce written judgments. The Judge Advocate General ('JAG') reviews of these trials (there were no appeals or appellate courts) are largely perfunctory with regard to legal issues, and in any event provide no substitute for a reasoned decision based upon factual and legal findings. The accounts too often relied upon by some judges and scholars in the Law Reports of Trials of War Criminals also are no substitute for final written decisions by the court and are merely the observations of observers of a very small and random selection of trials.

The French courts (again with a few exceptions) produced judgments that were simply forms that were filled out and hardly fulfilled the function of a reasoned decision or a discussion of jurisprudential issues. The Chinese courts did produce judgments but they are generally rather abbreviated except in the case of relatively few high profile trials. The problem of using cases from national tribunals that did promulgate written decisions was exacerbated by their bulk, but more importantly by their relative or absolute inaccessibility.

It was at the NMT that professional judges, assisted by a competent prosecution and an active professional defence, conducted trials that were for the most part adequate in scope to the crimes charged. These judges sifted through hundreds of hours of testimony and hundreds of thousands of pages of documents and written submissions in trials that lasted for many months, producing the lengthy and complex judgments that, far more than the IMT or Tokyo, actually carefully reviewed the evidence

---

[12] Yamashita case, see *supra* note 4.

and considered how it bore upon the liability of each individual accused. One only has to consider the brevity of the individual verdicts in the Tokyo Judgment or its Nuremberg counterpart, compared to the lengthy analysis afforded each accused in the Justice case,[13] the Ministries case,[14] the Pohl case,[15] and so on, to sense the enormity of the difference.

It was the NMT cases, then, that to the greatest extent considered the problems posed by attempting to develop the jurisprudential tools for analysing the liability of individuals. These included an architect employed by the Schutzstaffel ('SS'), who initialled a blueprint for a gassing installation at Auschwitz,[16] a functionary in the Foreign Ministry who assisted in negotiations with an allied government over deportations,[17] an accountant for the SS who, among a hundred other tasks, did the bookkeeping for confiscated valuables of deportees,[18] a staff officer on the Eastern Front who transmitted or in some cases reformulated the orders which his commanding officer had received from Berlin,[19] or a judge who was assigned cases where the applicable law was manifestly iniquitous, or finally, the chief dentist of the SS, who oversaw dental clinics for 1.1 million men but also was technically responsible for the dental gold extracted from corpses in extermination centres because that had been classified as a hygienic matter. Such examples could be multiplied and they were not confined of course to the NMT. Lower level national courts might consider the liability of a guard at Dachau or Mauthausen who merely patrolled the perimeter of the camp or of a low-

---

[13] Justice case, see *supra* note 1.

[14] Nuremberg Military Tribunal, *United States of America v. Ernst von Weizsaecker, et al.*, Case No. 11, Judgment, 11 April 1949, in *Trials of War Criminals Before the Nuremberg Military Tribunals Under Control Council Law No. 10*, US Government Printing Office vols. XII–XIV ('Green Series') ("Ministries case") (http://www.legal-tools.org/doc/eb20f6/).

[15] Nuremberg Military Tribunal, *United States v. Oswald Pohl, et al.*, Judgment, 3 November 1947, *Trials of War Criminals Before the Nuremberg Military Tribunals Uunder Control Council Law No. 10*, vol. V, US Government Printing Office ("Pohl case") (http://www.legal-tools.org/doc/84ae05/).

[16] *Ibid.*

[17] Ministries case, see *supra* note 14.

[18] Pohl case, see *supra* note 15.

[19] Nuremberg Military Tribunal, *United States of America v. Wilhelm von Leeb, et al.*, Case No. 12, Judgment, 27 October 1948, in *Trials of War Criminals Before the Nuremberg Military Tribunals Under Control Council Law No. 10*, vols. X–XI, US Government Printing Office ("High Command case") (http://www.legal-tools.org/doc/c340d7/).

level career technocrat in the bureaucratic maze of the Reichsbahn who was responsible for the scheduling of *Sonderzüge* (special trains).

The different trial chambers of the NMT grappled with these issues in different ways: some used the metaphor of cogs in the machinery of death, excusing those who were 'mere cogs'; others conceptualised a governmental system of organised criminality in which those who 'merely participated' were exculpated and those who participated in a manner that 'shocked the conscience' of humanity were convicted. But whatever the solution they adopted, in nearly all of the NMT cases one can sense that the judges struggled with a challenge for which their legal toolbox had not equipped them. This was also, then, the situation which judges in the early ICTY and ICTR cases found themselves as they faced the question of how municipal officials,[20] the manager of a tea factory,[21] a minister of education, and many others who were members of civilian, military, security, or paramilitary organisations could be held accountable for their various roles in mass murder and other serious international crimes. In cases like Tadić[22] and Čelebići,[23] they looked to the Second World War precedents as the only body of case law that had dealt with such issues.

I argue that if we view the situation from the perspective of these early cases, it is the Nuremberg Subsequent Proceedings, building upon the IMT's establishment of the principle of individual criminal responsibility, that create the most important body of jurisprudence to emerge from the Second World War trials. I also argue that in looking back to these 'historical foundations' what the new courts found was far from transparent and, for several reasons that will be elaborated below, could scarcely be regarded as providing an international customary law basis for defining key doctrines concerning modes of responsibility or defences (or elements of substantive crimes for that matter). It was,

---

[20] International Criminal Tribunal for Rwanda, *Prosecutor v. Jean Paul Akayesu*, Judgment, 2 September 1998, ICTR-96-4 ("Akayesu case") (http://www.legal-tools.org/doc/b8d7bd/).

[21] International Criminal Tribunal for Rwanda, *Prosecutor v. Alfred Musema*, Judgment, 27 January 2000, ICTR-96-13 ("Musema case") (http://www.legal-tools.org/en/doc/1fc6ed/).

[22] International Criminal Tribunal for the former Yugoslavia, *Prosecutor v. Duško Tadić et al.*, IT, Judgment, 7 May 1997, IT-94-1 ("Tadić case") (http://www.legal-tools.org/doc/0a90ae/).

[23] International Criminal Tribunal for the former Yugoslavia, *Prosecutor v. Zejnil Delalić et al.*, Judgment, 16 November 1998, IT-96-21 ("Čelebići case") (http://www.legal-tools.org/doc/6b4a33/).

however, precisely this lack of transparency and uniformity that allowed judges, like those in the Tadić case,[24] to find what they wanted to find. That is, to find what would enable them to make law while pretending that they were merely finding what already existed.

This is not surprising, of course, for it has a long history that goes back to the beginning of jurisprudence. But with regards to the issue of historical foundations it makes the point that is again not surprising: History is not fixed in stone and displayed on the mount. 'Historical foundations' in any society are constructed and contested, from the 'Norman Yoke' in early modern England to the Battle of Kosovo Polje in Serbia. History is a resource to be investigated and interpreted, to be used to fashion arguments, and to justify innovations that appear necessary for contemporary problems. Legal history is no different. For ICTY and ICTR judges confronting the difficult issues that responsibility for crimes of war and crimes against humanity inevitably pose, historical foundations were a resource to exploit for arguing that duress did or did not exist as a defence in customary international law, that a doctrine like JCE had established precedents and was already known to international customary law in the 1940s, or that civilian superior responsibility was an established doctrine in the Second World War jurisprudence.

This chapter will thus pursue two overarching themes. The first has to do with the problem with which I began above: How did the judges, when looking for ways to deal with the problems of responsibility they confronted look to a previous legal legacy on which they could draw? And how did they use and interpret that legacy to fashion legal doctrines and to reach decisions in concrete cases where the lives and liberty of accused persons were at stake? The second theme steps back from this doctrinal case analysis and asks: What does the analysis tell us about the way in which international criminal law develops?

In attempting to address these questions I will look at three substantive areas of legal development. (1) The problem of capturing collective action through doctrines like 'common design', being 'concerned in' a crime, conspiracy, participation in a criminal organisation, an 'organised system of criminality' or a systematic governmentally sponsored

---

[24] Tadić case, see *supra* note 22.

criminal policy or plan. Here I will examine NMT cases such as RuSHA,[25] Justice,[26] Ministries[27] and Pohl,[28] and refer to the way they are treated in JCE decisions at the Extraordinary Chambers in the Courts of Cambodia ('ECCC') and the ICTY. (2) The responsibility of military commanders and civilian superiors as reflected in a variety of Second World War cases and as discussed in the ICTY Čelebići trial judgment,[29] appeals judgment,[30] and the ICTR Musema trial judgment.[31] (3) The problem confronted when judges believe there is no historical foundation of case law for them to rely on. I here examine relatively briefly the attempt to define rape and sexual violence as international crimes. I argue that the different approaches taken to deal with this problem of definition reflects similar attitudes to the development of international criminal law as manifested in the situations addressed in (1) and (2), where the historical foundations exist. I will here consider the radically different approaches of the Akayesu,[32] Furundžija[33] and Kunarac[34] cases at the ICTY and ICTR.

2.2. The National Military Tribunals at Nuremberg and the Problem of Bureaucratic Responsibility or Collective Action

In this chapter I will, as noted above, largely turn to the NMT cases because Nuremberg and Tokyo are thin on doctrinal analysis and make little contribution to the jurisprudence of theories of responsibility or the

---

[25] Nuremberg Military Tribunal, *United States of America v. Ulrich Greifelt, et al.*, Case No. 8, Judgment, 10 March 1948, in *Trials of War Criminals Before the Nuremberg Military Tribunals Under Control Council Law No. 10*, vols. IV–V, US Government Printing Office ("RuSHA case") (http://www.legal-tools.org/doc/2bc719/).

[26] Justice case, see *supra* note 1.

[27] Ministries case, see *supra* note 14.

[28] Pohl case, see *supra* note 15.

[29] Čelebići case, see *supra* note 23

[30] *Prosecutor v. Zejnil Delalić et al.*, Appeals Judgment, 20 February 2001, IT-96-21 ("Čelebići case, Appeals Judgment") (http://www.legal-tools.org/doc/051554/).

[31] Musema case, see *supra* note 21.

[32] Akayesu case, see *supra* note 20.

[33] International Criminal Court for the former Yugoslavia, *Prosecutor v. Anto Furundžija*, Judgment, 10 December 1998, IT-95-17/1-T ("Furundžija case") (http://www.legal-tools.org/en/doc/e6081b/).

[34] International Criminal Court for the former Yugoslavia, *Prosecutor v. Dragoljub Kunarac et al.*, Judgment, 22 February 2001, IT-96-23 and IT-96-23/2 ("Kunarac case") (http://www.legal-tools.org/doc/fd881d/).

definition and elaboration of substantive offences.[35] On the one hand, the trials at the national level are severely limited in their jurisprudential importance because with regards to American, British and Australian cases there are, with scant exceptions, no judgments. The NMT judgments, on the other hand, are in important respects those that are most similar to the judgments of the contemporary tribunals such as the ICTY, ICTR, Special Court for Sierra Leone ('SCSL') and so on. They are comprehensive in scope and many of them at least, deal in some depth with substantive legal doctrines in a manner that provides the basis for the jurisprudence of the future. This is clearly the case, for example, with regard to command responsibility and the status and scope of crimes against humanity.[36] We will also consider here to what extent it is also true with regard to the foundations of other theories of responsibility such as JCE.

Many of the NMT judges were acutely aware of the unique moment in which they found themselves. How were 'historical foundations' regarded by the judges of the Nuremberg Subsequent Proceedings, and to what extent were they aware that they were engaged in the enterprise that was creating the foundation for the future? The judges in the Justice case, for example, regarded the judicial process in which they were participating as formative and transformative of international law:

> For the reasons stated by Lord Wright, this growth by accretion has been greatly accelerated since the First World War. The IMT Charter, the IMT judgment, and C. C. Law 10 are merely "great new cases in the book of international law". They constitute authoritative recognition of principles of individual penal responsibility in international affairs which, as we shall show, had been developing for many years.[37]

---

[35] The section of the Tokyo judgment on the Law of the Tribunal is convoluted, opaque and had little influence over subsequent developments. It is also inconsistent with the later portions of the judgment that deal with the legal standards of the tribunal. See David Cohen and Yuma Totani, *Law, Politics, and Jurisprudence at the Tokyo War Crimes Trial*, forthcoming. Nuremberg makes a significant contribution with regards to its qualifications of the treatment of conspiracy, superior orders and membership in a criminal organisation. None of these issues are, however, analysed in jurisprudential depth. The judges seem to have been aware that the historical significance of their judgment lay elsewhere.

[36] Compare, for example, the extended and detailed discussion of crimes against humanity in the judgment of the Justice case, see Nuremberg Military Tribunal, pp. 971–83, Justice case, see *supra* note 1, with the discussion in the IMT or IMTFE judgments.

[37] Justice case,, p. 968, see *supra* note 1.

How did this formative process of doctrinal development play itself out in cases where judges faced an assemblage of accused persons alleged to have played a wide variety of roles in a bureaucratic organisation that served criminal policies of the Nazi regime? Let us turn first to the RuSHA case,[38] which has often been cited as one of the important precedents for the contemporary doctrine of JCE.

Judges and prosecutors at the NMT were acutely aware of the ongoing process of establishing genocide as a new category of international crimes. The prosecution in the RuSHA case attempted to use genocide as a unifying concept for the various crimes against humanity that were charged. The way in which they did so reflects an attempt to conceptualise a theory by which a wide variety of individuals in a wide variety of roles can be held liable for contributing to the implementation of criminal policies of a government. Let us look first at the RusHA indictment:[39]

> Charges:
>
> Count 1: Crimes against Humanity
>
> 1. Between September 1939 and April 1945, all the defendants herein committed crimes against humanity as defined by Control Council Law No. 10, in that they were principals in, accessories to, ordered, abetted, took a consenting part in, *were connected with plans and enterprises involving, and were members of organizations* or groups connected with atrocities and offenses, including but not limited to murder, extermination, enslavement, deportation [...]
>
> 2. The acts, conduct, plans and enterprises charged in paragraph 1 of this count were carried out as part of a *systematic program of genocide*, aimed at the destruction of foreign nations and ethnic groups, in part by murderous extermination, and in part by elimination and suppression of national characteristics [...][40]
>
> 10. In carrying out the *plans and enterprises constituting a vast integrated scheme to commit genocide* and thereby

---

38 RuSHA case, see *supra* note 25.

39 *Ibid.*, Indictment ("RuSHA indictment") (http://www.legal-tools.org/doc/75ac90/).

40 *Ibid.*, vol. IV, pp. 609–10.

> to strengthen Germany, the defendants herein
> participated in criminal activities [...].[41]

The language of the indictment invokes genocidal plans and enterprises that were systematically carried out by the defendants, though in a variety of roles. The emphasis in the indictment, however, is on the roles of the accused in the *implementation* of the plan, not in the formulation or sharing of an intent that produced the criminal policies. We will see a similar emphasis in the Justice[42] and other cases.[43]

The prosecution opening statement takes up the genocidal enterprise in the first paragraph but does not attribute the plan or the intent to formulate or carry it out to the accused:

> [t]he crimes of these defendants, thirteen men and one woman
> for which they stand here accused, are the result of a vast and
> premeditated plan to destroy national groups in countries
> occupied by Germany. This *program of genocide* was part of
> the Nazi doctrine of total warfare, war waged against
> populations rather than against states and armed forces.[44]

The prosecution describes the plan to commit genocide in a way that defines the idea of genocide and employs a language that has overtones of a JCE-like notion, but again emphasises the role of the defendants in "helping" to implement the plan, though the usage of the phrase "they sought" implies that they shared the intent or purpose of the plan:

> This then was the program of genocide. It was a coordinated
> plan aimed at the destruction of the essential foundations of
> the life of national groups. This destruction can be and was

---

[41] *Ibid.*, vol. IV, p. 613.

[42] The Justice case also takes up the development of genocide but with a different inflection and without any reference to genocide as the product of an "organised system".

[43] Instead, the judgment uses the General Assembly Resolution as evidence that crimes against humanity (of which they take genocide to be an example) are part of international customary law:

> The General Assembly is not an international legislature, but it is the
> most authoritative organ in existence for the interpretation of world
> opinion. Its recognition of genocide as an international crime is
> persuasive evidence of the fact. We approve and adopt its conclusions.
> Whether the crime against humanity is the product of statute or of
> common international law, or, as we believe, of both, we find no
> injustice to persons tried for such crimes (Justice case, p. 982, see
> *supra* note 1).

[44] RuSHA case, vol. IV, p. 623, emphasis added, see *supra* note 25.

accomplished with the help of these defendants by a number of different means, which may be broadly classified as physical, political, biological, and cultural. They sought the "disintegration of the political and social institutions of culture, language, national feelings, religion, and the economic existence of national groups, and the destruction of the personal security, liberty, health, dignity, and even the lives of the individuals belonging to such groups".[45]

The defence counsel for defendant Greifelt objected that his client was being charged with a crime, genocide, which had not yet been established in international law.[46] The prosecution in its closing statement clarified the nature of the charges, specifying that genocide itself was not charged as the substantive offence, but the shared genocidal plan in which the accused participated was the unifying principle that underscored their liability.[47] The way in which they describe this plan is probably as close to JCE I as one will find in the Second World War literature. Their argument is really about how to assess responsibility in complex

---

[45] *Ibid.*, p. 626, citing Raphael Lemkin, *Axis Rule: In Occupied Europe: Laws Of Occupation, Analysis Of Government, Proposals For Redress*, Carnegie Endowment for World Peace, Washington, DC, 1944, p. 79. See also pp. 627–39: The prosecution goes on to describe the conduct of the accused in terms that clearly invoke what will be adopted as the enumerated genocidal acts in the 1948 Convention. Strikingly, however, he clearly considers the systematic destruction of a group's culture to be an integral part of the genocidal plan and the concept itself:

> The technique of these defendants was the mass deportation of oppressed peoples, the deprivation of their means of livelihood by the wholesale confiscation of property, the forced Germanization of citizens of occupied countries, and *the destruction of their national culture, folkways, and educational facilities* [...] The German cultural pattern and laws were imposed on the Polish country. Polish cultural life ceased to exist in the Eastern Territories. Polish schools, from the elementary schools to the universities, were closed. More than that, even German schools, theaters, libraries, lectures, and the like, were closed to the Poles. Religious services in the Polish language were discontinued [...] These procedures were designed to bring about a "selective Germanization" of the most healthy, able, and efficient elements of national groups of occupied countries, leaving only an amorphous group of people deprived of leadership, of real religion and spiritual life.

[46] RuSHA case, vol. IV, pp. 694, 701–4, see *supra* note 25. Other defence counsel echo this argument as in the opening statement for accused Brueckner, vol. V, pp. 4–5, see *supra* note 24.

[47] RuSHA case, vol. V, pp. 30–31, see *supra* note 25.

bureaucratic organisations where collective action is required to carry out tasks and implement policies:

> It has been shown that *a special office was set up to carry out this gigantic task*; that the office was known as the Office of the Reich Commissioner for the Strengthening of Germanism (later known as the Staff Main Office); and that the Nazi Party and SS agencies, RuSHA, VoMi, and Lebensborn, were detailed to assist in the execution of the program. It has been shown that these four offices, working in perfect harmony, in collaboration one with the other, and under the overall supervision of the Staff Main Office were responsible for the many criminal acts which were perpetrated in connection with the program. It has been shown that all of the defendants, as important and high ranking officials of these four offices, worked together to effectuate this criminal common plan. These defendants conferred together, discussed together, planned together, and worked together. Each was an expert in his own field. They comprised a team and each member was vital to the success of the whole enormous operation. Their tasks were so interwoven and so interrelated that without complete knowledge of the entire program, and without full collaboration on the part of all, they would not have been able to accomplish what they did in carrying out this criminal program. *So we repeat, these defendants constitute a team, they all were involved in one scheme. They are all responsible for the criminal acts which they committed in carrying out the program.*[48]

The emphasis here is equally upon planning and on execution of the commonly held plan. The prosecution ties together all of the disparate contributions of members of three complex bureaucratic organisations through their participation in a common scheme. Essentially, the prosecution is arguing that the accused were co-perpetrators who planned and carried out this criminal scheme and shared responsibility for all of the crimes it encompassed. What, however, is the legal basis on which the prosecution relies for grounding this far-reaching theory of responsibility? They quote only the modes of liability specified in Control Council Law No. 10[49] and do not specifically identify the grounds on which they are

---

[48] *Ibid.*, vol. V, p. 60, emphasis added.

[49] Control Council Law No. 10, 20 December 1945 (http://www.legal-tools.org/doc/ffda62/).

relying or explain how the notion of collective bureaucratic action it has just articulated so well falls under these provisions. The modes of liability provided for in Control Council Law No. 10 encompass anyone who acted as,

    (a) a principal, or

    (b) was an accessory to the commission of any such crime or ordered or abetted the same, or

    (c) took a consenting part therein, or

    (d) was connected with plans or enterprises involving its commission, or

    (e) was a member of any organization or group connected with the commission of any such crime.[50]

Having quoted these provisions of Control Council Law No. 10,[51] the prosecution merely states that they

> submit that the proof in this case shows beyond a reasonable doubt that all the defendants have *participated* in the crimes charged in the indictment in such a way as to bring them within the provisions above quoted, and that they therefore are guilty of having *committed* the crimes charged.[52]

In the end, the prosecution's interesting theory of responsibility dissolves into little more than traditional criminal law notions of perpetration and accessorial liability, perhaps supplemented by the vague provision of (d), being "connected with plans or enterprises". The latter hardly seems relevant, however, since the prosecution has argued that the defendants collaborated in planning, organising and committing the criminal acts charged. What, then, do the judges make of the case as presented by the prosecution?

It is striking that the judgment proceeds to basically ignore the prosecution's theory of the case with its invocation of a genocidal plan, and instead treats the indictment in conventional criminal law terms, focusing on the individual conduct and participation of each accused in the activities of the RuSHA. For example, with regards to kidnappings the judgment details the *direct participation* of accused in the implementation of the policy and their actual individual roles in assisting its execution.

---

[50] *Ibid.*

[51] *Ibid.*

[52] RuSHA case, vol. V, p. 60, see *supra* note 25.

Knowledge and participation are the criteria for liability.[53] In the case of Hildebrandt, head of RuSHA from 1943, the judgment concludes, "thus, not only did Hildebrandt have familiarity with the term 'special treatment', but he, and those deputized by him and under his express orders, actually handled special treatment cases".[54]

With regards to the prevention of births the judgment emphasises the direct involvement of particular offices and of particular individuals:

> The offices of RuSHA, VoMi, and the Staff Main Office bear particular responsibility for this criminal activity. Representatives of RuSHA and VoMi actively engaged in discussions and made suggestions concerning measures to be enacted. These representatives demanded, and received, the right for determination of individual cases by Higher SS and Police Leaders, which would result in a decisive intervention on the part of RKFDV. It was further agreed that in deciding cases it should be determined whether the child constituted a "desirable increase in population" (Poles suitable for Germanization); this will then be determined by the SS Race and Settlement Main Office.
>
> The Staff Main Office prepared decrees concerning marriages. *Greifelt under his own signature, forwarded decrees dealing with the question of prohibiting marriages; and representatives of the Staff Main Office participated actively in conferences in which drastic regulations were discussed and agreed upon. The defendant Greifelt bears full responsibility for the activities of the Staff Main Office, as well as his own individual acts,* which contributed in a large measure toward the program of hampering the reproduction of enemy nationals.[55]

With regards to the evacuation and resettlement programme the approach was similar.[56] I am quoting at length to dispel any question that evidence of participation was used to infer a shared purpose of intent in the manner now used in JCE I cases. The whole thrust of the judgment is to demonstrate "full knowledge" and "active participation" as the criteria on which liability is predicated. For example, with regards to accused

---

[53] *Ibid.*, p. 108.

[54] *Ibid.*, p. 120.

[55] *Ibid.*, p. 124, emphasis added.

[56] *Ibid.*, pp. 128–29.

Creutz, his "full knowledge of, and active participation in, deportation and resettlement actions is clearly shown by a report he made to Himmler's secretary on 7 August 1943".[57] The conclusions on two further accused are placed in the same frame:

> It has been established beyond any doubt by voluminous evidence that both Lorenz and Brueckner had knowledge of, and actively engaged in, actions carried out to evacuate and resettle· foreign populations, to Germanize enemy nationals, and to utilize enemy nationals as slave labor within the Reich.[58]

In the RuSHA verdicts,[59] on each individual accused the focus is solely upon the evidence that directly links them to the specific crimes charged, based upon their individual conduct, as assessed by their knowledge, their authority and the nature and scope of their participation. The prosecution had invited the judges to articulate a more expansive theory of responsibility to capture the liability of a group of individuals working in three related bureaucratic organisations in furtherance of a number of discrete governmental policies. While the judgment repeatedly refers to the co-operation of these offices in carrying out these policies the conclusions as to liability are based upon their conduct and not upon their shared intent or common design or purpose. The notion introduced by the prosecution of joint participation in a systematic programme aiming at genocide through a scheme consisting of related crimes against humanity under a unifying policy is left entirely fallow.

At the ECCC the Pre-Trial Chamber ('PTC') took up the issue of the status of JCE under international customary law in 1975. Rather than

---

[57] *Ibid.*, p. 131.

[58] *Ibid.*, p. 144. See also p. 124 on Greifelt:

> In the gigantic undertaking comprising evacuations and resettlements, Germanization, and commitment to slave labor of foreign nationals, the Staff Main Office, VoMi and RuSHA held significant roles. Greifelt, as chief of the Staff Main Office and also as deputy to Himmler, issued decree after decree concerning measures to be taken in the evacuation and resettlement of populations. Greifelt's intimate connection with, and active participation in, evacuations and resettlements as well as Germanization and slave labor, affecting the populations of various countries, may be clearly shown by reference to several decrees. These examples could be multiplied.

[59] RuSHA case, see *supra* note 25.

briefly reviewing the Tadić appeals judgment's[60] treatment of Second World War cases, the PTC conducted their own analysis of the Second World War jurisprudence. They conclude, in contradiction to the Tadić case, that JCE III was not part of customary international law as reflected in the Second World War jurisprudence. This conclusion is certainly well founded and is a welcome corrective to the flimsy evidence and misinterpretations on which the Tadić case reached its conclusion.[61]

In finding that JCE I was established under international customary law, the PTC focused on two of the subsequent proceedings cases that it found "particularly apposite".[62] These were the Justice[63] and RuSHA[64] cases. The PTC's interpretation of the RuSHA case focuses primarily only on the verdicts against two of the accused. But these portions of the judgment cited by the PTC do not really reflect the standards of liability used by the court in grounding their analysis and verdicts. Indeed, their theory of the case actually appears, when the whole judgment has been considered as above, to go in quite the opposite direction than that indicated by the PTC. Moreover, as we have seen, when looking at the prosecution's case, which could have provided a basis for the court to move towards a theory like JCE I or common design, one sees that the judgment in fact eschews such an approach in favour of a much more traditional conception of modes of liability.

In reaching its conclusion the PTC relies on the fact that the RuSHA judgment found that defendants, Hildebrandt and Hoffman, "enthusiastically participated' in the 'Germanisation' plan which the RuSHA helped to formulate, following decrees from Himmler.[65] What the PTC seems to have found persuasive in locating JCE I in this judgment was the Tribunal's finding that Hildebrandt and Hoffman bore responsibility for the kidnapping and forced abortion programmes because of their

---

[60] Tadić case, Appeals Judgment, 15 July 1999, see *supra* note 22 (http://www.legal-tools.org/doc/8efc3a/).

[61] Extraordinary Chambers in the Courts of Cambodia, *Prosecutor v. Nuon Chea et al.,* Decision on the Appeals against the Co-Investigating Judges Order on Joint Criminal Enterprise (JCE), Pre-Trial Chamber Decision (PTC JCE Decision), 20 May 2010, p. 45 (http://www.legal-tools.org/en/doc/320587/).

[62] *Ibid.*

[63] Justice case, see *supra* note 1.

[64] RuSHA case, see *supra* note 25.

[65] *Prosecutor v. Nuon Chea et al.*, see *supra* note 61.

knowledge of and participation in the execution of these programmes.[66] As stressed above in the discussion of the RuSHA judgment,[67] however, nowhere does the judgment stress that the participation of the defendants in a collective criminal activity reflected a common criminal purpose or that it was a common purpose or design that grounded their liability.

To be sure, Hildebrandt and Hoffman acted in a concerted manner. So did the other defendants. They were all civil servants in the same organisations, ordered to implement a policy that their superiors had tasked them with. This kind of co-operative activity can be captured by traditional notions of complicity or co-perpetratorship, where liability is based upon the elements of co-operation in planning, ordering and executing policies with knowledge of their criminal nature. I fail to see how one can read the RuSHA judgment[68] as predicating liability upon elements of a plurality of persons who share a common criminal purpose. There is no doubt that they were a plurality of persons and that they did actively engage in the activities of their organisations with the intention of implementing these policies. The problem is that the judgment eschews the language of the indictment[69] and the prosecution's arguments,[70] and does not make findings that liability is based upon the shared design or common purpose. Rather, the judgment's decision is based on assessment of the individual conduct of each accused person in formulating orders and directives, issuing orders to their subordinates, and actively overseeing the successful implementation of the goals they had been tasked by Himmler to achieve. The judgment portrays them as zealous and faithful German civil servants carrying out orders and directives that they have received from on high rather than demonstrating that they share a common criminal purpose with those at the policy level. Nor does the judgment articulate the grounds of liability, unlike in the Krstic appeals judgment,[71] which clearly stated that the defendants' liability rested on their aiding and abetting the shared criminal purpose of their superiors.

---

[66]   *Ibid.*, pp. 45–46.

[67]   RuSHA case, see *supra* note 25.

[68]   *Ibid.*

[69]   RuSHA Indictment, see *supra* note 39.

[70]   RuSHA case, see *supra* note 25.

[71]   International Criminal Tribunal for the former Yugoslavia, *Prosecutor v. Radislav Krstic; Srebrenica-Drina Corps*, Appeals Judgment, 19 April 2004, IT-98-33 ("Krstic Appeals Judgment") (http://www.legal-tools.org/doc/86a108/).

These were the directions in which the prosecution urged the Tribunal, but this was a path that the judges did not take.[72]

With regards to JCE II, the PTC finds the American concentration camp cases (trials conducted by American military commissions at Dachau) persuasive in establishing this systemic form of JCE. While it is certainly true that the American prosecutors (and British prosecutors in the Belsen case)[73] argued that the camps were systems of organised criminality and that all those individuals who worked in the camp were all responsible for the crimes committed there, it is far from certain that this was the basis on which convictions were handed down. What the PTC cites is the characterisation of the Dachau case (*USA v. Martin Gottfried Weiss and thirty-nine others*)[74] in the Tadić judgment[75] and in the United Nations War Crimes Commission (UNWCC) report on the trial in the Law Reports of the Trials of War Criminals.[76] The problem here, as noted above, is that these conclusions are not based upon a judgment of the Tribunal, but merely findings of the guilt or innocence of each accused. This is hardly a basis for analysing whether the judges accepted the prosecution's theory of the case in reaching a verdict.

What neither the PTC[77] nor the Tadić case[78] cites is a document that provides an authoritative view at least of how the American JAG

---

[72] RuSHA case, see *supra* note 25. See also the sceptical comments in the ICTR Rwamakuba case JCE decision which correctly notes that the Second World War cases do not fit into the neat categories of JCE I–III but float in the vagueness of being "concerned in" or "connected to" a crime. International Criminal Tribunal for Rwanda, *Prosecutor v. Édouard Karemera et al.*, Decision on the Preliminary Motions by the Defence of Joseph Nzirorera Édouard Karemera André Rwamakuba and Mathieu Ngirumpatse Challenging Jurisdiction in Relation to Joint Criminal Enterprise, 11 May 2004 (http://www.legal-tools.org/doc/56eebe/).

[73] United Kingdom (UK) Military Court, *Prosecutor v. Antoni Aurdzieg et al.*, Case No. 10, Judicial Summary, November 1945, National Archives, UK, WO235/19 ("Belsen case") (http://www.legal-tools.org/doc/15bccb/).

[74] United States of America (USA) Military Courts, *Prosecutor v. Martin Gottfried Weiss et al.*, Case No. 000-50-2, Dachau Concentration Camp Trials, Judicial Summary (http://www.legal-tools.org/en/doc/e3b89d/).

[75] Tadić case, see *supra* note 22.

[76] United Nations (UN) War Crimes Commission, *The Dachau Concentration Camp Trial: Trial of Martin Gottfried Weiss and Thirty-Nine Others*, Case No. 60, Law Reports of Trials of War Criminals, vol. XI, pp. 5–16 (http://www.legal-tools.org/doc/4d236c/).

[77] *Prosecutor v. Nuon Chea et al.*, see *supra* note 61.

[78] Tadić case, see *supra* note 22.

understood the basis of the American concentration camps cases. In 1948 the JAG issued a "Report of the Deputy Judge Advocate for War Crimes European Command, June 1944 to July 1948".[79] This report covered the American war crimes programme in Europe, which, apart from the NMT, was centred in Dachau where some 489 trials were held. One section of the JAG report is entitled "Common Design". The JAG understood this to be the section of Control Council Law No. 10,[80] which was applied by the prosecution in the American concentration camp cases. 'Common design' was understood by the JAG as a form of vicarious liability "in all material respects the same as conspiracy". Liability was based upon the nature of the positions the individuals held and the theory of liability was understood as participation in the execution of the common design:

> Common Design.
>
> 1. Most participants in the operation of concentration camps were tried under charges and particulars alleging participation in the execution of a common design, in the operation of concentration camps.
>
> *The legal characteristics of common design are in all materials respects the same as conspiracy.* As the latter is recognized in American municipal criminal law except that a previously conceived plan is not an essential element. *On the principle of vicarious liability*, accused convicted of participation in the execution of a common design were held responsible in varying degrees according to the positions held.[81]

From the standpoint of the JAG looking back at these American trials, it appears that the concentration camp cases were not based upon a theory of responsibility different from any of the other common design or conspiracy prosecutions. Instead, from the JAG's perspective, on the Tadić classification[82] there would be no reason to differentiate JCE I and

---

[79] Deputy Judge Advocate for War Crimes, European Command, Lieutenant Colonel Clio E. Straight, *Report of the Deputy Judge Advocate for War Crimes European Command, June 1944 to July 1948*, Office of the Judge Advocate General, 1948.

[80] Control Council Law No. 10, see *supra* note 49.

[81] *Report of the Deputy Judge Advocate for War Crimes European Command*, emphasis added, see *supra* note 79.

[82] Tadić case, see *supra* note 22.

JCE II for they would both simply be prosecutions under a conspiracy or common design theory, two terms which the JAG regarded as synonymous.

What basis, then, is there for reinterpreting the conspiracy and common design provisions employed at Nuremberg, Tokyo[83] and Control Council Law No. 10[84] as JCE I–III? The problem faced by the judges of the Tadić case[85] was that conspiracy theory could not be plausibly read into the ICTY Statute[86] which had deliberately omitted any reference to it despite the otherwise heavy reliance on the Nuremberg framework. So 'historical foundations' had to be sought for an alternative way of dealing with the complexities of the kinds of cases with which state-organised mass violence inevitably presented. While conspiracy was clearly the dominant theory of the prosecution's case at Nuremberg, Tokyo and beyond, another rubric had to be 'found' that would enable ICTY judges to deal with similar kinds of state-organised mass atrocity involving a multitude of actors in a variety of roles and levels of authority.

While in a sense I can agree that JCE II is better grounded than JCE III in the way that the prosecution framed some of the Second World War cases, the lack of judgments making specific factual and legal findings and articulating a standard of liability is crippling. Moreover, in many other camp cases, such as the British, American and Australian cases dealing with prisoner of war labour camps and civilian internment camps, the cases were argued on different bases altogether. But again these cases do not have judgments so we can only speculate as to what motivated the convictions handed down. This body of trial records without reasoned final decisions thus provides a rather flimsy basis for arriving at sweeping conclusions about the state of international customary law in the immediate post-war period. But of course the advantage of such a mixed record is that one can construct whatever doctrinal foundation one might seek. The Tadić case[87] did so in response to a perceived need for something to replace the conspiracy and common design language, or the crime of membership in a criminal organisation that had been provided

---

[83] Tokyo Trial, see *supra* note 5.

[84] Control Council Law No. 10, see *supra* note 49.

[85] Tadić case, see *supra* note 22.

[86] United Nations, *Updated Statute of the International Criminal Tribunal for the Former Yugoslavia*, 25 May 1993 ("ICTY Statute") (http://www.legal-tools.org/doc/b4f63b/).

[87] Tadić case, see *supra* note 22.

for the Second World War judges, [88] but was lacking in the ICTY Statute.[89]

We turn now to the other NMT case cited by the PTC of the ECCC and other courts as providing a foundation for JCE I. This case involved the trial of the German judiciary and ministerial bureaucracy.

2.2.1. The Justice Case[90]

As discussed in the JAG report,[91] common design and conspiracy were also considered as essentially synonymous in the Justice case.[92] The indictment[93] reveals, however, that they were not clearly distinguished from other modes of individual responsibility. The introduction of the indictment states that in the Justice case the defendants were charged with participation "in a common design or conspiracy to commit … war crimes and crimes against humanity, as defined in Control Council Law No. 10".[94] Some of the defendants were also "charged with membership in criminal organizations".[95]

Count one of the indictment, entitled "The Common Design and Conspiracy", charges the accused as follows:

> 1. Between January *1933* and April *1945* all of the defendants herein, acting pursuant to a common design, unlawfully, willfully, and knowingly did conspire and agree together and with each other and with diverse other persons, to commit war crimes and crimes against humanity, as defined in Control Council Law No. 10, Article 11.
>
> 2. Throughout the period covered by this indictment all of the defendants herein, acting in concert with each other and with others, unlawfully, willfully, and knowingly

---

[88] Nuremberg Charter, see *supra* note 8.

[89] ICTY Statute, see *supra* note 86.

[90] Justice case, see *supra* note 1.

[91] *Report of the Deputy Judge Advocate for War Crimes European Command*, see *supra* note 79.

[92] Justice case, see *supra* note 1.

[93] Justice case, see *supra* note 1; Justice case Indictment ("Justice indictment") (http://www.legal-tools.org/doc/90d563/).

[94] *Ibid.*, Indictment, p. 3

[95] Justice case, Judgment, p. 15, see *supra* note 1.

   were principals in, accessories to, ordered, abetted, took a consenting part in, and were connected with plans and enterprises involving, the commission of war crimes and crimes against humanity.

3. All of the defendants herein, acting in concert with each other and with others, unlawfully, willfully, and knowingly participated as leaders, organizers, instigators, and accomplices in the formulation and execution of the said common design, conspiracy, plans, and enterprises to commit, and which involved the commission of, war crimes and crimes against humanity, and accordingly are individually responsible for their own acts and for all acts performed by any person or persons in execution of the said common design, conspiracy, plans, and enterprises.

4. The said common design, conspiracy, plans, and enterprises embraced the commission of war crimes and crimes against humanity, as set forth in counts two and three of this indictment, in that the defendants unlawfully, willfully, and knowingly encouraged, aided, abetted, and participated in the commission of atrocities and offenses against persons and property.[96]

The opening statement of the prosecution dealing with count one concludes as follows: "Now that we have traced the steps in the *conspiracy*, it is timely that we examine the murders and other atrocities which were its intended and actual outcome".[97] The preceding discussion focused on what the accused persons did to pervert the system of justice in Germany, not on the common intent that they shared. When the judgment summarises the indictment, however, it characterises count one without mentioning common design and considers the charge as one of conspiracy: "The indictment contains four counts, as follows: (1) Conspiracy to commit war crimes and crimes against humanity".[98]

  As noted above, count one of the indictment seems to confuse conspiracy as a substantive offence rather than a theory of liability. This gave rise to a challenge of the jurisdiction of the court on the grounds that the Tribunal had no jurisdiction over such a substantive offence. The

---

[96] Justice Indictment, p. 5, emphasis added, see *supra* note 93.

[97] Justice case, vol. III, p. 57, emphasis added, see *supra* note 1.

[98] *Ibid.*, Judgment, p. 955.

Tribunal agreed and issued a decision that rules that in as far as count one alleged conspiracy as unlawful participation in the execution and actual commission of war crimes and crimes against humanity, that portion of the count could not be sustained. On the view of the Tribunal the part of count one that could be sustained was the allegation of participation in certain categories of crimes. As the Tribunal regarded these crimes as also subsumed under counts two and three, in the end no accused was convicted under count one. [99] What remained, of course, was the possibility of using conspiracy as a theory of liability for the perpetration of the crimes charged. The majority of judges declined to do this, and this led to Judge Blair writing a separate concurring opinion that is revealing of how these issues of liability were debated. [100]

Although the majority judges understood that the conspiracy charge in count one could be used as a mode of liability, nowhere in the judgment do they refer to the accused as having conspired or of having shared a common purpose or design. Instead, the judgment asserts that the accused are not being convicted of specific criminal acts but rather for their participation in a government-organised system of judicial terror. The terms by which they characterise this system seem to provide a basis for what the Tadić case will brand as the "systemic form of JCE", though in this case it is not a closed organisational system like a concentration camp, but the entire system of the administration of justice in Nazi Germany, encompassing the Ministry of Justice and major elements of the judiciary. What the judges do not refer to at all, however, is participation in a common design as alleged in the indictment. [101] As the judgment states:

---

[99]   *Ibid.*, Judgment, p. 1177:

> This Tribunal has held that it has no jurisdiction to try any defendant for the crime of conspiracy as a separate substantive offense, but we recognize that there are allegations in count one of the indictment which constitute charges of direct commission of war crimes and crimes against humanity. However, after eliminating the conspiracy charge from count one, we find that all other alleged criminal acts therein set forth and committed after 1 September 1939 are also charged as crimes in the subsequent counts of the indictment. We therefore find it unnecessary to pass formally upon the remaining charges in count one. Our pronouncements of guilt or innocence under counts two, three, and four dispose of all issues which have been submitted to us.

[100]   *Ibid.*, Judge Blair's Separate Opinion (http://www.legal-tools.org/doc/5a173c/).

[101]   Justice Indictment, see *supra* note 93.

The charge, in brief, is that of conscious participation in a nation wide government-organized system of cruelty and injustice, in violation of the laws of war and of humanity, and perpetrated in the name of law by the authority of the Ministry of Justice, and through the instrumentality of the courts. The dagger of the assassin was concealed beneath the robe of the jurist. The record is replete with evidence of specific criminal acts, but they are not the crimes charged in the indictment. They constitute evidence of the intentional participation of the defendants and serve as illustrations of the nature and effect of the greater crimes charged in the indictment. *Thus it is that the apparent generality of the indictment was not only necessary but proper. No indictment couched in specific terms and in the manner of the common law could have encompassed within practicable limits the generality of the offense.*[102]

Paradoxically, although stating at the beginning and at the end of the judgment that liability is based not on specific acts but rather on participation in the general system of criminality, the verdicts against the individual accused focus almost exclusively upon the nature and extent of their actual participation in specific events and actions. This paradoxical disparity reveals a tension in the judgment on the assessment of individual responsibility. On one hand, the Judgment clearly recognises that something larger is at stake because they are dealing with government-organised criminality that sets out to, and succeeds in co-opting the entire administration of justice in Germany. On the other hand, despite recognising the importance of this perspective, the judges ground the convictions of each accused on extremely detailed accounts of their individual roles as directly instigating, ordering, committing, encouraging or aiding and abetting the *specific crimes* that implemented the policies underlying the system rather than either sharing a common criminal purpose or their role in a conspiracy. The length and detail of the verdicts, focusing on the actions of the individual accused with regards to specific acts, stands in sharp contrast to the verdicts of the IMT and IMTFE.

This ambiguity over the doctrinal basis of the decision appears early in the judgment, when it turns to an articulation of the standards of liability. In referring to the legal basis for the modes of liability the

---

[102] *Ibid.*, Judgment, p. 985, emphasis added.

judgment does not specifically focus on the grounding of their notion of participation in a "government-organised system of cruelty" but instead quotes Control Council Law No. 10, Article 11, Paragraph 2, which provides that a person

> is deemed to have committed a crime as defined in paragraph 1 of this article, if he was (a) a principal or (b) was an accessory to the commission of any such crime or ordered or abetted the same or (c) took a consenting part therein or (d) was connected with plans or enterprises involving its commission or (e) was a member of any organization or group connected with the commission of any such crime.[103]

While one might have thought that (d) would prove to be a prominent component in assessing liability for participation in an organised system of criminality, in fact it does not. The phrase "connected with plans or enterprises" involving the commission of a crime is rather vague and the judgment never specifies whether the nature of that 'connection' is a shared intent or common purpose. When the judgment turns to an elaboration of the process by which the German judicial system was transformed into a system of terror, it frames the issue broadly and in terms of the nature and scope of the defendants' participation rather than on a mode of liability defined solely by a shared criminal purpose:

> [t]he evidence now to be considered will make clear the conditions under which the defendant[s] acted and will show knowledge, intent, and motive on their part, for in the period of preparation some of the defendants played a leading part in molding the judicial system which they later employed.[104]

In its detailed examination of the evidence the entire emphasis of the judgment is upon the actions of the individual defendants in working to make the German judiciary a subservient tool to the Nazi Party leadership and, more specifically, to the directives and wishes of Adolf Hitler, following the *Führerprinzip* (leadership principle). This stands in contrast, for example, to the more than 200 pages of the Tokyo judgment dealing with crimes against peace, which casts its narrative overwhelmingly in terms of the unfolding of the all-encompassing

---

[103] *Ibid.*, Judgment, p. 985; see also Control Council Law No. 10, see *supra* note 49.

[104] *Ibid.*, Judgment, p. 988.

conspiracy to wage aggressive war.[105] In that narrative the role of the individual accused is often obscured by repeated references to "the conspiracy" or "the conspirators" as the agents.[106] The Justice case, on the other hand, refers again and again to evidence of acts that demonstrate the participation of each of the accused in the direct implementation of the policy to pervert the administration of justice. For example, after detailing a whole series of specific actions and decrees the judgment concludes: "Among those of the Ministry of Justice who joined in the constant pressure upon the judges in favor of more severe or more discriminatory administration of justice, we find Thierack, Schlegelberger, Klemm, Rothenburger, and Joel".[107]

The judgment does not cite these actions as evidence from which a common design can be inferred in the way which has been used to ground findings of JCE I. Rather, these are specific examples of actions which ground the liability of the accused for their direct participation in the crimes. There are hundreds of examples of this in the massive judgment in the Justice case and they are enumerated for all the individual accused who were convicted. A central focus is defendant Schlegelberger, the highest-ranking defendant and *Staatssekretaer* (State Secretary) of the Ministry of Justice. For example, when he was informed of a decision regarded as unfavourable by the Nazi regime, "Schlegelberger ordered the responsible president of the appellate court and the judges concerned in the case to report to him on the next day, and on the third day of April 1941", when he informed them that the judges and the presiding judge of the criminal division had been replaced.[108] Or, to take another example, the Tribunal found that while some German judges resisted the incursions on their independence, "[there were] judges who with fanatical zeal enforced the will of the Party with such severity that they experienced no difficulties and little interference from party officials. To this group the defendants Rothaug and Oeschey belonged".[109] The judgment details

---

[105] Tokyo Trial, see *supra* note 5.

[106] See David Cohen, "Beyond Nuremberg: Individual Responsibility for War Crimes", in Carla Hesse and Robert Post (eds.), *Human Rights in Transition*, Zone Press, New York, 1999, pp. 53–92; and David Cohen, "Bureaucratic Responsibility in the World War II War Crimes Trials", in *Rechtshistorisches Journal*, 1999, pp. 313–42.

[107] Justice case, p. 1017, see *supra* note 1.

[108] *Ibid.*, p. 1021.

[109] *Ibid.*, p. 1025.

evidence adduced by the prosecution of specific instances that support this conclusion.

After reviewing the evidence the Tribunal concludes that: "The evidence conclusively establishes the adoption and application of systematic government-organised and approved procedures amounting to atrocities and offenses of the kind made punishable by C. C. Law 10".[110] While the judgment goes on to speak of these "procedures" as a plan, they also make clear that the liability of the accused is predicated upon the nature and scope of their participation in the implementation of the plan and not whether they shared a common purpose in the plan itself: "The remaining question is whether or not the evidence proves beyond a reasonable doubt in the case of the individual defendants, that they each consciously participated in the plan or took a consenting part therein".[111] It is by examining the individual verdicts then that we can determine on what basis individual accused were convicted and whether notions of common design, conspiracy or participation in a criminal system were employed in reaching judgment.

With regards to the most senior of the defendants, Schlegelberger, the Tribunal finds that he played a central role in developing this system of judicial terror. They accept that he did so in order to try and keep the judiciary out of the grasp of Himmler, but, however reluctantly, he was willing to pervert the administration of justice to do so:

> The evidence conclusively shows that in order to maintain the Ministry of Justice in the good graces of Hitler and to prevent its utter defeat by Himmler's police, Schlegelberger and the other defendants who joined in this claim of justification took over the dirty work which the leaders of the State demanded, and employed the Ministry of Justice as a means for exterminating the Jewish and Polish populations, terrorizing the inhabitants of occupied countries, and wiping out political opposition at home.[112]

Detailing the specific actions that Schlegelberger engaged in, the judgment enumerates the directives he signed, the orders he gave, the

---

[110] *Ibid.*, p. 1081.
[111] *Ibid.*
[112] *Ibid.*, p. 1086.

policies he carried out and so on. On the basis of his specific conduct they convict him on counts two and three.

In turning to defendant Klemm, who had occupied a series of offices in the Justice Ministry and elsewhere with steadily increasing responsibility, the Tribunal articulates its standard for liability:

> As heretofore pointed out in this opinion, the essential elements to prove a defendant guilty under the indictment in this case are that a defendant had knowledge of an offense charged in the indictment and established by the evidence, and that he was connected with the commission of that offense.[113]

The findings of the Tribunal implicate Klemm as much more intimately involved than Schlegelberger with what the judgment calls the "Nazi conspiracy". They also find him guilty under counts two and three. Given findings that make explicit that he shared the intention of the highest-level members of this conspiracy, it is striking that the Tribunal does not mention common design as a mode of liability. The conclusion as to Klemm's guilt makes clear that it is based upon his participation in the development of criminal policies and also in their execution:

> When Rothenberger was ousted as State Secretary because he was not brutal enough, it was Klemm who was chosen to carry on the Thierack program in closest cooperation with the heads of the Nazi conspiracy. Klemm was in the inner circle of the Nazi war criminals. He must share with his dead friend, Thierack, (with whom he had lived), and his missing friend, Bormann, the responsibility, at a high policy level, for the crimes committed in the name of justice which fill the pages of this record.[114]

The language of the "inner circle" and "high policy level" echoes the standard used by the Nuremberg (IMT) judgment[115] rather than a novel alternative theory of responsibility. The NMT predicated liability not on formal position but rather whether a defendant actually participated (not just was present) in meetings of Hitler's inner policy circle.

---

[113] *Ibid.*, p. 1093.

[114] *Ibid.*, p. 1107.

[115] International Military Tribunal, *Prosecutor* v. *Hermann Wilhelm Goring et al.*, Judgment, 1 October 1946 (http://www.legal-tools.org/doc/f41e8b/).

The court's treatment of the notorious Special Court Judge Oeschey casts further light on the criteria for their determination of liability. Oeschey was known for his abusive and cruel manner, his harsh sentences and his determination of guilt before the trial had even begun. The judgment states that the court will not convict a judge or other judicial official,

> merely because of the fact, without more, that he participated in the passing or enforcement of laws for the punishment of habitual criminals, looters, hoarders, or those guilty of undermining the defensive strength of the nation, but we also stated that these laws were in many instances applied in an arbitrary and brutal manner shocking to the conscience of mankind and punishable here.[116]

Oeschey, as the specific findings against him show, was convicted not for his participation in the system of state-organised injustice, but rather because of the cruel and arbitrary nature of the way in which he exercised his office of judge. The emphasis is on his individual conduct within the system.[117]

In sum, while the judgment states at the beginning and the end that what the defendants are being charged with is participation in a government-organised system of criminality (i.e., the judicial system of Nazi Germany), the focus of the individual verdicts and most of the judgment as a whole is on what each accused person did in specific instances that could ground their liability either as a perpetrator of the crimes charged or as an aider and abettor. Various defendants who participated in the judicial system were acquitted and the judgment provided that only participation that attained a certain degree of heinousness would suffice for conviction. Thus, even though they knowingly participated in the system of organised criminality this was not enough to justify conviction. This approach is quite unlike the theory of responsibility in the concentration camp cases where mere participation in the organised system of criminality that the camp represented was

---

[116] Justice case, p. 116, see *supra* note 1.

[117] For example, the judgment details his actions with regards to judicial proceedings involving Poles and concludes, "In this case Oeschey, with evil intent, participated in the government-organized system for the racial persecution of Poles. This is also a case of such a perversion of the judicial process as to shock the conscience of mankind", *ibid.*, p. 1161.

enough, provided that the accused was aware of the criminal nature of the camp. This discrepancy may be due to the difference in the relatively small closed system of a camp as opposed to the judicial bureaucracy and system of courts that was charged with the administration of justice in Nazi Germany. In the end, then, the Justice case seems ill-suited as a precedent for either JCE I or II and its somewhat confused approach to liability retains a certain ambiguity and opacity.

The reluctance of the Tribunal to convict on a theory of common design or conspiracy is underscored by the concurring opinion of Judge Blair who argues forcefully that it was on precisely such grounds that the accused should have been convicted:

> There is no material difference between a plan or scheme to commit a particular crime and a common design or conspiracy to commit the same crime. In legal concept there can be no material difference to plan, scheme, or conspire to commit a crime. But of them all, the conspiracy to commit the crimes charged in the indictment is the most realistic because the Nazi crimes are in reality indivisible and each plan, scheme, or conspiracy proved in the instant case was in reality an interlocking part of the whole criminal undertaking or enterprise.[118]

The broad terms in which he casts the conspiracy doctrine may be flawed but it is based upon an apprehension that when dealing with governmentally organised and criminal policies, all who participate in such criminal enterprises bear responsibility for the outcomes. Blair goes so far as to argue that anyone who implements or aids and abets such enterprises is guilty as a principal under a theory of conspiracy. The basis of such liability, he posits, is an agreement common to all those who so participate. This formulation of an underlying agreement that connects all of those who aid and abet the criminal enterprise in any manner does seem to operate on a register similar to that of JCE I:

> As a rule there can be no such thing as aiding and abetting without some previous agreement or understanding or common design in the execution of which the aider and abettor promoting that common design has made himself guilty as a principal.[119]

---

[118] *Ibid.*, p. 1195; see Judge Blair's Separate Opinion, see *supra* note 100.
[119] *Ibid.*, p. 1997.

Applying this principle in the final sentences of his opinion he concludes that all of the defendants should have been convicted under a theory of conspiracy, not because they all played a role in designing, planning, or executing the criminal plan but because they all knew of it and participated in some manner:

> [T]hey did knowingly aid, abet, and become connected with the plan, scheme, or conspiracy in aid of waging the war and committed those war crimes [and crimes] against humanity as charged in the indictment. A more perfect plan or scheme to show a conspiracy to commit crimes could hardly be written than was the agreement entered into by the OKW, Ministry of Justice, and the Gestapo to execute and carry out the Hitler Night and Fog decree. All the defendants who took a part in the execution and carrying out of the NN Decree knew of its illegality and of its cruel and inhumane purposes.[120]

Blair's view of the case, however, did not prevail and he was left to write his own concurring opinion. The majority in the Justice case did not disagree with Blair over the nature of the crimes and their systematic quality. The disagreement was instead over the theory of liability that should be used to convict. The majority differed with Blair in insisting that traditional notions of co-perpetration, and aiding and abetting were sufficient without introducing a theory of liability predicated upon a common design, agreement or conspiracy: "As we have said, the defendants are not charged with specific overt acts against named victims. They are charged with criminal participation in government organized atrocities and persecutions unmatched in the annals of history".[121] The majority thus clearly recognised the distinctive nature of state-organised criminality on a massive scale but they balked at using an all-embracing theory of liability of the kind advocated by Blair that would catch in its net anyone "connected with a plan, scheme or conspiracy"[122] and threatened to overshadow an inquiry into the individual conduct of each accused person. We turn now to a case that seems to even more clearly exemplify the reluctance of some of the Nuremberg Military Tribunals to tread the path advocated by Blair.

---

[120] *Ibid.*, p. 1199.

[121] *Ibid.*, p. 1177.

[122] Judge Blair's Separate Opinion, p. 1195, see *supra* note 100.

2.2.2. The Pohl Case (WVHA)[123]

The Pohl case,[124] far more than the hodgepodge of defendants assembled in the Justice [125] or Ministries [126] cases, seems to offer the perfect opportunity for conceptualising collective activity in a closed bureaucratic system driven by a criminal purpose.

Oswald Pohl was the head of the Wirtschafts-Verwaltungshauptamt ('WVHA', Economic Administrative Authority). The WVHA was one of the 12 main offices (*Hauptaemter*) of the SS. It essentially provided the administrative services, for instance bookkeeping, construction, vehicle maintenance and so on, for the entire SS organisation, including the Waffen-SS (Armed SS). The WVHA might have escaped prosecution at the NMT if not for an administrative reorganisation that placed the previously independent Directorate of Concentration Camps under the aegis of Pohl's rapidly expanding empire. As such, in addition to responsibility for all SS barracks, depots, bases, hospitals and so on from France to the USSR, the WVHA became responsible for the administration of the concentration camp system. Pohl and 17 section heads or deputy section heads of the WVHA bureaucracy were indicted for war crimes, crimes against humanity, conspiracy or common design, and membership in a criminal organisation. As in previous cases the charge of conspiracy as an independent offence was dismissed.

The Pohl case [127] presents a picture of a highly functional bureaucratic entity composed of divisions that had separate functions but each function was an interconnected and indispensable part of the administration of SS installations, and of concentration camps and killing centres. They all operated under the highly efficient direction of Pohl, whose ambition drove a continual expansion of WVHA enterprises. Moreover, the WVHA was one of the 12 principal subdivisions of an organisation that had been declared a criminal organisation by the NMT. Each of the accused was therefore also charged with membership in that criminal organisation and most of them were convicted on that charge. The combination of the authoritative designation of the WVHA as a

---

123 Pohl case, see *supra* note 15.

124 *Ibid.*

125 Nuremberg Military Tribunal, see *supra* note 1.

126 Ministries case, see *supra* note 14.

127 Pohl case, see *supra* note 15.

criminal organisation coupled with the nature of its activities with regards to concentration camps and the high degree of interconnectedness of its subdivisions, all co-operating to ensure the efficient running of the camps, would seem to provide fertile ground for employing a theory of liability such as common design or shared purpose in carrying out the programme of a criminal enterprise.[128]

Like the judges in the Justice and RuSHA cases, however, the Pohl case judges studiously avoided such an approach and focused on traditional criminal law criteria, identifying individuals as principals or accessories on the basis of their knowledge and the nature and degree of their participation. At the same time, however, the judges recognised the nature of collective action in such an organisation and repeatedly employed the metaphor of "cogs in a machine" to describe the co-ordinated operations of the WVHA bureaucracy. Those few individuals whom they found to be "mere cogs" in the implementation of the plans to commit mass murder, enslavement and spoliation were acquitted, whereas those who actively fulfilled, on the view of the court, important functions, were not "mere cogs" and were convicted.

It would have seemed natural to use the 'common design' language of the indictment to apply a JCE-like or conspiracy framework to the case, given that, as found in the judgment, all of the accused worked in an organisation where they not only knew of the criminal enterprises of the WVHA but were also organised into a smooth functioning unified whole that made the administration of the SS empire possible. Indeed, language in the IMT judgment on the nature of the charges against the six indicted criminal organisations appears to invite such a step:

> A criminal organization is analogous to a criminal conspiracy in that the essence of both is cooperation for criminal purposes. *There must be a group bound together and organized for a common purpose.* The group must be formed or used in connection with the commission of crimes denounced by the Charter.[129]

---

[128] See *ibid.*, pp. 993–94, which makes findings on the high degree of co-operation between the divisions of the WVHA, all in the service of a common enterprise.

[129] *Ibid.*, p. 1018, emphasis added. The IMT judgment limits the application of the crime of membership in a way that undermined the purpose for which the doctrine was conceived. The original idea behind the indictment of these six organisations and creation of a crime of membership in a criminal organisation was that tens or hundreds of thousands of

The Pohl Tribunal appears to have instead decided that such theories of responsibility were off the table and despite their accurate analysis of the way in which bureaucracies operate they relied on the conventional approach to liability. A few examples will suffice to demonstrate the judgment's analysis of liability.

With regards to the charge of employing slave labour under the most horrific conditions in the camps under his administrative umbrella, the Tribunal finds that Pohl

> cannot escape the fact that he was the administrative head of the agency which brought about these tragedies. His was more than a mere consenting part. It was active participation. On this count […] he is guilty of direct participation in a war crime and a crime against humanity.[130]

Or with regards to the WVHA's and Pohl's role in the collection of dental gold from concentration and extermination camp inmates, the judgment finds that

> [t]his was a broad criminal program, requiring the cooperation of many persons, and Pohl's part was to conserve and account for the loot. Having knowledge of the illegal purposes of the action and of the crimes which accompanied it, *his active participation* even in the after-phases of the action made him *particeps criminis* in the whole affair.[131]

Turning to defendant Frank, the chief of Amtsgruppe A, the Administrative Management Division of the WVHA, the Tribunal considered his liability for the looting of property of concentration and extermination camp victims as well as for the murder of these individuals.

---

members of the SS and other institutions could be subjected to assembly-line trials where it would suffice for the prosecution to prove their identity and their membership. The IMT, however, held that mere membership was not enough:

> Since the declaration with respect to the organizations and groups will, as has been pointed out, fix the criminality of its members, that definition should exclude persons who had no knowledge of the criminal purposes or acts of the organization and those who were drafted by the state for membership, unless they were personally implicated in the commission of acts declared criminal by article 6 of the Charter as members of the organization. Membership alone is not enough to come within the scope of these declarations.

[130] *Ibid.*, p. 984.
[131] *Ibid.*, p. 989, emphasis added.

They found that although Frank knew of the deaths they cannot be attributed to him and his liability is limited to the programme in which he participated, which was the distribution of the property of the victims. On a JCE or common design theory of liability it would be quite easy to connect the murders and the looting of the property, for the latter was so closely connected to the former and they both formed such essential parts of the extermination plan. The Tribunal's more conservative approach focused on an act requirement of direct participation (or aiding and abetting) and knowledge of the criminal activity.

Defendant Fanslau was head of the Personnel Department within Amtsgruppe A, and later headed that unit. His activities involved promotions, recruitment, replacements, transfers and so on, for the entire SS. Since this included concentration camp personnel, he was charged with and convicted of war crimes and crimes against humanity for knowing of and 'promoting and administering' slavery in the camps. The response of the judgment to Fanslau's protests that he was a mere personnel officer is telling:

> As the officer in charge of personnel he was as much an integral part of the whole organization and as *essential a cog* in its whole operation as any other of Pohl's subordinates. He was in command of one of the essential ingredients of successful functioning [...] He was not an obscure menial; he was a person of responsibility in the organization, who was charged with and performed important and essential functions.[132]

While the Pohl case presented the judges with perhaps the clearest opportunity to apply a doctrine of common purpose against the administrators of a single organisation who were charged with directly operating a system whose sole purpose was looting, enslavement and mass murder, they declined to do so. Despite their lucid explanation of how the WVHA operated as a machinery of death and criminal exploitation, and despite their findings that those convicted were all essential cogs in this machinery, they relied upon conventional standards of criminal liability rather than any theory that could plausibly be called a version of JCE. The judgments in the RuSHA,[133] Justice[134] and Pohl[135]

---

[132] *Ibid.*, p. 999, emphasis added.

[133] RuSHA case, see *supra* note 25.

[134] Justice case, see *supra* note 1.

cases all represent an apprehension of the nature of systemic state sponsored criminality, but they also demonstrate a reluctance on the part of the judges to follow through on this apprehension by creating a commensurate theory of responsibility. Even in the Justice case,[136] which comes closest to doing so, the majority appears reluctant to take the final step of actually convicting on the basis of the system of organised criminality they have identified. This, indeed, provides the basis for the criticism of the majority's reluctance in Blair's concurring opinion.[137]

With regards to the historical foundations of the modern doctrine of JCE, what we see in the three cases we have examined is Second World War era judges grappling with the same issues that confronted their later ICTY and ICTR brethren when dealing with state-organised mass atrocity. However, the solutions they found for dealing with these issues were very different. In the end, the judges in the NMT cases were more focused on justifying on an unassailable basis the convictions of each individual accused than they were in providing a jurisprudential legacy for the future. This is hardly surprising. It is also not surprising that while they went to great lengths to adequately acknowledge what they regarded as the unprecedented systematic inhumanity and atrocity perpetrated by the organs of the Nazi regime, they also fell back on conventionally accepted criminal law standards to justify the heavy sentences (including death) which they imposed upon the accused. They did this by carefully citing the evidence that demonstrated beyond a reasonable doubt that each accused had knowingly directly ordered, instigated, planned, perpetrated or assisted in the perpetration of specific crimes and the implementation of criminal orders and policies. We might note that all of these judges in the NMT cases had served as judges in the United States. As such it was natural for them to focus more narrowly on the case at hand and the justification of individual verdicts. This is quite unlike the far more mixed background of the ICTY judges, whose activities as professors and scholars of international law may have disposed them more to an approach that consciously sought to create new foundations for international criminal jurisprudence by inventing doctrines such as JCE. In doing so, however, these ICTY judges relied upon the traditional

---

[135] Pohl case, see *supra* note 15.

[136] Justice case, see *supra* note 1.

[137] Judge Blair's Separate Opinion, see *supra* note 100

judicial justificatory strategy of finding foundations in the past that could plausibly (or implausibly) serve as standards for the future.

2.3. Command and Superior Responsibility

Unlike JCE, command responsibility was a well-established category in international law when the ICTY and ICTR were created, and was enshrined in their statutes (Articles 7(3)[138] and 6(3)[139] respectively). When it came to defining the elements of command responsibility for military officers, or for civilian superiors, the judges of the new tribunals had a rich legacy of case law from Second World War to draw upon. For the judges of the Second World War courts, however, the situation was rather different and they were dealing with a relatively untested doctrine that had not been defined in a body of international case law. This is the likely explanation for why the Second World War cases created such a wide range of approaches to command responsibility. It was left to the contemporary tribunals to sift through this case law with regards to questions such as (1) the mental element; (2) the nature of the superior-subordinate relationship and whether it required *de jure* or could also encompass *de facto* authority; (3) the liability of civilian superiors under such theories; and (4) the liability of officers not in command positions, such as staff officers. These questions were all taken up in the Čelebići case,[140] where the Trial Chamber looked back to the historical foundations of command responsibility for answers to the question of how the customary law doctrine had been formulated. The Appeals Chamber judgment re-examined these questions and that judgment emerged as the leading ICTY/ICTR case on this issue. This section will consider the way in which the Čelebići judgments accessed the Second World War legacy and will examine aspects of that legacy anew. As we will see, the Second World War cases display a striking variety of standards on crucial issues. Many of the cases also display a frustrating opacity that has given rise to multiple and contested interpretations. This is nowhere more true than with regards to the Yamashita case.[141] As noted above, the enterprise of

---

[138] ICTY Statute, see *supra* note 86.

[139] United Nations, *Statute of the International Criminal Tribunal for Rwanda*, 8 November 1994 ("ICTR Statute") (http://www.legal-tools.org/doc/8732d6/).

[140] Čelebići case, see *supra* note 23.

[141] Yamashita case, see *supra* note 4.

interpreting the broad Second World War legacy is hampered by the absence of final written decisions that articulate the standards of liability that the court applied. It is also hampered by the fact that even when judgments were produced it was not the practice to analyse modes of liability or substantive offences in terms of elements or even, for the most part, to provide definitions.

2.3.1. Civilian Superiors and the Case of Hirota Kōki[142]

Let us begin with the appropriation of the IMTFE's conviction of Hirota Kōki as a supposed precedent for civilian superior responsibility. In the section of the Čelebići trial judgment[143] dealing with civilian superiors, the Trial Chamber asserts that the IMTFE relied on the principle of command responsibility in making findings of guilt against a number of Japanese civilian political leaders charged with having "deliberately and recklessly disregarded their duty" to prevent violations of the law of war.[144] The Trial Chamber analogises the treatment of Hirota to the conviction on command responsibility for failure to prevent war crimes of General Matsui, the commander of Imperial Japanese Army (IJA) forces at Nanjing: "The tribunal was also prepared to place such responsibility upon the Japanese Foreign Minister at the time, Hirota Koki".[145] The trial judgment quotes the full passage from the IMTFE judgment stating that while Hirota did make repeated inquiries to the IJA on the basis of the protests he was receiving from foreign governments about massacres in Nanjing, he was negligent in relying on these assurances. The IMTFE judgment concludes that Hirota, "was derelict in his duty in not insisting before the Cabinet that immediate action be taken to put an end to the atrocities [...] He was content to rely on assurances which he knew were not being implemented [...] His inaction amounted to criminal negligence".[146]

The Čelebići Trial Chamber[147] is not the only court that has relied on the conviction of Hirota as a prime example of the Second World War

---

[142] Tokyo Trial, see *supra* note 5

[143] Čelebići case, see *supra* note 23.

[144] *Ibid.*, p. 132.

[145] *Ibid.*

[146] *Ibid.*

[147] Čelebići case, see *supra* note 23.

era doctrine of command responsibility applied to civilian political officials. We may also note that the IMTFE judgment[148] characterised command responsibility as based upon a negligence standard. The Čelebići Trial Chamber also went further and pointed to the convictions of Foreign Minister Shigemitsu and Prime Minister Tōjō as further examples of the conviction of civilian superiors on this basis. This interpretation of the IMTFE judgment, however, is blatantly incorrect and points up one of the underlying problems of looking back to the Second World War historical foundations.

The IMTFE majority judgment[149] is a complex, poorly written and poorly argued document of some 500 pages in print. Reading a particular passage of the judgment without an understanding of the whole, and of the nature of the Japanese regime of the Second World War era, is not likely to produce sound results, but that is just what the Čelebići Trial Chamber did. If one reads the more than 200 pages of the judgment devoted to the conspiracy to commit crimes against peace, one of the overarching themes is the domination of Japanese policy in the 1930s by the IJA, and particularly by the faction in the IJA that from the late 1920s was pushing for Japanese expansion into China. This faction resorted to assassinations and military coups to advance the militaristic agenda, eventually gaining the upper hand and controlling Japanese military and political policy in China. What the IMTFE judgment points out over and over is that the civilian cabinet was unable to mount effective opposition to army policy and eventually most civilian members of the cabinet joined in the expansionist drive or were forced to resign.

One reason that the military came to dominate policy was that under the Japanese Constitution the army appointed the War Minister to the cabinet, as they did with General Tōjō Hideki. The army could bring about the downfall of any government that disagreed with its aggressive policies by simply having the War Minister resign. This dissolved the cabinet and a new government had to be appointed by the Emperor. In the section of the judgment on the conspiracy to commit crimes against peace, the IMTFE majority repeatedly finds that the cabinet was impotent in the face of the army's dominance and that whenever there was resistance in the cabinet they simply engineered its dissolution. Even in cases where, early

---

[148] Tokyo Trial, see *supra* note 5.

[149] *Ibid.*

on, the cabinet had objected to aggressive military action in China, or ordered the army to desist, the judgment found that the military simply ignored the civilian authorities. By the time of the Nanjing Massacre, when Hirota was Foreign Minister, outright war in China had begun and the dominance of the army was unassailable and only the Emperor possessed sufficient authority to influence the conduct of the war.

In this light, to read the verdict against Hirota as being based on his authority as a civilian superior is absurd. Not only was there no formal chain of command that gave the cabinet as a whole authority over the military, not only was Hirota as Foreign Minister certainly not in either a *de jure* or *de facto* position of having even a shred of authority over the army, but the judgment had in fact repeatedly concluded that the army blithely ignored any statements by the cabinet that went against its intentions in China and in fact dominated the formulation of governmental policy. If the cabinet as a whole had no authority to stop the army's actions, Hirota as a diplomat and Foreign Minister can in no sense be said to be a 'civilian superior'.

The interpretation of the IMTFE judgment's treatment of Hirota as based on his command authority or position as a superior also finds absolutely no support in the actual words of the judgment. The judgment finds him derelict in his duty because he did not insist that the cabinet take action. Nowhere does it imply that either he or the cabinet had the *de facto* authority to stop what the army was doing by issuing an order or directive, let alone stopping the army by such "insistence". Instead, modern commentators have read this into the judgment, starting with the assumption that Hirota must have been convicted on the basis of his authority, and this in turn is based on the assumption that the cabinet as a whole had such *de facto* authority.

However, I think that the basis of Hirota's conviction is actually quite different. The Tokyo judgment, to put it mildly, does not make a practice of clearly articulating its standards of responsibility. What a reading of the judgment as a whole indicates is that the Tribunal was operating with a loosely conceived and never clearly articulated theory of what we might call cabinet responsibility. Since the cabinet was in principle the policy-making body of the government of Japan, its members, on this view, were responsible for the actions of the state unless they did everything within their power to prevent crimes from occurring, however futile such actions might be. In the event the actions were futile, the IMTFE judgment requires them to resign their position. The judgment only seems to distinguish between cabinet members who had absolutely no connection to foreign affairs and policy and those who did, so the IMTFE did not go as far as creating a collective responsibility of the cabinet *per se*.

In the case of Hirota and Shigemitsu as Foreign Ministers, by virtue of their office they had a direct connection to Japan's aggressive foreign policy and were the recipients of the protests from foreign governments about Japanese war crimes. The tribunal's standard required them to do everything possible to prevent such crimes and to resign when they were unable to do so. It was not predicated on their authority or superior position with regards to the military. This might have been the case with the War Minister, who was a general appointed by the army, but certainly not of the civilian members of the cabinet. Indeed the very passage of the IMTFE judgment that convicts Hirota makes it clear that the army did not even deign to respond to Hirota's repeated inquiries, but contemptuously ignored them.[150] There was no need for the army to respond as Hirota had no authority to do more than politely inquire. He had no means to even compel them to answer, let alone to stop the massacres going on in Nanjing. From the standpoint of the army such inquiries or protests from civilian members of the cabinet were an annoyance to be brushed aside, nothing more. To use the modern terminology, unknown to the Second World War jurisprudence, there was no superior–subordinate relationship between Hirota or Shigemitsu and the IJA because there was no effective control in the form of the power to prevent or punish.

Reading the unpublished manuscript of the judgment which the President of the Tribunal, Sir William Webb, had drafted in the hope that the majority would adopt it, makes clear who did in fact have the authority to stop the tragedy playing out in Nanjing.[151] Webb's draft judgment is a model of clarity in comparison to the majority judgment and our view of the Tokyo trial would be far different and far more positive if the majority had adopted it. One reason why it was not is that Webb's judgment repeatedly made clear the ultimate authority of the Emperor.[152] As the American and British governments, over the vehement

---

[150] *Ibid.*, pp. 1158–61.

[151] W.F. Webb, (unpublished) Judgment, see *supra* note 6.

[152] *Ibid.*

protests of the Australians and Russians, had decided for reasons of political expediency not to permit the Emperor to be tried, the American and British prosecutors and judges were under strict instructions not to allow any reference to the responsibility of Hirohito.

In Webb's treatment of Hirota's role with regards to Nanjing, Webb also finds that Hirota should have taken the matter to the whole cabinet. But he goes on to point out that what Hirota should have done when the cabinet failed to take effective action was to have brought the matter directly to the Emperor. That was where authority over the army resided. Webb makes that point with regards to all the cabinet members convicted in relation to war crimes, saying that their duty was to take the matter to the Emperor.[153] The majority judgment, however, simply says that cabinet members like Hirota or Shigemitsu should have gone to the cabinet.[154] The majority judgment never mentions the Emperor in this regard. It was he who had the ultimate authority over the military, as indicated by his decision to go to war and his decision to end it. The cabinet as a whole, and certainly not the Foreign Minister as an individual, would have been in a position to do so.

2.3.2. The Mental Element in Command Responsibility

When the Čelebići Trial Chamber[155] took up the issue of the mental element in establishing command responsibility they inquired as to whether or not the contemporary 'knew or had reason to know' standard was the standard of the Second World War jurisprudence and whether it should be interpreted as a negligence standard. The Trial Chamber starts from the position that command responsibility is not based upon strict liability and that 'under customary law' a superior can be held liable when he either has actual knowledge or has information in his possession on the basis of which he was at least 'on notice of the risk' that such offences were being or might be committed by his subordinates.[156] They interpret this latter category as being based upon the Second World War jurisprudence that "affirmed the existence of a duty of commanders to

---

[153] *Ibid.*

[154] Tokyo Trial, p. 1160, see *supra* note 5.

[155] Čelebići case, see *supra* note 23.

[156] *Ibid.*, p. 143.

remain informed about the activities of their subordinates".[157] They cite a passage from the Hostage case[158] to support this based upon the duty of a commander of occupied territory to acquire knowledge of crimes being committed. Of course, as the High Command case[159] elaborates, the duty of a commander of occupied territory is a special duty by virtue of his responsibility for the well-being and security of the population of the occupied area. It is not the same duty that a commander engaged in military operations has. Be that as it may, the Trial Chamber concludes that the customary law standard developed by the Second World War jurisprudence was 'knew or has reason to know' as defined above. They do not clearly state, however, whether they regard the 'reason to know' standard as one of negligence or recklessness. Their reference to being 'on notice of the risk' would seem to suggest that it is a recklessness standard. Their treatment of accused Mucic, however, casts some doubt on this.[160]

In finding that Mucic possessed *de facto* authority sufficient to make him liable as a superior, the Trial Chamber considers the mental element as fulfilled based on the widespread nature of the crimes in the Čelebići camp. The one case they cite for this proposition, however, is the Yamashita case, and they quote the following passage from the decision of the US Military Commission that convicted Yamashita and sentenced him to death:

> Where murder and rape and vicious, revengeful actions are widespread offences, and there is no effective attempt by a commander *to discover and control the criminal acts*, such a

---

[157] *Ibid.*, p. 145.

[158] Nuremberg Military Tribunal, *United States of America v. Wilhelm List et al.*, Case No. 7, Judgment, 19 February 1948, *Trials of War Criminals Before the Nuremberg Military Tribunals Under Control Council Law No. 10*, US Government Printing Office, vol. XI ('Green Series') ("Hostage case") (http://www.legal-tools.org/doc/b05aa4/).

[159] High Command case, see *supra* note 19.

[160] The considerable confusion prevailing on this issue until it was clarified in the Čelebići Appeals Judgment (see Čelebići case, *supra* note 23) is reflected in the ICTR Musema trial judgment where the Trial Chamber states there are currently two opposing interpretations of the *mens rea* requirement for superior responsibility, one of which invokes a strict liability standard with no mental element, the other of which regards the required mental element as 'negligence' (see Musema case, para. 129, *supra* note 21). This is a rather astonishing interpretation because it totally ignores the very substantial body of jurisprudence that holds that the required mental element is 'knowledge'.

> commander may be held responsible, even criminally liable, for the lawless acts of his troops.[161]

This passage is ambiguous, but the language of "no effective attempt [...] to discover" seems to indicate a standard based on negligence rather than a standard based on a conscious disregard of a risk. Was negligence in fact the customary law standard in the Second World War jurisprudence? I would argue that it was not, and that in fact, there was no clear customary law standard for the mental element of command responsibility because of the wide variety of approaches that appear to have been employed by different tribunals.

We may start with the notorious conviction of General Yamashita Tomoyuki,[162] cited by the Čelebići decision. Without elaborating fully the nature of the kangaroo court trial of Yamashita, for present purposes it suffices to say that Yamashita was convicted under a strict liability standard. The brief and conceptually incoherent decision of the Military Commission in fact suggests different bases for liability and different points in its cursory and abbreviated treatment. What it does not do, however, is point to *any* evidence that Yamashita either had actual knowledge of crimes being committed by his subordinates or had actual information on the basis of which he was on inquiry notice. The commission merely concluded that the crimes were so widespread that Yamashita must have either "secretly ordered or wilfully permitted"[163] their commission.

"Secretly ordered" is a telling phrase, for what it actually means is that the prosecution introduced no evidence of any such orders. There was in fact absolutely no factual basis for the supposition that such 'orders' had ever existed. There was, however, evidence that Yamashita had issued orders to protect the civilian population and had ordered the naval garrison in Manila to leave the city prior to the American advance.

A review of the 3,000-page transcript of the trial shows that the prosecution never introduced one shred of evidence that Yamashita was aware of the crimes being committed or received any reports that would have put him on notice that such was the case. And in the case of the Rape of Manila, the naval garrison that committed the crimes did not

---

[161] Yamashita case, p. 279, emphasis added, see *supra* note 4.

[162] *Ibid.*

[163] *Ibid.*, p. 59.

acknowledge IJA General Yamashita as their commander and decided to disobey his explicit and repeated orders to withdraw from the city. In short, he had no effective control over these forces. Yamashita was convicted simply on the basis that he was the commander of Japanese forces and therefore responsible for the crimes they had committed.

That strict liability is the basis of the conviction of Yamashita is confirmed by comparison with the companion case, the trial of IJA General Homma Masaharu.[164] Homma was accused, among other things, of responsibility for the Bataan Death March. Although with regards to many of the crimes of which he was accused the prosecution was unable to provide direct evidence of his awareness, they did, for example, introduce testimony showing that Homma had driven along the route that the Death March had taken at a time when numerous corpses of those who had died or been murdered along the way were visible at the roadside. There was also some circumstantial evidence on the basis of which inferences could have been made as to his possession of information about other crimes. While the Homma trial was also more of a publicity campaign for vindicating the American commander, General Douglas MacArthur, than a fair trial, at least the prosecution did try to base its case on proving Homma's link to the crimes of which he was accused and his actual knowledge of these crimes. The prosecution in the case of Yamashita made no such attempt.[165]

---

[164] USA Military Courts, *United States of America v. Homma Masaharu*, US National Archives and Records Administration (NARA) RG 331, Box 1671–1672 ("Homma case").

[165] Observers of these two trials noted their media circus atmosphere. Homma, as commander of Japanese forces invading the Philippines, had humiliated MacArthur by inflicting perhaps the greatest defeat in US military history, with MacArthur escaping the Philippines while leaving his subordinates to the horrors of internment. Yamashita was the newly installed commander of Japanese forces defending the Philippines in 1944–1945, arriving some 10 days before the vastly superior American invasion force landed. Convicting Yamashita for all of the crimes committed across the Philippine archipelago simply on the basis that they had occurred in his command area offered a means of demonstrating to the Philippine population that the returning American colonial power, that had been so impotent to protect them in 1942, had returned to restore order. It is not coincidental that MacArthur intervened in the trial proceedings to speed things up so that the verdict against Yamashita could be handed down on 7 December 1945. For the classic account by one of Yamashita's defence counsel of the kangaroo court nature of the trial, see A. Frank Reel, *The Case of General Yamashita*, Octagon Books, New York, 1971, and more recently, largely following in Reel's footsteps, Allan A. Ryan, *Yamashita's Ghost: War Crimes, MacArthur's Justice, and Command Accountability*, University Press of Kansas, Lawrence, KS, 2012.

The conviction of Yamashita on this basis was not an isolated event. In the Australian war crimes programme a group of high-ranking commanders was put on trial largely based upon evidence introduced in previous trials against junior officers and enlisted personnel. The primary evidence introduced against many of the commanders was the transcripts of these previous proceedings. The problem was that those previous trials had generally not sought to establish linkage evidence connecting the distant commanders to the crimes charged against low-ranking subordinates.

Most of these accused generals had command authority over large geographical areas and the previous trials had dealt with crimes committed at prisoner of war ('POW') camps or other military bases within their command areas. The basic theory of the prosecution was that subordinates of the accused had been convicted of war crimes and therefore the accused, as their commanders, were responsible for these crimes. This was the basis, for example, on which Australian military courts convicted General Adachi Hatazō,[166] General Hirota Akira[167] and General Baba Masao.[168] In the Adachi and Hirota cases the documentary evidence submitted by the prosecution consisted of the transcripts from the previous trials, which for the most part only established that crimes had been committed. Indeed, the generals had not been accused in these previous trials and the evidence introduced by the prosecution bore upon the guilt of the lower-ranking individuals who were the accused, not on the responsibility of the high-level commanders in distant locations. These trials had not sought to establish the knowledge or other connection to the crimes of these commanders and of course they obviously had had no opportunity to confront the witnesses against them or contest the evidence introduced against them. There were no judgments in the trials of the subordinates so there had been no legal findings or conclusions that touched upon the responsibility of the generals. There were likewise no

---

[166] Australia Military Courts, *Prosecutor v. Hatazo Adachi*, Charge Sheet, 23 April 1947, National Archives UK, London, A-0471 No. 81652 ("Adachi case") (http://www.legal-tools.org/doc/041c46/).

[167] Australia Military Courts, *Prosecutor v. Akira Hirota*, Charge Sheet, 3 April 1947, National Archives UK, London, A-0471 No. 81653 ("Hirota case") (http://www.legal-tools.org/doc/22fd51/).

[168] Australia Military Courts, *Prosecutor v. Masao Baba*, Charge Sheet, 2 June 1947, National Archives UK, London, A-0471 No. 81631-A ("Baba case") (http://www.legal-tools.org/doc/32077f/).

judgments in the trials of the generals themselves, but in the cases where the prosecution had relied upon simply introducing the prior transcripts and did not introduce evidence that established the knowledge of the accused, the convictions can be seen as similar to that of Yamashita.[169] In addition to the conviction of Adachi, there is also the trial of General Baba Masao[170] where he was convicted and sentenced to death for the notorious Sandakan–Ranau Death March. In that trial the prosecution also failed to produce evidence that linked Baba to the criminal activity or that proved that he was aware of the conditions on the march.

At the other extreme from the strict liability standard of the Yamashita case,[171] we have the NMT High Command case,[172] which should be regarded as the leading Second World War case on command responsibility. Apart from the fact that there is a lengthy and on the whole carefully reasoned judgment which exhaustively reviews the evidence and makes specific findings, this judgment is one of the relatively few that also considers the legal standards of responsibility in some detail. It engages, for example, in a detailed and cogent discussion, under what conditions a commander may be held accountable for transmitting orders down the chain of command. The High Command case also has the best discussion in the Second World War case law of the liability of staff officers who did not have command authority. Comparison with the abbreviated and crude treatment of the liability of accused Mutō Akira at the IMTFE, for example, reveals not only a completely different standard, but also one that is nuanced, elaborate in detail, and based upon a logically developed argument. However, even in this closely reasoned judgment, it is not self-evident what the precise standard is for the mental element. For example,

> Modern war such as the last war entails a large measure of
> decentralization. A high commander cannot keep completely

---

[169] It is striking that only in the cases of three of these generals that the president of the Military Commissions that tried them wrote a memorandum explaining their finding of guilt. The memorandum is less than one and a half pages and basically seems designed to affirm the legitimacy of the proceedings by stating, without any supporting documentation, that the court was satisfied that the accused all had actual knowledge of the crimes for which they were charged under superior responsibility. See NAA MP 472/1, 336/1/1865.

[170] Baba case, see *supra* note 168.

[171] Yamashita case, see *supra* note 4.

[172] High Command case, see *supra* note 19.

> informed of the details of military operations of subordinates and most assuredly not of every administrative measure. He has the right to assume that details entrusted to responsible subordinates will be legally executed... The same is true of other high commanders in the chain of command. Criminality does not attach to every individual in this chain of command from that fact alone. There must be a personal dereliction. That can occur only where the act is directly traceable to him or where his failure to properly supervise his subordinates constitutes criminal negligence on his part. In the latter case it must be a personal neglect amounting to a wanton, immoral disregard of the action of his subordinates amounting to acquiescence.[173]

This paragraph comes in the section devoted to commanders of occupied territory, but it appears to set out a general standard. If that is the case, does the court mean 'negligence' in failing to supervise subordinates in the technical sense of the term? The next sentence seems rather to imply that recklessness, that is, a conscious disregard of risk is intended as the general standard: the phrase "wanton, immoral disregard of the action of his subordinates" seems to imply awareness of these actions is the standard, rather than a culpable failure to inform oneself about actions of which one is completely unaware. Further, in the next paragraph the judgment refers to the prosecution's argument that commanders of occupied territory are *per se* responsible (i.e. strict liability) and the judgment states that the prosecution relied on the Yamashita case[174] for this proposition. The judgment distinguishes that case and the judges seem anxious to avoid recognising that it might have any precedential or authoritative value. However, in reiterating their standard the court confusingly again refers to "criminal neglect" but goes on to articulate a standard based upon knowledge:

> We are of the opinion, however, as above pointed out in other aspects of this case, that the occupying commander must have knowledge of these offenses and acquiesce or participate or criminally neglect to interfere in their commission and that the offenses committed must be patently criminal.[175]

---

[173] *Ibid.*, Judgment pp. 543–44.

[174] Yamashita case, see *supra* note 4.

[175] High Command case, p. 545, see *supra* note 19.

The infelicitous choice of the word "neglect" causes needless confusion, but the fact that in the context of "having knowledge" it refers to neglecting "to interfere" in the commission of the crimes indicates awareness and a failure to act on the basis of that awareness rather than culpable ignorance.

The High Command judgment also considers liability of commanders of occupied territory in Russia for the operations of the Einsatzgruppen (SS paramilitary death squads) within their command areas. These units were under the operational command of SS headquarters in Berlin rather than under the Wehrmacht field commanders to whose command they had been attached for logistical support. The issue raised was whether the field commanders (for the most part generals or field marshals commanding armies or army groups) could be held liable for the actions of these SS and Sicherheitsdienst ('SD', Security Service) units over whom they had no operational command authority. The language of the judgment is instructive as to the mental element required: "The sole question then as to such defendants in this case is whether or not they knew of the criminal activities of the Einsatzgruppen of the Security Police and SD and neglected to suppress them".[176] Here again, "neglect" is based upon awareness of the crimes and should be interpreted as failure to act upon knowledge of the commission of war crimes.

This conclusion of knowledge as the required mental element is supported by the judgment's careful analysis of all the factors for and against the conclusion that because of the scale of the mobile killing operations the commanders must have been aware of these crimes. In direct contrast to the Yamashita case,[177] the High Command case[178] considers over several pages all the reasons why a commander might not have learned of such crimes. They conclude that there can be no general presumption that because of the widespread nature and scale of the crimes a commander must have known (i.e. that knowledge can on this basis be imputed to him). Rather, the judgment holds that each individual defendant's situation must be considered based on what they can actually

---

[176] *Ibid.*, p. 547.

[177] Yamashita case, see *supra* note 4.

[178] High Command case, see *supra* note 19.

be proved to have known or what facts were available to them. The conclusion is again drawn in terms of knowledge, not culpable ignorance:

> From this discussion it is apparent we can draw no general presumption as to their knowledge in this matter and must necessarily go to the evidence pertaining to the various defendants to make a determination of this question. And it is further pointed out that to establish the guilt of a defendant from connection with acts of the SIPO and SD by acquiescence, *not only must knowledge be established, but the time of such knowledge must be established.*[179]

Turning to analysis of the liability of each accused this is the standard the tribunal articulates. For example, with regards to defendant Wilhelm von Leeb,

> The evidence establishes that criminal orders were executed by units subordinate to the defendant and criminal acts were carried out by agencies within his command. But it is not considered under the situation outlined that criminal responsibility attaches to him merely on the theory of subordination and over-all command. He must be shown both to have had knowledge and to have been connected with such criminal acts, either by way of participation or criminal acquiescence.[180]

The standard here is knowledge and participation or acquiescence through not interfering. With regards to illegal executions of civilians by Einsatzgruppen, the judgment concludes that it was not established that von Leeb knew of or acquiesced to these executions that had taken place within his vast command area. The required standard of proof that the prosecution must meet directly contradicts the standard used to convict General Yamashita.[181] With regards to defendant Hermann Hoth, on the

---

[179] *Ibid.*, p. 549, emphasis added.

[180] *Ibid.*, p. 555.

[181] The later history of the Yamashita case also illustrates the malleability of historical foundations as they are interpreted and adapted for contemporary purposes. During the Vietnam War and after the My Lai massacre, Telford Taylor published *Nuremberg and Vietnam: An American Tragedy*, Quadrangle Books, Chicago, 1970. It was Taylor who, as chief prosecutor in the NMT Subsequent Proceedings, had prosecuted the High Command case (See High Command case, see *supra* note 19). But in the context of the American war in Vietnam he argued that because General Yamashita had been convicted and hanged by an American Military Commission on a strict liability standard, then the US had a duty to apply the same standard to its own commanders in Vietnam. Coming from a retired

other hand, the judgment concludes that he knew that the SD was operating in his command territory and he knew that they were conducting killing operations. It was on the basis of this knowledge and the fact that he then allowed the SD to continue operating that he was convicted with regards to the murder of civilians:

> Notwithstanding his knowledge of the character and functions of *the* SD, his possession of the power to curb *them* and his duty to do so, *he* washed his hands of his responsibility and let *the* SD take its unrestrained course in his area of command.[182]

We could continue to review the findings on each accused and compare them as to their consistency, but what seems clear is that the standard of responsibility applied here differs markedly from that in the Yamashita case and the Australian cases mentioned above.[183] Hoth, for example, was convicted because the court found he had the authority to prevent the crimes and had knowledge of the criminal activities, but took no action. We could continue this examination of the variety of command responsibility cases and consider the way in which command responsibility appears to have been dealt with in British and Australian cases involving the Death Railway labour camps or the Hell Ships. We could also consider the American trials of POW camp personnel and commanders. However, a significant obstacle would again be the lack of judgments, though the JAG reviews shed some light on what the JAG reviewers thought was the applicable legal standard. Therefore, to reach a sound conclusion as to the state of customary law would we not also have to consider the standards used in the thousands of other trials conducted by Norway, Denmark, the Netherlands, France, China, the Philippines and many more countries? Neither the Čelebići court nor any other

---

Brigadier General, famous author and Columbia law professor who had been the Deputy Prosecutor at the IMT and chief prosecutor at the NMT, Taylor's book was not exactly welcomed by the American military establishment. Military lawyers subsequently produced a series of articles purporting to show that Yamashita did not employ a strict liability standard and attempting to harmonise it with other Second World War cases such as the High Command (see *supra* note 19) and Hostage cases (see Hostage case, *supra* note 158).

[182] High Command case, p. 596, see *supra* note 19.

[183] Taking into account the lack of judgments in the Australian cases and the ensuing lack of specific factual findings or a statement of the standard of liability.

contemporary case dealing with the foundations of the doctrine of superior responsibility has done so.

With regards to the issue of the customary law standard for command responsibility in the Second World War era, what we confront is chaos, and a significant degree of ignorance. On one hand, the legal analysis that needs to be done has not been done, and indeed, cannot be done until the bulk of the Second World War cases become readily accessible. On the other hand, what the current state of our knowledge does reveal is a wide variety of approaches and a great deal of inconsistency in applying standards even within national war crimes programmes. The difficult state of the historical foundations of the contemporary doctrine of superior responsibility in Second World War jurisprudence was recognised by the Čelebići appeals judgment[184] when they reviewed the Trial Chamber's analysis of Second World War cases and found it sorely wanting. For example, with regards to the Trial Chamber's reliance on the Pohl case [185] they found that: "The Trial Chamber also quoted from the *Pohl* case. The phrase quoted is also meant to state a different point than that suggested by the Trial Chamber".[186]

The Appeals Chamber likewise found that the Trial Chamber misread the Hostage case [187] when they concluded that accused Field Marshal Wilhelm List had a duty to acquire knowledge. The Appeals Chamber finds that List actually had information in his possession from reports made to him that should have prompted him to investigate further. [188] The Appeals Chamber concludes more generally that: "Contrary to the Trial Chamber's conclusion, other cases discussed in the judgment do not show a consistent trend in the decisions that emerged out of the military trials conducted after the Second World War".[189] They further conclude that on the basis of their review of the case law referred

---

[184] Čelebići case, Appeals Judgment, see *supra* note 30.

[185] Pohl case, see *supra* note 15.

[186] Čelebići case, see *supra* note 23; for Appeals Judgment, see Čelebići case, Appeals Judgment *supra* note 30, p. 68.

[187] Hostage case, see *supra* note 158.

[188] Čelebići case, Appeals Judgment, pp. 68–69, see *supra* note 30.

[189] *Ibid.*, p. 68.

to by the Trial Chamber, it cannot be concluded that customary law at that time imposed a duty to know upon commanders.[190]

2.4. Defining Sexual Violence and the Construction of the International Crime of Rape

This section considers what happens when judges conclude that there is no body of international case law on which they can rely to define the elements of a core international crime. This was the situation when the first cases of prosecution for rape and sexual violence came before the ICTY and the ICTR. In the case of the ICTR this situation arose in the Akayesu case,[191] where in the midst of the trial the indictment had been amended to include the systematic sexual violence that had characterised the genocide in the Taba commune of which Akayesu was the *bourgmestre*. In the case of the ICTY it arose in the Furundžija case,[192] which rejected the approach of the Akayesu Trial Chamber and struck out on a completely different path.

At issue here is not just the definition of rape and sexual violence but rather the way in which the two Trial Chambers at the ICTY and ICTR set out to determine what was the applicable international law standard. The difference in their approaches as well as the contradictions in their respective definitions of rape gave rise to a series of conflicting decisions that was eventually resolved by the ICTY Appeals Chamber in the Kunarac appeals judgment.[193] We will not focus here on the definitions of the substantive offences but rather the approach of the respective courts as to how to arrive at such a definition. This, I will argue, raises the same issues of 'law-making' versus 'law-finding' that characterise the two previous sections of this paper.

The Akayesu Trial Chamber judgment proceeds from the statement that there is no previously established definition of rape on which the court can rely: "Considering the extent to which rape constitutes crimes against humanity, pursuant to Article 3(g) of the Statute, the Chamber

---

[190] *Ibid.*, p. 69–70.

[191] Akayesu case, see *supra* note 20.

[192] Furundžija case, see *supra* note 33.

[193] Kunarac case, Appeals Judgment, 12 June 2002 (http://www.legal-tools.org/doc/029a09/).

must define rape, as there is no commonly accepted definition of this term in international law".[194]

Rape had, of course, been the basis of convictions in Second World War cases but none of those cases defined the elements of that offence. The Akayesu judgment thus does not cite any previous cases. The Tribunal does note that there are many national jurisdictions that define rape through what they call a mechanical definition based upon the penetration of certain body parts.[195] The judgment considers, however, that such mechanical definitions are not suitable for defining rape in the context of state-sanctioned violence. What they propose instead is a conceptual definition[196] that proceeds from the principle that rape is an act of aggression and is systematically employed in conflicts as a weapon against the civilian population. Thus the Akayesu judgment quite clearly engages in law-making. They explicitly reject the notion that they should look to the domestic criminal law of national jurisdictions for a definition of rape. This is because they consider that systematic rape and sexual violence in the context of armed conflict or genocide requires its own definition suited to that context rather than the very different setting in which rape normally occurs in national jurisdictions. They proceed on the basis that since there is no accepted definition in the international setting they must create one by thinking about the nature of rape in the context of armed conflict as an international crime.

This manner of proceeding was clearly deeply troubling to the judges of the Furundžija Trial Chamber. They reject the Akayesu definition of rape as "a physical invasion of a sexual nature which is committed on a person under circumstances which are coercive".[197] The Furundžija court also proceeds from the starting point that "[n]o definition of rape can be found in international law".[198] In rejecting the Akayesu approach the Furundžija judgment merely states that resort cannot be had to any general principle of international law and implies that the Akayesu definition violates the principle of certainty (*Bestimmtheitsgrundsatz*).[199]

---

[194] Akayesu case, para. 596, see *supra* note 20.

[195] *Ibid.*, paras. 596–97.

[196] *Ibid.*, para. 597. The judgment states that they will focus on "the conceptual framework of state sanctioned violence".

[197] *Ibid.*, para. 598.

[198] Furundžija case, p. 68, see *supra* note 33.

[199] *Ibid.*, pp. 69–70.

What they state instead is that the proper way of defining an international crime where no definition exists is to look for "principles of criminal law common to the major legal systems of the world. These principles may be derived, with all due caution, from national laws".[200]

After noting the many fundamental differences in the definitions of rape in various national jurisdictions the Furundžija Tribunal nonetheless concludes that there is a clear standard that can be used for purposes of establishing the international norm:

> It is apparent from our survey of national legislation that, in spite of inevitable discrepancies, most legal systems in the common and civil law worlds consider rape to be the forcible sexual penetration of the human body by the penis or the forcible insertion of any other object into either the vagina or the anus.[201]

The Tribunal's finding that "forcible" penetration is required in most of the world's legal systems is particularly surprising in that the judgment had previously noted that in many legal systems the required element is the lack of consent of the victim.[202] In fact there is a major divide in national legal systems between those that have adopted the more progressive approach of focusing on the issue of consent as opposed to those that still require proof of an element of force, which makes some kinds of rape much more difficult to prove.

More importantly, we may note the way in which the judgment papers over this and other major discrepancies in order to arrive at the particular conclusion it reaches, following the method it has adopted for establishing the international norm. The Akayesu judgment represents the first contemporary case to convict for rape as a crime against humanity, to convict for rape as torture, to point to the importance of "coercive circumstances"[203] which preclude the possibility of consent, and to convict for rape as a genocidal act. Apart from these watershed substantive decisions, the Akayesu judgment had also taken a groundbreaking step in *how* it went about defining rape, looking to the nature of rape as an international crime in the context of armed conflict,

---

[200] *Ibid.*, p. 70.

[201] *Ibid.*, p. 72.

[202] *Ibid.*, p. 71.

[203] Akayesu case, p. 167, see *supra* note 20.

where it is used as a weapon of terror and dehumanisation. It was, however, precisely this step that so troubled the Furundžija Court.[204]

I would argue that what lay behind the Furundžija judgment's[205] vague reference to the *Bestimmtheitsgrundsatz* as a ground for rejecting Akayesu [206] was in fact the blatant manner in which the Akayesu judgment[207] created a norm without reference to traditional sources of international law. Or, we might say, without reference to the polite conventions by which judicial law-making is masked as law-finding. The most revolutionary step taken in Akayesu was perhaps not its definition of rape and sexual violence but rather, that they arrived at that definition simply by reflecting upon the role and meaning of systematic sexual violence in conflict contexts where it is used, "for such purposes as intimidation, degradation, humiliation, discrimination, punishment, control or destruction of a person". This definition and approach they characterised as "more useful in international law".[208] Indeed it is.

The split between the approaches and definitions in Akayesu[209] and Furundžija[210] gave rise to a series of decisions in other cases that created confusion as to what in fact were the elements of the crime of rape. This issue was ultimately resolved by the Kunarac appeals judgment based on appeals from the manner in which the Kunarac trial judgment had dealt with this issue.[211] The Trial Chamber addressed the definition of rape in a significantly more thorough and thoughtful manner than the Furundžija judgment. The Trial Chamber judgment argues that the proper method of proceeding where there is no established international norm is to inquire into "the general principles of law common to the major national legal systems of the world".[212] The justification for this manner of proceeding, they argue, "is whether it is possible to identify certain basic principles, or

---

[204] Furundžija case, see *supra* note 33.

[205] *Ibid.*

[206] Akayesu case, see *supra* note 20.

[207] *Ibid.*

[208] *Ibid.*, para. 597.

[209] *Ibid.*

[210] Furundžija case, see *supra* note 33.

[211] Kunarac case, see *supra* note 34.

[212] *Ibid.*, p. 147

in those legal systems which embody the *principles* which must be adopted in the international context".[213]

To carry out this task of identifying general principles the Kunarac trial judgment[214] surveys the domestic legislation of many national jurisdictions. Although adopting the same methodology as the Furundžija trial judgment,[215] it nonetheless arrives at a very different conclusion. In contradiction to the finding of Furundžija, the Kunarac trial judgment first notes: "In most common law systems, it is the absence of the victim's free and genuine consent to sexual penetration which is the defining characteristic of rape".[216] Discussing the common law jurisprudence at some length (which the Furundžija trial judgment refrains from doing) the Tribunal concludes that the international standard for defining rape is sexual penetration that "occurs without the consent of the victim".[217] This definition, of course, directly contradicts the standard articulated in Furundžija.[218] Nonetheless, the decision of the Trial Chamber was approved in the Kunarac appeals judgment.[219]

For present purposes the significance of these three cases resides in the way in which an international norm is established in the absence of a prior definition. We have seen in previous sections how various tribunals proceeded to define modes of liability with resort to a disparate body of Second World War case law that was so unsystematic that it allowed courts to find whatever standards they thought they needed to deal with the issues they were confronting. The situation with regards to the definition of rape and sexual violence is similar. The Kunarac and Furundžija Trial Chambers both survey the same body of domestic legislation but arrive at directly contradictory definitions. Both tribunals, however, agree that the national jurisdictions are divided. What actually motivates the Kunarac Trial Chamber, I would surmise, is their conviction

---

[213] *Ibid.*

[214] *Ibid.*

[215] Furundžija case, see *supra* note 33.

[216] Kunarac case, p. 152, see *supra* note 34.

[217] *Ibid.*, p. 156.

[218] In order to avoid blatantly rejecting the Furundžija definition, the Kunarac judgment politely states that the Furundžija judgment's standard also implicitly recognised the principle of sexual autonomy which also underlies the force requirement that had been adopted; *ibid.*, pp. 148, 155.

[219] *Ibid.*, Appeal Judgment, pp. 38–40, see *supra* note 193.

that lack of consent simply represents the better standard. Rather than directly stating this, however, they resort to unconvincing reasoning that because the principle of sexual autonomy underlies both the force and consent approaches there is in reality no contradiction. The fact that their articulation of the elements of rape only mentions consent, however, indicates the insubstantiality of this explanation.

The Akayesu Trial Chamber,[220] on the other hand, forthrightly makes clear how they are arriving at what they conceive to be the best standard for dealing with rape in situations of armed conflict. As I noted at the beginning of this paper, foundations of international criminal law are not simply 'there' to be found but are constructed through an interpretative process. It is this interpretative process in response to recognised needs that drives the constructive development of jurisprudence. That is to say that when a tribunal confronts an issue of establishing what is the relevant customary law standard it necessarily engages in a process of identifying, amidst the wealth of possible sources, those which it feels will be most useful for the case at hand.

2.5. Conclusion

As we saw above, the Čelebići appeals judgment concluded: "Contrary to the Trial Chamber's conclusion, other cases discussed in the Judgment do not show a consistent trend in decisions that emerged out of the military trials conducted after the Second World War".[221] This conclusion was well founded, and, as we have seen, this is true of many, if not most, of the key issues that arose in the Second World War cases. We have also seen how different tribunals confronted the situation of establishing a norm in the absence of prior case law, reaching different conclusions both as to the proper method of proceeding as well as the substantive result. We concluded that the underlying explanation for the divergences was in reality due to differing convictions as to what the definition *should be*.

What do these conclusions concerning how customary law standards are established reveal about the 'historical foundations' provided by the Second World War jurisprudence? Despite, or perhaps because of, the vast scope of the Second World War national war crimes

---

[220] Akayesu case, see *supra* note 20.

[221] Čelebići case, Appeals Judgment, p. 68, see *supra* note 30.

programmes the landscape is not a coherent or well-ordered one. A review of available Second World War jurisprudence indicates that what we have in most instances is not a clear customary law standard but rather an intellectual resource. The body of case law is simply too chaotic and too inconsistent to conclude, with regards to the kinds of issues discussed here, that there are standards and definitions that were almost universally, or even widely, adopted. Indeed, with regards to much of the corpus of case law we cannot even conclude what standards and definitions were in fact used as the basis of convictions. This is due, in the case of the British, American and Australian cases, to the fact that there are no judgments and hence no reasoned decision and no authoritative factual or legal findings. In the case of some other jurisdictions that did in fact produce judgments, they are, as in the French and Dutch cases, often so abbreviated and juristically impoverished that they are also of little use from the standpoint of jurisprudence.

What the Second World War cases do in fact provide is a wealth of material that represents the first large scale attempts of judges, prosecutors, defence counsel and the JAG reviewers to grapple with the complexities of locating responsibility in the context of massive state-sponsored violence involving all the major institutions of state, economy and society. On one hand, we have the major jurisprudential contributions of the NMT and, on the other hand, travesties of justice like the trials of Generals Yamashita[222] or Baba.[223] Both kinds of cases, however, are invaluable in framing the key issues that still shape the developing enterprise of international criminal law. The historical foundations represented by the Second World War legacy are thus an intellectual resource that can assist us in thinking through some of the most difficult issues of individual responsibility in international and comparative criminal theory. What they do not represent is a set of clear and coherent standards enshrined in customary law.

---

[222] Yamashita case, see *supra* note 4.

[223] Baba case, see *supra* note 168.

PART 1

Investigating Origins:
Going Beyond Conventional Historical
Narratives of International Criminal Law

3

International Law and International Humanitarian Law in Ancient China

LIU Daqun[*]

3.1. Introduction

The foundation stone of contemporary international law is generally regarded as the adoption of the Westphalia Treaties in 1648 in Europe, which marked the end of both the Thirty Years' War (1618–1648) in the Holy Roman Empire and the Eighty Years' War (1568–1648) between Spain and the Dutch Republic, with Spain formally recognising the independence of the Dutch Republic.[1] The Westphalia Treaties are considered to usher in the establishment of a new system of political order based upon the concept of a sovereign state. The Westphalia Treaties' regulations stood as a precursor to later major international treaties and thereby the development of international law in general. The precondition for the emergence and development of international law is the existence of sovereign states, which are equal in international law relations and their internal affairs should not be interfered with.[2] This is regarded as the beginning of contemporary international law in the modern world.

China's first contact with contemporary international law came through William Martin's 1865 translation of Henry Wheaton's book

---

[*] LIU Daqun is a Judge at the Appeals Chamber of the ICTY and ICTR (having been a Judge at the ICTY since 2000) and a Professor at the Centre of Cooperative Innovation and Judicial Civilization of China University of Political Science and Law. He is a member of the Institute of International law. He has been Deputy Director-General of the Department of the Treaty and Law Department, Ministry of Foreign Affairs of China. He has taught law at Peking University, the Chinese Academy of Social Sciences, Fudan University, and Wuhan University. He has participated in numerous delegations of the Chinese Government, including as Deputy Head and Chief Negotiator of the Chinese Delegation to the Rome Conference on the establishment of the ICC. He has also been Chinese Ambassador to Jamaica.

[1] Antonio Cassese, *International Law in a Divided World*, Oxford University Press, Oxford, 1986, pp. 36–37.

[2] See International Court of Justice, *South West Africa cases (Liberia v. South Africa, Ethiopia v. South Africa)*, Separate Opinion of Judge Bustamante, 21 December 1962, ICJ Reports (1962), p. 354.

Elements of International Law, 30 years after the book was first published.[3] Some years later, in his book entitled *Traces of International Law in Ancient China*, Martin pointed out two preconditions for the existence of international law: first, the existence of a group of independent states, so situated as to require or favour the maintenance of friendly intercourse; second, that those states should be so related as to conduct their intercourse on a basis of equality.[4] On that basis, Martin argued that the Spring and Autumn period in ancient Chinese history – which lasted from approximately 771 BC until 476 BC, or, according to some authorities, until 403 BC – had fulfilled those conditions, with hundreds of states functioning on the territory of present-day China. The following period, which is identified as the Warring States period, from 476 BC to 221 BC, is also a subject for discussion in this chapter. Here, both periods are collectively referred to as ancient China. This chapter examines the history of the ancient civilisation of China to find in its records evidence of the existence and practice of international law and international humanitarian law. This evidence is to be found in agreements and treaties, regulations and law, customs of usages, and in the works of philosophers and military leaders.

3.2. Evidence of the Existence of International Law or Interstate Law

Under contemporary international law, a state can be regarded as a 'legal person' only if it possesses the four following qualifications: 1) a permanent population; 2) a defined territory; 3) a government; and 4) a capacity to enter into relations with other states.[5] Population is the basic element for the existence of a state, while territory is the material basis on which the existence of a state is grounded.

During the Spring and Autumn period, the Eastern Zhou dynasty (770 BC–255 BC) entered into a period of decline, as a result of which

---

[3]   William Alexander Parsons Martin, also known as Ding Weiliang [丁韪良] (1827–1916) was an American Presbyterian missionary to China and translator, famous for having translated a number of important Western treatises and books into Chinese, such as Henry Wheaton's *Elements of International Law*.

[4]   William Martin, *Traces of International Law in Ancient China*, Industrial Review, New York, 1883, p. 65.

[5]   Article I of the Montevideo Convention on Rights and Duties of States, League of Nations Treaty Series, vol. 165, p. 19.

China's feudal system of *fēngjiàn* became largely irrelevant. As the power of the Zhou dynasty waned, the fiefdoms became increasingly independent states. Those newly independent states had a functioning government, could control a territory as well as a population, and could exercise their sovereignty effectively both domestically and internationally. The Prince of each fiefdom became *de facto* King and the fiefdoms became actual Princedoms. As a consequence of the increasing powers of the Princes, a new political situation emerged, in which "the ritual, music and military campaigns [were] initiated by the Princes".[6] The authority of the Zhou dynasty was no longer critical to the shaping of social and political processes. Although the Princes remained subject to the Zhou royal house in principle, in reality they enjoyed great political sovereignty. With the territorial expansion of each fiefdom and the increasing alienation from the kinship of the Zhou royal house, the Princes' independence became more and more apparent.[7] Each Princedom had its own territory and a reasonably sized population residing on this territory.[8] The biggest states – Chu, for example – had a population of up to 100,000, while the smallest states had only a few thousand people. Despite the fact that it was impossible for each state to have a defined territory – especially because of war and frequent changes of borders – each state had an effective control over certain areas. Furthermore, in each state there was a *de facto* head of state (though bearing titles such as Duke, Noble or Prince) effectively ruling over his territory and population by exercising effective administration and enacting legislation. Each state, regardless of its size, became independent with full sovereignty. According to historical records, there were over a hundred independent states in China in the Spring and Autumn period.[9] They created and

---

6   *Confucius: Confucian Analects* [孔子:论语], chapter 16, "Jishi", cited in Yang Bojun, *Interpretation of Confucian Analects*, Zhonghua Book Company, Beijing, 2005, p. 72. Confucius (551–479 BC) was the greatest philosopher, educator, politician and writer in China's history.

7   Lang Ye, Zhenggang Fei and Tianyou Wang (eds.), *China: Five Thousand Years of History and Civilization*, City University of Hong Kong Press, Hong Kong, 2007, p. 35.

8   "Zuo Zhuan: 19th Year of Prince Zhao", cited in Yang Bojun, *Chunqiu Zuo Zhuan Zhu [An Interpretation of Chunqiu]*, Zhonghua Book Company, Beijing, 1990, p. 24.

9   *Zuo Zhuan* [左传] (sometimes translated as *Chronicle of Zuo* or *Commentary of Zuo*) is among the earliest Chinese works of narrative history, covering the period from 722 BC to 468 BC. *Zuo Zhuan* is traditionally attributed to Zuo Qiuming (左丘明). The work was generally regarded as compiled during the Warring States period, with a compilation date

maintained functioning institutions of collective security, balance of power, diplomacy and interstate law to serve their common interests. Treaties, summit meetings, diplomatic conventions, court intermarriages became legitimate and normal practice. At the same time, each state had a very strong sense of sovereignty. For instance, in 655 BC Jin and Guo were separated from each other by a smaller state, Yu. Should it wish to attack Guo, Jin would need to seek permission from Yu in order to reach the territory of Guo.[10] The foregoing clearly shows the existence of a stable political community.

3.2.1. International Conferences and Summit Meetings

It was normal practice for those states to hold summit meetings and international conferences, to exchange ambassadors and envoys, to conclude treaties and agreements, to discuss the common norms of society and to establish rules of war with a humanitarian perspective. These practices are recounted in ancient sources such as the *Zuo Zhuan* and the eponymous *Chunqiu*,[11] which record the various diplomatic activities that characterised that period, such as court visits paid by one ruler to another, meetings of officials or nobles of different states, missions of friendly inquiries sent by the ruler of one state to another, emissaries sent from one state to another, and hunting parties attended by representatives of different states. Whilst the Spring and Autumn period in China's history was a period of turmoil, diplomatic activities were also very frequent. For instance, according to *Chunqiu*, during that period of time, over 500 international conferences and meetings were held. The Prince of Qi himself convened nine international conferences. The most important feudal Princes (known later as the 12 vassals) regularly discussed important matters, such as military action against foreign groups or offending nobles. During these conferences, one vassal leader was sometimes declared hegemon (伯, *bó*; later, 霸, *bà*) and given

---

    not later than 389 BC. Together with *Gongyang Zhuan* [公羊传] and *Guliang Zhuan* [古梁传], the work forms one of the surviving *Three Commentaries on the Spring and Autumn Annals* ["春秋三传"]. It recorded history according to the timeline of 12 princes in power in the state of Lu. In *Zuo Zhuan*, 128 princedoms are mentioned.

10   "5th Year of Prince Xi", in Yang, 1990, p. 26, see *supra* note 8.

11   One of China's oldest book on history, recording the period from 722 to 481 BC. It is said to have been written by Confucius.

---

leadership over the armies of all Zhou states. A clear political line also emerged, expressed through the slogan "supporting the Prince, and expelling the barbarians" (尊王攘夷, *zūn wáng rǎng yí*).[12] This slogan proved to be the basis for justifying Qi's dominance over the other states. The role of subsequent hegemons would also be framed in this way – as the primary defender and supporter of nominal Zhou authority and the existing order.

3.2.2. International Agreements and Treaties

More than 140 treaties are recorded in *Chunqiu*, including both bilateral and multilateral agreements, mainly for good relationships between states, joint defence, international trade and marriage alliances. This shows that the states dealt with each other on an equal footing. Normally, those agreements included three parts: the statement of purpose, substantive contents and an oath invoking the wrath of the most important deities upon anyone who transgressed the agreements. During the Spring and Autumn period, usage and custom were frequently referred to as a source of international law. In 651 BC the Prince of Qi met all other heads of state and signed the Agreement of Kuiqiu, which stipulated *inter alia* that "[a]ll the contracting parties shall not build dykes on a river; shall not store grain for speculation; shall not change successor; shall not make concubines as wives; shall not let women be involved in state affairs".[13]

The Agreement of Kuiqiu is a convincing illustration of the crystallisation of usage and custom into an international convention. The content of this Agreement looks very absurd and even ridiculous from a modern point of view, as it deals with moral precepts and domestic matters. However, at that time, those issues were very significant to the conduct of relations between states. Two thousand years ago, China was composed of agricultural states. Irrigation was the lifeline of each state. If an upstream state built a dyke on a river running through the territory of other states, the economy, even the daily life, of those downstream states could be greatly affected. The dramatic consequences of the construction of a dyke could amount to a pretext to war. In the same vein, since the output of the grain production was very low at that time, if a state stored grain for speculation, the shortage of food would be another reason for

---

[12] Yang, 1990, p. 28, see *supra* note 8.
[13] *Ibid.*, p. 36.

war. The succession issue in China's history was always a source for domestic disturbance and foreign interventions. At that time, interstate unions were widely celebrated and regarded as a means of strengthening the alliance between two states. If a head of state made his lover his wife, it would completely change the political balance and international relations. Since the wife of a head of state was from another country, if she was allowed to manage the state affairs, the other state's political will would be seen as the dictating factor in the domestic politics and international interchanges put forward by that particular wife. Therefore, the treaty specifically forbade women's involvement in political affairs.

In July 554 BC all the heads of states and the state of Zheng met in Hao and signed an agreement, which stated clearly that:

> The parties to the present Treaty agree to the following Articles: I. The exportation of corn shall not be prohibited; II. One party should not monopolise trade to the disadvantage of others; III. No one shall give protection to conspiracies directed against the others; IV. Fugitives from justice shall be surrendered; V. Mutual succour shall be given in case of famine; VI. Mutual aid shall be given in case of insurrection; VII. The contracting powers shall have the same friends and the same enemies; VIII. We all engage to support the Imperial House.[14]

The agreement concluded with the following:

> [w]e engage to maintain inviolate the terms of the foregoing agreement. May the gods of the hills and rivers, the spirits of former emperors and dukes, and the ancestors of our seven tribes and twelve states, watch over its fulfilment. If any one proves unfaithful, may the all-seeing gods smite him, so that his people shall forsake him, his life be lost, and his posterity cut off.[15]

Solemn formalities and ritual had to be performed before signing an agreement or a treaty. The participants had to bathe and change into decent clothes with incense burning. They also had to cut their hands and mingle their blood in a cup of wine. While laying their hands on the head of an ox or a white horse or goat to be offered in sacrifice, the participants

---

[14] W.A.P. Martin, *The Lore of Cathay*, Forgotten Books, London, 2013, pp. 440–41, originally published in 1901.

[15] Yang, 1990, p. 112, see *supra* note 8.

had to drink the cup of wine one by one and pronounce an oath. After the signature, the agreement was carefully kept in a sacred place called Meng Fu, the "Place of Treaties" – just like the depository in the United Nations system nowadays. Sometimes, hostages or other material guarantees were given in pledge or were guaranteed by a third party, which could intervene in order to punish a breach of faith.

With so many international agreements and treaties signed, each treaty in force was to be binding upon the parties to it and to be undertaken by them in good faith. The concept of *pacta sunt servanda* began to emerge at that time. In 681 BC, as a result of the defeat of the state of Lu by Qi, the Prince of Qi requested the Prince of Lu to attend a meeting in Ke in order to sign a covenant confirming the land transfer. During the meeting, at a point in the ritual when the Prince of Qi stood with the Prince of Lu on the ceremonial day, a minister of Lu assaulted the Prince of Qi and held him at sword point, demanding that he promise to return the borderlands to Lu. As his followers were helpless, the Prince of Qi was forced to take an oath. When he was released, the Prince of Qi immediately announced to his Prime Minister that he would not fulfil this coerced consent. The Prime Minister, however, counselled otherwise. The lands, he argued, were a minor affair, meaningful only to a small state. If the Prince were to consider a broader picture, he said, he would see that by abiding by an oath – regardless of the circumstances surrounding it or the cost to him – he would gain the trust of all other states. As a result, the Prince of Qi returned that piece of land to Lu and he gained great prestige and respect among other states and his title of hegemon was well recognised.[16]

3.2.3. Collective Security System

The league of states – seen to be the most effective way of upholding treaties and the rules of interstate law – emerged during that period. The members of the league were obliged to maintain security and solidarity

---

[16] The *Records of the Grand Historian* (now usually known as the *Shiji* [史记] – *Historical Records*) is a comprehensive history of ancient China that covers a 2,500-year period and completed by Sima Qian around 100 BC. The story is recorded in "Biography of Assassins", *Historical Records*. See *Shiji in Modern Chinese*, Harbin Publishing House, 2005, p. 626.

within their spheres of influence. As a result, the number of interstate wars was greatly reduced.

All historical sources agree that during the reign of the Prince of Qi, that state had a strong internal structure and conducted successful wars. In addition to ruling over an influential state, the Prince of Qi commanded such respect among the patrician Princes of the various states that he came close to becoming the *de facto* ruler of China. The Princes of almost all other states acknowledged him, explicitly and in assembly, as the chief among them. This prestigious role received a new epithet: hegemon. Although the title was unofficial, the 'office' of hegemon became the pivot around which multistate politics revolved during the remainder of the Spring and Autumn period.

In 679 BC, one year after the meeting in Ke, the Prince of Qi requested the other Princes to travel to the town of Juan in Lu to participate in a conference. At this meeting, which was attended by a great number of rulers and also by an envoy of the Prince of Zhou, the Prince of Qi was acknowledged as occupying a foremost role as overlord, qualified to issue orders to other Princes in the enterprise of stabilising the political balance.[17] Although the rulers of the other three great states were not present at the Juan conference, the co-operation among such a large number of Princes was unprecedented, and the presence of a royal envoy, who confirmed the Prince of Qi's role, gave legitimacy to the proceedings. Historians identify this meeting as the turning point of the Prince of Qi's career and of Spring and Autumn period politics.

The meeting in Juan initiated a new political practice, sometimes referred to as the "alliance system", which was essentially based on the idea of a collective security system – more or less like the modern United Nations or North Atlantic Treaty Organisation structure. Henceforth, for the remainder of the Spring and Autumn period, the patrician lords of China ruled in the expectation that there should exist a hegemon who would periodically summon them all to meetings, at which, ranked according to strict order of precedence, they would join in covenants aimed at maintaining a balance of power among the states of China. While rulers who were severely disaffected with the hegemon might

---

[17] Yang, 1990, p. 42, see *supra* note 8.

decline to participate, they always did so at the risk that armies levied by the allies could be directed against them as a consequence.[18]

The alliance system not only granted to the hegemon the implicit right to co-ordinate efforts to influence states outside the alliance but also the possibility to arbitrate conflicts between alliance members. The precedent for this was set for only two years after the meeting in Juan, when Zheng attacked Song, both being alliance members. The Prince of Qi, regarding Zheng as the aggressor and assuming his role as guardian of the peace, led troops in aid of Song and so forced Zheng to withdraw.[19] Using this kind of system, the Prince of Qi intervened in a power struggle in Lu, protected Yan from the encroaching western Rong nomads (664 BC), drove off northern Di nomads after they had invaded Wei (660 BC) and Xing (659 BC), provided the people with provisions and protective garrison units, and led an alliance of eight states to conquer Cai and thereby block the northward expansion of Chu (656 BC).[20]

During that period, hegemony did not necessarily mean rule by only one state. In 546 BC, in order to prevent an outbreak of renewed fighting between Jin and Chu, which was sure to engulf all the central states in another prolonged war, a minister of Song named Xiang Xu developed a plan. He proposed that an assembly of the patrician Princes be called with the goal of arranging a shared hegemony between Jin and Chu. At Song's invitation, the delegates of 11 Princedoms, including Jin and Chu reached a multilateral agreement. The agreement was to share the hegemon between Jin and Chu, and bound all the Princedoms to oaths rejecting offensive warfare in general. It was by far the most idealistic political initiative of the entire ancient period. For the next 40 years, the usual rhythm of incessant squabbling and border fighting among the states did indeed subside.[21] When peace was breached, it was not done by any of the parties to the agreement, but by the Princedom of Wu, a non-signatory to the agreement.

---

[18] *Ibid.*

[19] *Ibid.*

[20] "Chung Qiu Gong Yang Zhuan", in Yang, 1990, p. 68, see *supra* note 8.

[21] "27th Year of Prince Xiang", in Yang, 1990, p. 23, see *supra* note 8.

3.2.4. Respect for Diplomatic Envoys

Given the co-existence of numerous Princedoms during the period of ancient China, international activities were frequent and diplomatic envoys were very active. The duties of the diplomatic envoys were diverse. Some of them were trusted by the Prince to attend international conferences, and to negotiate and sign international treaties and agreements on behalf of the state. Some were sent to pay friendly visits to other states, for the purpose of establishing a good relationship between the two states. Other envoys were excellent negotiators or lobbyists, entrusted with a special mandate of persuading the Princes of other states to agree on certain diplomatic issues. For instance, Zhu Zhiwu, the special envoy of the Princedom of Zheng used his wisdom of reasoning and his persuasive powers to break down the alliance between the Princedoms of Jin and Qin and save his country from doom. According to *Zuo Zhuan*, on 10 September 630 BC the armies of Jin and Qin united to attack Zheng and put the capital of Zheng under siege. In this desperate situation, the Prince of Zheng entrusted an old man, Zhu Zhiwu, as his special envoy and brought him down by a rope from the city wall to meet the Prince of Qin. When he met with the Prince of Qin, he said:

> [i]f you want to lose your friend, Zheng, you may go ahead to attack. But Jin is located between Qin and Zheng. If Zheng is defeated and annexed by Jin, it could only increase Jin's territory, but not yours. If your neighbour, Jin becomes stronger, it will be a great threat to your own safety. If Zheng could survive this attack, it will at least serve as a stopover place for your envoys and provide supplies for them. In the past, Jin promised you to give you two pieces of territory in the morning, but on the same night, they broke their promise and built a fortress to resist your troops. The destruction of Zheng could only benefit Jin and your interest would be affected. You have to take this into consideration.

Following this meeting, the Prince of Qin was completely persuaded by the old man's views and signed a mutual non-aggression agreement with Zheng. He not only withdrew his troops but also left three of his generals to help Zheng defend itself against any potential aggressors.[22]

---

[22] "30th Year of Prince Xi", in Yang, 1990, p. 33, see *supra* note 8.

In the late Warring States period, when only seven big powers remained in existence after hundreds of years of armed conflict and competition, the most prominent diplomat was Su Qin. Among the seven remaining powers, the Princedom of Qin was the most powerful. The Prince of Zhao appointed Su Qin as his special envoy and successfully persuaded the other five states to form an alliance to resist Qin's advance. Later on, he became the Prime Minister of the six Princedoms and the head of this united front in 330 BC. For the next 15 years, the alliance successfully stopped Qin's advance to the east.[23] Later, the Princedom of Qin took the opportunity of internal disputes among the alliance members to send its own Prime Minister, Zhang Yi (who was also Su Qin's classmate and best friend) to exploit the differences between the six states and to persuade them individually not to form a common confrontation against Qin. Zhang, being an articulate man, combined persuasion with threat and coercion. He was well equipped with gold and distributed generously to make his argument even more convincing. His strategy worked well. The alliance of the six Princedoms collapsed, and they engaged in interstate conflicts among themselves.[24]

As a customary rule, diplomatic envoys had to be respected – especially during armed conflicts. In 596 BC Chu sent an envoy to Qi. In order to reach Qi, the envoy had to pass through the territory of Song. The Prince of Chu deliberately instructed the envoy not to ask the permission of Song. The Prime Minister of Song was very angry and regarded it as an insult to the sovereignty of Song. When this envoy passed the territory of the Princedom of Song, he was ambushed and killed. Furious, the Prince of Chu sent troops to attack Song. The troops besieged the capital for nine months. Song sent an envoy to Jin for help, but he was captured by Chu. The Prince of Chu sent the envoy back to the frontline to ask the army of Song to surrender. The envoy instead encouraged the army of Song to continue defending the capital. The Prince of Chu was advised by all his ministers to kill the envoy. After careful consideration, the Prince of Chu released him. In his view, the barbaric behaviour of the adversary was not an excuse to act reciprocally, and the envoy from a Princedom was to be respected, especially during an armed conflict.[25]

---

[23] "Biography of Su Qin", in *Shiji in Modern Chinese*, vol. 69, see *supra* note 16.

[24] *Ibid.* "Biography of Zhang Yi", vol. 70, p. 532.

[25] "14th Year of Prince Xuan", in Yang, 1990, p. 43, see *supra* note 8.

Humiliation of the diplomatic envoy could result in protest from the sending state, or even lead to war. In 591 BC the Prince of Jin sent his envoy to the Princedom of Qi. The mother of the Prince of Qi hid behind curtains to watch the scene during the audience. When she saw the envoy with one blind eye, she laughed at him. The envoy felt humiliated and swore that he would never cross the river, if he could not take revenge. When he came back to Jin, he reported this to his Prince who launched a war against Qi.[26]

3.2.5. Peaceful Settlement of Disputes

Over the course of the Spring and Autumn period, peaceful actions increasingly became a normal way to settle disputes among the states. Bilateral negotiations, consultations, mediation and arbitration were frequently resorted to. For instance, the Prince of Qi would meet with all the other heads of state to resolve the disputes amongst them and repair their relationships. During his 43-year-long reign, the Prince of Qi convened such meetings and conferences on 22 occasions.[27] In 579 BC, in order to put an end to the half-century-long armed conflict that opposed them, the heads of Chu and Jin met and signed an armistice agreement, thereby committing that in conducting the relations between the two states, peaceful means should be used. This agreement on armistice guaranteed peace for 40 years between the two Princedoms.[28]

In the winter of 587 BC the army of the Princedom of Zheng attacked the Princedom of Xu and annexed some of its territories. Later, the Prince of Jin helped Xu by taking possession of some territories of Zheng. Then, the Princedom of Chu sent troops in order to provide assistance to Zheng's army. Zheng and Xu decided to submit the territorial dispute to General Zi Fan from Chu. Zi Fan could not make any decision to solve the dispute. He told the two opposing Princes that they should first resolve the matter through a peaceful negotiation. He added that the Princes of Zheng and Xu would be entitled to submit to him the disagreement only if the matter could not be solved otherwise. The Prince of Chu and his ministers would then jointly hear the case and make a proper decision. After one year of unsuccessful negotiation, the Princes of

---

[26] "6th Year of Prince Xi", in Yang, 1990, p. 42, see *supra* note 8.

[27] "26th Year of Prince Xi", in Yang, 1990, p. 16, see *supra* note 8.

[28] *Ibid.*

Zheng and Xu submitted the case to the Prince of Chu. After hearing the two parties, the Prince of Chu ruled against Zheng, despite the fact that Chu supported Zheng during the territorial conflict. This case is a good illustration that disputes between two states could be submitted to a third party for arbitration or judicial process.[29]

Public opinion was also in favour of settling disputes through peaceful means. In this regard, one may think of the peace agreement proposed by the Princes of Lu and Qi to the Princedoms of Jü and Tan in 605 BC. Both Princes sent envoys to Jü, requesting it to agree to the idea of improving relations with Tan. Upon the refusal of Jü to comply, the state of Lu sent troops to attack the recalcitrant state. As a consequence of the attack, Lu occupied a piece of land belonging to Jü. This action was condemned by all other states. They called on the Princedom of Lu to make use of peaceful means in solving disputes between states, rather than resorting to armed force.[30]

3.3. Evidence of International Humanitarian Law

Before the unification of China in 221 BC, wars and armed conflicts were frequent phenomena. During the 255-year-long Warring States period (475–221 BC) there were more than 230 major wars and armed conflicts on record, which had the combined effect of causing great damage to human lives and the economy. Violence, chaos, brutality and social unrest prevailed over the whole of China. At that time, the winning side would not only massacre innocent civilians but they would also kill prisoners of war. For instance, as a consequence of the Princedom of Zhao's defeat to the Princedom of Qin in 260 BC, 400,000 prisoners of war were buried alive by Qin's army.[31] Another striking example of the widespread use of violence at that time was the attack carried out by the army of Qin against the capital of Wei in 225 BC. As part of the attack, the army of Qin broke a dam on the Yellow River to flood the city, as a result of which over 100,000 innocent people were drowned.[32] During the process of unification of China from 228 BC to 221 BC it is estimated that the army of

---

[29] "4th Year of Prince Cheng", in Yang, 1990, see *supra* note 8.

[30] "4th year of Prince Xuan", in Yang, 1990, see *supra* note 8.

[31] "Biography of Baiqi and Wangqian", in *Shiji in Modern Chinese*, pp. 553–58, see *supra* note 16.

[32] "Biography of Qin Shihuang", in *Shiji in Modern Chinese*, pp. 57–68, see *supra* note 16.

the Princedom of Qin exterminated one tenth of China's population, about 1.5 million at the time.

In response to these atrocities, humanitarian ideas and conceptions regulating armed conflicts emerged gradually (see below). These ideas and conceptions specifically prohibited or condemned unnecessary use of force and violence against civilians during armed conflicts. They slowly transformed into laws and regulations, akin to the modern concepts in the law of use of force (*jus ad bellum*) and the law governing the conduct of hostilities (*jus in bello*).

3.3.1. Perceptions of War

The writings of the most distinguished publicists at the time of ancient China significantly contributed to the advancement of the concept of humanity in war. Mencius (372–289 BC) – an ancient philosopher as famous as Confucius – pointed out that "the only invincible army is the army with humanity". He put forward the idea of the universal value of humanity, which was a break from traditional positivist thinking. He believed that "in this world, the most important thing is the people; governments and states are less important and the Kings, the least".[33]

In the same vein, Lao Zi, another great philosopher of ancient China and the founder of Daoism (Taoism) stated:

> Righteous man should do his best to avoid waging a war. Even if as the last resort, it should be treated as going through a funeral. Since war would bring great damage and death to human lives, even if one won the war, he should not be proud of it. If he were proud, he enjoyed killing lives, thus he could not realise his ambitions. If a lot of innocent people lost their lives, even if you won the war, you should cry for all those dead.[34]

The greatest Chinese military strategist, Sun Zi (515 BC), also pointed out that in this world, the most precious subject is the human being. He maintained that being prudent at waging war is better than being good at war, and no war at all is better than being prudent at war. In essence, he believed that to fight and conquer in all your battles is not supreme

---

[33] Wan Lihua, *Lanxu, Mencius*, Zhonghua Book Company, Beijing, 2006, p. 78.
[34] Lu Yulie, *Correction of Interpretation Lao Zi's Book of Dao*, Zhonghua Book Company, Beijing, 2008, p. 126.

excellence; rather, supreme excellence consists in breaking the enemy's resistance without fighting.[35] He also insisted that war could only be waged based on absolute necessity.[36]

The Methods of the Sima (*Sīmǎ Fǎ*), written by Sima Rangju (340 BC), laid out the basic principles of waging a war. It proclaimed that "in ancient times, humanity was the foundation for a state policy and to promote morality and rules is the guiding principle in managing the country".[37] He also stressed the principle of "not waging war unless absolutely necessary", which implied the principle of necessity and self-defence.

All the abovementioned authors believed that war was an evil thing and that a state should not engage in war unless absolutely necessary. Therefore, the skilful leader subdues the enemy's troops without any fighting. In this regard, *The Methods of the Sima* stipulated:

> [D]o not aggressively pursue the enemy who lost its ability to fight. For foot soldiers, do not pursue the defeated enemy for more than 100 metres, for those on horseback, not for more than 45 kilometres, so as to show some constraint. Take good care of the wounded and sick, to show the spirit of humanity; attacking until the enemy is in good order so as to show it is a fair play; to prisoners of war, with good treatment and pardon, so as to show our leniency.

It also stated:

> The Prime Minister should give the following order to his army: when entering enemy territory, show respect to the gods they deserve; do not hunt and do not ruin the buildings, especially the peasant's house, do not fell trees, do not loot the domestic animals, food and furniture. When coming across old people and children do not harm them and instead advise them to be away from the battlefields. When coming across able men, if they are not hostile to us, so do not harm them. Even when fighting with regular enemy army, among

---

[35] Sun Zi, *The Art of War*, cited in Hu Ping, *Strategy of Life, Nine Collections of Art of War*, Unity Publishing House, Beijing, 1995, p. 37.

[36] *Ibid.*, p. 40.

[37] *Ibid.*, pp. 189–194.

which there are wounded and sick, they should get medical
care and be released after the treatment.[38]

3.3.2. *Jus ad Bellum*

Jus ad bellum designates the branch of law that defines the legitimate
reasons for a state to engage in war against another state. In this respect,
jus ad bellum provides some criteria that render a war *just*. The concept of
a 'just war' emerged during the Spring and Autumn period, as illustrated
by sayings according to which "those who committed so many injustice
are doomed to destruction",[39] and that "humanity is the fundamental
principle for an armed force and using armed force is only for the purpose
of humanity".[40] Confucius also developed the theory of distinguishing
between a just war and an unjust war according to 'humanity'. He
believed that "the purpose of a Saint waging a war is to stop the killings
and get rid of tyranny".[41] During the Spring and Autumn period, custom
and law, especially humanity and benevolence, were the yardsticks for
whether to engage in a war. Accordingly, if a Prince committed an
aggression or a violation of custom and law, did not obey the orders of the
house of Zhou, usurped power by unlawful means, persecuted his
subordinates or exercised tyranny domestically, there were legitimate
reasons for waging a war or for intervening with the army.

Lao Zi thought that war was not a good thing, and should be waged
only when one must. In his view, one should subject the approach of
waging war to a bigger goal, and treat it with caution and deliberation.[42]

Winning without fighting is an important thought in ancient
Chinese military theory, which was advocated and promoted by the great
Chinese military strategist, Sun Zi. In *The Art of War*, he argued for first
employing strategies and then diplomacy to defeat the enemy. These were
followed by a military attack, and lastly laying siege to the enemy's cities
and castles.

---

[38] *Ibid.*, p. 192.

[39] "1st year of Prince Ying", in Yang, 1990, see *supra* note 8.

[40] *Ibid.*, p. 184.

[41] Confucius, *Dadai Liji* [《大戴礼记》], *on Using Armed Forces*, cited in Xu Jialu, *Dadai Liji Jiaobu* [Correction and Supplement to Dadai Liji], Chinese Publishing House, 2005, p. 22.

[42] Lu, 2008, p. 16, see *supra* note 34.

Chinese military culture used benevolence and justice as guidance, and would not let war escalate out of control. The emphasis was not on military strength nor engagement in uncontrolled violence – rather, a state strove to win without fighting.

According to *The Methods of the Sima*, "if it is beyond of the purpose of retaining peace for the whole population, then it is legitimate to kill the peace breakers; if it is beyond the purpose of protecting its people, it is legitimate to attack that state; if war is used to stop the war, it is legitimate".[43] Since the sovereign state had the right to engage in wars, the procedure for the declaration of war was strictly observed. Sima Rangju added: "When declaring a war, a state should notify all other sovereignties and condemn the wrongdoings of the targeted state. The supreme gods, the sun, the moon and stars should be witnesses, swearing before my territory, gods in the world and famous mountains and rivers, as well as the tombs of preceding Princes".[44] Although the procedure for the declaration of war had a very religious connotation, its purpose was to establish the justification of waging a war.

In ancient China's military culture, benevolence and justice, as well as the violation of the universally accepted norms and ethics, were used in an evaluation of a decision to go to war, in order to determine the probable benefit to the people. During an international conference, all the participating heads of state agreed on nine rules, which were ultimately enacted in a treaty:

1. If a head of state bullies the weak with his strength, he shall be condemned.

2. If he kills the innocent and massacres good people, then we shall send troops to attack him.

3. If he exercises cruel rule domestically and bullies other international states, he shall be forced to resign.

4. If he makes the land bare and people flee, his territory shall be reduced.

5. If he does not obey an order because he relies on fortress, we shall send troops to give him a warning.

6. If he kills his family members, he shall be punished according to law.

---

[43]   Hu, 1995, p. 189, see *supra* note 35.

[44]   *Ibid.*

7. If he drives the Prince out or murders the Prince, his conspirators shall be executed and his home shall be ruined.

8. If he violates the law and customs, he shall be sanctioned.

9. If he conducts adultery, his state shall be ruined.[45]

It is not difficult to see that most of the rules only relate to domestic matters, and certain customs and laws had become kinds of pre-emptive rules, like *jus cogens* in contemporary international law. If a Prince violated those norms, it would provide a good excuse for the intervention of other Princedoms, regardless of whether it was a domestic matter or not. The other Princedoms believed that the order of the society and their common interest were affected.

3.3.3. *Jus in Bello*

In contemporary international law, *jus in bello* is the set of laws that applies once a war has begun. It is meant to regulate the way wars are conducted, regardless of how or why they had begun. This set of laws relies on customary law, based on recognised practices of war, as well as treaty laws. It comprises two branches. One sets out the rules for the conduct of hostilities, such as the Hague Regulations of 1899 and 1907, and the other sets out rules on how to protect those who do not take an active part in the hostilities, such as the four Geneva Conventions of 1949, which protect war victims – the sick and wounded (First Geneva Convention); the shipwrecked (Second Geneva Convention); prisoners of war (Third Geneva Convention); and civilians in the hands of an adverse party and, to a limited extent, all civilians in the territories of the countries in conflict (Fourth Geneva Convention and the additional Protocols of 1977).

Over 4,000 years ago, in ancient China, the distinction between these two branches of law could be easily traced. The proper balance between military necessity and the protection of civilians began to emerge.

Xun Zi was one of the most sophisticated and influential philosophers of China's Warring States period.[46] In his book, he pointed

---

[45] Yang, 1990, p. 204, see *supra* note 8.

out that when using armed force, "do not kill or harm the old and weak persons, do not destroy the crops in the fields. Do not capture those who surrendered while fighting with those who continue to engage in the battle. Do not treat those who would like to join our troops as prisoners. We are not going to kill civilians, but to kill those who murdered civilians". He also added: "do not destroy the city walls and exterminate all the residents. Do not make a surprise attack and do not station troops in the occupied territories, and troops should be withdrawn within the prescribed time limits".[47]

As for starting wars, in his book *The Methods of the Sima*, Sima Rangju clearly pointed out that there were some limitations and that humanity should be the foremost consideration even if the war was justified. He stated:

> The principles of warfare are as follows: do not engage in a war when it is the time for agricultural cultivation or when there is a famine so as to protect its own people; do not attack an enemy state when it is in mourning after the Prince of the state died and when the enemy state is suffering from a famine, so as to protect the people in the enemy states. Do not wage a war in the seasons of winter and summer, so as to protect the people of both countries. Although a state is powerful, if it indulges in war, it is doomed.[48]

It was generally regarded as immoral or unfair to attack a Princedom when the Prince died, particularly because the whole country would be in a state of mourning. One striking example happened in March 569 BC, when the troops of the Princedom of Chu attacked the Princedom of Chen. However, when Chu heard that the Prince of Chen had died, it gave up the attack.[49] Another example is that in 552 BC troops from the Princedom of Jin invaded the territory of Qi. When the troops reached Yi,

---

[46] Xun Zi (荀子, ca. 312–230 BC) was a Confucian philosopher who lived during the Warring States period and contributed to one of the Hundred Schools of Thought during that period of time. He was one of the early central figures in the consolidation of what came to be thought of as the Confucian tradition.

[47] *Xunzi: Commentary on Using of Forces*, vol. 15, cited in Wang Xianqian, *An Interpretation of Xunzi's Work*, Zhonghua Book Company, Beijing, 1988, p. 73.

[48] Hu, 1995, p. 214, see *supra* note 35.

[49] Yang, 1990, p. 14, see *supra* note 8.

they learned of the death of the Prince of Qi, and similar to Chu's attack on Chen, they withdrew their troops.[50]

In 597 BC the army of Chu defeated the troops of Jin. The Prince of Chu saw Jin's soldiers retreating in boats to cross a river fighting with each other. He believed that the war was ignited by the heads of states of the two countries, and had nothing to do with the ordinary soldiers and so it was not necessary to kill more people. Therefore, he ordered his troops to stop the pursuit and allowed the defeated solders to retreat.[51]

The value of human lives was treasured even on the battleground. In 598 BC the army of Chu attacked Song and surrounded its capital for nine months. When the invading Chu force learned that the starving citizens of Song had begun to exchange children to be slaughtered for food, they voluntarily lifted the siege.[52]

As for behavioural standards on the battlefield, Sima Rangju pointed out:

> In the past, do not go more than 100 metres in pursuit of defeated enemy troops and 30 miles on horseback so as to show chivalry; do not kill enemy soldiers who have lost their ability to fight, and take good care of those wounded and sick, so as to show humanity; launch an attack when the enemy troops are in good order so as to show honesty; safeguard custom and law instead of interest so as to show the justification for the war; pardon the surrendered enemy so as to show the bravery of the army; predict the beginning and end of a war so as to show the wisdom of the commander. It is the principle by which to educate people, frequently teaching them with 'chivalry, humanity, honesty, justification, bravery and wisdom'.[53]

According to these six principles specific rules for conducting a war had emerged. For instance: declare war before raising arms; never slay envoys; do not make use of obstructions to hide from your enemy; do not fight in unsafe environments or ambush opponents – the battlefield should be on level ground; no battle should start without drumming; do not attack your opponent when they are unaware; do not maim your enemy; once

---

50 *Ibid.*, p. 19.
51 *Ibid.*, p. 32.
52 *Ibid.*
53 Hu, 1995, p. 189, see *supra* note 35.

your opponents are injured, do not continue to attack; do not capture grey-haired combatants – allow them to return home and retire; do not chase after an enemy that turns around and retreats, for it has admitted defeat.

According to historical records, some cases show that those principles were observed during a war. On 29 June 575 BC the Princedom of Jin defeated the united army of Chu and Zheng. General Han Jue was on a chariot chasing the Prince of Cheng. The driver of his chariot told General Han that "the coachman on the chariot of the Prince of Cheng looks back continuously. His mind is not on driving the wagon. Shall we speed up and catch the Prince of Cheng?" General Han replied: "We should not humiliate the Prince once again". He then ordered the halt of the pursuit.[54]

Specific orders were issued before a war:

> When entering an enemy state, do not blaspheme against the gods, do not hunt, do not destroy irrigation systems, do not burn houses, do not cut down trees, do not take domestic animals, grains and tools. When meeting with old people and children, do not harm them and escort them home; when meeting with young men, so long as they do not fight, do not treat them as an enemy; for wounded soldiers, give them medical treatment and release them. After the punishment of the principal violators, the Prince and other nobles should help the state for post-conflict reconstruction.[55]

After an armed conflict, post-conflict measures should also be taken in order to restore the normal political, economic and social life of the defeated states. As Confucius said: "He revived states that had been extinguished, restored families whose line of succession had been broken, and called to office those who had retired into obscurity, so that throughout the Princedom the hearts of the people turned towards him".[56]

3.3.4. Treatment of Prisoners of War

About 6,000 years ago, prisoners of war, as well as the weak and the old at the time of famine, would be killed and even eaten as food. In order to reduce such killings, the Law of the Shun Period, one of China's oldest

---

[54] Yang, 1990, p. 52, see *supra* note 8.

[55] *Ibid.*, p. 176.

[56] Lang *et al.*, 2007, p. 8, see *supra* note 7.

laws, prescribed that: "if someone killed other person and ate him, because of food shortage caused by natural disasters or consistent wars, he is not guilty. But if he killed more people [more than three people], he would get the death penalty by having his throat cut".[57]

During the Spring and Autumn period, captured soldiers, and even generals, were entirely at the mercy of their captors. Normally, they would be summarily killed or taken as slaves. Later, the treatment of prisoners of war changed. According to Zhou Yi: "If prisoners are captured, it will not cause any damage to take care of them. If we provide enough food for them, though there are changes, everything will be alright".[58]

In the early part of the Spring and Autumn period, the Princes of the various states were treated like heads of state, even after they had been captured by their opponents. On 17 June 589 BC the army of Jin and the army of Qi fought in a place called An. Jin's army – led by General Han Jue – defeated Qi. The chariot carrying the Prince of Qi fell and he was taken prisoner of war. General Han Jue chose not to mistreat or humiliate the Prince of Qi. Instead, he showed his respect to the Prince by kneeling down twice in front of him and presented the Prince with a cup of wine and a piece of jade. He also told the Prince of Qi: "My Prince sent troops to help the Princedoms of Lu and Wei and instructed us that we should not let our troops enter into the territory of Qi. Unfortunately, my troops could not avoid the encounter with Qi's army and won the battle. If I avoided your troops, then the Princes of Lu and Wei would be humiliated. So I just came here to show you that how impotent I was to avoid this situation".[59] It is clear that the defeated Prince was still regarded as a head of state and was to be respected by his opponents.

Normally, once a war ends, the two opposing sides will exchange prisoners of war. In ancient China, sometimes prisoners of war in the hands of one party would be exchanged for goods or the bodies of the dead nobles or generals. At the conclusion of the armed conflict between Chu and Jin, Jin proposed to the Prince of Chu to send back the bodies of his son and of another high official in exchange for General Zhiying who

---

[57] "Shang Shu: Yu's Law", cited in Sun Xinyan, *Interpretation of Shang Shu in Ancient and Contemporary Chinese*, Zhonghua Book Company, Beijing, 1986, p. 42.

[58] Guo Jian, *Understanding of Zhou Yi*, Zhonghua Book Company, Beijing, 2006, p. 25.

[59] Yang, 1990, p. 38, see *supra* note 8.

had been taken as a prisoner of war. Chu agreed to this proposal. The dialogues between the Prince of Chu and General Zhiying are worthy of note. The Prince asked General Zhiying if he hated him.

Zhiying answered: "Our two states engaged in a war and I was incompetent and could not function well as a commander, so I was taken as a prisoner of war by your troops. You did not kill me and put my blood on the war drums; instead, you send me back to Jin and let me get punished in my home country. All these are owing to my own fault and your grace. How could I possibly hate you?"

"You must be grateful to me", said the Prince.

Zhiying responded: "The two states engaging in war are for their respective national interest. Both sides would like to relieve the sufferings of civilians, control their own anger so as to reach a mutual understanding. Now, both sides decided to exchange the prisoners of war for the good of the relationship between our two countries. I did not take part in this effort. So to whom shall I be grateful?"

The Prince of Chu concluded: "Since Jin has this kind of general, we could not fight with Jin again". So the Prince of Chu held a big farewell ceremony to send Zhiying back to his home country.[60]

3.3.5. Military Law and Individual Criminal Responsibility

In order to secure military advantage, strengthen discipline among troops and punish violations of norms in the army, every Princedom introduced detailed military laws and regulations. The concept of individual criminal responsibility – that is to say, the possibility of holding an individual criminally liable for his own behaviour – began to emerge under those military laws and regulations. Some laws and regulations were at times very harsh and cruel. For instance, according to Wei Liao in his military text *Wei Liaozi*, if a commander who led thousands of troops was defeated in a battle, surrendered to enemy force, withdrew without permission or fled leaving his army behind, his military rank was to be revoked and he was to be sentenced to death. His family tombs were to be dug up and the bones of the dead displayed in the street. All his family

---

[60] *Ibid.*, p. 63.

members were to be made slaves. The same held true for all his subordinates, provided that they committed the same acts.[61]

What is more, almost all of the armies adopted the system of collective punishment. In the army, a squad was formed by five soldiers, a platoon was composed of 10 soldiers, a company was composed of 50 soldiers and a battalion had 100 soldiers. If one soldier committed a crime, the other soldiers in the same unit had a responsibility to report the crime. If reported, no one was to incur criminal responsibility. However, if not reported, all the soldiers were to be punished. The rule applied regardless of the size of the unit, be it a platoon, a company or a battalion.[62] This collateral punishment also applied to soldiers' relatives. If a soldier committed a crime, their relatives or anyone associated with the soldier were to receive the same punishment. In 356 BC, Shang Yang, the Prime Minister of Qin, even applied this martial system in a civilian context. In order to do so, he established a neighbourhood administrative system in which every 10 households formed a neighbourhood. If a person in one household committed a crime, the other nine would share the responsibility if they did not report or take any measures to prevent or stop the commission of the crime.[63]

Many military commentators and politicians at that time pointed out the problems of the collective punishment system. Wei Liao stated:

> in this situation, if 10 soldiers committed crimes, their parents and brothers and sisters, their relatives and their friends shall all be arrested and put into a cell, which will be populated with thousands of people. If an army of ten thousand soldiers fought abroad, but at home, the same numbers of the innocent civilians were in the prison. The wise Princes should know that this was a very dangerous situation.[64]

Out of humanitarian considerations, many philosophers and military strategists began to have doubts about the severity of the punishment. Mencius stated his criminal policy in the following terms:

---

[61] Hu, 1995, p. 501, see *supra* note 35.

[62] *Ibid.*, p. 212.

[63] "Biography of Shang Jun", in *Shiji in Modern Chinese*, p. 514, see *supra* note 16.

[64] Hu, 1995, p. 483, see *supra* note 35.

> If an ordinary person possesses some property, he will obey the law, and moral standards and legal education shall come first. If you waited until he committed a crime and then punished him, that is a policy of entrapment. The wise Prince should protect ordinary people's legitimate property rights so that they can support their parents, wives and children. For the whole, they would have food to eat and in a bad year they would avoid death. Only by doing so will the criminal rate and possibility of revolt be reduced.[65]

Some military strategists even challenged the cruel practice of torture. Wei Liao stated: "a military commander is also in charge of penalties, since he is the overall commander in the army. He should be impartial and not be biased against anyone, so that he could make a fair judgment [...] If whipping the back of the accused, burning his front and crushing his figures in interrogation, even if the accused is a strong man, he could not bear the torture and make the confession".[66]

Furthermore, the roots of superior responsibility – a well-established mode of liability in international criminal law designed to ensure that superiors comply with the laws and customs of war and international humanitarian law generally – can be traced back 2,300 years in China. In about 340 BC during the Warring States period in China, Wei Liao, the military commentator of the Princedom of Wei, published *Wei Liaozi*, in which he devoted a chapter on the law of army organisation. Commenting upon the duties of superiors in time of war, Wei Liao stated:

> All the officers – from the level of the squad of ten up to the top generals in command, superiors and inferiors – are mutually responsible for each other. If someone violates an order or commits an offence, those who report it will be spared from punishment, while those who know about it but do not report it will all share the same responsibility.[67]

This statement echoes the basic requirements of contemporary superior responsibility. Wei Liao's statement envisioned a superior's criminal responsibility as being equal to that of his subordinates who committed the crimes, if he knew of them and did not take any measures, which in that case, was the duty to report. Responsibility of commanders for the

---

[65] Wan, 2006, p. 245, see *supra* note 33.
[66] Hu, 1995, p. 502, see *supra* note 35.
[67] *Ibid.*, p. 518.

conduct of their troops is now recognised in many domestic jurisdictions, as well as in customary international law.

3.4. Conclusion

"It is the best of times, and it is the worst of times, it was the age of wisdom, it was the age of foolishness, it was the epoch of belief, it was the epoch of incredulity, it was the season of Light, it was the season of Darkness, it was the spring of hope, it was the winter of despair".[68] So Charles Dickens wrote at the beginning of *A Tale of Two Cities*. These words exactly describe the Spring and Autumn and Warring State periods in China, which were unique and paradoxical times. On the one hand, it was the most violent and divided period of time in China's history. From 771 to 221 BC the usurping of thrones, breaking of promises, brutal wars and mass massacres were common in society and millions of people died because of man-made disasters. As an author noted, this was a time of a "disintegration of propriety and ritual collapse".[69]

On the other hand, ancient China was the most splendid period in cultural terms. It was the golden age of Chinese philosophy and intellectual creativity. All Chinese philosophical ideologies, like Confucianism, Daoism, legalism and Moism, find their roots in that period. All these philosophical traditions still have an impact on every Chinese individual today. Ancient China was also a time when hundreds of schools flourished. As we have seen, international law and international humanitarian law were also developing during this period.

After the unification of China by the first emperor of the Qin dynasty in 221 BC, China became a totalitarian state,[70] where "all of the land under the Heaven belongs to the Prince and all of the people to the boundary of the earth are the Prince's subjects".[71] Given this ideology, one may argue that there is very little to say about the development of international law in China since international law is established on the basis of equality of the states. It is not submitted that the evidence of

---

[68] Charles Dickens, *A Tale of Two Cities*, Dover, Mineola, New York, 1999, p. 1, originally published in 1859.

[69] Bangu, *Hanshou, Biography of Emperor Wu*, vol. 6, Chinese Publishing House, 2007, p. 40.

[70] From the Qin Dynasty in 221 BC to 1911, when the monarchy was overthrown.

[71] Confucius, *Poems: Xiaoya*, Zhonghua Book Company, Beijing, 2006, p. 146.

international law found in ancient China is similar to modern international law. Nevertheless, ancient China is an example of one of the earliest systematic codes of international law and international humanitarian law. Some principles and practices during that period –summit meetings, the collective security system, the sharing of the hegemon for the balance of power, the respect for diplomatic mission and envoys, the principle of *pacta sunt servanda* and the rules and custom of humanitarian law in armed conflicts – still have contemporary significance to the present world.

4

The Tyrannicide Brief

Geoffrey Robertson QC[*]

4.1. The First Precedent

The trial of Charles I, back in 1649, was the first time in modern history that a head of state was charged with mass murdering his own people. The trial was conducted under common law and adversary procedures that 350 years later were, in their more developed form, adopted for international criminal courts. His case serves as the first modern precedent for a trial of a political or military leader at a moment of transition, after he has lost a war of his own making against his own people. Some of the dilemmas faced by "the regicides" – the King's judges and prosecutors – still confront their equivalents in The Hague today.

The indictment accused Charles of waging aggressive war against his subjects, and included allegations of ordering the torture of prisoners of war and pillage of civilian homes. It was, viewed today, an amalgam of war crimes and crimes against humanity committed against a civilian population, i.e. that part of the people of England which supported Parliament in a civil war against their King. This was called the crime of 'tyranny', which is still an accurate enough way of describing crimes against humanity committed by a head of state.[1] The trial terrified the

---

[*] **Geoffrey Robertson** QC has had a distinguished career as a trial counsel, human rights advocate and UN appellant judge. He has argued hundreds of death sentence appeals, defended Salman Rushdie, Mike Tyson and Julian Assange and acted for Human Rights Watch in the proceedings against General Pinochet. He served as first president of the UN's Special Court in Sierra Leone, and has authored landmark decisions on the limits of amnesties, the illegality of recruiting child soldiers and the legal protections for war correspondents and human rights monitors. He served as a 'distinguished jurist' on the UN Justice Council (2008–12) and in 2011 he was awarded the New York State Bar Association prize for Distinction in International Law and Affairs. Mr Robertson is founder and co-head of Doughty Street Chambers, the UK's largest human rights practice, and for many years held the office of Recorder (part-time judge) in London where he is a Master of the Middle Temple and visiting professor in human rights law at Queen Mary College and the New College of the Humanities. His books include *Crimes Against Humanity: The Struggle for Global Justice* (4th ed., 2012), *Mullahs Without Mercy: Human Rights and Nuclear Weapons* (2012); an acclaimed memoir, *The Justice Game*;

crowned heads of Europe, precisely because it shook their confidence in Westphalian sovereignty, newly minted in the Treaty of Westphalia just three months previously (October 1648) to end the Thirty Years' War. They, like Charles, also claimed "the divinity that hedges the crown" – they had been appointed as God's regents, and their sovereignty was absolute in law and guaranteed by the Church. Here was an indictment against a King that challenged their absolute rule: their regal power was held in trust for the people and they had a responsibility to protect – yes, those very words were used – the lives and property of those people. A head of state who attacked his own civilians, enslaved or tortured or killed them in significant numbers, was a tyrant in fact who could be tried in law for the crime of tyranny. European Kings and their courtiers were, consequently, frightened that this idea might catch on, and watched with horror the execution of Charles I after the unanimous verdict of guilt.

It is fascinating how many parallels there are between this trial and those today under international criminal law. There was the problem of sovereign immunity, for a start. Under Magna Carta, a man had to be tried by his peers – i.e. his equals – and his lawyers argued that a King had no peers, and hence could never be put on trial. There was the problem of the jurisdiction of the court – "by what power, and under what authority, do you try me?" asked Charles, in virtually the same words used by Slobodan Milošević and Saddam Hussein.[2] The answer given by the court – "by the authority of the people of England" – was not strictly true, as England was not a real democracy and the Parliament had been purged of the King's supporters. But there were, as we shall see, shards of common law, fragments of the Bible, arguments of international law professors like Grotius and Gentili that were melded into a kind of authority for these proceedings. "A King", said Charles defiantly, "cannot be tried by any superior jurisdiction on earth". But he *was* tried, by the first jurisdiction established by men determined to deter crimes against humanity.

That he was tried at all was something of a miracle. He could so easily have been shot whilst trying to escape from Carisbrooke Castle, or simply poisoned and then found dead in his bed. He could actually have

---

and in 2010 his Penguin Special *The Case of the Pope* was published in all major languages.

[1] See Geoffrey Robertson, *The Tyrannicide Brief*, Chatto & Windus, London, 2005.

[2] *Ibid.*, p. 6.

been court-martialled because he was the enemy commander in a war, and put before a firing squad immediately after capture. Or they could have set up a secret trial, as they did for Anne Boleyn and Mary Queen of Scots. But Cromwell and his Puritans simply did not think like this: they believed their actions had to be open and fair and in the sight of God. They wanted, as Clarendon put it, "to teach all Kings to know that they were accountable and punishable for the wickedness of their lives".[3] They wanted, in other words, to create a precedent, to establish that tyranny was a crime, anywhere in the world. They wanted to show, in effect, that the best thing about the Treaty of Westphalia was that England was not part of it.

4.2. The High Court of Justice

We can see this most vividly in the statute that established the High Court of Justice to try the King, "to the end that no Chief Officer or Magistrate whatsoever may hereinafter presume traitorously and maliciously to imagine or contrive the enslaving or destroying of the English nation, and expect *impunity* for so doing". This is the first time the word 'impunity' is used in its international criminal law sense, of living happily ever after one's crimes. The thinking behind establishing this court was that heads of state – and not only heads of the state of England – might be deterred from cruel actions if they knew that they might be punished for them, irrespective of sovereign immunity and without deference to any sacred protection that might be given to God's anointed.

This was a big step in a society where everyone believed in God,[4] but the Puritans believed in God so much that they found biblical passages which showed that God did not believe in Kings. Once that divine protection was withdrawn, the principle that the law was no respecter of persons could operate to fix heads of state with command responsibility for the barbarities they inflicted on the people they had a responsibility to protect.

---

[3] Edward Hyde, Earl of Clarendon, *History of the Rebellion and Civil Wars in England*, vol. 1, Oxford University Press, Oxford, 2001 (originally published in 1702–1704).

[4] See Austin Woolrych, *Britain in Revolution 1625–1660*, Oxford University Press, Oxford, 2002, p. 20. In *Calvin's Case* [1572] Eng. R. 64, all the judges – including Coke and Bacon – accepted that the King's authority came from God.

Finding a juristic basis for the trial of a King was hard enough in 1649, but as nothing compared to the practical problems of staging the trial. Suppose, Cromwell's lawyers said to themselves, he refused to plead – "guilty" or "not guilty" – or to recognise the court? He could go on and on about the illegitimacy of the tribunal, without ever being forced to face up to the charge. How might the trial then be perceived as fair? This was precisely what Charles did, of course, refusing over four hearings to enter a plea, and declining the services of the finest counsel in the land. (His judges did not think of the expedient, hit upon when Milošević used the same stance, of inviting *amicus* to take legal points for the defence.) If he refused to plead, should he be treated as having entered a plea of guilty? And if that was the law (as indeed it was – a refusal to plead was deemed a confession of guilt) how could the public and the court be satisfied that he was indeed guilty? This conundrum was solved by calling the prosecution's evidence after conviction, but before sentence, in a private hearing without the defendant's participation. The most difficult question of all – which United Nations (UN) courts today fortunately do not have to face, although it is a reason why post-revolutionary states like Libya refuse UN justice – was whether to execute him and run the risk of creating a martyr, or whether to exile and run the risk of his return at the head of an army.

4.3. The Legal Background

This unprecedented trial was held in a country that had laws, and a legal system, which had developed quite separately from Europe after 1215. That was when the Pope refused to lend the Church's authority to trials by ordeal – the superstitious system under which suspected wrongdoers were thrown into ponds and declared guilty if they swam but innocent if they sunk. To replace it, there developed a system of trial by jury, adapted from the medieval English colonial system, where members of the local community would squat around a dead body found in a ditch and discuss with the King's coroner who in the locality might be the murderer.[5] By the seventeenth century, trial by jury was highly regarded in England as a basic guarantee of fairness. It was always over quickly, and juries were culled from well-born men, but it gave the defendant at least the

---

[5]   See Geoffrey Robertson, *Freedom, The Individual and The Law*, Penguin, Harmondsworth, 1993, pp. 53, 349.

possibility of being found not guilty. Unlike the ordeal, or the European inquisition, it was an adversary system of criminal justice in which the prosecution's witnesses could be questioned by the defendant, who could not give sworn evidence, but could hire lawyers to speak for him on issues of law. There were many trials for treason and sometimes defendants were found not guilty.[6]

For nobles, aristocrats and persons of breeding who were found guilty of treason, death would come instantly and surgically, as the executioner's axe severed their cervical vertebrae: the silk-stockinged legs would twitch reflexively as the executioner's assistant displayed the aristocratic head to the crowd, with the awesome cry *"Behold – the head of a traitor"*. For those of common birth, however, there was a torture as barbaric as the times could devise, known as 'hanging, drawing and quartering'. The miscreant would be drawn on a sledge, facing backwards, to the place of execution: he would be forced up a ladder, hung from a rope for a few moments to the jeers of the crowd, then cut down whilst still conscious. His penis and testicles would first be cut off and dangled in his face. The executioner's knife would slit the stomach and deftly extract a few feet of bowel, which would be set alight by a torch, before his boggling eyes. Oblivion, in the stench and excruciating pain, was delayed as long as possible, and would be followed by cutting pieces off the carcass ('quartering') before it was dragged away behind the sledge: the severed head, arms, legs and torso would be boiled and preserved for exhibition on pikes at various public places in the city, *pour encourager les autres*. This obscene ritual was laid down in the law books: it was intended as the ultimate deterrent to any commoner who might think of deposing a King.

4.4. The Civil Wars

How then, did it come about that a group of lawyers under Cromwell could *dare* to envisage the ultimate treason – to put a King on trial? England had a Parliament, which the King could always ignore, except in one respect – it had the right to grant or approve taxation. Charles had come to the throne in 1624, at a time when MPs (themselves undemocratically elected men of wealth and substance) and the Lords

---

[6] See John Bellamy, *The Tudor Law of Treason: An Introduction*, Routledge & Kegan Paul, London, 1979, p. 171.

who sat in the Upper House were beginning to flex their muscles and demand a Bill of Rights. Charles was so infuriated by this that he suspended Parliament for 10 years, and only agreed to recall it in 1640 because he wanted it to vote him money. This was his big mistake, because these radical members of Parliament wanted to share power.

Charles believed he was divinely appointed and should have absolute authority, while Parliament insisted that they should have a say in government, that there should be more religious toleration, that the King's torture court, the Star Chamber, should be abolished, and that judges should be independent. Both factions raised armies, and the King attacked first. After four years of a bloody civil war, which killed one in 10 English males and left wounded beggars in every town, his army was beaten by Cromwell's Roundheads. He was captured and put under house arrest – or at least, castle arrest. It was a curious situation – he was the enemy commander, but he still held court, respected as the King by everyone and loved by some of his people. Then, from Carisbrooke Castle in the Isle of Wight in 1648, he started a second civil war – causing more bloodshed and more loss of life by Cromwell's army before they won again. These soldiers were sick of this 'man of blood' responsible for killing so many of their comrades. They wanted him tried, but the more conservative faction in Parliament wanted to do a deal to make him share power and give them lots of honours. (You have no idea how much the English love honours!) But Cromwell's Puritans were the real power in the land. So their army barred the conservatives from entering Parliament, and they voted to establish a court, with a real judge and jurors, to try the King in public and in the largest hall in London. This was on 6 January 1649, when the House of Commons passed that extraordinary statute saying that they were putting the King on trial so that heads of state who killed their own people should not have *impunity*.

4.5. The Trial Begins

On Saturday 20 January 1649, 60 black-gowned jurors, led by the judge, processed into the Great Hall at Westminster, for the public opening of the trial.[7] Accompanied by 120 soldiers with long pikes, they presented a

---

[7]   The descriptions of the trial are based on contemporary newspaper reports. The transcript, the first to be produced by the art of shorthand, is reproduced in the fourth volume of the State Trials series, from which the citations in this chapter are taken. See also C.V.

powerful tableau to thousands of citizens who crammed into the public galleries. Preceded by a clerk carrying the sword of state, Judge Bradshawe made his way to centre stage where his crimson velvet chair had been placed, behind a desk on which a crimson cushion bore the parliamentary mace. The jurors sat behind him, on benches hung with scarlet: the chair in which Charles would sit was directly in front of them. The government had learned, very quickly, the importance of Court choreography.

The assembly waited to see a sight that had no parallel: the bringing of a King to a place of public justice. When Charles did enter, it was with a certain dignity. The serjeant-at-arms, mace held aloft, escorted him towards his centre stage seat. This was no ordinary prisoner, as his behaviour immediately showed: resting upon his familiar silver-tipped cane, he looked with unblinking sternness at the judges, displaying his contempt for the court by refusing to remove his hat. He was, for these few moments, still a King in command.

"Charles Stuart, King of England [...]". Judge Bradshawe's words were respectful, his tone measured and polite: "the Commons of England have constituted this High Court of Justice before which you are now brought, and you are to hear your charge, after which the Court will proceed".[8]

This was the prosecution's cue. John Cooke, a poor sharecropper's son who had gone to Oxford on a scholarship and who was formally classed as a "plebeian" at the Inns of Court,[9] brandished the parchment upon which the charge had been written. "My Lord President", he began – at which point he felt a sharp tap on his shoulder. The King had hit the prosecutor with his cane, a walking stick with an ornate silver tip. "Hold", Charles commanded, and rose to speak, poking the low-bred lawyer again with his cane to emphasise his command to give way.

If Cooke had yielded, the entire enterprise would have faltered. But the barrister ignored the King, and continued to address the court: "My

---

Wedgwood, *The Trial of Charles I*, Collins, London, 1964 and J.G. Muddiman (ed.), *The Trial of King Charles the First*, The Notable Trials Library, Birmingham, AL, 1990. The editorial notes in the latter volume are notoriously biased but the trial transcript is accurate, as are the notes from Judge Bradshawe's journal.

8   Muddiman, 1990, p. 77, see *supra* note 7.

9   See Robertson, 2007, chapter 1, *supra* note 1.

Lord President", he went on, "according to an order of this High Court directed to me for that purpose [...]". At this point, he suffered a third blow from the cane, a palpable hit, hard enough to dislodge its silver tip, which rolled down the counsel's gown and clattered on to the floor between the two men. Their eyes met, and the King nodded for Cooke to bend and pick it up. But the barrister did not blink, much less stoop. Ignoring the little man beside him at the bar rail he continued, coldly and precisely: "I do, in the name and on the behalf of the people of England, exhibit and bring into this Court a charge of tyranny and other high crimes whereof I do accuse Charles Stuart, King of England, here present".[10] Slowly and painfully, under the astonished gaze of his people, the King stooped to pick up the silver tip from the floor at Cooke's feet.

The symbolism of this incident was plain to all. The King, the divine majesty, had bowed, powerless before the majesty of human law. In an age when everyone was on the lookout for signs and portents, this was taken as the direst of signals. The newspapers reported how Charles had been forced to stoop to retrieve the silver tip: "This it is conceived will be very ominous".[11] Few had really thought this unprecedented public spectacle would be taken seriously, but Cooke's resolve at its outset transformed expectations. It now had the appearance of a real trial in which the monarch would have no special favours. *"Be ye ever so high, the law is above you"* had been an empty aphorism for those who had tried to bring the Stuart Kings to the bar or the battlefield: this defining historical moment gave it meaning. It was, in retrospect, a Grotian moment for international criminal law.

4.6. The Defendant Refuses to Plead

It was a bad start, however, for the King. He was being treated, and beginning to look, like any ordinary prisoner. Now he had to listen to Cooke's lengthy indictment. There is a limit to body language for indifference but Charles did his best – rolling his eyes at the gallery, outstaring the judges, getting up to look behind him at the guards and the

---

[10] *R. v. Charles I*, State Trials Series, vol. 4, p. 995.

[11] *The Moderate*, No. 28, 16–23 January 1649, p. 228. Sir Thomas Herbert, in his self-serving (and hence Charles-serving) memoirs claims that he scrabbled around for the silver tip, but he was on the other side of the King and could not reach it. Thomas Herbert, *Memoirs*, British Library, London, 1815, p. 165.

spectators. At the description "tyrant, traitor, murderer [...]" he laughed loudly, as if trying to laugh the charge out of court.[12] It was not a predictable response and it seemed to rattle Bradshawe: Charles had the better of their next exchanges.[13] The judge began ponderously: "Sir, you have now heard your charge read [...] the court expects your answer".

Charles savoured the moment, delayed, then spoke (without his usual stammering) a carefully crafted, but none the less memorable, opening phrase:

> I would know by what power I am called hither [...]
>
> Now I would know by what authority, I mean lawful; there are many unlawful authorities in the world, thieves and robbers by the highways; but I would know by what authority I was brought from thence, and carried from place to place, and I know not what: and when I know by what lawful authority, I shall answer.

The judge responded that the court's authority was "the people of England" but this did not impress their King.

> KING: For answer, let me tell you, you have shown no lawful authority to satisfy any reasonable man.
>
> BRADSHAWE: That is in your apprehension – we think it reasonable, and we are your judges.

Bradshawe then uttered the magic words which for centuries in English courts have made the defendant disappear: "Take down the prisoner", he commanded the guards. "*The King*, you mean", corrected Charles, offended by the word 'prisoner'. There were voices in the Hall which now cried out as he left it "God save the King!", counterpointed with others which cried "Justice!"

The city of London that night was quiet, the public engaged – with curiosity, rather than anger or protest. The six licensed newspapers printed more copies, and three new papers had to be licensed immediately to cater for the public appetite to read about the trial. The royalist news-sheets failed to appear, as if cowered by the enormity of the event. This success was more than Cromwell could have hoped, but probably what he expected from providence – although providence had nothing to do with it. Justice always has its own momentum and one thing that was clear

---

[12] State Trials Series, vol. 4, pp. 995, 1073, see *supra* note 10.

[13] *Ibid.*, pp. 995–97, 1073–76.

from the proceedings of 20 January 1649 was that this trial was a deadly serious exercise: now that it had started, it would go on and on – to an end that no one could confidently predict.

Before the court's next session, the jurors – they were really commissioners – conferred about Bradshawe's inability to shut the King up. They thought he should be given some help, and drafted an answer for him to give when next Charles demanded to know their "lawful authority":

> That the Commons of England assembled in Parliament have constituted this court, whose power may not, nor should be permitted to be disputed by the King, and that they were resolved he should answer his charge.[14]

The common law rule that Acts of Parliament could not be questioned or investigated justified this answer, as a matter of law. As a matter of reality, this court had not been created by the Parliament, (1) because the Lords – the upper part of the Parliament – had adjourned rather than pass the ordinance, and (2) because the army had forcibly excluded from the Commons those MPs whose votes would have defeated it. But the 'Rump' Parliament that resulted was nevertheless a *de facto* authority, governing effectively with the support of the army. The interesting point is that in these circumstances its actions were not necessarily unlawful.

The right of a victorious army to detain enemy leaders and put them on trial by court martial was an accepted feature of the law of war. Fairfax, a general of considerable scruple, had satisfied himself that he had the power to detain the King, who had himself consulted with some of the best lawyers in the land and never once applied to any judge for *habeas corpus*, the remedy always available for unlawful detention. There were some judges, especially Presbyterians, who were more than capable of standing up to the army.[15] For all the complaints made by and on behalf of Charles about the unlawfulness of his treatment, he never once challenged it in courts before judges who were bound to entertain his

---

[14]   State Trials Series, vol. 4, pp. 1079–80, see *supra* note 10.

[15]   As William Prynne had proved on 10 January when his lawyers went to a Chancery judge to obtain *habeas corpus*. *Perfect Occurrences*, 5–12 January, entry for 10 January. Prynne had been committed to prison for contempt of Parliament. Whitelocke was back on the Bench, which granted the *habeus corpus* after he had conferred with the Commons. See Ruth Spalding (ed.), *The Diary of Bulstrode Whitelocke, 1605–1675*, Oxford University Press, Oxford, 1990, p. 228.

complaint.[16] It may be, of course, that a *habeas corpus* strategy was ruled out because an application to any court by the King could be interpreted as a concession that he *was* subject to the law.

In the likely event that the King continued his refusal to plead, Cooke reminded the commissioners that the common law had an invariable response: his silence would amount to a confession, and the charge would be "taken *pro confesso*", i.e. as an admission of every allegation made in it. Charles had three choices: to plead "guilty"; to plead "not guilty" and have his day in court; or to maintain his refusal to plead, in which case the charge would be taken *pro confesso*.

At the second session of the court, Bradshawe reminded the King of his objections at the previous hearing, and went on:

> Sir, the court now requires you to give a positive and particular answer to this charge that is exhibited against you: they expect you should either confess or deny it. If you deny, the Solicitor-General offers on behalf of the Commonwealth to make it good against you. Sir, the court expects you to apply yourself to the charge, so as not to lose any more time, and to give a positive answer.[17]

Charles was unfazed: he consulted his notes and managed to get some way through his prepared speech before Bradshawe interrupted:[18]

> KING: A King cannot be tried by any superior jurisdiction on earth [...] If power without law may make laws, may alter the fundamental laws of the Kingdom, I do not know what subject in England can be sure of his life, or anything that he calls his own. I cannot answer this till I be satisfied of the legality of it. All proceedings against any man whatsoever [...]
>
> BRADSHAWE: Sir, I must interrupt you. I do this unwillingly, but what you do is not agreeable to the proceedings of any court of justice, as all of us who are acquainted with justice know. It seems you are about to enter into argument and dispute concerning the authority of this

---

[16] Thus Fairfax was urged by Colonel White, one of his senior officers, to court martial the King rather than to put him on trial. See S.R. Gardiner, *History of the Great Civil War*, Windrush, London, 1987, p. 302.

[17] State Trials Series, vol. 4, pp. 1081–82, see *supra* note 10.

[18] *Ibid.*, pp. 1082–83.

court, before whom you appear as a prisoner and are charged as a high delinquent. You may not do it.

KING: Sir, I do not know the forms of law, but I do know law and reason. I know as much law as any gentleman in England. I do plead for the liberties of the people more than any of you do.

BRADSHAWE: I must again interrupt you. You must not go on in this course...

KING: I do desire to give my reasons for not answering: I require you give me time for that.

BRADSHAWE: Sir, it is not for prisoners to require.

KING: Prisoners! Sir, I am not an ordinary prisoner.

That was the understatement of the century. Bradshawe did not allow it:

BRADSHAWE: The commands of the court must be obeyed here. Sergeant, take away the prisoner.

KING: Well, Sir![19]

It was with this royal harrumph that the second session concluded. Charles was irritated and argumentative, involved now in the proceedings and anxious – against his own better judgment – to play the justice game. As he was taken down the stairs, he made a fatal mistake: he admitted his true feelings to his escorts, telling them he was untroubled by any of the thousands of deaths that had been laid to his charge, except for that of one man – his friend, the Earl of Strafford. This voluntary confession counted as admissible evidence of his remorseless state of mind: it was immediately reported to Cooke, and convinced him that this "hard-hearted man" was not only guilty of "so much precious Protestant blood shed in these three kingdoms" but would be happy to shed more in order to regain his prerogatives.[20] It was a turning point for the prosecutor, who had until now admired Charles's spirit and "undaunted resolution" at the trial and had thought him redeemable.[21] The King's insouciance about the casualties suffered by both sides in the Civil War also swayed the judges: it showed that the King was intractable and remorseless. So long as Charles lived, the country would be embroiled in war.

---

[19] *Ibid.*, p. 1084.

[20] John Cooke, "King Charles: His Case", in J.G. Muddiman (ed.), *Trial of Charles I (Notable British Trials)*, LexisNexis, London, 1928, p. 235.

[21] *Ibid.*, p. 250.

The third hearing day began ominously for the King: the House of Commons passed a law that writs should no longer go out under his name and royal seal, but by reference merely to the judge who had issued them. And the wording of criminal indictments, which since time immemorial had always accused offenders of acting contrary to "the peace of our Sovereign Lord the King, His Crown and Dignity" would be changed to accuse them, more rationally, of acting "against the Peace, Justice and Council of England". The great seal had already been altered to remove the King's emblems, along with any trace of Scotland, his original domain: it now featured a map of England and Ireland, with the cross of St George and the Irish harp. The flip side had an engraving by Thomas Simon of the House of Commons in session, with the proud legend: "In the first year of freedom, by God's blessing restored".

This was the first sign that Charles could not only be removed, but that he might not be replaced. Nonetheless, he would be given one last chance to co-operate. The judge was instructed to make one final attempt to have the King recognise the court, and this attempt was to be triggered by the prosecutor's request to proceed to judgment if he did not offer a plea. If the King remained contumacious, then the clerk was to put the charge to him for the last time. But if the King agreed to make answer, he would be given a copy of the indictment and allowed an adjournment until Wednesday at 1 p.m. Otherwise, that would be the time when the court would proceed to judgment and sentence.

It is little wonder that the King looked melancholy and distracted when he was brought into Westminster Hall. Cooke was ready this time to bring the King to the crunch: he leapt to his feet to make the speech which was later to hang him:[22]

> My Lord, to put an end to this great delay of justice, I shall now humbly move your Lordship for speedy judgement against him. I might press your Lordships, because according to the known rules of the law of the land, if a prisoner shall stand mute or contumacious and shall not put in an effective plea – guilty or not guilty – to the charge against him whereby he may come to a fair trial, that operates as an implicit confession – it may be taken *pro confesso*. The House of Commons has declared that the charge is true – and its truth, my Lord, is as clear as crystal

---

[22] State Trials Series, vol. 4, p. 1096, see *supra* note 10.

and as clear as the sun that shines at noon day. But if your Lordship and the court is not satisfied about that, then on the people of England's behalf, I have several witnesses to produce. And therefore I do humbly pray – and yet it is not so much I who pray, but the innocent blood that has been shed, the cry whereof is very great for justice and judgement – that speedy judgement be pronounced against the prisoner at the bar, according to justice.

Bradshawe picked up the "speedy justice" slogan canvassed by the Solicitor-General when he invited the King to enter a plea:

Sir, in plain terms – for justice is no respecter of persons – you are to give your positive and final answer, in plain English, whether you are guilty or not guilty of these treasons laid to your charge.

There was a long pause. Charles had reached the point of no return. He could make a last objection to the legality of the court, or he might have his day in it – listen to Cooke's evidence, belittle it and then present a defence that would establish for posterity the justice of his cause. That option he rejected, and for all his protestations that his stand was one of principle, he must have made the tough calculation that in any forensic battle, he would come off worst. Cooke was in command of all his secret correspondence captured at Naseby and from various messengers over the years, which would reveal his ongoing duplicity and traitorous dealings with the Scots, with the Irish and with continental powers. He simply did not dare contest the charge. His best and indeed only realistic tactic was to get in as many attacks on the legitimacy of the court as he could before he was stopped: [23]

BRADSHAWE: Sir, this is the third time that you have publicly disowned this court. How far you have preserved the fundamental laws and privileges of the people, your actions speak louder than your words [...] you have written your meaning in bloody characters throughout the whole Kingdom. Clerk, record the default. And gentlemen, you that brought the prisoner, take him back again.

KING: I will only say this one word more to you [...]

BRADSHAWE: Sir, you have heard the pleasure of the court. Notwithstanding your refusal to understand it, you

---

[23] *Ibid.*, pp. 1098–99.

will now find that you are before a court of justice.

"Well Sir, I find I am before a power" was the King's sarcastic rejoinder as he was led away.

4.7. The Prosecution Evidence

Both the court and the King recognised that the die had been cast: the last opportunity for Charles to make his defence was now irretrievable. He had given the court no way out: by law, it had now to convict him. The commissioners trudged back to their private room (the Chamber) grim-faced and angry that Charles had denied them for a third time. They were furious with the King for his offensive remarks but were more concerned by the fact that – as Cooke advised them – his refusal to plead would mean that the prosecution could not call its evidence. The common law required them to have the worst of all worlds: after three sessions in which Charles had insulted the court there would now be no opportunity to unveil the evidence of his responsibility for mass murder, treason and tyranny. So they hit upon an unusual compromise:

> notwithstanding the said contumacy of the King and his refusal to plead, which in law amounts to a tacit confession of the charge, and notwithstanding the notoriety of the facts charged, the court would nevertheless examine witnesses for the further and clearer satisfaction of their own judgement and consciences.[24]

This decision has often been interpreted as a device to stall for time: some historians speculate that it gave Cromwell the opportunity to persuade the commissioners to sentence the King to death, others that, on the contrary, it facilitated efforts behind the scenes to save him.[25] There is no need to

---

[24] See Muddiman, 1990, p. 211, *supra* note 7. Muddiman erroneously labels these minutes, taken by Phelps, as "Bradshawe's Journal".

[25] Sean Kelsey, for example, thinks that "somebody was playing for time" because "the colourful wartime recollections of a handful of non-entities ... constituted extremely weak evidence indeed". On the contrary, the evidence of common soldiers, from both sides, proved beyond doubt that the King bore command responsibility for the sufferings of ordinary people in the wars. The incriminating documents Cooke tendered for examination – the King's intercepted messages – provided the best evidence of his guilt. Kelsey's notion that "Parliamentary commanders and leading civilian politicians could have easily provided far better evidence" is also mistaken: what better cue for royalists to cry "victor's justice" had the likes of Cromwell or Haselrig testified against Charles? See Sean Kelsey,

impute a hidden agenda. Cooke, a stickler for due process, would have advised the judges that they could not hear the prosecution evidence as part of the trial, since the prisoner had been deemed to have confessed his guilt. There was, however, nothing to stop its being heard as part of a sentencing procedure – at a private session to satisfy their consciences that application of this *pro confesso* rule occasioned no injustice. It was unprecedented, but it did allow Cooke to take sworn statements from witnesses and present them to the judges. He recognised that it was an unsatisfactory expedient: it meant that the prosecution evidence against the King was not heard openly and did not become part of the public record. It would also mean, inevitably, that he could not make a closing speech.

In these final sessions, Cooke summoned no fewer than 33 witnesses to prove that the King had been a commander who had breached the laws of war.[26] Many of Cooke's witnesses were royalist soldiers whose identification of the King leading his troops at various battles could not be disputed. Charles had been a highly visible presence, fully armed and with his sword drawn, urging his men on with stirring speeches ("Stand to me this day for my crown lies upon the point of the sword. If I lose this day I lose my honour and my crown for ever".[27]) Witnesses depicted him in full command at Naseby and Copredy Bridge, at Edge Hill and Kenton and Newbury – all places referred to in the indictment. They usually added a description of the field after the battle, strewn with dead bodies. Cooke was able to prove that the King's preparations for war had begun as early as July 1642, and that his war crimes began soon afterwards. One eyewitness described the first act of plunder (the ransacking of civilian homes) committed on the King's orders and produced a royal command that stopped the food supply to Hull, a town that on the King's orders was starved unlawfully into surrender.[28] Cooke called a number of witnesses from Nottingham who

---

"Politics and Procedure in the Trial of Charles I", in *Law and History Review*, 2004, vol. 22, no. 1, pp. 19–21.

26   State Trials Series, vol. 4, pp. 1099–113, see *supra* note 10. The public turned up as usual at Westminster Hall, so Dendy and the usher were sent to tell them to depart – the Court was sitting in private in the painted chamber: *Perfect Occurrences*, 18–25 January, entry for 24 January.

27   *Ibid.*, p. 1108, Testimony of John Vinson.

28   *Ibid.*, Testimony of Will Cuthbert.

described the setting up of the King's standard and how his soldiers had extracted large sums of money from the inhabitants by threatening to plunder and fire the town.[29]

Much more serious were allegations that Charles had stood by and approved the beating and torturing of prisoners of war. Two witnesses claimed to have seen the King at Fowey in Cornwall, watching from his horse while his men stripped and stole from their prisoners, contrary to the surrender agreement and to the customary laws of warfare. One witness from Newark Fort, near Leicester, which had surrendered to the King and his forces in June 1645 on terms that no violence should befall its defenders, testified that "the King's soldiers, contrary to the [surrender] articles, fell upon the [surrendered] soldiers – stripped, cut and wounded many of them". They were rebuked by a royalist officer but the King "on horseback in bright armour" ordered the brutality to continue with the words, "I do not care if they cut them three times more for they are mine enemies". This was testimony that directly implicated Charles in ordering the torture of prisoners of war.[30]

What Cooke was presenting to the court over these two days was evidence that Charles was guilty of waging war against Parliament, personally and enthusiastically, that he bore command responsibility for the war crimes of his soldiers and that he was responsible as an individual for ordering and approving the torture of prisoners and plunder of towns. Even more damaging were his secret letters, full of double dealings and attempts to procure military assistance from Catholic powers and from Ireland and Scotland: this correspondence under his own hand would have been devastating if used to question him at Westminster Hall. There was damaging evidence from a Parliament agent, who had trapped Charles into making admissions about the support he had requested from the Irish.[31] The most damning testimony came from a barrister, Henry Gooch of Gray's Inn, who told of approaching the King during a negotiation with Parliament, under the pretence of being a supporter. The King arranged for the Prince of Wales to commission Gooch in the royalist army in exile, and expressed his "joy and affection" that so many of his subjects

---

29   *Ibid.*, pp. 1105–6, Samuel Lawson.

30   *Ibid.*, p. 1107, Humphrey Browne.

31   *Ibid.*, Richard Price (the scrivener who engrossed Cooke's charge, and who had met the King in 1643 as an emissary on behalf of the Independents).

were prepared to fight a third Civil War to restore him to power.[32]

The evidence, taken in private before a committee, was read back in public to the judges when each witness attended to swear to the truth of his statement. The 46 judges who sat through it to "satisfy their consciences" had so little doubt after reading the captured correspondence that they closed the doors and resolved to proceed to discuss the sentence.[33] Some thought that Charles should be deprived of his title of King once he had been convicted and before sentence, in which case he would face the commoner's death for treason, namely hanging, drawing and quartering. If he died as a king, he would be entitled to a relatively painless surgical exit from the world by beheading. It was a very important distinction: the difference between death with dignity and death by butchery.

4.8. Convicting the King

So, what was the intellectual basis for putting this head of state on trial? And, after a week of hearings at which he refused to plead, for cutting off his head and proclaiming England as a republic?

The key players in the end game were Bible republicans, not cynical regicides. The Puritan conviction that the institution of monarchy was antipathetic to God provided the moral force, which united with the dictates of human reason to turn the King's trial into the event that established a republic. The First Book of Samuel in the Bible clearly warned the Israelites that to seek an earthly King was to reject God: a King would oppress them and they would "cry out in that day because of your King which ye shall have chosen you; and the Lord will not hear you in that day" (8:18). Verses from the First Book of Samuel resounded from the pulpits of Puritan preachers to spread the word among their congregations that England, like Israel, would be better off without a King. To these biblical references they added the Magna Carta's guarantee of equal justice, and an idea drawn from the common law, although potentially revolutionary, that "the law was no respecter of persons". Of course it was – that was its function in the English class-stratified society, namely to keep the lower orders in their place, but it

---

[32] *Ibid.*, p. 1111, Henry Gooch.
[33] *Ibid.*, p. 1113.

was an ideal, or a least a conceit, developed by common law lawyers that "however high ye be, the law is above you". And then we can discern in the rhetoric of prosecutor Cooke and the sentencing remarks of Judge Bradshawe a pre-echo of the modern doctrine of 'responsibility to protect': the King is vouchsafed power to be exercised in trust for his people. By attacking or torturing them he is in breach of his responsibility to care for and protect them, and so they may remove him.

The King's tactic at the trial was to appear alone and defiant, to refuse to plead on the grounds that the court had no jurisdiction over him, and to refuse all legal assistance. The best criminal lawyer in the land – Matthew Hale – volunteered to represent him, but Charles wanted to appear as a martyr, in all his regal glory, confronting his accusers alone. The presence of defending lawyers always takes the spotlight away from their client. (The first head of state to be tried in an international court adopted this same tactic: Milošević ordered his lawyers to sit in the public gallery so that Serbian television would depict him as a solitary victim, alone against the world.)

The jury at the High Court of Justice contained the closest 'peers' of the King that could be found on Parliament's side – MPs, generals, civil and business leaders, county officials and mayors. It put Charles on trial but did not try him: it couldn't, because he refused to plead. That meant, by English law at the time that the court had to declare him guilty and proceed to sentence.

Even the prosecutor's closing speech was not necessary, because the King's guilt was "deemed" as a result of his refusal to recognise the court. But Cooke published it, to explain how, after the Treaty of Westphalia, 'tyranny' was a crime in any country. He invoked not only the common law of England, but international law – "the general law of all nations" – and natural law, "written in every rational man's heart with the pen of a diamond, in capital letters and a character so legible that even he that runs may read". The principle was simple:

> When any man is entrusted with the sword for the protection and preservation of the people, if this man shall employ to their destruction that which was put into his hand for their safety, then by the law of that land he becomes an enemy to that people and deserves the most exemplary and severe punishment. This law – *if the King become a tyrant he shall die for it* – is the law of nature and the law of God, written in

the fleshly tablets of men's hearts.[34]

It is important to understand that Cooke's indictment of 'tyranny' had a respectable pedigree, in so far as it was an elaboration of the laws of war which prohibited pillage and plunder, and torture of prisoners. The evidence implicated Charles in these atrocities. Although international lawyers had not gone so far as to impute command responsibility to princes, Grotius had argued that Kings were liable for wrongs they had known about and could have prevented. Erasmus had written extensively about the justification for regicide (in terms that Shakespeare applied to the accountability of Kings like Richard III and Macbeth) while Albert Gentili, the Oxford Regius professor, had pointed out that "unless we wish to make sovereigns exempt from the law and bound by no statutes and no precedents, there must also of necessity be someone to remind them of their duty and hold them in restraint".[35] That "someone" had to be a court, comprising judges empowered to enforce the law against the King.

Not for every crime – Cooke conceded the inconvenience of punishing a King for a single murder[36] – but for systematic breaches that resulted in the destruction of public lives and liberty. In this sense, 'tyranny' was a different crime to treason, which involved an attack on a lawful sovereign, or at least on a sovereign behaving lawfully, within his realm. The charge of tyranny might carry a consequence more momentous than treason or murder because it was against the law of nations and of nature. It would justify armed resistance, even invasion – what would now be termed 'humanitarian intervention'. As Gentili had put it: "Look you, if men clearly sin against the laws of nature and of mankind, I believe that anyone whatsoever may check such men by force of arms".[37]

For Cooke, tyranny was a crime committed by absolute rulers who became tyrants, not only when they took up arms against their own civilians, but by their fixed intention to govern without Parliament or an

---

[34] State Trials Series, vol. 4, p. 1032, see *supra* note 10.

[35] A. Gentili, *De Jure Belli Libri Tres* [1612], trans. by J.C. Rolfe as *Three Books on the Law of War*, Clarendon Press, Oxford, 1933, p. 74. See Theodore Meron, *War Crimes Law Comes of Age: Essays*, Oxford University Press, Oxford, 1998, p. 128.

[36] See Cooke, 1928, p. 248, *supra* note 20.

[37] Gentili, 1933, p. 122, see *supra* note 35.

independent judiciary or any other traditional check on their power. Kings were not invariably tyrannical: monarchical government was tolerated by God and by the law of nations, so long as the monarch did not abuse his power – by, for example (and it was the example to hand), waging war on the people in order to destroy their vested political rights to an independent judiciary and to a regular Parliament for the redress of their grievances. When the ruler's oppression becomes systematic and widespread, the people were entitled to have him arrested and put on trial. If he could claim to have acted from incompetence or honest misjudgment as to the public good, he might be pardoned or permitted to abdicate in favour of an heir bound to observe constitutional limits. But if his misconduct had been motivated by a desire for absolute power, a just sentence would be death and disinheritance. This was a revolutionary doctrine, which went further than the Dutch academics, and preceded by 40 years John Locke's argument that government was by social compact and the people's consent contingent on the governor's commitment to their liberties. As Locke was to explain, in his *Second Treatise on Government*:

> The end of government is the good of mankind. And which is best for mankind: that the people should always be exposed to the boundless will of tyranny, or that the rulers should be sometimes liable to be opposed when they grow exorbitant in the use of their power and employ it for the destruction and not the preservation of the properties of their people?[38]

4.9. The Follow-up Trials

Just as Nuremberg had follow-up trials, so did the trial of the King. His five leading military commanders, most notably the Duke of Hamilton, were next to be prosecuted. Several had surrendered to the army on promises of amnesty – or 'quarter'. The offer and grant of 'quarter' was a basic feature of the law of seventeenth-century warfare, accepted by all sides in the English civil wars.[39] A soldier who yielded and threw down

---

[38] John Locke, *Second Treatise of Government: Of the Beginning of Political Societies*, 1690, Hackett Publishing Company, Indianapolis, 1980, p. 115.

[39] "None shall kill an enemy who yields and throws down his arms, upon pain of death" was a rule of (a) the King's army in 1640, (b) the Earl of Essex's army in 1642 and (c) the Army of the Kingdom of Scotland in 1643. See (a) Francis Grose, *Military Antiquities*, S.

his arms could not be slain, and had thereafter to be treated humanely as a prisoner of war. But did it operate as a full-blown pardon for all crimes of war he might previously have committed, or was it a temporary expedient that saved him from being killed either on the spot or after an army court martial but did not prevent his subsequent prosecution for treason?

This argument, too, is reflected in current debates over whether amnesties granted in peace settlements prevent prosecution for crimes against humanity. Cooke's answer was that military law operated in a different dimension to criminal law: the grant of 'quarter' was a right that operated only in the former context, where it protected the beneficiary from further attack. It did not prevent his subsequent prosecution for serious war crimes. The court accepted Cooke's submission: 'quarter' meant freedom from execution in or after the heat of battle, but not freedom from justice. Cooke's insistence in these follow-up trials that military jurisdiction in the course of a war must not be allowed to subvert the jurisdiction of the common law remains of importance. Military and police authorities may offer expedient or unwise deals to prisoners guilty (it may subsequently turn out) of terrible offences, and Cooke's position, now accepted by international criminal law, was that such deals cannot prevent prosecution for heinous crimes that it is beyond the power of the military to overlook or forgive.

The trial of the King's courtiers lasted, in fits and starts, for a month. The appearance of defence counsel – the renowned Matthew Hale – gave the proceedings a genuine adversary flavour. The court strove to be fair and granted unheard-of indulgences to the prisoners. The Duke of Hamilton was permitted adjournments to gather evidence; he was allowed to instruct Hale in private, without being overheard by guards; the Earl of Holland's illness was accepted as a reason why he should not stand trial until his doctors certified that he was well enough to cope. These novel civilities may have reflected a lingering respect for high-born defendants, but they set standards which could not easily be ignored by the ordinary criminal courts in this new republican era. Within the constraints of the current rules of evidence, which denied defendants the right to testify on oath, this High Court's proceedings were remarkably fair.

Hooper, London, 1788, p. 118; (b) Charles M. Clode, *The Military Forces of the Crown: Their Administration and Government*, John Murray, London, 1869, pp. 422–25; (c) Grose (above) p. 136.

4.10. Ending Impunity

The instruction in Cooke's brief was to devise a lawful means of ending the impunity of a tyrant who happened to be a king. The republic came as a practical rather than a logical consequence of the trial: there was no viable alternative. That was also the case in revolutionary France over a century later, where the trial of Charles I assumed importance for all parties involved in the trial of Louis XVI. His lawyers advised him to adopt Charles's tactic of denying jurisdiction, since the constitution guaranteed his inviolability, but Louis doggedly insisted upon trying to establish his innocence – which was his big mistake. He was unanimously convicted by a National Assembly that had already declared his guilt. The vote to have him executed was close. Tom Paine, an honorary delegate, urged them to exile the King to America, where he might be reformed and become a democrat. Marat accused Paine of being a Quaker, Robespierre said humanity could not pardon mass-murdering despots, and St Just adopted Cooke's argument: all kings were tyrants, and this king must die so monarchy would die with him. The French had studied Charles's trial closely, and took care that Louis did not become a martyr: they even directed drummers to interrupt his speech from the guillotine.[40] Later the British took care not to put Napoleon on trial – they exiled him to St Helena so he could not be a martyr.

It was not until the twentieth century that head of state immunity was challenged, by a British government at Versailles determined to deliver on Lloyd George's promise to "Hang the Kaiser" for ordering the unprovoked invasion of Belgium and unrestricted submarine warfare. But the US insisted that sovereign immunity was central to Westphalian international law: the Kaiser remained in Holland, unhanged, as a guest of the Dutch government until his death in 1941. Had he been tried and punished, Hitler might have been given pause.

In 1945 the trial of Charles I cast a shadow over the US plans to put the Nazis on trial. Winston Churchill, an admirer of Cromwell, believed the trial had been a mistake: the King had exploited it to secure his own martyrdom. That, he feared, was exactly what Hitler would do if put on public trial. So he proposed that the top Nazis would be "outlawed" by name and once captured would be executed as soon as their identity could

---

[40] See Simon Schama, *Citizens: A Chronicle of the French Revolution*, Penguin, Harmondsworth, 1989, pp. 659–61.

be verified. President Harry S. Truman and his legal adviser, Justice Robert Jackson, objected:

> [S]ummary executions would not sit easy on the American conscience or be remembered by our children with pride. The only course is to determine the innocence or guilt of the accused after a hearing as dispassionate as the times and horrors we deal with will permit and upon a record that will leave our reasons and motives clear.[41]

So there was a deadlock over whether the Nazi leaders should be put on trial at all. Stalin had the casting vote, and he loved show trials – so long as every defendant was shot at the end. From this unpromising beginning, the Nazi leaders went to Nuremberg to face a new jurisdiction – that of international criminal law.

Hermann Goering advocated the Charles I gambit: at first he ordered his co-defendants to say only three words to their judges – the defiant catch-cry of one of Goethe's warrior heroes, loosely translated as "kiss my arse". This was to be the Nazi leader formula for denying jurisdiction. But as the pre-trial months passed, the Nazi leaders were inveigled by the fairness of Anglo-American trial procedures into playing the justice game.[42] It was because they entered so fully into the adversarial dynamics of the traditional criminal trial, testing the prosecution evidence and undergoing cross-examination, that the ensuing judgment at Nuremberg has the stamp of historical authority. It was this kind of judgment, of course, that Charles had skilfully pre-empted by challenging the court's jurisdiction and refusing all temptations to enter a defence. Goering cheated the hangman by taking poison: Charles, "the royal actor", would not for all the world have missed performing on the scaffold stage.

For the half-century following Nuremberg, tyrants of all types lived happily ever after their tyrannies. Although the US Supreme Court in 1946 in the Yamashita case [43] confirmed Cooke's "command responsibility" principle in relation to Japanese generals who connived at the war crimes of their troops, the allies covered up the responsibility of Emperor Hirohito for Japanese aggression. There was no accountability

---

[41] Report 1 June 1945, Jackson to Truman. Anne and John Tusa, *The Nuremberg Trial*, Skyhorse Publishing, London, 1983, p. 66.

[42] Robert E. Conot, *Justice at Nuremberg*, Basic Books, London, 1983, p. 68.

[43] Supreme Court of the United States, *In re Yamashita*, 327 US 1, judgment, 4 February 1946.

for Stalin, nor for other mass-murdering heads of state like Pol Pot and Emperor Bokassa and His Excellency Idi Amin VC and bar. It was not until General Pinochet's arrest in London in 1998 that an English court would again consider the scope of sovereign immunity, finding in the law of nations the basis for ruling that former heads of state who order the torture of prisoners – one of Cooke's allegations against Charles I – must face trial.[44] There was increasing acceptance, at the turn into the twenty-first century, that sovereign immunity would be lost if the sovereign bore command responsibility for a particularly heinous class of offence – a 'crime against humanity' – such as genocide or widespread torture, or plundering the property of innocent civilians. Milošević became in 2001 the first head of state since Charles I to face a panel of judges, at a court in The Hague set up by the UN Security Council.

Milošević opened with the King Charles gambit, refusing to plead on the ground that the court had been unlawfully established. The English presiding judge, Richard May, did not make Bradshawe's mistake of taking the plea *pro confesso*: he treated it as "not guilty" and appointed an *amicus* team to take legal points on Milošević's behalf. The defendant instructed his own lawyers but had them sit in the gallery so that he could appear in court like Charles, isolated and alone, and made rabble-rousing addresses which played well on television to his supporters back in Serbia. The problems that were encountered in attempting to try Milošević lend a kinder view to the way similar problems had to be approached by Cooke and Bradshawe back in 1649.

As for Saddam Hussein, there is no one who better fits the allegations of tyranny in Cooke's charge against the King. When he first appeared in court after his arrest, his language (in translation) was identical to that of Charles: "By what authority do you put me on trial?" This was a very good question, since he had been overthrown by a US invasion generally held by international lawyers to be unlawful.

Notwithstanding my doubts, I was conscripted to help train Iraqi judges in international criminal law. I began by telling them about the trial of Charles I, and they asked me what happened to the judges who convicted the tyrant. Reluctantly I had to tell them that when monarchy was restored and Charles II came to the throne, 11 years later, those who

---

[44] House of Lords, *R v. Bow Street Metropolitan Stipendiary Magistrate, Ex Parte Pinochet Ugarte (No. 3)*, 2 All ER 97, judgment, 25 November 1998.

had judged his father were taken out and disembowelled, expiring in the stench of their entrails being burned in front of their goggling eyes. That did not cheer them up.

At this time, whether the Iraq Tribunal would become an international court was a matter of debate. The Iraqi judges wanted to sit with international judges, but the Americans feared that they would not pass a death sentence. British lawyers did not want a death sentence, and so once again the two allies were at loggerheads. The Yanks wanted him dead, we wanted him in a prison in Finland. "Finland!" they expostulated. "Where he can watch 140 porn channels and have conjugal visits from his wives! No way!" So I suggested that we could do with him what we did with Napoleon, and send him to St Helena. The UK Foreign Office, to my surprise, took this suggestion seriously and enquired of St Helena's local council, who responded plaintively that "they were trying to start a tourist industry down here" and did not think Saddam would count as an attraction. So he went to the gallows, and his resting place in Takrit is a place of pilgrimage. I wish we had sent him – and the likes of Milošević – to the Falkland Islands, where they would commune with penguins and never be heard of again.

It is a problem – what to do with a convicted tyrant – and no solution is easy or necessarily right. The regicides who convicted Charles I made him a martyr by executing him, and he came back to haunt them after only 11 years. But what else could they have done, given that his followers were ready to die to restore him? This was their most intractable dilemma, at how to end the first trial of a head of state in modern times. In retrospect it did not end well.

5

Chinese Confucianism and Other Prevailing Chinese Practices in the Rise of International Criminal Law

SHI Bei,* ZENG Siqi** and ZHANG Qi***

5.1. Introduction

International criminal law contains the international aspects of national criminal systems and the criminal elements of international law,[1] which means the individual participation of states and international co-operation are intertwined as well as interconnected in the path of this discipline's development. Since the establishment of the first permanent International Criminal Court ('ICC'), people's expectations of international criminal justice have been increasingly high. Under the pressure of public opinion at home and abroad, China, as the only permanent member of the Security Council that has not yet signed the ICC Statute, is also considering its

* **SHI Bei** is currently working in the compliance department of an international bank. She holds an LL.M. in International Law and a Diploma of International Human Rights from Peking University. She has attended the Summer Courses in The Hague Academy of International Law. She also participated as a team member in the national round of the 2013 Philip C. Jessup International Law Moot Court Competition, and won the prize of "Best Oralist". She passed the National Judicial Examination of China in 2011 and attained an LL.B. degree from Southwest University of Political Science and Law in 2012.

** **ZENG Siqi** holds a Juris Master degree from Peking University Law School, majoring in Public International Law. She also graduated from the Lund University Raoul Wallenberg Institute's Master of Human Rights programme, and served as an editor of the website of the Research Centre for Human Rights and Humanitarian Law of Peking University. She graduated from Jinan University in 2011, majoring in English Literature.

*** **ZHANG Qi** is currently working at China United Credit Finance Group, which focuses on innovative finance. She holds an LL.M. degree in Public International Law from Peking University Law School. She was also enrolled in the Lund University Raoul Wallenberg Institute's Mater of Human Rights programme in 2013. In the same year she was awarded the Wang Tieya International Law Scholarship. In 2012 she was also awarded the Peking University Freshmen Scholarship. From 2010 to 2011, she was an exchange student at the School of Law, Renmin University of China. She holds a Bachelor of Laws from the School of Law, University of International Business and Economics.

[1] Ellen S. Podgor and Roger S. Clark, *Understanding International Criminal Law*, 2nd ed., LexisNexis, Newark, 2008, p. 4.

future relations with the ICC as well as its future status in the international criminal law arena.[2]

Retrospect is as important as prospect, however. Taking a look at the historical origins of international criminal law, we may acquire some inspiration and we may discover some hidden history or hidden efforts that are of contemporary relevance. This chapter will focus on China's early encounters with international criminal law in the Second World War and its aftermath. Chinese culture, represented by Confucianism, did have historical connections with the emergence of international criminal law, which, to a large extent, was facilitated by the Universal Declaration of Human Rights ('UDHR'). China did take an active part in the United Nations War Crimes Commission ('UNWCC') and played an important role in its Sub-Commission in Chungking, using international law as well as this war crimes forum to contain the aggression of Japan. Besides, the Chinese national prosecutions of Japanese war criminals in 1946 and 1956 displayed Chinese Confucianism – including the idea of justice, humanity and conscience – and demonstrated China's approach in dealing with war crimes, which also deserves to be discovered and understood by the world.

5.2. The Rise of International Criminal Law

In the regime of international law, where state sovereignty and state responsibility ensure the order of the international community, international criminal law is a special or even exceptional branch that emphasises the criminal liability of individuals, international criminal justice, as well as human rights protection. The embryo of international criminal law was formed in 1919, when the Commission on the Responsibility of the Authors of the War and on Enforcement of Penalties was established at the Paris Peace Conference. This Commission recommended an international tribunal to try violations of the laws of war and the laws of humanity.[3] However, for quite some time,

---

[2] The United States signed the ICC Statute in 2000. However, at the time of the ICC's founding in 2002, the United States said that it would not join the ICC. Russia signed but has not ratified the ICC Statute. France and the United Kingdom have both signed and ratified the ICC Statute.

[3] The Commission on the Responsibility of the Authors of the War and on Enforcement of Penalties, "Report Presented to the Preliminary Peace Conference", in *American Journal of International Law*, 1919, vol. 14, p. 95.

this concept remained a proposition with no actual established tribunal, no international prosecutions carried out and no practical actions taken.

The formal emergence of international criminal law was in the 1940s, when the extreme atrocities during the Second World War awakened the inner desire of people to punish war criminals. With the establishment of the UNWCC, an international co-operation forum committed to war crimes investigation, the punishment of war criminals was no longer empty talk but a reality with practical actions. Therefore, based on the preliminary exercise of the UNWCC, international criminal law soon deepened with the issuing of the London Charter and the onset of many of the post-Second World War international and national trials. Despite the Cold War's negative impact for a certain period, the United Nations Security Council's resolutions for setting up the International Criminal Tribunal for the Former Yugoslavia ('ICTY') and the International Criminal Tribunal for Rwanda ('ICTR'), followed by a number of mixed international and national tribunals in Sierra Leone, Timor Leste and Cambodia, pushed forward the maturing of international criminal law enormously. And now, with the first permanent international criminal court being established and in operation,[4] it is safe to conclude that international criminal law has evolved into a complete legal system.

Therefore, the period of the Second World War and its aftermath is significant for the rise of international criminal law. Those unprecedented international and national practices were the most necessary and difficult steps taken, and China participated fully in this process.

5.3. International Criminal Law and the UDHR

5.3.1. The Connection between International Criminal Law and the Law of Human Rights

The main idea in international criminal law has its origins in the concepts of natural rights and the inherent dignity of the human being. The UDHR and the later development of international human rights law during the preceding decades is of great significance in reinforcing the foundation of international criminal law.

---

[4]   Robert Cryer, "The Doctrinal Foundations of International Criminalization", in M. Cherif Bassiouni (ed.), *International Criminal Law*, vol. III: *International Enforcement*, Martinus Nijhoff, Leiden, 2008, p. 117.

First, international criminal law is an application of human rights standards in the way of criminal prosecutions, which ultimately intends to protect values that have been written into the UDHR and other human rights instruments. Modern human rights law emerged at the end of the Second World War in response to the atrocities and massive violations of human rights.[5] The horrors of the Nazi Holocaust and the ruthless abuse of human rights awakened the international community to the importance of human rights and strengthened the demands for international protection of human rights. It became necessary that states could no longer use domestic jurisdiction arguments to defend themselves against international scrutiny.[6] In 1945 the United Nations brought human rights firmly into the sphere of international law in its own constituent document, the UN Charter. And then the UDHR was adopted, with a series of human rights treaties subsequently concluded.

It was also against this background that international criminal law emerged, which intended to establish the criminal responsibility of individuals for international crimes, including war crimes, crimes against humanity, genocide, torture, aggression and some extreme forms of terrorism.[7] As the last and most effective resort in protecting human rights, it ultimately intends to ensure the actual realisation of ideas that have been written down in the UDHR, by preventing severe violations of human rights by even the most authoritarian regimes. There is no doubt that international crimes are subject to these rules and are protecting values that are considered important by the whole international community. Most of these values have been laid down in international instruments, especially in the 1948 UDHR.[8] The rules of international criminal law do not proclaim these values directly, but prohibit conduct that infringes them. Therefore, the development of human rights protection pushes forward the efforts of the international community to

---

[5] United Nations, *The United Nations and Human Rights, 1945–1995*, The United Nations Blue Books Series, vol. VII, United Nations Department of Public Information, New York, 1995, p. 3.

[6] Asbjørn Eide and Gudmundur Alfredsson, "Introduction", in Gudmundur Alfredsson and Asbjørn Eide (eds.), *The Universal Declaration of Human Rights: A Common Standard of Achievement*, Martinus Nijhoff, The Hague, 1999, p. xxxi.

[7] Antonio Cassese, *International Criminal Law*, Oxford University Press, Oxford, 2003, p. 23.

[8] *Ibid.*

prohibit and prevent international crimes, so as to ensure world peace and the fundamental rights of human beings.

Second, international criminal law ensures the protection of human rights in criminal proceedings. Many human rights in the civil and political category are of direct concern to those involved in the criminal justice process, whether at the national or international level.[9] These human rights include the right to a speedy and fair trial, the right to the presumption of innocence, the right to confront witnesses and evidence, the right to appeal one's conviction[10] and so on.

In addition, its principles and concepts, which are of crucial importance, originate from human rights law. First, the individual being a subject of international law has been carefully woven into the UN Charter and the UDHR, both of which tend to reaffirm the faith in fundamental human rights as well as human dignity. Public international law traditionally focused on the rights and obligations of states, but the progress of human rights law promoted the development of a whole new field of public international law, focusing on the status of individuals. Based on this, international criminal law attaches great importance to the criminal responsibility of those individuals who commit international crimes.[11] It has now been recognised that international law can speak to individuals directly, as indicated by the Nuremberg Trials, the Tokyo Trials, Nuremberg Principles, the ICC Statute and the Convention on the Prevention and Punishment of the Crime of Genocide. Second, the UDHR set the framework for the "Law of Non-Retroactivity" principle in subsequent treaties of international criminal law. Later, the principle of legality in the UDHR and human rights treaties was applied to crimes under international law, and has created a solid legal foundation to support later prosecutions of war crimes, crimes against humanity and crimes against peace[12]. These two principles are the leading instances of

---

[9]   Podgor and Clark, 2008, p. 187, see *supra* note 1.

[10] David Weissbrodt and Kristin K. Zinsmaster, "Protecting the Fair Trial Rights of the Accused in International Criminal Law: Comparison of the International Criminal Court and the Military Commission in Guantánamo", in Bartram S. Brown (ed.), *Research Handbook on International Criminal Law*, Edward Elgar, Northampton, MA, 2011, pp. 261–83.

[11] Bartram S. Brown, "International Criminal Law: Nature, Origins and a Few Key Issues", in Bartram S. Brown, 2011, p. 4, see *supra* note 10.

[12] Kenneth S. Gallant, *The Principle of Legality in International Comparative Criminal Law*, Cambridge University Press, Cambridge, 2009, pp. 156–159.

many principles and ideas that human rights law and international criminal law both share.

5.3.2. The Role of the UDHR in the Law of Human Rights

International human rights law is defined as the law that deals with the protection of individuals and groups against violations of their internationally guaranteed rights. It also deals with the promotion of these rights.[13] As an international legal instrument, the UDHR is not only the earliest and the most influential document in the field of international human rights but also the most comprehensive and systematic account of the concept of human rights. Therefore, it is necessary to have a close analysis of the status of the UDHR in order to better understand human rights law and international criminal law.

First, the UDHR is the most comprehensive human rights instrument to be proclaimed by a global international organisation,[14] a milestone in mankind's struggle for freedom and human dignity. It was adopted by the General Assembly as a resolution in 1948. It took 18 more years before the two core Covenants were adopted by the Assembly and opened for signature. Another 10 years elapsed before the two Covenants entered into force in 1976. Thus in those 28 years, the only instrument that acquired unparalleled legal and political importance was the UDHR. It laid the conceptual and legal foundations for the future development of international measures to protect human rights.[15]

Second, the UN endorsed a list of recognised human rights in the UDHR, which remains the cornerstone of expression of global human rights values.[16] The UDHR was the first instrument to establish a detailed list of human rights encompassing not only civil and political rights, but also economic, social and cultural rights. These rights are interrelated, constituting the basic system for international human rights law, and have

---

[13] Thomas Buergenthal, Dinah Shelton and David P. Stewart, *International Human Rights in a Nutshell*, 3rd ed., West Group, St Paul, 2004, p. 1.

[14] Asbjørn Eide, Gudmundur Alfredsson, Göran Melander, Lars Adam and Allan Rosas (eds.), *The Universal Declaration of Human Rights: A Commentary*, Scandinavian University Press, Oslo, 1992.

[15] United Nations, 1995, p. 3, see *supra* note 5.

[16] Sarah Joseph and Joanna Kyriakakis, "The United Nations and Human Rights", in Sarah Joseph and Adam McBeth (eds.), *Research Handbook on International Human Rights Law*, Edward Elgar, Northampton, MA, 2010, p. 2.

served, since their adoption, as a framework for subsequent international human rights treaties as well as many regional human rights instruments and national constitutions[17].

Third, as laid out in its preamble, the purpose of the UDHR is to provide "a common understanding" of the human rights and fundamental freedoms referred to in the UN Charter. Therefore, the UDHR plays an important role in 'standard-setting' activities.[18] It not only provides an authoritative interpretation of the provisions on human rights in the UN Charter but also becomes an important part of customary international law, or in other words, it has come to be crystallised as customary international law.[19] Thus, not surprisingly, the UDHR is the most frequently cited standard of international human rights.[20]

5.3.3. Drafting Debate of the UDHR

After the adoption of the UN Charter, the Commission on Human Rights was established in 1946 with the mandate to develop the framework for the international bill of human rights,[21] to clearly set out the specific contents of the international human rights recognised under the Charter. The Commission appointed a drafting committee chaired by Eleanor Roosevelt, which drafted the UDHR in 1948.[22] Although the UDHR was adopted unanimously as a resolution of the UN General Assembly on 10 December 1948, there were many essential and controversial issues to tackle in the process of the drafting.[23]

---

[17] Mashood A. Baderin and Manisuli Ssenyonjo, "Development of International Human Rights Law Before and After the UDHR", in Mashood A. Baderin and Manisuli Ssenyonjo (eds.), *International Human Rights Law: Six Decades after the UDHR and Beyond*, Ashgate, Farnham, 2010, p. 8.

[18] *Ibid.*

[19] Louis B. Sohn, "The New International Law: Protection of the Rights of Individuals Rather than States", in *American University Law Review*, 1982, vol. 32, no. 1, pp. 15–17.

[20] Brown, 2011, p. 9, see *supra* note 11.

[21] Ed Bates, "History", in Daniel Moeckli, Sangeeta Shah and Sandesh Sivakumaran (eds.), *International Human Rights Law*, Oxford University Press, Oxford, 2010, p. 35.

[22] Baderin and Ssenyonjo, 2010, p. 7, see *supra* note 17.

[23] Ashild Samney, "The Origins of the Universal Declaration of Human Rights", in Gudmundur Alfredsson and Asbjørn Eide (eds.), *The Universal Declaration of Human Rights: A Common Standard of Achievement*, Martinus Nijhoff, The Hague, 1999, p. 5.

One of the important debates was the form or status of the planned document, whether it should take the form of a binding convention or become a declaration that is not formally binding. This difference had an obvious effect on the attitudes towards substantive questions.[24] Apart from the issue of form, there were many controversies concerning the substance. The representatives of some states advocated the inclusion of social and economic rights in the UDHR, which was met with intense opposition.[25] Also, the drafting participants put varying degrees of emphasis on the freedom of individuals as distinct from the interests of states. And there were highly diverse interpretations on the origin of human rights, the rule of law, the meaning of democracy, the freedom of marriage and the right to change one's religion.[26]

According to related materials, many of the substantial controversies and disagreements were derived from deep-rooted cultural differences of the different countries, and the struggle to make the UDHR suitable for universal application.[27] It was necessary to achieve a compromise on the form and content of the UDHR, and to go beyond the linguistic, cultural, political, and even personal differences of the commissioners themselves to produce a document of broad applicability, making the idea of an international human rights standard a reality.[28]

5.4. Confucianism and the UDHR: The Participation and Contribution of Chang Peng Chun

The Commission comprised 18 intelligent and great minds of that time, including Eleanor Roosevelt (Chairwoman of the UN Human Rights Commission), John Peters Humphrey (the first Director of the United Nations Human Rights Division), Charles Malik (the Rapporteur of the Commission and the then president of the General Assembly), as well as Chang Peng Chun ('P.C. Chang') and other brilliant people. However, regretfully, most of these contributors are seldom remembered. It is worth

---

[24] *Ibid.*, p. 10.

[25] *Ibid.*, p. 11.

[26] *Ibid.*, pp. 12–13.

[27] Craig Williams, "International Human Rights and Confucianism", in *Asia-Pacific Journal on Human Rights and the Law*, 2006, vol. 1, p. 44.

[28] Mary Ann Glendon, "John P. Humphrey and the Drafting of the Universal Declaration of Human Rights", in *Journal of the History of International Law*, 2000, vol. 2, p. 251.

recalling and reassessing the role as well as the contribution of the forerunners, especially Confucianism's function in the drafting of the UDHR, in order to attain the wisdom to develop international criminal law even further, with an open outlook, making it more inclusive of diverse cultures.

P.C. Chang was the Chinese delegate participating in the drafting of the UDHR. His work was of great significance for the adoption of the UDHR as the Vice-Chairman of the Human Rights Commission. It was he who managed, in a Confucian way, to diffuse the conflicts between different delegates from diverse cultures and ideologies. P.C. Chang's Confucian ideas "often provided the formula which made it possible for the Commission to escape from some impasse".[29] What's more, through his efforts, core Confucian concepts were included in the UDHR and created impetus for human rights and the development of international criminal law in subsequent years.

As a Confucian intellectual, P.C. Chang also had a western educational background. He was a diplomat, a renowned educator and a playwright. As a diplomat, he had travelled to various regions of the world, including but not limited to the Far East, Latin America and some Western countries, which enabled him to cultivate a profound understanding of different cultures and the reality of the world. Therefore, he subsequently managed to co-ordinate delegates with divergent beliefs during the drafting of the UDHR and propose several far-reaching suggestions.

5.4.1. Facilitating the Adoption of the UDHR in a Confucian Manner

The two World Wars had caused many people to fall into the belief that "[r]ights [were] only a question between equals in power. The strong do what they can while the weak suffer what they must".[30] However, P.C. Chang observed this issue from another perspective, believing that certain human rights principles were so fundamental that every state in this world was obliged to comply with them. However, it was not an easy task to determine the scope of principles that ought to be included into the

---

[29] Mary Ann Glendon, *A World Made New: Eleanor Roosevelt and the Universal Declaration of Human Rights*, Random House, New York, 2002, p. 44.

[30] *Ibid.*, pp. 250–60.

UDHR. It was not doubted that the UDHR should contain diverse cultures and beliefs. Only in this way could the human rights document epitomise the whole of humanity. However, this faced the dilemma of surmounting the political, cultural and ideological differences of all negotiators and states.

P.C. Chang played an essential role in conciliating the different participants' opinions. From Eleanor Roosevelt's memoirs, we know that:

> Dr. P.C. Chang, who was a great joy to all of us because of his sense of humor, his philosophical observations and his ability to quote some apt Chinese proverb to fit almost any occasion. Dr. Chang was a pluralist and held forth in charming fashion on the proposition that there is more than one kind of ultimate reality. The Declaration, he said, should reflect more than simply Western ideas and Dr. Humphrey would have to be eclectic in his approach. His remark, though addressed to Dr. Humphrey, was really directed at Dr. Malik, from whom it drew a prompt retort as he expounded at some length the philosophy of Thomas Aquinas. I remember that at one point Dr. Chang suggested that the Secretariat might well spend a few months studying the fundamentals of Confucianism![31]

P.C. Chang was a pluralist influenced by Confucianism. He attempted to convince others that Western thoughts could not be foisted on other cultures. Confucius once said that men with noble characters might hold different opinions while understanding each other at the same time. The Commission finally accepted this view. P.C. Chang used Confucian wisdom in solving many diplomatic problems in the drafting process of the UDHR. What is more, he also quoted some Chinese proverbs to promote communication. For instance, Chang utilised the phrase about how one should "sweep the snow in front of one's door, overlook the frost on other's roof tiles" to settle the contentions and disputes among raging delegates.[32]

---

[31]   Eleanor Roosevelt, *On My Own*, Hutchinson, London, 1959, p. 95.

[32]   Huang Jianwu, "Confucian Tradition and the Construction of Modern Human Rights – From the Perspective of P.C. Chang's Contribution to Drafting the Universal Declaration of Human Rights", in *Journal of Sun Yat-Sen University, Social Science Edition*, 2012, vol. 52, no. 6, p. 169.

The sources of human rights have yielded many controversies throughout history and this was also the case during the drafting process of the UDHR. The debates mainly focused on whether God should be expressed. Several countries such as Brazil and Canada maintained that God should be included as the Creator. The Belgian delegate contested such a practice as ambiguous and believed it would risk leading to an endless philosophical debate. P.C. Chang endorsed this opinion by pointing out that such theoretical elements may damage its universal application. The age of religious intolerance had already terminated. The Commission accepted P.C. Chang's idea and the delegation from Brazil withdrew their amendment.[33]

The controversy about whether the UDHR should be legally binding was huge. The UN Charter authorised the Human Rights Commission to enact the bill of human rights without stipulating its nature. Delegates from Australia, India and the United Kingdom asserted that the document should be legally binding. On the other hand, China, the Soviet Union, the United States and Yugoslavia preferred to enact a declaration without binding efficiency. Chile, Egypt, France and Uruguay held eclectic standpoints. They thought a convention associated with a declaration was better. Debate was so fierce that the Commission could not draw a unanimous conclusion.[34]

During the course of the above conflicts, it was P.C. Chang who proposed to enact a declaration as the first step. There were three specific reasons for this idea. First, a convention imposing legal obligations may provide excuses for great powers to intervene in other countries. Second, the most urgent need of the international community was to make a document to protect human rights after the two World Wars, while a binding convention would lead to a very time-consuming process. Lastly, the imposing of legal obligations would limit the universality of the document, since some countries might be put off by the compulsory contents. Based on these considerations, he suggested enacting the bill of human rights in the following order: a declaration, a convention and an enforcement measures text. This was exactly the final decision made by

---

[33] Lu Jianping, Wang Jian and Zhao Jun, "Chinese Representative Peng Chun Chang and the Universal Declaration of Human Rights", in *Journal of Human Rights*, 2003, vol. 6, p. 21.

[34] *Ibid.*

the Commission. Because of P.C. Chang's solution, the drafting of the UDHR had a clear and useful process.[35]

It was proved that P.C. Chang's opinion, derived from the Confucian thought of unity, was constructive and practical. Considering the historical background, the primary need was to end the divisions of the world. To achieve a common understanding was far more important than adhering to different narrow views.

5.4.2. Confucianism as a Historical Origin of the UDHR

Article 1 of the UDHR contains the core concept of Confucianism: "Conscience". It states: "All human beings are born free and equal in dignity and rights. They are endowed with reason and conscience and should act towards one another in a spirit of brotherhood".[36]

During the preliminary arrangements of the drafting, P.C. Chang advocated adopting the concept of benevolence. Actually, the meaning of this term was so complex that it could not be clarified in simple words. It was first posed by Confucius and emphasised sympathy and understanding towards others. P.C. Chang translated the term as "conscience".[37] He delivered this opinion in the speech, "A New Loyalty", at the opening meeting of the first session of the Economic and Social Council in London on 23 January 1946:

> A new loyalty must be cultivated. A deeper mutual understanding must be promoted. A saying from the Chinese thinker, Mencius, may be appropriate. "Subdue people with goodness" – this is already one step higher than subdue people with force – "Subdue people with goodness, people can never subdued. Nourish people with goodness, the whole world can be subdued".[38]

---

[35] *Ibid.*

[36] Universal Declaration of Human Rights, G.A.Res. 217A (III), U.N. Doc A/810, 71 ("UDHR"), 1948.

[37] Mireille Delmas-Marty, "Present-day China and the Rule of Law: Progress and Resistance", in *Chinese Journal of International Law*, 2003, vol. 2, no. 1, p. 28.

[38] Peng Chun Chang, "A New Loyalty-War Against Microbes (Three Speeches Delivered to the United Nations Economic and Social Council), 1946", in Ruth H.C. Cheng and Sze-Chuh Cheng (eds.), *Peng Chun Chang 1892–1957: Biography and Collected Works*, Chinese Theatre Press, 1995, p. 150.

Confucianism had long valued the ordinary people's livelihood. P.C. Chang observed the necessity of establishing a fair economic order to protect the less developed parts of the world. He believed that poverty and ignorance were usually the source of authoritarianism and totalitarianism.[39] However, the Commission's members had different attitudes towards the so-called 'second generation of rights', namely economic, social and cultural rights. Western countries espoused liberal values and focused on civil and political rights, and did not think that economic, social and cultural rights should be included.[40] Two years later after the adoption of the UDHR, the European Convention on Human Rights ('ECHR') did not include economic, social and cultural rights.[41]

P.C. Chang gave a speech at a meeting of the Second Session of the Economic and Social Council on 4 June 1946. He asserted:

> We must learn to envisage the world as a whole, giving due consideration to the economically less developed areas not only because of the huge populations and potential resources, not only because they supply the raw materials and furnish the markets for the manufactured goods of the industrialized countries, but also because they serve as the meeting places for conflicts and contentions of the industrialized powers. It is in these economically "low pressure" areas that we can detect and delineate the shape of things to come in international struggles, actual and potential. It is significant that most of the countries in Latin America depend upon exports of a single product such as coffee, petroleum, sugar, meats, copper and other minerals. The single product for export often account for fifty percent of the values of these countries. This type of economy is most sensitive to shifts in world market demand and to changes in world prices. Prosperity and depression seem to be altogether outside of the possibility of rational control. These countries with the specialized products for export deserve our sympathetic understanding and support. In the past, the various agricultural, mining, pastoral, and forest

---

[39] Peng Chun Chang, "World Significance of Economically 'Low-Pressure' Areas", in Ruth H.C. Cheng and Sze-Chuh Cheng, 1995, p. 152, see *supra* note 38.

[40] Lu *et al.*, 2003, p. 20, see *supra* note 33.

[41] Zhao Jianwen, "Cornerstone of International Human Rights Law", in *Chinese Journal of Law,* 1999, no. 2, pp. 93–107.

resources have been exploited to meet the needs of the industrial countries.[42]

He especially appealed to the Commission to pay much attention to the right to education. As an educator himself, he understood the values and propulsive effect of education on the whole of society. His proposal that "[e]lementary education shall be compulsory; technical and professional education shall be made generally available; and higher education shall be equally accessible to all on the basis of merit"[43] was accepted. It resembled the final authorised text of the UDHR that formulated the right to education in Article 26:

> (1) Everyone has the right to education. Education shall be free, at least in the elementary and fundamental stages. Elementary education shall be compulsory. Technical and professional education shall be made generally available and higher education shall be equally accessible to all on the basis of merit; (2) Education shall be directed to the full development of the human personality and to the strengthening of respect for human rights and fundamental freedoms. It shall promote understanding, tolerance and friendship among all nations, racial or religious groups, and shall further the activities of the United Nations for the maintenance of peace; (3) Parents have a prior right to choose the kind of education that shall be given to their children.[44]

5.4.3. The Connection between Confucianism and International Criminal Law

It may be said that without being legally binding outlook and ideals have no significant meaning. Is that true? In fact, if we focus on the long-term effect, we will discover that the power of thought is easily overlooked. Confucianism and international criminal law have common values towards humanity. International criminal law aims at punishing criminals who infringe human rights and also aims at maintaining world peace. Individuals who committed crimes were usually in the position of an

---

[42] Chang, 1995, pp. 151–52, see *supra* note 40.
[43] Sun Pinghua, *The Study of the Universal Declaration of Human Rights*, Peking University Press, Beijing, 2012, p. 8.
[44] UDHR, see *supra* note 36.

official with authoritarian power. International criminal law calls on the governments to restrain power and to rule benevolently, so that grave violations of human rights law can be avoided. International criminal law could find ideas in Confucianism as its historical origin to attain this goal. What is more, Confucianism could promote communication between diverse cultures.

The Confucian philosopher Lo Chung-Shu, whom the Human Rights Commission had consulted, interpreted Confucian ideas concerning human rights as follows:

> The problem of human rights was seldom discussed by Chinese thinkers of the past, at least in the same way as it was in the West. There was no open declaration of human rights in China, either by individual thinkers or by political constitutions, until this conception was introduced from the West [...] [However], the idea of human rights developed very early in China, and the right of the people to revolt against oppressive rulers was very early established [...] A great Confucian Mencius (372–289 BC) strongly maintained that a government should work of the will of the people. He said "People are of primary importance. The State is of less importance. The sovereign is of least importance".[45]

The Chinese intellectual Koh Hong-Beng asserted that the Chinese people preserved democracy espoused by Westerners for thousands of years. Mencius believed that "a ruler should be subject to his people. Thus the Heavenly Mandate can be lost if a leader loses the hearts of the people; Mencius was of the opinion this justifies regicide".[46] The core concept of Confucianism was benevolence and conscience. As a result, Confucianism inherently concentrated on the common people. The practice of P.C. Chang convinced the world that Chinese Confucianism is a living tradition and could provide solutions to solve contemporary problems.

---

[45] Glendon, 2002, p. 74, see *supra* note 29.

[46] D.W.Y. Kwok, "On the Rites and Rights of Being Human", in Wm. Theodore de Bary and Tu Weiming (eds.), *Confucianism and Human Rights*, Columbia University Press, New York, 1998, p. 89.

5.5. China and the UNWCC

During the period of the Second World War and its aftermath, China's practical actions in war-crimes-related issues also deserve much more contemporary attention. There are other Chinese encounters with early international criminal law, in which Chinese people's wisdom and their approach to international crimes all indicate that China and its people should not be forgotten in the course of international criminal law.

5.5.1. The UNWCC's Historical Importance

Compared to the major historical significance attached to the London Charter as well as the Nuremberg and Tokyo Trials in the aftermath of the Second World War, the work of the UNWCC and its participating states was routinely ignored by international criminal law scholars, practitioners and publications until recently when more and more archival information has been made available, such as by making the UNWCC's archive freely accessible through the ICC Legal Tools database.[47]

During the Second World War unprecedented sufferings were imposed on civilians. Hitler's and other arch-criminals' incredible multiplication of cruelties and atrocities not only violated domestic criminal laws but also flagrantly trampled on international law. The Allied Powers made various declarations to condemn those evils, while the UNWCC was the first institution that transferred those declarations into practice and the first forum where war crimes issues as well as international criminal justice were systematically discussed.[48]

On 20 October 1943, with the resolution of the Allied Nations to punish Second World War criminals, the UNWCC was founded in London,[49] embarking on its operation for five years (from 1943 to 1948). Indeed, its primary powers were confined to war-related crimes and the

---

[47] UN War Crimes Commission's archive is now available at the ICC Legal Tools Database (http://www.legal-tools.org/).

[48] Lai Wen-Wei, "Forgiven and Forgotten: The Republic of China in the United Nations War Crimes Commission", in *Columbia Journal of Asian Law*, 2012, vol. 25, no. 2, p. 308.

[49] United Nations War Crimes Commission (UNWCC), United Nations Archives Predecessor Archives Group: United Nations War Crimes Commission 1943–1949 PAG-3/Rev. 1, 1987 (http://www.legal-tools.org/en/go-to-database/record/336bd1/).

finding of evidence, making investigations, reporting and advising.[50] The
UNWCC was the first practical scheme for war criminal issues. Just 10
days after its establishment, the Moscow Declaration was issued with its
final section especially making a statement on atrocities:

> Germans would be sent back to the countries where they had
> committed their crimes and judged on the spot by the
> peoples whom they have outraged. As for those Germans
> whose criminal offenses had no particular geographical
> localization, they would be punished by joint decision of the
> governments of the Allies.[51]

The days of mere condemnation or preaching no longer existed, and under
the authority of the Moscow Declaration, the London Charter was born to
guide the trials of the criminals, ushering in a new era of human history
where international criminal law was formally resorted to, for the respect
of humanity as well as the maintenance of world peace.

Besides, since the inception of the UNWCC, the proposal for
setting up an international criminal court was brought up and incurred
serious discussions among the member states. On 22 February 1944 the
UNWCC referred this issue to its Committee on Enforcement for
immediate consideration.[52] Most of the members held this kind of
international criminal court should be *ad hoc*, while some of the members
suggested a permanent international criminal court, which was strongly
opposed by the United States and the United Kingdom.[53] Later, the Draft
Convention for the Establishment of a United Nations War Crimes Court
was issued on 19 September 1944, though it was later largely ignored.[54]

---

[50] The terms of reference of the UNWCC were as follows: (i) to collect, investigate and
record evidence of war crimes, identifying where possible the individual responsible; (ii)
to report to the government concerned cases where the criminal available appear to
disclose a *prima facie* case; (iii) to act as a committee of legal experts charged with
advertising the government's concerned upon matters of a technical nature, such as the
sort of tribunals to be employed in the trial of war criminals, the law to be applied, the
procedure to be adopted and the rules or evidence to be followed.

[51] Moscow Conference, "Joint Four-Nation Declaration, Statement on Atrocities", 30
October 1943.

[52] United Nations War Crimes Commission, Minutes of Tenth Meeting of 22 February 1944
(http://www.legal-tools.org/uploads/tx_ltpdb/File%20531-537.pdf).

[53] Arieh J. Kochavi, *Prelude to Nuremberg: Allied War Crimes Policy and the Question of
Punishment*, University of North Carolina Press, Chapel Hill, 1998, p. 117.

[54] Lai, 2012, p. 326, see *supra* note 48.

Almost 60 years later, this long-dreamed permanent international criminal court finally became a reality.

The discussions, statements, debates and actual practice of the UNWCC and its members on war crimes issues, facilitated the formal emergence of international criminal law and played an integral as well as indispensable part in its developmental course, which shall no longer be forgotten in contemporary academic study and criminal practice.

5.5.2. China's Active Participation in the UNWCC

As the state that suffered the most and longest during the Second World War, China was resolute in wanting to punish the Japanese criminals and called for international co-operation. In 1942 China sent Wunsz King[55] as a representative to the conference at St James's Palace in London, after which King issued a statement which largely agreed with the main principles of this conference and insisted that Japanese atrocities should not go unpunished.[56] As for the invitation asking China to join the proposed United Nations Commission on atrocities, China showed its strong desire of using this platform to contain Japanese aggression with a special interest in setting up a Sub-Commission in Chungking (the wartime capital of China). Additionally, in order to illustrate a co-operative spirit, Vi Kyuin Wellington Koo ('Koo') was appointed as the Chinese representative to the inaugural meeting of the UNWCC on 20 October 1943.

Koo was then the Chinese Ambassador to the United Kingdom and his educational background was quite similar to P.C. Chang's. Koo was born in a traditional Chinese family. Many of his family members acquired the first (*hsiu-ts'ai*) and the higher (*chü-jen*)[57] degrees through civil examinations, and his father was a successful merchant who also had

---

[55] Wunsz King was a Chinese diplomat who received his LL.B. from Tianjin Northern University in 1915 and went to Columbia University to study international law as well as diplomacy. In the Second World War, he was the Chinese ambassador to some European states occupied by Germany, including the Netherlands, Belgium, Czechoslovakia, Poland and Norway.

[56] Wunsz King, *Memories of My Diplomatic Work*, Biography Literature Press, Beijing, 1968, p. 119.

[57] *Hsiu-ts'ai* [秀才] and *chü-jen* [举人] are the products of China's *keju* [科举] system, which are closely related to the Confucianism's prosperity since the Han Dynasty.

studied Confucian Classics.[58] Not surprisingly, he was brought up in the finest Chinese tradition. At the age of five, Koo was sent to the school of Master Chu (a scholar with a *hsiu-ts'ai* degree) where he learned the *Trimetric Classic*[59] as well as the *Hundred Family Surnames*,[60] and gradually progressed to the Confucian Classics in the subsequent seven years.[61] At the same time, Koo also started his Western education at an early age, and later went to Columbia University, receiving a B.A., M.A. and Ph.D. His traditional family background and the deep cultivation of Confucianism constantly influenced Koo's personality while his Western study equipped him with an exceptional competence[62] in the field of international law. Koo was therefore the best choice to speak for China at the UNWCC, to defend China's state interests through professional negotiation with the Western powers.

Koo's efforts in the UNWCC mainly concerned two important issues with regards to China, i.e. the Japanese atrocities committed in the period from 1931 to the eruption of war in Europe and the necessity of establishing a Sub-Commission in Chungking.[63] Later, Koo submitted a formal proposal from China to the UNWCC's meeting of 25 April 1944, recommending a Far Eastern Commission to be set up immediately and that it should enjoy the greatest level of autonomy. After some fierce debates with his foreign counterparts, the UNWCC finally adopted most of China's suggestions and decided to establish its Far Eastern and Pacific Sub-Commission in Chungking.

As to the substantial issues discussed in the UNWCC, Koo expressed China's strong desire to try the Japanese Emperor, arguing that

---

[58] Pao-Chin Chu, *V.K. Wellington Koo: A Case Study of China's Diplomat and Diplomacy of Nationalism, 1912–1966*, Chinese University Press, Hong Kong, 1981, p. 4.

[59] *Trimetric Classic*, also called *San Zi Jing* [三字经], is one of the classic Chinese texts. It was probably written in the thirteenth century and attributed to Wang Yinglin during the Song Dynasty. The work is not one of the traditional six Confucian classics, but rather the embodiment of Confucianism suitable for teaching young children.

[60] The *Hundred Family Surnames*, also named *Bai Jia Xing* [百家姓], is a classic Chinese text composed of common Chinese surnames. The book was composed in the early Song Dynasty.

[61] Chu, 1981, p. 5, see *supra* note 58.

[62] Stephen G. Craft, *V.K. Wellington Koo and the Emergence of Modern China*, University Press of Kentucky, Lexington, 2004, p. 29.

[63] United Nations War Crimes Commission, Minutes of Fifteenth Meeting of 25 April 1944, (http://www.legal-tools.org/uploads/tx_ltpdb/File%20559-565.pdf).

"men like Hirohito should not go unpunished", [64] though this failed due to political reasons. China's lack of interest in crimes against humanity issues had repercussions. At that time, China was focusing on war crimes, while the crimes committed by the Japanese in Taiwan (then a colony of Japan) were almost ignored, resulting in the Taiwan "comfort women" incidents going unpunished.

The treaty-based international court or international tribunal to try war criminals was another important issue raised by Koo in the UNWCC. On the one hand, this indicated China's endorsement of the principles of the London Charter and, on the other hand, showed China's eagerness to create a legal basis for the Far East trials since the London Charter only applied to European criminals. Unfortunately, the International Military Tribunal for the Far East (IMTFE) was established under a special proclamation issued by Douglas MacArthur, the Supreme Commander of the Allied Powers, with no treaty-making process for China to express its opinions on Japanese war criminal issues. China should have had more say than any other state during these processes, for it was a major victim of Japan's aggression and suffered enormous losses in the Second World War. What is worse, some of the major war criminals who were chosen for trial by China were not prosecuted by the IMTFE in the end. [65]

In 1943 to 1948, China, as an invaded and victimised state, did take an active part in the UNWCC to call on the common conscience deeply rooted in the international community, to request the trial of Japanese war criminals and to defend the interests of every Chinese compatriot.

5.6. Chinese National Trials of Japanese War Criminals

It is well acknowledged by all that after the Second World War, Nazi Germany's war criminals were tried at the Nuremberg International Military Tribunal and that Japanese war criminals were tried at the IMTFE. Despite the importance of both these trials, it is still of great significance that we reveal the history and practice of China's national trials of Japanese war criminals in 1946 and 1956, a hidden history that needs to be discovered and understood.

---

[64] United Nations War Crimes Commission, Minutes of Thirty-third Meeting of 26 September 1944 (http://www.legal-tools.org/uploads/tx_ltpdb/File%20711-718.pdf).

[65] Lai, 2012, p. 328, see *supra* note 48.

During 1946 and 1947, the Nationalist government of the Republic of China ('the Nationalist government') held trials of Japanese war criminals in 10 cities: Nanjing, Shanghai, Hankou, Guangzhou, Shenyang, Beijing, Xuzhou, Jinan, Taiyuan and Taipei.[66] The trials were conducted under the leadership of the War Crimes Processing Committee, established in December 1945 by relevant departments in the Nationalist government as well as the UNWCC Far Eastern and Pacific Sub-Commission.[67] The legitimacy of the trials was based on the Potsdam Declaration, Special Proclamation for Establishment of an International Military Tribunal for the Far East, Regulations for Processing War Criminals, War Crimes Trial Procedure and the Detailed Rules of the War Crimes Trial Procedure.[68]

The war crimes trials carried out by the Nationalist government in the immediate post-war period primarily focused on the case of the Nanjing massacre as well as other crimes that were committed by the Japanese. The trials in 10 cities were conducted in accordance with international law and Chinese domestic law with reference to the legal proceedings of the Nuremberg and Tokyo trials.[69] It resulted in 145 death sentences and more than 500 total convictions prior to 1949.[70] Because of the trials, the war criminals received deserving punishments.[71] What is more, the main facts of the crimes committed during the Nanjing

---

[66] Weng Youli, "Comments on the National Government's Disposal of Japanese War Criminals", in *Journal of Southwest China Normal University: Philosophy & Social Science Edition*, 1998, vol. 6, p. 112.

[67] *Ibid.*

[68] Zhao Lang, Liao Xiaoqing and Zhang Qiang, "A Comparative Study of the Trial in Shenyang and the Trials in Nuremberg, Tokyo and Nanjing", in *Journal of Liaoning University: Philosophy and Social Science Edition*, 2009, vol. 37, no. 6, p. 65; Song Zhiyong, "Chinese Foreign Policy Towards Japan and the Trial of Japanese War Criminals at the Years Immediately After the Second World War", in *Nankai Journal*, 2001, vol. 4, p. 44; Jing Shenghong, "On the Trial of Nanjing Massacre Conducted by the Nanjing War Crimes Tribunal", in *Nanjing Social Science*, 2013, no. 6, p. 146.

[69] Zhao *et al.*, 2009, p. 68, see *supra* note 68.

[70] Justin Jacobs, "Preparing the People for Mass Clemency: The 1956 Japanese War Crimes Trials in Shenyang and Taiyuan", in *The China Quarterly*, 2011, vol. 205, p. 153; Weng, 1998, p. 112, see *supra* note 66.

[71] Zhao Sheming and Meng Guoxiang, "Comment on the PRC Trials of the Japanese War Criminals", in *Social Science in Nanjing*, 2009, vol. 8, p. 100.

massacre were confirmed, based on the evidence provided and invaluable materials uncovered through years of investigation.[72]

Ten years later, the government of the People's Republic of China ('PRC') established a Special Military Tribunal of the Supreme People's Court to put the remaining Japanese prisoners on trial in two separate proceedings held in Shenyang (9 June 1956) and Taiyuan (12 June 1956).[73] This is viewed as the high point of the PRC prosecutions against Japanese war criminals, coinciding precisely with China's unmistakable push for diplomatic normalisation with Japan.[74] As the site of the 18 September incident, Shenyang was chosen as the site of the trial due to its deep historical symbolism.[75] This trial prosecuted 36 criminals, including eight Japanese generals or field officers and 28 high-ranking officials of the puppet state of Manchuria set up by Japan in northeastern China in 1932.[76] According to the verdicts handed down by the Special Military Tribunal in the Shenyang and Taiyuan trials, only 45 of the "most heinous offenders" were sentenced to prison, and of these none were handed a life imprisonment sentence or a death sentence. Prison sentences ranged from eight to 20 years. Following a retroactive application of 11 years that had already passed since the end of the war, most prisoners were freed within a few years of their sentencing. The remaining 1,017 Japanese war criminals were released upon confessing to their crimes.[77]

It is worth noticing that Chinese Confucianism was displayed clearly in the way China dealt with the war criminals during the 1946 and 1956 national trials. First, we are of the opinion that justice and human dignity were upheld at the national tribunals, and the trials reflected a common aspiration to peace and justice. We also argue that China's national trials were, without doubt, in line with the purpose and spirit of

---

[72] Yan Haijian, "A Re-understanding of the Trial on the Case of the Nanjing Massacre", in *Journal of Nanjing Normal University: Social Science*, 2008, no. 3, p. 67; Song, 2001, p. 42, see *supra* note 68.

[73] Zhao *et al.*, 2009, p. 67, see *supra* note 68.

[74] Adam Cathcart and Patricia Nash, "War Criminals and the Road to Sino–Japanese Normalization: Zhou Enlai and the Shenyang Trials, 1954–1956", in *Twentieth-Century China*, 2008, vol. 34, no. 2, p. 89.

[75] *Ibid.*, p. 102.

[76] Shen Zongyan, "A Summary of the Trial Against Japanese War Criminals in the Shenyang Special Military Tribunal", in *Journal of Liaoning Institute of Socialism*, 2009, vol. 1, no. 38, p. 95.

[77] Jacobs, 2011, p. 153, see *supra* note 70.

international criminal law, which aims at punishing criminals who infringe human rights and at maintaining world peace. Under the direct control of the Department of Defence of the Nationalist Government and the Supreme Court of the PRC Government, the national military tribunals for war criminals met the requirements of justice and maintain national interests and dignity.[78] Relevant historical documents of the trials, including the judgments, memoirs and all the materials that this chapter is based on, provide a compact summary of the trials and their subsequent influence in the practice of war crimes trials. Soon after the establishment of the PRC, the preparations for the trial of Japanese war criminals were initiated. More than 4,000 pieces of evidence were collected in Beijing, Changchun, Harbin and Fushun.[79] The historical verdicts were based on a large amount of evidence collected through years of preparatory work.[80] Written in the verdicts, it was stated that the conducting of germ and chemical warfare, and a series of inhuman atrocities legitimately constituted war crimes and crimes against humanity.[81] From a procedural standpoint, the 1946 and 1956 trials, evoking previous judicial proceedings against Japanese defendants, were conducted in accordance with international law and Chinese domestic law.[82] During the legal proceedings, defendants were ensured due process,[83] and hundreds of spectators attended the trials.[84] What is more, not a single prisoner revoked their confession or claimed that it had been made under duress.[85]

Second, China treated the post-war Japanese prisoners in custody with a policy of magnanimous and lenient treatment. Both the Nationalist Government and the PRC Government limited imprisonment to only a

---

[78] Yan, 2008, p. 67, see *supra* note 72.

[79] Chen Jing, "The Trial of Japanese War Criminals in China: The Paradox of Leniency", in *China Information*, 2009, vol. 23, no. 3, p. 452.

[80] Song, 2001, p. 43, see *supra* note 68.

[81] Sui Shiying, "On the Trial and Release of the Japanese War Criminals by the Chinese Government in the 1950s", in *Journal of Yantai University: Philosophy and Social Science Edition*, 2006, vol. 19, no. 4, p. 460.

[82] Long Xingang and Sun Jun, "On the Special Military Tribunals Trials of Shenyang and Taiyuan in 1956", in *Literature on Party Building*, 2009, vol. 2, p. 10; Cathcart and Nash, 2008, p. 97, see *supra* note 74.

[83] Zhao *et al.*, 2009, p. 68, see *supra* note 68.

[84] Cathcart and Nash, 2008, p. 102, see *supra* note 74.

[85] Shen, 2009, p. 59, see *supra* note 76; Zhao and Meng, 2009, see *supra* note 71.

small selected group of heinous offenders. The trials conducted by the PRC Government might be one of the most humanitarian trials in world history in the sense that none of the criminals was sentenced to death.[86]

The Nationalist Government insisted on a spirit of benevolence and magnanimity towards Japanese war criminals, keeping an ideal balance between a policy of justice and a policy of lenient treatment.[87] It must also be pointed out that the trials demonstrated the traditional virtues of kindness and humanitarian spirit.[88] As for the PRC Government, Premier Zhou Enlai was determined to adopt a policy of leniency towards the Japanese prisoners, and he directly led the formulation and implementation of the policies adopted for resolving the cases of these Japanese war criminals.[89] According to Zhou, there were two main reasons for the PRC's leniency. The first concerned the characteristics of the Japanese war criminals imprisoned at the time. Zhou observed that the war criminals had already been in prison for about ten years, so this term of imprisonment could be seen as the penalty for their crimes. Among them, only those who had committed graver atrocities deserved to be given extended prison sentences. Second, a lenient policy would be more beneficial to the overall peaceful construction of China, and strengthen post-war relations with Japan.[90] In the end, the lenient policy extended towards Japanese war criminals proved to be a real success. Those Japanese war criminals who had received such generous treatment did not dispute the issue of their culpability and they pleaded guilty without any objection.[91] None of the other tribunals had ever achieved such a profound effect on their indicted war criminals.[92]

Third, the humane treatment of Japanese war criminals, in keeping with the ideas of Confucianism, was the proper way to handle Japanese war criminals while still upholding justice in the trials. Humane treatment

---

[86] Chen, 2009, p. 448, see *supra* note 79.

[87] Sui, 2006, p. 459, see *supra* note 81.

[88] Weng, 1998, p. 113, see *supra* note 66.

[89] Sui, 2006, p. 461, see *supra* note 81.

[90] Chen, 2009, p. 451, see *supra* note 79.

[91] *Ibid.*, p. 448.

[92] Wang Heli, Zhang Jia'an and Zhao Xinwen, "The Special Military Tribunal's Trials of Japanese War Criminals in Shenyang", in *Jianghuai Culture History*, 2001, vol. 1, p. 20; Zhao *et al.*, 2009, p. 68, see *supra* note 68; Chen, 2009, pp. 21–22, see *supra* note 79; and Zhao and Meng, 2009, p. 100, see *supra* note 71.

included the safeguarding of adequate standards of living in the prisons, medical care, cultural activities and so on. It was also emphasised by Zhou that humane treatment was not only demonstrated in the care shown to prisoners in their daily lives but also in the respect for their human dignity.[93] There is no doubt that the education received by these criminals in prison led them to the realisation and confession of their guilt in the court of law, and helped restore their conscience.[94] The newly converted pacifists in the Shenyang and Taiyuan trials returned home to Japan, organised a group known as the Liaison for the Returnees from China,[95] and promptly began to spread the word about a benevolent and progressive Chinese Communist Government in Beijing.[96]

In the end, the trials evoked patriotism and the pursuit of peace, and the policy of leniency towards Japanese war criminals reinforced people's desires for peace and love, instead of stirring up hatred between China and Japan. The humane treatment of the Japanese war criminals also enhanced the political stature and progressive reputation of the PRC in the international arena.

Looking back, the inhumane atrocities and the series of crimes that were committed in China deserved universal condemnation. The former Chinese President, Hu Jintao, said on 3 September 2005 that in the war crimes military tribunals, "those arch criminals who launched the wars of aggression and had their hands blotted with the blood of the people around the world received their due punishment".[97] However, due to the outbreak of the Chinese Civil War and the isolation of the PRC Government at the international level afterwards, the contribution of the Chinese national trials to international criminal law has not been known, and little has been written about the proceedings.[98]

The Japanese war crimes trials that occurred in China should be discussed not only from the perspective of history and foreign policy but

---

[93] Sun Hui and Lin Xiaoguang, "The PRC Trials and Rehabilitation of Japanese War Criminals", in *Hundred Year Tide*, 2005, vol. 7, pp. 49–50.

[94] Chen, 2009, p. 449, see *supra* note 79; Sui, 2006, p. 462, see *supra* note 81; Zjao and Meng, 2009, p. 101, see *supra* note 71.

[95] Chen, 2009, p. 466, see *supra* note 79.

[96] Jacobs, 2011, p. 154, see *supra* note 70.

[97] BBC, "Chinese Leader Says Trials of Japan, Germany War Criminals Allow No Challenge", in *BBC Monitoring Asia Pacific*, 3 September 2005.

[98] Cathcart and Nash, 2008, p. 89, see *supra* note 74.

also from a legal point of view. Peace, co-existence, humanity, morality and justice are the core values of Confucianism in Chinese culture.[99] The hidden stories here make it an unprecedented opportunity for China to enhance its influence in international affairs.[100] More specifically, China's national trials embraced international law, demonstrating China's approach in dealing with war crimes and its efforts in building a connection between international justice and its own national tribunals.

5.7. Conclusion

International criminal law publications tend to regard the emergence and development of international criminal law as a result of Western ideology and Western values. Little mention is made of China. But, with more attention drawn to China's connections to international criminal law, we may find that such arguments are oversimplified or biased. Focusing on Chinese Confucianism's influence on international human rights law as well as international criminal law, China's concrete actions in the UNWCC and its Sub-Commission and China's early application of international criminal norms or procedures in its national trials, it is plausible to conclude that China was an indispensable participating state in the rise of international criminal law. Chinese culture and prevailing values, to some extent, flowed into international criminal law and will constantly act as a link between China's future participation and the development of international criminal law. It was precisely because of those early encounters that China continuously recognised the core values of international criminal law, which may have facilitated China's subsequent involvement in international criminal law in the late twentieth century. Especially since China recovered its status as a permanent member of the Security Council of the UN, it has acceded to many conventions that contain provisions on international crimes and corresponding criminal procedures. [101] In addition, as a permanent

---

99 Sun and Lin, 2005, p. 55, see *supra* note 93.

100 Song, 2001, p. 47, see *supra* note 68.

101 China has ratified the Convention on the Prevention and Punishment of the Crime of Genocide; the Geneva Convention for the Amelioration of the Condition of the Wounded and Sick in Armed Forces in the Field (Geneva Convention I); the Geneva Convention for the Amelioration of the Condition of the Wounded, Sick and Shipwrecked Members of the Armed Forces at Sea (Geneva Convention II); the Geneva Convention Relative to the Treatment of Prisoners of War (Geneva Convention III); the Geneva Convention Relative

member of the Security Council wielding veto power, China supported the establishment as well as operation of the ICTY and ICTR. Further, China actively joined in the Preparatory Committee for the Establishment of the ICC and made statements to support the founding of the ICC, despite finally deciding not to sign the ICC Statute.

As scholars, it is important to discover China's early encounters with international criminal law and to draw worldwide attention to their contemporary importance. However, our research into the period of the Second World War and its aftermath has so far only established a historical connection between China and international criminal law. More concrete Chinese contributions, more details of those Chinese Confucian scholars and a more specific assessment of China's influence are still hidden away in history. There is a need for efforts by historians, international criminal law scholars, international organisations and non-governmental organisations to explore, to analyse and to summarise in order to fill the void of what is missing. Therefore, the discussion in this chapter may also be a starting point for more archival research about China's historical participation in international criminal law, and the drawing of new conclusions about the past contributions China has made to the field of international criminal law.

---

to the Protection of Civilian Persons in Time of War (Geneva Convention IV); Protocol Additional to the Geneva Conventions of 12 August 1949, and Relating to the Protection of Victims of International Armed Conflicts (Geneva Protocol I); Protocol Additional to the Geneva Convention of 12 August 1949, and Relating to the Protection of Non-International Armed Conflicts (Geneva Protocol II); the Convention Against Torture and other Cruel, Inhuman or Degrading Treatment or Punishment.

PART 2

A Critical Examination of Investigatory and Prosecuratorial Efforts in the Aftermath of the First World War

6

The 1919 Paris Peace Conference and the Allied Commission: Challenging Sovereignty Through Supranational Criminal Jurisdiction

Jackson Nyamuya Maogoto[*]

6.1. Introduction

The first major effort to curb international crimes through international penal process arose after the First World War. In 1914 Europe, divided by competing military alliances, was a powder keg waiting to explode. The fuse was lit when a Serbian nationalist assassinated Austrian Archduke Franz Ferdinand on the bridge at Sarajevo. Lacking any institution with authority to maintain peace, the disputing parties had no choice but to call upon their allies and resort to force. The First World War witnessed one of the largest military mobilisations in history, with the Allied Powers mobilising over 40 million soldiers and the Central Powers mobilising close to 20 million soldiers. Four years later, with the armistice in force, the war came to an abrupt halt. The smoke cleared slowly and the devastation of cities, the loss of life, mangled bodies and scattered families lay revealed. The facts of the death, destruction and the financial cost of the war staggered the 'civilised' world. The total cost in human life was estimated at 22 million dead and eight million casualties. In monetary terms, the war cost US\$202 billion, with property destroyed in the war topping US\$56 billion.[1]

The end of the First World War marked 300 years since the start of the Thirty Years' War in 1618 that had ended with the Peace of

---

[*]   **Jackson Nyamuya Maogoto** is a Senior Lecturer in the Department of Law, University of Manchester, UK. He is the author of six books, most recently *Public International Law* (with B. Clarke) and *The Militarization of Outer Space and International Law*, several book chapters, and more than three dozen refereed articles in general and specialist Australian, American, European and African journals. He attained a Doctorate in Law from the University of Melbourne, Australia.

[1]   For war costs at a glance, see Charles Horne (ed.), *The Great Events of the Great War*, vol. II, National Alumni, New York, 1923. A table of the cost in human life and money is reproduced in Harold Elk Straubing (ed.), *The Last Magnificent War: Rare Journalistic and Eyewitness Accounts of World War I*, Paragon House, New York, 1989, pp. 402–3.

Westphalia. The war "to end all wars" was premised on the same general goals as that conflict 300 years earlier – military and political hegemony. In the closing years of the nineteenth century and the opening years of the twentieth century, a number of countries had extended their sovereignty through the acquisition of territories and dominions usually through military conquest but occasionally through treaty. The war afforded other nations the chance to extend their sovereignty through conquest of other countries as well as the opportunity to assert themselves as military and political powers. Essentially then, the war was the result of sovereign excesses, a result of the old 'war system' which the treaties of Versailles and Sèvres sought to transplant with a new democratic order of peace, in which sovereignty of the nation state was abridged. The period after the end of the war had many important repercussions, key among which was a gradual imposition of legal restraints on resort to military force by states, but more significantly, an attempt to devise means of enforcing violations of international obligations. There was a general feeling that the emerging multilateralism would usher in a new political order less dominated by ultranationalism and its pull to unilateralism.

In a dramatic break with the past, and in a bid to build a normative foundation of human dignity, the chaos and destruction of the war gave rise to a yearning for peace and a popular backlash against impunity for atrocity. The devastation of the war provided a catalyst for the first serious attempt to crack the Westphalian notion of sovereignty. This dramatic new attitude was encapsulated in the enthusiasm for extending criminal jurisdiction over sovereign states (Germany and Turkey) with the aim of apprehension, trial and punishment of individuals guilty of committing atrocities under the rubric of 'war crimes' and 'crimes against humanity'.

This chapter focuses on the Commission on the Responsibilities of the Authors of War and on Enforcement of Penalties ('the Commission') through a nuanced consideration of the commission's mandate: the responsibility of the authors of the war; breaches of the laws and customs of war committed by the Central Powers; the degree of responsibility for these offences attaching to particular members and the constitution; and procedure of a tribunal appropriate to the trial of these offences. The underlying central theme of the chapter is an exposition on how the Commission sought to advance international criminal justice through new elucidations and re-evaluation of principles, doctrines and modes of criminal liability under international law that challenged sovereignty.

6.2. Germany and Turkey: Championing Nationalism Through Destruction

The first major offence that Germany committed, which was to return to haunt it at the end of the war, happened at the very start of the war – the violation of Belgian neutrality of which Germany was one of the guarantors. In the case of the invasion of Belgium, it was felt that the violation of an international obligation by a country that guaranteed it was so flagrant that the conscience of the public would not be satisfied if that act were treated in any other way than as a crime against public law.[2] Germany was to commit further violations of the rights of combatants and civilians. Not even prisoners, or wounded, or women or children were respected by a nation which deliberately sought to strike terror into every heart for the purpose of repressing all resistance. Murders, massacres, tortures, human shields, collective penalties, arrest and execution of hostages formed part of a long list of violations of laws and customs of war exhibiting cruel practices which primitive barbarism, aided by all the resources of modern science, could devise. Concomitantly, the First World War witnessed the first active application of new modes of warfare, notably, submarine naval warfare and aerial bombing. Germany initially required submarine commanders to attempt to identify neutral shipping within the area of war. By January 1917 Germany had declared unrestricted submarine warfare within the war zone.[3] Consequently, all sea traffic (military or non-military) was torpedoed on sight by the German navy without warning. This German strategy of unrestricted submarine warfare saw German U-boats sink tens of thousands of both

---

[2] The attributes of neutrality were specifically defined by the Hague Convention (V) of 18 October 1907 in Articles 1, 2 and 10. Belgium's neutrality was not the only neutrality that was violated. Germany also violated Luxembourg's neutrality which was guaranteed by Article 2 of the 1867 Treaty of London. For comments by the French and British leaders at the Paris Peace Conference concerning the public outrage at Germany's violation of Belgian neutrality, see Paul Mantoux, "Paris Peace Conference 1919", in Arthur S. Link and Manfred F. Boemeke (eds.), *The Deliberations of the Council of Four, March 24–June 28, 1919*, vol. 1, Princeton University Press, Princeton, 1992, pp. 189–90.

[3] D.P. O'Connell, *The Influence of Law on Sea Power*, Manchester University Press, Manchester, 1975, pp. 46–47.

Allied and neutral shipping.[4] Regarding aerial bombing, the Zeppelin and Gotha offensives by Germany and Allied counteroffensives were largely indiscriminate.[5]

Regarding Turkey, on 16 December 1914, five months after the start of the First World War, an Imperial Rescript by the Ottoman Empire (precursor of Turkey) cancelled the Armenian Reform Agreement of 8 February 1914 containing international stipulations for the respect of the rights of the Armenian minority, which the Turkish Government had undertaken to protect.[6] This reflected a general determination to abrogate the international treaties that had resulted from the application of the principle of 'humanitarian intervention' because the treaties imposed "political shackles" on the Ottoman Empire, which wanted to deal with its "troublesome" Christian minority – a majority of which was opposed to the predatory tendencies of the Ottoman State.[7]

The decisive stage of the process of reducing the Armenian population to helplessness came five months after the 1914 Imperial

---

[4] See for example, W.T. Mallison Jr., *Studies in the Law of Naval Warfare: Submarines in General and Limited Wars*, US Government Printing Office, Washington, DC, 1966, pp. 62–65.

[5] See for example, Walter Raleigh and Henry Jones, *The War In The Air: Being The Story Of The Part Played In The Great War By The Royal Air Force*, vol. 1, Clarendon Press, Oxford, 1922; Joseph Morris, *The German Air Raids on Great Britain, 1914–1918*, Sampson Low, Marston and Co., London, 1925; Kenneth Poolman, *Zeppelins Against London*, John Day, New York, 1961; Colin White, *The Gotha Summer: The German Daytime Air Raids on England, May to August 1917*, R. Hale, London, 1986.

[6] The Armenian Reform Agreement signed on 8 February 1914 between Turkey and Russia, with the concurrence of the other powers, contained international stipulations with regard to Turkish governmental measures to respect and uphold the rights of the minority Armenians. This agreement was seen by Turkey as placing shackles on the government with regard to exercise of sovereign prerogatives and governmental policy. See Vahakn Dadrian, "Genocide as a Problem of National and International Law: The World War I Armenian Case and Its Contemporary Legal Ramifications", in *Yale Journal of International Law*, 1989, vol. 14, no. 2, p. 263.

[7] *Ibid.* Halil departed for Berlin on the same day to seek German support for the annulments. In informing his government of this move in his 5 September 1916 report, the German ambassador Metternich directed attention to the Turkish concern for Article 61 of the Berlin Treaty involving Turkey's "engagements for Armenia", and to Halil's justification of the act on grounds of "the effect of war" (*Kriegszustand*). A.A. Turkei, 183/44, A24061 (Ottoman Archives, Istanbul Research Centre). The full text of the repudiation of the treaties in German is in Friedrich von Kraelitz-Greifenhorst, "Die Ungültigkeitserklärung des Pariser und Berliner Vertrages durch die osmanische Regierung", in *Osterreichische Monatsschrift für den Orient*, 1917, vol. 43, pp. 56–60.

Rescript. In a memorandum dated 26 May 1915, the Interior Minister requested from the Grand Vezir the enactment through the cabinet of a special law authorising deportations. The memorandum was endorsed on 30 May and a new emergency law, the Temporary Law of Deportation, was enacted.[8] Pursuant to this law, alleging treasonable acts, separatism, and other assorted acts by the Armenians as a national minority, the Ottoman authorities ordered, for national security reasons, the wholesale deportation of Armenians, a measure that was later extended to virtually all of the Empire's Armenian population. The execution of this order, ostensibly a wartime emergency measure of relocation, actually masked the execution of the Armenian population. The deportations proved to be a cover for the ensuing destruction. The massive, deliberate and systematic massacres by Turkey of its Christian subjects under the cover of war did not go unnoticed. As early as 24 May 1915, during the course of the war, the Entente Powers solemnly condemned these atrocities.[9]

6.3. The Paris Peace Conference

In settling upon the terms for the Germans, it was not possible wholly to ignore the responsibility of those who were deemed to have first drawn the sword and therefore might be held accountable for the horror that ensued. Nor could the violation of Belgian neutrality in 1914 by a power that had guaranteed it be overlooked. The major Allied Powers were also confronted with Germany's resort to submarine atrocities and to other forms of terror, all in disregard of the restraint theretofore imposed by custom upon the conduct of hostilities by civilised nations. Britain was of the opinion that the ex-Emperor of Germany, Wilhelm II, be brought from his asylum in Holland and arraigned before an inter-Allied tribunal. France and Italy voiced support for this position with the United States agreeing to co-operate. However, European politicians and diplomats raised fundamental questions. Would the Government of the Netherlands give up the German Emperor? If the Allied governments set up a tribunal, would the world at large accept the jurisdiction of such a court to try and

---

[8]   For the English text of the law, see Richard G. Hovannisian, *Armenia on the Road to Independence, 1918*, University of California Press, Berkeley, 1967, p. 51.

[9]   France, Great Britain and Russia Joint Declaration, 24 May 1915, cited in Egon Schwelb, "Crimes Against Humanity", in *British Year Book of International Law*, 1946, vol. 23, p. 181; See also Dadrian, 1989, p. 262, *supra* note 6.

to punish seemingly *ex post facto* crimes? Would not lawlessness on the part of the enemy find an excuse in the lawlessness of the victors?[10]

The President of the United States, Woodrow Wilson, representing the major power that was credited through its involvement with hastening the end of the war, suggested that the question of national and individual crimes against decency be settled in the comparative privacy of the Supreme Council – the Paris Conference's highest organ. However, at the insistence of the British Prime Minister, David Lloyd George, it was decided to place the subject on the agenda of a plenary session. As a result, the Peace Conference decided on 25 January 1919 to create a commission – the first international investigative commission – to study the question of penal responsibility.[11] The official intergovernmental commission subsequently established by the Paris Peace Conference was named the Commission on the Responsibilities of the Authors of War and on Enforcement of Penalties.[12] It was composed of delegates of the five great powers and five minor powers – Belgium, Greece, Poland, Romania and Serbia. Its mandate was ambitious for that time. It encompassed:

    a.   The responsibility of the authors of the war;

---

[10] See for example, David A. Foltz, *The War Crimes Issue at the Paris Peace Conference 1919–1920*, Ph.D. Dissertation, American University, 1978, pp. 49ff.

[11] The Provisional Government of Germany, representing a people told by their rulers that war had been forced on them in 1914 by conspiring enemies, persistently urged the creation of a neutral commission to inquire impartially into the origins of the conflict. The German Foreign Minister, addressing the foreign offices of the major Allies, conjured up the ideals of lasting peace and international confidence. From London and Paris, however, he received blunt rebuffs, asserting that the responsibility of Germany for the war had long ago been incontestably proved. The American State Department, after communicating with the peace mission at Paris, replied in the same tenor. See for example, U.S. Department of State, "Papers Relating to the Foreign Relations of the United States", *Paris Peace Conference – F.R., P.P.C.*, vol. 2, pp. 71–72; Dispatch from Solf to the State Department, forwarded to the House on 11 December 1918, *Yale House Collection and Related Papers* (Manuscripts and Archives Room, Yale University Library, "Y.H.C.").

[12] The Commission comprised two members from each of the five great powers: the United States of America, the British Empire, France, Italy and Japan. The additional states composing the Allied and Associated Powers were Belgium, Bolivia, Brazil, China, Cuba, Czechoslovakia, Ecuador, Greece, Guatemala, Haiti, the Hedjaz, Honduras, Liberia, Nicaragua, Panama, Peru, Poland, Portugal, Romania, the Serb-Croat-Slovene State, Siam and Uruguay. Carnegie Endowment for International Peace, *The Treaties of Peace 1919–1923*, Carnegie Endowment for International Peace, New York, 1924, p. 3. The additional states, having a special interest in the matter, met and decided that Belgium, Greece, Poland, Romania and Serbia should each name a representative to the commission as well, see *Commission Report*, 1919, p. 20.

---

    b.   The fact as to breaches of the laws and customs of war
committed by the forces of the German Empire and
their allies;

    c.   The degree of responsibility for these offences
attaching to particular members of the enemy forces;

    d.   The constitution and procedure of a tribunal appropriate
to the trial of these offences.[13]

6.4. The 1919 Commission on the Responsibilities of the Authors of War and on Enforcement of Penalties

6.4.1. New Understandings: Extending the Frontiers of International Law and Justice Paradigms

The Commission on the Responsibilities of the Authors of War and on Enforcement of Penalties was charged with an onerous responsibility. It held closed meetings for two months and conducted intensive investigations.[14] Its work was to culminate in the charging of named individuals for specific war crimes. Besides German responsibility for the war and its breaches of the laws and customs of war, the Commission also sought to charge Turkish officials and other individuals for "crimes against the laws of humanity"[15] based on the so-called Martens Clause contained in the preamble of the 1907 Hague Convention (IV).[16] That clause states:

> Until a more complete code of the laws of war has been issued, the High Contracting Parties deem it expedient to declare that, in cases not included in the Regulations adopted

---

[13] Arthur Walworth, *Wilson and His Peacemakers: American Diplomacy at the Paris Peace Conference 1919*, vol. 3, Norton, New York, 1986, p. 699; *Violations of the Laws and Customs of War: Report of the Majority and Dissenting Reports of The American and Japanese Members of The Commission on Responsibilities, Conference of Paris, 1919*, no. 32, Carnegie Endowment For International Peace, New York, 1919 ("Report of the Majority and Dissenting Reports"), p. 23.

[14] James F. Willis, *Prologue to Nuremberg: The Politics and Diplomacy of Punishing War Criminals of the First World War*, Greenwood Press, Westport, CT, 1982, p. 68.

[15] Schwelb, 1946, p. 178, see *supra* note 9.

[16] Convention (IV) Respecting the Laws and Customs of War on Land, The Hague, 18 October 1907, 36 Stat 2277, preamble, 2779–80. See also *The Proceedings of The Hague Peace Conferences: Translation of the Original Texts*, Oxford University Press, New York, 1920, p. 548.

> by them, the inhabitants and the belligerents remain under the protection and the rule of the principles of the law of nations, as they result from the usages established among civilized peoples, from the laws of humanity, and the dictates of the public conscience.[17]

It was in this context that Nikolaos Politis, a member of the Commission and Foreign Minister of Greece, proposed the adoption of a new category of war crimes meant to cover the massacres against the Armenians, declaring: "Technically these acts [the Armenian massacres] did not come within the provisions of the penal code, but they constituted grave offences against the law of humanity".[18] Despite the objections of American representatives Robert Lansing (the United States Secretary of State and chairman of the Commission) and James Brown Scott (an eminent international jurist), who challenged the *ex post facto* nature of such a law, the majority of the Commission hesitatingly concurred with Politis.[19] On 5 March 1919 the preliminary report by the Commission specified the following violations against civilian populations as falling within the purview of grave offences against the laws of humanity: systematic terror; murders and massacres; dishonouring of women; confiscation of private property; pillage; seizing of goods belonging to communities, educational establishments and charities; arbitrary destruction of public and private goods; deportation and forced labour; execution of civilians under false allegations of war crimes; and violations against civilians as well as military personnel.

The Commission's final Report, dated 29 March 1919, concluded that the war had been premeditated by Austro-Hungary and Germany; that they had deliberately violated the neutrality of Belgium and Luxembourg; and that they had committed massive violations of the laws and customs of war.[20] It determined that "rank, however exalted", including heads of state, should not protect the holder of it from personal responsibility.[21] In addition, the Commission's final Report also spoke of "the clear dictates

---

[17] Hague Convention (IV), preamble.

[18] Willis, 1982, p. 157, see *supra* note 14.

[19] *Ibid.*

[20] Commission on the Responsibility of the Authors of the War and on Enforcement of Penalties, "Report Presented to the Preliminary Peace Conference (29 March 1919)", reprinted in *American Journal of International Law*, 1920, vol. 14, pp. 113–14.

[21] *Ibid.*, pp. 112–17.

of humanity" which were abused "by the Central Empires together with their allies, Turkey and Bulgaria, by barbarous or illegitimate methods" including "the violation of [...] the laws of humanity". The Report concluded that "all persons belonging to enemy countries [...] who have been guilty of offences against the laws and customs of war or the laws of humanity, are liable to criminal prosecution".[22]

Prompted by the Belgian jurist Rolin Jaequemyns, the Commission included, albeit did not sharply highlight, the crimes which Turkey was accused of having perpetrated against her Armenian citizens.[23] The Commission concluded that "[e]very belligerent has, according to international law, the power and authority to try the individuals alleged to be guilty of [war crimes] [...] if such persons have been taken prisoners or have otherwise fallen into its power".[24] The Commission recommended that any peace treaty provide for an international tribunal to prosecute war criminals.[25] The Commission proffered a series of acts deemed war crimes and grouped those acts into four categories: (1) offences committed in prison camps against civilians and soldiers of the Allies; (2) offences committed by officials who issued orders in the German campaign against Allied armies; (3) offences committed by all persons of authority, including the German Kaiser, who failed to stop violations of laws and customs of war despite knowledge of those acts; and (4) any other offences committed by the Central Powers that national courts should not be allowed to adjudicate.[26]

---

[22] Report of the Majority and Dissenting Reports, see *supra* note 13. The dissenting American members were Robert Lansing and James Scott, who felt that the words "and the laws of humanity" were "improperly added", pp. 64 and 73. In their Memorandum of Reservations, they maintained that the law and principles of humanity were not "a standard certain" to be found in legal treatises of authority and in international law practices. They argued that these laws and principles do vary within different periods of a legal system, between different legal systems, and with different circumstances. In other words, they declared that there is no fixed and universal standard of humanity, and that a judicial organ only relies on existing law when administering it.

[23] See Her Majesty's Stationery Office, British Foreign Office Papers, FO, FO 608/246, Third Session, folio 163, 20 February 1919, p. 20.

[24] Commission on the Responsibility of the Authors of the War and on Enforcement of Penalties, 1920, p. 121, see *supra* note 20.

[25] *Ibid.*

[26] *Ibid.*, pp. 121–22. At the end of the First World War in 1919, the major international instruments relating to the laws of war were the two Hague Conventions on the Laws and Customs of War on Land of 1899 and 1907. Willis, 1982, p. 5, see *supra* note 14. Other

6.4.2. Old Understandings: The Lingering Legacy and Tenacity of Classical International Law

The American and Japanese representatives (two of the major powers) on the Commission objected to several key aspects of the Allied Commission's Report. Lansing (chairman of the committee) and Scott, the American members of the Commission on the Responsibilities of the Authors of War and on Enforcement of Penalties, dissented. In view of the vigour of the dissent of the American delegates, it is deemed appropriate to consider the areas of disagreement in some detail.

The Commission proposed the establishment of a high tribunal to try

> all authorities, civil or military, belonging to enemy countries, however high their positions may have been, without distinction of rank, including the heads of state, who ordered, or, with knowledge thereof and with power to intervene, abstained from preventing or taking measures to prevent, putting an end to repressing, violations of the laws or customs of war (it being understood that no such abstention should constitute a defense for the actual perpetrators).[27]

In their reservation to the Commission's Report, the American representatives stated, among other things, that

> there were two classes of responsibilities, those of a legal nature and those of a moral nature, that legal offenses were justiciable and liable to trial and punishment by appropriate tribunals, but that moral offences, however iniquitous and infamous and however terrible in their results, were beyond the reach of judicial procedure, and subject only to moral sanctions.[28]

Concerning crimes against humanity, they said:

> [The Report of the Commission] declares that the facts found and acts committed were in violation of the laws [and customs of war] and of the elementary principles of humanity. The laws and customs of war are a standard

---

sources of information on the laws of war included national military manuals and Geneva Conferences beginning in 1864.

[27] Commission on the Responsibility of the Authors of the War and on Enforcement of Penalties, 1920, p. 121, see *supra* note 20.

[28] *Ibid.*, p. 128.

certain to be found in books of authority and in the practice
of nations. The laws and principles of humanity vary with
the individual, which, if for no other reason, should exclude
them from consideration in a court of justice, especially one
charged with the administration of criminal law [...] The
American representatives are unable to agree with this
inclusion, in so far as it subjects to criminal, and, therefore,
to legal prosecution, persons accused of offences against
"the laws of humanity," and in so far as its subjects chiefs of
state to a degree of responsibility hitherto unknown to
municipal or international law, which no precedents are to be
found in the modern practice of nations.[29]

The American representatives, therefore, objected to the references to the
laws and principles of humanity, to be found in the Report, in what they
believed was meant to be a judicial proceeding. In their opinion, the facts
found were to be violations or breaches of the laws and customs of war,
and the persons singled out for trial and punishment for acts committed
during the war were only to be those persons guilty of acts which should
have been committed in violation of the laws and customs of war. The
United States (and Japan), opposed 'crimes against humanity' on the
grounds that the Commission's mandate was to investigate violations of
the laws and customs of war and not the uncodified, so-called 'laws of
humanity'.[30]

Concerning the criminal liability of heads of state, they argued:

This does not mean that the head of state, whether he be
called emperor, king, or chief executive, is not responsible
for breaches of the law, but that he is responsible not to the
judicial but to the political authority of his country. His act
may and does bind his country and render it responsible for
the acts which he has committed in its name and its behalf,
or under cover of its authority; but he is, and it is submitted
that he should be, only responsible to his country as
otherwise to hold would be to subject to foreign countries, a
chief executive, thus withdrawing him from the laws of his
country, even its organic laws, to which he owes obedience,
and subordinating him to foreign jurisdictions to which

---

[29] *Ibid.*, pp. 134–35.
[30] *Ibid.*, p. 134.

> neither he nor his country owes allegiance or obedience, thus
> denying the very conception of sovereignty.[31]

Concerning war crimes trials in general, they said:

> The American representatives know of no international
> statute or convention making a violation of the laws and
> customs of war-not to speak of the laws of humanity-an
> international crime affixing a punishment to it, and declaring
> the court which has jurisdiction over it.[32]

Finally, concerning the establishment of an international tribunal, Lansing and Scott, representing a nation that had suffered less than the Allies from the misconduct of Germans during the war, were not so ready as their European colleagues to cloak the exercise of power in what they considered to be "dubious" legal form. Lansing and Scott proposed that it "should be formed by the union of existing military tribunals or commissions of admitted competence in the premises".[33] The Japanese delegation shared American opposition to the penal responsibility advocated by the rest of the Commission. However, in the author's opinion, there were two difficulties that the American delegates seemed not to have considered thoroughly. First, which national procedure would the tribunal apply and how would attempts to develop a uniform procedure be addressed by national courts? Confusion was bound to emanate from any attempt to amalgamate or adjust the varying procedures of the different tribunals without careful previous preparation. Second, if the laws and customs of war were to be applied, did such implementation exist in domestic legislation of the Allies and, if not, was it necessary that it did?[34] Lansing and Scott maintained the strong position that to create an international tribunal to try war crimes committed during the First World War "would be extralegal from the viewpoint of international law [...] contrary to the spirit both of international law and of the municipal law of civilized states and [...] would, in reality, be a political and not a legal creation".[35]

---

[31] *Ibid.*, pp. 134–35

[32] *Ibid.*, p. 146.

[33] *Ibid.*, p. 129.

[34] Sheldon Glueck, "By What Tribunal Shall War Offenders be Tried?", in *Harvard Law Review*, 1943, vol. 56, pp. 1075–76.

[35] Memorandum by Miller and Scott, ca. 18 January 1919, published in David Miller, *My Diary at the Conference of Paris with Documents*, vol. 3, Appeal Printing Company, New

The rest of the Commission rejected the American (and Japanese) opposition, and insisted on the insertion of penal responsibility provisions in the eventual peace treaty. Having overruled its chairman, Lansing, a large majority of the Commission agreed that at the next renewal of the armistice the Germans should be required to deliver certain war criminals and also relevant documents. Furthermore, Allied commanders in occupied territory should be ordered to secure such wanted persons as lived in regions under their control. However, Lansing refused to transmit these suggestions to the Supreme Council, arguing that as appointees of a plenary session the Commission could report only to the full Peace Conference. The Secretary of State preferred that the Conference, instead of trying Germans, issue a severe reprimand. He proposed that a committee of inquiry be appointed to consider the question in the light of documents in the archives of the enemy, and to report to the participating governments.

The work of the Commission was to feature prominently in the subsequent treaties of peace negotiated by the representatives of the Allies and those of Germany and Turkey. In a dramatic break with past precedence, the peace treaties were to contain penal provisions as opposed to blanket amnesties characteristic of past instruments. Much of the debate among the Allies addressed issues concerning the prosecution of Germany's Kaiser Wilhelm II, German war criminals and Turkish officials for "crimes against the laws of humanity".[36]

The majority and minority positions, as noted, were coloured by a tussle between legality and realpolitik. The preliminary reflections by the Supreme Council on 2 April in relation to the Commission's Report encapsulated the quandary in the late-afternoon discussions of the US, French, British and Italian leaders.[37] The British Prime Minister, Lloyd George, castigated the US position which was based on the apprehension

---

York, 1921, pp. 456–57. It is to be noted that the vigorous dissent of the American and Japanese delegations split the Commission and was later to play itself out amongst the Allies who ultimately pandered towards political expedience by incorporating only limited penal provisions in the peace treaties of Versailles and Sèvres.

[36] For information on the Armenian genocide, see generally, Vahakn N. Dadrian, *The History of the Armenian Genocide: Ethnic Conflict from the Balkans to Anatolia to the Caucasus*, Berghahn Books, Providence, 1995; Dadrian, 1989, p. 35, see *supra* note 6.

[37] Mantoux, 1992, p. 91, see *supra* note 2.

of creating a precedent where one had not existed before.[38] He noted that Britain had assembled a cast of distinguished jurists to debate the legalities and who were of the opinion that there were no insurmountable legal hurdles. President Wilson countered that the German Emperor's guilt was difficult to determine as it was too great.[39] Most significantly in addressing the main legal aspect of establishing a supranational tribunal, Wilson noted:

> It would be creating a dangerous precedent to try our enemies before judges who represent us. Suppose that, in the future, one nation alone should be victorious over another which had attacked it in violation of a rule of law. Would that nation, the victim of a crime against the *droit des gens*, be the only one to judge the guilty?[40]

Lloyd George countered that the League of Nations (a landmark institution which was to mark the move from balance of parochial power military frameworks to a universal collective military framework) would be wounded *ab initio* by appearing "as just a word on a scrap of paper".[41] The French Prime Minister, Georges Clemenceau, was to later intercede assertively siding with Lloyd George by reiterating that trials were essential and that the conscience of people would not simply rest on political condemnation.[42] In his vigorous statement Clemenceau thundered:

> Is there no precedent? There never is a precedent. What is a precedent? I shall tell you. A man comes along; he acts, for good or evil. Out of what is good, we create a precedent. Out of what is evil, the criminals, whether individuals or heads of State, create a precedent of their crimes.[43]

The exchanges between the members of the Supreme Council outlined above aptly sum up the political, legal and philosophical regarding the recommendations of the Commission and reflected the same split between the majority and minority of the Commission. The discussion now turns to the responsibility clauses of the main peace

---

[38] *Ibid.*

[39] *Ibid.*

[40] *Ibid.*

[41] *Ibid.*, p. 92.

[42] *Ibid.*, pp. 147–50.

[43] *Ibid.*, p. 149.

treaties after the Anglo–French position regarding legality as the sanction rather than political denunciation prevailed.

6.5. The Failure to Establish Prosecutions Pursuant to the Peace Treaty of Versailles

The Commission's final Report came to the Supreme Council (which had the final authority on negotiating the peace treaty) on 29 March 1919. The American members attached a statement to the effect that the views of the majority contravened American principles. Lansing, the Commission's chairman, thought that the British knew the practical impossibility of the action that they were forced by public opinion to advocate and were depending on the US to block it. Lansing found his boss – President Wilson – even more strongly opposed to trying the Kaiser than he was himself. Both feared that physical punishment of Wilhelm II would make him a martyr and would lead to the restoration of the dynasty.[44]

On 8 April the Big Four discussed the question of penal responsibility for wartime atrocities at great length. Wilson, the chairman of the Supreme Council, opined: "I am afraid, it would be difficult to reach the real culprits. I fear that the evidence would be lacking".[45] The President thought that in the violation of Belgium's neutrality a crime had been committed for which eventually the League of Nations would find a remedy. He warned against dignifying a culprit by citing him before a high tribunal, and against stooping to his level by flouting the principles of law that were already accepted. When Lloyd George told the Council of Four that he wanted "the man responsible for the greatest crime in history to receive the punishment for it", Wilson replied: "He will be judged by the contempt of the whole world; isn't that the worst punishment for such a man?" He thought the German militarists doomed to "the execration of history".[46] Although Wilson agreed that the Allied

---

[44] US Department of State, vol. 11, pp. 93–94; Lansing, "Memorandum of Reservations", 4 April 1919; Lansing to Wilson, in "Wilson Papers", 8 April 1919; Foltz, 1978, pp. 135–74, see *supra* note 10; Letter from Lansing to Polk, 14–15 March 1919, Y.H.C.; Geneviève Tabouis, *The Life of Jules Cambon*, trans. by C.F. Atkinson, Jonathan Cape, London, 1938, pp. 319–20.

[45] Wilson had said on the *George Washington* in December that probably the Kaiser had been "coerced to an extent" by the General Staff, see Swern Book manuscript, chapter 21 at 9, Princeton University Library.

[46] Mantoux, 1992, p. 83, see *supra* note 2.

peoples might not understand if the Kaiser were allowed to go free, he stated: "I can do only what I consider to be just, whether public sentiment be for or against the verdict of my conscience". In the face of a likelihood of political censure rather than criminal prosecutions of the Kaiser and German law of war violations, Clemenceau asserted:

> For me, one law dominates all others, that of responsibility. Civilization is the organization of human responsibilities. Mr. Orlando [the Italian Prime Minister] says: 'Yes, within the nation. I say: In the international domain. I say this with President Wilson who, when he laid the foundations of the League of Nations, had the honour to carry over into international law the essential principles of national law [...] We have today a glorious opportunity to bring about the transfer to international law of the principle of responsibility which is at the basis of national law.

Even in the face of the French Prime Minister's impassioned plea, Wilson demurred, mostly in terms of broader realpolitik, pointing out that the legal basis or other means of forcing Holland to give up the Kaiser were tepid.[47] The basis for this was Lord Maurice Hankey's (the *de facto* secretary of the Supreme Council) pointed observation to the political leaders after they had settled on the matter of formal criminal proceedings regarding the breaches of the laws of war, that the standpoint would involve difficult legislation in reconciling the view with the basic tenets of American and British legal frameworks.[48] This observation seemingly reignited Wilson's initial obstinate resistance to the Anglo–French position.[49] Interestingly, Lloyd George disagreed with Hankey (who incidentally was his personal aide as well). He declared that the question of the Kaiser's prosecution before an international tribunal, like that of reparations, interested British opinion "to the highest degree", and this public opinion could not accept a treaty that left it unsolved. Lloyd George noted:

> [...] the Kaiser is the arch-criminal of the world, and just as in any other sphere of life when you get hold of a criminal you bring him to justice, so I do not see, because he is an

---

[47] *Ibid.*, p. 193.

[48] Lord [Maurice] Hankey, *The Supreme Control at the Paris Peace Conference 1919: A Commentary*, Allen and Unwin, London, 1963, p. 114.

[49] *Ibid.*

> Emperor and living in exile in another country, why should
> he be saved from the punishment which is due.[50]

It was in this regard that Lloyd George suggested that they should bring pressure to bear on Holland to deliver Wilhelm II by threatening its exclusion from the League of Nations. This position was also enthusiastically supported by Clemenceau. Under this well-directed attack Wilson, who at this very time was about to go into the final meetings of the Commission on the League of Nations to seek approval of an amendment in respect of the Monroe Doctrine, yielded. The next morning he read to the Supreme Council a draft that he had prepared. It satisfied Clemenceau and Lloyd George, and provided the substance for Articles 227 and 229 of the Peace Treaty of Versailles.[51] In withdrawing from his opposition to the war crime clauses, Wilson recognised that they were too ineffectual to warrant any determined resistance to them.[52] When he was asked by the American ambassador to Paris, John Davis, whether he expected to "catch his rabbit", he replied in the negative, quipping that "was all damned foolishness anyway". [53] Similarly Lloyd George's enthusiasm was to wane after a strong protest from the South African Prime Minister, Louis Botha, in the face of a rapidly subsiding vindictive feeling among the British public.[54]

On 25 June, three days before the conclusion of the Peace Treaty of Versailles, Wilson brought up the matter of the Kaiser's extradition from his refuge in Netherlands where he had fled to at the end of the war. Lansing drafted a note that was sent to the Dutch government requesting compliance with Article 227 of the Peace Treaty of Versailles, under

---

[50] David Lloyd George, *The Truth About the Peace Treaties*, vol. I, Gollancz, London, 1938, p. 98.

[51] Wilson to Lansing, 9 April 1919. Wilson's text with minor changes became Part VII of the Peace Treaty of Versailles. See Foltz, 1978, pp. 201, see *supra* note 10. A diary letter of Edith Benham from 9 April 1919 records that it was at the suggestion of Mrs Wilson that the President prepared his compromise formula and secured the signature of his colleagues.

[52] Mantoux, 1992, pp. 151–54, see *supra* note 2.

[53] Diary of John W. Davis, 5 June 1919, Y.H.C.

[54] On the anniversary of the Treaty of Vereeniging, Botha pointedly reminded the British delegation of the incendiary effect upon the Boers of an English proposal that he and Smuts be tried for the crime of causing the Boer War. Ambassador Davis noticed a marked cooling in the eagerness to try the Kaiser and a growing disinclination to have the trial staged in London, see J.W. Davis to Lansing, 30 July 1919.

which the five great victorious powers were to try Wilhelm II before a 'special tribunal' on the charge of "a supreme offence against international morality and the sanctity of treaties". The response from the Netherlands, whose sitting monarch was the Kaiser's cousin, was not positive. The Dutch insisted that the usage of political asylum should be respected. The Dutch rejected not only the concepts of 'international policy' and 'international morality' upon which the Allies proposed to try and punish the Kaiser, but they also invoked the domestic laws and national traditions of Holland as further justification. The Dutch defined the offence with which the Kaiser was charged as "political" and hence exempt from extradition.[55] As a result, the Allies did not formally request his extradition, and there was no formal judicial or administrative process in which the Kaiser's extradition was denied.[56] No further action was taken, but the British and French leaders could appease their constituencies with evidence that they had tried to satisfy the prevailing demand for retributive 'justice'.[57] Nevertheless, the assertion by the Peace Conference of a right to punish war criminals was a novel departure from tradition, one that set a precedent for action at the end of the next world war.

After much compromise, the Allied representatives finally agreed on the terms of the Treaty of Peace between the Allied and Associated Powers and Germany ('Peace Treaty of Versailles'), concluded at Versailles on 28 June 1919.[58] Besides other important matters including reparations, in Article 227 it provided for the creation of an *ad hoc* international criminal tribunal to prosecute Kaiser Wilhelm II for initiating the war.[59] It further provided in Articles 228 and 229 for the prosecution of German military personnel accused of violating the laws

---

[55] See Quincy Wright, "The Legal Liability of the Kaiser", in *American Political Science Review*, 1919, vol. 13, p. 120; *New York Times*, 22 January 1920.

[56] See Telford Taylor, *The Anatomy of The Nuremberg Trials: A Personal Memoir*, Knopf, New York, 1992, p. 16. The legal grounds for denying the request were that the "offence charged against the Kaiser was unknown to Dutch law, was not mentioned in any treaties to which Holland was a party, and appeared to be of a political rather than a criminal character". Also Wright, 1919, p. 120, see *supra* note 55. The Netherlands discouraged formal extradition requests because extradition treaties applied only to cases in which a criminal act occurred.

[57] See Mantoux, 1992, vol. 1, pp. 144–51 and vol. 2, pp. 524–25, *supra* note 2.

[58] Peace Treaty of Versailles [1919] UKTS 4 (Cmd. 153).

[59] *Ibid.*, Article 227.

and customs of war before Allied Military Tribunals or before the Military Courts of any of the Allies.[60] The limited incorporation of the recommendations of the Allied Commission with regard to penal provisions was to prove fatal because the treaty provisions pertaining to war crimes ultimately proved unworkable in the post-war political context.[61] The attempt to try war criminals failed for a number of reasons, including: the enormity of the undertaking; deficiencies in international law and in the specific provisions of the Peace Treaty of Versailles, which proved to be unworkable owing to the failure of the Allies to present a united front to the Germans by taking strong measures to enforce the treaty.

The victors' lack of control over affairs within Germany ultimately defeated the Allied attempt to bring accused war criminals to justice.[62] The Peace Treaty of Versailles did not link the 1919 Commission to eventual prosecutions recognised under its Articles 228 and 229, resulting in an institutional vacuum between the investigation and prosecution

---

[60]   Article 228 states:

> The German Government recognizes the right of the Allied and Associated Powers to bring before military tribunals persons accused of having committed acts in violation of the laws and customs of war. Such persons shall, if found guilty, be sentenced to punishments laid down by law. This provision will apply notwithstanding any proceedings or prosecution before a tribunal in Germany or in the territory of her allies.
>
> The German Government shall hand over to the Allied and Associated Powers, or to such one of them as shall so request, all persons accused of having committed an act in violation of the laws and customs of war, who are specified either by name or by the rank, office, or employment which they held under the German authorities.

Article 229 states:

> Persons guilty of criminal acts against the nationals of one of the Allied and Associated Powers will be brought before the military tribunals of that Power. Persons guilty of criminal acts against the nationals of more than one of the Allied and Associated Powers will be brought before military tribunals composed of members of the military tribunals of the Powers concerned. In every case the accused will be entitled to name his own counsel.

[61]   Willis, 1982, pp. 52–62, see *supra* note 14.

[62]   See generally Elizabeth L. Pearl, "Punishing Balkan War Criminals: Could the End of Yugoslavia Provide an End to Victors' Justice?", in *American Criminal Law Review*, 1993, vol. 30, no. 4, pp. 1389–90.

stage.[63] Subsequently, the two major provisions of the Peace Treaty of Versailles, Articles 227 and 228, were not implemented as geopolitical considerations dominated the post-First World War era. Regarding prosecution of the Kaiser under Article 227, the Allies blamed the Dutch government for its refusal to extradite him and some saw this as a way to avoid establishing a tribunal pursuant to Article 227. The Allies were not ready to create the precedent of prosecuting a head of state for a new international crime.

By 1920 the Allies had compiled a list of approximately 20,000 Germans who were to be investigated for war crimes.[64] These crimes included torture, use of human shields, rape and the torpedoing of hospital ships by German submarines.[65] However, the Allies were apprehensive of trying so many German officials and personnel, as this posed a political problem since Germany was trying to reconstruct and the extensive trials might jeopardise the stability of an already vulnerable Weimar Republic and, more galling, expose it to revolutionary Bolshevik influence.[66] "Many politicians argued against prosecution, preferring instead to look to the future".[67] However, since many of these crimes were truly heinous, complete freedom from prosecution was also unacceptable. An alternative solution was therefore reached. Instead of setting up an international tribunal, Germany would conduct the prosecutions. An agreement was thus made, allowing the German Government to prosecute a limited number of war criminals before the Supreme Court of Germany (*Reichsgericht*) in Leipzig instead of establishing an Allied tribunal, as provided for in Article 228.

---

[63] See for example, M. Cherif Bassiouni, "From Versailles to Rwanda in Seventy-five Years: The Need to Establish a Permanent International Criminal Court", in *Harvard Human Rights Journal*, 1997, vol. 10, p. 18.

[64] M. Cherif Bassiouni, "Former Yugoslavia: Investigating Violations of International Humanitarian Law and Establishing an International Criminal Tribunal", in *Fordham International Law Journal*, 1995, vol. 18, p. 1194.

[65] Willis, 1982, pp. 137–39, see *supra* note 14.

[66] *Ibid.*, p. 113.

[67] M. Cherif Bassiouni, "The International Criminal Court in Historical Context", in *St Louis-Warsaw Transatlantic Journal*, 1999, vol. 99, p. 57.

6.6.   The Failure to Establish Prosecutions Pursuant to the Peace Treaty of Sèvres

Based on the recommendations of the 1919 Allied Commission on the Responsibilities of the Authors of War and on Enforcement of Penalties, several articles stipulating the trial and punishment of those responsible for the Armenian genocide were incorporated into the Peace Treaty of Sèvres.[68] Under Article 226, "the Turkish government recognized the right of trial and punishment by the Allied Powers, notwithstanding any proceedings or prosecution before a tribunal in Turkey".[69] Moreover, Turkey was obligated to surrender "all persons accused of having committed an act in violation of the laws and customs of war, who are specified either by name or by rank, office or employment which they held under Turkish authorities".[70] Under Article 230 of the Treaty, Turkey was further obligated to hand over to the Allied Powers the persons whose surrender may be required by the latter as being responsible for the massacres committed during the continuance of the state of war on territory which formed part of the Turkish Empire on 1 August 1914. The Allied Powers reserved to themselves the right to designate the tribunal which would try the persons so accused, and the Turkish Government was obligated to recognise such a tribunal.[71] The Peace Treaty of Sèvres, therefore, provided for international adjudication of the crimes perpetrated by the Ottoman Empire against the Armenians during the First World War.

The Allies, pursuant to their earlier warning in May 1915, were committed to prosecutions of Turkish officials and personnel responsible for the Armenian massacres. This initial commitment was reflected in the fact that beginning in January 1919, prior to the conclusion and signing of the Peace Treaty of Sèvres, Turkish authorities, directed and often pressured by Allied authorities in Istanbul, arrested and detained scores of Turks. Those arrested comprised four groups: (1) the members of Ittihat's Central Committee; (2) the two war-time cabinet ministers; (3) a host of provincial governors; and (4) high ranking military officers identified as organisers of wholesale massacres in their zones of authority. The

---

[68]   Gr. Brit. T.S. No. 11, 1920.

[69]   *Ibid.*

[70]   Willis, 1982, pp. 180–81, see *supra* note 14.

[71]   Peace Treaty of Sèvres, Article 230, see *supra* note 47.

suspects were first taken to the Military Governor's headquarters and were subsequently transferred to the military prison maintained by the Turkish Defence Ministry. Their custody and the disposal of their case by the Turkish judiciary, however, posed serious problems.[72]

The Turkish response to the demand by the Allies for the surrender of arrested criminal suspects for trial before an international tribunal or inter-Allied tribunal paralleled the German response. Not only did the Government object to surrendering Turkish nationals to the Allies, Mustafa Kemal, the head of the antagonistic Ankara Government, rejected the very idea of "recognizing a kind of right of jurisdiction on the part of a foreign government over the acts of a Turkish subject in the interior of Turkey herself".[73] The claim was that such a surrender of Turkish subjects contradicted the sovereign rights of the Ottoman Empire as recognised in the armistice agreement.[74] Despite this argument, the Commission on Responsibilities and Sanctions of the Paris Peace Conference held that trials by national courts should not bar legal proceedings by an international or an inter-Allied national tribunal.

The Allies began to bicker among themselves. Delays in the final peace settlement with Turkey complicated this volatile situation. France and Italy began to court the Kemalists in secret; the Italians lent the new regime substantial military assistance, and both the French and the Italians sabotaged British efforts to restore and strengthen the authority of

---

[72] Bilal N. Simsir, *Malta Surgunleri* [The Malta Exiles], Milliyet Yayinlari, Istanbul, 1976, p. 113. Of these, 26 were ordered released by the court martial itself with the assertion, "there is no case against them", in *Spectateur d'orient*, 21 May 1919, Istanbul. Admiral Calthorpe informed London regarding the 41 Turks released from military prison by Ottoman authorities that, "there was every reason to believe, [they] were guilty of the most heinous crimes [...] mainly in connection with massacres", in *British Foreign Office Papers*, 72, FO 371/4174/88761, folio 9, 30 May 1919. Referring to the Malta exiles, the Foreign Office Near East specialist Edmonds declared, "there is probably not one of these prisoners who does not deserve a long term of imprisonment if not capital punishment", FO 371/6509/E8745, folios 23–24.

[73] Speech delivered by Mustafa Kemal in Ataturk in 1927 (Istanbul, 1963). The speech lasted six days, 15–20 October 1927, and was delivered before the Deputies and Representatives of the Republican Party that was founded by him. The volume containing the speech is published under the auspices of the Turkish Ministry of Education.

[74] See for example, British Foreign Office Papers, FO 608/244/3749, folio 315 (Rear Admiral Webb's 19 February 1919 telegram to London, quoting from the Turkish Minister's 16 February note whose original, full text in French is in British Foreign Office Papers, FO 608/247/4222, folio 177).

the Sultan and his Government.[75] In the face of these developments, the resolve to secure justice in accordance with the 24 May 1915 Allied note was progressively attenuated. This was not helped by a defiant Germany. Just as the Netherlands had refused to extradite the Kaiser, a request to Germany to arrest and surrender Talaat Paşa, Grand Vezir and *de facto* head of the Ottoman State who had fled to Germany at the end of the war, was rebuffed by Germany.

Rising political tensions within the Allied Powers and nationalistic passions in Turkey eventually led to the scrapping of the Peace Treaty of Sèvres and its subsequent replacement in 1923 by the Peace Treaty of Lausanne,[76] which wiped out the provisions in the Peace Treaty of Sèvres relating to international penal process. The Peace Treaty of Lausanne did not contain any provisions on prosecutions, but rather had an unpublicised annex granting Turkish officials amnesty.[77] This effectively granted Turkish officials impunity for both war crimes and crimes against humanity, and effectively buried any hope of prosecutions. Although ultimately ineffectual, the attempted prosecution of some of the Turkish leaders implicated in the Armenian genocide before Turkish Courts Martial, which resulted in a series of indictments, verdicts and sentences, was of extraordinary, though unrecognised, significance.

6.7. Conclusion

The policymakers at Paris desired that their deliberations crystallise in policies rooted in the idealism of liberal international relations theory. The problem was not just to build a peace but also to construct a peaceful

---

[75] David Lloyd George, *Memoirs of the Peace Conference*, vol. 2, H. Fertig, New York, 1972, pp. 871, 878. Willis in *Prologue to Nuremberg* (1982, see *supra* note 14) summed up the situation as follows: "During the two years between the armistice and Mudros and the signing of the treaty of Sèvres, the Turkish nationalist movement grew into a major force, and the Allied coalition virtually dissolved. By 1920 most of the victors no longer included among their aims the punishment of Turkish war criminals. The Italians evaded a British request for the arrest of former Young Turk leaders then reported as meeting within their territory. The French and Italians hoped to secure concessions in Asia Minor and did not want to antagonise powerful factions in Turkey unnecessarily". See also Bassiouni, 1999, p. 63, *supra* note 67.

[76] Treaty with Turkey and Other Instruments (Peace Treaty of Lausanne), 24 July 1923, reprinted in *American Journal of International Law*, 1924, vol. 18, suppl. 18, pp. 92ff.

[77] *Ibid.* See also M. Cherif Bassiouni, "The Time Has Come for an International Criminal Court", in *Indiana International and Comparative Law Review*, 1991, vol. 1, pp. 2–4.

international order that would successfully manage all international conflicts of the future.[78] Peace treaties must be signed, of worldwide range, and affecting an unprecedented number of nations. Before the terms could be determined in detail, the victorious powers would have to reach a general understanding among themselves before they could do so, secret negotiation among the great powers would have to run its course.

Ultimately, the Peace Treaty of Versailles provided for the prosecution of Kaiser Wilhelm II and for an international tribunal to try German war criminals. After the war, the Kaiser fled to the Netherlands where he obtained refuge, but the Allies, who had no genuine interest in prosecuting him, abandoned the idea of an international court. Instead, they allowed the German Supreme Court sitting in Leipzig to prosecute a few German officers. The Germans criticised the proceedings because they were only directed against them and did not apply to Allied personnel who also committed war crimes. More troublesome, however, was the Allies' failure to pursue the killing of a then estimated 600,000 Armenians in Turkey. The 1919 Commission recommended the prosecution of responsible Turkish officials and by doing so, the notion of 'crimes against humanity' became a legal reality. Interestingly, from a contemporary perspective, the US and Japan's vocal opposition to the idea with the technical legal argument that no such crime yet existed under positive international law killed off the idea with the Peace Treaty of Sèvres, which was to serve as a basis for Turkish prosecutions, being replaced by the Peace Treaty of Lausanne which gave the Turks amnesty.

---

[78] Kalevi Holsti, *Peace and War: Armed Conflicts and International Order, 1648–1989*, Cambridge University Press, Cambridge, 1991, pp. 175–76, 208–9.

7

Trying the Kaiser: The Origins of International Criminal Law

Kirsten Sellars[*]

International criminal law can be said to have come of age in 1945, when jurists and policymakers decided to prosecute the defeated German leaders for crimes connected with the Second World War. Robert Jackson captured the general mood when he argued that to let them go free would "mock the dead and make cynics of the living". [1] A variety of justifications for a trial were forthcoming. The war had been uniquely barbaric, necessitating new legal methods to deal with perpetrators (Bohuslav Ečer).[2] Germany's actions had placed her outside international society, so her leaders should be treated as outlaws (William Chanler).[3] States had every right to instigate new customs and agreements as the source of future law (Robert Jackson).[4] Preceding decades had seen the crystallisation of customary law validating the aggression charges (Sheldon Glueck).[5] Prosecutors could transpose modes of liability from domestic security law into international law (Aron Trainin and Murray

---

[*] **Kirsten Sellars** is a Research Fellow at the Centre for Asian Legal Studies at the National University of Singapore's Faculty of Law. She focuses on Asian perspectives on public international law, with a particular interest in uses of force, international criminal law and law of the sea. Her most recent books, *'Crimes against Peace' and International Law* (2013) and the edited volume, *Trials for International Crimes in Asia* (forthcoming, 2015), are published by Cambridge University Press.

[1] Robert Jackson, "Report to the President", in *Report of Robert H. Jackson, United States Representative, to the International Conference on Military Trials*, Department of State, Washington, DC, 1949, p. 46.

[2] Bohuslav Ečer, "Minority Report", 27 September 1944, p. 2: The National Archives, UK ('TNA'), FO 371/39003.

[3] William Chanler, "Memo", 30 November 1944, reprinted in Bradley Smith, *The American Road to Nuremberg: The Documentary Record 1944–1945*, Hoover Institution Press, Stanford, 1982, pp. 69–70.

[4] Jackson, 1949, p. 52, see *supra* note 1.

[5] Sheldon Glueck, *The Nuremberg Trial and Aggressive War*, Knopf, New York, 1946, pp. 37–38.

Bernays).[6] Prosecutors would not be transgressing the legality principle by adding new punishments to pre-existing offences (Hersch Lauterpacht and Hartley Shawcross).[7] Prosecutors could not breach the principle of legality because it had not been incorporated into international law (Hans Kelsen).[8] And so on.

Although they appeared new, the Nuremberg arguments were not wholly original. The revolution that gave birth to international criminal law had already taken place a quarter century earlier in the aftermath of the previous world war. In late 1918 the Entente powers proposed trying the just-abdicated Kaiser and his subordinates for starting the war and committing crimes during its course. Policymakers and jurists not only set out an *international* jurisdiction over war crimes for the first time; they also proposed new categories of crimes (the precursors to 'crimes against peace' and 'crimes against humanity'). In the process, they engaged in sophisticated debates about the implications of these steps – arguments that would later be rehashed at Nuremberg. Here, we will examine these original perspectives, focusing on the work of the official advisors to the British and French governments – including John Macdonell, John Morgan, Ferdinand Larnaude and Albert Geouffre de Lapradelle – as well as three influential commentators: the French jurist, Louis Le Fur, the American lawyer, Richard Floyd Clarke, and the British official, James Headlam-Morley. Over the course of just eight weeks, from late October to early December 1918, they turned their attention to the proposed trial of Wilhelm II, and offered strikingly prescient insights into the issues that shaped – and would continue to shape – international criminal law.

7.1. The Official Approach

Trying the ex-Kaiser was an Anglo-French idea. After the two powers sounded each other out in November 1918, David Lloyd George formally placed the proposal on the Entente's agenda when he met with Georges Clemenceau, Vittorio Orlando, and their respective ministers in London

---

[6] Aron Naumovich Trainin, *Hitlerite Responsibility Under Criminal Law*, A.Y. Vishinsky (ed.), Hutchinson, London, 1945, p. 84; and Murray Bernays, "Memo", 15 September 1944, reprinted in Smith, 1982, p. 36, see *supra* note 3.

[7] International Military Tribunal, *Trial of the Major War Criminals before the International Military Tribunal*, The Blue Series (42 vols.), vol. 3, IMT, Nuremberg, 1947–1949, p. 106.

[8] Hans Kelsen, *Peace Through Law*, University of North Carolina Press, Chapel Hill, 1944, p. 87.

on 2 December. The British and the French (joined rather more reluctantly by the Italians)[9] decided that Wilhelm II, who had abdicated on 9 November, should be surrendered to an international court for "being the criminal mainly responsible for the War" and for presiding over the German forces' violations of international law.[10] The reasons for doing so were set out in a British Foreign Office telegram:

> (a) That justice requires that the Kaiser and his principal accomplices who designed and caused the War with its malignant purpose or who were responsible for the incalculable sufferings inflicted upon the human race during the war should be brought to trial and punished for their crimes.
>
> (b) That the certainty of inevitable personal punishment for crimes against humanity and international right shall be a very important security against future attempts to make war wrongfully or to violate international law, and is a necessary stage in the development of the authority of a League of Nations.
>
> (c) That it will be impossible to bring to justice lesser criminals... if the arch-criminal, who for thirty years has proclaimed himself the sole arbiter of German policy, and has been so in fact, escapes condign punishment.[11]

When coming to their decision in London, the delegates had to hand two officially sanctioned legal reports making the case for the indictment of the ex-Kaiser and his subordinates. The first was a British report, produced by a Special Sub-committee on Law answerable to the Attorney General F.E. Smith and presided over by the jurists Sir John Macdonell and Adjutant General John Morgan. (This report, presented to Smith on 28 November, was distributed to the London conference attendees on their arrival.) The sub-committee members were aware that the Imperial War Cabinet had pre-empted their own discussion by debating the desirability of prosecuting Wilhelm II, and that Lloyd George

---

9 Vittorio Emanuele Orlando, "On the Aborted Decision to Bring the German Emperor to Trial", in *Journal of International Criminal Justice*, 2007, vol. 5, no. 4, p. 1023.

10 Foreign Office to Washington and New York, 2 December 1918, TNA, FO 608/247.

11 *Ibid.*

strongly favoured a trial.[12] Hemmed in by these political constraints, their report occupied the middle ground by accepting the idea of trying the ex-Kaiser in principle while expressing doubts about Lloyd George's most subversive proposal: prosecuting him for the hitherto unknown crime of embarking on war.

Their arguments in favour of trying him rested on negative bases. First, if he were not tried for the violation of the principles of international law, then these principles would never be completely vindicated.[13] And second, if he were not tried for breaches of the laws of war, then the case against his subordinates would be weakened.[14] Perhaps aiming to spread the responsibility for creating a new jurisdiction, they rejected the idea of trying him under domestic jurisdiction, and advised instead the establishment of an international tribunal, which, they argued, would be free from national bias, would produce authoritative decisions and fortify international law.[15]

Some members of the sub-committee nevertheless expressed strong reservations about trying Wilhelm II for starting an aggressive war.[16] The first difficulty, they argued, was that it might raise unwanted issues about the behaviour of the Entente powers, and thus distract attention away from the other charges against him. Mindful of the arms races, provocations and bad faith on both sides during the pre-war period, they warned that courtroom proceedings

> might involve a prolonged examination of the whole political situation, the political difficulties and controversies preceding August 4th, 1914 and, indeed, the entire political history of Europe for some years before that date. It might be difficult to set limits to such enquiries [...][17]

The second difficulty was the possibility that Wilhelm II, however reprehensibly he had behaved when in power, had nonetheless been acting constitutionally. Some members argued that his conduct "might be

---

[12] See for example, Imperial War Cabinet 37, 20 November 1918, TNA, CAB 23/43.

[13] "Report of Special Sub-committee on Law" (as part of *First Interim Report from the Committee of Enquiry into Breaches of the Laws of War*), presented 28 November 1918, dated 20 December 1918, p. 95, TNA, CAB 24/85.

[14] *Ibid.*

[15] *Ibid.*, p. 96.

[16] *Ibid.*, p. 97.

[17] *Ibid.*

said to be a political act, the guilt of which is shared by the German nation, the representatives of which were the Bundesrath and Reichstag".[18] Others countered that his conduct "might be constitutionally correct and, nevertheless, might be a grave breach of International Law".[19] Beset with doubts of his personal culpability, the sub-committee members divided over whether to advise the Attorney General to charge him for aggressive war. After taking a vote on the question, they decided by the narrowest margin – four to three – in favour of bringing this charge against him.[20] It was one of the earliest debates on an issue that continues to exercise legal minds to this day.

7.2. New Law to Meet Changed Circumstances

The second official report, *Examen de la responsabilité pénale de l'empereur Guillaume II*, was written by the French jurists Larnaude and de Lapradelle, and published by the French Ministry of War in November 1918.[21] This so impressed Clemenceau that he insisted on it being distributed to all the delegates at the preliminary Peace Conference convened in Paris in January 1919.

Larnaude and de Lapradelle had no doubt that Wilhelm II was criminally responsible for crimes committed during the course of the war, but they were compelled to confront the significant implications of placing a one-time head of state on trial. On the one hand, they reasoned, the Kaiser when in power enjoyed the international rights of legal immunity, honours and precedence; on the other, he bore international responsibilities – "*Ubi emolumentum, ibi onus esse debet.*"[22] They left it to the reader to make the logical connection: that by renouncing his responsibilities when he abdicated, he thereby lost his rights, and could thus be compelled to account for himself in a court of law.

Should it be a military court, a criminal court or a specially constituted international tribunal? They argued that while military courts

---

[18] *Ibid.*

[19] *Ibid.*

[20] *Ibid.*

[21] Ferdinand Larnaude and Albert Geouffre de Lapradelle, *Examen de la responsabilité pénale de l'empereur Guillaume II*, Ministère de la Guerre, Paris, 1918. My thanks to Julien Anglade for translating the French materials in this chapter.

[22] *Ibid.*, p. 17.

were the most appropriate arrangement for dealing with alleged war criminals captured by belligerent parties during hostilities, they were *not* suitable for trying the ex-Kaiser. Even if he had been captured in such circumstances he could not have been considered a prisoner of war, because he had abdicated and had therefore "ceased to be a soldier".[23] A further problem, they observed, was that while military courts could pass judgment during a war, they could not do so after the suspension or termination of hostilities – in this case, the armistice with Germany.

Given that the ex-Kaiser was now hypothetically no more than a "vulgar malfeasant",[24] could he perhaps be tried by an ordinary criminal court? Here the authors were confronted with a double bind relating to the distinction between the Kaiser and the man. On the one hand, had Wilhelm II *not* abdicated, then, as Kaiser, he would have been protected by sovereign immunity, and would therefore have escaped all responsibility. This was because immunity "still covers the acts of duty [...] over which the courts, traditionally, refuse to exercise jurisdiction".[25] On the other hand, given that he had indeed abdicated, then as a mere man he could not be pursued in the criminal courts for crimes committed in relation to his official functions. He could therefore be tried only for personal crimes unconnected to those roles.

Despite its limitations, domestic criminal law did offer some guidelines for potential charges. For example, the authors considered charging the ex-Kaiser for complicity in plans to commit crimes of war:

> Criminologists might ask themselves if complicity – which [...] must entail *an abuse of power* constituting an incitement to commit a *special act* – can still be applied in regard to the German emperor who, manifestly, was only giving a general order. To which they will no doubt reply that, for complicity, the necessary and sufficient condition is the *relation between cause and effect* between the accomplice and the principal perpetrator, a relation that clearly exists between the order or directives emanating from the German emperor and the charges made against such-and-such officer or soldier within his troops: the leader of a band of brigands is their accomplice as soon as he gives the

---

[23]   *Ibid.*, p. 5.

[24]   *Ibid.*, p. 6.

[25]   *Ibid.*, p. 8.

> general order to commit theft, murders, set light or pillage, even if he hasn't specifically ordered this or that murder or arson.[26]

They admitted, however, that there were difficulties in bringing complicity charges against groups of people for acts committed in the course of the war. Even if the Entente powers managed to capture both the ex-Kaiser (who had given the general orders) and the military personnel who had carried them out, this might prove to be counterproductive, because "we would only manage, and not without difficulty, to restrict the scope of [Wilhelm II's] personal responsibility by limiting it to a few specific cases, where in fact these cases are countless, and make him appear to be an accessory when in fact he holds a principal role".[27] Criminal law was thus no more suitable than military law for dealing specifically with the ex-Kaiser's responsibility for orchestrating crimes that were in "singular defiance of the essential laws of humanity, of civilisation, of honour".[28]

Larnaude and de Lapradelle considered it unthinkable that such crimes should go unpunished,[29] so they turned to the international sphere for a possible solution. It was immediately apparent that the old approaches to crimes of war – which had emerged in response to the old conception of war "as simply a means of political coercion"[30] – were no longer adequate. A new approach was required, involving legal responsibilities, and in the process, the authors declared, "A new international law is born."[31]

The most urgent task for this new regime was the establishment of an international tribunal to hold the ex-Kaiser to account for his embarking upon a premeditated and unjust war, violating the neutrality of Belgium and Luxembourg, and breaching customary and Hague law.[32] Beginning with his responsibility for launching the war, they wrote:

> Given that the violation of the public peace of a state gives

---

[26] *Ibid.*, p. 9 (original emphases).

[27] *Ibid.*, p. 10.

[28] *Ibid.*, p. 9.

[29] *Ibid.*, p. 8.

[30] *Ibid.*, p. 12.

[31] *Ibid.*

[32] *Ibid.*, pp. 18-19.

rise to the gravest of penalties, it would not be understandable that an attack on the peace of the world might go unpunished. The corporeal responsibility of the emperor, if one might call it that, presents itself first and foremost, and we must seize upon it – as we emerge from war – lest we should fail to bring about from this new international law its most necessary consequences.[33]

Although Larnaude and de Lapradelle referred on several occasions to the ex-Kaiser's responsibility for embarking on an aggressive and premeditated war, and although they paid lip service to the views of Vattel, Vitoria and Bellini on unjust wars, they did not go into the details of this proposed charge. They clearly felt themselves to be on firmer legal ground when dealing with the ex-Kaiser's liability for the conduct of the war, rather than for starting it – although they were careful to leave the door ajar for a charge of aggression, just in case the issue was raised at a later date.

7.3. The Kaiser as an 'Outlaw'

While the British and French governments took their lead from the commissioned reports, those with more independent or critical views also sought to influence official opinion. Among them was the New York-based lawyer, Richard Floyd Clarke (1859–1921), the author of *The Science of Law and Law-making* and an American authority on international law. As well as representing private companies against Venezuelan and Cuban interests, and the US government against Mexico over land claims in Texas, he was one of the earliest contributors to the *American Journal of International Law*.[34] Like many jurists after the First Wold War, he embraced naturalism (and derided the Analytical School's "exploded theories").[35] In his view, sovereign states summoned nationalism and positivism to march the world into war; now, a community of states guided by higher ideals would advance towards peace.

Clarke took a lively interest in the settlement of the war, and not only advocated trying the ex-Kaiser, but also hanging him. This stance

---

[33] *Ibid.*, pp. 16–17.

[34] Richard Floyd Clarke, "A Permanent Tribunal of International Arbitration: Its Necessity and Value", in *American Journal of International Law*, 1921, vol. 1, no. 2, pp. 342–408.

[35] Richard Floyd Clarke, *In the Matter of the Position of William Hohenzollern, Kaiser of Germany: Under International Law*, 1918, p. 13, TNA, FO 371/3227.

was sharply at odds with the official American position – set out by Robert Lansing and Woodrow Wilson at the Paris Peace Conference – that trying a head of state would establish an unwelcome sovereignty-breaching precedent. Undeterred, in November 1918 he wrote a paper entitled "In the Matter of the Position of William Hohenzollern, Kaiser of Germany: Under International Law," which he sent to each of the major Entente leaders. In this, he made arguments that strikingly prefigured those advanced after the Second World War.

He began by decrying the paucity of international law when it came to dealing with the ex-Kaiser: "That in spite of his many atrocious crimes [...] he must now go free because there is no law according to the principles of our municipal or international law under which jurisdiction can be obtained of his person, or under which he may be convicted, is a conclusion absolutely shocking to the moral sense."[36] He proposed several solutions to this problem. The first was to invoke customary international law as the basis for a prosecution. While conceding that treaties dealing with conduct of war might have expired, he nonetheless argued that:

> If Moses, in accepting the decalogue, had declared that the Jewish nation should not be bound thereby beyond ten years, the expressions of truth contained in that Code would have remained the same without regard to this express limitation. It follows, therefore, that the civilized nations of the world, prior to 1914, had, by common consent at The Hague Tribunal, declared certain moral rules to exist in respect to the conduct of nations in war.[37]

In other words, Clarke was contending that the Hague Conventions generated customary international law. Although subsequently vindicated, his claim was premature: states' actions deriving from the Conventions signed in 1899 and 1907 did not – because too recent – meet one of the tests of customary law, namely, long-standing practice. (The Nuremberg Tribunal was more cautious about timescale, stating, for example, that "by 1939" the rules laid down by the 1907 Convention "were regarded as being declaratory of the laws and customs of war".[38]) But Clarke's assertion of a customary basis for the conventions served a further

---

[36] *Ibid.*, pp. 1–2.

[37] *Ibid.*, p. 14.

[38] IMT, vol. 1, 1947–1949, p. 254, see *supra* note 7.

purpose: to get around the fact that the relevant treaties had either expired or lacked sanctions. If customary norms were present, however, then all that was required was "the consent of the majority of nations recognizing them to prescribe a sanction for their violation".[39] So, after summoning custom from thin air, he proceeded in the same fashion to summon a punishment for its transgression.

Who or what would be punished? Clarke argued that by violating customary international law, Germany had placed itself outside the society of nations, and hence beyond the law itself: "She has placed herself beyond the pale,"[40] he wrote; "She has become an outlaw in the truest sense."[41] But if Germany was outside the law, then so too, by the same logic, were Germany's leaders. *Ergo*,

> The Kaiser, as the representative of Germany and the author of the acts which have been done by her as a sovereign state, stands in the same relation to the nations of the world as a pirate, and as an outlaw stood under the old law. He is *hostis humani generis*, and has no standing as the representative of a nation or state so far as concerns the rest of the Society of Nations.[42]

If the German leaders were mere pirates, then the question about jurisdiction appeared to be solved: whoever captured them had the right to deal with as they saw fit. But bringing a head of state or his senior minsters before an international court on unprecedented charges smacked of retroactivity, and Clarke knew it. He addressed this by first claiming that the prohibition on retroactivity was merely "an American stipulation obtaining in American Constitutions" and that "no constitution limits the activities of the Allied Nations in this case".[43] (In 1944, Hans Kelsen made a similar point about the absence of the legality principle from

---

[39] Clarke, 1918, p. 15, see *supra* note 35.

[40] *Ibid.*, p. 24.

[41] *Ibid.*, pp. 15.

[42] These arguments were echoed by 1944 by the American official, William Chanler, who proposed trying the German leaders for starting the Second World War. He argued that they had effectively placed themselves outside international law and thus forfeited the rights and protections afforded those engaged in legitimate wars – they were, he wrote, "on no better footing than a band of guerillas who under established International Law are not entitled to be treated as lawful belligerents". (Smith, 1982, p. 71, see *supra* note 3).

[43] Clarke, 1918, p. 26, see *supra* note 35.

international law.[44]) Second, he argued that the law forbidding murder in war was already in existence, and that the German perpetrators must have *foreseen* that a penalty might be added to the prohibition. A wrongdoer "took his chances with his eyes wide open" and could hardly complain if a penalty were imposed upon him.[45] (Again, Kelsen made a similar point about foreseeability, this time in 1945.[46]) Be that as it may, the fact remained that the prosecuting powers would still have been transgressing the legality principle by adding not-yet-determined punishment to a pre-existing offence, whether doing so was foreseeable or not.[47]

7.4. The Irresponsibility of Sovereignty

Although originally interested in federalism and constitutional law, Louis Le Fur (1870–1943), a Catholic natural law advocate based at the University of Strasbourg at the end of the war, was also part of the naturalist movement that gained momentum in public international law during the 1920s. He believed that states' pursuit of sovereign aims was at odds with the world order ordained by God, criticised the formalism of positive law, and contributed to discussions about both dispute settlement and theological issues during the interwar years.[48] In late 1918 he wrote the piece 'Guerre juste et juste paix', published in *Revue générale de droit international public* in 1919,[49] which raised the perennial question: Was there no basis in international law for bringing Wilhelm II to justice? To admit the possibility that there was not, he wrote, "would give reason to those that see in international law only a colossal denial of justice, a series

---

44   Kelsen, 1944, p. 87, see *supra* note 8.

45   Clarke, 1918, p. 26, see *supra* note 35.

46   Hans Kelsen, "The Rule Against Ex Post Facto Laws and the Prosecution of the Axis War Criminals", in *The Judge Advocate Journal*, 1945, vol. 2, no. 3, p. 10.

47   When the British prosecutor Hartley Shawcross made similar claims at Nuremberg, the German jurist Hans Ehard complained: "A law which fills a gap is new law; a law which creates a jurisdiction not hitherto existing is also new law". ("The Nuremberg Trial Against the Major War Criminals and International Law", in *American Journal of International Law*, 1949, vol. 43, no. 2, p. 241.)

48   Le Fur's post-war books include *Des représailles en temps de guerre* (1919), *La théorie du droit naturel depuis le XVIIe siècle et la doctrine modern* (1928) and *Les grands problèmes du droit* (1937).

49   Louis Le Fur, "Guerre juste et juste paix", in *Revue générale de droit international public*, 1919, vol. 26, pp. 268–405.

of rules dreamt up by jurists that are incapable of protecting those who trust in it against the injustice and barbarity of sovereigns".[50]

The problem was that there was no precedent for putting a head of state on trial. There were no rules and no tribunal: "There's nothing, in other words."[51] Surely, then, the announcement of a new jurisdiction would violate the principle of non-retroactivity? No, he argued, "the fact that no precedent exists proves nothing; it can simply signify, as is the case here, that during these last centuries no war has witnessed such a multiplicity of crimes, nor provoked such universal indignation".[52] It was clear where Le Fur was going with this argument: the unprecedented horror of the latest war demanded unprecedented action to prevent the next. (Bohuslav Ečer would make similar claims based on the uniqueness of the Second World War.)[53] Indeed, he stated, it was nothing less than "the vital duty of international society" to protect itself from those who would "tear down the social fundaments".[54]

But in case this argument was not sufficiently persuasive, he adopted a belt and braces approach by additionally asserting the existence of customary international law as the grounds for punishment:

> [F]or centuries, war, even when justly declared, has no longer been an enterprise for brigands in which everything is permitted. There exists – without even mentioning the regulations of the Hague – customary rules of war that impose themselves on all civilised states. Those who violate them [...] place themselves outside of the laws of war and the law of nations in general; their acts become criminal once again and can be pursued as such.[55]

If, as Le Fur claimed, the creation of a new jurisdiction was supported by either an international duty to take action, or by customary international law, then surely there were no further impediments to prosecution? He admitted that in fact there were. The first, he noted, was the view that sovereigns enjoyed immunity – what he describes as "the principle of

---

[50] *Ibid.*, p. 367.
[51] *Ibid.*, p. 377.
[52] *Ibid.*
[53] Ečer, 1944, see *supra* note 2.
[54] Le Fur, 1919, p. 377, see *supra* note 49.
[55] *Ibid.*, p. 368.

irresponsibility of public power".[56] In the domestic context, he argued, sovereign power may have diversified from King to Parliament, but there was still an entity not answerable to anyone, and therefore not subject to *internal* control. At the same time, in the international arena, sovereignty was expressed as independence from – and thus equality with – other states, so the sovereign entity was not subject to *external* control either. This absolute sovereignty was, he claimed, essentially an anarchic state of affairs, because sovereigns, like anarchists, wrote their own rules and refused to accept restraints on their actions. (Small wonder, he added, that some French publicists had compared Wilhelm II to the anarchist Jules Bonnot,[57] who had led *La bande à Bonnot* before dying in a police shoot-out in Paris in 1912.) Nation states, like anarchists, considered freedom to be an absolute; they saw waging war as an expression of their sovereignty – "as anarchists of public law, there is no law, there is only force, be that individual or collective, and triumph over the adversary is proof of that law".[58]

The outcome was a fundamental absence of responsibility. When it came to adhering the rules of war, a sovereign power, whether King or Parliament, could exercise discretionary power because they were not answerable to a higher authority – "he or they are thereby irresponsible".[59] At the same time, the subordinates to this sovereign were duty-bound to carry out orders, so they could not be held personally responsible for their actions either.

> So it is that [...] even in the case of a blatant crime, nobody is responsible: neither the author of the decision, because he is sovereign, nor the lesser agents, because responsibility and the power of decision are not in their hands and it would be unjust to take against the simple executors of orders that emanate from a superior authority.[60]

---

[56] *Ibid.*, p. 369.

[57] *Ibid.*, p. 373.

[58] *Ibid.*, p. 374.

[59] *Ibid.*, p. 370.

[60] *Ibid.* In 1945 Robert Jackson argued the same: "With the doctrine of immunity of a head of state usually is coupled another, that orders from an official superior protect one who obeys them. It will be noticed that the combination of these two doctrines means that nobody is responsible. Society as modernly organized cannot tolerate so broad an area of official irresponsibility." Jackson, 1949, p. 47, see *supra* note 1. This repetition of Le Fur's

So how might this cycle of irresponsibility be broken? After all, he wrote: "Positive law is not designed to go against justice, to assure the triumph of evil, but, quite the opposite, to satisfy social needs, first and foremost of which is the maintenance of public order."[61] These needs could be met by focusing on the perpetrators' knowledge about the criminality of their actions, even if the crimes had not yet been codified in international law. He argued that it must have been plain to everyone that acts committed in the inception and during the course of the war were crimes. Even the perpetrators, despite their lack of moral scruples, were perfectly well aware of their illegality. So, if there was no doubt in anyone's minds about the criminality of the action, there was also no doubt about the right to punish the perpetrators.[62] (The Nuremberg Tribunal drew a similar conclusion, stating that the defendants *must have known* that they were doing wrong.[63]) Drawing together the threads of the argument, Le Fur concluded:

> [T]he Emperor, the chancellor, the army chiefs and the commanders on the ground, are all authors of criminal orders – orders, certainly, that they issue knowing full well that they are covered by their sovereign, but that they have nevertheless taken on their own authority, while exercising the power invested in them, such that their personal responsibility is not in doubt. For all of them, there exists no legal impediment to their being punished for their crimes; for all of them, any criminal pursuit now depends solely on the capacity to bring them to justice. Now the Allies are victorious and such issues are accounted for in the treaty; there is nothing, in this regard, to oppose the pursuit of justice.[64]

7.5. Crimes, Moral and Legal

The final commentator considered here is James Headlam-Morley (1863–1929), the English classicist and historian on Germany who joined the

---

point and the reference to "official irresponsibility" suggests that Jackson may have borrowed from Le Fur without attribution.

61   *Ibid.*, p. 375.
62   *Ibid.*, p. 374.
63   IMT, vol. 1, 1947–1949, p. 219, see *supra* note 7.
64   Le Fur, 1919, p. 376, see *supra* note 49.

Foreign Office's Political Intelligence Department during the First World War, and advocated internationalised approaches to the Saar, Danzig and minorities questions at the Paris Peace Conference.[65] While a strong believer in the League of Nations, he was more sceptical about the prospects of successfully trying the ex-Kaiser. Unlike the aforementioned lawyers, who sometimes attempted to downplay the perils of a prosecution, Headlam-Morley, while not a lawyer, was sensitive to the pitfalls, and warned against mounting a potentially unsuccessful case. In particular, he recognised the difficulties of ascribing sole blame to Germany for starting the war – one of his books, *The History of Twelve Days*, published in 1915, had probed the origins of the conflict – and while accepting charges on the basis of war crimes, he opposed charges on grounds of aggression.

He raised these issues in an official memorandum dated 12 December 1918, written at the height of a general election campaign during which Lloyd George promised to prosecute Wilhelm II for starting the war.[66] (Two days later, the electorate returned Lloyd George's government by a landslide.) Headlam-Morley was under no illusion that this charge was anything other than a leap into the unknown. He noted that prior to the war, international relations were conducted on the premise that in certain circumstances wars were "the legal and natural method" for settling disputes.[67] At the same time, he added, there was a growing sentiment that war should be avoided – especially wars in which states attempted to coerce other states. When this happened, the statesmen responsible for initiating these assaults were regarded "morally as criminal" – but no more than that, because a "moral crime is [...] quite different from a legal crime".[68]

What prospect, then, was there of bringing criminal charges against the ex-Kaiser on grounds of aggression? The proposal was "something absolutely new" because there was no precedent for such charges, and no

---

[65] His books, written under the name James Wycliffe Headlam, included *The German Chancellor and the Outbreak of War* (1917), *Bismarck and the Foundation of the German Empire* (1926) and *Studies in Diplomatic History* (1930).

[66] See for example, "Coalition Policy Defined, Mr. Lloyd George's Pledges", in *The Times*, 6 December 1918, p. 9.

[67] "Memorandum by Mr. Headlam-Morley", 12 December 1918, p. 1, TNA, FO 371/3227.

[68] *Ibid.*, p. 2.

court with jurisdiction over them.[69] This, he thought, was an important – though not an insurmountable – impediment, because the creation of a jurisdiction might be justified as precedent on which future law could be founded[70] (an argument revived by Robert Jackson in 1945).[71]

A far greater stumbling block, in his view, was the weakness of the case against the ex-Kaiser. He argued that if the prosecuting powers charged the ex-Kaiser for mere recklessness, incompetence or folly in foreign affairs, then an injustice might be perpetrated against him. "[I]t has often been said that the punishment for the Emperor is only just, for kings should no more be regarded as immune than lesser men," he explained. [72] But "if he were to be punished merely for folly and recklessness, then far from enjoying immunity denied to other men, he would himself be subjected to a responsibility from which statesmen and politicians are free".[73] For this reason, he stated that it was not enough for the prosecution to prove only that Wilhelm II was reckless or foolish; it also had to prove that he had *intended* to start the general war in Europe[74] (as distinct from merely supporting a localised war between Austria and Serbia). The question was: Could it be established that he deliberately brought about the general war, and in doing so, betrayed both his own country and the other European states? Based on the evidence, Headlam-Morley thought this was "extremely doubtful".[75] The Germans, he wrote a few months later, "knew that they were taking the risk of a European war, but this is a very different thing from deliberately intending it".[76]

7.6. Conclusion

Moving forward to 1945, the factual case against the Nazi leaders appeared more clear-cut. Yet the legal questions stubbornly refused to go away. In the event, the architects of the Nuremberg Tribunal sought

---

[69] *Ibid.*, p. 1.

[70] *Ibid.*, p. 3.

[71] Jackson, 1949, pp. 51–52, see *supra* note 1.

[72] "Memorandum", p. 1, see *supra* note 67.

[73] *Ibid.*

[74] *Ibid.*, pp. 3–4.

[75] *Ibid.*

[76] James Headlam-Morley, "Note on the Report of the Sub-commission", 19 March 1919, p. 2, TNA, FO 608/246/1.

solutions in the discussions of their predecessors in 1918, and ended up relying heavily on their ideas. Yet they consistently failed to acknowledge this debt, which is one reason why their ideas were erroneously assumed to be new.

This was not a matter of forgetfulness. Rather, they had a strong incentive *not* to publicise the earlier debates. The Americans (the greatest advocates of trying the Nazi leaders) had previously been the greatest critics of proposals to try the ex-Kaiser for newly minted crimes. At the same time, the British and French (the greatest advocates of trying the ex-Kaiser) were now the most opposed to charging the Nazi leaders for these same crimes. Small wonder then that no official was particularly interested in referring back to earlier positions, thus drawing attention to their own nation's policy reversals.[77] This expediency, coupled with the monumental historical impact of the tribunal at Nuremberg, in which national leaders actually *were* put on trial, has helped consign to relative obscurity the groundbreaking ideas of an earlier era in which influential voices called for the very same thing.

---

[77] At the 1945 London Conference, for example, there was just one exchange about the change of American policy, prompted by the French delegate, André Gros (who, incidentally, made no reference to his own nation's about-turn). *Report of Robert Jackson*, 1949, p. 297, see *supra* note 1.

8

Hang Kaiser Wilhelm! But For What?
A Criminal Law Perspective

Paul Mevis[*] and Jan Reijntjes[**]

On 28 July 1914, when Austria-Hungary declared war on Serbia, the First World War (also known as the Great War) started, "the cruellest and most terrible war that has ever scourged mankind".[1] The causes of this tragic conflict are still under sometimes venomous debate. One cannot expect lawyers to provide the answers. But they enter the picture as soon as individuals are accused of bearing more than only moral responsibility for the outbreak of, and acts committed during, the war. And of course accusations did not fail to be uttered. After such an upheaval it is but natural to look for culprits, and it would be amazing if the citizens of the victorious states did not find them among former opponents. There would be a strong demand for bringing them to court and trying them. If the criminal laws turned out to be insufficient, there would be an urge to enlarge them.

As a result of this phenomenon, the wish to try 'war criminals' will nearly always cause a struggle between the rather conservative doctrinarians on one side, and lawyers who are willing if not eager to 'stretch' the law on the other. This is why in such cases, a trial often has such a strong influence on the development of law. But lawyers who are

---

[*] **Paul Mevis** is a Professor in the Department of Criminal Law, Erasmus School of Law, Erasmus University Rotterdam, the Netherlands. His research interests include the rule of law in the era of globalisation, judicial guarantees of the rule of law, and monitoring safety and security. Professor Mevis has published in Dutch "De berechting van Wilhelm II" [Prosecuting Wilhelm II], in which he addresses some of the questions illuminated in this chapter. He is the co-author of *Modaliteiten van betekening in rechtsvergelijkend perspectief* (2013) among many other scholarly publications.

[**] **Jan Reijntjes** is Professor of Criminal Procedure at the University of Curaçao. He has published on international criminal law (especially mutual assistance), developed a course on international criminal law in English and taught on human rights in China, at the invitation of the Chinese Public Prosecution Service.

[1] The British Prime Minister David Lloyd George in the House of Commons, 11 November 1918. See David Lloyd George, *War Memoirs*, vol. 2, Odhams Press, London, 1938, p. 1984.

willing to burst the old chains have, at the same time, to define new borders: is that not what law is about?

From the earliest days, the main accused was the German Kaiser, Wilhelm II of Hohenzollern. Britain and France especially left no doubt that they would try to prosecute him. Although the Americans and Japanese did their utmost to prevent a formal trial at the end of the war, the cry for retribution (and, at the same time, the wish to grant the Kaiser a fair trial) had the upper hand.[2] This led to Article 227 of the Versailles Treaty:

> The Allied and Associated Powers publicly arraign William II of Hohenzollern, formerly German Emperor, for a supreme offence against international morality and the sanctity of treaties.
>
> A special tribunal will be constituted to try the accused, thereby assuring him the guarantees essential to the right of defence. It will be composed of five judges, one appointed by each of the following Powers: namely, the United States of America, Great Britain, France, Italy and Japan.
>
> In its decision the tribunal will be guided by the highest motives of international policy, with a view to vindicating the solemn obligations of international undertakings and the validity of international morality. It will be its duty to fix the punishment which it considers should be imposed.
>
> The Allied and Associated Powers will address a request to the Government of the Netherlands for the surrender to them of the ex-Emperor in order that he may be put on trial.

This meant a totally new development in the approach to international responsibilities. It was not politicians who would be charged with deciding on the guilt of the defeated, but a (special) Tribunal; not politics, but the law would be decisive. Against Wilhelm no administrative measures would be taken, as they were against Napoleon: no imprisonment or banishment without more ado, no execution without trial – the solution Churchill would propose in 1945. And, for the time

---

[2] It seems that the Americans would not have objected to simple reprisals, in the form of banishment, imprisonment or maybe even summary execution. See also Walter Schwengler, *Völkerrecht, Versailler Vertrag und Auslieferungsfrage*, Deutsche Verlags-Anstalt, Stuttgart, 1982, pp. 84–87; and James F. Willis, *Prologue to Nuremberg. The Politics and Diplomacy of Punishing War Criminals of the First World War*, Greenwood Press, Westport, CT, 1982, especially pp. 66–68.

being, those who had the intention that the Tribunal should be composed of civilians formed a majority. Questions of war would no longer be reserved for military justice. Nevertheless it may be assumed that the Americans would not have remained satisfied with a civilian court – and the wording of the Treaty provided sufficient openings for bringing in the military, after all. Whose point of view would have won remains highly speculative.

However, the creation of the Tribunal in itself, whether civil or military, would already have been a gigantic step forward. Of course a permanent court would have been preferable, with permanent members who were not tempted to regard themselves as representatives of their native countries or, worse, as representatives of their governments (like some members of the Tokyo Tribunal did later). But it could have been a first step in that direction, just as in recent decades the International Criminal Tribunal for the Former Yugoslavia ('ICTY') and the International Criminal Tribunal for Rwanda ('ICTR') were the first steps towards the creation of the International Criminal Court ('ICC'). In any case, membership from different countries would have been a guarantee against the prevalence of nationally inspired fears and beliefs ('national honour'!), like in the Leipzig trials, where judges simply could not believe that German officers had done what the evidence clearly showed they had done.[3]

Monarchs had been tried before: Mary Queen of Scots, Charles I, Louis XVI ... but never by victorious enemies from without. What would happen next? Would the Tribunal be able to wrestle itself free from the clusters of doctrine prevalent in national criminal law? It had no other choice! A prosecution based on the laws of the defendants would mean that norms of international origin could only be taken in consideration as far as they were included in German national laws – unless one would force the young German Republic to enact fresh, retroactive, criminal law. If that had been the intention, it would have been in the Treaty – but it was not. At the same time it was clear that without applying norms of international origin, a trial could never lead to a conviction – in any case not for "supreme offences against international morality and the sanctity

---

[3] See, for example, Gerd Hankel, *Die Leipziger Prozesse: Deutsche Kriegsverbrechen und ihre strafrechtliche Verfolgung nach dem Ersten Weltkrieg*, Hamburger Edition, Hamburg, 2003, p. 138.

of treaties". From the onset the Tribunal would have but one option available: applying international criminal law. But did this exist? First it had to be found.

At the end of the war the position of Kaiser Wilhelm had become untenable. He could not trust his army any more, and had to fear for his life if he were to fall into the hands of the rabble in the Berlin streets. This was probably the main reason why he abdicated[4] and, on 10 November 1918, fled to the Netherlands where he asked the government of his relative, Queen Wilhelmina, to grant him asylum.[5] An Allied request for his surrender became necessary, but took a rather long time to materialise.[6] Maybe the problem was that the Allies had to base their claim on the Versailles Treaty itself and – as would turn out, rightly – feared that the Netherlands, because it was not a party to the Treaty, would not feel bound by it. At last the French Prime Minister, Georges Clemenceau, acting on behalf of the Allied and Associated Powers ('Allied Powers'), addressed himself in due form to the Dutch government on 15 January 1920. The text of his request was rather amazing. He wrote, among other things,

> il ne s'agit pas dans la circonstance d'une accusation publique ayant le caractère juridique quant au fond, mais d'un acte de haute politique internationale imposée par la conscience universelle dans lequel les formes du droit ont été prévues uniquement pour assurer à l'accusé un ensemble de garanties tel que le droit publique n'en a jamais connu.

In other words: What we are dealing with is a question of politics, only clothed in the forms of the law in order to offer the accused guarantees (more than ever before) – so do not think of using juridical arguments

---

[4]   Another motive could have been that the Allied powers were unwilling to accept an armistice as long as the Kaiser was still in function. His abdication, however, had already been published on 9 November 1918 in the *Reichs-Anzeiger*, but only signed by the Reichskanzler and, as the ex-Kaiser later stated, without his knowledge. See Wilhelm II, *Ereignisse und Gestalten 1878–1918*, Koehler, Leipzig, 1922, pp. 243–44. It was followed by a more formal abdication on 28 November 1918, published on 30 November 1918 in the *Reichs-Anzeiger*.

[5]   See, for example, Nicolaas Japikse, *Die Stellung Hollands im Weltkrieg, politisch und wirtschaftlich*, Nijhoff, The Hague, 1921, pp. 287–94.

[6]   However, a first move had already been made shortly after the conclusion of the Treaty, in a telegram to the Dutch government dated 26 June 1919.

against us. This opened the door for a polite refusal. The Dutch government answered:

> *Il* [the government] *repousse avec énergie tout soupçon de vouloir couvrir de son droit souverain et de son autorité morale des violations des principes essentiels de la solidarité des nations, mais il ne peut reconnaître un devoir international de s'associer à l'acte de haute politique internationale des Puissances; si dans l'avenir, il serait institué par la Société des Nations une juridiction internationale compétente de juger, dans le cas d'une guerre, des faits, qualifiés de crimes et soumis à des sanctions par un statut antérieur aux actes commis, il appartiendra aux Pays-Bas de s'associer à ce nouveau régime.*[7]

Of course the Allied Powers could have tried Wilhelm *in absentia*, but obviously they did not want to do so. Although it has never been clarified whether they even discussed this option, it may be assumed that it was highly repulsive to American and British legal minds.[8]

What would have happened *had* the Kaiser been surrendered? For the Allied Powers there would have been no way back; without any doubt the Kaiser would have been put on trial.

8.1. What If?

Historians usually try to describe sequences of events and determine their causes. The results will always be somewhat distorted, by lack of information (vital facts remain undiscovered), by leaning on subjectively coloured information (sources are intentionally misleading or unintentionally defective because they are themselves leaning on incomplete information or information coloured by emotions), or – mostly – by a combination of these. Memoirs offer a fine example of sometimes

---

[7] Letter by foreign minister Van Karnebeek, 21 January 1920. A further request, signed by Lloyd George, was made on 16 February 1920, this time based on "*des revendications du Droit*"; it was refused on 2 March 1920. Lloyd George in a final note of 24 March 1920 made the Dutch government responsible for all the consequences that might follow from the presence of the ex-Kaiser in the Netherlands. Texts in Japikse, 1921, pp. 373–80, see *supra* note 5.

[8] Clemenceau however thought a trial *in absentia* quite possible. See David Lloyd George, *The Truth About the Peace Treaties*, Gollancz, London, 1920, vol. 1, p. 98.

intentional, sometimes unintentional combinations of facts and fancies.[9] This can be countered by concentrating on subjective impressions alone, in the same way as criminologists do when they supplement quantitative research with qualitative research. But in history a third option is available: asking the 'what if' question. What would have happened if? When one is more interested in developments than in static facts, it can be especially challenging to wrestle free from the clusters of fact and look at events in a more speculative way. However, not just any 'what if' question is useful; it should be well defined and to the point. The question, for example, of what would have happened if the Axis had won the Great War leads nowhere – not because the Axis could never have vanquished the Entente (it nearly did), but because a war can be won in a thousand different ways, each leading to a different result. Trying to answer a 'what if' question only makes sense when its subject is clear-cut. For example, what would have happened if Kaiser Wilhelm, after having been surrendered by the Netherlands to the Allied Powers, had been put on trial?

This is exactly the question we will address and try to answer. For what kind of crimes would he have been tried? Could there have been a possibility that he would not be convicted? How could the Tribunal have guaranteed a fair trial? And what would have been the most probable sentence? Answering these questions will not amount to pure speculation,[10] especially because the problems do not primarily lie in the facts, but in the law. The facts can be accepted as historians of today present them, under the assumption that a well-equipped court could have found them in, say, 1920. As for the law, the same sources are available to the researcher that the court established to try the ex-Kaiser would have used itself: legal texts and authoritative publications. Nevertheless it will be no easy task. It requires some knowledge of the history of the Versailles Treaty, but above all it requires knowledge of the opinions of the academic community in the field of international (criminal) law in those times. These opinions are buried in many books. Most of them cannot be found on the internet, and they are not in the libraries of the

---

[9] See, for example, those of Wilhelm II, 1922, *supra* note 4.

[10] Unless one opts for the method used by Georg Sylvester ('Swastika') Viereck, *The Kaiser on Trial*, Greystone Press, New York, 1937. The author reports in his book the trial of Wilhelm II as he imagined it would have been, witness statements included.

younger universities. Important sources also exist in books that nobody reads anymore.

We think such an exercise is not only exciting but also useful. It will reveal the 'prehistory' of international criminal law, and can also provide information about the way it could have developed, if the Kaiser had been surrendered – and in this way clarify the actual situation of today. Putting the ex-Kaiser on trial would have sped up developments, especially in the field of international criminal law. As a result of the Dutch refusal to surrender him, many of the problems that would have faced the court have in fact been solved but many years later – and some are troubling us until today. Our experiment should provide a better understanding of the ways in which the trial of the ex-Kaiser would have accelerated, and maybe even changed, the development of international criminal law. In our chapter we will try to give an outline of what could be expected from this kind of research.

For the Tribunal one of the first questions to answer would be: Was there a common opinion on the content of international law, or were the opinions within the Axis states contrary to those of Entente experts? In the latter case, the Tribunal would have been confronted with a problem that it could hardly solve: Is there any law at all, if no written law, and no common opinion on the content of unwritten law exist? Some nationalist German authors, who dreamed about "*der welterlösenden Sendung des Deutschtums*",[11] pretended that a deep and unbridgeable gap existed between opinions in *Kulturstaat* Germany and the decadent Entente states. They were mistaken. We found that before 1914, on most subjects there really *was* a common opinion between authoritative authors – maybe the typically German doctrine of military necessity (*Not kennt kein Gebot*) excepted.[12] But was this doctrine not specially developed to defend and, later, excuse the German way of making war? Indeed, during and shortly after the war, texts were published that were strongly influenced by the recent conflicts and were therefore to a high degree partisan. This not only applies to German, but also French and some English texts. Before the war, however, German authority was not less trustworthy and respectable than British, French, Swiss or American – to mention but a

---

[11] Walter Flex, *Der Wanderer zwischen beiden Welten: Ein Kriegserlebnis*, Beck, Munich, p. 100.

[12] See on this subject, for example, Hankel, 2004, pp. 244–47, *supra* note 3.

few. So, in general, the opinion of James Wilford Garner that German authority in the field of international law is untrustworthy has to be rejected.[13]

For us it is clear that the Tribunal could have relied to a large extent on German sources. This would have facilitated a decision that was convincing, even in German eyes – as far as under the existing circumstances a convincing decision was conceivable.

We have to ask ourselves, however, what criminal judges do exactly when trying to solve complicated problems of fact in order to apply the rules of the law. And how do they decide what the law is, if its contents are contested? Judges will first try to reduce a too complex reality by elimination, keeping only the facts needed to answer the central question: Is the defendant guilty of the crimes he is accused of having committed? They will not try to find 'causes' of these facts, neither will they be concerned about purely moral guilt. They will in a way 'recreate' happenings of the past as outlined and defined by the indictment, drawn up by the prosecutor. Lawyers can do no more; only historians have the competence to go a step further in 'reconstructing the truth' – but nevertheless their 'truth' again is nothing more than a reconstruction. It is only more complete than what lawyers provide.

Moreover, judges are always to a certain degree 'reasoning towards their goal', when deciding whether the *indictment* (and only the indictment) is 'true'. In doing so they are not only plying the facts; they will ply the law as well, when it leaves room for interpretation (as it usually does) and it seems suitable to do so. This is called 'development of the law', and it means progress. The quality of justice does not depend on the extent to which the judges followed 'the letter of the law'; attempts to apply rules more or less automatically to given facts never inspire respect. Justice means that the law has been presented, better: has been 'recreated', in an acceptable form. When determining acceptability, the catchwords are usefulness, fitting into the generally accepted system of the law, and respecting the position of the defendant. Only decisions sufficiently complying with these conditions will be accepted and will contribute to further development of the law; all others are to be rejected.

---

[13] James Wilford Garner, *International Law and the World War*, Longman, Green and Co., London, 1920, vol. 1, p. viiii.

We have to take the position that our Tribunal will satisfy these conditions.

All this makes it more difficult to predict what judges would do in a given case. One never knows how far they would be willing to go; their thinking process is not purely scientific, but also oriented to what they suppose society needs most. In some cases they will even not recoil from a certain 'massage' of their sources. Especially in highly contested cases, this makes their personality extremely important, and their standing as well, for two different reasons: it is determinative of their willingness to explore new approaches, but also (and they are fully aware of this fact) of the willingness of their contemporaries to accept their decisions. But the personality and standing of the individual judge are not decisive. More powerful and therefore decisive will be the group process within the court. That is the secret of collegiate justice.

8.2. Hanging the Kaiser

Shortly after the war, prosecution of the Kaiser was an important issue in French and British politics. The British Prime Minister H.H. Asquith and his successor Lloyd George were especially clamorous. In December 1918 Lloyd George did not even shrink from going into the elections under the cry: Hang the Kaiser! This created the impression that for him the result of a trial would be a sentence of death. Obviously he thought this was what the voters also wished. Another outcome would have been rather embarrassing. Could a trial under such circumstances have been fair and impartial? It is true that many others were less intransigent. So, for instance, Lord George Curzon, a member of the British war cabinet, who, on 15 October 1918 in a memorandum about the conditions of an armistice,[14] demanded the "trial and punishment of the principal criminals, *possibly* including the Kaiser, *unless he abdicated*". But notice again the peculiar combination of trial and punishment – as if the one would be the logical consequence of the other. If ever a prosecution would have deserved the disqualification 'political', it was the prosecution of the ex-Kaiser. When requesting his surrender, however, the Allied Powers did not invoke the existing extradition treaties with the Netherlands, probably on the – quite justified – supposition that these were not applicable in the case, because they were not written for requests to bring someone before

---

[14] Lloyd George, 1938, pp. 1963–64, see *supra* note 1.

an *international* court applying *international* criminal law. As a result the Dutch government had no need to refuse surrender on the generally accepted political offence exception, nor on its later offshoot, the prospective unfairness of the prosecution for its political character. Maybe it was quite happy it did not have to irritate the Allied Powers by using such arguments.

Probably not all the Allies deplored the Dutch refusal very much. In any case they had the Kaiser out of their way and his prosecution could only have led to embarrassment. Even Lloyd George, when confronted with his former election cry, seems to have answered: I only wanted to hang him to the electoral gallows.[15]

8.3. The Indictment

In the Versailles Treaty, the Allied Powers stated that the Kaiser should be prosecuted "for a supreme offence against international morality and the sanctity of treaties". What did they mean, and where did this formula come from?

The Preliminary Peace Conference decided at its plenary session of 25 January 1919 to create, for the purpose of inquiring into the responsibilities relating to the war, a Commission on the Responsibility of the Authors of the War and on Enforcement of Penalties ('Commission on Responsibility'), composed of 15 members.[16] It was charged to inquire into and report on the following points:

1. the responsibility of the authors of the war;
2. the facts as to breaches of the laws and customs of war committed by the forces of the German Empire

---

[15] Alexandre Ribot, *Journal d'Alexandre Ribot et correspondances inédites, 1914–22*, Plon, Paris, 1936, p. 294 ("*une potence électorale*").

[16] See, for example, Willis, 1982, pp. 68–79, *supra* note 2, and M. Cherif Bassiouni, "World War I: 'The War to End All Wars' and the Birth of a Handicapped International Criminal Justice System", in *Denver Journal of International Law and Policy*, 2002, vol. 30, pp. 253–55. An interesting detail: from the French government the Preliminary Conference received a detailed report by two eminent lawyers on the difficulties connected with prosecuting the Kaiser, later published as A. de Lapradelle and F. Larnaude, "Examen de la responsabilité pénale de l'Empereur Guillaume II d'Allemagne", in *Journal de Droit International*, 1919, vol. 46, pp. 131–59.

and their Allies, on land, on sea, and in the air during the present war;

3. the degree of responsibility for these offences attaching to particular members of the enemy forces, including members of the General Staffs, and other individuals, however highly placed;

4. the constitution and procedure of a tribunal appropriate for the trial of these offences; and

5. any other matters cognate or ancillary to the above which may arise in the course of the enquiry, and which the Commission finds it useful and relevant to take into consideration.

In its Report[17] of 29 March 1919 the Commission on Responsibility stigmatised the Central Powers for authoring the war, for violating the neutrality of Belgium and Luxembourg, guaranteed by treaty, and for carrying on the war by illegitimate methods in violation of the established laws and customs of war and the elementary laws of humanity. However, the Commission found that it would not make much sense to prosecute for starting an aggressive war in itself:

> [T]he premeditation of a war of aggression, dissimulated under a peaceful pretence, then suddenly declared under false pretexts, is conduct which the public conscience reproves and which history will condemn, but by reason of the purely optional character of the institutions at The Hague for the maintenance of peace (International Commission of Inquiry, Mediation and Arbitration) a war of aggression may not be considered as an act directly contrary to positive law, or one which can be successfully brought before a tribunal.[18]

For that reason the Kaiser, in the opinion of the Commission, should not be prosecuted for the acts which brought about the war, neither for the breaches of the neutrality of Belgium and Luxembourg. Although the Commission held the opinion that these breaches were "a high-handed outrage [...] upon international engagements, deliberately, and for a

---

[17] Commission on Responsibility, "Report Presented to the Preliminary Peace Conference", in *American Journal of International Law*, 1920, vol. 14, pp. 95–154.

[18] *Ibid.*, p. 118.

purpose which cannot justify the conduct of those who were responsible", it thought that they should only be made the subject of a formal condemnation by the Peace Conference – that is, by politicians, not by judges. Unmistakably, the Commission saw breaches of the *ius ad bellum* not yet as a criminal act, but as an act that should be made so. "It is desirable that for the future penal sanctions should be provided for such grave outrages against the elementary principles of international law".[19] But with regard to the *ius in bello* the Commission found:

> All persons belonging to enemy countries, however high their position may have been, without distinction of rank, including Chiefs of States, who have been guilty of offences against the laws and customs of war or the laws of humanity, are liable to criminal prosecution.[20]

Here the ex-Kaiser had been included because "the trial of the offenders might be seriously prejudiced if they attempted and were able to plead the superior orders of a sovereign against whom no steps had been or were being taken".[21] Although this is an interesting point of view, we may leave it here for what it is worth, because there was but one person who could never plead superior orders, to wit the ex-Kaiser himself.

Meanwhile the politicians[22] kept to their opinion that the former Kaiser should (also) be tried for his responsibility as author of the war. They shared "a growing feeling that war itself was a crime against humanity";[23] thus they thought that bringing the case against the ex-Kaiser to court also stood for "a new world order".[24] That is a rather hazardous starting point for a fair trial. Obviously they belonged to those who expected that his prosecution would inevitably be followed by

---

[19] *Ibid.*, p. 120.

[20] *Ibid.*, p. 117.

[21] *Ibid.*

[22] The British Attorney-General Sir Frederick Smith (see Lloyd George, 1920, pp. 98–99, see *supra* note 8) and Lord Birkenhead included. See the interesting opinion of the latter, reprinted in Lloyd George, 1920, pp. 102–12, see *supra* note 8. There is more in Willis, 1982, chapter 5, see *supra* note 2; Lloyd George, 1920, pp. 102–12, see *supra* note 8; and, for example, Margaret MacMillan, *Peacemakers: The Paris Conference of 1919 and Its Attempt to End War*, Murray, London, 2001.

[23] Lloyd George, 1920, p. 96, see *supra* note 8.

[24] Willis, 1982, pp. 3–4, see *supra* note 2.

conviction. The French especially did not doubt such an outcome.[25] As to the question of whether waging an aggressive war was a criminal act, they were in good company: the American members of the Commission, disagreeing with the majority, believed that

> any nation going to war assumes a grave responsibility, and that a nation engaging in a war of aggression commits a crime. They hold that the neutrality of nations should be observed, especially when it is guaranteed by a treaty to which the nations violating it are parties, and that the plighted word and the good faith of nations should be faithfully observed in this as in all other respects.[26]

The only reason why the Americans did not formally dissent from the conclusions of the Commission on the *ius ad bellum* was "the difficulty of determining whether an act is in reality one of aggression or of defence". As an afterthought they added that a head of state is responsible only to the law of his own country, unless he has abdicated or has been repudiated by his people (by then both applied to the Kaiser). What to do with defeated heads of state was a question for statesmen, not for judges to decide; their offences were of a political nature and should therefore be met by political sanctions.[27] (Obviously they had in mind the option of sending the Kaiser to a place like the Falkland Islands, as Napoleon had been sent to Saint Helena.) In Britain, Lord Birkenhead said:

> the ex-Kaiser ought to be punished, either by way of trial or as Napoleon was punished. (Some people incline) to the first of those courses, namely that he should be tried. I am not at present wholly convinced upon this point (but) I say quite plainly that I should feel the greatest difficulty in being responsible in any way for the trial of subordinate criminals if the ex-Kaiser is allowed to escape.[28]

---

[25] Obviously they leaned heavily on de Lapradelle and Larnaude, who solved many problems by declaring: *"Un droit international nouveau est né"* (de Lapradelle and Larnaude, 1919, p. 144, see *supra* note 16). Exemplary for the French post-war literature on the subject is their sneer about the ex-Kaiser, *"déserteur de sa propre armée"* (*ibid.*, p. 137). In the same style A. Mérignhac and E. Lémonon, *Le droit des gens et la guerre de 1914-1918*, Sirey, Paris, 1921.

[26] Commission on Responsibility, 1920, p. 140, see *supra* note 17.

[27] *Ibid.*, p. 136.

[28] Lloyd George, 1920, pp. 112–13, see *supra* note 8.

In any case, a judgment by politicians was what the politicians, after some debate, decided *not* to give. They thought that the ex-Kaiser should be prosecuted ("publicly arraigned") for his breaches of the *ius ad bellum,* to wit *supreme offences against international morality and the sanctity of treaties,* before an independent international court, and that he should have a fair trial. Some authors (Garner and Schwengler, for instance) insist that the result would not be a *criminal* trial. But what else could it be? Obviously the politicians thought that even after a four-year war and millions of deaths, such a court could be found, and fairness of the procedure could be guaranteed. Clemenceau seems to have answered the American President Woodrow Wilson, when Wilson expressed his fear that a trial would be infected by emotions: "Nothing is accomplished without emotion. Was Jesus Christ not carried away by passion the day he chased the moncy changers from the Temple?"[29] In other words, even emotional actions can be just, and have just results. In any case a judgment by Entente politicians would be sheer 'victor's justice', and should be avoided – as far as possible. Lloyd George in particular thought that fair proceedings, in which the rights of the defence were sufficiently guaranteed, would help in further developing international criminal law. He even suggested inviting the young German Republic to participate in the Tribunal that would be formed and added: "I have no doubt she will send men, in her present state, who will judge the ex-Kaiser very impartially".[30]

At the same time, as advised by the Commission on Responsibilities, the Kaiser would be prosecuted, together with other 'war criminals', for breaches of the *ius in bello,* that is for *acts in violation of the laws and customs of war.* This was based on Article 228 of the Versailles Treaty:

> The German Government recognises the right of the Allied and Associated Powers to bring before military tribunals persons accused of having committed acts in violation of the laws and customs of war. Such persons shall, if found guilty, be sentenced to punishments laid down by law. This provision will apply notwithstanding any proceedings or prosecution before a tribunal in Germany or in the territory of her allies.

---

[29] Cited in Willis, 1982, p. 78, see *supra* note 2.

[30] Lloyd George, 1920, p. 100, see *supra* note 8.

> The German Government shall hand over to the Allied
> and Associated Powers, or to such one of them as shall so
> request, all persons accused of having committed an act in
> violation of the laws and customs of war, who are specified
> either by name or by the rank, office or employment which
> they held under the German authorities.[31]

Retribution was the main object of these clauses. At the same time they emphasised, as a clear-cut – but certainly not completely new – principle of international criminal law, that not only states were responsible for the maintenance of the rules of war, but individuals were directly subject to the duties imposed by these rules as well. The Allied Powers had already brought captive German officers[32] to justice for what – from the Allied point of view – constituted breaches of the laws and customs of war. Now they wanted to try culprits who were not (yet) in their power as well. But another motive would be that they wanted to affirm the validity of the pre-war *ius in bello*, as it had been written in the Hague Conventions and as it would be found in customary law. It all came to nothing. On 3 February 1920 the Allied Powers delivered a 'provisional' list to the German authorities with the names of those who in any case should be surrendered to be tried. The Germans refused, and within a very short time the Allied Powers accepted that the culprits would be tried in Germany, by German courts: the infamous Leipzig trials. But that is quite another story.

The Commission on Responsibility found that the war had been carried on "by barbarous or illegitimate methods in violation of the established laws and customs of war and the elementary laws of humanity".[33] Its report leaves no doubt that, in the opinion of its majority, the Kaiser should not be prosecuted for breaches of the *ius ad bellum*, but for the German infringements upon the *ius in bello*. Only the American and the Japanese members disagreed even on this point, mainly because

---

[31] Both Article 227 and Article 228 were included in Part VII of the Treaty, on *Penalties*. Stipulations comparable with Article 228 were included in the Treaties of Saint Germain (with Austria, 10 September 1919), Neuilly (with Bulgaria, 27 November 1919) and Sèvres (with Turkey, 1920, never ratified).

[32] For example, Lieutenants Von Schierstaedt and Von Strachwitz, sentenced on 1 October 1914 for looting. See R. Poincaré, *Au service de la France: Neuf années de souvenirs*: *Les tranchées*, Plon, Paris, 1930, pp. 145–46. The Germans prosecuted some French soldiers as well; see Hankel, 2004, pp. 92–97, see *supra* note 3.

[33] Commission on Responsibility, 1920, p. 115, see *supra* note 17.

they did not want to prosecute for offences that had not been directly ordered by the Kaiser. They strongly disliked what they called the doctrine of negative criminality, based on criminal liability for mere abstention from preventing violations of the laws and customs of war and of humanity. There is no reason why the politicians would not have followed the Commission on this point. That the Kaiser is only mentioned in Article 227 of the Treaty, and not in Article 228, may not be used as an argument as to why it would not be acceptable to also prosecute him under Article 228. [34] But did the politicians also adopt negative responsibility?

The Commission on Responsibility recommended to base a prosecution for violations of the laws and customs of war on "the principles of the law of nations as they result from the usages established among civilized peoples, from the laws of humanity and from the dictates of public conscience".[35] Unmistakably, these criteria had been inspired by the so-called Martens clause in the preamble of the second 1899 Hague Treaty, repeated in the preamble of the fourth 1907 Hague Treaty:

> *En attendant qu'un Code plus complet des lois de la guerre puisse être édicté, les Hautes Parties contractantes jugent opportun de constater que, dans les cas non compris dans les dispositions réglementaires adoptées par Elles, les populations et les belligérants restent sous la sauvegarde et sous l'empire des principes du droit des gens, tels qu'ils résultent des usages établis entre les nations civilisées, des lois de l'humanité et des exigences de la conscience publique.*

It was probably to appease the Americans that the laws of humanity in the end did not appear in the Versailles Treaty. They thought that "the laws of humanity do not constitute a definite code with fixed penalties which can be applied through judicial process".[36] Nevertheless we have to

---

[34] The request for his extradition mentioned in so many words: the breach of Belgian and Luxembourg neutrality, taking of hostages, mass deportations, abduction of young girls in Lille, France, systematic devastation of whole regions without any military necessity, unlimited submarine war, including the abandonment of victims on the high seas, and breaches of the rules of war against non-combatants. See Japikse, 1921, p. 374, *supra* note 5.

[35] Commission on Responsibility, 1920, p. 122, see *supra* note 17.

[36] Robert Lansing, "Some Legal Questions of the Peace Conference", in *American Journal of International Law*, 1919, vol. 13, pp. 631–50, especially p. 647.

conclude that the Versailles Treaty, as far as it concerns the adjudication of Wilhelm II, was not an American show.[37] When the Versailles Treaty, in this respect, had its influence on the Nuremberg trials, this means that Nuremberg was not a completely American show either – contrary to what has sometimes been asserted.

Taken together, this means that the indictment against Wilhelm II with a certain degree of probability could have been:

A. Ius ad bellum

Count 1   Starting an aggressive war against Russia, France and other countries (according to Article 227: *a supreme offence against international morality*).

Count 2   Ordering or at least condoning violation of the neutrality of Belgium and Luxembourg (according to Article 227: *a supreme offence against international morality and the sanctity of treaties*).

B. Ius in bello

Count 3   Ordering or at least not preventing violations of the laws and customs of war, especially in Belgium, France, Poland, Serbia and Romania.[38]

Count 4   Declaring an unlimited submarine war.

Count 5   Ordering or at least not preventing violations of the laws and customs of war at sea.

Before we ask ourselves what the Tribunal would have decided, another question has to be answered: Was a trial not superfluous? Had the new German Republic not already accepted its war guilt? Article 231 of the Versailles Treaty reads:

> The Allied and Associated Governments affirm and Germany accepts the responsibility of Germany and her allies for causing all the loss and damage to which the Allied

---

[37]   More on the American position in, for example, Binoy Kampmark, "Sacred Sovereigns and Punishable War Crimes: The Ambivalence of the Wilson Administration Towards a Trial of Kaiser Wilhelm II", in *Australian Journal of Politics and History*, 2007, vol. 53, no. 4, pp. 519–37.

[38]   The Commission gave a list of 32 categories. Commission on Responsibility, 1920, pp. 114–15, see *supra* note 17. For their basis in law see Bassiouni, 2002, pp. 260–61, see *supra* note 16.

> and Associated Governments and their nationals have been
> subjected as a consequence of the war imposed upon them
> by the aggression of Germany and her allies.

Some Allied politicians eagerly used this text to assure their adherents that the time to discuss German guilt had passed: they had the German confession in black and white. This, however, is utter nonsense. Of course an extorted confession is worthless, even when extorted by treaty, and never could the Republic confess on behalf of the ex-Kaiser; but neither did they confess on behalf of the former Reich. It is not without importance that Article 231 is a part of Chapter 8 of the Treaty, on reparations, and not of Chapter 7, on penalties. The Republic only promised to pay the bill for (all the damages of) the war and (therefore) conceded that they had started the actual fighting (which was quite clear) and could therefore be called 'aggressors'. Article 231 thus created a title to have Germany pay for all damages – and not specifically those caused by breaches of the laws and customs of war.[39] Guilt – criminal or only moral guilt – is quite something else. All that may be deduced from Article 231 is civil responsibility.[40]

8.4. Preliminary Decisions: Competence and Jurisdiction

The Tribunal would certainly have to make some preliminary decisions, at least on its own competence and jurisdiction, but also on the applicable norms, on *nulla poena* and on the possible immunity of the ex-Kaiser. Would the Tribunal be able to pass these hurdles? The answer would possibly be even more interesting than its later decision on the Kaiser's guilt.

The Tribunal, however, could be expected to take the validity of the Treaty, by which it had been founded, for granted. Many years later the military tribunals after the Second World War and the ICTY would do the same. That the Versailles Treaty needed implementation before the Tribunal could come into existence does not seem to make a difference. It is also clear that the Tribunal would have to find that it should base its

---

[39] See also Schwengler, 1982, p. 123, *supra* note 2.

[40] Compare Carl Schmitt, *Das international-rechtliche Verbrechen des Angriffskrieges und der Grundsatz 'Nullum crimen, nulla poena sine lege'*, 1945, especially Part II, "Kriegsverbrechen und Kriegsschuld im Versailler Vertrag", republished with notes and an introduction by Helmut Quaritsch, Duncker and Humblot, Berlin, 1994, p. 157.

decisions not on rules of national law, but purely on international law. The consequences of this position would be of the utmost importance. The first, and maybe the main consequence, would be that the simple fact that an international norm had not (yet) acquired written form, for example, in a duly ratified treaty, nor been implemented in national law, would not offer a valid defence. In international law a norm does not have to be written down to be valid; general acceptance is sufficient. When there was (a sufficient degree of) general acceptance, the next question would be answered at the same time: What is generally accepted will be generally known, too. We will see that the *ius ad bellum*, as far as it really existed, would be completely customary. In the field of the *ius in bello*, however, there existed a rather large corpus of written law, but here a punitive sanction was missing.

In former times, anyone who went down in battle and could not save himself by flight had to surrender unconditionally. The victorious party could freely dispose of its captive enemies. Usually there was no hesitation to incarcerate, banish or even execute the former opponents without any form of procedure when it was thought that this would serve the victor's interests; even more so, when the captives were accused of evil deeds. Thus Napoleon Bonaparte was banished to Elba, and later imprisoned on Saint Helena. From this a rule of customary law could be derived, that whoever misbehaved in war and succumbed to his opponent could be sanctioned by him. In that case, it would be a step forward to not simply imprison the ex-Kaiser for life on the Falkland Islands, but to try him before an independent court under strict rules of procedure, guaranteeing his rights to defend himself effectively.[41]

Victor's justice? Yes, to a certain degree. It is not very realistic to expect victors to try themselves! The alternative, victim's justice, is even more unattractive; it would amount to lynchings.

8.5. Preliminary Decisions: The Norms; *Nulla Poena*

In this line of reasoning it becomes clear why under such circumstances the *nullum crimen* rule does not apply – in any case not in the strict sense

---

[41] Some authors draw attention to what they define as a different development, the offering of amnesty in peace treaties: "No real peace without forgiveness". That, however, is quite another discussion, the opposing point of view being: "No real peace without justice". This would bring us to cases in South Africa and South America.

in which it is used by criminal lawyers and in which it was invoked by the Dutch government when refusing the Allied request for the surrender of the ex-Kaiser. Of course there has to be a clear norm of behaviour; nobody should be punished for his activities when he could not know that these were not allowed. But why does international law require that these norms should be written down in treaties or statutes? Why would it not be sufficient that one is aware of the consequences that his acts could have if he were caught? In fact he benefits by being granted a criminal trial, instead of a lynching. But what about the punishment? Again it seems sufficient when it lies within the range of possibilities that could be foreseen: a fine, imprisonment for some time or for life, or execution.

This underlines that here international law has to define the limits of liability, not (classic) criminal law. It is axiomatic that prosecutions under international law are not subjected to legality in the strict sense of a requirement of well-defined prohibitions. Foreseeability is sufficient. Criminal law, in such cases, only has to provide a procedure. As soon as international customary law has developed into clear, well-defined rules, supplemented by formal criminal liability and provided with well-defined penalties, it has lost its own peculiar character and has moved into the sphere of criminal law – in the same manner as (the law on) extradition has moved from international (interstate) to (national) criminal law. This prospect could also help to accept prosecutions under international law: they contribute to finding a more clear definition of the behaviour to be punished and thus open the door to formal criminal law, with its stricter application of the *nullum crimen* rule.[42] This construction of trial and punishment under international law has been recognised in 1954, in Article 7(2) of the European Convention on Human Rights:

> This article shall not prejudice the trial and punishment of any person for any act or omission which, at the time when it was committed, was criminal according to the general principles of law, recognised by civilised nations.[43]

---

[42] Jonas Nilsson, "The Principle Nullum Crimen Sine Lege", in Olaoluwa Olusanya (ed.), *Rethinking International Criminal Law: The Substantive Part*, Europa Law Publishing, Groningen, 2007, pp. 41, 64, with further literature.

[43] See also International Covenant on Civil and Political Rights, 16 December 1966, Article 15, and, for example, Kenneth S. Gallant, *The Principle of Legality in International and Comparative Criminal Law*, Cambridge University Press, Cambridge, 2009, pp. 175–200 and 202–11.

What was the discussion on whether the Kaiser could be prosecuted for waging war really about? We already distinguished the *ius in bello* from the *ius ad bellum*. An important part of the *ius in bello* had been defined in the 1907 Hague Treaties. The treaties laid down clear and mostly unambiguous norms – but could infringements of these norms be punished criminally? And maybe there was still an unwritten part of the *ius in bello* left, especially with regard to the war on sea. Could breaches of unwritten law also be punished criminally? In relation to the *ius ad bellum*, which had never been defined in any treaty, this was an urgent question. Some authors even denied the existence of this part of the law (they thought that the decision to start a war was not governed by law at all, as further explained below). But if it really existed, the same question had to be answered: Could infringements be punished criminally? The 'special tribunal', as foreseen in Article 227 of the treaty, would have to make its own way, leaning on the existing literature. Inspecting this literature, it would find that, although the famous Emer de Vattel (probably the most studied and the most cited author after Hugo Grotius) did indeed defend the principle that the victor could punish the waging of an unjust war[44] – but the Tribunal would also find that this view soon lost most of its support. In the nineteenth century it was even an issue whether infringements upon the *ius in bello* could be punished. Authors like G.F. von Martens,[45] J.C. Bluntschli[46] and Cornelis van Vollenhoven[47] defended this, and it was confirmed by the *Manuel des lois de la guerre sur terre*, drawn up in 1880 by the Institut de Droit International in Brussels, but others flatly denied the point.

However, as soon as we find that breaches of the *ius ad bellum* can be prosecuted criminally, it cannot be denied that we have to deal with the most serious category of criminal behaviour that can be imagined. Whoever acts in this way knows that, if he is caught, he can expect a

---

[44] Emer de Vattel, *Le droit des gens, ou Principes de la loi naturelle appliqués à la conduite et aux affaires des Nations et des Souverains*, Leiden, 1758, for example Book 2, § 52 and Book 3, § 185.

[45] G.F. von Martens, *Précis du droit des gens moderne de l'Europe*, 1788; we used the edition published in Paris by Guillaumin, 1864, vol. 2, p. 232.

[46] J.C. Bluntschli, *Das moderne Kriegsrecht der civilisirten Staaten*, 2nd ed., Beck, Nördlingen, 1874, I.1, first pub. in 1866.

[47] Cornelis van Vollenhoven, *Omtrek en inhoud van het internationale recht*, Ph.D. Thesis, University of Leiden, 1898.

severe – maybe even the most severe – punishment. It would be highly unpractical, for that reason unacceptable and moreover dogmatically erroneous, to require that prospective war criminals should be able to calculate beforehand exactly the punishment they could expect. It would be useless too. Maybe people can be prevented from committing war crimes by the knowledge that they will be caught and prosecuted, but they surely will not be kept back by knowledge of the sanction they can expect. In this field, sanctions will not have a preventative effect; they are purely retributive.

As we already explained, as soon as international criminal law, as part of international law, has developed into common criminal law, one may expect more, especially clear-cut rules which punishments may be given, and in what measure, and also what kinds of aggravating or alleviating circumstances could be accepted.[48]

In short, the *nullum crimen, nulla poena* rule *does* apply in international law, but only in so far that suspects should be able to foresee what kind of activities they will be punished for, if caught, and what their punishments could be. So it has a far less specific content, and will be satisfied much easier, than in (traditional) criminal law.[49] That, we think, would also have been the opinion of the Tribunal in the proceedings against Wilhelm II.

8.6. Preliminary Decisions: Immunity of (Former) Heads of State

Under general international law, a head of state enjoys immunity in principle. He can be prosecuted neither in his own country nor elsewhere, not for what he did in his official capacity, nor for what he did in private ("the King can do no wrong"). In England, King Charles I even refused to recognise the court before which he was brought after his defeat in the civil war against the Roundheads under Fairfax and Cromwell. He considered himself King by the grace of God – so how could there be a worldly power above him?[50] This implied that abdication was as

---

[48] See also Christoph Safferling, *Towards an International Criminal Procedure*, Oxford University Press, Oxford, 2001, pp. 314–18.

[49] Compare, for example, Gallant, 2009, p. 57, see *supra* note 43.

[50] As a result of his point of view, he refused to answer the indictment, which resulted in his condemnation without further proof and his execution on 9 February 1649 (continental chronology). C.V. Wedgwood, *The Trial of Charles I*, Collins, London, 1964.

unthinkable as a trial. Abdicating, however, was exactly what Wilhelm II had done, in this way preventing his disposition by his compatriots. Nevertheless, in the period immediately after the Great War, immunity of heads of state still formed a clear-cut rule, more so than nowadays;[51] the motives, however, had changed somewhat. Although the question who would try the head of a sovereign state (*par in parem non habet imperium*) still had not found a definite answer, the real problem seemed to be that trying a head of state for what he had done in his supreme quality in fact is the equivalent to trying the state itself.

Anyhow, with his abdication, Wilhelm II's immunity had come to an end. But did it also end for what he *had* done in his former capacity as head of state? Some authors answered in the negative. Hankel[52] thought there was around 1918 so much discussion on this subject that it would have been a sufficient reason for a trial of Wilhelm II to run aground. We doubt this. Had Wilhelm II really been surrendered to a court that the Allied Powers had constituted specially to try him, it seems highly improbable that judges who accepted their nomination would abort the trial beforehand. But they would have had better arguments than just that. In a trial before an international criminal court, none of the reasons given for immunity really applies: the international court would be of a higher order than the individual head of state, and why could it be a problem that (supposedly) criminal acts of state would come under discussion in his trial? Whatever might have been its reasoning, in our opinion it is highly improbable that the Tribunal would have granted Wilhelm II immunity for what he did as head of the German Reich. Although the American members of the Commission on Responsibility dissented, their own President Wilson after all accepted that Wilhelm II would be prosecuted, and the Dutch government did not refuse Wilhelm II's extradition by reason of his immunity.[53] Actually it took some time before a court made clear that former heads of state could not invoke immunity. Although

---

51 More in, for example, Rosanne van Alebeek, *The Immunity of States and Their Officials in International Criminal Law and International Human Rights Law*, Oxford University Press, Oxford, 2008.

52 Hankel, 2004, pp. 83–87 (with literature), see *supra* note 3.

53 N. Ashton and D. Hellema, "'Hang the Kaiser!'; De Brits-Nederlandse betrekkingen en het lot van ex-Keizer Wilhelm II, 1918–1920", in D.A. Hellema, C. Wiebes and B. Zeeman (eds.), *Buitenlandse Zaken: Vierde Jaarboek voor de geschiedenis van de Nederlandse politiek in the 20ste eeuw*, SDU, The Hague, 1998, p. 75–93.

Article 7 of the Statute of the International Military Tribunal (IMT) stated: "The official position of defendants, whether as Heads of State or responsible officials in Government Departments, shall not be considered as freeing them from responsibility or mitigating punishment", Hitler's suicide prevented the Tribunal from deciding whether this would really apply for heads of state. The world had to wait for the ICTY to ratify the conclusions of the 1919 Commission on Responsibility.[54]

But *can* supreme offences against international morality and the sanctity of treaties and serious infringements upon the law and customs on war be committed in an official capacity? We fear that the answer has to be affirmative[55] – another reason for not granting immunity. Nevertheless, the Amsterdam Court of Appeals in a recent case decided otherwise. It found that committing such offences can never be the *task* of a head of state;[56] but task and capacity are quite different notions. Obviously the reasoning of the Allied Powers had been that it was no longer acceptable to let this kind of criminal go scot-free. It is clear that the Allies not only denied them immunity after their abdication or disposal but even wished to prosecute them when they were still in power.[57] There was some relation with the exception of superior orders (to be discussed below): when one did accept such an exception, it would be unacceptable that the source of

---

[54] ICTY, *Prosecutor v. Milosevic and others*, Case No. IT-99-37-I, Decision on Review of Indictment and Application for Consequential Orders, Judge Hunt, 24 May 1999; André Klip and Göran Sluiter (eds.), *Annotated Leading Cases of International Criminal Tribunals*, vol. 3, Intersentia, 2001, p. 39; and ICTY, *Prosecutor v. Milosevic and others*, Case No. IT-99-37-PT, Decision on Preliminary Motions, 8 Nov. 2001.

[55] In the same sense, de Lapradelle and Larnaude, 1919, p. 141, see *supra* note 16.

[56] Court of Appeal Amsterdam, *Bouterse Case*, LJN AA8395, Judgment, 20 November 2000, on the Surinam 'December murders'.

[57] Insofar they were supported by German authors, for example O. Poensgen, who made clear that (in his opinion) immunity only applied in constitutional law, not in international law. "*Bei uns in Deutschland tragen unsere Herrscher ... dem Feinde gegenüber auch mit ihrer eigenen Person die Verantwortung [...] und wir würden daher eine Ausnahmestellung fremder Staatsoberhaüpter [...] nicht verstehen*". O. Poensgen, "Strafe gegen Verletzungen des Völkerrechts", in *Deutsche Strafrechts-Zeitung*, 1914, vol. 1, cols. 634–639. Article 7 of the Charter of the Nuremberg Tribunal also excluded immunity; the same applies to Article 27 ICC Statute. The warrant against Omar al-Bashir was the first against a serving head of state. Compare the opinions of the British Law Lords in the Pinochet case (House of Lords, *Regina v. Bartle and the Commissioner of Police for the Metropolis and Others Ex Parte Pinochet*, Judgment, 24 March 1999) and, with a different result, the ICJ in the Congo case (ICJ, *Democratic Republic of the Congo v. Belgium*, Judgment, 14 February 2002).

---

these orders would enjoy immunity. For a head of state this would result in a special legal responsibility as supreme commander.[58]

8.7. *Ius ad Bellum*

What would have been the result of the prosecution under counts one and two as defined above? Since Aquinas, a large majority of authors, including Thomas Hobbes, Niccolò Macchiavelli, Grotius, de Vattel and Montesquieu, held that every state has the right to go to war against other states. Yes, they did try to restrict the actions of the state to a *bellum iustum* (to be translated as a *justified* war), but were nearly unanimous that the (heads of) states themselves were the only authorities who could decide if the war they started *was* justified. Immanuel Kant at least admonished the states *"ihre Streitigkeiten auf civile Art, gleichsam durch einen Proceß, nicht auf barbarische (nach Art der Wilden), nämlich durch Krieg, zu entscheiden"*,[59] but G.W.F. Hegel, the Prussian state philosopher, somewhat ingenuously thought that war would purify the nation. Neither did later authors, like Bluntschli,[60] Max Huber[61] and Emanuel von Ullmann,[62] deny the state a right to go to war if it saw fit to do so. Some of them, like Josef Kohler, thought that war is something *"jenseits von Recht und Unrecht"*;[63] Ernest Nys and W.T. Hall defended the thesis that war is not a subject of international law at all and therefore *cannot* be prohibited.[64] In any case a denial of *ius ad bellum* is not to be found in the pre-war literature nor in treaty law.[65] Article 1 of the second 1907 Hague Convention (*Convention concernant la limitation de l'emploi de la force*

---

[58] See Garner, 1920, vol. 2, p. 497ff., *supra* note 13.

[59] Immanuel Kant, *Die Metaphysik der Sitten*, 1797, §61.

[60] Bluntschli, 1874, see *supra* note 46.

[61] Max Huber, *Die Staatssuccession: Völkerrechtliche und Staatsrechtliche Praxis im XIX. Jahrhundert*, Duncker and Humblot, Leipzig, 1898.

[62] Emanuel von Ullmann, *Völkerrecht*, vol. 3 in the series *Das öffentliche Recht der Gegenwart*, Mohr, Tübingen, 1908.

[63] Josef Kohler, *Grundlagen des Völkerrechts: Vergangenheit, Gegenwart, Zukunft*, Enke, Stuttgart, 1918, p. 10.

[64] This seems to be an example of circular reasoning: by prohibiting war it would become automatically a subject of law!

[65] See also Paul Heilborn, "Völkerrecht", in Josef Kohler (ed.), *Encyklopädie der Rechtswissenschaft*, Duncker und Humblot, Leipzig, 1904, vol. 2, p. 973–1074, on p. 1056. More literature in Wilhelm G. Grewe, *Epochen der Völkerrechtsgeschichte*, Nomos Baden-Baden, 1984, pp. 623–28.

pour le recouvrement de dettes contractuelles, or Drago-Porter Convention) stipulated:

> *Les Puissances Contractantes sont convenues de ne pas avoir recours à la force armée pour le recouvrement de dettes contractuelles réclamées au Gouvernement d'un pays par le Gouvernement d'un autre pays comme dues à ses nationaux.*

This is unmistakably formulated as an exception to a general rule. We conclude that the Special Tribunal under Article 227 could not have found that waging war was a criminal act. In that case Wilhelm II had to be acquitted from count one of the indictment.

But would it have been as simple as that? During the war, in Great Britain, the US and the Netherlands, for example, plans had been contrived to lay a ban on war. But "[n]one of them proposed that war, following the slave trade, should cease to be a recognised and legitimate practice in international relations. None of them *prohibited* recourse to war, still less treated it as a crime or a common nuisance, to be visited with appropriate penalties".[66] This, however, changed after the Great War, when several highly respectable authors *did* defend the view that waging war was a criminal act, but mainly when looking for a way to punish Wilhelm II. They used simplifications like: "*Alors que l'infraction à la paix publique d'un Etat entraîne les peines les plus graves, on ne comprendrait pas qu'une atteinte à la paix du monde demeurât sans sanction*".[67]

Here we see the risks of criminal trials under international law *in optima forma*: without the strict *nullum crimen* rule, as rejected by us, it would be difficult not to give in to public opinion by creating new law and applying it retrospectively. The time was ripe for such a step. In 1927, at a Polish proposal, the General Assembly of the League of Nations adopted a resolution expressing the conviction that "a war of aggression can never serve as a means of settling international disputes and is, in consequence, an international crime" – as the last war had learned. In 1928 it found expression in the General Treaty for Renunciation of War

---

[66] Sir Alfred Zimmern, *The League of Nations and the Rule of Law, 1918–1935*, Macmillan, London, 1936, pp. 162–63.

[67] De Lapradelle and Larnaude, 1919, p. 149, see *supra* note 16. In the same style, Mérignhac and Lémonon, 1921, see *supra* note 25.

(better known as the Kellogg-Briand Pact). It is not quite unimaginable that the Tribunal would have taken the same point of view.

And what about infringement of the neutrality of Belgium and Luxembourg?[68] The neutrality of both countries had been guaranteed by the German Reich: in the case of Belgium by a treaty of 19 April 1839, concluded between Austria, France, Great Britain, Prussia and Russia; in the case of Luxembourg on 11 May 1867, in the Treaty of London, between the same countries, Belgium, Italy, Luxembourg and the Netherlands. Was the Reich nevertheless free to attack these countries at will, and make the given guarantees no more than scraps of paper? Or, from a somewhat different point of view, could a qualified kind of waging war be defined as a crime: attacking another country, only because this would be useful in conducting war against a third party? And would this breach of the law be more qualified by an explicit guarantee of neutrality? Some authors thought that even in such a case it could only be for the state itself to decide whether it should honour its word; but much support for this point of view cannot be found, at least not in the law. The international respect for and value of treaties as instruments for the arrangement of mutual relations as well as the act of violating an explicit guarantee would – in our view – be enough to conclude that Wilhelm II could at least foresee the wrongfulness of this action under the *nullum crimen* rule as developed above. For that reason we think it probable that Wilhelm II would have been convicted for committing *a supreme offence against international morality and the sanctity of treaties* by not respecting the international instruments guaranteeing the neutrality of Belgium. That also would have been something new, but not quite as revolutionary as criminalising the waging of war in general.

On 4 August 1914, a short time after the invasion of Belgium, the German Chancellor Theobald von Bethmann Hollweg said in parliament:

> *Wir sind in der Notwehr und Not kennt kein Gebot. Unsere Truppen haben ... vielleicht schon belgisches Gebiet betreten. Das widerspricht den Geboten des Völkerrechts. Die französische Regierung hat zwar in Brüssel erklärt, Belgiens Neutralität respektieren zu wollen, solange der Gegner sie respektiere. Wir wuszten aber, dasz Frankreich zum Einfall bereit stand. Frankreich konnte warten; wir*

---

[68] Compare Larry Zuckerman, *The Rape of Belgium: The Untold Story of World War 1*, New York University Press, New York, 2004.

aber nicht! Ein französischer Einfall in unsere Flanke am unteren Rhein hätte verhängnisvoll werden können. So waren wir gezwungen, uns über den berechtigten Protest der [...] belgischen Regierung hinwegzusetzen. Das Unrecht, das wir damit tun, werden wir wieder gutmachen, sobald unser militärisches Ziel erreicht ist. Wer so bedroht ist wie wir und um sein Höchstes kämpft, der darf nur daran denken, wie er sich durchhaut![69]

In other words, he disqualified the invasion as a wrong, which should be repaired after the expected Allied defeat, but at the same time he invoked a justification: military necessity or maybe even self-defence. Although he has been blamed later by many of his compatriots for the lack of clarity in and the inner contradictions within this statement, its purport was unmistakably that the invasion was justified by the circumstances. This defence had to be answered by the Tribunal.

In the *Instructions for the Government of the Armies of the U.S. in the Field* (General Order No. 100), drafted during the American Civil War for the armies of the Northern States by Professor Francis Lieber and confirmed by President Abraham Lincoln on 24 April 1863, we find in Article 15:

> Military necessity admits of such deception as does not involve the breaking of good faith either positively pledged, regarding agreements entered into during the war, or supposed by the modern war to exist.

In other words, military necessity does not justify breaking a solemn treaty. The leader of the German delegation to the Hague Peace Conference of 1907, Baron Marschall von Bieberstein, agreed:

> All conventional promises are obligatory in virtue of the general and almost commonplace principle that man must fulfil his contractual engagements.[70]

Nevertheless, many authors supported the opinion that military necessity

---

[69] A somewhat abridged version, cited in *Die deutschen Dokumente zum Kriegsausbruch*, vol. 4, p. 65; see also a more completely version in *American Journal of International Law*, 1914, no. 4.

[70] Cited in Arthur Eyffinger, *The 1907 Hague Peace Conference: 'The Conscience of the Civilized World'*, JudiCap, The Hague, 2007, p. 105.

may justify otherwise unlawful behaviour. For example, W.E. Hall[71] and the Permanent Court of Arbitration found:

> L'exception de la force majeure [...] est opposable en droit international public [...]; l'obligation pour un Etat d'exécuter les traités peut fléchir, si l'existence même de l'Etat vient à être en danger, si l'observation du devoir international est [...] self-destructive.[72]

However, in the case of a treaty that had been recently and solemnly confirmed, the Tribunal probably would require very cogent reasons of necessity, and it would not accept the German position that only the state concerned itself may decide whether such a situation exists. We think it highly improbable that the Tribunal would have found such very cogent reasons of necessity.

What about self-defence as a justification? Such a defence had not yet been developed under international law, but there is no reason why the Tribunal would use other criteria different to that under traditional criminal law: defence against an immediate, unlawful attack. The position would be that Germany had to defend itself against the imminent French attack by invading Belgium. Would the Tribunal have found such a defence proportionate? And would it have accepted such a justification after Germany itself had declared war on France? Probably not.

8.8. War Crimes: Command Responsibility

When speaking about the *ius in bello* we have to deal first with an objection against its binding force, as far as it was accumulated in the (fourth) Hague Convention respecting the Laws and Customs of War on Land, of 1907. Article 2 of this Convention said:

> Les dispositions contenues dans le Règlement (on the laws and customs of war on land) ainsi que dans la présente Convention, ne sont applicables qu'entre les puissances contractantes et seulement si les belligérants sont tous parties à la Convention.

---

[71] William Edward Hall, *A Treatise on International Law*, 7th ed. revised by A.P. Higgins, Clarendon Press, Oxford, 1917, p. 281, referring to Hugo Grotius, *De Jure Belli ac Pacis*, Book 2, Chapter 2, § 10.

[72] PCA, *Rusland v. Turkey*, Award, 11 November 1912; *Reports of International Arbitral Awards XI*, p. 443; *Scott's Hague Court Reports*, pp. 318, 546.

According to this *general participation clause* or *si omnes clause*, if taken literally, the *ius in bello*, as fixed by the Convention, would only apply in a war where all warfaring states were parties to and had ratified the Convention. The problem was that some of the states that took part in the Great War did *not* ratify the Convention, such as Brazil, Montenegro and Turkey. Should this lead to the conclusion that the Convention did not apply in the First World War? No. In our opinion, the Tribunal would have dismissed such an objection without much hesitation. It could mention three different reasons for doing so. In the first place we have to ask ourselves what the meaning of the *si omnes* clause was exactly. On this point hardly any doubt is possible: it had to prevent the situation where one state had to apply the Convention, while one of its opponent states was under no obligation to do so. In other words, it was a rather complicated way of expressing an extended requirement of reciprocity. When the war in Europe started, all states opposing each other (Austria-Hungary, Serbia, Russia, Germany, France and Great Britain) had ratified the Convention, so at least in that period the Convention was applicable. Did this change from the moment Turkey and Montenegro joined the struggle? We do not see an acceptable reason why this would be so as regards theatres of war where the extended reciprocity was not lacking. A second ground for dismissing the objection was that all the warfaring states were parties to the comparable Hague Convention with Respect to the Laws and Customs of War on Land of 1899, which did not contain a *si omnes* clause. From our point of view, for that matter, this could not make much of a difference, since reciprocity would have been a condition for the applicability of the 1899 Convention as well. A third reason for dismissing the objection would be that nearly all the rules that would have been breached belonged to the field of customary law.

There was another problem. The Germans often tried to justify their actions with a claim of reprisal, thus creating a vicious circle: a reprisal provokes another reprisal from the other side. The so-called 'right' of reprisal includes the right to decide whether the reprisal is justified and whether it is proportionate. This often leads to the situation that 'reprisal' is a mere justification for breaches of international law that one would have committed anyhow. Nevertheless in the first half of the twentieth century the existence of a right of reprisal was hardly contested, and such a right was invoked not only by Germany, but also by Great Britain (for example, when proclaiming Germany to be blockaded).

Germany especially invoked the right of reprisal with regard to the actions of so-called *franc-tireurs*. Obviously they labelled *franc-tireur* anyone who, not being a regular soldier or, if a regular soldier, not being in uniform, defended his country. This, however, is clearly wrong. Article 2 of the Regulations concerning the Laws and Customs of War on Land stated:

> *La population d'un territoire non occupé qui, à l'approche de l'ennemi, prend spontanément les armes pour combattre les troupes d'invasion sans avoir eu le temps de s'organiser conformément à l'article premier* [of these Regulations], *sera considérée comme belligérante si elle porte les armes ouvertement et si elle respecte les lois et coutumes de la guerre.*

In many cases, reprisals seem to have been taken in reaction to a legitimate defence by non-uniformed persons, and so contrary to Article 2 of the Regulations. The German point of view is only acceptable after the enemy country has been occupied. Often its source seems to have been not sheer malice, but a lack of knowledge, the German general staff having neglected to disseminate the text of the Regulations within the army. It simply abhorred the fact that warfare had been subjected to the law.

Neither during nor after the Great War has other evidence been found of state organised crime, although strong suspicions that the Germans intentionally terrorised the Belgians in order to induce them to give up their initial resistance have always lingered. However, proof of a shocking number of breaches of the rules of war – especially of war on land – has been supplied. In the words of the Commission on Responsibility "abundant evidence of outrages of every description" existed:[73] for example, killing or wounding enemies who had surrendered, declaring that no quarter would be granted, the destruction of enemy property without sufficient military necessity (all in Article 23 of the Regulations concerning the Laws and Customs of War on Land), pilfering (Article 47; see also Article 28) and the inflicting of collective punishments (Article 50). However, the only action of the ex-Kaiser himself that clearly constituted a breach of the Regulations was his public

---

[73] Commission on Responsibility, 1920, p. 113, see *supra* note 17.

incitement not to take prisoners and to grant no quarter.[74] How far would the Kaiser have been responsible for acts, not of his own doing, but of others under his command? He had superior command over all German forces, including those which breached the laws and customs of war – but would this have been sufficient?

Where there is no direct criminal act, criminal liability has to be based on indirect actions – or lack of actions. One could reason that the ex-Kaiser was obliged to 'prove' his command, and already for that reason alone was responsible. In this view a commander would simply have to bear all consequences of his function. This kind of general responsibility was defended by the German patriot Poensgen, who wanted to punish

> die Leitung der Polizei, die Ausschreitungen geduldet hat, Verwaltungsbehörden, welche den Franktireurkrieg unterstützt haben, Befehlshaber, in deren Truppen- oder Flottenteilen völkerrechtswidrige Handlungen vorgekommen sind.[75]

Of course he had his eye on the Belgian and French authorities, but this does not alter the principle. Even in this view, however, with its far-reaching consequences, an exception should be made for acts committed in secret, which the commander could not reasonably know, and which did not result from or were at least favoured by structures for whose existence he was directly responsible. But even such an amended version of general criminal responsibility is difficult to accept, and would probably not have been endorsed by the Tribunal. Of course, there were more possibilities. We mention three of them:

- Variant 1: Gross negligence in preventing infringements upon the laws of war more generally, for example by not taking care that all soldiers would know these laws (the written instructions to the German soldiers even denied the fourth 1907 Hague Convention its force of law) or, more specifically, by not acting on reported violations. This form of responsibility could be deduced from the

---

[74] See Admiral Georg von Müller in Walter Görlitz (ed.), *Regierte der Kaiser? Kriegstachebücher, Aufzeichnungen und Briefe des Chefs des Marine-Kabinetts*, 2nd ed., Musterschmidt, Göttingen, 1959, p. 65. The Admiral noted with disgust: "*Wie muß es im Kopfe dieses Mannes aussehen, dem der Krieg im Grunde genommen ganz zuwider ist? Was hat der Deutsche Kaiser dem Volke schon geschadet?*"

[75] *Ibid.*

1907 Hague Conventions. Those who accept such treaties, like the German Reich did, not only accept the obligation to follow the rules given therein, but also to enforce its fulfilment by anyone under their command. The personal negligence of Wilhelm II, however, would be rather hard to prove.

- Variant 2: Gross negligence by not properly investigating possible infringements and not combating and punishing reported misbehaviour. Already at the end of September 1914, the circles around the Kaiser knew from Allied sources of serious misbehaviour in Belgium. The head of the Kaiser's *Marine-kabinett*, Admiral Georg von Müller, confronted by what he saw as Allied propaganda, proposed an objective international investigation by the Hague Court of Arbitration. Although he was supported by the Reichskanzler, the Secretary of State Gottlieb von Jagow refused to follow him *"weil wir schon zu viel auf dem Kerbholz haben"*.[76] Would a court doubt that the Kaiser himself knew about all this and leave it at that? Or would the later German investigations, which resulted in a highly apologetic report that laid all blame on the Belgians and their government,[77] be accepted as a sufficient measure?

- Variant 3: Restricted (or indirect) command (or superior) responsibility: responsibility for any acts one could have known and could have prevented (but, by one's own fault, did not know, and in any case did not prevent).[78] Roots of this point of view can be found in the report of the Commission on Responsibility. The Commission held responsible

---

[76] Görlitz, 1959, pp. 62–63, see *supra* note 74.

[77] Germany, Ministry of Foreign Affairs, *Die völkerrechtswidrige Führung des belgischen Volkskrieges*, Berlin, 1915.

[78] See, for example, the Yamashita case after the Second World War. United States Military Commission, "Trial of General Tomoyuki Yamashita", in UN War Crimes Commission, *Law Reports of Trials of War Criminals*, vol. IV, p. 1; Elies van Sliedregt, *The Criminal Responsibility of Individuals for Violations of International Humanitarian Law*, T.M.C. Asser Press, The Hague, 2003; Robert Cryer, Hakan Friman, Darryl Robinson and Elizabeth Wilmshurst, *An Introduction to International Criminal Law and Procedure*, Cambridge University Press, New York, 2007, chapter 15.8; A.H.J. Swart, "De strafrechtelijke aansprakelijkheid van meerderen in het internationale humanitaire recht", in M. Dolman, P. Duyx and S. Stolwijk (eds.), *Geleerde Lessen: Liber amicorum Simon Stolwijk*, WLP, Nijmegen, 2007, pp. 213–34; and Maarten Daman, "Aansprakelijkheid van militaire en civiele leiders", in *Internationaal Humanitair recht in de Kijker*, Flanders Red Cross, Mechelen, 2008, pp. 57–68 (all with further literature).

> all authorities, civil or military, belonging to enemy countries, however high their position may have been, without distinction of rank, including the heads of states, who ordered, or, with knowledge thereof and with power to intervene, abstained from preventing or taking measures to prevent, putting an end to or repressing, violations of the laws or customs of war (it being understood that no such abstention should constitute a defence for the actual perpetrators).

This underlines that command responsibility is definitely not a post-Second World War concept. For this kind of command responsibility, one could require evidence that the breaches of the laws and customs of war resulted from, or at least were favoured by, structures or decisions for which the commander was directly responsible. The ex-Kaiser could be reproached because he did not take care that the army received sufficient instruction on the Regulations concerning the Laws and Customs of War on Land, or maybe that he did partake in spreading wrong conceptions of these Regulations. Another relevant reproach could be that he accepted the use of insufficiently trained and insufficiently commanded troops. And a third could be that he, after breaches of the Regulations had been reported, neglected to instigate a thorough and impartial investigation into the truth of the allegations that were made against the German army. Whatever position the Tribunal would have taken, it would have created something new.

8.9. Submarine Warfare

The discussions on the war at sea would have been very difficult. To give but one example: Was submarine warfare against the *ius in bello*? Did a *ius in bello* exist for war on and under the seas? Great Britain had been successful in preventing treaty law on this subject. It became a great naval power without substantial treaty rules. Doubts as to whether such rules would become cumbersome in maintaining its supreme position led many Englishmen to reject any rules at all. In general, the attitude of the British government was hesitant. It took the initiative, for instance, for the London Naval Conference of 1908 and 1909, which led to the Declaration of London, containing 71 articles on the laws of naval warfare. The British government accepted the Declaration, but under pressure of public opinion a bill embodying its provisions was rejected by the House of

Lords. In his memoirs Lloyd George later commented that it was "luckily rejected, for had it been in operation during the War, it would have deprived us of our most effective weapon against Germany"[79] – probably meaning the blockade of German ports. As a result, at the outbreak of the war in 1914, not one of the parties represented at the Conference had ratified this instrument in accordance with the prescribed procedure. After the declaration of war, the German Reich notified its willingness to apply the London Declaration on the basis of reciprocity, but Britain refused to promise that it would observe all the rules it contained (22 August 1914). France and Russia followed this bad example.[80] Nevertheless, all warring states did recognise parts of the Declaration as being binding – but not always the same parts, and not without changing their position from time to time. Given these facts, it is highly doubtful whether a sufficiently clear and generally accepted *corpus* of customary law on this subject could be defined. However, if it found so, the Tribunal was sure to be severely criticised by the general public. It probably could not convict Wilhelm II on these points without creating new law on naval warfare, and it would have crossed the limits of the *nullum crimen* principle as described above.

Thus far about this question in general. More specifically, the Tribunal would be faced with the question of whether declaring unconditional submarine warfare, given its terrible consequences, was a crime under international law, while declaring war in general was not. The Tribunal would certainly be confronted with the sinking of the *Lusitania* on 7 May 1915, which resulted in the death of more than 2,000 passengers and crew. Although it could be aware of the fact that, because of a shortage of shipping, the Dutch government loaded strategic goods (brass, nickel) on passenger steamers as well,[81] it would probably have accepted the British and American position that the *Lusitania* was only carrying peaceful passengers, and no contraband. And maybe it would find that the carrying of contraband did not make much of a difference: Is torpedoing ships with thousands of passengers not always a crime? And what about special aspects, like the intentional destruction of neutral ships, and the order to German submarines not to rescue enemy crews,

---

[79] Lloyd George, 1938, vol. 1, p. 59, see *supra* note 1.

[80] Garner, 1920, vol. 1, pp. 28–30, see *supra* note 13.

[81] Acknowledged in the memoirs of the former Dutch War Minister Nicolaas Bosboom, *In moeilijke omstandigheden*, Noorduyn, Gorinchem, 1933, p. 111, but certainly no secret for the American authorities.

because this would endanger themselves in too high a degree?

8.10. Remarks on Procedural Aspects

When discussing the applicable rules of procedure in a trial before the Tribunal, we have to be aware that the ex-Kaiser would possibly have followed the example of Charles I and not have defended himself against the accusations, because in doing so he would have accepted and justified, or at least legitimated, the trial against him, including a possible conviction as the outcome of it.[82] His first line of defence would in any case have been a denial of the jurisdiction of the Tribunal.

Substantive (criminal) law has to be realised and applied in specific criminal cases in a criminal procedure on the basis of a detailed indictment, and a criminal procedure and its outcome are only legitimate if the trial has been fair. At the time of the Versailles Treaty, there were no primary or secondary sources of international law that contained any rule about criminal procedure before an international tribunal, as foreseen in Article 227 of the Treaty. For example, there were no rules of procedure or rules on the use of evidence (including a guilty plea and the use of hearsay evidence). The Commission on Responsibility, dealing with the Tribunal as meant by Article 228 of the Treaty, wrote succinctly: "The tribunal shall determine its own procedure".[83] The authors of the Treaty obviously took the same approach with regard to Article 227: the procedure had to be "judge made".

As such, the fact that the procedure had to be "judge made" would not have been a strong judicial, fundamental obstacle in offering the ex-Kaiser a fair and legitimate trial. There was no international obligation to only use foreseeable and accessible rules of procedure, well codified or otherwise elaborated prior to the trial – nor does such an obligation exist in our times.[84] The principle of non-retroactivity of penal law, the dogma

---

[82] Was the trial against Jesus not the more unsatisfactory for those who accused him, just because he did not defend himself?

[83] Commission on Responsibility, 1920, p. 122, see *supra* note 17.

[84] Article 7 ECHR and Article 15 ICCPR require that a court should be established by law. However, neither treaty incorporates an article on the prohibition of retroactivity as far as procedural law is concerned. In the ICCPR such a prohibition is expressly refrained from: Safferling, 2001, p. 87, see *supra* note 48. He admitted that another outcome could not be expected because otherwise the ICCPR would have been disapproving Nuremberg and Tokyo. Only the American Convention of Human Rights stated differently on this point

of *nullen crimen sine lege*, relates to substantive criminal law only.[85] Moreover, an open procedure and the use of more implicit and/or inherent judge made rules and decisions on the specific facts and circumstances of the case, for instance on criminal evidence, may even lead to a fairer trial than the 'closed' use of well-codified previous procedure rules. This openness in creating and applying rules of evidence and procedure to create a fair process during trial would have been of some importance for the unique international tribunal, as was foreseen in Article 227 of the Treaty. The Tribunal had no predecessors to rely on; it had to find its own way to a fair trial.

What would have been the best way to secure Wilhelm II a fair trial? In his case, the fairness of the procedure might even be of more importance than it seems at first sight. As stated above, there is a certain ambiguity in Article 227 of the Treaty: it is an attempt to constitute a criminal charge, based on moral and political grounds (supreme offence against international morality and the sanctity of treaties), but in legal proceedings. In this way, the Allied Powers sought to strengthen the case for further 'outlawry' of war (*ius ad bellum*) and towards the introduction of penal sanctions and the possibility of applying them, thus trying to establish the notion of (individual) responsibility for starting a war itself. In this attempt and in this approach, the fairness of the procedure and its legitimacy is a vital element. As Cornelis A. Pompe states the French position:

> According to which the ex-Emperor could be brought to trial for violations of international law before a special tribunal

---

("competent, independent and impartial tribunal, *previously* established by law"). The conclusion of Safferling, *ibid.*, pp. 87–88, that it is from the perspective of human rights law advisable that the prohibition of retroactivity by procedural law is incorporated, even before the incriminated crime is committed, can be questioned. It is interesting that by the ICTY the formation of the procedural law by codification is dedicated to the judges, as was envisioned by the Commission of the trial of Wilhelm II. The judges of the ICC have also the possibility of changing the rules by codification. Reportedly, this flexibility has worked in favour of the substantive and dynamic development of the (international) criminal procedure, certainly because the judges also involved prosecutors and defenders by further designing the procedural law.

[85] Germany, in offering the Allied Powers criminal procedures before the *Reichsgericht* in Leipzig as an alternative to extradition of the Germans on the Article 228 list, expected to ignore the influence of statute-related limitations and even the outcome of former criminal procedures, may they have ended in conviction or acquittal, thus accepting a violation of the *ne bis in idem* principle. Schwengler, 1982, p. 319, see *supra* note 2.

> which by its composition and authority would at the same time, in a most solemn verdict, advance the moral and political importance of proceedings that would never the less be legal.[86]

Apart from composition and authority, the fairness of the proceedings is the third important pillar of making the trial against Wilhelm 'legal'; moving forward towards the crime of launching war could only be done successfully if the procedure were fair and legitimate.

The Treaty contained two different elements of legitimate criminal procedure. The Tribunal should be composed of five judges, appointed by each of the Member States mentioned in Article 227. In the view of the Allied Powers, obviously, the demand for 'judges' seemed to be enough guarantee for the independence and impartiality of the Tribunal, a guarantee that is an important element for a fair, that is non-political, trial in the meaning of not being influenced by politicians. The demand for 'judges' of (only) the five main powers under the victors seemed to be enough guarantee against '*Siegerjustiz*' (victor's justice). As stated earlier, Lloyd George even suggested inviting the young German Republic to participate in the Tribunal. That is an interesting option in the light of the further development of international criminal law and criminal procedure.

For Lloyd George, a sufficient guarantee of the right of defence was a specific and vital element of the trial to come. This guarantee for procedural rights is expressed in Article 227 of the Treaty: "thereby assuring him the guarantees essential to the right of defence". The authors of the Treaty took the above quoted remark of the Commission on Responsibility rather literally!

As far as the accusation against Wilhelm II was based on Article 228 of the Treaty, we may assume that the guarantee of Article 229 ("In every case the accused will be entitled to name its own counsel") would also be applicable. The right to choose one's own defence counsel can be seen as a guarantee "essential to the right of defence". But which other guarantees would be covered by the Treaty? The Treaty was, apart from the quoted parts, silent on this point. It is easily conceived why in the days immediately after the Great War, no international sources or rules existed for criminal procedures before an international tribunal as indicated in the

---

[86] Cornelis A. Pompe, *Aggressive War: An International Crime*, Martinus Nijhof, The Hague, 1953, p. 168.

Treaty, nor for essential procedural rights of the accused. Not before 1950 was a clear text available.[87] Nevertheless, in those days, some constitutions and other fundamental documents contained some rudimentary provisions. However, there is a big difference between, for instance, the American tradition (fundamental rights on criminal procedure in the Constitution of 1787 and its Amendments) and the French/continental tradition (hardly any of these rights can be found in the *Declaration des droits de l'homme et du citoyen* of 1789). But the Tribunal could have inferred or derived its procedural provisions from the different Codes of criminal procedure.

It would have been possible to line up a catalogue of fundamental rights of the accused in criminal procedure that, back in 1919–1920, already belonged to the common opinion of the different national systems of law. It can be argued that in 1919 there were already certain established, generally derived principles of fair trial found in every national regulation, which incorporated rules on criminal procedure based on common sense. Christoph Safferling[88] mentions the right of a public hearing, the doctrine of an oral hearing which guarantees that all the relevant documents are accessible to the accused, the right of the presence of the accused (see earlier stated comments on the (im)possibility of a trial *in absentia* of Wilhelm II), the doctrine of equality of arms, the presumption of innocence, and the guarantee of a trial within reasonable time. In this respect of fundamental rights of the accused in criminal procedure, the principle of publicity of proceedings (not behind 'closed doors') and of the pronouncement of the judgment can also be mentioned. A right to appeal seems not to be part of this catalogue in those days, at least not as a right for the accused to a complete new hearing of the case and to a new decision on points of facts and points of law equally.

A more important, non-legal obstacle is that these elements can be implicated by entirely different process models and traditions (inquisitorial or accusatorial process; trial by professionals or a jury trial, etc.). The question arises whether the principal signatory states could have come to a compromise. In elaborating these fundamental rights of the accused in criminal procedure, the Tribunal would have had the 'challenge' of choosing between the different ways these rights existed in

---

87   See Article 6 ECRM and Article 14 ICCBPR.
88   Safferling, 2001, pp. 372–74, see *supra* note 48.

the laws on criminal procedure in the different law families and traditions.[89] A jury trial is excluded in the Treaty as such, but would the Tribunal have chosen an accusatorial or adversarial or a more inquisitorial, or even a mixed approach? It might be relevant to note that a criminal procedure is not as such 'fairer' in one of the approaches than in another.[90] Nevertheless, if Wilhelm II were confronted with a model of procedure that would be completely new or 'strange' to him, the right to have the time and facilities to prepare the trial and the right to defend himself in trial might be at stake. Here, the question arises whether boundaries are reached or exceeded when Wilhelm II, in the context of the Treaty-established right of defence, was to be confronted with a process model that entirely diverged from the German legal tradition.

For the exercise of Willhelm II's right of defence, it would be vital that the defence counsel be seen and accepted as an 'organ of the Tribunal', having such access to the powers of the Tribunal as mentioned in Article 227 of the Versailles Treaty, to co-operate with the States and possibly use the authority of the Tribunal in this respect, for instance in obtaining relevant documents: a 'defence request' should be considered as a 'court request'.[91]

In conclusion, the specific way in which the Tribunal operated would have been as important as general rules in guaranteeing Wilhelm II a fair trial. The (lack of) procedural law cannot be considered as the main obstacle to the implementation of Article 227 of the Treaty of Versailles.

8.11. The Sanctions

The Versailles Treaty left it to the Tribunal "to fix the punishment which it considers should be imposed" (*Il lui appartiendra de determiner la peine qu'il estimera devoir être appliquée*). This covers all sanctions from a simple fine to imprisonment for life and even death. But the Tribunal not only had to determine what types of sanctions could be imposed but also to fix their terms, for instance in case it decided that (temporary)

---

[89] The procedural order for the Nuremberg Tribunal was exclusively based on the Anglo-American (adversarial) system; *ibid.*, p. 33.

[90] See, among others, ECHR, *Taxquet v. Belgium*, App. No. 926/05, Judgment, 16 November 2010, paras. 83–84.

[91] Interestingly enough, most international courts of 'our' days do not recognise the defence as an organ of the court.

imprisonment "should be imposed". It is clear that in this respect Article 227 differed from Article 228. As Article 227 dealt with new and, up to those years, unknown crimes, an international tribunal had to be introduced, and there was no sanction prescribed in any national or international law. Article 228, on the contrary, in dealing with violations of the laws and customs of war, not only regarded a much more clearly defined part of the law but could also rely on existing military tribunals that could apply existing national laws. Therefore, in Article 228, the tribunal could also refer to punishments "laid down by law". It is to be noted that, in those days, military law in nearly all countries relied rather heavily on the death penalty.

Article 227 might be criticised for violation of legality, especially of the *nullum poena sine lege* principle. However, this principle has not the same theoretical 'weight' concerning sanctions as it has concerning criminal liability as such. Under Article 27 of the Charter for the Nuremberg Tribunal, and even under Article 77 of the Rome Statute of the ICC, there is a certain open discretion for the tribunal to fix the penalty, although in the ICC Statute some boundaries have been fixed. The criticism from the Japanese and American members of the Commission on Responsibility on Article 227, derived from this *nullum crimen sine lege* principle, was indeed directed at the definition of the (proposed) 'crimes', not the determination of sanctions. Nevertheless, that Article 227 of the Treaty did not even indicate what kind of sanction the Tribunal might fix is, in today's view, a rather weak point.[92]

Are there any more specific indications about the sanction(s) that might have been at stake? The Allied Powers wanted to assure Wilhelm II of a fair trial, as part of their attempt to put him on trial in a judicial (criminal) process for allegations on – more or less – moral grounds. One can argue that the guarantee that the sanction would not be (too) disproportionate in relation to the facts and crimes to which an accused has been found guilty may come within the scope of fair trial, where the "guarantees essential to the right of the defence", underlined in Article 227 of the Treaty, are also related to the fact finding and discussion about these facts during trial, the determination of the appropriate sanction, the

---

[92] For elaboration and discussion of the pros and cons of the *nulla poena* rule as applicable to the discussed provision of Article 227 of the Versailles Treaty and to (modern) crimes under international law in general, see Gallant 2009, pp. 56–59 and chapter 7.C. respectively, see *supra* note 43.

extent of punishment and the terms of imprisonment, etc.[93]

Could the deportation of Wilhelm II to – for instance – the Falkland Islands have been an appropriate sanction, and a sanction that he might have expected? This would hardly be the case. Except in France, at that time deportation was not a criminal punishment under any national criminal law any more. Moreover, the deportation of Napoleon was mainly a safety measure because this French ex-Emperor was still considered a danger to international order and peace.

Given the situation in Germany and Wilhelm II's exile in the Netherlands, it is understandable that this was not an argument that was in any way taken into consideration.[94] We hear from Lloyd George that Clemenceau, in particular, was not very interested in punishments. His main wish was that Wilhelm II would be branded and ostracised as a "universal outlaw".[95] Garner came to the same conclusion by simple legal reasoning. He took the view that Wilhelm II, if he was not prosecuted and convicted for a crime under the Penal Code as (in his view) required by Article 228 of the Versailles Treaty, could not be sentenced to "punishments laid down by law", "and since the law of nations prescribes no penalties for offences against international morality or the sanctity of treaties", the Tribunal would have but one option, to wit "a formal pronouncement, stigmatizing [Wilhelm II] as a treaty breaker [...] and holding him up to the execration of mankind".[96] But Garner was wrong. The Commission on Responsibility asked for "such punishment or punishments as may be imposed for such an offence or offences by any court in any country represented on the tribunal or in the country of the convicted person"[97] – and there is no reason to suppose that the Treaty makers took another position, although they also wanted to try Wilhelm II for supreme offences against international morality and the sanctity of treaties.

Had the Tribunal, in the case of a conviction, to apply any sanction? Or might a conviction without sanction have been an option too? Do the

---

[93] Safferling, 2001, pp. 314–18, see *supra* note 48.

[94] Pompe, 1953, p. 169, see *supra* note 86.

[95] *Ibid.*, p. 98.

[96] James Garner, "Punishment of Offenders Against the Laws and Customs of War", in *American Journal of International Law*, 1920, vol. 14, pp. 70–94, on p. 92.

[97] Commission on Responsibility, 1920, p. 122, see *supra* note 17.

words "fix the punishment which it considers should be imposed" allow for this possibility? One might argue that the Allied Powers were primarily interested in making clear that waging war and breaching a guaranteed neutrality were criminal under international law and would have accepted "a formal condemnation", as had been proposed by the Commission on Responsibility. But would this, at that time, really have been a realistic option? Anyway, the combination of Articles 227 and 228 gave the Tribunal as much liberty as the Nuremberg Tribunal[98] and the ICTY would later have. It really is a pity that we do not know how it would have used this liberty.

8.12. Conclusion

It seems clear that, barring the (rather improbable) possibility of a complete acquittal, the Tribunal would have created an important piece of international (criminal) law. What we have presented only offers a very global outline of what might have been expected. That Kaiser Wilhelm II was never tried, and that the intended Tribunal was not even constituted, meant that a number of important and interesting questions rested unanswered until after the Second World War. We mention but two: the status of *Not kennt kein Gebot*, and the status of *Befehl ist Befehl*. It also meant that even in 1949, lawyers could insist that until 1945 crimes against peace and crimes against humanity were not generally accepted as such, and therefore according to international law could not be punished.[99]

Does this mean that the decisions of the Tribunal could have made history take a different turn? We do not think so. The power of the Courts, and of law in general, is limited. The deterrent effect of convictions in the field of crimes against humanity is probably not much more than zero. But the Tribunal would certainly have levelled the path for the

---

[98] The Charter of this Tribunal (Article 27) mentioned the death penalty or any other punishment that the Tribunal would think fit. See the comment by Quaritsch, 1994, p. 162, see *supra* note 40: "*Das Kriegsvölkerrecht enthält jedoch keine 'poena', nämlich keinen Strafrahmen, der Richter ist in diesen Fällen auf die Strafdrohungen des nationalen Rechts angewiesen. Man kann nicht annehmen, das (Gericht) könne die Strafe zwischen Geldbusse und Tot durch Erhängen frei und ohne normative Grundlage wählen und festsetzen*".

[99] For example, Günther Lummert, *Die Strafverfahren gegen Deutsche im Ausland wegen 'Kriegsverbrechen'*, ARKD, Hamburg, 1949, p. 26.

Nuremberg and Tokyo Tribunals; and perhaps it could have boosted morality. In any case it would have considerably accelerated developments in criminal law.

A last word. The Second World War was waged against an evil that had overwhelmed Germany: racism and its proponents. Although Allied propaganda often presented the Great War as being waged against comparable evils, militarism and Pan-Germanism,[100] it was in fact rather different, being carried on against the aspirations of a large majority of the German people. Although Pan-German thinking had a strong influence on German politics in the decade before 1914, and the German Constitution, in comparison with most other European states, left much power in the hands of the Kaiser, as commander in chief and at least a *symbol* of militarism, it can hardly be denied that the Pan-Germans formed a (albeit noisy) minority without real power, and that the militarists only took over the reins during the war.

The decision to engage in a deadly struggle with the Entente was backed by a large majority in parliament and in the streets, mainstream socialists included. As a consequence, the political and military leadership was much more representative of public opinion than during the Second World War. For that reason, prosecution of political and military leaders would have felt like a prosecution of Germany itself. This has been amply demonstrated by the reactions of the German army, the German government and the German parliament to the Allied list of persons who should be extradited under Article 228. In itself, it would be insufficient reason not to prosecute, but it would give the trial quite another character compared to the later Nuremberg trials. Perverted nationalistic ideas like those propagated by Kohler, and those uttered sometimes by Wilhelm II himself, really started prospering in the time of Hindenburg and Hitler; the turn of their protagonists to stand trial still had to come. So one has to keep in mind that the type of defendants in Nuremberg was quite different from the people the Allied Powers intended to prosecute after 1918. In our opinion it is highly improbable that this would not have influenced the outcome – like it did in Leipzig.

---

[100] Pan-German theories denoted that German *Kultur* and *Blut* were superior, implying that Germans should rule the world.

Postscript: Not Elba, But Doorn!

In 2013–2014 a small group of Dutch lawyers and historians organised a mock trial of ex-Kaiser Wilhelm II, as they thought it could have been held around 1925. The ex-Kaiser was acquitted from starting an aggressive war, but convicted for ordering the invasion of Belgium, qualified as being a supreme offence against international morality and the sanctity of treaties under Article 227 of the Treaty. He was sentenced to a lifelong stay in the castle of Doorn (Netherlands), under prohibition of fulfilling official charges of any kind.

9

The Istanbul and Leipzig Trials:
Myth or Reality?

Joseph Rikhof[*]

9.1. Introduction

The narrative most commonly associated with the efforts to bring persons accused of war crimes to justice after the First World War goes something likes this. Pursuant to the provisions of the progressive peace treaties of Versailles[1] and Sèvres,[2] the victorious powers in this conflict could put on trial nationals of Germany and Turkey before their military tribunals, and where war crimes were committed against the nationals of more than one Allied Power, these treaties envisaged the possibility of an international tribunal. However, due to the general public post-war fatigue in Britain and France, combined with the return to the traditional policy of international isolationism on the part of the United States (US), nationals of Germany and Turkey were not tried by these tribunals but instead handed over to their own states to be put on trial there. The outcome of these trials was wholly unsatisfactory in terms of providing appropriate justice for the serious war crimes committed by these nationals, resulting directly in the creation of the International Military Tribunal ('IMT') in Nuremberg.[3]

---

[*] **Joseph Rikhof** is a part-time Professor at the University of Ottawa. He received his Ph.D. from the Irish Centre for Human Rights. He teaches the course International Criminal Law at the University of Ottawa. He is Senior Counsel, Manager of the Law with the Crimes against Humanity and War Crimes Section of the Department of Justice, Canada. He was a visiting professional with the International Criminal Court in 2005 while also serving as Special Counsel and Policy Advisor to the Modern War Crimes Section of the Department of Citizenship and Immigration between 1998 and 2002. He has written over 40 articles as well as his book, *The Criminal Refugee: The Treatment of Asylum Seekers with a Criminal Background in International and Domestic Law*.

[1] Treaty of Peace between the Allied and Associated Powers and Germany, 9 July 1919, Articles 227–29.

[2] Treaty of Peace Between the Allied and Associated Powers and the Ottoman Empire, Articles 226–27, 230.

[3] Part of this narrative can be found in the following writings: M. Cherif Bassiouni, "International Criminal Investigations and Prosecutions: From Versailles to Rwanda" and William A. Schabas, "International Sentencing: From Leipzig (1923) to Arusha (1996)", in M. Cherif Bassiouni (ed.), *International Criminal Law*, vol. III. *International*

The purpose of this chapter is to critically examine this narrative in all its aspects. In order to do so, the political and legal developments leading up to those trials, including the negotiations of not only the Versailles and Sèvres treaties but also the 1923 Treaty of Lausanne between the new Turkish government and the Allied Powers, which contained no provisions regarding trials at all, will be addressed. A similar approach will be taken in respect to similar contexts after the trials, such as the climate leading up to the London Charter[4] after the Second World War. The largest portion of this chapter, however, will be occupied with an analysis of the Istanbul and Leipzig trials themselves. This will be both from the more general aspects, such as of the number of trials, their outcome, the legal issues decided and their reasoning, but also more specifically concerning the possible application of the nascent war crimes law and the impact of these decisions on the future development of international criminal law.

9.2. Prologue

The notion that persons involved in the commission of war crimes and crimes against humanity should be held personally responsible was not new when the Statute of the **International Criminal Court ('ICC')** was agreed upon in 1998. It was not a novel approach when the international criminal tribunals for the former Yugoslavia and Rwanda were established by the United Nations Security Council in 1993 and 1994 respectively. It was not even a revolutionary concept after the Second World War when the International Military Tribunals in Nuremberg and Tokyo began their work. No. The idea that violations of the laws of war

---

Enforcement, Brill, Leiden, 1999, pp. 38–39 and pp. 171–72; Margaret MacMillan, *Paris 1919: Six Months That Changed the World*, Random House, Toronto, 2001, pp. 163–65; Claus Kreß, "Versailles – Nuremberg – The Hague: Germany and International Criminal Law", in *International Lawyer*, 2006, vol. 40, pp. 16–20; Shane Darcy, *Collective Responsibility and Accountability Under International Law*, Brill, Leiden, 2007, pp. 191–92; Steven R. Ratner, Jason S. Abrams and James L. Bischoff, *Accountability for Human Rights Atrocities in International Law: Beyond the Nuremberg Legacy*, Oxford University Press, Oxford, 2009, p. 6; Robert Cryer, Hakan Friman, Darryl Robinson and Elizabeth Wilmshurst, *An Introduction to International Criminal Law and Procedure*, Cambridge University Press, Cambridge, 2010, p. 110; Kai Ambos, *Treatise on International Criminal Law*, vol. 1, *Foundations and General Part*, Oxford University Press, Oxford, 2013, pp. 2–4.

4   London Agreement of 8 August 1945 attaching the Charter of the International Military Tribunal.

---

or the dictates of humanity could be separated from the normal reach of public international law by holding states responsible, and instead could be levelled against the very individuals who had breached those norms by other institutions than the states of which they were nationals, is almost a hundred years old.

Like the first calls to provide solace to the millions of victims of Germany and Japan during the Second World War, the call to put perpetrators of very serious crimes on trial galvanised during the First World War as a result of a number of atrocities already committed by German and Turkish nationals very early during this conflict. In particular, the crimes against the Armenian population in 1915 by Turkey, which later came to be known as genocide, as well as the unlimited U-boat warfare in the Atlantic, the treatment of British prisoners of war in internment camps and the abuse of civilians in France and Belgium throughout the war, caused a popular outcry taken over by the Allied negotiators of the peace treaties with Germany and Turkey.[5]

The issue of responsibility for the commission of war crimes was of such great importance to the Paris Peace Conference that in January 1919 a special Commission on the Responsibility of the Authors of the War and on Enforcement of Penalties ('Commission') was established by the Supreme Council of the Paris Peace Conference, with the purpose of both setting out the legal parameters of responsibility as well as charging named individuals

---

[5] James F. Willis, *Prologue to Nuremberg: Politics and Diplomacy of Punishing War Criminals of the First World War (Contributions in Legal Studies)*, Greenwood, Westport, CT, 1982, pp. 27–33, 38–39; Jackson Nyamuya Maogoto, *War Crimes and Realpolitik: International Justice from World War I to the 21st Century*, Lynne Rienner, Boulder, CO, 2004, pp. 43–44; Gary Jonathan Bass, *Stay the Hand of Vengeance: The Politics of War Crimes Tribunals*, Princeton University Press, Princeton, NJ, 2000, pp. 58–59, 60–64, 83, 94–96; Samantha Power, *'A Problem from Hell': America and the Age of Genocide*, Basic Books, New York, 2002, pp. 5–14; Vahakn N. Dadrian and Taner Akçam, *Judgment at Istanbul: The Armenian Genocide Trials*, Berghahn Books, New York, 2011, pp. 19–22. The outrage with respect to massacres of the Armenian population was reflected at the official level by a statement by the governments of France, Britain and Russia on 24 May 1915 denouncing these acts as "crimes against humanity and civilisation", for which the members of the Turkish government would be held responsible; see United Nations War Crimes Commission, *History of the United Nations War Crimes Commission and the Development of the Laws of War*, His Majesty's Stationery Office, London, 1948, p. 35; Willis, 1982, pp. 25–27; Alan Kramer, "The First Wave of International War Crimes Trials: Istanbul and Leipzig", in *European Review*, 2006, vol. 14, no. 4, p. 442; Bass, 2000, pp. 114–17; Dadrian and Akçam, 2011, pp. 17, 22, 134.

for specific war crimes.[6] The final Report of this Commission provided a lengthy list of behaviour, which violated the laws of war, based on the 1907 Hague Convention,[7] as well as, for the first time, setting out criminal liability for the offence of conducting aggressive war (with respect to Germany)[8] and the violations of the clear dictates of humanity or crimes against humanity (with respect to Turkey).[9] In addition to providing liability for particular crimes, the Commission also recommended the establishment of an international tribunal to prosecute war criminals.[10]

While the majority of the Commission clearly intended to develop international law beyond the 1907 confines, this approach was by no means unanimous as two members of the Commission, Japan and especially the US, expressed concerns about a number of aspects of the majority Report, such as the notion of 'crimes against humanity' as a legal concept and putting on trial a head of state for starting a war.[11] In

---

[6]   The Commission had 15 members (hence the other name used for it, the Commission of Fifteen): two from Britain, France, Italy, Japan and the US and one from Belgium, Greece, Poland, Romania and Serbia. For a background of the work of the various subcommittees of this Commission and the approaches taken by its members, see United Nations War Crimes Commission, 1948, pp. 32–33, see *supra* note 5; Willis, 1982, pp. 69–74, see *supra* note 5; John Horne and Alan Kramer, *German Atrocities, 1914: A History of Denial*, Yale University Press, New Haven, 2001, pp. 330–32; Jürgen Matthäus, "The Lessons of Leipzig: Punishing German War Criminals after the First World War", in Patricia Heberer and Jürgen Matthäus (eds.), *Atrocities on Trial: Historical Perspectives on the Politics of Prosecuting War Crimes*, University of Nebraska Press, Lincoln, 2008, pp. 3–9; Harry M. Rhea, *The United States and International Criminal Tribunals: An Introduction*, Intersentia, Cambridge, 2012, pp. 21–41.

[7]   Reprinted in *American Journal of International Law*, 1920, vol. 14, pp. 112–15; see also London International Assembly, *Reports of Commission I (formerly Commission II) on the Trial and Punishment of War Criminals* ('Reports of Commission I'), London, 1944, pp. 142–44; United Nations War Crimes Commission, 1948, pp. 33–41, 236–38, see *supra* note 5; James W. Garner, "Punishment of Offenders Against the Laws and Customs of War", in *American Journal of International Law*, 1920, vol. 14, nos. 1/2, pp. 90–94; Rhea, 2012, pp. 36–38, see *supra* note 6; Maogoto, 2004, p. 48, see *supra* note 5; Matthew Lippman, "Nuremberg: Forty Five Years Later", in *Connecticut Journal of International Law*, 1991/92, vol. 7, p. 1, reproduced in Guénaël Mettraux, *Perspectives on the Nuremberg Trial*, Oxford University Press, Oxford, 2008, pp. 495–96.

[8]   *American Journal of International Law*, 1920, pp. 116–17, see *supra* note 7.

[9]   *Ibid.*, pp. 122–23.

[10] *Ibid.*, pp. 121–24; see also United Nations War Crimes Commission, 1948, pp. 263–64, 436, see *supra* note 5.

[11] *American Journal of International Law*, 1920, pp. 135–36 (for the US) and pp. 151–52 (for Japan), see *supra* note 7; for the US position, see also United Nations War Crimes Commission, 1948, pp. 36–37, 39–40, 238–39, 437, *supra* note 5; Willis, 1982, pp. 75–77,

---

addition, they opposed the establishment of an international tribunal but would rather have had a union of existing national military tribunals.[12] The final text of the peace treaties represented a compromise between the majority and minority views in that the reference to crimes against humanity was maintained, as was a special tribunal to try the Kaiser, Wilhelm II, but the latter only on the charge of "the supreme offence against international morality and the sanctity of treaties", while the tribunals to try lesser war criminals became limited to inter-Allied tribunals or national courts martial of any of the Allied countries.[13]

In practice, the ideal of trials of persons involved in war crimes or other crimes outside their country of origin was frustrated for a number of reasons: the enormity of the undertaking of setting up military tribunals; the refusal of the Netherlands to hand over the Kaiser to stand trial; the resistance in Germany due to public anger as well as the need to send a message about German sovereignty; the vague language in the peace treaties; domestic issues in the Allied countries; the changing political situation in Germany and Turkey; the delay in bringing accused to trial; the failure of the Allies to present a united front to the Germans and Turks and to take strong measures to enforce the treaties; and the lack of control of the Allied states within Germany and Turkey.[14]

9.3. The Leipzig Trials

Originally, a list had been drawn up by the Commission on the organisation of mixed tribunals under the auspices of the Paris Peace Conference, which was responsible for implementing Articles 228 to 230 of the Versailles Treaty and which had asked individual countries to provide names of

---

supra note 5; Rhea, 2012, pp. 38–41, *supra* note 6; Maogoto, 2004, pp. 49–50, *supra* note 5; Bass, 2000, pp. 100–4, *supra* note 5; Mettraux, 2008, pp. 496–98, *supra* note 7.

[12] *American Journal of International Law*, 1920, pp. 139–50 (for the US) and p. 152 (for Japan), see *supra* note 7; see also Reports of Commission I , 1944, pp. 144–47, *supra* note 7; United Nations War Crimes Commission, 1948, pp. 264–65, see *supra* note 5; Sheldon Glueck, "By What Tribunal Shall War Offenders Be Tried?", in *Harvard Law Review,* 1943, vol. 56, pp. 1079–81.

[13] Articles 227 and 229 of the Versailles Treaty and Article 227 of the Treaty of Sèvres.

[14] Reports of Commission I, 1944, p. 119, see *supra* note 7; United Nations War Crimes Commission, 1948, pp. 46, 52, see *supra* note 5; Willis, 1982, pp. 77–82, 107–12, see *supra* note 5; Horne and Kramer, 2001, pp. 340–41, see *supra* note 6; Bass, 2000, pp. 78–80, see *supra* note 5; Maogoto, 2004, pp. 55–56, 104–5, see *supra* note 5; Kramer, 2006, p. 449, see *supra* note 5; Matthäus, 2008, p. 19, see *supra* note 6.

---

individuals to be extradited by Germany for trial before the various tribunals. The number of names on this list reached eventually 1,590 names (from about 20,000 on the national lists). But given the impracticality of trying that many individuals, the list was pared down to 862 suspects, which was broken down to 334 each from the French and Belgian lists, 97 from the British list (including nine Turks involved in the Armenian genocide), 57 from the Polish list, 41 from Romania, 29 from Italy and four from a list submitted by Croatia, Serbia and Slovenia (for a total of 896 persons but some people appeared on more than one list). The list was slightly reduced, but on 3 February 1920 it was handed over to the German ambassador in Paris with 853 German names. In the face of very strong opposition in Germany to extraditing their nationals to foreign tribunals, the Allies, primarily Britain, decided to switch their approach. This was the result of a proposal by the German government, which was examined by a commission set up by the Allied governments and which declared this proposal compatible with Article 228 of the Versailles Treaty. The Allied countries then submitted on 7 May 1920 a much-reduced list of 45 cases, with the most serious charges for trials to be conducted in Germany. Of the 45 cases, 11 originated from France, 15 from Belgium, seven from Britain and 12 cases together from Italy, Poland, Romania and Yugoslavia.[15]

Because of the fact that most of the evidence related to these cases was in the hands of the Allied governments and because some of the accused had disappeared, it was decided at another conference in July 1920 that the Allied governments would collect and provide statements of the evidence against persons on the abridged list.[16] Of the 45 cases selected for prosecution in 1921 before the Supreme Court of Germany,

---

[15] Reports of Commission I, 1944, p. 9, see *supra* note 7; United Nations War Crimes Commission, 1948, pp. 46, see *supra* note 5; Kramer, 2006, pp. 446–47, see *supra* note 5; British Parliamentary Command Paper No. 1450, "German War Trials: Report of Proceedings before the Supreme Court in Leipzig" ('British Parliamentary Command Paper No. 1450'), reprinted in *American Journal of International Law*, 1922 [1921], vol. 16, pp. 628–40, p. 4; Willis, 1982, pp. 117–25 and 148–53, see *supra* note 5 (discussing attempts to put on trial war criminals from other countries, such as Austria, Hungary and Bulgaria); Horne and Kramer, 2001, pp. 341–45 and 448–50, see *supra* note 6; Bass, 2000, pp. 68 and 87–88, see *supra* note 5; Maogoto, 2004, p. 55–56, see *supra* note 5; Chantal Meloni, *Command Responsibility in International Criminal Law*, T.M.C. Asser Press, The Hague, 2009, pp. 41–42.

[16] British Parliamentary Command Paper No. 1450, p. 5, see *supra* note 15; United Nations War Crimes Commission, 1948, pp. 46–47, see *supra* note 5.

---

nine (with 12 accused) proceeded to trial resulting in six convictions. There were five (involving six accused) cases involving British victims, resulting in five convictions; three French cases (involving five persons), resulting in one conviction; and one Belgian case where an acquittal was entered. These trials started on 23 May 1921 and ended in July of the same year.[17]

The details of the British cases, the first three of which dealt with prisoner of war ('POW') situations while the other two addressed issues related to naval warfare and submarines, are as follows.[18]

9.3.1. Sergeant Karl Heynen[19]

In autumn 1915 Heynen was in charge of 200 British and 40 Russian POWs in a working camp at a mine in Germany. He was charged with maltreatment of these POWs on a number of occasions. There had been a

---

[17] The main sources for the British cases are the summaries in British Parliamentary Command Paper No. 1450, 1921, see *supra* note 15 and *American Journal of International Law,* 1922, vol. 16, pp. 674–724, see *supra* note 15 for the actual text of the judgments. Claud Mullins, *The Leipzig Trials: An Account of the War Criminals' Trials and a Study of German Mentality*, H.F. & G. Witherby, London, 1921 provides detailed descriptions of all the trials while more general summaries can be found in Reports of Commission I, 1944, pp. 11–12, see *supra* note 7 and United Nations War Crimes Commission, 1948, pp. 48–51, see *supra* note 5. See the chapter by Wolfgang Form, "Law as Farce: On the Miscarriage of Justice at the German Leipzig Trials: The *Llandovery Castle* Case", pp. 299–331. Based on German records, this refers to the case of Dieter Lottman, Paul Niegel and Paul Sangershausen which took place in January 1921 and which was not based on the Allied list, and to the case of Karl Grüner, which was held in November 1922.

[18] The British cases had one aspect not seen in the Belgium or French cases, namely that some witnesses, who had been reluctant to testify in Germany, had given their depositions before a British court in London, attended by representatives of the accused and the German government, which were then used in the German proceedings; this approach was achieved at a conference in February 1921. United Nations War Crimes Commission, 1948, p. 47, see *supra* note 5; Mullins, 1921, p. 36, see *supra* note 17; Horne and Kramer, 2001, p. 347, see *supra* note 6. For the procedure followed at the trials, see British Parliamentary Command Paper No. 1450, 1921, p. 5–8, see *supra* note 15; Mullins, 1921, pp. 37–41, see *supra* note 17; Willis, 1982, pp. 132–34, see *supra* note 5 (while also indicating that the trials attracted a great deal of press coverage).

[19] Heynen had already been found guilty by the German military authorities in a court martial and sentenced to 14 days arrest. These proceedings were set aside as a result of the new jurisdiction of the Supreme Court and this file was selected as a test case to see if a civilian court would follow the precedent of a German military court during the war. British Parliamentary Command Paper No. 1450, 1921, p. 8, see *supra* note 15. Three British witnesses testified in Britain and 16 at the trial in Leipzig.

concerted resistance on the part of the prisoners to work in the mine, and Heynen had ordered the guard to use the butt end of their rifles as well as their fists to get the prisoners to work. The court was of the view that in light of the orders given to him by his superiors and the subordination on the part of the prisoners he was entitled to use force, which was not seen as excessive in these circumstances.[20] However, in some 15 individual cases the force used against the prisoners was considered to be violent and excessive.[21] On 26 May 1921 Heynen was sentenced to 10 months imprisonment,[22] but he only served five months.[23]

9.3.2. Captain Emil Müller[24]

Müller was a commander of a prisoner of war camp in France for five weeks in early 1918 and was convicted for individual acts of brutality. The camp was heavily overcrowded while more POWs kept arriving. The situation resulted in increase of various diseases, lack of food and terrible sanitary conditions. The court found that Müller had sought assistance from his superiors, but to no avail. The court said he was not responsible for the poor conditions but it did imply that the German Military Staff knew of these conditions. The court found Müller guilty of deliberate personal cruelty, allowing a subordinate to ill-treat a POW, minor breaches of the law and two cases of insults, as well as forcing some prisoners to work while they were in no condition to do so.[25] He was sentenced to six months of imprisonment on 30 May 1921, for which the court weighed the facts that he tried to improve situation at the camp, that none of the prisoners whom he had abused had suffered serious consequences against the fact "that there has been an accumulation of offences, which show an almost habitually harsh and contemptuous and

---

[20] British Parliamentary Command Paper No. 1450, 1921, p. 9, see *supra* note 15; *American Journal of International Law*, 1922, vol. 16, pp. 677–78, see *supra* note 15.

[21] *Ibid.*, pp. 680–82.

[22] *Ibid.*, pp. 683–84.

[23] Willis, 1982, p. 141, see *supra* note 5.

[24] Eight British witnesses had testified in London while 19 did so in person in Germany.

[25] British Parliamentary Command Paper No. 1450, 1921, pp. 10–11, see *supra* note 15; *American Journal of International Law*, 1922, vol. 16, pp. 685–94, see *supra* note 15.

even frankly brutal treatment of prisoners entrusted in his care. His conduct has some times been unworthy of a human being".[26]

9.3.3. Private Robert Neumann[27]

Neumann was a labourer who was in charge of the British POWs from March until December 1917 at a chemical plant in Germany. He was charged with ill-treatment of these POWs. Neumann did admit to occasionally hitting soldiers because they kept refusing orders. The court ruled he could not be held responsible as he was acting upon the order of his superior, Trinke, who could not be arrested by the German government,[28] or, in the words of the court, "He was covered by the order of his superior which he was bound to obey […] It is of course understood that the use of force in any particular case must not be greater than is necessary to compel obedience".[29] The court concluded Neumann did not know his orders constituted criminal acts. He was sentenced to six months in prison on 2 June 1921.[30]

9.3.4. Lieutenant Captain Karl Neumann (*Dover Castle* Case)

Neumann, the commander of a German submarine, was charged with sinking a British hospital ship, the *Dover Castle*, without warning in May 1917. He knew the boat was a hospital ship. There were 842 people on the ship, including 632 patients, all of whom were rescued, although six crew members perished. These facts were admitted and as a result no witnesses were called. The only issue was whether the defence of superior orders could lead to an acquittal. It was undisputed that the German Admiralty had issued orders that a certain portion of the Mediterranean was subject to a blockade, which included hospital ships, and that any such ships that found themselves in that area were to be attacked by submarines. The

---

[26] *American Journal of International Law*, 1922, vol. 16, p. 695; he served three months, see Willis, 1982, p. 141, see *supra* note 5.

[27] Four British witnesses had testified in London while there were 25 British and 14 witnesses in Leipzig.

[28] British Parliamentary Command Paper, No. 1450, 1921, p. 12, see *supra* note 15.

[29] *American Journal of International Law*, 1922, vol. 16, p. 699, see *supra* note 15.

[30] *Ibid.*, pp. 703–4.

court ruled Neumann did not go beyond the orders issued by the German Staff and he could not be held responsible for following those orders.[31]

With respect to the issue of superior orders, the court said:

> It is a military principle that the subordinate is bound to obey the orders of his superiors. This duty of obedience is of considerable importance from the point of view of the criminal law. Its consequence is that, when the execution of a service order involves an offence against the criminal law, the superior giving the order is alone responsible [...] The Admiralty Staff was the highest service authority over the accused. He was in duty bound to obey their orders in service matters [...] there are two exceptional cases in which the question of the punishment of a subordinate who has acted in conformity with his orders can arise. He can in the first place be held responsible, if he has gone beyond the orders given him [...] a subordinate who acts in conformity with orders is also liable to punishment as an accomplice, when he knows that his superiors have ordered him to do acts which involve a civil or military crime or misdemeanor. There has been no case of this here. The memoranda of the German Government about the misuse of enemy hospital ships were known to the accused.[32]

Neumann was acquitted on 4 June 1921.[33]

9.3.5. First Lieutenants Ludwig Dithmar and John Boldt (*Llandovery Castle* Case)[34]

The initial accused was Commander Patzig, First Lieutenant of U-boat 86, who could not be found for the trial. The factual background of the case was that in June 1918 the ship was on the way from Halifax to Britain,

---

[31] *Ibid.*, pp. 706–7.

[32] *Ibid.*, p. 707.

[33] *Ibid.*, pp. 704–5.

[34] *Ibid.*, pp. 13–14; Elbridge Colby, "War Crimes", in *Michigan Law Review*, 1924–1925, vol. 24, pp. 615–16; see also Willis, 1982, pp. 137–38, *supra* note 5; Matthäus, 2008, pp. 11–18, *supra* note 6. One witness testified in Britain while 12 British witnesses came to Leipzig to attend court and a number of German witnesses were heard as well. This case was unusual in that the person on the list submitted by the British government, Patzig, could not be found by the German government, which decided on its own accord to put Patzig's subordinates on trial instead.

carrying 164 men, 80 officers, 14 nurses and men of the Canadian Medical Corps, 258 people in total. There were no soldiers on board and no ammunition. Patzig was convinced the ship was carrying eight American soldiers and some arms, so he decided to sink the ship, including two of the three lifeboats, in which a number of people had been able to escape from the sinking ship. Only 24 persons survived. Patzig was aware that he was acting against orders of the German Military Staff, but he firmly believed that the ship was used for military purposes. The court determined that Patzig had committed murder, as he killed people on the lifeboats. Two other accused knowingly assisted Patzig by executing his orders.

The court was of the view that killing defenceless shipwrecked people was contrary to ethical principles as well as German and international law. With respect to international law, the court phrased the applicable principles as follows:

> The firing on the boats was an offence against the law of nations. In war on land the killing of unarmed enemies is not allowed (compare the Hague regulations as to war on land, para. 23(c)), similarly in war at sea, the killing of shipwrecked people, who have taken refuge in life-boats, is forbidden. It is certainly possible to imagine exceptions to this rule, as, for example, if the inmates of the life-boats take part in the fight. But there was no such state of affairs in the present case, as Patzig and the accused persons were well aware, when they cruised around and examined the boats. Any violation of the law of nations in warfare is, as the Senate has already pointed out, a punishable offence, so far as in general, a penalty is attached to the deed. The killing of enemies in war is in accordance with the will of the State that makes war, (whose laws as to the legality or illegality on the question of killing are decisive), only in so far as such killing is in accordance with the conditions and limitations imposed by the law of nations. The fact that his deed is a violation of international law must be well-known to the doer, apart from acts of carelessness, in which careless ignorance is a sufficient excuse. In examining the question of the existence of this knowledge, the ambiguity of many of the rules of international law, as well as the actual circumstances of the case, must be borne in mind, because in war time decisions of great importance have frequently to be

made on very insufficient material. This consideration, however, cannot be applied to the case at present before the court. The rule of international law, which is here involved, is simple and is universally known. No possible doubt can exist with regard to the question of its applicability. The court must in this instance affirm Patzig's guilt of killing contrary to international law.[35]

The court also refined further the defence of superior orders, which it had started to develop in the Heynen and two Neumann cases by saying:

Patzig's order does not free the accused from guilt. It is true that according to para. 47 of the Military Penal Code, if the execution of an order in the ordinary course of duty involves such a violation of the law as is punishable, the superior officer issuing such an order is alone responsible. According to No. 2, however, the subordinate obeying such an order is liable to punishment, if it was known to him that the order of the superior involved the infringement of civil or military law. This applies in the case of the accused. It is certainly to be urged in favor of the military sub- ordinates, that they are under no obligation to question the order of their superior officer, and they can count upon its legality. But no such confidence can be held to exist, if such an order is universally known to everybody, including also the accused, to be without any doubt whatever against the law. This happens only in rare and exceptional cases. But this case was precisely one of them, for in the present instance, it was perfectly clear to the accused that killing defenceless people in the life-boats could be nothing else but a breach of the law. As naval officers by profession they were well aware, as the naval expert Saalwiachter has strikingly stated, that one is not legally authorized to kill defenceless people. They well knew that this was the case here. They quickly found out the facts by questioning the occupants in the boats when these were stopped. They could only have gathered, from the order given by Patzig, that he wished to make use of his subordinates to carry out a breach of the law. They should,

---

[35] British Parliamentary Command Paper No. 1450, 1921, vol. 16, pp. 721–22, see *supra* note 15; see also Sheldon Glueck, *The Nuremberg Trial and Aggressive War*, Alfred A. Knopf, New York, 1946, partially reproduced in Mettraux, 2008, pp. 100, 152, see *supra* note 7, as well as Willis, 1982, p. 138, see *supra* note 5.

therefore, have refused to obey. As they did not do so, they
must be punished.[36]

The two accused present at trial were sentenced to four years of
imprisonment on 16 July 1921. However, Boldt escaped from custody on
18 November 1921 with the help of German officials while Dithmar left
prison on 31 January 1922.[37]

The following are details of the one Belgian and three French cases.

9.3.6. Max Ramdohr

Ramdohr was an officer of Secret German Military Police in Belgium and
was accused of cruelty towards Belgian children in 1917–1918. The
background of the case was that train signals were frequently interrupted
and German trains had to stop often, resulting in the plundering of
provisions as well as affecting the transport of troops. The accused
arrested several Belgian children who admitted their guilt but only after
they had been mistreated in order to obtain confessions or further
intelligence. At the time there was an army order in place to the effect that
secret police could circumvent normal arrest procedures and that any
conduct pursuant to those orders would not be questioned by the court.
However, this order did not apply to children. As a result the court found
that "there can be no question of the accused having rendered himself
guilty of deliberate illegal arrest when he kept children in confinement
until the necessary inquiries were over".[38]

However, this conduct was not part of the charges brought against
Ramdohr. With respect to those accusations, the court was of the view
that the testimony of the children who were witnesses during the trial was
on the whole not reliable, and while the court had a suspicion that
Ramdohr "employed measures which were legally forbidden" the
evidence was insufficient to meet the criminal standard of a finding of
guilt.[39]

---

[36] British Parliamentary Command Paper No. 1450, 1921, vol. 16, pp. 721–22, see *supra* note 15.

[37] Reports of Commission I, 1944, p. 11, see *supra* note 7; United Nations War Crimes Commission, 1948, p. 49, see *supra* note 5; Willis, 1982, pp. 140–41, see *supra* note 5.

[38] Mullins, 1921, p. 141–43, see *supra* note 17.

[39] *Ibid.*, pp. 149–50; see also Willis, 1982, pp. 134–35, *supra* note 5.

9.3.7. Lieutenant General Karl Stenger and Major Benno Crusius[40]

It was alleged that in August 1914 in northern France and in Germany, General Stenger, on two occasions, issued an order to kill all French POWs under his control, while Crusius was charged with personally killing several French soldiers while passing on Stenger's order to his subordinates to do the same. The court was not sure whether Stenger wanted to kill only those who were abusing the privileges of captured or wounded men, or whether his order was to the effect that all were to be put to death. The court ruled that the former type of order was in accordance with international law by saying:

> Such an order, if it were issued, would not have been contrary to international principles, for the protection afforded by the regulations for land warfare does not extend to such wounded who take up arms again and renew the fight. Such men have by so doing forfeited the claim for mercy granted to them by the laws of warfare. On the other hand, an order of the nature maintained by the accused Crusius would have had absolutely no justification.[41]

The court found that the evidence did not show that General Stenger had issued an order to kill wounded and unarmed POWs, and that Crusius had been mistaken in thinking that such an order existed as a result of his mental state or in the words of the court:

> The accused Crusius acted in the mistaken idea that General Stenger, at the time of the discussion near the chapel, had issued the order to shoot the wounded. He was not conscious of the illegality of such an order, and therefore considered that he might pass on the supposed order to his company, and indeed must do so. So pronounced a misconception of the real facts seems only comprehensible in view of the mental condition of the accused. Already on 21st August he was intensely excited and suffered from nervous complaints. The medical experts have convincingly stated, that these complaints did not preclude the free exercise of his will, but were, nevertheless, likely to affect his powers of

---

[40] Reports of Commission I, 1944, pp. 12–13, see *supra* note 7; Willis, 1982, pp. 135–36, see *supra* note 5; Horne and Kramer, 2001, pp. 348–51, see *supra* note 6; Meloni, 2009, pp. 41–42, see *supra* note 15.

[41] Mullins, 1921, p. 153, see *supra* note 17.

comprehension and judgment. But this merely explains the error of the accused; it does not excuse it [...] Had he applied the attention which was to be expected from him, what was immediately clear to many of his men would not have escaped him, namely, that the indiscriminate killing of all wounded was a monstrous war measure, in no way to be justified.[42]

As a result Crusius was found guilty of negligent killing and the court sentenced him to two years imprisonment for the first incident on 21 August, but acquitted him of a second killing a week later because at that time his mental state had deteriorated to such an extent (had "a morbid derangement" and "complete mental collapse") that he could not be held responsible for his actions.[43]

9.3.8. First Lieutenant Adolph Laule

Laule was charged with intentional murder of a French Captain in August 1914 during the German offensive while being a company commander. The pertinent issue was whether he had issued an order or killed the Captain himself. The court ruled that Laule did not give an order nor did he kill the Captain himself. The Captain was killed by German soldiers during an attempt to convince the French officer to surrender but who instead offered resistance. As such the "French officer was not yet a prisoner, as he persistently resisted capture. He was killed by the German soldiers of their own accord as he would not cease continuing to struggle".[44] Laule was found not guilty.

9.3.9. Lieutenant General Hans von Schack and Major General Benno Kruska[45]

In September 1914 the German Ministry of War issued an order establishing a prisoner camp in Cassel for 15,000 men. The camp accommodated Belgians, French and Russians. In March 1915 the number went up to 18,300 men. The camp faced severe medical problems, as a result of which 1,280 men died (most of them French). The court

---

[42] *Ibid.*, pp. 160–61.

[43] *Ibid.*, pp. 165–67.

[44] *Ibid.*, p. 173.

[45] Willis, 1982, p. 136, see *supra* note 5.

ruled that the biggest problem was that Russian soldiers (who had brought the diseases) were commingled with healthy prisoners, and that the accused were not able to separate the two groups due to the orders of the High Command of the Army, which they had to follow. The court absolved both accused from guilt in these strong terms: "General Kruska, as well as General von Schack, is, as the State Attorney has himself said, to be acquitted absolutely. That the fatal epidemic broke out during his command was a misfortune which could not be averted, even by the most strenuous fulfilment of duty". The court continued: "the trial before this Court has not revealed even the shadow of proof for these monstrous accusations".[46]

9.4. The Istanbul Trials

All the trials were related to the 1915 deportations and massacres of the Armenian population in Turkey by representatives of the government then in power, the Committee of Union and Progress ('CUP'), also known as the Young Turks. After the First World War, the Allied countries warned the re-established government of the Ottoman Empire to seek out and prosecute suspects for this genocide and put them on trial or face harsh consequences, including the division of Turkey. The first government after the war, that of Ahmet Izzet, was reluctant to do so (with as a result that a number of high level CUP officials fled to Germany), but it was forced to resign for this lack of co-operation less than three weeks after it had come to power. The new government of Tevfik Paşa, which took over on 8 November 1918, was more serious about taking steps to bring perpetrators to justice and a month later special courts martial were established for this purpose. A parliamentary commission produced files with evidence on 130 suspects, which was handed over to the courts in January 1919 while the trials began under the next government of Damad Ferid, which had come to power in March 1919. One hundred and seven arrests were made by April 1919, of which 98 were put on trial. While these trials were ongoing, the British made efforts to prosecute Turkish war criminals who had abused British POWs before their own courts in British-occupied territory, while also demanding the extradition of other suspects from Ottoman territory for trial before an international tribunal pursuant to the provisions of the Treaty of Sèvres. To that end, on 26 May

---

[46]   Mullins, 1921, p. 189, see *supra* note 17.

1919 the British arrested 41 prominent prisoners, arrested several more later, and eventually interned, by August 1920, 118 men on Malta for trials on crimes against humanity before the to-be-established international tribunal. The government in Istanbul protested and arrested some of the suspects accused by the British government of the mistreatment of British POWs.[47]

There were 10 main trials (or 11 as the trial pertaining to the cabinet ministers and CUP members was divided into two separate phases with one verdict) before the Extraordinary Courts Martial (Extraordinary Military Tribunals or Special Military Tribunals) between 5 February 1919 and 29 July 1920. These can be divided into three major groups: cabinet ministers and members of the CUP Central Committee; secretaries and delegates of the CUP; and middle level and minor officials in various geographic regions.[48]

9.4.1. The Trial of Cabinet Ministers and Top CUP Leaders

This trial pertained originally[49] to 18 cabinet ministers (four of which were *in absentia*)[50] and 11 members of the CUP Central Committee (four of which were *in absentia*), where nine became the subject of a verdict.

---

[47] Willis, 1982, pp. 153–56, 158–159, see *supra* note 5; Kramer, 2006, pp. 443–44, see *supra* note 5; Maogoto, 2004, p. 57–60, see *supra* note 5; Bass, 2000, pp. 118–28, see *supra* note 5; Dadrian and Akçam, 2011, pp. 57–69, 78–91, 251–64, see *supra* note 5.

[48] Bass, 2000, pp. 124–25, see *supra* note 5 (while indicating that more trials were planned but never held); Dadrian and Akçam, 2011, pp. 108–24, see *supra* note 5. The latter book makes it clear that these 10 or 11 trials with 98 accused were the ones reported in the *Takvîm-i Vekâyi*, the official journal of the tribunals, while in the estimation of the authors, based on contemporary newspaper reporting, there were likely to have been a total of 63 cases between April 1919 and July 1921, which, apart from the reported ones, involved another over 120 accused, and of which 22 cases came to a judicial decision including 17 acquittals, eight cases being dismissed due to lack of evidence while the result of 21 files remains unknown, see pp. 201–2 with more details at pp. 219–42; this book also reports one other trial at pp. 122 and 208, but that trial does not deal with the Armenian massacres and rather with persons who helped escape from prison one of the convicts in the CUP Secretaries trial, Ahmet Midhat. For contemporary legal views on the Armenian genocide, see *International Criminal Law Review*, Special Issue: Armenian Genocide Reparations, 2014, vol. 14, no. 2.

[49] The British removed a number of these accused to Malta on 26 May 1919. Bass, 2000, p. 128, see *supra* note 5; Dadrian and Akçam, 2011, p. 120, see *supra* note 5.

[50] Dadrian and Akçam, 2011, see *supra* note 5. The main source for this information is not clear as at p. 120 the numbers are respectively 13 and 3 while at p. 203 the numbers are 14 and 4.

The trial began on 28 April 1919 and ended on 19 July 1919, divided between the first phase, which dealt with CUP component from 28 April to 17 May 1919, while the second phase dealing with the cabinet ministers took place from 3 June to 25 June 1919. The tribunal sentenced to death four persons, all of whom had been both cabinet ministers as well as members of the CUP Central Committee: Küçük Talaat, Ismail Enver, Ahmet Cemal and Mehmed Nazim. All four had been tried *in absentia* and were not present when the verdict was announced. Three others were sentenced to 15 years hard labour, of whom two, Mustafa Şeref and Mehmet Cavit, were not present either, while for the third, Musa Kazim, the sentence was later commuted to exile. Finally, two others, Rif'at and Haşim, were acquitted.[51]

The central theme in the charges against the ministers and CUP members was the crime of mass murder against the Armenians[52] while mention was also made of "calamities",[53] "deportation with the goal of annihilation",[54] "slaughter",[55] and "massacres",[56] while accusations of plunder figured prominently[57] as did those of destruction of property, rape, torture,[58] forced displacement and deportation and, interestingly, "altering the form of government by force and compulsion, by sowing fear and terror among the populace".[59]

In the opening statement of the Attorney General it was said:

> The principal subject matter of this investigation has been the event of the disaster befalling the deported Armenians

---

[51] Willis, 1982, pp. 155–56, see *supra* note 5; Bass, 2000, pp. 129–30, see *supra* note 5; Dadrian and Akçam, 2011, pp. 121, 202–3, 330–31, see *supra* note 5 (for the subsequent fate of the four sentenced to death *in absentia*, see p. 196). The result of this trial prompted the British Acting High Commissioner in Istanbul to say: "It is interesting to see how skilfully the Turkish penal code has been manipulated to cover the acts attributed to the accused and the manner in which the sentences have been apportioned among the absent and the present so as to effect a minimum of real bloodshed", see Bass, 2000, p. 129, see *supra* note 5.

[52] Dadrian and Akçam, 2011, p. 120, see *supra* note 5.

[53] *Ibid.*, pp. 273, 278, 279.

[54] *Ibid.*, p. 274.

[55] *Ibid.*, p. 275.

[56] *Ibid.*, pp. 277, 282, 284, 286.

[57] *Ibid.*, pp. 284, 286.

[58] *Ibid.*, p. 286.

[59] *Ibid.*, p. 289.

> […] The disaster visiting the Armenians was not a local or isolated event. It was the result of a premeditated decision taken by a central body composed of the above-mentioned persons; and the immolations and excesses which took place were based on oral and written orders issued by that central body.[60]

The judgment came to this conclusion:

> The evidence shows that the crimes of massacre that occurred in Trabzon, Yozgad, and Boğazhyan, and that were verified as a result of the trials that were held by the Military Tribunal, were ordered, planned and carried out by persons among the leadership of the CUP. Furthermore, as was presented during the defence's case, although there were those who became aware of the crimes after their occurrence, these persons made no effort whatsoever to prevent their repetition or stop the perpetrators of the previous crimes.[61]

9.4.2. The Trial of Secretaries and Delegates of the CUP

This trial started on 12 June 1919 and completed on 8 January 1920 when the judgment was issued. The verdict was appealed on 13 February and overturned by the Appellate Court, which sent the case back to the Trial Court but there it is not clear what happened at the rehearing.[62]

The main feature of this trial, which comprised 29 accused, of whom only 11 appeared at trial, was that these persons had gained control of the state apparatus, both in the capital and in the regions where the deportations and killings had taken place. The charge against the members of the CUP in Istanbul was that they were responsible for the enactment of the Temporary Law of Deportation, which was the legal vehicle for the massacres to occur. The regional secretaries were accused of replacing local governors, who had opposed the harsh measures against the Armenian population, in order to put into effect the deportations and killings.[63]

---

[60] Bass, 2000, pp. 126–27, see *supra* note 5.

[61] Dadrian and Akçam, 2011, p. 327, see *supra* note 5.

[62] *Ibid.*, pp. 116, 202–6.

[63] *Ibid.*, pp. 116–17 (there is also a reference to the 30 accused on p. 116).

Only four persons were found guilty of committing massacres, plunder and other crimes under the pretext of organising deportations (although seven others were convicted of the crime of altering the legitimate government). The court held that there was not sufficient evidence to convict some of the others, while for two persons further examination was ordered, and the case of yet two others was severed from the main case. The four accused who had been convicted were spared the death penalty as they were considered accessories to the crimes rather than principals. Two of the accused, Hasan Fehmi and Ahmet Midhat, were sentenced to 10 years hard labour, while a third, Avni, was sentenced to two months incarceration, but he was released immediately as he had already served this time during the trial. The sentence of the fourth person, Abdülgani, was held in abeyance until the completion of another trial, in which he was also an accused.[64]

9.4.3. The Trials of Regional Functionaries

There were regional trials in the districts of Yozgad, Trabzon, Harput, Bayburt, Erzincan, Büyükdere, Izmit and Çankiri. The accused had all been directly involved in the massacres of the local Armenian population, either at a high level, such as district governors or with a senior military or police rank, or at lower levels, such as businessmen, local party or government officials or lower-ranking soldiers and police officers. While in most cases the allegations of carrying out a massacre was the main count, other criminal acts, such as pillage, plunder and rape were also frequently mentioned as were the purpose of these crimes, namely the "extermination of the deportee population" or "annihilation of the population". The sentences for the accused varied from the death penalty to one-year imprisonment while a number were also acquitted.

The Yozgad trial was the first to be held and ran from 5 February to 8 April 1919. There were three defendants, namely the Yozgad Deputy Governor, Mehmet Kemal; the gendarmerie Commander Major Manastirli Mehmet Tevfik bin Halil Osman; and Abdül Feyyaz Ali, an employee of the group Religious Foundations. The latter was removed from the trial and ordered to be processed separately, while Kemal received a death sentence and Tevfik a sentence of 15 years' hard

---

[64] *Ibid.*, pp. 118–19, 314–16, 320–23.

labour.[65] When Kemal was executed on 10 April 1919, there was a very large nationalist demonstration during his funeral.[66]

The judgment contains this telling assessment of the situation in the Yozgad district in 1915:

> The deportation of all of the Armenians, even their helpless wives and children, thereby discounting the officially allowed exceptions, was ordered through the auspices of Boğazliyan County Executive and Acting District Governor of Yozgad, Kemal Bey, and Gendarmerie Commander for the provincial district of Yozgad, Major Tevfik Bey, whose convictions are being demanded. Driven by their own personal ambition and greed, and after accepting the secret, illegal communications and instructions of a few evil individuals, they undertook the deportations after first taking all of the money and valuable possessions from these persons who made up the departing convoys, in complete disregard for their individual rights. Not only did they fail to adopt the necessary measures to ensure the protection of the aforementioned deportees, so that might reach their destination point in comfort and ease, they bound the hands of the men, thus allowing these premeditated tragic events to take place, causing all manner of slaughter, looting, and pillage, such are entirely unacceptable to human and civilized sensibilities and which, in Islam's views of the severity of the crimes are considered among the greatest of offences. The defendants even blocked attempts at preventing their occurrence by concealing the truth from their superiors, who have testified how they repeatedly asked for reports concerning the aforementioned tragedies. What is more, they supported and facilitated the realization of the accursed aims by dispatching irresponsible persons without any official authority as supervisors over the officials and guards responsible for the deportations.[67]

---

[65] *Ibid.*, pp. 110–11, 218–19.

[66] *Ibid.*, pp. 195, 219; Bass, 2000, pp. 125–26, see *supra* note 5.

[67] Dadrian and Akçam, 2011, p. 291, see *supra* note 5; see also Bass, 2000, p. 125, see *supra* note 5, who uses the words "against humanity and civilization", based on a number of other sources (in his footnote 133) where Dadrian and Akçam in the above excerpt say "unacceptable to human and civilized sensibilities". The excerpt of the verdict is a translation by one of the authors, Vahakn Dadrian (footnote 1 on p. 332), in describing the judgment earlier in the book the same author, states: "The crimes were committed with a

Kemal and Tevfîk were found guilty as principal co-perpetrators for these crimes, while Kemal was also considered the principal perpetrator because he was the highest official in the district. He planned the manner in which the crimes were to be carried out, ordered a group of individuals without title or authority to accompany the convoys, and encouraged the official in charge of the convoy to obey the commands of this group of individuals while bypassing the official chain of command.[68]

The Trabzon trial was held from 26 March and 22 May 1919 and involved 10 accused, two of whom *in absentia*. These two had been the main organisers of the massacres in this province, namely the Governor-General and the CUP representative in the province. Among the allegations were the separation from men and women, the latter becoming the subject of sexual crimes, even girls at a young age, and the transport of male and female infants, who were loaded on barges and boats and then drowned, in addition to the systematic killing of adults and the plunder of their properties. Six of the accused were convicted, two acquitted and two persons were separated from this proceeding and deferred for further clarification for another trial. Two were given the death penalty *in absentia*, namely Cemal Azmi, the Governor-General and Yenibahćeli Nail, the CUP representative. Mehmet Ali, the Director of Customs and the trustee of the Trabzon Red Crescent Hospital, was given 10 years hard labour; Ahmet Mustafa, an agent for a maritime company in Trabzon, and Nuri, the police chief, were each given one-year imprisonment.[69]

The difference between the death penalties and hard labour were explained by the tribunal on the basis of involvement as principal co-perpetrator or accessory in the following terms:

> If several persons unitedly commit a felony or misdemeanour
> or if a felony or misdemeanour is composed of several acts

---

firm intention. Equally important, the method of 'deportation' was a subterfuge for the ultimate objective of 'exterminating the deportee population'. About this 'there can be no doubt and no hesitation'. Referring to the method of incapacitation the male victims at the very start of the deportation operations, the verdict speaks of the standard procedure of 'tying together the arms of several men. In order to intensify the scale of the atrocities, the perpetrators incited the religious hatreds 'not only of Yozgat Muslims but Muslims in general'" (on pp. 110–11), thereby providing further insight into the term 'premeditated' used in the excerpt.

68 Dadrian and Akçam, 2011, p. 293, see *supra* note 5.

69 *Ibid.*, pp. 111–13, 196, 218, 294–99; see also Bass, 2000, p. 128, see *supra* note 5.

---

and each of a gang of persons perpetrates one or some of such acts with a view to the accomplishment of the offence, such persons are styled accomplices and all of them are punished as sole perpetrators [...] who knowingly assist the principal perpetrator in acts which are means of preparing, facilitating, or completing a felony or misdemeanour are deemed accessories in the commission of such felony or misdemeanour.[70]

The Harput trial started on 28 July 1919 and was completed on 13 January 1920. It involved four accused, two of whom *in absentia*, against the persons most responsible, namely high officials of the CUP in Harput province, Dr. Bahaeddim Şakir and Resneli Boşnak Nazim. The two persons *in absentia* were convicted and given the death penalty and five years hard labour respectively; the two persons present for the trial were acquitted.[71] As with the previous two cases, the verdict concentrated on the "massacre" while making reference to the "Special Organizations, which had been formed for the purpose of destroying and annihilating the Armenians".[72]

The Bayburt trial began on 15 March 1920 and ended on 20 July 1920. It involved two defendants, Mehmet Nusret, the District Governor of Bayburt, and Mehmet Necati, a reserve officer in the army, who were, again, accused of massacres against Armenians. Both were found guilty and sentenced to death, Necati *in absentia*. Nusret was executed on 5 August 1920.[73]

The Erzincan proceeding took place from 18 May 1920 to 29 July 1920. It involved seven accused, including the District Governor, Mehmet Memduh bin Tayar. Of these seven, one passed away during the trial. The trial of Tayar was separated as he was detained in Malta, while guilty verdicts and death sentences were pronounced against the other five, of whom only one, Hafiz Abdulah Avni, a businessman, was present. He was executed on 29 July 1920.[74]

---

[70] Dadrian and Akçam, 2011, p. 297, see *supra* note 5.

[71] *Ibid.*, pp. 113–14, 196, 212–16, 299–303.

[72] *Ibid.*, p. 300.

[73] *Ibid.*, pp. 114–15, 197, 207–8, 304–10.

[74] *Ibid.*, pp. 115–16, 196–97, 211–12, 310–13.

The Büyükdere trial was held from 23 April to May 24 1919 with four accused, two of whom were convicted and two acquitted, resulting in sentences of hard labour for two and one year.[75]

The Izmit trial involved eight defendants, four of whom received terms of imprisonment of 15 (*in absentia*), three, two and one year, as well as four months for two persons, while two others were acquitted. The trial ran from 27 October 1919 to 29 February 1920.[76]

The Çankiri trial pertained to Cemal Oğuz, a provincial party secretary, and Nureddin Bey, a Captain in the army, held between 27 October 1919 and 5 February 1920. Oğuz was originally the subject of a separate investigation but then his file was merged with the CUP secretaries' trial, only to be separated again. Both were accused of deporting Armenians from Istanbul to Çankiri and murdering them. Oğuz was sentenced to five years and four months hard labour, and Nureddin to six years and eight months hard labour but *in absentia*.[77]

9.5. The Aftermath

With respect to the Leipzig trials, the Belgian, British and French governments sent representatives to their respective trials. But the Belgian delegation left Leipzig very dissatisfied while the French delegation did not even attend the last trial, that of von Schack and Kruska.[78] The files submitted by Italy were discarded in that no action was undertaken. On 15 January 1922 the Commission of Allied Jurists, which had been appointed by the Supreme Council to inquire into the Leipzig trials, recommended that it was useless to proceed with further trials, and that the German

---

[75] *Ibid.*, pp. 121–22, 209–10.

[76] *Ibid.*, p. 122 (although the Izmit trial mentioned here pertains to three accused with different names than the ones referred to later, pp. 216–18). There is a discrepancy in the account of this trial as on p. 216 it refers to six defendants while on pp. 217–18 it appears that eight people received a sentence.

[77] *Ibid.*, pp. 122–24, 210–11.

[78] Reports of Commission I, 1944, pp. 10, 13, see *supra* note 7; United Nations War Crimes Commission, 1948, p. 47, see *supra* note 5; Bass, 2000, p. 89, see *supra* note 5; Matthäus, 2008, pp. 9–10, see *supra* note 6. Neutral observers in Leipzig were of the view that the French had overreacted, see Willis, 1982, p. 137, see *supra* note 5, where it also stated that: "A Dutch judge who had watched the Stenger trial wrote that the court acted in a 'perfectly correct manner' and that the 'fairly general disapproval of the judgment is misplaced'. British officials agreed and refused the French request to end British participation".

government should be made to hand over the remaining accused to Allied countries for trial. The reasons given were that the persons who had been acquitted should have been convicted, while the sentences given to the persons convicted had been too lenient. In June 1922 the Leipzig court decided to proceed with the remainder of the trials, which was done without the presence of Allied representation. In that same month, the first trial commenced on this basis against Dr. Oskar Michelson, who had been accused of having beaten and ill-treated several French prisoners in his hospital and having caused the death of several of them. But he was acquitted on 3 July 1922 (after the 14 French witnesses scheduled to testify did not show up). In December 1922 another 93 accused (out of the original 1920 list of 853) were brought to trial, followed by the remainder in the next three years, but only six proceedings led to a conviction, bringing the total number of convictions to 12 (out of 901 files), of which a number escaped, often in collusion with their jailers.[79] At the same time, France and Belgium conducted a large number of courts martial *in absentia* against German soldiers on the original list, as well as others. This resulted in over 1,200 guilty verdicts (out of 2,000 proceedings) by December 1924 in France alone, as well as an approximately 80 in Belgium by May 1925, frequently reaching different results to the proceedings in Germany for the same suspects.[80]

The immediate reaction to the Leipzig trials differed. While, as indicated earlier, the Belgian and French observers at the trials left the proceedings in disgust because of the unwillingness of the courts to sentence most of the German soldiers involved in crimes against their nationals, the British assessments of the trials were more positive on a number of levels. One commentator, Claud Mullins, a lawyer who spoke German and who had been present during the British trials in 1921 as part of the British delegation, was of the view that the trials had been markedly fair given the overwhelming negative public and government

---

[79] Reports of Commission I, 1944, pp. 9, 13, 199, see *supra* note 7; United Nations War Crimes Commission, 1948, pp. 47–48, 51, see *supra* note 5; Willis, 1982, p. 140–45, see *supra* note 5; Ann Tusa and John Tusa, *The Nuremberg Trial*, Atheneum, New York, 1984, p. 19; Maogoto, 2004, p. 56, see *supra* note 5; Lippman, 1991–1992, p. 1, see *supra* note 7, reproduced in Mettraux, 2008, p. 500, see *supra* note 7; Horne and Kramer, 2001, pp. 352–53, see *supra* note 6. Form, 2014, p. 17, see *supra* note 17 suggests that the vast majority of these proceedings were not trials but summary rulings by the courts.

[80] Willis, 1982, p. 146, see *supra* note 5; Horne and Kramer, 2001, pp. 353–55, see *supra* note 6; Kramer, 2006, p. 449, see *supra* note 5; Bass, 2000, p. 90, see *supra* note 5.

attitude in Germany.[81] When venturing for an explanation why the British trials had been more successful than the Belgian or French ones, he came

---

[81] Mullins, 1921, pp. 42–43, 196, see *supra* note 17 states: "Never have trials taken place amidst more difficult surroundings", "No judges have ever had a more difficult task than to act judicially under such circumstances" and "At the time of the trials, The Times described them as 'a travesty of justice' and the Evening Standard said that 'Leipzig, from the Allies' point of view, has been a farce'; but I do not think that any Englishman who was present was of that opinion. However much we may criticise the judgments of the Court, and however much we may deplore their inadequacy from the point of view of jurisprudence, the trials were not a farce and the seven German judges endeavoured throughout to be true to the traditions of fairness and impartiality which are the pride of all judicial courts". Along the same lines, see Lord Cave, "War Crimes and Their Punishment" in *Problems of Peace and War, Papers Read before the Society in the Year 1922, Transactions of the Grotius Society*, vol. 8, p. xxix. "The results, so far, of our efforts to bring the war criminals to justice are far from encouraging. No doubt it is worth something that a German Court has convicted and sentenced German soldiers and sailors for flagrant inhumanity and breach of the laws of war and it appears to me that for this achievement credit is due to the British lawyers who prepared and watched the cases with so much ability and judgment. Nor would it be fair to pass by the fact that German judges and law officers were found who had the courage to listen carefully to evidence which was given by their late enemies against their own nationals and (however inadequately) to condemn and sentence some of the most flagrant offenders. Further, we have gained some experience which will be of assistance in considering what steps can be taken to ensure better results in the event (which God forbid) of our being again involved in war. But that some such steps should be taken, and that promptly, will, I think, be plain to everyone". See also comments by Sir Ernest Pollock, the head of the British delegation to Leipzig, who was "much impressed by the Supreme Court of Leipzig – the trials were conducted very impartially with every desire to get to the truth", as reproduced by Bass, 2000, p. 81, see *supra* note 5 (who does point out on the same page that this sentiment was not necessarily shared by everyone in the British Foreign Office); Colby, p. 616, see *supra* note 34 ("There were many difficulties to be surmounted in instituting and conducting such trials. The marvel is that they were held at all. Instances to the contrary must be very numerous".); Horne and Kramer, 2001, p. 346, see *supra* note 6 ("The court president, Dr. Karl Schmidt, conducted the trials with punctilious fairness and courtesy towards the both Allied witnesses and top-level delegations from Britain, France, and Belgium which attended the prosecution of 'their' cases"); Willis, 1982, p. 138, see *supra* note 5 ("Although the French and Belgians were outraged over the results of the Leipzig trials, the British viewed the proceedings with some satisfaction. *The Times* called them a 'scandalous failure of justice' but other newspapers and journals thought that the principle of punishment had been observed, despite the light sentences. Several members of parliament fumed over the 'farce' but most politicians had lost interest. The House of Commons by a large majority decisively defeated a motion to hold a special debate on the trials [...] The British gratefully accepted the opinion of the law officers who pronounced themselves satisfied. Sir Ernest Pollock told the cabinet, and later the House of Commons, that the *Reichsgericht* 'acted impartially' and that the 'moral effect of the condemnation' outweighed the leniency of the sentences"); Reports of Commission I, 1944, pp. 13–14, see *supra* note 7 ("In the beginning the trials seem to have been conducted impartially: the

---

to the conclusion that, on the whole, the British cases were stronger from an evidentiary perspective, because the British witnesses were generally better prepared and more credible and objective.[82] He also did not view the sentences handed out to be too light, as these sentences were going to be served in the harsh conditions of German military prisons.[83] Lastly, British commentators were also in agreement with the international law applied by the German judges in these cases, specifically the parameters of the defence of superior orders.[84]

---

presiding judge showed a real desire to ascertain the truth and expressed the disgust at the horrors revealed, paying tribute to the objective sincerity of the British witnesses. This did not, however, prevent the Court from accompanying its findings by considerations that show a wide gulf between the German conception of honour and our own, and soon it allowed itself to be ruled by motives of opportunism. The German public showed indignation that German judges could be found to sentence the war criminals and the press brought all possible pressure to bear on the court, how successfully, its decisions showed. What the more enlightened section of the audience found most shocking was not the horrors brought to light but the fact that those truly responsible were escaping punishment"); Matthäus, 2008, p. 10, see *supra* note 6 ("The verdicts leave no doubt that the Leipzig court's attempt at professional impartiality found its limitation where political interest and national honor were at stake"); see also United Nations War Crimes Commission, 1948, p. 51, see *supra* note 5.

[82] Mullins, 1921, p. 192, 195–96, see *supra* note 17; he also alludes to the fact that the conduct of the British mission during the trials might have had a positive effect on the proceedings at pp. 48–50.

[83] *Ibid.*, pp. 202–8. This sentiment is shared by Sir Ernest Pollock, who states in the "Introduction" of Mullins's book at pp. 10–11: "These sentences were, to our estimate, far too light; but as the following pages show, they must be estimated according to their values in Germany. To the Germans a sentence of imprisonment upon an officer carries a special stigma, and imports a blot upon the service to which belongs"; see also along the same vein the report by Pollock to the British cabinet and parliament in 1921, as set out in Horne and Kramer, 2001, pp. 347–48, see *supra* note 6.

[84] British Parliamentary Command Paper No. 1450, 1921, p. 13, see *supra* note 15; Mullins, 1921, pp. 218–21, see *supra* note 17, after comparing the German, British and French Military Manuals; see also in the same vein Colby, pp. 606–13, see *supra* note 34; Hersch Lauterpacht, *The Law of Nations and the Punishment of War Crimes*, 1944, partially reproduced in Mettraux, 2008, pp. 26–27, 42, see *supra* note 7; the United Nations War Crimes Commission, 1948, pp. 274–182, see *supra* note 5. With respect to international law in general, Mullins was of the view at p. 200 that "in the fluid state in which International Law was in 1921, it could scarcely be expected that a German Court would define for the first time principles which, however generally accepted as maxims of morality, had never hitherto been regarded as laws, the breaches of which involved penalties" while going in more detail at pp. 212–215 and saying this on pp. 223–24 (after questioning on pp. 221–22 why the general order in the *Dover Castle* case to restrict routes for hospital ships to travel or in the Ramdohr case the suspend normal arrest procedures for the secret police were accepted by the court without question): "If it had been possible

Academic and political opinion hardened considerably as the distance in time between the occurrence of the trials and the assessment of them increased. A study of the United Nations War Crimes Commission ('UNWCC'), which was published shortly after the Second World War, deplored in strong terms the outcome of the Leipzig judgments.[85] It was a sentiment followed in modern times when terms such as a "sorry mess",[86] "failed effort",[87] "farce",[88] "fiasco",[89] "debacle"[90] and "disaster"[91] were used to describe these proceedings, although these statements were almost exclusively used in relation to the number of people tried and the

---

to carry out the intentions embodied in the Versailles Treaty, there might have resulted decisions of real value in building up both International Law and the Laws of War. On the other hand, we may reasonably doubt whether such problems can be settled by any national court. It certainly could scarcely be expected that the Court at Leipzig would lay down principles on these points which could be generally accepted. If these problems are to be settled, they are essentially suited for the consideration of the League of Nations and of the new Permanent Court of International Justice. The Leipzig experiment has not been valueless, even from the legal point of view, but, nevertheless, the problem of punishing crimes committed either in beginning or in conducting wars has yet to be solved". Both documents address the question why in the *Llandovery Castle* case a verdict of manslaughter rather than murder was arrived at by explaining that German law has a more exacting standard for the crime of murder than British law, see British Parliamentary Command Paper No. 1450, 1921, p. 15, *supra* note 15; Mullins, 1921, pp. 200–1, *supra* note 17.

[85] United Nations War Crimes Commission, 1948, pp. 51–52, see *supra* note 5 states that "the demand by public opinion that the war criminals of 1914–1918 should be made to answer for their crimes had ended in failure", that Leipzig court issued "findings that were contrary to the principles of all civilised nations" and that "the most shocking was not the horrors brought to light but the fact that those truly responsible were escaping punishment". It is interesting to note that the first and last ones of these quotes are taken almost verbatim from the Reports of Commission I, 1944, p. 13, see *supra* note 7 while at p. 119 in the same document the term 'disastrous' is used; this publication of the London International Assembly was a combination of submissions and comments by individuals as well as conclusions by its commission and the negative comments made about the Leipzig trials came from a both a submission and a comment by the same person, Dr. de Baer, Chief of the Belgian Court of Justice in Britain at that time.

[86] Sheldon Glueck, *The Nuremberg Trial and Aggressive War*, 1946, partially reproduced in Mettraux, 2008, p. 96, fn. 91, see *supra* note 7.

[87] Horne and Kramer, 2001, p. 350, see *supra* note 6; Lippman, 1991–1992, p. 1, see *supra* note 7, reproduced in Mettraux, 2008, p. 501, see *supra* note 7.

[88] Maogoto, 2004, p. 57, see *supra* note 5; Matthäus, 2008, p. 18, see *supra* note 6.

[89] Tusa and Tusa, 1984, p. 19, see *supra* note 79.

[90] Bass, 2000, p. 104, see *supra* note 5.

[91] *Ibid.*, p. 80.

---

sentences handed out rather than with respect to the validity of the legal principles espoused in these judgments.

With respect to the Istanbul trials, after a promising beginning with the first trials conducted in a fair manner with large numbers of witnesses,[92] these same trials also showed an underlying strong fracture in Turkish society and leadership. Kemal Bey, one of the accused in the Yozgad trial, was sentenced to death. But his execution resulted in serious nationalist unrest to the extent that supporters of the political party responsible for the Armenian massacres protested against this measure and other trials still to be held.[93] In later proceedings fewer and fewer people were arrested, charged or convicted, or escaped Turkish custody before the trials even started.[94] Moreover, a combination of a nationalist upsurge in Turkey and eventual British reluctance to either try themselves the persons in their own custody or hand them over to Turkey resulted in the new nationalist or Kemalist government of Kemal Atatürk resisting the provisions of the Treaty of Sèvres and renegotiating a new treaty without any provisions relating to trials, the Treaty of Lausanne.[95] While this rebellion had originally started to paralyse the Ottoman government in Istanbul from taking further action against the perpetrators of the Armenian massacres by releasing some of the prisoners in their custody in June 1919,[96] the influence of Atatürk started to spread as his armies

---

[92] Dadrian and Akçam, 2011, pp. 108–24, see *supra* note 5.

[93] *Ibid.*, pp. 195, 219; Bass, 2000, pp. 125–26, see *supra* note 5.

[94] Bass, 2000, pp. 124 –30, see *supra* note 5; at pp. 128–29 he indicates that this process was viewed by the British authorities in Istanbul as a 'farce'.

[95] As a matter of fact, the Declaration of Amnesty, which was attached as Part VIII to this treaty says the following in Article IV: "Turkish nationals, and reciprocally nationals of the other Powers signatory of the Treaty of Peace signed this day who may have been arrested, prosecuted or sentenced by the authorities of the said Powers or by the Turkish authorities respectively, for reasons of a political or military nature previous to the 20th November, 1922, on territory which remains Turkish in accordance with the said Treaty of Peace, shall benefit from the amnesty, and, if they are detained, shall be handed over to the authorities of the States of which they are the nationals. This stipulation is similarly applicable to Turkish nationals arrested, prosecuted or sentenced by the authorities of the Powers who have occupied a portion of the above mentioned territory even for a transgression of the ordinary law committed before that date, and even if they have been removed from Turkey, excepting those who have committed, against a person belonging to the armies of occupation, an assault which has entailed death or a grievous wound". The Treaty was signed in July 1923.

[96] Bass, 2000, p. 129, see *supra* note 5.

---

started to occupy more and more of Turkey and to defeat Allied forces. This decline in the interest in trials on the part of the British culminated in 1920, when the nationalists had taken prisoner a small group of British soldiers, and the subsequent negotiations about an exchange of the British prisoners in Turkish custody and the Turkish internees on Malta eventually resulted in all perpetrators of the Armenian genocide being released by 1 November 1921.[97] A number of these perpetrators were hunted down and assassinated by a radical wing of the Armenian Revolutionary Federation ('ARF', also known as 'the Dashaks'),[98] while in 1926 the new Kemalist government also tried, convicted and executed a number of architects of the genocide, namely high CUP officials, but on different charges relating to the overthrow of this government.[99]

Subsequent assessments of the Istanbul trials have not been as negative[100] as was the case for the Leipzig trials after the Second World War. But oblivion seems to have been their fate instead, at least until recently. For instance, while there had been some references to the Leipzig trials in the report issued by the UNWCC in 1948, the Istanbul trials were not mentioned at all in these materials.[101]

The issue of how to deal with the atrocities committed during the Second World War came to the fore as a result of statements issued by the US President, Franklin D. Roosevelt, and the British Prime Minister, Winston Churchill, on 25 October 1941, to the effect that "retribution for these crimes must henceforward take its place among the main purposes

---

[97] *Ibid.*, pp. 139–43; Willis, 1982, pp. 161–63, see *supra* note 5; Maogoto, 2004, pp. 60–61, see *supra* note 5.

[98] Bass, 2000, p. 145, see *supra* note 5; Dadrian and Akçam, 2011, pp. 178, 196, see *supra* note 5.

[99] Dadrian and Akçam, 2011, pp. 178–82, see *supra* note 5; at pp. 182–87 this book also refers to the killing of perpetrators without trial by the CUP itself in 1915 and by the new government in 1925.

[100] Willis, 1982, p. 148, see *supra* note 5; Bass, 2000, p. 127, see *supra* note 5 refers to "a promising start" while Maogoto, 2004, p. 61, see *supra* note 5 discusses "good intentions" and Dadrian and Akçam, 2011, p. 1, see *supra* note 5 states that "the tribunal gradually lost its effectiveness".

[101] Apart from the historical overview of these proceedings, the United Nations War Crimes Commission, 1948, pp. 286–87, see *supra* note 5 also refers to these trials in respect to the notion of superior orders. The fate of the Istanbul trials has been silence, which was commented by Hitler in a 1939 speech where he said: "Who after all is today speaking about the destruction of the Armenians". Rhea, 2012, p. 53, see *supra* note 6.

of the war".[102] This followed by the similar sentiment of the Minister of Foreign Affairs of the Soviet Union, V.M. Molotov, on 7 November 1941. The impetus to take action against war criminals gained momentum by the issuance of the Declaration of St James's Palace of 13 January 1942, signed by nine occupied countries,[103] and culminated in the Moscow Declaration of 1 November 1943, signed by Britain, the US and the Soviet Union. The latter provided details as to the modalities of taking legal action against such perpetrators. It stated that "they may be judged and punished according to the laws of these liberated countries" and "they will be brought back to the scene of their crimes and judged on the spot by the peoples they have outraged". It ended by saying that "the above declaration is without prejudice to the case of the major criminals whose offences have no particular geographical location and who will be punished by a joint declaration of the Governments of the Allies".[104] Neither the Leipzig nor the Istanbul trials were referred to in these various statements.[105]

While there had been some discussions at the non-governmental level regarding the established of an international criminal court dealing with war crimes and other crimes committed during the war, the issue was first raised in a government setting on 20 October 1943 at the newly established UNWCC,[106] with further discussions between February and

---

[102] United Nations War Crimes Commission, 1948, pp. 87–88, see *supra* note 5; see also Rhea, 2012, pp. 53–54, see *supra* note 6.

[103] Belgium, Czechoslovakia, France, Greece, Luxembourg, the Netherlands, Norway, Poland and Yugoslavia while the conference leading to this declaration was also attended by representatives of Britain, the US, the Soviet Union, Australia, Canada, India, New Zealand, South Africa and China.

[104] United Nations War Crimes Commission, 1948, pp. 107–8, see *supra* note 5; Rhea, 2012, pp. 55–56, see *supra* note 6.

[105] Tusa and Tusa, 1984, p. 24, see *supra* note 79.

[106] United Nations War Crimes Commission, 1948, pp. 441–43, see *supra* note 5; Rhea, 2012, pp. 59–60, see *supra* note 6. While an international conference dealing with the crime of terrorism had prepared in November 1937 a Convention for the Repression of Terrorism, to which was attached a Convention for the Creation of an International Criminal Court, the jurisdiction of this court was limited to the subject matter of terrorism and the convention never came into force due to the deteriorating international situation, see United Nations War Crimes Commission, 1948, pp. 440–41, see *supra* note 5; "Historical Survey of the Question of International Criminal Jurisdiction: Memorandum Submitted by the Secretary General", U.N. Doc. A/CN.4/7/Rev. 1, U.N. Sales No. 1949, V.8, 1949, pp. 17–18. For a detailed overview of the work of the UNWCC, see *Criminal Law Forum*

September 1944, and resulting in draft Convention for the Establishment of a United Nations Joint Court on 20 September 1944.[107] Because of concerns from Britain and the US that the UNWCC had gone beyond its mandate in terms of setting out its jurisdiction, which went as far as to include crimes committed in Germany against its own nationals, the UNWCC on 6 January 1945 made the following recommendations regarding the prosecution of war criminals:

(1) that the cases should be tried in the national courts of the countries against which the crimes have been committed;

(2) that a convention be concluded providing for the establishment of a United Nations court to pass upon such cases as are referred to it by the Governments;

(3) that pending the establishment of such a court there be established mixed military tribunals to function in addition to the United Nations Court when the latter is established.[108]

The last issue in this recommendation had already been the subject of discussion in the UNWCC since August 1944, because it had become clear that the creation of an international court would be subject to long delays and it was considered desirable to have other interim institutions in place. Articles 228 and 229 of the Versailles Treaty as well as Allied national practice were cited as precedents for such a solution.[109]

However, the two tribunals dealing with major war criminals, the International Military Tribunals in Nuremberg and Tokyo, were both initiated by the US, the first as a result of negotiations with France, Britain and the Soviet Union, resulting in the London Agreement of 8 August 1945, the second as a result of a Special Proclamation of the Supreme Commander for the Allied Powers, the US General Douglas MacArthur, on 19 January 1946.[110] The UNWCC only played an indirect part in the drawing up of the London Agreement although the statutes of

---

Symposium: The United Nations War Crimes Commission and the Origins of International Criminal Justice, 2014, vol. 25, nos. 1–2.

[107] United Nations War Crimes Commission, 1948, pp. 443–50, see *supra* note 5; Rhea, 2012, pp. 60–62, see *supra* note 6.

[108] Rhea, 2012, pp. 63–64, see *supra* note 6.

[109] United Nations War Crimes Commission, 1948, pp. 450–54, see *supra* note 5.

[110] *Ibid.*, pp. 454–61.

both institutions incorporated concepts of its draft Convention for the Establishment of a United Nations Joint Court and its work done on the mixed tribunals.[111]

9.6. Legal Findings

While most of the legal findings in the Leipzig and Istanbul trials are related to the application of either the German or Ottoman criminal codes in force at the time, there are some statements which had international legal significance at the time or which still have some resonance in modern times.

In the Istanbul trials, the language used in a number of the verdicts along the lines of massacres, extermination or annihilation of a civilian population mirror the words used in the Treaty of Sèvres. There Article 230 refers to massacres, as well as the later notion of crimes against humanity, while the use of the term "premeditation", and references to Armenian Christians as a religious group foreshadowed similar terminology in the 1948 Genocide Convention,[112] the wording of which was repeated in the statutes of the International Criminals Tribunals for

---

[111] *Ibid.*, pp. 454, 461; for detailed accounts of the conceptualisation and negotiations of the Nuremberg tribunal, see Bradley F. Smith, *Reaching Judgment at Nuremberg*, Basic Books, New York, 1977, pp. 20–45; Tusa and Tusa, 1984, pp. 50–67, see *supra* note 79; Bass, 2000, pp. 149–203, see *supra* note 5.

[112] Convention on the Prevention and Punishment of the Crime of Genocide, Article 2, 1951 (http://www.legal-tools.org/en/go-to-database/record/498c38/). Genocide as a war crime or crime against humanity was recognised by various tribunals after the Second World War, such as the International Military Tribunal at Nuremberg where it was included in the indictment as part of murder and ill-treatment of the civilian population. In the United Nations War Crimes Commission, "Justice Trial: Trial of Josef Altstötter and Others", in *Law Reports of Trials of War Criminals*, 1948, vol. 6, p. 99, the accused Rothaug was actually convicted of this crime and also found guilty of the charges of crimes against humanity. Other examples where the crime of genocide was recognised can be found in "Trial of Hauptsturmführer Amon Leopold Goeth", in *Law Reports of Trials of War Criminals*, 1948, vol. 7, pp. 7–9; "Trial of Ulrich Greifelt and Others", in *Law Reports of Trials of War Criminals*, 1949, vol. 13, pp. 37–42 and "Trial of Obersturmbannführer Rudolf Franz Ferdinand Hoess" in *Law Reports of Trials of War Criminals*, 1948, vol. 7, pp. 24–26. It appears that the tribunals treated genocide as the end result of a series of war crimes and crimes against humanity, rather than an independent crime. This was probably done in order to achieve a balance between recognising genocide as a crime on one hand and fitting the crime within the confines of their constituting instruments on the other.

the former Yugoslavia ('ICTY'), International Criminal Tribunal for Rwanda ('ICTR') and the ICC.[113]

Similarly, the wording used in the very first trial, the Yozgad trial, where the court convicted Tevfik Bey for issuing orders to his subalterns for the deportation of the Armenians, resembles the notion of command responsibility as does the judgment in the trial against the cabinet ministers, including in the latter case the element of not preventing crimes from occurring after having become aware of them. This became an ingredient of the notion of command responsibility in jurisprudence after the Second World War,[114] as well as at the ICTY and ICTR.[115] Lastly, there are some references to the concept of co-perpetration in the Yozgad and Trabzon cases, the explanation of which resemble a similar discussion at the ICC, even though these two verdicts discuss co-perpetration from a Turkish domestic law perspective.[116]

The judgments at the Leipzig trials not only discuss concepts, which bear a similarity to contemporary and present international law, they go further than the Istanbul trials by actually placing their discussions in an international law context. The *Llandovery Castle* and *Dover Castle* judgments were quite clear about this connection between

---

[113] Articles 4, 2 and 6 respectively; for a recent overview of the jurisprudence pertaining to genocide in these institutions, see Robert J. Currie and Joseph Rikhof, *International & Transnational Criminal Law,* 2nd ed., Irwin, Toronto, 2013, pp. 108–20.

[114] For an overview, see *Law Reports of Trials of War Criminals*, 1949, vol. 15, pp. 65–76.

[115] Currie and Rikhof, 2013, pp. 662–64, see *supra* note 113. The most recent iteration of this concept is included in the ICC Statute which states the following in Article 28(a):

> A military commander or person effectively acting as a military commander shall be criminally responsible for crimes within the jurisdiction of the Court committed by forces under his or her effective command and control, or effective authority and control as the case may be, as a result of his or her failure to exercise control properly over such forces, where
>
> a) that military commander or person either knew or, owing to the circumstances at the time, should have known that the forces were committing or about to commit such crimes; and
>
> b) that military commander or person failed to take all necessary and reasonable measures within his or her power to prevent or repress their commission or to submit the matter to the competent authorities for investigation and prosecution.

[116] For a discussion of the concept of co-perpetration in the ICC jurisprudence, see Currie and Rikhof, 2013, pp. 658–62, *supra* note 113.

German and international law. The first case stated that firing at boats with civilians on board was a crime under international law resulting in criminal responsibility for the perpetrator of such an act. With respect to the legal determination regarding naval warfare, the same principles as set out in the *Llandovery Castle* case were applied after the Second World War when both the International Military Tribunal in Nuremberg and the British Military Court in Germany convicted a number of German naval officers of similar activities, including Admiral Karl Dönitz, the head of the German naval forces during that time period.[117]

Both cases, as well as the Robert Neumann case, already stated the essential elements of the defence of superior orders by indicating that while in principle following orders to commit a crime would absolve a person from liability, there are also exceptions to this rule, namely that the

---

[117] Judgment of the IMT, pp. 309–14 (http://www.legal-tools.org/en/go-to-database/record/f41e8b/); the same tribunal also convicted Admiral Reader for violations of naval warfare provisions, *ibid.*, pp. 314–16. As a matter of fact, the IMT was more equivocal with respect to the rules of naval warfare than the Leipzig court had been even though the violations of the laws of war had been remarkably similar, by making comments such as "In the actual circumstances of this case, the Tribunal is not prepared to hold Dönitz guilty for his conduct of submarine warfare against British armed merchants ships" (p. 311) and "In view of all the facts proved, and in particular of an order of the British Admiralty announced on May 8, 1940, according to which all vessels should be sunk in the Skagerrak, and the answer to interrogatories by Admiral Nimitz that unrestricted submarine warfare was carried out in the Pacific Ocean by the United States from the first day that nation entered the war, the sentence of Dönitz is not assessed on the ground of his breaches of the international law of submarine warfare" (p. 312). For further background on these ambiguous statements, see Tusa and Tusa, 1984, pp. 461–62, *supra* note 79 and Smith, 1977, pp. 248–65, *supra* note 111. The British Military Court in Hamburg had less compunction in convicting senior officers of a submarine and an armed raider ship in the cases of Karl-Heinz Moehle and of Helmuth von Ruchtestell, *Law Reports of Trials of War Criminals*, 1947, vol. 9, pp. 75–82 and pp. 82–90. While some of these principles have found their way into international instruments such as the Second Geneva Convention of 1949 and the San Remo Manual on International Law Applicable to Armed Conflicts at Sea (1994) (see also Wolff Heintschel von Heinegg, "Maritime Warfare", in Andrew Clapham and Paola Gaeta (eds.), *The Oxford Handbook of International Law in Armed Conflict*, Oxford University Press, Oxford, 2014, pp. 145–81), neither the modern international(ised) tribunals nor the ICC have dealt with such issues nor have they been on the radar of domestic courts with one exception in the Netherlands, where a district court addressed naval blockade questions during the Iran–Iraq war in the context of a refugee exclusion proceeding. Rb, Den Bosch, Awb 10/32882, 14 November 2011, discussed in Joseph Rikhof, "Exclusion Law and International Law: Sui Generis or Overlap?", in *International Journal on Minority and Group Rights*, 2013, vol. 20, pp. 211–12.

person has to act within the limitations of his authority[118] and the person must not be aware that these orders were illegal.[119] While this defence was not given the same absolute character (it only went to mitigation of sentence) in the Charters of the International Military Tribunals in Nuremberg[120] and Tokyo,[121] nor the Statutes of the ICTY[122], the ICTR[123] and the Special Court for Sierra Leone,[124] a reflection of this position can be found in the ICC Statute with respect to war crimes, which were the crimes under discussion during the Leipzig trials.[125]

---

[118] This is expressed in the Neumann case by saying that a person cannot use force which is greater than necessary in the circumstances while in this case and in the *Dover Castle* case the statement is made that a person cannot go beyond the order given to him.

[119] The *Dover Castle* case states this principle by saying that a person is liable if he knows that his superiors have ordered him to carry illegal acts, which language is also used in the *Llandovery Castle* case.

[120] Article 8 of the Statute of the IMT (http://www.legal-tools.org/en/go-to-database/record/64ffdd/). It states: "The fact that the Defendant acted pursuant to order of his Government or of a superior shall not free him from responsibility, but may be considered in mitigation of punishment if the Tribunal determines that justice so requires".

[121] Article 6 of the Charter of the IMTFE with the same text as the Statute of the IMT (http://www.legal-tools.org/en/go-to-database/record/a3c41c/).

[122] Article 7.4 with again a similar text as the IMT (http://www.legal-tools.org/uploads/tx_ltpdb/statute_sept09_en_02.pdf).

[123] Article 6.4 with the same text as the ICTY Statute (http://www.legal-tools.org/en/go-to-database/record/8732d6/).

[124] Article 6.4 with the same text as the ICTY and ICTR Statutes (http://www.legal-tools.org/en/go-to-database/record/797850/).

[125] Article 33, paragraph 1 (http://www.legal-tools.org/en/go-to-database/record/7b9af9/): "The fact that a crime within the jurisdiction of the Court has been committed by a person pursuant to an order of a Government or of a superior, whether military or civilian, shall not relieve that person of criminal responsibility unless: (a) the person was under a legal obligation to obey orders of the Government or the superior in question; (b) the person did not know that the order was unlawful; and (c) the order was not manifestly unlawful" while continuing in paragraph 2: "For the purposes of this article, orders to commit genocide or crimes against humanity are manifestly unlawful". While this defence was raised on a number of occasions after the Second World War and the jurisprudence as to its constituting elements had been generally along the same lines as the Leipzig judgments (see in general *Law Reports of Trials of War Criminals*, vol. 15, pp. 157–60) while for a specific mention of the *Llandovery Castle* case as used by prosecutors, see "The Peleus Trial", in *Law Reports of Trials of War Criminals*, 1947, vol. 1, pp. 7–11, 15, 19–20; "The Belsen Trial", in *Law Reports of Trials of War Criminals*, 1947, vol. 2, p. 107; "Trial of Lieutenant-General Shigeru Sawada and Three Others", in *Law Reports of Trials of War Criminals*, 1948, vol. 5, p. 15; "Trial of Friedrich Flick and Five Others", in *Law Reports of Trials of War Criminals*, 1949, vol. 15, p. 50; "Trial of Max Wielen and 17 others, the Stalag Luft III Trial", in *Law Reports of Trials of War Criminals*, 1949, vol. 11, pp. 48–50;

In addition to the British cases, the French Stenger and Crusius case contained a principle, which, while expressed in general terms, reflects existing international law at the time, namely the prohibition of the killing of wounded soldiers, which was set out in the 1906 Convention for the Amelioration of the Condition of the Wounded and Sick in Armies in the Field.[126]

The same case also addressed two other defences, mistake of fact (which was also alluded to in the Robert Neumann case) and insanity, to the effect that if a person was under the mistaken impression that an order to execute wounded and unarmed soldiers existed he could rely on the defence of mistake of fact if he carried out such an order while a complete mental collapse could be a reason not to convict a person for the carrying out of such killings. While the Charters of the International Military Tribunals in Nuremberg and Tokyo did not specifically mention these defences, the jurisprudence after the Second World War did apply the same principles to similar situations in a few cases.[127] The international

---

"Trial of Hans Renoth and Three Others", in *Law Reports of Trials of War Criminals*, 1949, vol. 11, p. 78. The *Dover Castle* case is mentioned in the Peleus case, above, and the "Trial of General von Mackensen and General Maelzer", in *Law Reports of Trials of War Criminals*, 1949, vol. 8, p. 8. There has been no interpretation of this defence provided at the international level since that time (except briefly by the Extraordinary Chambers in the Courts of Cambodia in Judgment, *Kaing Guek Eav alias Duch*, Case File 001/18-07-2007/ECCC/TC, Trial Chamber, 26 July 2010, pp. 551–52). At the national level, reference was made to these two Leipzig cases in the decisions of the High Court of Australia in *Polyukhovich v Commonwealth* (War Crimes Act case) [1991] HCA 32 (Brennan, para. 56; Dawson, para. 87) and of the Supreme Court of Canada in *R v. Finta*, [1994] 1 SCR 701 at 834.

[126] Article 1 states "officers, soldiers, and other persons officially attached to armies, who are sick or wounded, shall be respected and cared for, without distinction of nationality, by the belligerent in whose power they are" (http://www.legal-tools.org/en/go-to-database/ltfolder/0_804/#results) and which became Article 1 in the 1929 (http://www.legal-tools.org/en/go-to-database/record/c613cf/) and Article 6 in the 1949 (http://www.legal-tools.org/en/go-to-database/record/baf8e7/) conventions of the same name, the latter also known as First Geneva Convention of 1949, where a violation of this norm is also a war crime under its Article 50. The provisions of the 1929 Convention were addressed in "The Abbaye Ardenne Case. Trial of S.S. Brigadeführer Kurt Meyer", in *Law Reports of Trials of War Criminals*, 1948, vol. 4, pp. 97–112, but the similar provision in later instruments has not been the subject of judicial consideration since that time.

[127] For the defence of mistake of fact, see "The Almelo Trial: Trial of Otto Sandrock and Three Others", in *Law Reports of Trials of War Criminals*, 1947, vol. 1, pp. 35–41 and the "Trial of Carl Rath and Richard Thiel", in *Law Reports of Trials of War Criminals*, 1949, vol. 15, p. 184, fn. 4, while for the defence regarding the mental incapacity of the accused,

---

institutions since the Second World War have not incorporated these defences in their statutes with the exception of the ICC, [128] and no jurisprudence has emanated yet from these institutions. [129]

9.7. Conclusion

The general narrative set out in the introduction of this chapter does not correspond in all aspects to the reality of the events, which took place between 1915 and 1945. To begin with, during the negotiations for the two original peace treaties, the inclusion of tribunals to deal with perpetrators who had committed their offences against nationals of more than one state, as well as the inclusion of trials for the persons involved in the Armenian genocide, caused disagreement between the majority and

---

see "Trial of Wilhem Gerbsch", in *Law Reports of Trials of War Criminals*, 1949, vol. 13, pp. 131–37.

[128] Articles 32.1 and 31.1(a) respectively.

[129] In general, the ICTY has discussed four defences, namely duress, the *tu quoque* defence, reprisals and self-defence. Duress was discussed in *Prosecutor v. Erdemović*, IT-96-22, Appeals Chamber, Joint Separate Opinion of Judge McDonald and Judge Vohrah, 7 October 1997, para. 88, which was accepted by the majority of the Chamber in *Prosecutor v. Erdemović*, IT-96-22, Appeals Chamber, Judgment, 7 October 1997, para. 19. The *tu quoque* defence, which stands for the proposition that if one party commits atrocities the other party should be justified in doing the same was rejected in a number of decisions, such as *Prosecutor v. Kupreškić et al.*, IT-95-16, Trial Chamber, Decision on Evidence of the Good Character of the Accused and The Defence of Tu Quoque, 17 February 1999, and Trial Judgment, 14 January 2000, paras. 511, 515–20 and 765; *Prosecutor v. Kunarac et al.*, IT-96-23/IT-96-23/1, Appeals Judgment, 12 June 2002, para. 87; *Prosecutor v. Limaj et al.*, IT-03-66-T, Trial Judgment, 30 November 2005, para. 193; *Prosecutor v. Stanišić and Župljanin*, IT-08-91-T, Trial Judgment, 27 March 2013, para. 16. The defence of reprisals was examined in Kupreškić et al., Trial Judgment, paras. 527–36; *Prosecutor v. Martić*, IT-95-11-T, Trial Judgment, 12 June 2007, paras. 464–68 while self-defence was discussed in *Prosecutor v. Kordić and Čerkez*, IT-95-14/2, Trial Judgment, 26 February 2001, paras. 448-452 (which was accepted as long as it is raised on a personal level rather than as an issue of military self-defence); *Prosecutor v. Bagosora, Kabiligi, Ntabakuze and Nsengiyumva*, ICTR-98-41-T, Trial Judgment, 18 December 2008, para. 1999; *Prosecutor v. Boškoski and Tarčulovski*, IT-04-82-A, Appeals Judgment, 19 May 2010, paras. 31–36, 45–46, 51 (although the latter discussed the issue of self-defence at the state level against terrorist attacks). At the Special Court for Sierra Leone, the minority of a trial chamber raised the prospect of the defence of state necessity (*Prosecutor v. Fofana and Kondewa*, SCSL-04-14-T, Separate Concurring and Partially Dissenting Judgment of Justice Bankole Thompson, 2 August 2007, paras. 68–92) but this was rejected on appeal (*Prosecutor v. Fofana and Kondewa*, SCSL-04-14-A, Appeals Judgment, 28 May 2008, para. 247).

---

the minority of the special Commission on the Responsibility of the Authors of the War and on Enforcement of Penalties, resulting in the watering down of the provisions for international tribunals and instead the setting up of mixed military tribunals.

The assessment and criticism of the Leipzig and Istanbul trials have centred around four themes, namely the weakness of domestic trials in general; the small number of persons on trial; the light sentences or acquittals given for very serious crimes; and the international law applied by these tribunals.

It was clear that the Allied countries would have preferred to put the major German and Turkish war criminals on trial before international or mixed military institutions. But apart from the eventual lack of political will on their part, due primarily to the emerging nationalist sentiments in the two countries, an argument can be made that, when the trials were held in Germany and in Turkey, these trials were conducted, especially in the beginning, in a fair and even-handed manner and with regard to the appropriate rules of evidence. It is telling that the first international statement during the Second World War dealing with exacting justice from the Germans, the Moscow Declaration, called for trials to be conducted again by national courts rather than by a tribunal at the international level.

With respect to the second issue, the number of people put on trial for the Leipzig proceedings could be questioned, as only 12 people were convicted from a much larger list provided to the German authorities. However, this argument holds less water with respect to the Istanbul trials as over 200 people were arrested and made subject to criminal proceedings. Additionally, with respect to the Turkish trials, the rank of perpetrators varied from low officials and individuals to the highest decision-makers in the land at the time of the commission of the crimes. The trial of the cabinet members and CUP leaders, in particular, was similar in importance to the International Military Tribunals in Nuremberg and Tokyo when taking into account the defendants with influence within their respective governments.

The observations with regard to sentencing are also only partially accurate. While a proportionally large number of accused in both the Leipzig and Istanbul trials were acquitted or convicted *in absentia*, the sentencing practice in Turkey especially was commensurate with the crimes committed, as can be seen from the number of death penalties, namely 13 with three actual executions, and long periods of hard labour handed out.

Lastly, reliance on and application of international law principles during the Istanbul and especially the Leipzig trials were not only appropriate in the circumstances at the time of the trials but have been applied in later proceedings as well. While the reference to international law were rather embryonic in Turkey, the German judges were conversant with the principles of international law in the area of naval warfare and the treatment of wounded soldiers, while the defences of mistake of fact, mental capacity and especially superior orders were used correctly when comparing these principles to the international law at the time. During the discussions for the establishment of the two International Military Tribunals it was acknowledged that the defence of superior orders still existed at that time and while the naval warfare doctrines and the other defences set out in Leipzig have been lost to later commentators they were applied in the same manner after the Second World War and are still useful for modern times.

10

Law as Farce:
On the Miscarriage of Justice at the German
Leipzig Trials: The *Llandovery Castle* Case

Wolfgang Form[*]

In many respects the First World War was a *novum*. It was the first time in history that war was spoken of as world event. War was waged in a way that had never before happened, an internationalised war, and if one were to take a look at the world map, there was hardly a country that was not involved. But above all, the methods of warfare changed fundamentally. New technologies were deployed: submarines, airplanes, tanks, motorised vehicles and, last but not least, chemical warfare (poison gas). By the end of the war on 11 November 1918 (signing of the armistice at Compiègne[1]), more than 8 million soldiers had died.[2] Furthermore, the dimensions of the brutality of the war[3] contributed to the Allies' demand for penal consequences. From today's perspective it was a largely unspectacular transitional justice[4] reaction. However, in 1918 it was a completely new demand: prior to this there were rarely penal

---

[*] **Wolfgang Form** studied political science, sociology, social and economic history, and public law in Marburg, and received his doctoral degree on political criminal justice during National Socialism in Germany from the University of Marburg. In 2003 he co-founded the International Research and Documentation Centre for War Crimes Trials, Marburg, and has been its project co-ordinator since. From 1992 he has been lecturer in political science and peace and conflict studies at the University of Marburg, and member of the Austrian Research Centre for Post-War Trials Advisory Board. His main fields of research are political, criminal and military justice, history of international criminal law, peace and conflict studies, and local and regional history of National Socialism.

[1] Edmund Marhefka, Hans Hammerstein and Otto Stein (eds.), *Der Waffenstillstand 1918–1919: Das Dokumentenmaterial der Waffenstillstandsverhandlungen von Compiègne, Spa, Trier und Brüssel. Notenwechsel, Verhandlungsprotokolle, Verträge, Gesamttätigkeitsbericht*, Deutsche Verlagsgesellschaft für Politik und Geschichte, Berlin, 1928.

[2] Michael Salewski, *Geschichte Europas: Staaten und Nationen von der Antike bis zur Gegenwart*, C.H. Beck, Munich, 2000, p. 993; Volker Berghahn, *Der erste Weltkrieg*, 6th ed., C.H. Beck, Munich, 2006, p. 10; Katharina Lacina, *Grundbegriffe der europäischen Geistesgeschichte: Tod*, Facultas, Vienna, 2009, p. 48.

[3] See John Horne and Alan Kramer, *German Atrocities, 1914: A History of Denial*, Yale University Press, New Haven, 2001.

[4] See Ruti G. Teitel, *Transitional Justice*, Oxford University Press, New York, 2000.

---

consequences for individual soldiers – and heads of state were never held to account.[5]

The basis for international customary law up until the First World War goes back to the Peace of Westphalia in 1648.[6] Prior to that there was fundamentally no account of the law in war (*jus in bello*).[7] Questions regarding the protection of civilians and combatants were, practically, unregulated.[8] As the first interstate agreement in Europe, the Peace of Westphalia introduced the international law of state sovereignty.[9] Contemporary commentators of that time[10] combined the traditional laws of war and customary law in a legal corpus, which have had an effect right up to modern international law.[11] Amongst them were the first beginnings of protection of the civilian population.[12] Above all was the regulation that the sovereign of a nation had the right to go to war (*jus ad bellum*). Other important aspects of the Peace of Westphalia were the payment of reparations, immunity for heads of state and amnesties for both of the warring sides.[13] No soldier or officer had to answer for atrocities committed. These basic principles were to shape post-conflict times for the next 250 years.

---

[5]   See Frank Neubacher, "Die Relativierung von Normen bei Verbrechen des Staates – wie selbst schwerste Verbrechen möglich (gemacht) werden", in Gerd Hankel (ed.), *Die Macht und das Recht: Beiträge zum Völkerrecht und Völkerstrafrecht am Beginn des 21. Jahrhunderts*, Hamburger Edition, Hamburg, 2008, pp. 23–49. The first documented case of a special military court for the prosecution of war crimes took place in 1473 in Breisach, Germany. Peter von Hagenbach was brought before a board of 27 judges and sentenced to death for murder, chain of command responsibility and unlawful requisitioning of property. See Kelly Dawn Askin, *War Crimes Against Women: Prosecution in International War Crimes Tribunals*, Martinus Nijhoff, The Hague, 1997, pp. 28–29; Elizabeth Neuffer, *The Key to My Neighbor's House: Seeking Justice in Bosnia and Rwanda*, Picador, New York, 2002, p. 67.

[6]   See Stéphane Beaulac, *The Power of Language in the Making of International Law: The Word Sovereignty in Bodin and Vattel and the Myth of Westphalia*, Martinus Nijhoff, Leiden, 2004.

[7]   Theodor Meron, *Henry's Wars and Shakespeare's Laws: Perspectives on the Law of War in the Later Middle Ages*, Clarendon Press, Oxford, 1993, p. 125.

[8]   *Ibid.*, p. 209.

[9]   *Ibid.*, p. 211.

[10]   For example, Hugo Grotius. See Norberg Konegen and Peter Nitschke (eds.), *Staat bei Hugo Grotius*, Nomos, Baden-Baden, 2005.

[11]   Meron, 1993, pp. 212–13, see *supra* note 7.

[12]   Askin, 1997, p. 26–27, see *supra* note 5; Meron, 1993, p. 112, see *supra* note 7.

[13]   See Fritz Dickmann, *Der Westfälische Frieden*, Aschendorf, Munich, 1998.

The events of the mid-nineteenth century accelerated the development of international humanitarian law. In 1859 Henry Dunant was a witness to the Battle of Solferino in which 40,000 wounded and fallen soldiers remained unattended to on the battlefield. He narrated his impressions in his book *A Memories of Solferino*.[14] His initiatives throughout the years that followed coalesced in several thrusts to make acts of war "more humane" and in veritable demands for universally valid rules. One result is the Geneva Convention for the Amelioration of the Condition of the Wounded and Sick in Armed Forces in the Field where the central article stated:

> Persons taking no active part in the hostilities, including members of armed forces who have laid down their arms and those placed hors de combat by sickness, wounds, detention, or any other cause, shall in all circumstances be treated humanely, without any adverse distinction founded on race, colour, religion or faith, sex, birth or wealth, or any other similar criteria.[15]

One must note that only the rights of the wounded and of prisoners of war ('POWs') were regulated. Questions regarding the consequences of breaches of rules were ignored. The Lieber Code of April 1863 is not to be forgotten in the overall context.[16]

At the end of the nineteenth century (1898), at the invitation of Tsar Nicholas II, all of the accredited states came together for a disarmament conference in St Petersburg.[17] From this came the programme for a peace conference, which took place from 18 May until 29 July 1899 in The Hague ('The First Hague Peace Conference'), at which the first version of the Hague Convention was designed.[18] Eight years later (1907), a second

---

[14] Jean-Henry Dunant, *Eine Erinnerungen an Solferino*, Verlag von H. Georg, Basel, 1863.

[15] Geneva Convention for the Amelioration of the Condition of Wounded and Sick Armed Forces in the Field, 12 August 1949, Article 3, and Geneva Convention relative to the Treatment of Prisoners of War, 12 August 1949, Article 3.

[16] Instructions for the Government of Armies of the United States in the Field ('Lieber Code'), 24 April 1863. See Burrus M. Carnahan, "Lincoln, Lieber and the Laws of War: The Origins and Limits of the Principle of Military Necessity", in *American Journal of International Law*, 1998, vol. 92, no. 2, pp. 213–31.

[17] Jost Dülffer, "Regeln im Krieg? Kriegsverbrechen und die Haager Friedenskonferenzen", in Wolfram Wette and Gerd R. Ueberschär (eds.), *Kriegsverbrechen im 20. Jahrhundert*, Wissenschaftliche Buchgesellschaft, Darmstadt, 2001, pp. 35–49.

[18] *Ibid.*

peace conference took place in The Hague and another version of the Hague Convention was adopted.[19] Aside from that, an addition to the implementation of the Geneva Convention regarding the Armed Forces at Sea was effected in 1907. "A central idea was an unspoken guideline, which could be applied to directly reduce legitimate deadly use of force at the core of war".[20]

In the Hague Convention four categories of international legal obligations for war were established: 1) weapons bans (like dumdum bullets,[21] gas war, etc.); 2) the protection of neutral states; 3) the definition of various modes of combatants plus the marking of military persons in order to distinguish them from the civilian population; and finally, 4) granting those no longer in combat (wounded, POWs) rights and entitlements (however, here it referred to the Geneva Convention). The right to wage war remained unchallenged, even wars of aggression. In 1907 there was no concrete regulation on the consequences of violating the rules. No level of jurisdiction was introduced which could have decided such matters.

The question of what could be understood to be a crime was discussed in the run up to the Hague Convention, because if a war were to be placed under the norm of equality, there must inevitably be penal regulations for any violation of the law. The new law was to be universally applicable, disconnected from the victor/loser scheme. The regulations were valid in war regardless of who initiated it or who won. The international regulations were valid upon declaration, but despite this, there were already the beginnings of further-reaching deliberations. Practically at the last minute, on the evening before the Hague Convention, the British military lawyer Lassa Oppenheim introduced the term 'war crime' with a handful of delict groups.[22] Additionally, he compiled, for the first time, a list of 20 violations of the law of war, which

---

[19] *Ibid.*, p. 83.

[20] *Ibid.*, p. 39.

[21] See Karl G. Sellier and Beat P. Kneubüehl, *Wound Ballistics and the Scientific Background*, Elsevier, Amsterdam, 1994, p. 182.

[22] Lassa F.L. Oppenheim, "Conception of War Crimes", in *International Law, War and Neutrality*, Longmans, Green and Co., London, 1906, pp. 264–66.

he classified as 'war crimes'.[23] Oppenheim's explanations were revolutionary. His ideas found their way into many national military handbooks.[24] The British Manual of Military Law and the American Rules of Land Warfare correspond with regard to material and procedure.[25]

From the outset of the First World War there were voices demanding that German war crimes be punished.[26] Many of the crimes mentioned (brutal treatment of civilians, killing of POWs, plundering and arson, and rapes, among others) took place in 1914, and moreover deportations took place throughout the course of the war.[27] However, it proved difficult to establish a united (international) procedural method within one administrative framework. The various national legal foundations and ideas about which groups of people ought to be prosecuted differed greatly.[28] As the war advanced, the French and British sides considered national and international strategies for prosecution.[29]

Following the armistice of 1918, the British Minister of the Marines, Winston Churchill, avowed that persons who had contravened the laws and usages of war would be indicted and brought before court, particularly those who had committed atrocities against helpless prisoners. If they had made themselves guilty, then they were to be punished, as they deserved – regardless of which military rank they held.[30] Churchill's demands were welcomed by many in the ranks of the

---

[23] *Ibid.*; see also Lassa F.L. Oppenheim, "Punishment of War Crimes", in *International Law: A Treatise*, vol. 2, *Disputes, War and Neutrality*, Longmans, Green and Co., London, 1937, pp. 452–60.

[24] J.E. Edmonds and Lassa F.L. Oppenheim, *Land Warfare: An Exposition of the Laws and Usages of War on Land, for the Guidance of Officers of His Majesty's Army*, His Majesty's Stationery Office, London, 1912, p. 163.

[25] Gerd Hankel, *Die Leipziger Prozesse: Deutsche Kriegsverbrechen und ihre strafrechtliche Verfolgung nach dem Ersten Weltkrieg*, Hamburger Edition, Hamburg, 2003, p. 164.

[26] John Horne and Alan Kramer, *Deutsche Kriegsgreuel 1914: Die umstrittene Wahrheit*, Hamburger Edition, Hamburg, 2004, pp. 482–83.

[27] *Ibid.*, appendix 4, pp. 656–57.

[28] *Ibid.*

[29] James F. Willis, *Prologue to Nuremberg: The Politics and Diplomacy of Punishing War Criminals of the First World War*, Greenwood Press, Westport, CT, 1982, pp. 50–52, 77–82; Daniel Marc Segesser, "'Aggression is the Most Dangerous International Crime': Die internationale Debatte zur Frage der Ahndung von Kriegsverbrechen 1919–1945", in Timm C. Richter (ed.), *Krieg und Verbrechen: Situation und Intentionen: Fallbeispiele*, Martin Meidenbauer, Munich, 2006, pp. 219–30, p. 221.

[30] Hankel, 2003, p. 26, see *supra* note 25.

Allies, and so the definitional clarification of war crimes was taken up once again and successfully developed from there. The French government was also heading in the same direction in a statement on 5 October 1918: "acts so contrary to International Law, and to the very principles of human civilisation, should not go unpunished".[31] In 1919 the Allies called for a peace conference in Paris to negotiate the modalities of a peace treaty.[32]

> At one of the earliest sittings of that commission in Paris, on 7th February, 1919, British delegates pointed out, unless immediate steps were taken to arrest War Criminals, the labours of the commission might prove fruitless.[33]

A commission of the negotiating parties was to find a way to discuss the many questions which had arisen with regard to an original international criminal law.[34] In the course of the proceedings of the committee sittings[35] – which were not without tension – and following the study of a great number of documents,[36] a comprehensive 32-point list of war crimes was produced (see Table 1).[37] Many of the points are as valid today as they were in 1919.[38]

---

[31] Claud Mullins, *The Leipzig Trials: An Account of the War Criminals Trials and a Study of German Mentality*, H.F. & G. Witherby, London, 1921, p. 5. See also Walter Schwengler, *Völkerrecht, Versailler Vertrag und Auslieferungsfrage: die Strafverfolgung wegen Kriegsverbrechen als Problem des Friedensschlusses 1919/20*, Deutsche Verlags-Anstalt, Stuttgart, 1982, pp. 72–74.

[32] The War Crimes Commission Report, which was presented to the Preliminary Peace Conference, is reproduced in *American Journal of International Law*, 1920, vol. 14, pp. 95–154. See also Schwengler, 1982, pp. 71–124, *supra* note 31.

[33] Mullins, 1921, p. 6, see *supra* note 31.

[34] The "Commission des responsabilités des auteurs de la guerre et sanctions" created with 15 members (Chair : US Foreign Minister Robert Lansing). James B. Scott, "The Trial of the Kaiser", in Edward M. House and Charles Seymour (eds.), *What Really Happened at Paris: The Story of the Peace Conference, 1918–1919*, Charles Scribner's Sons, New York, 1921, pp. 232–33.

[35] See Willis, 1982, pp. 70–71, *supra* note 29; Horne and Kramer, 2004, pp. 484–87, *supra* note 26.

[36] The War Crimes Commission Report, 1920, p. 112, see *supra* note 32.

[37] *Ibid.* "In spite of the explicit regulation, of established customs, and of the clear dictates of humanity, Germany and her allies have piled outrage upon outrage [...] it is impossible to imagine a list of cases so diverse and so painful".

[38] See Askin, 1997, p. 45, *supra* note 5; William A. Schabas, *Genocide in International Law: The Crime of Crimes*, Cambridge University Press, Cambridge, 2000, p. 17; Seth P.

Table 1: War Crimes Identified by 1919 Allied War Crimes Commission

War Crimes[39]
1   Murder and massacres, systematic terrorism
2   Putting hostages to death
3   Torture of civilians
4   Deliberate starvation of civilians
5   Rape
6   Abduction of girls and women for the purpose of enforced prostitution
7   Deportation of civilians
8   Internment of civilians under inhuman conditions
9   Forced labour of civilians in connection with the military operations of the enemy
10   Usurpation of sovereignty during military occupation
11   Compulsory enlistment of soldiers among the inhabitants of occupied territory
12   Attempts to denationalise the inhabitants of occupied territory
13   Pillage
14   Confiscation of property
15   Exaction of illegitimate or of exorbitant contributions and requisitions
16   Debasement of the currency and issue of spurious currency
17   Imposition of collective penalties
18   Wanton devastation and destruction of property
19   Deliberate bombardment of undefended places
20   Wanton destruction of religious, charitable, educational, and historic buildings and monuments
21   Destruction of merchant ships and passenger vessels without warning and without provision for the safety of passengers or crew

Tillman, *Anglo-American Relations at the Paris Peace Conference of 1919*, Princeton University Press, Princeton, NJ, 1961, p. 312.

[39] US National Archives and Records Administration ('NARA'), microfilm series M-1891, roll 1. See also The War Crimes Commission Report, 1920, pp. 114–15, *supra* note 32; United Nations War Crimes Commission, *History of the United Nations War Crimes Commission and Development of the Laws of War*, Her Majesty's Stationery Office, London, 1948, pp. 34–35; Harald Wiggenhorn, *Verliererjustiz: Die Leipziger Kriegsverbrecherprozesse nach dem Ersten Weltkrieg*, Studien Zur Geschichte des Völkerrechts, Nomos Verlag, Baden-Baden, 2005, pp. 18–19.

	War Crimes[39]
22	Destruction of fishing boats and of relief ships
23	Deliberate bombardment of hospitals
24	Attack on and destruction of hospital ships
25	Breach of other rules relating to the Red Cross
26	Use of deleterious and asphyxiating gases
27	Use of explosive or expanding bullets and other inhuman appliances
28	Directions to give no quarter
29	Ill-treatment of wounded and prisoners of war
30	Employment of prisoners of war on unauthorized works
31	Misuse of flags of truce
32	Poisoning of wells

In their explanatory statement, the 15 editors cited:

> Violations of the rights of combatants, of the rights of civilians, and of the rights of both, are multiplied in this list of most cruel practices which primitive barbarism, aided by all the resources of modern science, could devise for the execution of a system of terrorism carefully planned and carried out to the end.[40]

War criminals stop at nothing, not even women and children, to destroy resistance with terror and cruelty:

> Murders and massacres, tortures, shields formed of living human beings, collective penalties, the arrest and execution of hostages, the requisitioning of services for military purpose [...] the destruction of merchant ships without previous visit and without any precautions for the safety of passengers and crew, [...] attacks on hospital ships, the poisoning of springs and wells, [...] deliberate destruction of industries with no other object than to promote German economic supremacy after the war, constitute the most shame of those who committed them.[41]

---

[40] The War Crimes Commission Report, 1920, pp. 113, see *supra* note 32.
[41] *Ibid.*, pp. 113–14.

Spurred on by a backdrop of various crimes, a special commission for the comprehensive collation of war crimes was established.[42]

> A commission should be created for the purpose of collecting and classifying systematically all the information already had or to be obtained, in order to prepare as complete a list of facts as possible concerning the violation of the laws and costumes of war committed by the forces of the German Empire and its Allies, on land, on sea and in the air, in the course of the present war.[43]

According to the recommendation, it should have been an international commission, as no other undertaking could have implemented it. All affected states would have been obligated to assist in comprehensively documenting all wartime atrocities. It did not come to that, but the idea itself remained in the "collective diplomatic memory" of the Allies. During the Second World War the Allies and the exile-governments of countries occupied by Germany once again took up those ideas and founded the United Nations War Crimes Commission in 1943.[44]

The commission that was convened by the Paris Peace Conference was also responsible for other tasks. Amongst others they were to determine "the responsibility for these offences attaching to the enemy forces, including members of the General Staffs and other individuals, however highly placed".[45] In their explanation it was clearly emphasised that there could be no position and no military rank which could be excluded from potential prosecution – not even a head of state. Even if the prosecution of a head of state was not foreseen on a national level, from an international perspective this was not a procedural bar.[46] Accordingly, the establishment of an international court seemed to be a reasonable decision because respecting the immunity of a head of state "would shock

---

[42] *Ibid.*, p. 114.

[43] *Ibid.*, p. 115, para. 2 of the conclusions.

[44] Wolfgang Form, "Planung und Durchführung west-alliierter Kriegsverbrecherprozesse nach dem Zweiten Weltkrieg", in Thomas von Winter and Volker Mittendorf (eds.), *Perspektiven der politischen Soziologie im Wandel von Gesellschaft und Staatlichkeit: Festschrift für Theo Schiller*, Verlag für Sozialwissenschaften, Wiesbaden, 2008, pp. 238–39; United Nations War Crimes Commission, 1948, see *supra* note 39.

[45] The War Crimes Commission Report, 1920, p. 116, see *supra* note 32.

[46] *Ibid.* See also James W. Garner, "Punishment of Offenders against the Laws and the Customs of War", in *American Journal of International Law*, 1920, vol. 14, pp. 71–73.

the conscience of civilized mankind".[47] Deciding against the criminal responsibility of the German Kaiser[48] would have had fatal consequences for the implementation of sentences against less high-ranking war criminals. Every accused would have been able to imply "superior orders of a sovereign against whom no steps had been or were being taken".[49] If Kaiser Wilhelm II were sentenced, this defence strategy would be obsolete.

10.1. The Treaty of Versailles

The delegates of the Allied and Associated Powers took on board the suggestions of the commission and completed the work on the peace treaty in the following weeks. It ended with a unique and comprehensive body of legislation: the Treaty of Versailles of 28 June 1919. Its revolutionary Articles 227 to 230 founded a new era of international relations.[50]

Article 227. The German Kaiser was to be arraigned.

> A special tribunal will be constituted to try the accused, thereby assuring him the guarantees essential to the right of defence. It will be composed of five judges, one appoint by each of the following Powers: namely, the United States of America, Great Britain, France, Italy, and Japan. In its decision the tribunal will be guided by the highest motives of international policy, with a view to vindicating the solemn obligations of international undertakings and the validity of international morality. It will be its duty to fix the punishment which it considers should be imposed.[51]

The German Kaiser had fled to the Netherlands.[52] The Treaty dictated that his extradition would be applied for (Article 227, para. 4). For all intents and purposes Wilhelm II was seen as being responsible for the war. The

---

[47] The War Crimes Commission Report, 1920, p. 116, see *supra* note 32.

[48] Alan Kramer, "Versailles, deutsche Kriegsverbrechen und das Auslieferungsbegehren der Alliierten, 1919/20", in Wette and Ueberschär, 2001, pp. 75–76, see *supra* note 17.

[49] The War Crimes Commission Report, 1920, p. 117, see *supra* note 32.

[50] In general, see Schwengler, 1982, pp. 125–232, *supra* note 31; Hankel, 2003, pp. 19–40, *supra* note 25; Horne and Kramer, 2004, pp. 488–96, *supra* note 26.

[51] Treaty of Versailles, Article 227, paras. 2–3. *Deutsches Reichsgesetzblatt 1919*, p. 980. See also Garner 1920, pp. 91–92, *supra* note 46.

[52] Kramer, 2001, pp. 75–76, see *supra* note 48.

British Foreign Minister, Lord Curzon, summarised what many politicians thought at the end of the First World War:

> We know that the war was started by the Kaiser, and we have reason to believe that all the cruelty, the inequities, and the horrors that have been perpetrated, of not directly inspired by him, have been countenanced and in no way discouraged by him. In my view the Kaiser is the arch-Criminal of the world, and just as in any other sphere of life when you get hold of criminal you bring him to justice, so I do not see, because he is an Emperor and living in exile in another country, why he should be saved from the punishment which is his due.[53]

Article 228. "The German Government recognise[d] the right of the Allied and Associated Powers to bring before military tribunals persons accused of having committed acts in violation of the laws and customs of war" (Article 228, para. 1). Should it come to a conviction, the sentence would be implemented without regard to possible trials before courts in Germany or its confederates. German war criminals were not entitled to the use of the *ne bis in idem* principle,[54] which excluded double penalties. In Article 228, the question of extradition was also addressed: Germany was obligated to accommodate all relevant petitions made by the Allies (Article 228, para. 2). Thereby an alleged war criminal did not necessarily have to be mentioned by name. A summary list – related approximately to rank or official position in a specific context – would suffice.

Article 229 referred to the application of the principle of territoriality. "Persons guilty of criminal acts against the nationals of one of the Allied and Associated Powers will be brought before the military tribunals of that Power" (Article 229, para. 1). As for different cases in which obvious regional attribution could not be proven, an international military tribunal would be established (Article 229, para. 2). This purported a similar direction to that of the 1943 Moscow Declaration.[55]

---

[53] Schwengler, 1982, pp. 74–75, see *supra* note 31. See also Schabas, 2000, p. 17, *supra* note 38; David Lloyd George, *The Truth about the Peace Treaties*, vol. 1, Victor Gollancz, London, 1938, pp. 93–114.

[54] See Magdalena Sepúlveda, T. van Banning, G.D. Gudmundsdottir, C. Chamoun and W.J.M. van Genugten (eds.), *Human Rights Reference Handbook*, University of Peace, Ciudad Colon, 2004, p. 173.

[55] Form, 2008, p. 236, see *supra* note 44.

Article 230. It was clear to the Allies that without further records (evidence, documents, orders, etc.) the war crimes trials could not be initiated. Thus, in Article 230 they explicitly referred to the obligation of the German government to hand over all records and information, "the production of which may be considered necessary to ensure the full knowledge of the incriminating acts, the discovery of offenders and the just appreciation of responsibility".

These, then, were the regulations of the Treaty of Versailles. However, the legal reality was much more complex. On the one hand, the Netherlands declined to extradite the ex-Kaiser Wilhelm II to Germany.[56] Therewith, the legitimacy of bringing war criminals before Allied courts or international tribunals was damaged.[57] In particular, the German military vehemently opposed any extradition of other war criminals.[58] At the beginning of February 1920, the Allies forwarded an extradition list of more then 850 persons – in their view this concerned the most serious war criminals.[59] Most of the men were to be extradited to France and Belgium (over 300 each).[60] Many of the crimes mentioned took place in 1914 (brutal treatment of civilians, killing of POWs, plundering and arson, and rapes amongst others), and moreover deportations throughout the course of the war.[61]

10.2. German War Crimes Trials Law

Heated discussion about the extradition demands broke out, and became increasingly explosive as Germany broke new ground at the end of 1919, threatening to undermine – or raise structural questions about – Articles 227 to 230. On the one hand, the German government alluded to the general danger of a revolution of political order – in other words leftist or right-wing conservative subversion. Had this proven to be true, it would have been bad for reparations. Any political change would have led to the

---

[56] Kramer, 2001, pp. 75–76, see *supra* note 48.

[57] Horne and Kramer, 2004, p. 498, see *supra* note 26.

[58] Schwengler, 1982, pp. 246–50, see *supra* note 31.

[59] *Ibid.* pp. 303–5; Hankel, 2003, p. 42, see *supra* note 24; Wiggenhorn, 2005, pp. 57–62, see *supra* note 39.

[60] Hankel, 2003, p. 41, supra note 25; Horne and Kramer, 2004, pp. 500, 656–57 (Appendix 4), see *supra* note 26.

[61] Horne and Kramer, 2004, pp. 656–57 (Appendix 4), see *supra* note 26.

interruption or even the cancellation of monetary obligations arising from the Treaty of Versailles.[62] On the other hand the German Constituent National Assembly declared the Law on the Prosecution of War Crimes and War Offences on 18 December 1919 ('German Prosecution Law').[63]

§ 1 regulated the jurisdiction of the *Reichsgericht* (German Supreme Court) for the inquiry and adjudication of crimes and offences committed by Germans both nationally and abroad against enemy citizens or their property during the First World War. As a result, the reach of the sentencing powers of German criminal law had to be extended to other states (§ 2). The trials were to be held as trials of the first instance, as was usual under the *Reichsgericht*.[64] No separate 'war criminal' chamber was established, but rather the regular criminal chamber was to be responsible (§ 4 Abs. 2). As stated in § 1, in parallel to German criminal law, war delicts were distinguished into crimes and offences. The result of which was that not all of the prescribed offences were automatically crimes. According to the German criminal code, crimes were to be punished with more than one year of *Zuchthaus*[65] or the death penalty (§ 1 Abs. 1 StGB – German Penal Code). In contrast, an offence would be punished by *Gefängnis*[66] (one day to five years), *Festungshaft – custodia honesta*[67] (less than five years) or a fine (over 150 Reichsmark, § 1 Abs. 2 StGB).[68] Consequently, the trials before the *Reichsgericht* were not war crimes

---

[62] Schwengler, 1982, pp. 298–99, supra note 31.

[63] *Deutsches Reichsgesetzblatt 1919*, pp. 2125–26. The law was signed by Reichspräsident (Reich President) Ebert and Minister of Justice Eugen Schiffer.

[64] § 3 Kriegsverbrechergesetz (War Crimes Law).

[65] *Zuchthaus* was a hard labour penal facility. A *Zuchthaus* was a type of prison for prisoners in penal servitude. This meant that the prisoners were subjected to much harsher living conditions than in a regular prison, their civil rights were taken away from them and they were made to work at hard labour. Communication with the outside world was extremely limited both in terms of letter writing and visits from family members and/or friends. German Penal Code 1871, 16 April 1871, p. 14. See Karl Lorenz *et al.*, *Justus von Olshausens's Kommentar zum Strafgesetzbuch für das Deutsche Reich*, 11th ed., Berlin, 1927, pp. 90–94.

[66] Regular prison. A *Gefängnis* is a prison. Prisoners in a *Gefängnis* lost their civil freedoms but were not subjected to hard labour and living conditions were markedly better than in a *Zuchthaus*. Regular prisoners could write and receive letters and receive visitors; *ibid.*

[67] George Sigerson, *"Custodia Honesta": Treatment of Political Prisoners in Great Britain*, The Woman's Press, London, 1913.

[68] See Ludwig Ebermayer, Adolf Lobe and Werner Rosenberg, *Leipziger Kommentar zum Reichsstrafgesetzbuch*, Walter de Gruyter, Berlin, 1929, pp. 115–19.

---

trials in today's sense. If one compares the prescribed terminology of the Allies – which universally operated using the term crime – this deviation is striking.[69] The most serious form of crime as defined according to the French legal system was a crime (French: *crime*). In contrast to this, less serious criminal actions were offences (French: *délit*). If the German Prosecution Law differentiated between a crime and an offence, then this must have had an impact on the verdicts reached by the *Reichsgericht*. If all of the punishable actions had exclusively been crimes, this would have led to minimum sentences of one-year *Zuchthaus* (for the perpetrators, though not the abettors § 49 StGB). Under German law, further consequences were to be expected, for example the loss of civil rights or the so-called unworthiness to do military service (§ 34 No. 2 StGB).[70]

The prevailing anti-Allies mood in Germany against the war crimes trials did not just manifest itself in pubs and discussions of the ordinary people. There was also vehement criticism of the Treaty of Versailles from the ranks of lawyers.[71] Those who pointed out that the German invasion of Belgium in 1914 constituted a breach of international treaties were punished with exclusion from the judicial academic community. Only a few academics and men of letters demanded a complete clarification of war guilt and the consequences of war.[72] The article in the Treaty of Versailles on reparations seemed less contentious than the threat of extradition of German citizens.[73] At the end of 1919, the Allies responded to the apparent lack of German co-operation in writing.[74]

§ 6 para. 1 of the German Prosecution Law after all allowed the possibility of civil claims. As § 1 defined the nationality of the victim, they could only deal with foreigners (crimes or offences which were committed against enemy citizens). However, there was another possibility. According to § 6 para. 2, the Minister of Justice could admit

---

[69] Schwegler, 1982, see *supra* note 31; Hankel, 2003, see *supra* note 25; Horne and Kramer, 2001, see *supra* note 3; Wiggenhorn, 2005, see *supra* note 39.

[70] German Penal Code, pp. 32–34, see *supra* note 65. See Ebermayer, Lobe and Rosenberg, 1929, pp. 183–87, see *supra* note 68. See also *Wehrgesetz*, 24 March 1921, pp. 44, 48. See Martin Rittau, *Wehrgesetz vom 21.3.1921 in der Fassung des Gesetzes vom 18.6.1921 nebst Anlagen 1 bis 8*, Verlag Kameradschaft, Berlin, 1924.

[71] Wiggenhorn, 2005, pp. 39–41, see *supra* note 39.

[72] *Ibid.*, p. 40.

[73] Kramer, 2001, pp. 79–82, see *supra* note 48.

[74] See Schwengler, 1982, pp. 268–70, *supra* note 31.

other persons as civil parties. It is assumed that this passage was thought to facilitate co-operation with the Allies by allowing them to appoint their own representatives.[75]

The Minister of Justice, Fritz Scheffer, tabled the German Prosecution Law at the beginning of December 1919 with the intention of having a political parliamentary discussion on devolving the prosecution of war crimes and offences to the *Reichsgericht*. This too was perceived to be a signal to the Allies, as it admitted that German wartime atrocities merited punishment.[76] The *Reichsgericht* was the only high judicial alternative. Military jurisdiction (Supreme Military Court – *Reichskriegsgericht*) no longer existed: it had been dissolved and could only be reinstated in the event of war.[77] As a result of the German Prosecution Law, there were dogmatic criminal law problems in Germany: 1) which legal basis should be used, as neither German criminal law nor military law recognised crimes under international law? 2) criminal proceedings were aimed exclusively at German perpetrators, even if foreigners (Allies) too committed crimes under the jurisdiction of German criminal law.[78]

The discussion in the German National Assembly about the proposed German Prosecution Law was emotionally charged.[79] When a parliamentarian remarked that it was nothing more than a belated attempt to conciliate with the Allies,[80] the government vehemently rebuffed it.[81] There was an interesting amendment from Oskar Cohn (*Unabhängige Sozialdemokratische Partei Deutschlands* [Independent Social Democratic Party of Germany]). He pleaded for the setting up of a People's Court, which should mainly be made up of non-jurists.[82] The petition was not followed and the suggested law at the end of the

---

75 Wiggenhorn, 2005, p. 43, see *supra* note 39.

76 *Ibid.*, p. 7.

77 Weimar Constitution, 11 August 1919, Article 106. See also *Gesetz betrifft Aufhebung der Militärgerichtsbarkeit*, 17 August 1920.

78 See Kramer, 2001, pp. 79–82, *supra* note 48; Willis, 1982, pp. 1–125, *supra* note 29.

79 See *Verhandlungen der verfassungsgebenden Deutschen Nationalversammlung*, vol. 331, pp. 4041–48.

80 *Ibid.*, p. 4043.

81 *Ibid.*, pp. 4044–45 (Scheffer, Minister of Justice), p. 4046 (Müller, Foreign Minister). See Wiggenhorn, 2005, pp. 45–47, *supra* note 39.

82 *Ibid.*, p. 4041.

---

deliberations on 13 December 1919 was adopted unanimously.[83] The Allies were immediately informed of the new state of affairs.[84]

Shortly after the German Prosecution Law came into effect, the advocates responsible for the criminal proceedings indicated that there were problems with personnel. The permanent staff would not have been able to cope with the expected volume of work. There was also fundamental criticism of the accuracy of the wording of the law.[85] Some legal commentators spoke of an obvious connection between the law and the extradition debate. Due to the fact that the German side had not spoke of war crimes since the armistice from 1918, this sudden change of tack could only be judged as a final attempt, at the last minute, to impede the imminent extraditions.[86]

The National Liberal Party Member of Parliament and legal scientist, Wilhelm Kahl, hit the nail on the head: if the permanent removal of Article 228 could not be achieved, then the German Prosecution Law had not fulfilled its aim and must be cancelled.[87] The law initiative was not an attempt to punish wartime atrocities, but was merely a means to an end.[88] The history of what became known as the Leipzig trials shows that the law was not representative of an individual opinion, but rather a consensus on avoiding the worst evil.

10.3. The Leipzig Trials

Shortly after the German Prosecution Law came into effect, the Allies and the Germans agreed, after long and difficult negotiations, to the implementation of the Treaty of Versailles on 10 January 1920. As regulated by Article 3 of the final protocol, the Allies had one month to

---

[83] *Ibid.*, p. 4048.

[84] Wiggenhorn, 2005, p. 48, see *supra* note 39.

[85] Albert Feisenberger, "Die Verfolgung von Kriegsverbrechen und -vergehen", in *Deutsche Strafrechts-Zeitung*, 1920, vol. 7, pp. 20–23.

[86] Wiggenhorn, 2005, p. 42, see *supra* note 39.

[87] *Ibid.*, p. 51.

[88] *Ibid.*, p. 52. See also Hermann Wittmaack, *Über die Verantwortlichkeit von Angehörigen der Armee im Feindesland (Artikel 228 des Friedensvertrages)*, Ferdinand Enke, Stuttgart, 1920; Heinrich Klemens von Feilitsch, "Deutsche Kriminalpolitik: Das Gesetz zur Verfolgung von Kriegsverbrechen und Kriegsvergehen vom 18. Dezember 1919", in *Goltdammers Archiv für Strafrecht und Strafprozess*, 1920, vol. 69, pp. 29–33.

hand over the extradition lists.[89] As has already been mentioned, there were 850 persons on the list, which was handed over at the beginning of February.[90] Prior to this, attempts were made, from within the ranks of the military, to help potentially affected officers to go into hiding or flee to other countries.[91] The danger of a military coup can be substantiated – and there were even plans to reignite the war.[92] At the same time, the German diplomacy sought to explain to the Allies that it was at the moment administratively impossible to implement the extraditions. The Reichs Government felt affronted by the naming of well-known persons like Hindenburg, Ludendorff and other military, political and noble dignitaries. The situation appeared to escalate and Germany was threatening to collapse into chaos. Aware of the precarious political situation, the politicians of the Entente Powers kept an observant distance. Additionally, the Allies were no longer as at one among themselves as they had been at the end of the war and in 1919.[93]

Ultimately, the German move to enact the German Prosecution Law proved to be advantageous as a face-saving solution for all sides.[94] The redemptory news from the British Foreign Minister Lloyd George to the Reich President Friedrich Ebert came on 17 February 1920. The Allied Powers declared that they were prepared to accept Germany's offer.[95] All those named on the extradition list could, without delay, be indicted before the *Reichsgericht*.[96]

The prosecution of war criminals by Allied Tribunals was made possible by Article 228 of the Treaty of Versailles but was not compulsory: "The German Government recognise the right of the Allied [...] to bring before military tribunals persons accused of having

---

[89] Wiggenhorn, 2005, p. 53, see *supra* note 39.

[90] Horne and Kramer, 2004, pp. 656–57, see *supra* note 26; Hankel, 2003, pp. 42–43, see *supra* note 25; Kramer, 2001, p. 81, see *supra* note 48; Wiggenhorn, 2005, pp. 53–54, see *supra* note 39; Willis, 1982, pp. 117–20, see *supra* note 29.

[91] Schwengler, 1982, p. 295, see *supra* note 31; Wiggenhorn, 2005, p. 55, see *supra* note 39.

[92] Schwengler, 1982, pp. 314–16, see *supra* note 31.

[93] Hankel, 2003, p. 48, see *supra* note 25.

[94] Schwengler, 1982, pp. 316–17, see *supra* note 31; Wiggenhorn, 2005, pp. 60–61, see *supra* note 39; Willis, 1982, pp. 124–26, see *supra* note 29.

[95] German Note January 25, 1920. *Verhandlungen der verfassungsgebenden Deutschen Nationalversammlung*, 1920, vol. 341, p. 2391.

[96] *Ibid.*

---

committed acts in violation of the laws and customs of war".[97] An automatism did not arise out of the formulation. It was clear to all parties to the Treaty at the time it was signed that the extradition of German war criminals could be demanded. Lloyd George explicitly emphasised that the mutual decision would be compliant with the Treaty of Versailles.[98] At the same time the Allies assured Germany that they would not become involved in German jurisprudence and "the German government would be left fully responsible".[99] However, they also pointed out that they would vigilantly observe the latter on the so-called Leipzig Trials and would take it upon themselves to verify the will to prosecute depending on the outcome of the proceedings. If it came to it and the German judiciary did not sentence the perpetrators appropriately, then the favourable allowances could be revoked.[100] What the Germans should have done was to arrest all of the accused. In order to support the Reich Attorney General (*Reichsanwalt*) in its inquiries, the Allied Commission considered collating all of the evidence against war criminals and then handing it over to Germany.[101]

Now there was no going back and Germany had to begin the promised trials. However before that could happen they had to make some clarifications of the German Prosecution Law. On the 24 March 1920 the German National Assembly passed a law amending the German Prosecution Law.[102] Amnesty regulations,[103] problems regarding readmission and the statute of limitations were smoothed out (§ 2). Further regulations incorporated into the law were obviously for the 'benefit' of the accused. On the one hand the Reich Attorney General could petition to terminate a trial if he ascertained that the evidence was not sufficient for a conviction. The *Reichsgericht* could also take the

---

[97] *Reichsgesetzblatt 1919*, p. 980 (English version).

[98] *Verhandlungen der verfassungsgebenden Deutschen Nationalversammlung*, 1920, vol. 341, p. 2391.

[99] *Ibid.* (my translation).

[100] *Ibid.*, p. 2392. The original text in French: "*Les Puissances se réservent d'apprécier si les procédures proposées par l'Allemagne pour assurer suivant elle aux inculpés toutes les garanties de la justice n'ont pas en définitive pour effet de les soustraire au juste châtiment de leurs forfaits. Les Alliés exerceraient leurs propres tribunaux.*"

[101] *Ibid.*

[102] *Reichsgesetzblatt 1920*, pp. 341–43. See also *Verhandlungen der verfassungsgebenden Deutschen Nationalversammlung*, 1920, vol. 332, pp. 4659–74, 4694–702.

[103] *Reichsgesetzblatt 1918*, p. 1415.

decision of stay of procedure on the basis of the documents presented. From today's perspective, § 4 is incomprehensible, whereby in the case of a conviction the costs for the trial could be paid in full or in part by the state.[104] Through the suspension of the regular codes of procedure, the risk of litigation was reduced. It was also a clear sign to all potential defendants that they would be treated differently to 'normal' criminals. Given that there would be legal costs for the accused in the case of a conviction, the special treatment of war criminals can only be understood as a type of exculpation by the state. Therewith the "Farce Leipzig Trials" began months before the first court case. In March 1920 it should have been clear to the Allies that the German will to prosecute was threatening to tend in the direction of taking on a symbolic character.

The extradition list from February 1920 was still valid. In May 1920, however, the Germans received a new list: 45 names were put together with the instruction that the promise of criminal prosecution was to be honoured.[105] The list was the result of the appointment of an interim inter-Allies mixed commission and was proclaimed, and applied as, a 'test list' to check how prepared the Germans were to prosecute. As there were no 'big names' aside from General Feldmarschall von Bülow, it can be assumed that the upper ranks of the military leadership were taken out of the line of fire.[106]

Between 1921 and 1927 the *Reichsgericht* ruled on hundreds of cases of war crimes and offences. However, there were only 12 trials with a total of 17 accused (see Table 2) before Court. "Large proportions were adjudicated in closed hearing by order of the Court or were terminated by order of the Court by the Reichs Attorney General".[107] Three clusters of cases can be ascertained: 1) January 1921; 2) May to July 1921; and 3) July to November 1922 (see Table 2).

The first trial took place on 10 January 1921. However, it did not deal with any accused from the Allied list. Moreover the charge was rather lapidary, it related to 800 Reichsmark and a few valuables.[108]

---

[104] See Wiggenhorn, 2005, p. 65, *supra* note 39.

[105] Hankel, 2003, p. 56, see *supra* note 25.

[106] Schwengler, 1982, pp. 341–43, see *supra* note 31.

[107] Hankel, 2003, p. 91, see *supra* note 25 (my translation).

[108] Schwengler, 1982, p. 345, see *supra* note 31.

Doubtlessly, many comparable crimes happened during the occupation of Belgium.[109]

What the Allies actually wanted to see tried as war crimes were offences of an entirely different level:

- killing of civilians,
- rape,
- ill-treatment of POWs and civilians,
- pillage,
- arson,
- massacres,
- felonious orders,
- cannonade of unfortified cities and towns,
- cultural abhorrence,
- atrocities in POW camps,
- deportations,
- forced labour,
- and last but not least crimes on the sea.[110]

Despite this, the most severe punishment of all the Leipzig Trials was four to five years of *Zuchthaus* (handed down in the case against Lottmann *et al.* – see Table 2). The public interest in the trial was relatively big. Many daily papers published reports on the trials. However, with the exception of the left-wing press, they abstained from critical comments.[111]

Above all, German politicians and military personnel attentively observed the trial, as they were aware of the volatility of the trials. In further proceedings, high-ranking government ministers agreed to a course of action: cases that would obviously lead to convictions should be alternated, where possible, with cases that were less clear. In this way, acquittals or very mild punishments would not accumulate.[112] Moreover, the 'test list' of May 1920 was to be binding. Against the backdrop of the

---

[109] Hankel tells of 1,500 cases. Hankel, 2003, p. 91 footnote 1, see *supra* note 25.

[110] See Horne and Kramer, 2004, pp. 656–57 (Appendix 4), *supra* note 26.

[111] Hankel, 2003, p. 97, see *supra* note 25; Schwengler, 1982, p. 345 *supra* note 31.

[112] Schwengler, 1982, p. 345, see *supra* note 31.

criminal offence in the *Lottmann et al.* case and the register of crimes on the 'test list', one would assume that the expected penalty must be quite severe. It did not, however, come to that.

In spring 1921, within the framework of the second cluster of trials, the Reich Attorney General submitted nine charges (see Table 2). The Second Chamber of the *Reichsgericht* would be responsible. Charges were pressed against some of the accused on the extradition list of February 1920.[113] In a further five cases the prosecuting body applied to terminate the case. At practically the same time, the German Government received a diplomatic note from the Allies which addressed, among other things, the slow developments at the war crimes trials.[114] The Allies demanded the immediate indictment of more war criminals. Germany was given an ultimatum: the Allies threatened to occupy the Rhineland if their demands were not met. The Reich Government immediately accepted the ultimatum.[115]

There was, however, a passage in the amending act of 24 March 1920 that opposed the demand for the quick indictment of all 45 accused listed on the 'test list': Article 1 § 1 para 1. If the Reich Attorney General concluded that there was not enough evidence to convict the accused, he could apply to the *Reichsgericht* to drop the charges. Pressing charges on the basis of the Allied assessment ('test list') was not intended. This imperative offered a direct flank for further criticism by the Allies. The second amending act of 12 May 1921[116] mitigated the hitherto existing regulations. The Reich Attorney General could apply to the *Reichsgericht* to open the trial even if he was not personally convinced that the accused were guilty – without an indictment! Evidently this measure was supposed to pacify tense relations – especially with Great Britain.[117] It was, in the end, nothing but a sham – how would one expect the prosecutor to convincingly press charges in a case where he was convinced that the accused was innocent? This was another part of the "Farce Leipzig Trials".

This impression was intensified by the many acquittals (seven out of 17 cases), particularly when it dealt with a direct war incident. For

---

[113] Hankel, 2003, p. 98, see *supra* note 25.

[114] Schwengler, 1982, p. 346, fn. 15, see *supra* note 31.

[115] *Ibid.*

[116] *Reichsgesetzblatt 1921*, p. 508.

[117] Wiggenhorn, 2005, pp. 141–42, see *supra* note 39.

example, Lieutenant Commander Karl Neumann was acquitted although he, as a submarine commander, was responsible for the death of six sailors.

> On the basis of Article 228, para. 2 of the Peace Treaty […] of the list made by the Allies, he was charged with torpedoing the English hospital ship 'Dover Castle' and sinking it under exceeding brutality on the 26 May 1917.[118]

The Court explicitly pointed out that the main trial was arranged under the new regulations from May 1921. Undoubtedly, the trials would never have taken place without the amendment to the war criminals law. Wiggenhorn stated:

> In fact it formed a trial merely in the appearance of a regular criminal trial but exclusively aimed for an acquittal […] The term show trial must therefore take on a new facet. There is not just the show trial *against* but also the show trial *for* the accused.[119]

If and how far deviations from the criminal proceedings were acceptable, cannot be more specifically demonstrated here.[120]

In one trial, both of the possible criminal proceedings were applied: Lieutenant General Karl Stenger[121] stood before the *Reichgericht* without an indictment. Conversely Major Benno Crusius, the second in the trial, was arraigned. Stenger was acquitted and Crusius was sentenced to two years in prison (see Table 2).[122] In two further 'indictment-less' trials (Adolph Laule[123] and Hans von Schack/Benno Kruska[124]) the Court also sentenced the accused as expected: acquitted. In light of this, the previously quoted judgment by Wiggenhorn that there was a show trial *for* the accused gains empirical proof. Even more, these trials give rise to another puzzle in the "Farce Leipzig Trials": the strict will to acquit.

---

[118] *Reichsgericht, Trial of Commander Karl Neumann*, Judgment, 4 June 1921, p. 1; *Verhandlungen des Reichstags: I. Wahlperiode 1920*, vol. 368, p. 2556 (my translation).

[119] Wiggenhorn, 2005, p. 141, see *supra* note 39 (my translation).

[120] See *Ibid.*, pp. 140–47.

[121] *Reichsgericht, Trial of Lt. Gen. Karl Stenger and Maj. Benno Crusius*, Judgment, p. 2; *Verhandlungen des Reichstags: I. Wahlperiode 1920*, vol. 368, p. 2564.

[122] *Ibid.*, pp. 2563–72.

[123] *Ibid.*, pp. 2572–74.

[124] *Ibid.*, pp. 2573–79.

The accused at the three trials arranged by Great Britain were charged with abuse of POWs (amongst others, forced labour).[125] Heynen, Müller and Neumann were accused of committing acts of violence and being responsible for the miserable living conditions in camps – POWs died as a result of those conditions.[126] There was a world of difference between the body of evidence of the British and the facts relevant to the *Reichsgericht*. In the case of Müller, for example, the judges found that the condition of camps which he was in charge of was the responsibility of his superiors – and even the responsibility of the British themselves: "The camp, which had just been taken over by the English in the so called March offensive, was found to be in a pitiful state".[127] Basically the arguments made by the Allies were not taken seriously, the facts were played down and accountability was assigned to persons who were not seizable. The penalties (between 6 and 10 months *Gefängnis* – see Table 2) turned out to be mild. There was no comparison to the theft of 800 Reichsmark like in the first trial.

The judicial assessment schemata functioned smoothly for war crimes which had an equivalent in peacetime. However, this was not so for criminality contingent to war. Judges argued conspicuously, often referring to the behaviour of the opposing side or to the sense of duty of the accused:

> After all his excesses were [...] only an outlet for his officiousness [...] They were inconsiderations and privations [...] not personal appetite for cruelty [...] or [...] a conscious disregard for the laws of humanity.[128]

The incidents that the Allies assessed as war crimes seemed to be 'normal' concomitant phenomena which accompanied armed conflict, and they were punished mildly by the *Reichsgericht*.

---

[125] *Ibid.*, pp. 2543–56. See Hankel, 2003, pp. 333–41, *supra* note 25.

[126] Hankel, 2003, p. 333, see *supra* note 25.

[127] *Reichsgericht, Trial of Capt. Emil Müller*, Judgment, p. 2 (my translation); *Verhandlungen des Reichstags I. Wahlperiode 1920*, vol. 368, p. 2548.

[128] *Reichsgericht, Trial of Capt. Emil Müller*, Judgment, p. 7 (my translation); *Verhandlungen des Reichstags I. Wahlperiode 1920*, vol. 368, p. 2552.

Table 2: Trials before the *Reichgericht* in Leipzig

10.01.1921	Dieter Lottmann (Soldier) Paul Niegel (Soldier) Paul Sangershausen (Soldier)	Pillage	5 years *Zuchthaus* 4 years *Zuchthaus* 2 years *Gefängnis*
28.05.1921	Karl Heynen (Corporal)	Ill-treatment, deformation	10 months *Gefängnis*
30.05.1921	Emil Müller (Captain)	Ill-treatment, deformation	6 months *Gefängnis*
02.06.1921	Robert Neumann (Soldier)	Ill-treatment, deformation	6 months *Gefängnis*
04.06.1921	Karl Neumann (Lieutenant Commander)	Killing of soldiers (on sea)	Acquittal
11.06.1921	Max Ramdohr	Deprivation of liberty, bodily harm	Acquittal
06.07.1921	Karl Stenger (Lieutenant General) Benno Crusius (Major)	Superior responsibility, manslaughter	Acquittal 2 years *Gefängnis*
07.07.1921	Adolph Laule (First Lieutenant)	Killing of Captain Migat	Acquittal
09.07.1921	Hans von Schack (Lieutenant General) Benno Kruska (Major General)	Superior responsibility, murder	Acquittal
16.07.1921	Ludwig Dithmar John Boldt	Aiding and abetting a manslaughter	4 years *Gefängnis* 4 years *Gefängnis*
03.07.1922	Dr. Oskar Michelsohn	Killing of POWs	Acquittal
17.11.1922	Karl Grüner	Pillage, theft	2 years *Zuchthaus*

Sources: Gerd Hankel, *Deutsche Kriegsverbrechen des Weltkrieges 1914–18 vor deutschen Gerichten*, in Wette and Ueberschär, 2001, pp. 85–98, see *supra* note 17; Schwengler, 1982, pp. 345–59, see *supra* note 31; Wiggenhorn, 2005, pp. 153–283, 329-341, 350-352, see *supra* note 39; *Verhandlungen des Reichstags I. Wahlperiode 1920*, vol. 368, pp. 2543–86 (Judgments).

10.4. The *Llandovery Castle* Case

The last and perhaps most spectacular trial in the second cluster from 1921 is also the most well known: the *Llandovery Castle* case.[129] The commander of the Germany submarine U-86 (Helmut Brümmer-Patzig) was number one on the 'test list' from May 1921. The British were particularly concerned with his conviction. On 27 June 1918 Patzig torpedoed and sank the hospital ship *Llandovery Castle*. The steamship had brought wounded Canadian soldiers to their homeland.

> The ship was equipped for this purpose and was marked [...] as stipulated for military hospital ships [...] in the Haag Convention. Its name was communicated to the opposing powers.[130]

At the end of June 1918 the ship was on its way from Halifax, Canada to Britain. Aside from the 164-man crew, there were 80 medical corps soldiers and 14 nurses on board. On 27 June 1918 the submarine U-86 sank the *Llandovery Castle* with a torpedo. Of the 258 people on board, only 24 survived. Interrogations of survivors established that there had been no non-medical personnel aboard, apart from the crew. In order to eradicate all evidence of his misdeed, Patzig and two of his officers proceeded to machine gun the hospital ship's lifeboats with the result that only the personnel on one lifeboat escaped and survived.[131]

According to international criminal law of the time, it was forbidden for submarines to torpedo hospital ships.[132] What made this case so significant[133] was the circumstance. Not only did Patzig attack a hospital ship, he also put the lifeboats under fire, thus the high number of deaths. According to the judges, the lifeboats were attacked in order to

---

[129] See Wiggenhorn, 2005, pp. 256–83, *supra* note 39; Hankel, 2003, pp. 452–70, 500–5, *supra* note 25; Schwengler, 1982, pp. 348–59, *supra* note 3. In detail: National Archives, UK, London Record Group TS 26 no. 907, pp. 1–30.

[130] *Reichsgericht, Trial of Ludwig Dithmar and John Boldt*, Judgment, p. 2 (my translation); *Verhandlungen des Reichstags I. Wahlperiode 1920*, vol. 368, p. 2580.

[131] See Mullins, 1921, p. 107, *supra* note 31.

[132] *Reichsgericht, Trial of Ludwig Dithmar and John Boldt*, Judgment, p. 2; *Verhandlungen des Reichstags I. Wahlperiode 1920*, vol. 368, p. 2580.

[133] For other attacks of submarines see Hankel, 2003, pp. 452–54, *supra* note 25.

cover up the crime. Not only did Patzig fail to enter the episode in the ship's log, he also falsified the route taken by the submarine.[134]

Patzig was never caught. It was, however, certain that both of the accused (Ludwig Dithmar and John Boldt) were present at the sinking of the lifeboats. Two of Patzig's officers came before the *Reichsgericht* in July 1920, but neither of them was on the 'test list'. The prosecuting body held an investigation without any demand by the British. Both officers made great use of the right to refuse to give evidence.[135] Their defence was based on them being forced to follow the orders of their commanding officer.[136] The *Reichsgericht* firmly referred to § 47 Nr. 2 MStGB[137] (Militärstrafgesetzbuch [Military Penal Code]), that such orders should only be implemented if they were not intended to commit a civilian or military crime.[138] Aside from that, the Court stated that it was obvious to the accused and everyone in their situation that it was a criminal order. Furthermore, they would not have had to fear insufferable consequences if they had refused to carry out the order. Therefore, the plea of superior orders was not deemed a reason to waive the sentence.[139]

The judges dealt predominantly with Patzig's actions. He was built up as a perpetrator. The participation of the two accused in a crime against international law – the judges did not use the term war crime – was explained in detail at the end of sentencing. Beforehand, fundamental questions of the trial were addressed:

1. The attack on the hospital ship was a contravention of international criminal law;

2. Commander Patzig had wilfully attempted to cover up the sinking of the *Llandovery Castle*;

---

[134] *Reichsgericht, Trial of Ludwig Dithmar and John Boldt*, Judgment, p. 6; *Verhandlungen des Reichstags I. Wahlperiode 1920*, vol. 368, p. 2583.

[135] *Ibid.*

[136] See Karin Hassel, *Kriegsverbrechen vor Gericht: Die Kriegsverbrecherprozesse vor Militärgerichten in der britischen Besatzungszone und der Royal Warrant vom 18. Juni 1945 (1945-1949)*, Nomos, Baden-Baden, 2009, pp. 39–43.

[137] See Antonius Maria Romen and Carl Rissim, *Militär-Strafgesetzbuch für das Deutsche Reich vom 20. Juni 1872 nebst Einführungsgesetz*, 3rd ed., Guttentag'sche Sammlung deutscher Reichgesetze, Berlin, 1918, pp. 184–89.

[138] *Reichsgericht, Trial of Ludwig Dithmar and John Boldt*, Judgment, p. 6; *Verhandlungen des Reichstags I. Wahlperiode 1920*, vol. 368, p. 2584.

[139] *Verhandlungen des Reichstags I. Wahlperiode 1920*, vol. 368, p. 2585.

---

3. Responsibility for the deaths of over 230 people.[140]

In this case the rules of international law were clear; Patzig's unlawful actions were easily identified. Therefore, it was established that Patzig, as a perpetrator, was responsible for his actions. The question with regard to the severity of the penalty was: Which delict had he committed? The judges eliminated murder (§ 211 StGB) and examined manslaughter (§ 212 StGB).[141]

Now for the other two accused whom the trial actually dealt with it had a very cursory outline of their participation in the sequence of events.[142] It is simply outlined that Ludwig Dithmar and John Boldt aided the perpetrator in a homicide. The view of the court was that they were not responsible for operation of the ordnance on the submarine. This was the responsibility of another participant (Meißner) who had died in the meantime.[143] "They had [...] limited themselves to observation during the shooting".[144] However, this raised the question of whether the observations were necessary to find the lifeboats at sea.

In the reasons given by the *Reichsgericht* for the judgment, Ludwig Dithmar and John Boldt were found to lack personal intent. Seen subjectively, they did not want to endanger the lives of the ship's crew. They helped the perpetrator to commit a crime. Thus, they were only punished as abettors (§ 49 StGB). Therefore the judges had to occupy themselves in detail with Patzig. As soon as Patzig's perpetration could be proven, it was possible to get the other two accused out of the line of fire.

Experts, who were heard, saw it differently. Vice Admiral Adolf von Trotha, for example, represented the point of view that higher authority – particularly in a war situation – could not be challenged. In the German fleet, the firm conviction that a commander in battle would be allowed to go beyond the bounds of the law prevailed. The Court retorted to this appraisal by pointing out that shooting at helpless castaways was not an act of war.[145] In sentencing, the culpable action of both of the

---

[140] *Ibid.*, pp. 2584–85.

[141] *Ibid.*, p. 2585.

[142] Hankel, 2003, p. 458, see *supra* note 25.

[143] *Reichsgericht, Trial of Ludwig Dithmar and John Boldt*, Judgment, p. 6; *Verhandlungen des Reichstags I. Wahlperiode 1920*, vol. 368, p. 2584.

[144] *Verhandlungen des Reichstags I. Wahlperiode 1920*, vol. 368, p. 2585 .

[145] *Ibid.*, p. 2586.

accused was explicitly pointed out: they had carried out a criminal order. Under these circumstances, both of them would have been sentenced for aiding and abetting (§ 49 StGB)[146] manslaughter (§ 212 StGB). The inevitable consequence would be a sentence of several years' imprisonment (*Zuchthaus*).

The German Penal Code envisioned a lesser sentence for aiding and abetting than for the perpetrator. This reduction in the sentence was regulated by § 44 StGB. The range of punishments depends on the crime that was carried out. If the perpetrator had committed manslaughter then according to the penal provisions the abettor would be sentenced for manslaughter.[147] According to § 44, the punishment could be reduced to a quarter of the atonement expected for the perpetrator. Generally this meant that if the main crime was punished with *Zuchthaus*, then the abettor would also be sentenced to *Zuchthaus* – but less severely.[148] In the case at hand the minimum sentence for manslaughter (§ 212 StGB) was five years in a *Zuchthaus*. Accordingly the minimum sentence, which could be imposed, was one and a quarter years in a *Zuchthaus*. For Patzig, who was responsible for the deaths of over 200 people, the minimum sentence for manslaughter would not have even come into question. "The killing of helpless castaways is a serious and notably morally disturbing crime".[149]

The punishment for the two accused was four years in *Gefängnis*. How can this be explained? According to the calculation just made, they expected a delicate *Zuchthaus* sentence. The judges specifically spoke about manslaughter and moreover (see quotation above) about a particularly abhorrent crime. Without further explanation the *Reichsgericht* returned to its usual practice of imposing only minimal sentences for war criminals. It deviated from § 49 StGB and allowed the abettors, rather than the perpetrator, extenuating circumstances: "The pressure of the military authority under which they (had) acted, [...] justified the extenuating circumstances (§§ 213, 49 para. 2, 44 StGB)".[150]

---

[146] For section 49 German Penal Code, see Ebermayer, Lobe and Rosenberg, 1929, pp. 257–65, *supra* note 68.

[147] *Ibid.*, p. 264.

[148] See *ibid.*, pp. 228-31.

[149] *Reichsgericht, Trial of Ludwig Dithmar and John Boldt*, Judgment, p. 6 (my translation); *Verhandlungen des Reichstags I. Wahlperiode 1920*, vol. 368, p. 2586.

[150] *Ibid.* (my translation).

The elements of the crime from § 212 StGB (manslaughter) were changed to the less serious case according to § 213 StGB. This should only have been able to happen in the case of the perpetrator. Abettors were always tied to the crime of the perpetrator. For Dithmar and Boldt, this circumstance brought the possibility of a *Gefängnis* sentence. How far this was legally valid is irrelevant as the court passed sentence in the first and last instance. There was no appeal and the judges were well aware of this situation.

The *Llandovery Castle* trial had effects on several levels. 1) For the first time the killings were categorised as violating international law and therefore, implicitly sentenced as war crimes. 2) Acting on orders did not automatically exclude personal liability.[151] Whoever carried out an order in violation of the law is not a perpetrator but an abettor. The new court ruling was, despite all criticisms, thoroughly revolutionary and because of this lent an air of ambivalence to the events. 3) The German judiciary was signalling to the Allies that it was willing and capable of taking national responsibility. 4) Ultimately, the attempt to find a fitting punishment failed.

The *Llandovery Castle* episode led to criticism by the Allies.[152] Above all, the sentence and the application of the lesser case of manslaughter carried weight. Naturally, the British observed the trial.[153] What had been a clear case of mass murder became a 'delict' before the *Reichsgericht*, the minimum sentence for which was six months' imprisonment.[154] This was incomprehensible to anyone who had seen the legal text. At the core of it, the less serious case of manslaughter goes back to a provocation that resulted in the offence.[155]

10.5. After the Trials

For a broad German public and, above all, the military, the entire case was a scandal, but for different reasons to that of the British observers. From their point of view, the *Reichsgericht* judgment was to be dismissed because a subordinate could plead wholesale to have acting on superior

---

[151] Oppenheim, 1937, pp. 454–56 (in particular p. 455, fn. 1), see *supra* note 23.

[152] Hassel, 2009, p. 40, see *supra* note 136; Hankel, 2003, p. 462, see *supra* note 25.

[153] Wiggenhorn, 2005, pp. 277–78, see *supra* note 39; Mullins, 1921, p. 134, see *supra* note 31.

[154] Hankel, 2003, p. 462, see *supra* note 25.

[155] See Ebermayer, Lobe and Rosenberg, 1929, pp. 673–74, *supra* note 68.

order. The generals were over-sensitively shocked; they said the judgment put the writing on the wall that the troops could no longer be disciplined.[156] The Germany Admiralty and conservative politicians did not want to overcome their misgivings and defiantly defended the war criminals. [157] Arguments were not admitted: critique "based almost entirely on sentiment and not on facts".[158]

What had been a – bitterly fought – diplomatic conflict between the Allies and the Germans over the question of whether German soldiers would be sentenced for their deeds in their own country was now depicted as trials being imposed by the victorious Allies on the Germans. [159] Moreover, the ability of the judges to properly judge was discussed. If a judge had never travelled on a submarine, then he could not understand the conditions on board, said an expert.[160] Here, one could ask: Does, for example, only a bank robber understand his crime adequately? Must the court also be made up of bank robbers? Furthermore it was noted that while indeed, at the time of their distress, the castaways from the *Llandovery Castle* were defenceless, they could have joined enemy combat units again after they had been saved. Thus, one may kill them "preventatively".[161]

On balance, the criticisms aimed to prove that the case was not about a violation of international law. Additionally, they gave the impression that the judiciary had retroactively stabbed the military in the back in a double sense: 1) vilifying the honour of German soldiers who had risked their lives for Germany; and 2) recognising the British charges that German soldiers had violated existing international law. Up to the *Llandovery Castle* case, one spoke of war criminality or violations of discipline of the troops.[162] Now a new category was added: crimes against international law. This made the case so volatile, and triggered criticisms by both the proponents and opponents of the new crime category.

---

[156] See Wiggenhorn, 2005, p. 280, *supra* note 39.

[157] *Ibid.*

[158] Lord d'Abernin (27 July 1921), cited by Wiggenhorn, 2005, p. 279, see *supra* note 39.

[159] Andreas Michelsen (ed.), *Das Urteil im Leipziger Uboot-Prozeß ein Fehlurteil? Juristische und militärische Gutachten*, Staatspolitischer Verlag, Berlin, 1922, p. 5.

[160] Dethleffsen, "Das Urteil gegen die Ubootoffiziere", in Michelsen, 1922, p. 9, see *supra* note 159.

[161] *Ibid.*, p. 10.

[162] Michelsen, 1922, p. 3, see *supra* note 159.

The reaction of the German Government to the criticisms of the war crimes trials was unambiguous: the *Reichsgericht*'s work was beyond reproof and was absolutely in accordance with the rule of law. The highest levels of government joined in the discussion in February 1922, in the person of the Minister of Justice Gustav Radbruch. He artfully began by explaining his criticism of the *Reichsgericht* and its legal practice.[163] He assessed the judicial handling of the Kapp rebels in comparison to the sentencing of communists[164] as one of "the worst sources of resentfulness yielded towards the judiciary in recent years".[165] Radbruch identified the *Reichsgericht* as a "small world of its own" which, above all, could be characterised by its corporate self-confidence and a "defiant feel for judicial independence".[166] Then he stressed his unbowed respect for the highest German court – which he also demanded abroad – particularly with regard to the war crimes trials.[167] Radbruch identified the Leipzig Trials as one of the most difficult tasks a court had ever had to deal with. Under no circumstances was the work of the *Reichsgericht* to be compared with a laughable comedy (*caractère dérisoire* [168]). Underpinning his evaluation Radbruch quoted a book by Claud Mullins:[169]

> At the time of the trials, The Times described them as 'a travesty of justice' and the Evening Standard said that 'Leipzig' from the Allies' point of view, has been a 'farce'; but I do not think that any Englishman who was present was of that opinion. However much we may criticise the judgements of the court and however much we may deplore their inadequacy from the point of view of jurisprudence, the trials were not a farce and seven German judges endeavoured throughout to be true to the traditions of fairness and impartiality which are the pride of all judicial courts. To my mind this is a hopeful sign in these days when

---

[163] *Verhandlungen des Reichstags I. Wahlperiode 1920*, vol. 353, p. 6063. See *Entscheidungen des Reichsgerichts*, 1922, pp. 259–72.

[164] Arthur Kaufmann (ed.), *Gustav Radbruch Gesamtausgabe Reichstagsreden*, vol. 19, C.F. Müller, Tübingen, 1998, p. 192.

[165] *Verhandlungen des Reichstags I. Wahlperiode 1920*, vol. 353, 1922, p. 6063.

[166] *Ibid.*

[167] *Ibid.*

[168] *Ibid.*

[169] Mullins, 1921, see *supra* note 31.

more and more international problems have to be settled by argument before judicial tribunals. As a lawyer myself, I felt and feel proud of the legal mind, which seeks justice even through the heavens fall. [...] It is a British characteristic to give honour where honour is due. Speaking for myself and of the trials which I witnessed, I say frankly that Dr. Schmidt[170] and his Court were fair. Fully neutral at the start, I learnt to respect them, and am convinced that they performed their difficult task without fear or favour. Personally I should be willing to be tried by Dr. Schmidt on any charge, even on one which involved my word against that of a German.[171]

The Mullins statement quoted by Radbruch was aimed more at the *Llandovery Castle* case than any of the other trials. With this focus, the criticism of the critique seems to have a certain justification. This particular case does in fact stand out. However, the appealingly outward eloquence of the judgment cannot be unreservedly taken out of the context of the whole trial complex. The fundamental reluctance of the German judiciary – and politics – to prosecute war crimes is also reflected in the *Llandovery Castle* case.

10.6. Conclusion

An appraisal of the Leipzig Trials is not an easy undertaking. Many different facets lead to a multifaceted general view. On the level of the actors, there are Allied and German stakeholders. On the victor's side of the First World War, the governments fighting against Germany formed a strong bastion and codified a new type of peace treaty. The Treaty of Versailles did not just regulate reparations and territorial changes. There was also the revolutionary endeavour by the Allies to prosecute war crimes themselves. However, the basic consensus to actually do this amongst Allies changed between summer 1919 and spring of 1920. In the process they did not depart from the framework of the peace treaty because no imperative for prosecution was set down, but only the possibility to.

---

[170] President of the Chamber was Carl Ludwig Schmidt.
[171] *Verhandlungen des Reichstags I. Wahlperiode 1920*, vol. 353, 1922, p. 6063. The original text as cited see Mullins, 1921, pp. 43–44, see *supra* note 31.

On the side of the losers of the war, there was a multilayered network of actors. In politics, the opposition and the government acted according to their own patterns. The military – often the personnel overlapped with politics – feared for its own reputation as a champion of the honour of the nation. In contrast to this, the jurists worked on the guidelines of politics, both as the executor (public prosecutors' office/prosecution) as well as the formally independent force (judge). The end result of the clash between internal and external influences was that the German side won.

These structures are again reflected on an administrative level. The Allies tried to establish their own court for German war criminal, but they did not have the political will to find a way to see it through to the end (trial). They investigated German atrocities and demanded that the Ebert Government extradite the accused. Divided on how Article 228 of the Treaty of Versailles should be implemented, verbal attacks were the weapon of choice for (a lack of) diplomacy. Germany, for its part, reacted cunningly to the pressure from abroad. The German government implemented the War Crimes Law before the Treaty of Versailles came into force. Thus the Ebert Government showed the will to take the prosecution of war crimes into its hands. Through the amendments and firm establishment of the regulations, it reacted to domestic and foreign political criticism.

The main aim of the German prosecution of war criminals was to minimise prosecutions. Of the initial hundreds, and then 45, Germans accused of war crimes by the Allies, only 17 were brought before the *Reichsgericht*. Of those, five were not actually intended for trial and were dealt with by the court for the sake of appearances. There were not even indictments, just references to the accusations by the Allies. All five were acquitted.

The "Farce Leipzig Trials" was a multidimensional event. It was composed of various subdivisions: 1) legal regulations; 2) measures of criminal proceedings; 3) show trials; 4) disproportionately mild sentences or, as the case may be, acquittals; 5) protection of the military; and 6) masked diplomacy.

11

When Justice Is Left to the Losers:
The Leipzig War Crimes Trials

Matthias Neuner[*]

In the period from 10 January 1921 to 3 July 1922, the German Supreme
Court (*Reichsgericht*) in Leipzig conducted 12 trials involving 17 accused
Germans on charges relating to allegations of criminal conduct by
German citizens during the First World War ('Leipzig War Crimes
Trials'). Apart from few exceptions,[1] these proceedings found a consistent
critical echo, whether within the then Weimar Republic or outside
Germany, in the countries of the Allied Powers. The French Prime
Minister, Aristide Briand, saw these trials as a comedy, a parody of
justice and a scandal, and was not the only one to voice such harsh
criticism.[2] *The Times* wrote that these proceedings were "little better than
a farce";[3] others spoke of a "judicial farce".[4] Alexander Cadogan, then a

---

[*] **Matthias Neuner** has been a Trial Counsel at the Office of the Prosecutor, Special
Tribunal for Lebanon (STL) since 2009. Prior to that he was a Trial Attorney at the Office
of the Prosecutor, International Tribunal for Crimes committed in the Former Yugoslavia
('ICTY') for almost 10 years. He holds a German First State Exam in Law from the Free
University Berlin, Germany, and a German Second State Exam in Law, from the Berlin
Higher Regional Court, Berlin.

[1] Ernest Pollock, then British solicitor general declared to be "much impressed by the
Supreme Court of Leipzig – the trials were conducted very impartially with every desire to
get to the truth". Ernest Pollock, *Memorandum about the Leipzig Trials*, 2 June 1921, The
National Archives, UK ('TNA'), CAB 24/125, C.P.-3006); Claud Mullins, *The Leipzig
Trials: An Account of the War Criminals Trials and a Study of German Mentality*, H.F. &
G. Witherby, London, 1921; G. van Slooten, "Beschouwingen naar aanleiding van het
geding Stenger – Crusius voor het Reichsgericht te Leipzig", in *Militair-rechtelijk
Tijdschrift*, Mouton & Co., The Hague, 1921, vol. 17, p. 7; G. van Slooten,
"Betrachtungen aus Anlass des Prozesses Stenger-Crusius", in *Zeitschrift für Völkerrecht*,
Duncker & Humblot, Berlin, vol. 12, 1923, p. 174.

[2] Aristide Briand, Declaration before the French Parliament, printed in *Journal du Droit
International*, 1921, vol. 48, pp. 442 ff. The Belgian Minister of Justice criticised the
proceedings in Leipzig in a similar way. Kai Müller, "Oktroyierte Verliererjustiz nach dem
Ersten Weltkrieg", in *Archiv des Völkerrechts*, 2001, vol. 39, p. 217. Sheldon Glueck calls
these trials a "trago-comedy" in *War Criminals: Their Prosecution and Punishment*, A.A.
Knopf, New York, 1944, p. 34.

[3] *The Times*, London, 2 June 1922.

British Foreign Office official who later served as the British Permanent Under-Secretary for Foreign Affairs during the Second World War, expressed the British view that the Leipzig "experiment has been pronounced a failure".[5] More recently, Gary Jonathan Bass labelled these proceedings a "disaster".[6] Moving beyond such emotional assessments, this chapter analyses the facts surrounding these war crimes proceedings and presents them in seven sections.

11.1. If the *Reichsgericht* Convicted, Then Sentences Were Lenient

None of the 12 war crimes trials conducted in front of the *Reichsgericht* in Leipzig resulted in sentences that exceeded five years' detention. Each trial and its result (conviction or acquittal) are listed in chronological order in Table 1:

Table 1: War Crimes Trials at the *Reichsgericht*, Leipzig, 1921–1922

Trial No.	Accused	Charge(s)	Result	Sentence
1	Dietrich Lottmann	Plunder[7]	Convicted	5 years
	Paul Niegel			4 years
	Paul Sangerhausen			2 years[8]

---

4   Yoram Dinstein, *The Defence of 'Obedience to Superior Orders' in International Law*, Oxford University Press, Oxford, 2012, p. 11.

5   British Foreign Office, FO 371/7529/C17096, Allied-German Negotiations on War Criminals, 9 December 1922 (TNA).

6   Gary Jonathan Bass, *Stay the Hand of Vengeance: The Politics of War Crimes Trials*, Princeton University Press, Princeton, NJ, 2000, p. 80.

7   Bundesarchiv (BA) Berlin-Lichterfelde R3003 ORA/RG a J 8/20, vol. 6, p. 5, Indictment from 19 November 1920.

8   Reichsgericht, the Case of Lottmann, Niegel and Sangerhausen, Judgment, dated 10 January 1921 ("Lottmann, Niegel and Sangerhausen Judgment") a J 8/1920 – IX.52/1921, reprinted in German in BA Berlin-Lichterfelde R3003 ORA/RG a J 8/1920, vol. 4, pp. 44–50; see also R3003 ORA Generalia 62.

Trial No.	Accused	Charge(s)	Result	Sentence
2	Karl Heynen	47 acts of mistreatment of prisoners of war ('POWs')[9]	Partial conviction for 15 acts of mistreatment and three acts of insult of subordinates;[10] otherwise partial acquittal	10 months[11]
3	Emil Müller	14 acts of mistreatment and/or slander of POWs as well as six insults[12]	Convicted for 13 acts of slander/ mistreatment of POWs and for 2 insults; otherwise partial acquittal[13]	6 months[14]
4	Robert Neumann	17 acts of mistreatment of POWs[15]	Partially convicted (for 12 acts); otherwise partial acquittal[16]	6 months[17]

---

[9] BA Berlin-Lichterfelde R3003 ORA/RG, vol. 4, pp. 43–46, Indictment from 12 May 1921; BJ 903/20, ORA bJ 903/20-3 of 14 May 1921 to the Second Senate of the Reichsgericht with Indictment 903/20 from 14 May 1921, also vol. 8, pp. 26, 29.

[10] Reichsgericht, the Case of Karl Heynen, Judgment, dated 26 May 1921 ("Heynen Judgment"), reprinted in German in Weißbuch, *Deutscher Reichstag, Reichstagsprotokolle*, 1920/24,25, ("Weißbuch") pp. 2542–43; reprinted in English in *German War Trials, Report of Proceedings Before the Supreme Court in Leipzig*, presented to the British Parliament by Command of his Majesty, 1921, His Majesty's Stationery Office, London, ("UK Report"), appendix II, p. 19.

[11] Heynen Judgment, sections XII and XIV, see *supra* note 10.

[12] PA AA R 48432z b J 588/20-31, Indictment from 11 April 1921; BA Berlin-Lichterfelde R3003 ORA/RG b J 901.20, Indictment from 12 May 1921, p. 15; Reichsgericht, the Case of Emil Müller, Judgment, dated 30 May 1921 ("Müller Judgment"), reprinted in German in Weißbuch, p. 2547, see *supra* note 10; reprinted in English language in UK Report, appendix III, p. 27, see *supra* note 10.

[13] Müller Judgment, p. 2547, see *supra* note 12.

[14] *Ibid.*

[15] PA AA R 48433j: ORA b J 589/20, Indictment from 11 April 1921; ORA b J 902.20, Indictment from 9 May 1921.

[16] Reichsgericht, the Case of Robert Neumann, Judgment, 2 June 1921 ("Robert Neumann Iudgment"), reprinted in German in Weißbuch, pp. 2552–53, see *supra* note 10; reprinted in English in UK Report, appendix IV, p. 36, see *supra* note 10.

[17] *Ibid.*

Trial No.	Accused	Charge(s)	Result	Sentence
5	Karl Neumann (*Dover Castle* case)	Murder of six men[18]	Acquittal[19]	—
6	Max Ramdohr	Several acts of illegal deprivation of liberty, of prolonging such illegal deprivation of liberty and/or of assault in exercise of the office[20]	Acquittal[21]	—
7	Karl Stenger	Misuse of official position by instigating subordinates to criminal acts	Acquittal[22]	—
	Benno Crusius	Also attempted manslaughter and intentional killing of at least seven wounded soldiers or POWs	Conviction (for negligent manslaughter); otherwise partial acquittal[23]	2 years[24]
8	Adolph Laule	Manslaughter[25]	Acquittal[26]	—

[18] PA AA R 48433i: ORA b J 586/20, application dated 28 May 1921 to hold a main trial.

[19] Reichsgericht, the Case of Karl Neumann (also referred to as the "*Dover Castle* case"), Judgment, dated 4 June 1921 ("Karl Neumann Judgment"), reprinted in German in Weißbuch, p. 2556, see *supra* note 10; reprinted in English in UK Report, appendix V, p. 43, see *supra* note 10.

[20] BA Berlin-Lichterfelde R3003 ORA/RG b J 46/20, vol. 6, Indictment from 21 March 1921, pp. 29–35.

[21] Reichsgericht, the Case of Ramdohr, Judgment, 11 June 1921 ("Ramdohr Judgment"), reprinted in German in Weißbuch, p. 2558, see *supra* note 10.

[22] Reichsgericht, the Case of *Stenger and Crusius*, Judgment, 6 July 1921 ("Stenger and Crusius Judgment"), reprinted in German in Weißbuch, p. 2563, section I, see *supra* note 10.

[23] *Ibid.*

[24] Stenger and Crusius Judgment, section II, see *supra* note 22.

Trial No.	Accused	Charge(s)	Result	Sentence
9	Hans von Schack Benno Kruska	Murder of more than 3,000 men[27]	Acquittal[28]	—
10	Ludwig Dithmar John Boldt Helmut Patzig (*Llandovery Castle* case)	Murder[29]	Conviction	Dithmar and Boldt: 4 years for aiding and abetting manslaughter[30] No proceedings against Patzig
11	Oskar Michelson	Mistreatment of wounded[31]	Acquittal[32]	—
12	Karl Grüner	Theft and plunder[33]	Conviction for plunder, otherwise acquittal[34]	2 years[35]

The Leipzig War Crimes Trials resulted in convictions of 10 men. The sentences imposed ranged from six months (twice),[36] ten months

---

[25] Compare Albert Feisenberger, "Zusammenstellung der bisher durch das Reichsgericht abgeurteilten Kriegsverbrechen", in *Deutsche Strafrechtszeitung*, 1921, col. 267.

[26] Reichsgericht, the Case of Laule, Judgment, 7 July 1921 ("Laule Judgment"), reprinted in German in Weißbuch, p. 2572, see *supra* note 10.

[27] BA Berlin-Lichterfelde R3003 ORA/RG b J 296/20, vol. 1, pp. 142–47, RS: ORA b J 296/20 application dated 9 July 1921 to hold a main trial.

[28] Reichsgericht, the Case of von Schack and Kruska, Judgment, 9 July 1921 ("von Schack and Kruska Judgment"), reprinted in German in Weißbuch, p. 2573, see *supra* note 10.

[29] PA AA R 48429l, Indictment from 11 June 1921 (a J 95/21).

[30] Reichsgericht, the Case of Dithmar and Boldt, Judgment, 16 July 1921 ("*Llandovery Castle* case"), reprinted in German in Weißbuch, pp. 2579–80, see *supra* note 10.

[31] PA AA R 48432v, ORA b J 512/20-72, Indictment from 23 March 1922, pp. 9–10.

[32] Reichsgericht, the Case of Dr. Oskar Michelson, Judgment, 3 July 1922 ("Michelson Judgment"), BA Berlin-Lichterfelde R3003 ORA Gen. 62: b J 512/20 – IX.281/22.

[33] PA AA R 48427i, ORA a J 13/21-57, Indictment from 18 September 1922.

[34] Reichsgericht, the Case of Karl Grüner, Judgment, 17 November 1921 ("Grüner Judgment"), BA Berlin-Lichterfelde R3001 RMJ 2017, p. 278: ORA Gen. I 8-191 of 9 February 1923; PA AA R 48427i, R 48427j and R 48427j and R48427m.

[35] *Ibid.*

[36] Namely against Emil Müller and Robert Neumann.

(once),[37] two years (three times)[38] and a sentence of five years (once) that was imposed for plunder.[39] A four-year sentence was imposed for plunder[40] in the Lottmann, Niegel and Sangerhausen case, and twice for aiding and abetting murder in the *Llandovery Castle* case.[41] In 1922 the Conference of Ambassadors, which contained among others representatives from Belgium, France, Italy and Britain, regarded these sentences as too lenient.[42] Georg Schwarzenberger called the proceedings at the *Reichsgericht* fair, but criticised the sentences imposed as "lenient beyond any justification".[43]

11.2. Quashing of Sentences, Amnesty and a Practice of Suspensions (*Nolle Prosequi*)

The Leipzig War Crimes Trials drew criticism not only for their lenient sentences, but also for the ineffective policy of the German authorities to secure the imposed sanctions in the execution of sentences phase following the judgments.

11.2.1. The Shadow of the *Llandovery Castle* Case[44]

The *Llandovery Castle* case deserves further scrutiny. After the Second Senate of the *Reichsgericht* had convicted Dithmar and Boldt in 1921, they served their sentences in different detention facilities, but both managed to

---

[37] Namely against Karl Heynen.

[38] Namely against Crusius, Grüner and Sangerhausen.

[39] Namely against Lottmann (see also Lottmann, Niegel and Sangerhausen Judgment, see *supra* note 8).

[40] Namely against Niegel (*ibid.*).

[41] Namely Dithmar and Boldt, see *supra* note 30.

[42] Note issued by French Prime Minister Poincaré on 23 August 1922, Conference of Ambassadors, sent to Dr. Mayer, para. 5 (MAE Paris 580, pp. 35–37: Conférence des Ambassadeurs, Le Président; PA AA R 48415j: telegram Paris Pax of 23 August 1922, note of Conference of Ambassadors, re question of war suspects; BA Berlin Lichterfelde R3003 ORA Gen. 47, pp. 71–76: note of the conference of ambassadors; Conference of Ambassadors to German Embassy in Paris, 23 August 1922, FO 371/7529 (C16860/555/18), Confidential Print 11990; compare Woods to Foreign Office, 16 August 1922, FO 371/7529 (C11741/555/18).

[43] Georg Schwarzenberger, *International Law and Totalitarian Lawlessness*, Jonathan Cape, London, 1942, p. 72.

[44] *Llandovery Castle* case, see *supra* note 30.

escape from detention.[45] Notwithstanding these ongoing flights, in 1926 the German President (Reichspräsident) Hindenburg informed Wilhelm Marx, the German Minister of Justice, that he would consider pardoning both Dithmar and Boldt if they would return to the law enforcement authorities.[46] Marx refused to countersign this request.[47] Only months after this attempt to pardon Dithmar and Boldt had failed, on 5 and 10 July 1926 the defence of both convicted persons requested the *Reichsgericht* to reopen the proceedings. Without expressing any reasons, the Fifth Senate of the *Reichsgericht* reopened the proceedings, which resulted in a ruling suspending the further imposition of the "outstanding" sentences against Dithmar and Boldt.[48] Almost two years later, on 4 May 1928, the Fifth Senate proceeding in closed session quashed the initial judgment of the Second Senate convicting Dithmar and Boldt on 16 July 1921 and acquitted both men.[49] Dithmar and Boldt also obtained financial compensation for their periods of detention.[50]

The third co-accused in the same proceeding, Patzig, had absconded before the trial against the co-defendants, Dithmar and Boldt, had begun

---

[45] Glueck, 1944, p. 33, see *supra* note 2, referring to a telegraph of a correspondent of the *Daily Mail* from 20 November 1921; Peter Maguire, *Law and War: An American Story*, Columbia University Press, New York, 2002, p. 82; Harald Wiggenhorn, *Verlierjustiz: Die Leipziger Kriegsverbrecherprozesse nach dem Ersten Weltkrieg*, Nomos, Baden-Baden, 2005, pp. 304–5, 325–26; Bass, 2000, pp. 80–81, see *supra* note 6.

[46] PA AA R 48429l: RP.1075/26, 8 March 1926.

[47] PA AA R 48428t: Marx, Reichsminister of Justice to the Reich President, Hindenburg, correspondence dated 17 March 1926.

[48] PA AA R 48433o, Decision b j 585/20-60/XI. 182, pursuant to § 112, 123, 124, German Criminal Procedural Code.

[49] BA Berlin Lichterfelde R3003 ORA/RG a J 95/21, vol. 2, p. 1: reprint RG, V. senate a J 95/21/XII. 117 of 4 May 1928; R 3003 ORA Generalia 62; PA AA R 48429l; compare Albert Feisenberger, *Strafprozessordnung und Gerichtsverfassungsgesetz*, Gruter & Co., Berlin, 1926, p. 302, remark 3 to § 371 German Code of Criminal Procedure. Peter Maguire, 2005, p. 82 sees this procedure as a "crude form of strategic legalism – post-trial, *nonjudicial* sentence modification", see *supra* note 45, emphasis added. However, Maguire overlooks that in this case a *judicial* sentence modification of Dithmar and Boldt occurred through a *judicial* body: by quashing the convictions of the Second Senate, the Fifth Senate of the *Reichsgericht* set the four-year sentences of Dithmar and Boldt aside and completely acquitted both men. The amnesty in favour of Patzig was also declared by the Fourth Senate of the *Reichsgericht*, again a judicial body.

[50] Wiggenhorn, 2005, p. 381, see *supra* note 45.

in 1921.[51] German law not providing for trial proceedings *in absentia* in criminal matters barred the *Reichsgericht* from litigating the question of guilt or innocence of Patzig. Thus, this court could only try and convict Dithmar and Boldt, who had been accused of the same transaction as Patzig. However, even before the Fifth Senate of the *Reichsgericht* quashed the convictions rendered in 1921 by the Second Senate, the German authorities made attempts to avoid pursuing proceedings against Patzig. On 19 July 1926 the Fifth Senate decided to suspend the warrant of arrest against Patzig, claiming that no urgent suspicion existed.[52] The reasoning of this decision consisted of two sentences only.

Other attempts by the judiciary and political actors to suspend or dispose of the pending proceedings against Patzig met with opposition from the German Foreign Office as it feared a critical echo from the international community, particularly from Britain, whose citizens had been killed as a result of actions ordered by Patzig.[53] However, in October 1930 the German Parliament amended the amnesty law adopted initially in 1928 to also provide amnesties for criminal procedures instituted for politically motivated killings.[54] Relying on this law, five months later on 20 March 1931, the Fourth Senate of the *Reichsgericht* decided to suspend and thereby terminate the criminal proceedings relating to war crimes against Patzig.[55] Thereby, the Fourth Senate dismissed the Second Senate's earlier *obiter dictum* relating to Patzig, which contained indirect findings about the criminality of his behaviour. The Second Senate had made these findings on the occasion of the conviction of Dithmar and Boldt.[56]

11.2.2. Practice of Suspensions (*Nolle Prosequi*)

That only 12 war crimes trials could be conducted in Leipzig was the result of a practice of the German authorities to issue suspensions or *nolle*

---

[51] James F. Willis, *Prologue to Nuremberg: The Politics and Diplomacy of Punishing War Criminals of the First World War*, Greenwood Press, London, 1982, p. 137.

[52] PA AA R48433o, Decision a J 95/21-183/XI. 183, pursuant to §§ 359 Nr. 5, 360, paras. 2, 366, 367 and 369 German Code of Criminal Procedure.

[53] Wiggenhorn, 2005, pp. 382–88, see *supra* note 45.

[54] RGBl. 1928 I, p. 195, Law about amnesty from 14 July 1928; RGBl 1930 I S.467: Law amending the Law about amnesty/impunity of 14 July 1928 (RGBl. I, p. 195).

[55] PA AA R 48433o: Decision Fourth Senate for Criminal Matters, *Reichsgericht*, Reprint b J 585/20-101/XII Tgb. 56/1931.

[56] Wiggenhorn, 2005, p. 390, see *supra* note 45.

---

prosequi decisions during the investigation stage (before a case could reach the indictment or trial stage in front of the *Reichsgericht*). 'Beneficiaries' of these suspensions were those persons who had been on lists of German suspects handed over by the Allied Powers to the German authorities.

The prosecutor's office at the *Reichsgericht* in Leipzig requested suspensions or *nolle prosequi* decisions of many proceedings relating to suspected war criminals. However, the pace of such suspensions varied. In the first three years following the adoption of the law for the prosecution of war crimes and war felonies,[57] the prosecutor's office only suspended 12 criminal proceedings.[58] In mid-September 1922 Ludwig Ebermayer, the senior prosecutor at the *Reichsgericht*, suggested that if suspension of criminal proceedings against war criminals would be possible without causing too much attention, then the files should be submitted to the *Reichsgericht* which would then decide. Forwarding such files should not be done in great numbers all at once, but should be done gradually, because the German Minister of Justice wanted to avoid the appearance of a campaign of *nolle prosequi* decisions that could spark negativity from a foreign policy point of view.[59] Within the next four months, until 30 January 1923, the number of suspensions increased significantly to 210 cases.[60] Thereafter until 26 April 1923, an average of two and a half proceedings were suspended daily, followed by a further increase of suspensions of an additional 122 cases between April and July 1923.[61] Again, between July and October 1923, the number of suspended proceedings increased to 127 cases.[62]

---

[57] German *Reichstag, Gesetz zur Verfolgung von Kriegsverbrechen und Kriegsvergehen* (Law to prosecute war crimes and war misdemeanour), German Parliamentary gazette (*Reichsgesetzblatt*) 1919, 18 December 1919; published in RGBl. 1919, ("Law to prosecute war crimes"), pp. 2125–26.

[58] BA Berlin Lichterfelde, R 3001 RMJ 7689, pp. 239–40: ORA Gen. I 30-80 from 25 October 1922 to Reichsministry of Justice.

[59] PA AA R 48415j: Note relating to F 6376u; V F 6485 from 18 September 1922 (von Levinski) relating to consultation on 15 September 1922 in the Ministry of Justice Germany.

[60] BA Berlin Lichterfelde, R 3001 RMJ 7689, p. 7: ORA Gen. I 30-86 from 30 January 1923 to Reich Ministry of Justice.

[61] BA Berlin Lichterfelde, R 3001 RMJ 7689, p. 35: ORA Gen. I 30-100 from 27 July 1923.

[62] BA Berlin Lichterfelde, R 3001 RMJ 7689, p. 41: ORA Gen. I 30-108 from 20 October 1923.

The *nolle prosequi* decisions included also high profile personalities. On 7 June 1923 the *Reichsgericht* suspended the criminal proceeding against Crown Prince Eitel Friedrich of Prussia who had fled with his father, the former Emperor Wilhelm II, to the Netherlands.[63] Independently of these suspensions by the German authorities, the new French Prime Minister, Raymond Poincaré, requested until 1924 the surrender of the prince as a war criminal, but this proved unsuccessful because the British Cabinet refused[64] to support this French initiative. Finally, France gave up on their demand regarding the prince who remained in the Netherlands without ever standing trial for war crimes.[65]

In early 1925, the Fourth Senate of the *Reichsgericht* suspended and thereby terminated criminal proceedings against Ludendorff, who had been on the initial Allied list handed over to the Germans in February 1920.[66] In May 1925 the same Senate terminated the proceedings against Hindenburg, whose name had also been on the same list.[67]

Not only the German, but also the judicial authorities in Belgium and France suspended criminal proceedings against German war criminals. For example, after Hindenburg had been elected as Reich President, the Belgian authorities also suspended criminal proceedings against him.[68] Also the French authorities suspended their own prosecutions against notable public figures, such as Hindenburg, Crown Prince Rupprecht of Bavaria and General Erich Ludendorff, to avoid unwanted reactions from Germany.[69]

---

[63]   PA AA R 484727m: Decision of the Reichsgericht b J 507-20/II 67-25 from 7 June 1923.

[64]   Cabinet meeting, No. 55(23), 14 November 1923, CAB 23/46 (TNA).

[65]   Willis, 1982, p. 143, see *supra* note 51.

[66]   PA AA – R 48427n, reprint b J 540/1920 – X 24/25.

[67]   Decision of the Fourth Senate in Criminal Matters, Reichsgericht, 9 April 1925, PA AA R 48430u: reprint b J 539/1920 – X.128/25.

[68]   MAE Paris, vol. 585, p. 166, note of M. Corbin dated 29 April 1925 C/42.

[69]   Poincaré to Ministry of War, No. 1578, 20 July 1922, La Série Europe, 1918–1929, Allemagne, vol. 579, "Sanctions aux violations du droit des gens: Punition des coupables, 1–13 juillet 1922", MAE; Ministry of War to Poincaré, 25 August 1922, La Série Europe, 1918–1929, Allemagne, vol. 580, "Sanctions aux violations du droit des gens: Punition des coupables, 1 août-31 décembre 1922," MAE.

11.2.3. Amnesty

On 20 March 1931, based on the German amnesty law,[70] the Fourth Senate of the *Reichsgericht* decided to suspend the criminal proceedings relating to war crimes against the absconded Patzig.[71] Thereby the only remaining accused of the *Llandovery Castle* case[72] no longer had to face penal sanctions.

11.3. Could the War Crimes Proceedings Initiated in Leipzig Have Any Deterrent Effect?

Since a great number of proceedings against war crimes suspects were terminated by way of suspensions and the remaining 12 criminal trials resulted in acquittals or sentences by the *Reichsgericht* which were perceived to be lenient, the question arises whether these war crimes proceedings could have any deterrent effect.

Deterrence is an "act or process of discouraging certain behavior, particularly by fear; especially as a goal of criminal law, the prevention of criminal behavior by fear of punishment".[73] Thus, the existence of prisons is a major deterrent to crime. As such the concept of deterrence has two key assumptions: that a prison sentence will prevent the convicted offender from committing further crime, and that the abstract fear of punishment will prevent *others* from committing similar crime. In essence, deterrence aims to reduce crime.[74]

Generally, it is hard to measure whether and which particular deterrent effect the prosecution of international crimes has on (potential) perpetrators. Scholars admit that at best there is only anecdotal data on the deterrent effect the prosecutions and judgments may have on criminals in

---

[70] RGBl. 1928 I, p. 195, Law about amnesty from 14 July 1928; RGBl 1930 I S.467: Law amending the Law about amnesty from 14 July 1928.

[71] PA AA R 48433o: Decision of the fourth senate of the Reichsgericht, b J 585/20-101//XII Tgb. 56/1931.

[72] *Llandovery Castle* case, see *supra* note 30; cf. *supra* section 11.2.1.

[73] Bryan A. Garner (ed.), *Black's Law Dictionary*, 9th ed., West, St Paul, 2009, p. 514.

[74] Compare David Ormerod, *Smith and Hogan's Criminal Law*, 13th ed., Oxford University Press, Oxford, 2011, p. 39.

---

one conflict, let alone on other potential authors of international crimes in future conflicts.[75]

11.3.1. Trials in Leipzig

Against a deterrent effect the Leipzig War Crimes Trials may have had on the German population, or at least on the members of the German Army and Navy, is the fact that the prosecutor's office at the *Reichsgericht* suspended many criminal proceedings even before they could reach the stage of issuance of arrest warrants against suspects, or of confirming an indictment against alleged suspects of violations of war crimes. Furthermore, the 12 proceedings that were finally litigated in front of the *Reichsgericht* resulted in six acquittals[76] and the sentences of the 10 convictions were low, none exceeding five years.[77]

On the other hand, the Leipzig War Crimes Trials had extensive press coverage, not only in Germany but also abroad, because journalists from several nations attended the proceedings and Belgium, France, the Netherlands and Britain sent observers, who then produced reports about the outcome of these proceedings.[78] Ernest Pollock, the British Solicitor General, predicted the Leipzig War Crimes Trials would have "a wide reaching and permanent effect" in Germany.[79]

That Dithmar and Boldt, the two navy officers sentenced to four years each in the *Llandovery Castle* case, absconded[80] during the first part

---

[75] M. Cherif Bassiouni, "Reflections on Contemporary Developments in International Criminal Justice", in Bartram S. Brown (ed.), *Research Handbook on International Criminal Law*, Edward Elgar, Northampton, MA, 2011, pp. 414–15; compare also Dawn L. Rothe and Isabel Schoultz, "International Criminal Justice: Law, Courts and Punishment as Deterrent Mechanisms?", in Willem de Lint, Marinella Marmo and Nerida Chazal (eds.), *Criminal Justice in International Society*, Routledge, New York, 2014, pp. 155–63.

[76] See the penultimate column of Table 1.

[77] *Ibid.*, last column.

[78] UK Report, see *supra* note 10, pp. 3–18; van Slooten, 1921, see *supra* note 1; Mullins, 1921, see *supra* note 1; Edouard Clunet, "Les Criminels de guerre devant le Reichsgericht à Leipzig", in *Journal du Droit International*, 1921, vol. 48, pp. 440–47; British Parliamentary Command Paper, "Judicial Decisions Involving Questions of International Law – German War Trials", reprinted in *American Journal of International Law*, 1920, vol. 16, pp. 674–724.

[79] Pollock, 1921, see *supra* note 1.

[80] See text preceding fn. 45.

of their prison sentences does not militate against the deterrent effect this criminal proceeding had on both men and on the Germany navy. Members of the German navy argued repeatedly against the judgment rendered by the Second Senate in July 1921.[81] These concerns suggest that the German Navy and Army took the pronouncements of the *Reichsgericht* in criminal matters seriously. Furthermore, until the Fourth Senate finally quashed the judgment in the *Llandovery Castle* case, Dithmar and Boldt had to live a life in hiding.

Whether the proceedings against Patzig, the third accused in the *Llandovery Castle* case,[82] had any deterrent effect on him is questionable. Patzig had absconded before the trial against Dithmar, Boldt and himself could begin. Since German criminal procedural law does not provide for a trial *in absentia*, the Second Senate could therefore not convict him. However, the judges made at least certain *obiter dictum* findings regarding Patzig in the judgment convicting Dithmar and Boldt for the same transaction. Hence, Patzig continued his flight from the German judicial organs. Only after the Fourth Senate suspended his case based on the amendment to the German amnesty law[83] did the inherent threat to resume judicial proceedings against him stop. When the Second World War broke out, Patzig reported to the German navy command and served again from 1940 as commander of a German submarine.[84] It is not known whether Patzig again engaged in war crimes. However, though the Allied Powers instituted judicial proceedings against many members of the German navy after 1945, they did *not* institute proceedings against Patzig for any war crime committed during the Second World War.

11.3.2. *In Absentia* Trials in France and Belgium

To assess whether war crimes trials after the First World War had any deterrent effect, the Leipzig War Crimes Trials have to be seen in the wider context of (criminal) proceedings instituted by other nations against

---

[81] Andreas Michelsen (ed.), *Das Urteil im Leipziger Uboots-Prozess ein Fehlspruch? Juristische und militärische Gutachten*, Staatspolitischer Verlag, Berlin, 1922; compare Wiggenhorn, 2005, pp. 372–78, see *supra* note 45.

[82] *Llandovery Castle* case, see *supra* note 30.

[83] PA AA R48433o, Decision a J 95/21-183/XI. 183, pursuant to §§ 359 Nr. 5, 360, paragraph 2, 366, 367 and 369 German Code of Criminal Procedure.

[84] Rainer Busch and Hans Joachim Röll, *German U-Boat Commanders of World War II: A Biographical Dictionary*, Greenhill Books, London, 1999, p. 41.

German Army members, Navy members and senior civilian leaders. On 18 April 1922 Poincaré ordered the French Ministry of War and Justice to consider prosecuting some 2,000 Germans named in the initial French list, and not only the 334 suspects named in the list furnished to Germany on 3 February 1920.[85] On 23 August 1923, following the initiative of France, the Conference of Ambassadors declared to resume the rights granted by Articles 228 to 230 of the Treaty of Versailles, namely to prosecute war criminals by way of *in absentia* proceedings.[86] In order to not let impunity reign, the French and Belgian authorities conducted trials *in absentia* in Nancy, Lille, Châlons-sur-Marne and Belgian towns where they convicted many German authors of war crimes.[87]

In particular, in January 1919 the Belgian Ministry of Justice adopted a decree that provided for the arrest of suspects of war crimes in Belgium. Most ensuing trials related to mere property issues such as Germans purchasing requisitioned Belgian machinery, with only a few trials relating to war crimes.[88]

French law at that time provided for trials *in absentia* by Articles 145 to 170 of the *Code de Justice Militaire* and Articles 224, 465 to 478 of the *Code d'instruction criminelle*.[89] By December 1924, the Conseil de Guerre of the 1st, 6th and 20th Corps of the French Army had convicted

---

[85] Note for the President of the Council, 24 June 1922, La Série Europe 1918–1929, Allemagne, vol. 578, *Sanctions aux violations du droit des gens: Punition des coupables, 1 avril–30 juin 1922*; unsigned memorandum on prosecution of Germans, 20 December 1924, La Série Europe 1918–1929, Allemagne, vol. 584, *Sanctions aux violations du droit des gens: Punition des coupables, 1 décembre 1924–31 mars 1925*, MAE.

[86] Note issued by French Prime Minister Poincaré on 23 August 1922, Conference of Ambassadors, sent to Dr. Mayer, paragraph 8 (MAE Paris 580, pp. 35–37: Conférence des Ambassadeurs, Le Président) PA AA R 48415j: telegram Paris Pax of 23 August 1922, note of Conference of Ambassadors, re question of war suspects; BA Berlin Lichterfelde R3003 ORA Gen. 47, pp. 71–76: note of the conference of ambassadors; Conference of Ambassadors to German Embassy in Paris, 23 August 1922, FO 371/7529 (C16860/555/18), Confidential Print 11990; compare Woods to Foreign Office, 16 August 1922, FO 371/7529 (C11741/555/18).

[87] Willis, 1982, p. 142, see *supra* note 51; Jody M. Prescott, "In Absentia War Crime Trials: A Just Means to Enforce International Human Rights?", Thesis, Judge Advocate General's School, United States Army, 4 April 1994, pp. 34–36.

[88] Larry Zuckermann, *The Rape of Belgium: The Untold Story of World War I*, New York University Press, New York, 2004, p. 257.

[89] MAE Paris: 583, p. 57: Ministère de Guerre à Président du Conseil/MAE, No. 1192 from 18 July 1922.

between 941 and 1,200 Germans *in absentia*.[90] For example the Conseil de Guerre of the 20th Corps convicted the General Adolf von Oven and Major Richard von Keiser *in absentia* and imposed the death penalty.[91] Germans who were convicted *in absentia* in France were arrested when they entered French territory. In particular, in November 1924 the German General Wilhelm von Nathusius was arrested in Alsace by the French authorities and was convicted in the course of a retrial in Lille to serve a one-year prison sentence in France for pillaging cloth and a table service.[92] Following a diplomatic intervention by the German authorities, who promised to release a French citizen in return, the French Prime Minister Édouard Herriot pardoned von Nathusius after he had served one month of his sentence in a French prison.[93] Furthermore, Herriot instituted several measures regarding Germans who had been convicted *in absentia* by French courts: secretly he ordered French customs officials and the police to no longer arrest Germans convicted in France for war crimes, but to return them 'discreetly' to German territory. Generally, the French authorities no longer issued this category of Germans any visa to re-enter France.[94]

In mid-October 1925 the French Foreign Minister Briand and his Belgian counterpart agreed in principle to stop *in absentia* trials against Germans for war crimes.[95] By early November 1925 the Belgian government stopped its authorities, having conducted some 80[96] war crimes

---

[90] The numbers vary between 941 and 1,200: MAE Paris 584, pp. 71 ff., note of 20 December 1924; Wiggenhorn, 2005, p. 366, see *supra* note 45; Zuckermann, 2004, p. 260, see *supra* note 88; Poincaré to Ministry of Justice, No. 148, 24 March 1924, La Série Europe 1918–1929, Allemagne, vol. 577, *Sanctions aux violations du droit des gens: Punition des coupables, 1 janvier–31 mars 1922* MAE; Ministry of War to Poincaré, No. 1386, 9 October 1924, La Série Europe 1918-1929, Allemagne, vol. 578, *Sanctions aux violations du droit des gens: Punition des coupables, 1 avril–30 Novembre 1924*, Willis, 1982, p. 142, see *supra* note 51, particularly text surrounding fn. 106.

[91] Both suspects had also been on the French list of 45 persons submitted to Germany. Wiggenhorn, 2005, p. 360, see *supra* note 45.

[92] Conseil de Guerre permanent de la 1ère region séant à Lille, Jugement par defaut, Nr. 616 du Jugement Art. 140 du code de justice militaire; Willis, 1982, p. 144, see *supra* note 51.

[93] Wiggenhorn, 2005, p. 368, see *supra* note 45, referring to PA AA R 48433d: AA e.o. VF 1751 from 4 December 1924: note regarding the pardoning of General von Nathasius.

[94] Willis, 1982, p. 144, see *supra* note 51; Zuckermann, 2004, p. 260, see *supra* note 88.

[95] Wiggenhorn, 2005, pp. 367–68, see *supra* note 45.

[96] Peter W. Guenther, *A History of Articles 227, 228, 229 and 230 of the Treaty in Versailles*, M.A. Thesis, University of Texas, Austin, 1960, p. 180, referring to George Callier,

---

trials *in absentia* against Germans, from pursuing further proceedings.[97] In early 1926 Briand gained support from other French politicians to 'quietly' let war crimes trials *in absentia* slide as opposed to officially stopping them, a move which did not affect the policy of denying entry visas to Germans convicted *in absentia*.[98] This visa policy was only abandoned in October 1929 when the French authorities replaced it with the policy that Germans convicted as a result of *in absentia* proceedings could enter French territory, but were put under police surveillance during their stay.[99]

11.3.3. Conclusion on Deterrent Effect

In hindsight, a comparison of the French and the German approaches to war crimes' suspects reveals that the German authorities suspended too many criminal investigations. Also, the *Reichsgericht*, by imposing lenient penalties and by silently quashing the judgment convicting Boldt and Dithmar,[100] did not rigorously ensure the deterrent effect of their judgments. Nevertheless, when the efforts of the *Reichsgericht*, the Belgian and French authorities against suspected war criminals are combined, and when one considers the coverage these proceedings had in academic circles as well as in the media of Germany and the Allied states, the deterrent effect these judicial proceedings had on Germans who committed war crimes on French or Belgium territory, and on those who committed crimes during naval warfare,[101] becomes more apparent.

Minister of Belgium in Washington D.C. to Peter Guenther, 26 January 1959; Zuckermann, 2004, p. 261, see *supra* note 88.

[97] MAE Brussels 324 VIII: communiqué, Brussels 7 November 1925; compare PA AA R 28596, p. 430: AA VF 2013 from 21 November 1925 to German Embassy Paris; p. 433: German embassy Paris to foreign office Germany, nr. 884, from 23 November 1925; Friedrich von Keller to Foreign Ministry of Germany, No. 177, 29 October 1925, AA (T-120/1567/D685128); MAE Brussels 324 IX: MAE Direction P/B No. 560; Wiggenhorn, 2005, p. 368, quotes passages of this letter, see *supra* note 45.

[98] Willis, 1982, p. 145, see *supra* note 51.

[99] *Ibid.*, referring in note 126 to Briand to the French Minister of Interior, No. BC/19, 28-Oct-1929 and a Memorandum of a conversation between German Ambassador and Philippe Berthelot, 13 November 1929.

[100] See *supra* note 48.

[101] Compare Wiggenhorn, 2005, pp. 372–78, see *supra* note 45.

11.4. Hardly Any German Senior Leader Had to Stand Trial in Leipzig

No senior civilian and no member of the German Supreme Command of the Army or of the Admiralty had to stand trial in front of the *Reichsgericht*.

11.4.1. The German Emperor, Wilhelm II

Article 227 of the Treaty of Versailles provided that the German Emperor Wilhelm II of Hohenzollern, should be "publicly arraigned" in front of an international tribunal for a "supreme offence against international morality and the sanctity of treaties". Regarding the nature of this "supreme offence" the Allied Powers clarified:

> *Enfin, ells entendent indiquer clairement que la mise en accusation publique décrétèe contre l'ex Empereur allemande aux termes de l'article 227 n'aura pas le caractère juridique quant au fond, mais seulement quant à la forme. Cette mise en Accusation est une question de haute politique international, le minimum que l'on puisse exiger pour le plus grand des crimes contre la morale international, le caractère sacré de Traitès et les règles essentielles de la justice. Les Puissanxes allies et associés ont voulu des forms et une procedure judiciaires ainsi qu'un tribunal régulierement constitué afin d'assur l'accusé, pour sa défense, la plaine jouissance de ses droits et de ses libertés et d'entourer le jugement du maximum de solennité possible.[102]*

Thus, the Allied Powers intended to put the Emperor on trial as an act of high policy, presented in the form of judicial proceedings. However, the United States and Japan objected to this approach.[103] The US made a formal reservation against an option to subject "to criminal and therefore to legal prosecution, persons accused of offences against the 'laws of humanity' and in so far as it subjects chiefs of states to a degree of responsibility hitherto unknown to municipal or international law, for

---

[102] Report of the Allied Powers accompanying the ultimatum of 16 June 1919, reprinted in Kraus-Rödiger, *Urkunden zum Friedensvertrag von Versailles vom 28. Juni 1919*, 1920–1921, vol. I, p. 622.

[103] M. Cherif Bassiouni, *Introduction to International Criminal Law*, 2003, Transnational Publishers, Ardsley, p. 398.

which no precedents are to be found in the modern practice of nations".[104]
Also, the Japanese delegates objected that charges could be brought
against "heads of state".[105]

Trying a head of state for having violated norms of international
criminal law during the First World War would have been a novelty that
would have faced legal complexities. Until the Treaty of Versailles, heads
of state were granted immunity from criminal prosecutions.[106] At the
beginning of the First World War, a prohibition on going to war did not
exist. In 1912, two years before war broke out, Lassa Oppenheim stated
that international law "at present cannot and does not object to States
which are in conflict waging war upon each other instead of peaceably
settling their differences".[107] The prohibition to go to war did not exist
until the Kellogg-Briand Pact was codified in 1928 and subsequently
ratified.[108] Thus, creating this "supreme offence against international
morality and the sanctity of treaties" after the First World War via a peace
treaty and attempting to set the Emperor up for a criminal trial was a
"hazardous adventure".[109]

A different situation existed regarding the Emperor's responsibility
for violations of the *jus in bello*, meaning his responsibility for war
crimes. Since the Emperor had fled to the Netherlands and German law
did not provide for proceedings *in absentia*, trying the Emperor on
German territory for violations of *jus in bello* was not possible. However,
the Emperor could have changed his mind during his exile and may one
day have chosen to return to Germany. To adequately react to this

---

[104] Commission on the Responsibility of the Authors of the War and on Enforcement of
Penalties, "Report Presented to the Preliminary Peace Conference" ("Commission
Report"), 29 March 1919, reprinted in *American Journal of International Law*, 1920, vol.
14, Annex II, USA, *Memorandum of Reservations Presented by the Representatives of the
United States to the Report of the Commission on Responsibilities*, p. 135.

[105] *Ibid.*, Annex III, Reservation by the Japanese Delegation, 4 April 1919, p. 152. The
objection is directed at eliminating the phrase "including the heads of states" on p. 143 of
the Commission Report.

[106] Christian Tomuschat, "The 1871 Peace Treaty between France and Germany and the 1919
Peace Treaty of Versailles", in Randall Lesaffer (ed.), *Peace Treaties and International
Law in European History*, Cambridge University Press, Cambridge, 2008, pp. 393–94.

[107] Lassa Oppenheim, *International Law: A Treatise*, 2nd ed., Longmans, Green & Co.,
London, 1912, p. 60.

[108] Tomuschat, 2008, pp. 384, 395, see *supra* note 106.

[109] *Ibid.*, p. 393.

situation it would have mattered that the German authorities would have scrutinised the Emperor's potential responsibility for war crimes in order to arrest him in case he would have returned to German territory. However, original German source material, documents from the Allied Powers and secondary academic literature reviewed by the author do not suggest that the *Reichsgericht* and its attached prosecutor's office attempted to investigate the Emperor for his responsibility for crimes committed during the First World War (*jus in bello*).

11.4.2. Other Senior Civilian Superiors and Senior Military Commanders

Though the first and second Allied lists[110] communicated to the Germans contained also senior political and military leaders[111] suspected of war crimes, the German prosecutor's office furnished no prosecutions of senior German leaders to the *Reichsgericht*. Neither a member of the German supreme command (whether from the military or the admiralty) nor of the senior civilian leadership was indicted by the prosecutor's office attached to the *Reichsgericht*.

11.4.2.1. Karl Stenger

This left Lieutenant General Karl Stenger, a mere brigade commander, whom the French had initially put forward on their list sent to the Germans, together with Benno Kruska as the second highest German to

---

[110] Friedrich Karl Kaul refers to lists from France, Britain, Italy, Poland, Rumania and Yugoslavia in *Die Verfolgung deutscher Kriegsverbrecher nach dem ersten Weltkrieg*, Zeitschrift für Geschichtswissenschaft, 1966, vol. 14, pp. 25–26.

[111] The initial Allied list communicated on 3 February 1920 to the German Baron von Lersner, the German delegate at the Peace Conference in Versailles and then to the German Government, contained 896 names of suspects. Among them were at least three German generals (Hindenburg, Ludendorff and von Mackensen), and a number of admirals including von Tirpitz as well as Crown Prince Rupprecht of Bavaria, the Duke of Württemberg, ex-chancellor Bethman Hollweg, the Imperial Crown Prince of Germany and Count Bismarck, grandson of the "Iron Chancellor". Compare Alexandre Mérignhac and E. Lémonon, *Le droit des gens et la guerre de 1914–1918*, Recueil Sirey, Paris, 1921, p. 593; Robert K. Woetzel, *The Nuremberg Trials in International Law*, Stevens & Sons, London, 1962, pp. 31–32; George A. Finch, "Editorial Comment: Retribution for War Crimes", in *American Journal of International Law*, 1943, vol. 37, p. 83, fn. 7.

stand trial in Leipzig.[112] The prosecutor alleged that in August 1914 Stenger misused his official position as brigade commander by instructing subordinates to commit crimes, namely to issue orders to kill wounded French soldiers or POWs. The prosecutor further alleged that one of the subordinates receiving this order was Major Benno Crusius who then, among other acts, misused his official position by instructing subordinates to directly implement the aforementioned order and thereby commit the killings.[113] As such, the case against Stenger and Crusius related to command responsibility for an order not to give pardon, meaning not to take any prisoners and to kill the wounded.

On 6 July 1921, after a six-day trial, the *Reichsgericht* acquitted Stenger because it considered the allegation that he had given an order not to give pardon as "refuted".[114] This was surprising because witnesses at trial made contradictory statements as to the existence or non-existence of such an order. The written reasons reflect the fact that the judges relied on denials by certain insider witnesses, officers of the immediate staff of Stenger, as to whether such an order was ever given. However, the judgment also acknowledged that two witnesses testified otherwise: the co-accused Crusius testified to have obtained an oral order not to give pardon and the witness Major Müller testified to have forwarded the order from Crusius to others.[115] The judgment of the *Reichsgericht* was silent as to why the judges favoured the denials of witnesses forming Stenger's inner circle over the different version advanced by Crusius and Müller. The latter mutually confirmed each other's version, but also explained why killings of French wounded soldiers and POWs had occurred. Faced with such contradictory versions, the judges should have discussed in

---

[112] The so-called French list of 45 contained Stenger, the commander of the 58th Brigade, and four other members of this brigade (Captain Crusius, Lieutenant Laule, Commander Müller and Captain Schröder) who were alleged to be involved in passing on or carrying out the order of Stenger not to give pardon to French prisoners (Kaul, 1966, pp. 25–26, see *supra* note 110). However, Schröder and Müller had been killed during the First World War (Wiggenhorn, 2005, pp. 214–15, see *supra* note 45).

[113] Stenger and Crusius, Judgment, reprinted in Weißbuch, see *supra* notes 10 and 22, containing the judgments pronounced due to the German Laws of 18 December 1919 and 24 March 1920, in Negotiations of the German *Reichstag*, I. election period, 1920, vol. 368, dossier number 2584, p. 2563 (2564); Feisenberger, 1921, col. 267, see *supra* note 25.

[114] Stenger and Crusius, Judgment, p. 2566, see *supra* notes 10 and 22.

[115] *Ibid.*

their written reasoning the probability of each version including the reliability of each witnesses supporting it. Instead, the judges simply asserted that the allegations regarding the existence of an order were "refuted" because it would have to be given in written form. This in itself is not convincing, even more so since a French witness from Alsace, where the crimes occurred, testified that a third officer, Captain Schröder, a subordinate of Major Müller, would have also announced the order.[116] Neither the written judgment nor its oral pronouncement in Leipzig mentioned this witness testimony at all,[117] though it contradicts a central finding of the court that no order was ever given by Stenger. Instead of labelling the alleged existence of an order of Stenger as "refuted",[118] the *Reichsgericht* should have discussed in more detail *all* contradictory evidence and assessed the reliability of evidence more carefully. And this should have included a detailed assessment of the credibility of all witnesses on this issue. Moreover, since at least three witnesses, two insiders and one French witness, testified as to the existence of an order not to give pardon, it would have at least been better to base an acquittal of Stenger only on the principle *in dubio pro reo*.

11.4.2.2. Hans von Schack and Benno Kruska

Kruska, a camp commander, was a Major General, the second highest German to stand trial in war crimes proceedings in Leipzig. His superior was von Schack, a Lieutenant General who was the highest commander to stand trial in front of the *Reichsgericht*. The French authorities alleged that both men had been negligent, had intentionally suppressed hygienic measures,[119] and were therefore responsible for the spreading of typhus in a camp in Kassel-Niederzwehren, which caused the deaths of up to 3,000 detained persons. Von Schack had issued an explicit order to Kruska to

---

[116] Witness Alfred Rubrecht (see stenograhic protocol of the Stenger and Crusius trial, printed in German Federal Archive Berlin-Lichterfelde, R 3003 ORA/RG b J 92/20, vol. 3 and Political Archive German Foreign Office, R 48436q, p. 230. However, this version appears to be contradicted by three witnesses who claimed that Captain Schröder was on holiday in the relevant period of time. Political Archive German Foreign Office, R 48436q, p. 235 (witness General Major Neubauer), p. 236 (witness Dr. Döhner) and p. 341 Senior Lieutenant Laule).

[117] Wiggenhorn, 2005, pp. 227–28, see *supra* note 45.

[118] Stenger and Crusius, Judgment, reprinted in Weißbuch, p. 2566, see *supra* notes 10 and 22.

[119] Von Schack and Kruska Judgment, p. 2574, see *supra* note 28.

---

mix detainees with Russians who had been infected with lice: "It appears quite harmless, if the French and Brits get from their fellow brothers lice" because it is "in our interest that the Allies mutually know and appreciate one another".[120] Due to the wording of this order Harald Wiggenhorn suggests that the lice plague was spread intentionally.[121] The *Reichsgericht* referred to an order from the German War Ministry from 18 October 1914 in which the wish was expressed to mix the nationalities among the detainees.[122] Throughout the judgment it was pointed out which measures Kruska tried to implement (disinfection, isolation of the affected detainees and destruction of infected mattresses).[123] The judgment omitted a critical report that alleged negligence in combatting this plague on the part of Kruska, and mentioned that countermeasures had been implemented too late.[124] Otherwise the judgment was full of positive assessments of Kruska's personality and was generally critical of those witnesses who produced incriminating evidence.[125] The *Reichsgericht* acquitted both Kruska and von Schack. Seeing in which direction the judges were heading, the French observer delegation departed Leipzig before the judgment was officially pronounced.[126] The French would not return to observe further war crimes proceedings in Leipzig.

---

[120] Command of garrison Kassel to Command detention camp, diary Nr. 2642, dated 29 October 1914 (BA Berlin-Lichterfelde R 3003 ORA/RG b J 296/20, vol. 1 p. 63) (my translation).

[121] Wiggenhorn, 2005, p. 240, see *supra* note 45.

[122] Von Schack and Kruska Judgment, p. 2577, see *supra* note 28.

[123] These measures were implemented in consultation with the medical staff of the camp. At the same time the judges acknowledged that these measures were "insufficient and could not realize its objective because they could not reach the causative agent of the typhus fever, the louse", *ibid.*, pp. 2576, 2578 (my translation).

[124] Inspection of the Detention Camp, XI. Army Corps, T.B. Nr. 54, Kassel 4 May; see also p. 4: General Major von Tettau, 9 Aug 1919 to Generalstaff, XI. Corps (BA Berlin-Lichterfelde R3003 ORA/RG b J 296/20, vol. 4, pp. 13 *et seq*); Door Heather Jones pointed out that key evidence was ignored by the court. See *Violence Against Prisoners of War in the First World War: Britain, France and Germany – 1914–1920*, Cambridge University Press, Cambridge, 2011, pp. 108–9.

[125] Von Schack and Kruska Judgment, 1921, pp. 2574–79, see *supra* note 28.

[126] Wiggenhorn, 2005, pp. 243–44, see *supra* note 45.

11.5. The Leipzig War Crimes Trials Against the Background of the Criminalisation of Violations of International Humanitarian Law

The Leipzig War Crimes Trials have to be seen in the context of the international humanitarian law existing during the First World War and its subsequent evolution. Prior to 1921 and 1922, when these trials were conducted, several international treaties prohibiting certain methods of warfare on land and on sea had been signed and ratified by up to 37 nations. States agreed in The Hague to three instruments of international humanitarian law: 1) the Convention concerning Bombardment by Naval Forces in Time of War ('1907 Hague Naval Convention'); 2) the Convention respecting the Laws and Customs of War on Land ('1907 Hague Land Convention') which contained in its Annex; 3) the Regulations concerning the Laws and Customs of War on Land ('1907 Hague Regulations') of 18 October 1907.[127] On that day, Germany had signed all three instruments and ratified them on 27 November 1909 with one reservation.[128]

The 1907 Hague Regulations prohibited certain means of warfare on land,[129] while the 1907 Hague Naval Convention prohibited certain conduct at sea.[130] However, a mere prohibition of certain conduct may stop short of criminalising this act or omission. For instance, a certain conduct may be prohibited by certain international norms, but their violation does not automatically amount to a commission of an international crime, because a crime under international law is *only* given if three distinct requirements are met:

a)   A prohibition forms part of international law (either conventional or customary international law);[131]

---

[127] Thirty-six states ratified the 1907 Hague Naval Convention (http://www.legal-tools.org/doc/5d3857/); 37 states ratified the 1907 Hague Land Convention and its annexed 1907 The Hague Regulations (http://www.legal-tools.org/doc/fa0161/).

[128] Compare James Brown Scott, *The Hague Conventions and Declarations of 1899 and 1907*, Oxford University Press, New York, 1915, pp. 132, 162. The reservation related to Article 44 of the annexed 1907 The Hague Regulations and to Article 1(2) of the 1907 Hague Naval Convention, see *supra* note 127.

[129] See Articles 23, 25, 28, 44, 45, 47 and 50, *supra* note 127.

[130] See Articles 1, 4 and 7, *supra* note 127.

[131] Compare Antonio Cassese, *International Criminal Law*, Oxford University Press, New York, 2008, p. 11, no. 1; Kai Ambos, "Judicial Creativity at the Special Tribunal for

b)   The breach of this prohibition is serious, because it affects certain universal values;[132] and

c)   The breach entails individual criminal responsibility [133] and is punishable regardless of its incorporation into domestic law.[134]

The two 1907 Hague Conventions and the 1907 Hague Regulations contained prohibitions[135] that protected universal values such as life and well-being. However, whether the 1907 Hague Conventions and Regulations also satisfied the third requirement to provide for individual responsibility is questionable.

A textbook example of an international provision providing for individual criminal responsibility of the violator is Article 1 of the Genocide Convention which states: "The Contracting Parties confirm that genocide […] is a crime under international law which they undertake to

---

Lebanon: Is There a Crime of Terrorism under International Law?", in *Leiden Journal of International Law*, 2011, vol. 24, no. 1, p. 16.

[132]   Cassese, 2008, p. 11, no. 2, see *supra* note 131; Bassiouni, 2003, p. 114, no. 1, see *supra* note 103; Ambos, 2011, p. 16, no. 1, see *supra* note 131; Robert Cryer, Hakan Friman, Darryl Robinson and Elizabeth Wilmshurst, *An Introduction to International Criminal Law and Procedure*, Cambridge University Press, New York, 2008, pp. 3–4; Bruce Broomhall, *International Justice and the International Criminal Court: Between State Sovereignty and the Rule of Law*, Oxford University Press, Oxford, 2003, pp. 44–51; Gerhard Werle, *Principles of International Criminal Law*, 2nd ed., T.M.C. Asser Press, The Hague, 2009, para. 95.

[133]   ICTY, Appeals Chamber, *Decision on the Defence Motion for Interlocutory Appeal on Jurisdiction*, IT-94-I-T ("Tadić case"), 2 October 1995, para. 94, in section (IV) ("Tadić Jurisdiction Decision") (http://www.legal-tools.org/doc/866e17/); Special Tribunal for Lebanon, Appeals Chamber, *Interlocutory Decision on the Applicable Law: Terrorism, Conspiracy, Homicide, Perpetration, Cumulative Charging*, STL-11-01/I, 16 February 2011, paragraph 103, ("STL Interlocutory Decision") (http://www.legal-tools.org/doc/4c16e9); Cassese, 2008, pp. 33–34, see *supra* note 131; Hans Heinrich Jescheck, *Die Verantwortlichkeit der Staatsorgane nach Völkerstrafrecht: eine Studie zu den Nürnberger Prozessen*, Lothar Röhrscheid, Bonn, 1952, p. 374; Claus Kress, "International Criminal Law", in Rüdiger Wolfrum (ed.), *The Max Planck Encyclopedia of Public International Law*, Oxford University Press, Oxford, 2008, paras. 10–11; Ambos, 2011, p. 16, no. 3, see *supra* note 131; Michael Cottier, "Article 8 ICC Statute", in Otto Triffterer (ed.), *Commentary on the Rome Statute of the International Criminal Court: Observer's Notes, Article by Article*, 2nd ed., C.H. Beck, Hart Publishing and Nomos, Munich, 2008, para. 1; Werle, 2009, para. 84, see *supra* note 132.

[134]   Ambos, 2011, p. 16, no. 3, see *supra* note 131; Paolo Gaeta, "International Criminalization of Prohibited Conduct", in Antonio Cassese (ed.), *The Oxford Companion to International Criminal Justice*, 2009, Oxford University Press, Oxford, pp. 69–70; Werle, 2009, para. 84, see *supra* note 132.

[135]   See *supra* notes 129–30.

---

prevent and to punish".[136] The language of the 1907 Hague Conventions and Regulations is not that clear-cut. The Preamble to the 1907 Hague Land Convention talks about "High Contracting Parties" meaning the states themselves as opposed to individuals. Article 3 then continues that a "belligerent party which violates the provisions of the said [1907 Hague] Regulations shall, if the case demands, be liable to pay compensation. It shall be responsible for all acts committed by persons forming part of its armed forces". This indicates that the focus of the 1907 Hague Land Convention and its attached Regulations were the obligations of States to pay *compensation* for violations of their armed forces,[137] as opposed to the individual criminal liability of individuals for their own conduct. On the other hand, Article 3 of the Hague Land Convention does also not exclude individual personal responsibility, but acknowledges it only vis-à-vis the perpetrators own state.[138]

The closest provisions of the 1907 Hague Regulations come to introducing individual (criminal) responsibility are Articles 41 and 56(2). The former reads: a "violation of the terms of the armistice by private persons acting on their own initiative only entitles the injured party to demand the punishment of the offenders or, if necessary, compensation for the losses sustained". This provision does not explicitly clarify which authority has the right to sanction, but the context suggests that it is at least the State whose citizens had violated the armistice. Article 56(2) of the 1907 Hague Regulations prohibits seizure, damage and destruction to religious, charity or educational institutions, and directs that such acts "should be made subject of legal proceedings".[139] By contrast, all other prohibitions contained in the 1907 Hague Regulations[140] do *not* contain similar language suggesting punishments, whether by the State whose citizens had carried out the violations, or by the affected state.

The 1907 Hague Naval Convention, which also contains similar prohibitions, clarifies in Article 8 that its provisions "do not apply except

---

[136] Convention on the Prevention and Punishment of the Crime of Genocide, adopted by Resolution 260 (III) A of the United Nations General Assembly on 9 December 1948 (http://www.legal-tools.org/doc/498c38/).

[137] Bassiouni, 2003, p. 92, see *supra* note 103; Cottier, 2008, para. 3, see *supra* note 133.

[138] Jescheck, 1952, pp. 37–38, see *supra* note 133.

[139] See *supra* note 127.

[140] See Articles 23, 25, 28, 44, 45, 47 and 50, see *supra* note 127.

between Contracting Powers", meaning the states themselves as opposed to individuals.[141]

Cherif Bassiouni proposes ten penal characteristics which, if found, would be sufficient to characterise the conduct prohibited by a convention as an international crime.[142] However, having developed these criteria he acknowledged that the 1907 Hague Conventions and Regulations had at best only "limited penal relevance".[143] In conclusion, except for the limited situations provided for in Articles 41 and 56(2) of the 1907 Hague Regulations, all 1907 Hague Conventions and Regulations *only* dealt with obligations of states and did not provide for individual responsibility, let alone for individual criminal responsibility.[144] The only other exception is Article 28 of the Convention for the Amelioration of the Condition of the Wounded and Sick in Armies in the Field ('1906 Geneva Convention').[145]

However, following the 1907 adoption of these Hague Conventions and Regulations and the 1906 Geneva Convention, consideration may be given as to whether the individual (criminal) responsibility of individuals violating these codified prohibitions may have acquired the status of customary international law. This would require that: 1) an *opinio juris*; and 2) a practice to attach individual criminal responsibility to the prohibitions existed.

---

[141] See *supra* note 127.

[142] Bassiouni, 2003, p. 115, see *supra* note 103.

[143] *Ibid.*, p. 137.

[144] Cottier, 2008, Article 8, para. 1, see *supra* note 133. Compare Tomuschat, 2008, p. 394: "During the relevant period from 1914 to 1918, no international penal law had existed. To be sure, Germany had violated Belgium's neutrality, but its military operations on Belgium territory amounted to nothing more – but also nothing less – than a breach of international law for which Germany was responsible as a collective entity. Individual criminal responsibility is a different matter altogether", see *supra* note 106. Also compare Dirk von Selle, "Prolog zu Nürnberg – Die Leipziger Kriegsverbrecherprozesse vor dem Reichsgericht", *Zeitschrift für neuere Rechtsgeschichte*, 1997, p. 205, fn. 83.

[145] Article 28 (1) of the 1906 Geneva Convention states: "In the event of their military penal laws being insufficient, the signatory governments also engage to take, or to recommend to their legislatures, the necessary measures to repress, in time of war, individual acts of robbery and ill treatment of the sick and wounded of the armies, as well as to punish, as usurpations of military insignia, the wrongful use of the flag and brassard of the Red Cross by military persons or private individuals not protected by the present convention". The 1906 Geneva Convention was adopted in Geneva on 6 July 1906 (http://www.legal-tools.org/doc/90dd83/).

Two international criminal tribunals accepted this two-prong test: the International Criminal Tribunal for the former Yugoslavia ('ICTY') Appeals Chamber required in the Duško Tadić case:

> The following requirements must be met for an offence to be subject to prosecution [...] (iv) the violation of the rule must entail, under customary or conventional law, the individual criminal responsibility of the person breaching the rule.[146]

Also, the Special Tribunal for Lebanon ruled,

> to give rise to individual criminal liability at the international level it is necessary for a violation of the *international rule to entail the individual criminal responsibility of the person* breaching the rule. The criteria for determining this issue were again suggested by the ICTY in that seminal decision: the intention to criminalise the prohibition must be evidenced by statements of government officials and international organisations, as well as by punishment for such violations by national courts. Perusal of these elements in practice will establish whether States intend to criminalise breaches of the international rule.[147]

We will now explore whether customary international law existed during the First World War to attach individual criminal responsibility to the prohibitions of international humanitarian law.

11.5.1. *Opinio Juris*

During the First World War governments and academics voiced their opinion to hold perpetrators accountable. For example, in France, the law professors Louis Renault and René Garraud, as well as the practitioners Juda Tchernoff, an advocate, and Jacques Dumas, deputy prosecutor in Versailles, argued that French courts could adjudicate violations of the laws and customs of war committed by foreign troops on French territory.[148] At the same time, no debate occurred in the German Reich as

---

[146] Tadić Jurisdiction Decision, para. 94, section IV, see *supra* note 133.

[147] STL Interlocutory Decision, para. 103, see *supra* note 133 (emphasis added).

[148] Louis Renault, "Dans quelle mesure le droit pénal peut-il s'appliquer à des faits de guerre contraires au droit des gens?", in *Revue pénitentaire et de droit pénal*, 1915, vol. 39, pp. 423–24, 475–77; René Garraud, "L'application du droit pénal aux faits de guerre", in *Revue Pénitentaire et de Droit Pénal*, 1916, vol. 40, pp. 20–32; Juda Tchernoff, "Les sanctions pénales des abus de la Guerre", in *Revue politique et parlementaire*, 1915, vol. 84, pp. 59–60; Jaques Dumas and Andre Weiss, *Les sanctions pénales des crimes*

to whether to punish senior civilian or military leaders from enemy states.[149] Rather, the debate in Germany focused on whether it would be possible to try ordinary soldiers of enemy states. Initially, the notion was advanced that an enemy soldier could only be tried for crimes *after* his arrest, but not for violations of international humanitarian law before his captivity.[150] However, when French military courts began convicting German soldiers, a German court martial in the field responded by confirming their competence also for crimes committed by enemy soldiers *before* their captivity.[151]

In 1915, neither the British First Lord of the Admiralty, Winston Churchill, nor Prime Minister H.H. Asquith wanted to exclude the possibility that German submarine naval staff arrested by the British forces could face criminal proceedings at the end of the war.[152] Asquith told the British House of Commons that careful records were taken by the British government so that "when the proper hour comes the technical difficulties be as few as possible and the means of convicting and punishing the offenders, whatever the appropriate mode of punishment may turn out to be, may be put in force".[153] Even British academics had mixed reactions to this proposition.[154] For his part, the British elder statesman Sir Arthur Balfour warned that violations of international law

---

Allemands, Librairie Arthur Rouasseau, Paris, 1916, pp. 7–38; compare Jescheck, 1952, pp. 42–46, see *supra* note 133.

[149] Jescheck, 1952, p. 49, see *supra* note 133.

[150] German Military Court of the Reich (Reichsmilitärgericht), *Deutsche Juristen Zeitung*, Berlin and Leipzig, 1915, col. 129; Willis, 1982, p. 14, see *supra* note 51.

[151] Alfred Verdroß, *Die völkerrechtswidrige Kriegshandlung und der Strafanspruch der Staaten*, H.R. Engelmann, Berlin, 1920, p. 18.

[152] Willis, 1982, p. 17, text preceding fn. 59, see *supra* note 51; Daniel Marc Segesser, *Recht statt Rache oder Rache durch Recht? Die Ahndung von Kriegsverbrechen in der internationalen wissenschaftlichen Debatte (1872–1945)*, Ferdinand Schöningh, Paderborn, 2010, pp. 178–79; Bass, 2000, pp. 61–62, see *supra* note 6.

[153] House of Commons, United Kingdom, *Parliamentary Debates*, vol. 71, 1915, pp. 651–64, cols. 1201–8.

[154] Segesser, 2010, p. 178, see *supra* note 152, referring to Graham Bower, "The Laws of War: Prisoners of War and Reprisals", in *Transaction of the Grotius Society*, 1916, vol. 1, pp. 23–37; Thomas Erskine Holland, *Letters to 'The Times' upon War and Neutrality (1881–1920)*, Longmans, Green and Co., London, 1921, pp. 70–72; Hugh H. Bellot, "War Crimes and War Criminals", in *Canadian Law Times*, 1916, vol. 36, p. 765; Sir Herbert Stephen, Letters, *The Times*, 11 March 1915, p. 9, 19 March 1915, p. 10; Sir Harry Poland, Letter, *The Times*, London, 17 March 1915, p. 9.

---

would not be dealt with "in isolation, and that the general question of personal responsibility shall be reserved until the end of the war".[155] In hindsight, the British call for justice for German war criminals developed as follows: Churchill, who had contested the POW status of detained German navy members in order to hold them accountable for war crimes, was removed from office. In order to protect British POWs in German hands, the government had to mute its own demands for trials on war crimes charges.[156] Even weeks before the conclusion of the war, the British Cabinet was cautious regarding war crimes trials:

> It was suggested that we might make it a condition of the peace that those individuals who had been responsible for the ill-treatment of our prisoners should be tried by a court of law. It was pointed out, however, that it would be very difficult to fix responsibility. In addition, no nation, unless it was beaten to dust, would accept such terms. If England had been beaten in this war, we should never agree to our officers being tried by German tribunals.[157]

In the US at the beginning of the war, President Woodrow Wilson was more concerned with keeping American neutrality than with remanding German leaders with criminal responsibility for their deeds. Despite Republican outrage over German atrocities in their use of poison gas, and regardless of criticism from Henry Stimson or Theodore Roosevelt, Wilson emphasised American neutrality. This meant that the US had no obligations unless its own citizens were affected by German actions.[158] Only after German or Austrian submarines sank the *Lusitania*, the *Ancona* and the *Sussex*, killing American citizens each time, did Wilson begin to criticise submarine warfare. However, the main American politicians said little, if anything, about war crimes trials.[159] Bass observes: "Despite America's occasional rumbles about war crimes trials the Wilson administration did not associate itself with the war crimes provisions of the Treaty of Versailles".[160]

---

[155] House of Commons, United Kingdom, *Parliamentary Debates*, vol. 72, 1915, pp. 267– 68.

[156] Bass, 2000, pp. 61 ff., see *supra* note 6.

[157] CAB 23/8, War Cabinet 484 and Imperial War Cabinet 35, 11 October 1918, 16 hours (TNA)

[158] Bass, 2000, p. 94, see *supra* note 6.

[159] *Ibid.*, pp. 95–99.

[160] *Ibid.*, p. 100.

The Allied Commission on the Responsibility of the Authors of the War and on Enforcement of Penalties not only created a list of 32 possible charges but also dealt in a special chapter entitled "Personal Responsibility" with issues of command responsibility, the non-immunity of a sovereign, and the responsibility of the German Emperor.[161] The US made a formal reservation against an option to subject

> to criminal and therefore to legal prosecution, persons accused of offences against the 'laws of humanity' and in so far it subjects chiefs of states to a degree of responsibility hitherto unknown to municipal or international law, for which no precedents are to be found in the modern practice of nations.[162]

Furthermore the American representatives argued that

> nations should use the machinery at hand, which had been tried and found competent, with a law and procedure framed and therefore known in advance, rather than to create an international tribunal with a criminal jurisdiction for which there is no precedent, precept, practice, or procedure.[163]

In essence, the US would neither participate in the creation of the envisaged international tribunal nor would it send cases relating to their citizens before it.[164] In a similar manner to the US, the Japanese delegates also formulated their reservations and posed the following question: "It may be asked whether international law recognizes a penal law as applicable to those who are guilty".[165]

Sheldon Glueck commented regarding the efforts of the Allied Powers to create an *opinion juris*: "for the Allies to have made several solemn pronouncements that war criminals would be punished and then to have let the entire matter go by default was worse than if they had said nothing about war criminals".[166]

---

161 Commission Report, 1919, pp. 114–17, see *supra* note 104.

162 *Ibid.*, Annex II, USA, *Memorandum of Reservations Presented by the Representatives of the United States to the Report of the Commission on Responsibilities*, p. 135.

163 *Ibid.*, p. 142.

164 Bass, 2000, pp. 102–3, see *supra* note 6.

165 Commission Report, 1919, p. 152, see *supra* note 104.

166 Glueck, 1944, p. 34, see *supra* note 2.

11.5.2. Practice: To Attach Individual Criminal Responsibility to the Prohibitions of International Humanitarian Law including to the 1907 Hague Law[167]

During the First World War, France had set up special military courts to try German prisoners of war and in October 1914, three Germans were convicted for pillage with further trials following.[168] However, when the German Reich 'retaliated'[169] by arresting French citizens, France stopped its proceedings until the end of the First World War, engaged with Germany in secret talks about an exchange of prisoners and otherwise negotiated in secret with the UK about the establishment of a war crimes tribunal to be established after the end of the hostilities.[170]

In 1915, the German authorities tried the British nurse Edith Cavell, then head of the school for training purposes, for having participated in a scheme to shelter enemy soldiers from the occupation authorities in Brussels.[171] The nurse's behaviour was considered a crime under the German Military Penal Code (*Militärstrafgesetzbuch*) and incurred sanctions. Yet it is doubtful whether her behaviour was prohibited under international humanitarian law and even more doubtful whether international law attached penal responsibility for such conduct. Therefore, this trial by the German authorities does not qualify as a valid 'practice' of attaching individual criminal responsibility to norms of international humanitarian law.[172]

On 7 May 1915, a German U-boat torpedoed and sunk the British ocean liner *RMS Lusitania* some 11 miles south of the Old Head of Kinsale in the county of Cork in Ireland, resulting in 1,198 dead persons.[173] A day later, Dr. Bernhard Dernburg, a German spokesman claimed that the *Lusitania* had "carried contraband of war" and "was

---

[167] See *supra* note 127.

[168] Bass, 2000, p. 83, see *supra* note 6; Jescheck, 1952, p. 46, see *supra* note 133.

[169] Bass, 2000, p. 83, see *supra* note 6; Verdroß, 1920, see *supra* note 151.

[170] Bass, 2000, p. 83, see *supra* note 6.

[171] Willis, 1982, pp. 27–28, see *supra* note 51.

[172] Even Britain's law officers considered that Edith Cavell had been treated fairly, although harshly, by the German authorities. "Committee of Enquiry into Breaches of the Laws of War", *Third Interim Report*, 26 February 1926, CAB 24/111. C.P. 1813, pp. 418–28 (TNA).

[173] Bass, 2000, p. 62, see *supra* note 6.

classed as an auxiliary cruiser". He continued that "vessels of that kind" could be stopped, seized and destroyed under the Hague rules and that a prior search would not have been necessary.[174] Notwithstanding such allegations, a British coroner's jury of Kinsale confirmed an indictment against the German Emperor and the German government only days later:

> This appalling crime was contrary to international law and the conventions of all civilized nations and we therefore charge the officers of the submarine and the German Emperor and the Government of Germany, under whose orders they acted, with the crime of wilful and wholesale murder.[175]

In late July 1916, the German Reich tried and executed the British Captain Charles Fryatt, a commander of an unarmed cross-channel steamer, for attempting to ram a German submarine with his ship in 1915.[176] The trial and the execution of Fryatt marked a further escalation. Earlier in 1915, the Germans had protested against what they considered to be illegal attacks on submarines by merchantmen who they alleged had been armed by British authorities to resist U-boats.[177] However, the execution of Fryatt caused an outrage in the British public, concerned the official authorities and prompted the British Prime Minister Asquith to warn to "bring to justice the criminals".[178] Still, British courts did *not* conduct any war crimes trials against German citizens during the First World War.[179] Similarly during the First World War, the US also did not conduct any war crimes trials against Germans suspected of having committed war crimes.[180]

---

[174] Francis W. Halsey, *The Literary Digest History of the World War: Compiled from Original and Contemporary Sources: American, British, French, German, and Others*, Funk & Wagnalls, New York, 1919, p. 255.

[175] "Kaiser is Accused in Ship Inquest Verdict", *Chicago Examiner*, vol. 13, no. 120, 11 May 1915, p. 1.

[176] Sir Archibald Hurd, *Official History of the War: The Merchant Navy*, Longmans, Green & Co., London, 1921–1929, vol. 2, pp. 308–36; British Admiralty to Foreign Office, 18 July 1916, FO 383/195/140584 (TNA); Maxse to Foreign Office, 28 July 1916, FO 383/195/147519 (TNA).

[177] Willis, 1982, pp. 30–31, see *supra* note 51.

[178] House of Commons, United Kingdom, Parliamentary Debates, vol. 84, 1916, pp. 2080–81.

[179] Compare Willis, 1982, pp. 31–36, see *supra* note 51; Bass, 2000, pp. 62–64, see *supra* note 6.

[180] Compare Bass, 2000, pp. 92–105, see *supra* note 6.

In conclusion, during the First World War there was some limited, but certainly no consistent practice of states trying enemy soldiers, navy staff or civilians on allegations of international war crimes originating from the 1907 Hague Conventions and Hague Regulations or any other international humanitarian law in force at this time.

11.5.3. Application of International Humanitarian Law in the German Reich: Between 1907 and the Leipzig War Crimes Trials

On 27 November 1909 the German Reich ratified the 1907 Hague Conventions and Hague Regulations.[181] Following the conclusion of the First World War on 18 December 1919, the German Parliament adopted the law to prosecute war crimes and war misdemeanours.[182] Its Article 1 determined that the *Reichsgericht* would be *exclusively* competent to investigate and adjudicate crimes and misdemeanours that a German citizen within or outside Germany had committed against enemy citizens during the war until 18 June 1919. Article 2 further determined that the prosecutor at the *Reichsgericht* is obliged to prosecute *according to German law* criminal conduct mentioned in Article 1, even if the transaction occurred abroad and was there subject to penal sanctions according to the local laws in force.

With both provisions the German Parliament cemented the German demand to request exclusive jurisdiction for war crimes possibly committed by its own citizens, providing the *Reichsgericht* in Leipzig as the only appropriate forum. Regarding possible war crimes proceedings in Leipzig, the German legislator made the fundamental decision that *only* German law and not international treaty law or international customs would be the applicable law. In the eyes of the German legislator the *Geltungsgrund*, meaning the basis for validity, of penal sanctions was not that a certain conduct may have violated international law prohibiting such conduct, but that it was the mere *will* of the German state that certain international rules should be adhered to. As such, at the beginning of the Weimar Republic, the German legislator adopted a strict dualistic

---

[181] See *supra* note 128.

[182] Law to Prosecute War Crimes, pp. 2125–26, see *supra* note 57.

approach regarding the relationship of German domestic law and international (humanitarian) law.[183]

The *Reichsgericht*, bound by this political decision of the German legislator, further elaborated in its judgments the relationship between international law and German law. Overall, the judges of the Second Senate observed the parameters set by the German legislator but managed to expand the influence of international law as follows:

In the Stenger and Crusius judgment the Second Senate elaborated that "the application of the ordinary domestic Penal Code [...] to war acts which meet the elements of an offence sanctioned with a penalty raises no concerns".[184] So far the judges mirrored the approach of the German legislator. They then continued:

> Regarding the evaluation of the lawfulness or illegality of war acts, the provisions of international law are authoritative. The will of a state which conducts war and whose laws as to the question of legality or illegality are decisive, corresponds to the killing of an enemy during war only insofar as these acts meet the requirements and observe the conditions and limits imposed by international law. The state which enters the war against another state submits itself regarding the international law at least as far as he is obligated by international agreements with the adversary. Every action, including the negligent killing of a human being, which occurs under violation of provisions of international law, is therefore objectively illegal. It is also subjectively illegal, if the perpetrator was conscious regarding his duty to act otherwise, or, by negligent commission, was not aware of this out of negligence. That the killing of a defenceless wounded person runs contrary to international law needs no further explanation.[185]

Further, in the *Llandovery Castle* case, the Second Senate stated that the

> firing on the [life]boats was an offence against the law of nations. In war on land the killing of unarmed enemies is not

---

[183] Wiggenhorn, 2005, p. 228, see *supra* note 45.

[184] Stenger and Crusius Judgment, p. 2568, see *supra* note 22 (my translation).

[185] *Ibid.* (my translation). The first part of this argumentation was repeated in the judgment against Dithmar and Boldt, *Llandovery Castle* case, see *supra* note 30, Weißbuch, p. 2585, see *supra* note 10, and "Judicial Decisions involving Questions of International Law", in *American Journal of International Law*, 1920, vol. 16, p. 721.

allowed (compare the [1907] Hague Regulations as to the war on land, section 23(c)[186]), similarly in war at sea, the killing of shipwrecked people, who have taken refuge in lifeboats, is forbidden. It is certainly possible to imagine exceptions to this rule, as, for example, if the inmates of the lifeboats take part in the fight. But there were no state of affairs in the present case [...] Any violation of the law of nations in warfare is, as the Senate has already pointed out, a punishable offence, so far as in general, a penalty is attached to the deed.[187]

During the First World War and thereafter during the time of the Leipzig War Crimes Trials, the German Criminal Code only contained very few offences[188] that would penalise conduct relating to international humanitarian law. The *Reichsgericht* adjudicated according to ordinary German criminal law conduct such as killing of hostages or of the wounded, mistreatment of prisoners, destruction of houses and sinking of (hospital) ships.[189] Thus, in all trials in which convictions occurred, the *Reichsgericht* based these on offences codified in German law, either in the domestic Criminal Code or the Military Penal Code. For example, in the first trial related to the First World War, the *Reichsgericht* convicted all three accused for plunder, an offence under German law, namely § 129 of the Military Penal Code.[190] The latter section protects the army's discipline and fulfils the obligations under international law as contained in Articles 28 and 47 of the 1907 Hague Regulations which prohibit plunder.[191]

---

[186] See *supra* note 127.

[187] *Llandovery Castle* case, p. 2585, see *supra* note 30, and "Judicial Decisions involving Questions of International Law", in *American Journal of International Law*, 1920, vol. 16, p. 721.

[188] Jescheck, 1952, p. 51, see *supra* note 133, notes that at least some German provisions of the ordinary German Penal Code (namely § 87, 89–91) and of the Military Penal Code (namely § 57, 58, 160 and 161) provided for punishment of offences for violations of the laws and customs of war.

[189] Compare Ludwig Ebermayer, *Fünfzig Jahre Dienst am Recht: Erinnerungen eines Juristen*, Gretlain, Leipzig, 1930, p. 190.

[190] Lottmann, Niegel and Sangerhausen Judgment, see *supra* note 8.

[191] A.M. Romen and C. Rissom, *Militärstrafgesetzbuch*, 3rd ed., J. Guttentag, 1918, para. 3; Gerd Hankel, "Deutsche Kriegsverbrechen des Weltkrieges 1914-18 vor deutschen Gerichten", in Wolfram Wette and Gerd R. Ueberschär (eds.), *Kriegsverbrechen im 20. Jahrhundert*, Wissenschaftliche Buchgesellschaft, Darmstadt, 2001, p. 88.

The following offences of German law were adjudicated at the *Reichsgericht* during the Leipzig war crimes trials: insults,[192] illegal deprivation of liberty,[193] theft and plunder,[194] misuse of official position by instigating subordinates to criminal acts,[195] assault (of POWs),[196] assault in exercise of the office,[197] (negligent) manslaughter,[198] killing[199] and murder.[200]

11.6. Defence of Obedience to Superior Orders

The Leipzig War Crimes Trials mark a significant step in the history of international criminal law because at least four judgments developed the defence of obedience to superior orders making it the first significant body of case law. The defence of superior orders is today recognised in the statutes of all *ad hoc* international criminal tribunals as well as in Article 33 of the ICC Statute.[201] Generally, national systems obligate subordinates to obey orders or instructions from their superiors or military commanders who assume (co-)responsibility for the subordinate's act in carrying out the order. As long as the content of the order or instruction is in accordance with the current domestic and international law, this system functions seamlessly. However, the responsibility of the subordinate is

---

[192] Müller Judgment, see *supra* note 12; Heynen Judgment, see *supra* note 10.

[193] Ramdohr Judgment, see *supra* note 21.

[194] Lottmann, Niegel and Sangerhausen Judgment, see *supra* note 8; Grüner Judgment, see *supra* note 34.

[195] Stenger and Crusius Judgment, see *supra* note 22.

[196] Heynen Judgment, see *supra* note 10; Müller Judgment, see *supra* note 12; Robert Neumann Judgment, see *supra* note 16; Michelson Judgment, see *supra* note 32.

[197] Ramdohr Judgment, see *supra* note 21.

[198] Stenger and Crusius Judgment, see *supra* note 22; Laule Judgment, see *supra* note 26.

[199] Stenger and Crusius Judgment, see *supra* note 22.

[200] Karl Neumann Judgment, see *supra* note 19; Schack and Kruska Judgment, see *supra* note 28; Dithmar and Boldt Judgment, see *supra* note 30.

[201] Statute of the International Criminal Court (http://www.legal-tools.org/doc/7b9af9/). Compare Article 7 (4) Statute of the International Criminal Tribunal for crimes committed in ex-Yugoslavia (http://www.legal-tools.org/doc/b4f63b/), Article 6 (4) Statute of the International Criminal Tribunal for Rwanda (http://www.legal-tools.org/doc/8732d6/); Article 6 (4) Statute for the Special Court for Sierra Leone (http://www.legal-tools.org/doc/aa0e20/); Article 29 (4) Law on the Establishment of the Extraordinary Chambers, with inclusion of amendments as promulgated on 27 October 2004 (NS/RKM/1004/006) (http://www.legal-tools.org/doc/9b12f0/).

---

more problematic when the order or instruction he or she received is contrary to existing (domestic or international) laws.

In Leipzig, several accused persons attempted to defend and thereby absolve themselves from criminal responsibility by seeking recourse to superior orders. The *Reichsgericht*'s rulings on this defence constitute landmark decisions. They are one of the origins for what was later termed the *conditional liability* theory.

11.6.1. Origin of the Conditional Liability Theory

In 1915, the Austro-Hungarian Military Court ruled that

> penal responsibility of a subordinate if it has not exceeded the received task, is limited to those actions which clearly and manifestly are in conflict not only with criminal law but also with the customs of war of civilised nations and which cannot be excused by a situation of duress.[202]

The Austro-Hungarian Military Court had accepted the principle that a superior order can amount to a complete defence, if *objective* criteria such as the action carried out by the subordinate was not in clear and manifest conflict with existing domestic and international law (the customs of war of civilised nations).

11.6.2. Absolute Liability Theory

By contrast, both International Military Tribunals after the Second World War followed the so-called "absolute liability theory", according to which obedience to superior orders or instructions *cannot* be a complete defence, but can be considered only in mitigation of penalty. Namely, Article 8 of the London Agreement stated:

> The fact that the defendant acted pursuant to the order of his Government or of a superior shall not free him from responsibility, but may be considered in mitigation of

---

[202] My translation. The excerpt of the original judgment states: "[d]ienststrafrechtliche Verantwortlichkeit des Untergebenen, den Fall der Überschreitung des erhaltenen Auftrages ausgenommen, ist nur auf jene Handlungen beschränkt, die klar und offenbar nicht nur gegen das Strafgesetz, sondern auch gegen die Kriegsgebräuche gesitteter Völker verstoßen und durch eine Zwangslage nicht entschuldigt werden können" (*Entscheidungen des kaiserlichen und königlichen Obersten Militärstrafgerichtshofes*, 30 December 1915, reprinted in Albin Schager, vol. III 1, 1920, No. 184, 17 (at 20)).

punishment if the Tribunal determines that justice so requires.[203]

Article 6 of the Charter of the International Military Tribunal for the Far East provided similar language.[204]

11.6.3. Defence of Superior Orders in the Leipzig War Crimes Trials

At least four judgments of the *Reichsgericht* developed the defence of superior orders along the lines of the conditional liability theory. The legal basis for the *Reichsgericht* was § 47 of the German Military Penal Code which stated:

> If the execution of an order pertaining to the service violates a penal law, then the superior issuing the order is alone responsible. The obedient subordinate is to be punished as an accomplice
>
> a)   If he went beyond the order issued to him, or
>
> a)   If he knew that the order of the superior concerned an act which aimed at a civil or military crime or misdemeanour.[205]

11.6.3.1. Case Against Robert Neumann

At the *Reichsgericht*, the defendant Robert Neumann was charged with ill-treatment of British POWs. Most of these instances related to

---

[203]   Charter of the International Military Tribunal – Annex to the Agreement for the prosecution and punishment of the major war criminals of the European Axis, Decree issued on 8 August 1945, London, reprinted in United Nations Treaty Series, No. 251, 1951, pp. 280 ff. (http://www.legal-tools.org/doc/64ffdd/).

[204]   General Douglas MacArthur, Supreme Commander of the Allied Powers in Allied occupied Japan, Decree dated 19 January 1946, containing the Charter of the International Military Tribunal for the Far East; see also USA Treaties and other International Acts Series, 1589, reprinted in C.F. Bevans (ed.), *Treaties and Other International Agreements of the USA (1776–1949)*, vol. 4, Department of State, Washington, DC, 1970, p. 20.

[205]   My translation. The original German law read: "Wird durch die Ausführung eines Befehls in Dienstsachen ein Strafgesetz verletzt, so ist dafür der befehlende Vorgesetzte allein verantwortlich. Es trifft jedoch den gehorchenden Untergebenen die Strafe des Teilnehmers: 1) wenn er den ihm erteilten Befehl überschritten hat, oder 2) wenn ihm bekannt gewesen, daß der Befehl des Vorgesetzten eine Handlung betraf, welche ein bürgerliches oder militärisches Verbrechen oder Vergehen bezweckte". Militär Strafgesetzbuch für das Deutsche Reich, 20 June 1872 (Military Penal Code for the German Reich).

Neumann's behaviour *without* any prior authorisation or order from his commander. Only in one instance did Neumann have such authorisation: on 1 April 1917 the British POWs announced they would not go to work. Neumann's superior, Sergeant Trienke, tried in vain to get them to give in, and attempted to persuade them with friendly means to give up their resistance before phoning his superior commander for instructions. Trienke then gave the order to his subordinates, including Neumann, to "set about" the POWs. Robert Neumann participated in this event and mistreated Florence, a Scottish POW, with his fist and feet. The judges in the Second Senate ruled:

> The accused can*not*, however, be held responsible for these events. He was covered by the order of his superior which he was bound to obey. According to §47 of the [German] Military Penal Code a subordinate can only be criminally responsible under such circumstances, when he *knows* that his orders involve an act which is a civil or military crime. This was not the case here. Before the non-commissioned officer Trienke gave this order [to "set about" the POWs] he made telephone inquiries of the commandant of the camp at Altdamm. Therefore he himself clearly acted only upon the order of a superior. As matters stood there could be no doubt about the legality of the order. Unless there is irreparable damage to military discipline, even in a body of prisoners, disorderly tendencies have to be nipped in the bud relentlessly and they have to be stamped out by all the means at the disposal of the commanding officer and if necessary even by the use of arms. It is of course understood that the use of force in any particular case must not be greater than is necessary to compel obedience. It has not been established that there was excessive use of force here.[206]

Similar to the Austro-Hungarian Military Court, the *Reichsgericht* in Leipzig also accepted the principle that a superior order can amount to a *complete* defence. However, different than the Austrian-Hungarian precedent, the German judges did not explicitly check whether the order from Trienke could have been "*clearly and manifestly*"[207] in conflict with

---

[206] Robert Neumann Judgment, p. 2554, see *supra* note 16 (emphasis added). English translation taken from "Judicial Decisions involving Questions of International Law", in *American Journal of International Law*, 1920, vol. 16, p. 699.

[207] See *supra* note 202.

law. Rather, the judges (only) considered whether the force used to reinstate discipline was proportional. The *Reichsgericht* required that the subordinate himself had to *know* that the order requires an act from him which is a crime. Hence, the *Reichsgericht*'s test for illegality of an order is a subjective one (focusing on the *mens rea* of the subordinate). In contrast, the Austro-Hungarian court had focused on an objective test, namely whether the order was "clearly and manifestly" illegal.

11.6.3.2. The *Dover Castle* Case[208]

In the *Dover Castle* case, Karl Neumann, a commander of a German submarine admitted to having torpedoed and thereby sunk the hospital ship *Dover Castle*, but claimed that he had done so on instructions of the German Admiralty. His defence relied on a 1917 declaration of the German government that claimed that foreign hospital ships had been used for military purposes in violation of the 1907 Hague Naval Convention. The *Reichsgericht* acquitted Karl Neumann:

> It is a military principle that the subordinate is bound to obey the orders of his superiors. This duty of obedience is of considerable importance from the point of view of the criminal law. Its consequence is that, when the execution of a service order involves an offence against the criminal law, the superior giving the order is alone responsible [...]
>
> The Admiralty Staff was the highest service authority over the accused. He was duty bound to obey their orders in service matters. So far as he did that, he was free from criminal responsibility [...]
>
> According to § 47 Nr. 2 of the [German] Military Penal Code a subordinate who acts in conformity with orders is also liable to punishment as an accomplice, when he *knows* that his superiors have ordered him to do acts which involve a civil or military crime or misdemeanour. There has been no case of this here. The memoranda of the German government about the misuse of enemy hospital ships were known to the accused. The facts set out in them he held to be conclusive, especially as he had received, as he explained, similar reports from his comrades. He was therefore of the opinion that the measures taken by the German government

---

[208] *Dover Castle* case, see *supra* note 19.

> against the misuse of enemy hospital ships were not contrary
> to international law, but legitimate reprisals [...]
>
> The accused accordingly sank the *Dover Castle* in
> obedience to a service order of his highest superiors, an
> order which he considered to be binding. He cannot,
> therefore, be punished for his conduct.[209]

Again, consistent with its previous ruling in the Robert Neumann
case, the *Reichsgericht* accepted that an order (here in form of a manual
from the German Admiralty) could have the effect of completely
exempting the subordinate. Consistent with its previous ruling, the
judgment in the Neumann case applied a *subjective* test regarding the
possible illegality of the order: it focused on the *mens rea* of the
subordinate. Since Neumann believed that the memorandum was in
accordance with the law, he was acquitted.

11.6.3.3. The *Llandovery Castle* Case[210]

In the *Llandovery Castle* case, the Second Senate for the first time held
that an order could not absolve a subordinate from guilt. In this case, the
German submarine commander Patzig, who had absconded before the
trial in Leipzig began, had ordered an attack on the hospital ship
Llandovery Castle in the Atlantic Ocean, southwest of Ireland, on 27 June
1918. After the ship sank, three lifeboats remained. Patzig then ordered
his subordinates to open fire on the lifeboats, sinking two of them. While
this action was underway, Dithmar and Boldt, two officers, had been on
their observation post on the submarine. When they stood trial in Leipzig
they defended themselves by referring to the order of Patzig. The judges
of the second senate held:

> Patzig's order does not free the accused from guilt. It is true
> that according to section 47 of the [German] Military Penal
> Code, if the execution of an order in the ordinary course of
> duty involves such a violation of the laws as is punishable,
> the superior officer issuing such an order is alone
> responsible.

---

[209] Karl Neumann Judgment, p. 2557, emphasis added, see *supra* note 19. English translation
taken from "Judicial Decisions involving Questions of International Law", in *American
Journal of International Law*, 1920, vol. 16, pp. 707–8.

[210] *Llandovery Castle* case, see *supra* note 30.

> According to [section 47] No. 2 [of the German Military Penal Code] however, the subordinate obeying such an order is liable to punishment, if it was known to him that the order of the superior involved the infringement of civil or military law. This applies in the present case of the accused. It is certainly to be urged in favor of the military subordinates, that they are under no obligation to question the order of their superior officer, and they can count upon its legality. But no such confidence can exist, if such an order is *universally known to everybody, including also the accused, to be without any doubt whatever against the law* [...] [I]t was perfectly clear to the accused that the killing defenceless people in the life-boats could be nothing else, but a breach of the law [...]
>
> They could only have gathered, from the order given by Patzig, that he wished to make use of his subordinates to carry out a breach of the law. They should therefore, have refused to obey. As they did not do so, they must be punished.[211]

With this ruling the Second Senate no longer relied only on the subjective views of the accused Boldt and Dithmar on the legality of Patzig's order to sink the *Llandovery Castle* and its lifeboats. Rather, emphasising the universal rules [212] in effect at the time, the judges *supplemented* the accused's personal knowledge regarding the legality of Patzig's order with universal knowledge on the same subject.[213] Still, the accused's knowledge of the illegality of the order was the litmus test to hold him criminally responsible, but the fact that an order is directed at something that is universally known to be illegal, was an auxiliary test to

---

[211] Dithmar and Boldt Judgment, *Llandovery Castle* case, p. 2586, see *supra* note 30 (emphasis added). English translation taken from "Judicial Decisions involving Questions of International Law", in *American Journal of International Law*, 1920, vol. 16, pp. 721–22.

[212] "The firing on the [life-]boats was an offence against the law of nations. In war on land the killing of unarmed enemies is not allowed (compare the [1907] Hague Regulations as to the war on land, section 23(c)), similarly in war at sea, the killing of shipwrecked people, who have taken refuge in life-boats, is forbidden [...] Any violation of the law of nations in warfare is [...] a punishable offence, so far as in general, a penalty is attached to the deed" (Dithmar and Boldt Judgment, *Llandovery Castle* case, p. 2585, see *supra* note 30) and "Judicial Decisions involving Questions of International Law", in *American Journal of International Law*, 1920, vol. 16, p. 721.

[213] Dinstein, 2012, pp. 16–17, see *supra* note 4.

---

establish an accused's personal knowledge about the illegality of an order.[214]

11.6.3.4. Stenger and Crusius Case[215]

In the Stenger and Crusius case, the latter claimed to have acted under an order from Stenger to kill wounded French POWs in August 1914. The Second Senate ruled that Crusius had the

> illegality of such an order not included in his consciousness [...] The incorrectness and impossibility of his notion *should have come to his consciousness* [...] Under application of the necessary care expected of him, he could have not missed what was immediately apparent to many of his people, namely that the indiscriminate killing of all wounded was a monstrous, in no way justifiable war measure.[216]

The *Reichsgericht* further clarified that

> for the evaluation of the legality or illegality of war measures the provisions of international law are relevant [...] That the killing of defenceless wounded runs contrary to the provisions of international law requires no further explanation.[217]

The judges for the first time argued that an accused *should have* been aware that an order (here to kill wounded prisoners) was apparently illegal. Thereby, the judges no longer focused on what the accused *actually* had in mind when committing the criminal act he was charged with. Rather, the judges relied on external evaluations, such as the parameters of international law, to come to the conclusion that the accused *should have* been aware of the manifest illegality of an order given to him. Hence, with the Stenger and Crusius judgment, the *Reichsgericht* turned the consideration of manifest illegality of an order into the principal touchstone.[218] It can be further argued that the *Reichsgericht* used the principal illegality of an order under domestic or international law as an "auxiliary, technical contrivance of the law of

---

[214] *Ibid.*, p. 17.

[215] Stenger and Crusius Judgment, see *supra* note 22.

[216] *Ibid.*, reprinted in German language in Weißbuch, p. 2567, see *supra* note 10 (my translation, emphasis added).

[217] *Ibid.*, p. 2568.

[218] Dinstein, 2012, p. 18, see *supra* note 4.

evidence, designed to ease the burden of proof lying on the prosecution, insofar as the subjective knowledge of the accused is concerned".[219]

11.7. Conclusion

The Leipzig War Crimes Trials relating to violations of Germans during the First World War were at least an attempt in the history of international criminal law to carry out justice. In tandem with the *in absentia* trials in Belgium and France, these trials caused a limited deterrent effect, although the sentences imposed were lenient.

The judges clarified the relationship between national law and international law. The German Reich, belonging to the continental law tradition and having adopted a strict dualistic approach, refrained from prosecuting war crimes on the basis of existing international humanitarian law. In fact, with the exception of a few international provisions,[220] the prohibitions of international humanitarian law during and immediately after the First World War did not (yet) provide for personal criminal responsibility. Hence, at the *Reichsgericht* international law was not used as a basis to prosecute, but merely as a benchmark to assess the legality or illegality (*Rechtswidrigkeit*) of offences defined by German law. The prohibitions of international humanitarian law were relevant to create an exception to the defence of superior orders. Insofar the *Reichsgericht* produced significant case law forming a basis for the conditional liability theory. Generally, the *Reichsgericht* considered obedience to superior orders as a complete defence.

However, due to restrictive case selections the war crimes proceedings in Leipzig were limited in so far as they targeted only either civilians or low- and middle-ranking soldiers and Admiralty staff. Seldom did military superiors stand trial. Keeping in mind which cases were *not* selected and prepared for trials, the entirety of procedures conducted in Leipzig signalled an unwillingness of an otherwise able German state to vigorously pursue criminal behaviour during the First World War: The prosecutions and trials in Leipzig did *not* even touch the German civilian leadership regarding its responsibility for any of the crimes committed in the First World War. Also, the highest military leaders of the German

---

[219] *Ibid.*, p. 29.
[220] See text preceding *supra* notes 139, 144 and 145.

Reich, the members of the supreme Army command and Admiralty, were not prosecuted at all. Thus, the twelve judgments focusing on isolated cases and targeting only low- or mid-level Army staff or civilians were unable to distil the widespread or systematic nature of certain wrongdoing by the German Army leadership, whether in the conduct of hostilities[221] or in overall policy of the German Army staff or civilian leadership.

Since the domestic judicial authorities could conduct investigations and trials on German territory against German citizens, and since the Allied Powers rendered assistance and co-operation in legal matters, *access* to documentary evidence, witnesses or crime scenes would *not* have been an impediment to prosecute more senior civilian and military leaders. Thus, the German state was clearly *able* to effectively prosecute and punish a greater totality of the criminal wrongdoing by the German authorities during the First World War. Instead, the German authorities pursued a silent campaign of suspensions or *nolle prosequi* decisions. In hindsight, these *in camera* procedures and the 12 public trials at the *Reichsgericht* were part of an "appeasement measure" designed to "provide symbolic justice and little more".[222]

---

[221] Namely the issue of use of chemical agents at the Western Front, for example, in France.

[222] Maguire, 2002, p. 80, see *supra* note 45.

12

The Forgotten:
The Armenian Genocide 100 Years Later[*]

Lina Laurinaviciute,[**] Regina M. Paulose[***] and Ronald G. Rogo[****]

12.1. Armenia: Then and Now

"My conscience does not accept the denial of the great catastrophe that the Ottoman Armenians were subjected to in 1915. I reject this injustice and [...] empathise with the feelings and pain of my Armenian brothers. I apologise to them".[1] Approximately 200 Turkish[2] intellectuals orchestrated an internet campaign to apologise for the Armenian genocide[3] carried out by the

---

[*] The authors would like to thank the Armenian Mission to the United Nations in Geneva for their support of this article. This chapter is dedicated to those who long for justice with regards to the Armenian genocide.

[**] **Lina Laurinaviciute** is a Chief Specialist of International Relations Division of the National Courts Administration of the Republic of Lithuania. She holds an LL.M. in International Crime and Justice from the United Nations Interregional Crime and Justice Research Institute ('UNICRI'), Turin, Italy.

[***] **Regina Paulose** holds a LL.M. in International Crime and Justice from the University of Torino/UNICRI (2012) and Juris Doctorate from Seattle University (2004). She is an attorney in the US. She is a former Prosecutor in Arizona and Washington state. She is the creator and co-founder of A CONTRARIO ICL, a blog community devoted to international criminal justice issues (www.acontrarioicl.com).

[****] **Ronald G. Rogo** is a Lecturer at the University of Nairobi, and a Partner at Rogo & Associates. He holds an LL.M. in International Crime and Justice from UNICRI, Turin, Italy. He also holds an M.A. in Organizational Leadership from Eastern University and a LL.B. (Honours) from the University of Nairobi, Kenya.

[1] Nicholas Birch, "Turkish Academics to Apologize for Armenian Genocide", in *Huffington Post*, 15 January 2009.

[2] "Turkey" and "Ottoman Empire" have been used interchangeably since the period of the Ottoman Empire. The current government in Turkey does not disavow itself from the Ottoman Empire. See Vahakn N. Dadrian, *The Key Elements in the Turkish Denial of the Armenian Genocide: A Case Study of Distortion and Falsification*, Zoryan Institute, Cambridge, MA, 1999, pp. 5–6.

[3] We use the definition of "genocide" as found in Article 6 of the Rome Statute of the International Criminal Court, where it means "any of the following acts committed with intent to destroy, in whole or in part, a national, ethnical, racial or religious group, as such:

    a) Killing members of the group;

    b) Causing serious bodily or mental harm to members of the group;

Ottoman Turks, which remains controversial to this day.[4] The online apology was quickly dismissed by the Turkish Prime Minister Tayyip Erdoğan, who stated that there was no necessity for Turkey to apologise.[5] The discussion and recognition of these events have continued to cause tension between Armenia and Turkey. Turkey's position has been to deny the genocide by "minimizing statistics" and "blaming" the victims.[6] Nonetheless, recent speeches by Turkish leaders indicate a possible change in attitude towards Armenia over the genocide is taking place within the government and among its people.[7] Despite Turkey's contention, there are an increasing number of countries stepping forward out of a "moral duty" to recognise the genocide.[8]

The historical road leading up to the Armenian genocide (considered the first modern genocide)[9] is a story that contains multiple accounts from different viewpoints.[10] It is also a difficult story to narrate because of the limited access to the documents that exist from the time period.[11] It is important for us to consider the historical aspect of this

---

      c) Deliberately inflicting on the group conditions of life calculated to bring about its physical destruction in whole or in part;

      d) Imposing measures intended to prevent births within the group;

      e) Forcibly transferring children of the group to another group".

[4]   Birch, see *supra* note 1.

[5]   *Ibid.*

[6]   Gregory Stanton, "The Cost of Denial", in *Genocide Watch*, 23 April 2008. For a full view of Turkey's position on the genocide, see Republic of Turkey, Ministry of Foreign Affairs, "The Armenian Allegations of Genocide: The Issue and Facts".

[7]   Constanze Letsch, "Turkish PM Offers Condolences over 1915 Massacre", in *The Guardian*, 23 April 2014; see also Cengiz Aktar, "Armenian Genocide: Turkey Has Lost the Battle of the Truth", Al Jazeera, 24 April 2014.

[8]   For a historical list of entities that recognised the genocide, see Vahakn N. Dadrian, "Genocide as a Problem of National and International Law: The World War I Armenian Case and Its Contemporary Legal Ramifications", in *Yale Journal of International Law*, 1989, vol. 14, no. 2, pp. 221–334; see "Israeli Parliament to Prepare Armenian 'Genocide' Recognition Law", in *Today's Zaman*, 24 April 2013. For a list of countries that have recognised the genocide, see Armenian National Committee of America, "Genocide Recognition".

[9]   Donald Bloxham, *The Great Game of Genocide: Imperialism, Nationalism, and the Destruction of the Ottoman Armenians*, Oxford University Press, Oxford, 2005, p. 94.

[10]   We have consulted numerous sources and have found that, depending on the location, texts have different dates for various events that have occurred during this particular time period.

[11]   Most of the documents are in the possession of the Turkish Government archives.

---

genocide prior to our discussion of how the trials came to fruition and their lasting contribution to international criminal law. Through this historical analysis, we suggest that the Armenian genocide is the groundwork upon which the Nuremberg Trials and subsequent tribunals were built.[12] Further, we emphasise importance of recognising that the events which occurred in Armenia were the crucial turning point in solidifying "genocide" as the crime of all crimes.[13] As with all the tribunals that have been in existence since the late twentieth century, historical events cannot be separated from the actual trials and determination of the elements to the crimes cannot be completed without proper contextual analysis.

Under the rule of Sultan Abdülhamid II, Christians in the Ottoman Empire in the latter part of the nineteenth century faced enormous persecution.[14] The Armenians were mainly Christians who were afforded second-class citizenship due to their religion.[15] Long before the Congress of Berlin after the Russo-Ottoman War of 1877, the Armenians were seeking to redress inequalities targeting them.[16] During the late 1890s the Sultan carried out the "Hamidian massacres" to dissuade Armenians from encouraging Western reforms.[17] From 1894 to 1896 approximately 100,000 to 300,000 Armenians were killed.[18] The United States ('US') President Grover Cleveland, in a statement to the US Senate in 1895, said that such "fanatical brutality" against the Armenians would justify intervention by

---

[12] Justice Robert H. Jackson was the Chief of Counsel for the US during the prosecution of Nazi war criminals at the Nuremberg Trials. He eloquently stated that prior to the Second World War, leaders got away with crimes against humanity. Robert H. Jackson Center, "The Influence of the Nuremberg Trial on International Criminal Law".

[13] We dispense with any debate as to whether there was a genocide. The term was in fact created because of the Armenian genocide. Further, the consequence for denying the genocide exonerates those responsible for it. See Roger W. Smith, Eric Markusen and Robert Jay Lifton, "Professional Ethics and the Denial of Armenian Genocide", in *Holocaust and Genocide Studies*, 1995, vol. 9, no. 1, p. 13.

[14] Alfred de Zayas, "The Genocide Against the Armenians 1915–1923 and the Relevance of the 1948 Genocide Convention", in *Armenian Review*, 2012, vol. 53, nos. 1–4, pp. 85–120.

[15] Arthur Grenke, *God, Greed, and Genocide: The Holocaust Through the Centuries*, New Academia Publishing, Washington, DC, 2005, p. 51.

[16] Taner Akçam, *A Shameful Act: The Armenian Genocide and the Question of Turkish Responsibility*, Henry Holt, New York, 2006, p. 36.

[17] Rouben Paul Adalian, "Hamidian (Armenian) Massacres", Armenian National Institute.

[18] Michael Bobelian, *Children of Armenia: A Forgotten Genocide and the Century-long Struggle for Justice*, Simon and Schuster, New York, 2009, p. 20.

European countries, as "agents of the Christian world" to prevent "dreadful occurrences" that have "lately shocked civilizations".[19] European countries such as Britain, France and Russia asked Sultan Abdülhamid II to change his treatment of the Armenians. Eventually, the Sultan's acquiescence caused the Committee of Union and Progress ('CUP', also known as the Ittihat Party), whose nucleus were the Young Turks, to rise up and stage a coup in 1908.[20] Turkish nationalism had been gaining power before the coup.[21] The CUP was led by the "Father of Turkish Nationalism", Ziya Gökalp.[22] His interpretation of nationalism envisioned a "mystical vision of blood and race".[23] For their part, the Young Turks were led by the "great triumvirate" of Ismail Enver Paşa, Ahmet Cemal Paşa and Mehmet Talaat Paşa.[24] With this leadership in place, the Young Turks began a massive propaganda campaign against the Armenians in 1908. In particular, the Armenians were portrayed as "saboteurs" and "pro-Russian".[25]

In April 1915 the Turkish government claimed that the Armenians were in a "nationwide revolt" and ordered the deportation of the Armenians from Turkey.[26] Two bills were introduced in Parliament. The first was the Temporary Law of Deportation which authorised the mass deportation of the Armenians; the second, the Temporary Law of Expropriation and

---

[19] "President Statements", Seventh Annual Message to Congress by President Grover Cleveland, 2 December 1895, Armenian National Committee of America.

[20] Grenke, 2005, p. 53, see *supra* note 15.

[21] *Crimes Against Humanity and Civilization: The Genocide of the Armenians* ('*Crimes Against Humanity and Civilization*'), Facing History and Ourselves National Foundation, 2004, p. 65.

[22] Guenter Lewy, *The Armenian Massacres in Ottoman Turkey: A Disputed Genocide*, University of Utah Press, Salt Lake City, 2005, pp. 44–45. See also *Crimes Against Humanity and Civilization*, p. 61, *supra* note 21.

[23] Lewy, 2005, p. 45, see *supra* note 22. Gökalp was also interested in creating the state of "Turan" which would only have Turkish language and Turkish peoples. Talaat Paşa supported this idea. Plans to create Turan were abandoned when the war began. See Akçam, 2006, p. 112, *supra* note 16.

[24] Lewy, 2005, p. 45, see *supra* note 22.

[25] "Q & A: Armenian Genocide Dispute", in BBC News, 5 March 2010.

[26] Richard Hovannisian, *The Armenian Genocide, History, Politics, and Ethics*, St Martin's Press, New York, 1992, p. 105. Donald Bloxham notes: "The solution to the empire's nationality problems was ultimately directed at 'problem' populations themselves rather than their grievances and aspirations"; see Donald Bloxham, *The Great Game of Genocide*, Oxford University Press, Oxford, 2005, p. 29.

Confiscation took property that belonged to the Armenians and resold it "for profit".[27] The Young Turks blamed the Armenians for their own removal, and stated that any deaths that resulted from this "preventative measure" would be considered the first casualties of the First World War.[28] Turkey's allies, Germany and Austria-Hungary, denied that an Armenian revolt took place.[29] In fact, German commanders stated that "no proof" existed that the Armenians were staging an uprising, but that they were "improvised acts of self-defence".[30] Further documentation corroborates that the Ottomans had a "pre-arranged scheme" to relay "alarming reports" of a supposed Armenian uprising.[31] Various sources document different horrific acts against the Armenians. The first missionaries, who had arrived by 1830, documented mass deportations and "calculated domestic genocide".[32] Missionary eyewitness accounts indicated that the Turkish government intended that the Armenians die "en route" to "desert communities".[33] The Armenians were transported to "isolated, uninhabited places in order to be massacred".[34] German Army commanders described "killing squads" which were placed where the deportees passed and massacred them.[35] By 1915 Armenian soldiers were "deported, put into labor camps, and killed", and Armenian political and intellectual leaders were gathered and killed.[36] Armenians who were left after passing through this killing machine were placed in concentration camps in the desert, where they died from resulting calamities such as heat, starvation or were thrown into the sea.[37] Many massacres took place at the beginning of 1915.

---

[27] Crimes Against Humanity, p. 120, see *supra* note 21.

[28] Hovannisian, 1992, p. 105, see *supra* note 26.

[29] Dadrian, 1999, p. 12, see *supra* note 2.

[30] *Ibid.*

[31] Hovannisian, 1992, p. 291, see *supra* note 26.

[32] *Ibid.*, pp. 103, 105–6.

[33] *Ibid.*, p. 121. One of the most well-known places of execution was the Deir ez-Zor, where countless Armenians were slaughtered. See Lucine Kasbarian, "Der Zor Diary: A Pilgrimage to the Killing Fields of Armenian Genocide", in *The Armenian Reporter*, 26 August 2010.

[34] Aida Alayarian, *Consequences of Denial: The Armenian Genocide*, Karnac Books, London, 2008, p. 15.

[35] *Ibid.*, p. 12.

[36] *Ibid.*, p. 14.

[37] *Ibid.*

The largest massacres are reported to have occurred in Sivas (7,000 deaths), in Baku (30,000) and in the Deier ez-Zor area (60,000).[38]

The leadership of the Ottoman Turks justified their own actions. In 1917, when Talaat became the Grand Vizier of the CUP, he unapologetically explained: "once it became obvious that the flanks and rear of the army were in jeopardy, we proceeded to carry out deportations from the war zone for the good of our troops".[39] Talaat further justified these actions and referred to Britain's treatment of the Irish and the "concentration camps in the Transvaal" where women and children were starved to death.[40]

The number of Armenians who were killed as a result of these policies (known as Turkification) is hard to determine because no consensus surrounds the surveys during that time period.[41] Most of the figures show that around one million Armenians were deported.[42] Men were taken first and killed by death squads, leaving women and children to be victims of kidnapping, rape and murder.[43] The deaths of the Armenians involved an indecent amount of depravity.[44] Although the killing of the Armenians stopped around 1923 the destruction of Armenian property and historical memory continued.[45] By the autumn of 1918, Allied forces were advancing towards Turkey. On 30 October 1918

---

[38] Armenian National Institute, "Chronology of the Armenian Genocide – 1916 (July–December)", 5 July 1916 and 7 September 1916. For another narrative which details intent to commit a genocide, see Smith, Markusen and Lifton, 1995, see *supra* note 13.

[39] Raymond Kévorkian, *The Armenian Genocide: A Complete History*, I.B. Tauris, London, 2011, p. 701.

[40] *Ibid.*, pp. 701–2. See also John L. Scott, "British Concentration Camps of the Second South African War (The Transvaal, 1900–1902)", M.A. Thesis, Florida State University, 2007.

[41] Lewy, 2005, p. 233, see *supra* note 22, p. 233. There are those who argue that the numbers of Armenians versus the numbers who died cannot be mathematically calculated. See Assembly of Turkish American Associations, "Armenian Issue Revisited". The Armenian side argues that between 1 and 1.5 million died as a result of the genocide; see Adalian, *supra* note 17.

[42] Lewy, 2005, p. 234, see *supra* note 22.

[43] Bobelian, 2009, p. 26, see *supra* note 18.

[44] Individual doctors were involved in the massacre of the Armenians, which involved poisoning infants, killing children and issuing false death certificates attributing the cause of death to "natural causes". Jeremy Hugh Baron, "Genocidal Doctors", in *Journal of the Royal Society of Medicine*, 1990, vol. 92, no. 11, p. 590.

[45] De Zayas, 2012, p. 99, see *supra* note 14.

the Mudros Armistice was concluded between the Allied Powers and the Ottoman Empire.[46] The new Ottoman government, led briefly by Ahmet Izzet Paşa, passed a resolution to bring those responsible for war crimes before court.[47] As we discuss below, the attempted trials did not bring justice for the victims who were tormented by their perpetrators.

12.2. The Military Tribunals

As early as 24 May 1915, the Entente Powers – Russia, Britain and France – threatened the Ottoman Empire with prosecution and punishment for the mass murders of the Armenians.[48] Subsequently, the 1918 Mudros Armistice agreement "marked the first step toward prosecuting the perpetrators of the massacres". This happened in three steps.[49] First, at the Paris Peace Conference of 1919 "proposals were submitted to try suspects [...] ultimately came to nothing".[50] The second step came in 1920 when the Ottoman Empire began a series of courts martial, beginning a historical precedent in prosecuting those responsible for war crimes.[51] The third step was the British attempt to try cases in Malta, which, as we discuss below, also amounted to nothing.[52]

The Ottoman authorities set up various Extraordinary Courts Martial (Special Military Tribunals) to try perpetrators at the encouragement of the Allies. These locations included Leipzig in Germany and a tribunal in Istanbul (Constantinople).[53] The Mazhar Inquiry Commission spearheaded the investigation.[54] Between 50 and 100

---

[46] Erik Jan Zurcher, "The Ottoman Empire and the Armistice of Mudros", in Hugh Cecil and Peter H. Liddle (eds.), *At the Eleventh Hour: Reflections, Hopes, and Anxieties at the Closing of the Great War, 1918*, Leo Cooper, London, 1998, pp. 266–75.

[47] Meher Grigorian, "The Role of Impunity in Genocide: An Analysis of War Crimes Trials Within the Context of International Criminal Law", in Colin Tayz, Peter Arnold and Sandra Tatz (eds.), *Genocide Perspectives II: Essays on Holocaust and Genocide*, Brandl & Schlesinger, Sydney, 2003, p. 135.

[48] Dadrian, 1999, p. 35, see *supra* note 2.

[49] Akçam, 2006, p. 221, see *supra* note 16.

[50] *Ibid.*, p. 221.

[51] Peter Balakian, *The Burning Tigris: The Armenian Genocide and America's Response*, Harper Collins, New York, 2013, p. 331.

[52] Akçam, 2006, p. 221, see *supra* note 16.

[53] Balakian, 2013, p. 332, see *supra* note 51.

[54] *Ibid.*, p. 333.

CUP leaders were arrested. However, Talaat and Enver avoided arrest and fled to Germany where they were given refuge.[55] There were four major trials dealing with the Armenian massacres: one at Yozgat, one at Trebizon, one for lower-level CUP leaders who were in the Special Organisation, and one for Turkish cabinet members.[56] The Ottoman leadership's attempt to create Tribunals and try the former leaders seemed to have been motivated by the desire to placate the Allied forces and prevent them from "dismembering" the Ottoman Empire.[57] The Tribunals started and stopped their work as a result of pressure from nationalists, who considered those guilty of mass deportations to be heroes.[58] Eventually, the Treaty of Sèvres proved to Mustafa Kemal (Atatürk) and his followers that with or without the Tribunals, the Allied forces would continue with their plan to dismember the Empire.[59] By August 1920 the Tribunals were abolished.[60]

However, even if they had continued, certain trials showed the problems that the Tribunals would have faced. In the trial of Talaat and his inner circle, none of the defendants were in custody.[61] They were tried and sentenced *in abstentia*.[62] Germany refused to extradite defendants, making it impossible for victims to properly confront the accused and for justice to be dispensed in a meaningful manner.[63] As the examples from the Yozgat trials and Malta Tribunal show, the trials themselves struggled not only with the political climate and resistance from society, but also with their internal organisation. The lack of a serious structure inevitably caused fatigue on the part of the Allied Powers to enforce provisions of the Treaty of Sèvres, while the lack of accountability was another reason why further destruction of the Armenian historical memory continued.[64]

---

[55] *Ibid.*, p. 334.

[56] *Ibid.*, p. 334. The author notes that there were "lesser trials" that were planned at sites such as Harput, Mosul, Baiburt and Erzinjan. The trials that were planned in places such as Aleppo, Marash and Van were never held.

[57] Bobelian, 2009, p. 54, see *supra* note 18.

[58] *Ibid.*, p. 55.

[59] *Ibid.*, p. 56.

[60] *Ibid.*

[61] *Ibid.*, p. 55.

[62] *Ibid.*

[63] *Ibid.*

[64] De Zayas, 2012, p. 100, see *supra* note 14. The author notes "that the Turkish government allowed the decay and destruction of Armenian buildings by denying building permits

The Yozgat trials, spearheaded by the Ottoman Empire, and the Malta Tribunal, spearheaded by the British, represent two radically different examples of miscarriages of justice. Despite the shortcomings discussed below, Sir Hartley Shawcross, the British Chief Prosecutor at Nuremberg would later declare that the "World War I genocide of the Armenians was the foundation for Nuremberg law recognising crimes against humanity".[65]

12.2.1. Yozgat Trials

The Yozgat trials held in Istanbul were composed of a series of trials, each with its own distinct characteristics. The Tribunal focused on the massacre of Armenians in the district of Yozgat (Ankara Province), which began on 5 February 1919 and lasted for two months.[66]

The complexity and range of the crimes are acknowledged and revealed in the discrepancies of the numbers of the Armenian victims. The Ottoman statistics show that the total pre-war Armenian population was 33,133 in Yozgat district.[67] The Yozgat trials documented that 61,000 of the 63,605 Armenians of Ankara Province (about 96 per cent) had been deported. The trials also revealed that the word "deport" in fact meant "to massacre", which denoted that most of the persons identified as deportees were killed.[68] Subsequently, the real scale of the Armenian victimisation may also be illustrated by the authenticated ciphers introduced in the trial, which disclosed that of about 1,800 Armenians from the town of Yozgat only 88 survivors could be accounted for.[69]

In addition to the massive scale of atrocities, the Armenian survivors during their testimonies at the trials revealed the crimes of robbery, plunder and pillage before, during and after the initiation of the genocide. Young Armenian women were also the victims of rape, often serial rape. A few of the Armenian witnesses testified that they were able

---

needed to carry out repairs. The scale of destruction of the Armenian cultural heritage has been so widespread and systematic over the decades".

[65] *Crimes Against Humanity and Civilization*, 2004, p. 157, see *supra* note 21.

[66] Lewy, 2005, p. 75, see *supra* note 22.

[67] Vahakn N. Dadrian, "The Turkish Military Tribunal's Prosecution of the Authors of the Armenian Genocide: Four Major Court-Martial Series", in *Holocaust and Genocide Studies*, 1997, vol. 11, no. 1, p. 33.

[68] Balakian, 2013, p. 339, see *supra* note 51.

[69] Dadrian, 1997, p. 33, see *supra* note 67.

---

to survive by converting to Islam and concealing their Armenian identity.[70] In fact, the policy of Islamicisation was abandoned as a result of this gesture.[71]

The Yozgat trials were unique in so far as "for the first time in history, a deliberate mass murder, *designated as a crime* under international law was adjudicated in accordance with domestic penal codes thus substituting national laws for the rules of international law".[72]

12.2.1.1. Trial Proceedings

The Yozgat trials consisted of 18 sittings and three officials were charged: Mehmet Kemal, the 35-year-old interim District Governor of Yozgat (the principal defendant); Major Manastirli Mehmet Tevfik bin Halil Osman, the 44-year-old commander of Yozgat's gendarmerie battalion (the co-defendant) and Abdül Feyyaz Ali, the 36-year-old governmental estates official, whose trial at a later stage (17th sitting) was detached for inclusion in a projected second series of Yozgat trials.[73] It is also worth mentioning that at the 12th sitting (6 March 1919), the trials were interrupted in connection with the installation of Damad Ferid's[74] first Cabinet. The trials continued when the Chief Judge and the Attorney General were replaced and new court martial statutes were introduced (24 March 1919). Such a situation may lead to the presumption that the trial lacked a clear structure and was shaped by sensitive political decisions.

Despite the challenges, the trial proceedings were opposed to "victor's justice" – one common objection in the criticism of them. The defendants were represented by six attorneys. The defence was aggressive in arguing about the court's jurisdiction: "the defense counsel challenged the jurisdiction of the Tribunal, arguing that since the alleged crimes were

---

[70] Annette Hoss, "Trial of Perpetrators by the Turkish Military Tribunals: The Case of Yozgat", in Hovannisian, 1992, p. 217, see *supra* 26.

[71] Akçam, 2006, p. 175, see *supra* note 16.

[72] Dadrian, 1989, p. 308, see *supra* note 8 (emphasis added). See also Aram Kuyumjian, "The Armenian Genocide: International Legal and Political Avenues for Turkey's Responsibility", in *Revue de droit de l'Université de Sherbrooke*, 2011, vol. 11, p. 264.

[73] Dadrian, 1997, p. 33, see *supra* note 67.

[74] Damad Ferid was an Ottoman statesman who held the office of Grand Vizier during two periods during the reign of the last Ottoman Sultan Mehmed VI (Vahideddin), the first time between 4 March 1919 and 2 October 1919 and the second time between 5 April 1920 and 21 October 1920.

perpetrated in distant Yozgat they could not be tried in Istanbul".[75] Further sources show that the challenges put forward by the defence counsel were reasonably considered by the Tribunal. It ruled against the defence, however, and stated that it was the proper venue for the trial as the orders for the massacres had come from Istanbul.[76]

The legal defence of superior orders was also prominent during the trials.[77] The defence raised an argument that some of the accused persons were following higher orders. The prosecutor in Kemal's case, for example, stated that "an order from above is only then executable when it is in accord with one's conscience".[78] This principle would, of course, be significant during the Nuremberg Trials after the Second World War,[79] and has now become a part of international criminal law.

The indictment of the defendants alleged conduct of deportations, pillage and plunder of the victims' goods, and the abduction and rape of many members of the convoys.[80] Characterising these offences under the Ottoman Penal Code,[81] the Prosecutor General explicitly used the term "anti-human" and demanded severe punishment for the perpetrators.[82] The pre-trial stage of the proceedings included written and oral interrogations.[83] These interrogations were prepared by the examining magistrates, as was customary in the Ottoman criminal justice system. Accordingly, they encompassed answers from the defendants regarding

> their backgrounds; their relationship to the Ittihad Party [CUP]; their official duties before and during the war; their hierarchy of command; the nature of the orders and instructions they received; their *modus operandi* in the treatment of the Armenians; their rewards in terms of amassing personal fortunes at the expense of victims.[84]

---

75 Dadrian, 1997, p. 33, see *supra* note 67.

76 *Ibid.*, p. 14.

77 *Ibid.*, p. 33.

78 *Ibid.*

79 Silva Hinek, "The Superior Orders Defence: Embraced at Last?", in *New Zealand Post Graduate Law E-Journal*, 2005, issue 2, p. 14.

80 Hoss, 1992, p. 213, see *supra* note 70.

81 Under Articles 45, 170 and 180 of the Ottoman Penal Code.

82 Hoss, 1992, p. 213, see *supra* note 70.

83 Dadrian, 1997, p. 33, see *supra* note 67.

84 Hoss, 1992, p. 214, see *supra* note 70.

Concerning the evidence used in the trial proceedings, most authentic documents were destroyed by CUP members.[85] Therefore, documents from different countries were used as evidence to refute their neutrality. Although all evidence found in the archives of several countries leads to the same conclusion, those in Austria and Germany are the most compelling and reliable.[86] In order to bypass any uncertainty, before being introduced as accusatory exhibits, each official document was authenticated by officials of the Interior Ministry and marked: "It conforms to the original".[87]

The Yozgat atrocities were thoroughly pre-planned and secured by the coded orders, instructions and other materials pertaining to the Armenian deportations and massacres in the region, as well as correspondence to and from the Ministry of War, headed by Enver.[88] These records were of a crucial importance during the trial as they revealed the roles of the defendants.[89] Accordingly, "the documents introduced as prosecution exhibits consisted of decoded cipher telegrams mainly involving the gendarmerie and military officials in charge of implementing the deportation measures. The ciphers contained the number of deportees in a particular convoy, their place of origin, destination, and actual fate".[90] The documentation gathered revealed the euphemisms that were used to conceal the killing operations disguised as deportations.[91] During the 9th sitting of the trial (22 February 1919), the prosecutor introduced 12 cipher telegrams[92] which demonstrated that "the word '*deportation*' meant '*massacre*'".[93]

---

[85]   Kuyumjian, 2011, p. 277, see *supra* note 72.

[86]   *Ibid.*, p. 266; see also Vahakn N. Dadrian, *German Responsibility in the Armenian Genocide: A Review of the Historical Evidence of German Complicity*, Blue Crane Books, Watertown, MA, 1996, pp. 45, 73, 74.

[87]   Dadrian, 1997, p. 35, see *supra* note 67.

[88]   Hoss, 1992, p. 212, see *supra* note 70.

[89]   *Ibid.*

[90]   *Ibid.*, p. 214.

[91]   *Ibid.*, p. 216.

[92]   A cipher telegram of 22 July 1915, by which Mustafa, the Military Governor and Chief of the Recruitment Bureau of Boghazliyan, informing Colonel Redjai that a group of Armenians were "sent off to their destination". When Redjai asked for the clarification as to the meaning of the word "destination", Mustafa replied that the word meant "murdered"; see Hoss, 1992, p. 216, see *supra* note 70.

[93]   Dadrian, 1997, p. 35, see *supra* note 67 (emphasis added).

Beside the documentary exhibits, witness testimony was also introduced as evidence, and in such a way that refuted the criticism of the trial from the supporters of the culprits, complaining that no witnesses testified to the crimes committed.[94] The information gathered reveals that during the trial proceedings 27 witnesses testified under oath (seven Turks, 18 Armenians and two of other nationalities).[95] It is important to mention that the testimonies of the witnesses summoned not only corroborated the charges against the defendants but also provided elements in favour of the defence. Indeed, four of the Turks testified for the prosecution and three for the defendants.[96] Therefore, the right to present incriminating as well as exculpatory evidence in the trial was secured. Additionally, the incriminating evidence was also included in for example, the written depositions of the chief of Yozgat's post and telegraph office.[97]

Finally, all three defendants were repeatedly examined and cross-examined. These examinations were conducted on the basis of the pre-trial testimony, the documentary evidence, prosecutorial witness testimony and the admissions made by the other defendants. Some authors observe that "this method proved fruitful in terms of compelling the defendants to modify, amend, and at times reverse parts of their testimony".[98] However, as has been well noted, Armenian survivors' testimony "sometimes appeared to be at a disadvantage because partisan Turks were unwilling to rely on such testimony and therefore upon the objectivity of the court".[99] Subsequently, in order to answer this kind of criticism, the Prosecutor General informed the court in his closing arguments that he intentionally excluded all evidence provided by the Armenian witnesses and, therefore, concentrated his closing arguments on the authenticated documents in the possession of the court, especially on the testimony of former government officials.[100]

---

[94] Vahakn N. Dadrian, "Legal Proceedings as a Conceptual Framework", in Vahakn N. Dadrian and Taner Akçam (eds.), *Judgment at Istanbul: The Armenian Genocide Trials*, Berghahn, Oxford, 2011, p. 133.

[95] Hoss, 1992, p. 214, see *supra* note 70.

[96] *Ibid.*

[97] *Ibid.*

[98] *Ibid.*

[99] *Ibid.*, p. 220.

[100] *Ibid.*

As a result, the verdicts pronounced by the Tribunal were based almost entirely on the authenticated official documents. Hence, as Vahakn N. Dadrian suggests: "As in Nuremberg, so in Istanbul, the tribunal relied largely on authenticated documents in its possession rather than on courtroom testimony",[101] which also had an effect on the whole picture and weight of the crimes committed. In this respect, the documents proved incontrovertible evidence of the intention of the Ottoman Empire, which cannot be discredited as mere propaganda, as was done during the trials.

12.2.1.2. Verdicts and Sentencing

After stating that the evidence on both sides had been carefully reviewed and assessed on 8 April 1919, the Tribunal found Mehmet Kemal and Mehmet Tevfik guilty.[102] Invoking "the precepts of Islam", "the impartial Ottoman laws and rules of law" and "the sentiments of humanity and civilization", the Tribunal denounced the "premeditated" character of these crimes and agreed unanimously on its verdicts and its sentences.[103] Kemal was condemned to death as a principal perpetrator and Tevfik was found guilty of being an accessory to the crime and was sentenced to 15 years' hard labour.[104] Feyyaz, the third defendant, had a very different fate. As was mentioned earlier, he was excluded from this series of trials. Further, he was released on bail and became a Deputy for the Kayseri District in the Turkish national legislature and, subsequently, in the Grand National Assembly.[105] Kemal's death by hanging took place on 10 April 1919.[106] Kemal's funeral turned into a large-scale nationalist demonstration and created a new atmosphere of tension around the trials.[107] On 14 October 1922 he was proclaimed a "national martyr" by the Grand National Assembly via special legislation.[108]

---

[101] Vahakn N. Dadrian, "The Documentation of the World War I Armenian Massacres in the Proceedings of the Turkish Military Tribunal", in *International Journal of Middle East Studies*, 1991, vol. 23, no. 4, p. 566.

[102] Hoss, 1992, p. 218, see *supra* note 70.

[103] *Ibid.*, pp. 218–19.

[104] *Ibid.*, p. 219.

[105] *Ibid.*, p. 218.

[106] Balakian, 2013, p. 339, see *supra* note 51.

[107] *Ibid.*

[108] Hoss, 1992, p. 219, see *supra* note 70.

It is evident that the trials received limited support not only from the Turkish population at large but also from the state authorities.[109] This is illustrated in the Tribunal's verdict when it pointed to crimes that appeared to be inseparable from the massacres. These crimes included the complete plundering of the money and valuable goods of the deportees, which were then handed over to the perpetrators who received secret and illegal instructions for their disposal.[110] In this regard, the pre-trial investigations revealed that inspectors of the crimes were not authorised to investigate massacres, but "limited their investigations to wide-ranging abuses involving plunder and fraud".[111] Indeed, this was precisely why Kemal was originally taken to court. It was not because of the massacres that he organised but the "irregularities" in handling the goods and possessions of the Armenians.[112] A 1999 Report by the Zoryan Institute for Contemporary Armenian Research has claimed: "In other words, the authorities were not in the slightest interested to prosecute and punish massacres, but to stop the massive embezzlements. By virtue of these abuses, the vast riches of the Armenian victim population were being personally appropriated by the organizers and executioners of the massacres instead of being transferred, as was their duty to do, to the Treasury of the state".[113] Writing less than a decade later, Ahmed Emin concluded, "the whole thing amounted more to a demonstration rather than a sincere attempt to fix complete responsibility".[114] Such a "simplified" standpoint about the nature of the crimes not only spread a perception of compassion towards the defendants, recognising them as martyrs and fuelling Turkish society with the further hatred for enemies (Christian Armenians), but also distorted the perception of justice *per se*.

Despite these circumstances, the Tribunal was able to secure, authenticate and compile an array of documents, including formal and informal orders for the massacre. Finally, nearly all of its verdicts were based upon these documents rather than courtroom testimony.[115] The

---

[109] Lewy, 2005, p. 77, see *supra* note 22.

[110] Hoss, 1992, p. 218, see *supra* note 70.

[111] Dadrian, 1997, p. 39, see *supra* note 67.

[112] *Ibid.*

[113] "The Key Distortions and Falsehoods in the Denial of the Armenian Genocide (A Response to the Memorandum of the Turkish Ambassador)", Zoryan Institute, 1999

[114] Ahmed Emin, *Turkey in the World War*, Yale University Press, New Haven, 1930, p. 221.

[115] Dadrian, 1991, p. 566, see *supra* note 101.

Tribunal emphasised in its verdict the probative and legal nature of the evidence. Scholars agree that one of the most important features of the verdict was its conclusion that "the escorts of the deportee convoys were provided not for the purpose of protecting the convoys as repeatedly claimed. Their handwritten documents confirm the nature of the real purpose of these guards – the massacre of the people of these convoys. *There can be no hesitation or doubt about this*".[116] Further, "the court used the term 'intent' to direct attention to the premeditated character of the annihilation scheme under the cover of deportation or relocation".[117]

Moreover, the Tribunal exonerated the vast majority of the Armenian population of Yozgat, rejecting the Prosecutor General's proposal to assume a kind of civil war involving mutual hostilities and excesses and therefore to rely on Article 56 of the Ottoman Penal Code, which stated:

> Whosoever dares, by making the people of the Ottoman dominions arm themselves against each other to instigate or incite them to engage in mutual slaughter, or to bring about acts of rapine, pillage, devastation of country or homicide in divers places is, if the matter of disorder comes into effect entirely or if a commencement of the matter of the disorder has been made, likewise put to death.[118]

Supporting this position, as Dadrian points out, the Tribunal had "proven [Armenian] dedication and loyalty to the Ottoman State".[119]

12.2.1.3. The Legacy of the Yozgat Trials

As Aram Kuyumjian notes, "the establishment of courts-martial was an experiment which illustrated the difficulty in prosecuting criminals for genocide and other crimes against humanity (such as pillage, rape and torture) through domestic processes without the complete commitment of the international community".[120] We can agree that the practice of not allowing effective immunity to perpetrators of international wrongful acts

---

[116] Hoss, 1992, p. 218, see *supra* note 70.

[117] *Ibid.*, p. 219.

[118] John A. Bucknill and Haig Apisoghom S. Utidjian (trans.), *The Imperial Ottoman Penal Code: A Translation*, Oxford University Press, Oxford, 1913.

[119] Dadrian, 1997, p. 39, see *supra* note 67.

[120] Kuyumjian, 2011, p. 266, see *supra* note 72.

can only arise from political will, dialogue and negotiations among states.[121] In the opposite situation, the absence of an effective international penal response to those crimes limits the significance of the acknowledgement of customary international law and leaves the substantive content of the crime, covered by the provisions of such law, unclear.[122]

12.2.2. Malta: Turkish–British Divide

While the Tribunals in Istanbul were steadily falling apart, the British, who felt "morally bound" to "redress the wrong [they] had perpetrated"[123] began to transfer prisoners to the island of Malta for eventual prosecution.[124] Some argue that Britain was motivated to punish perpetrators because of the mistreatment of British prisoners during the war.[125] This is perhaps true in light of the British "blacklists" that were created.[126] This motive is further underscored by the detainee policy that the British undertook, having no formal evidence to pursue charges against detainees who were shipped to Malta.[127] However, mass demonstrations as a result of the Greek occupation of the port of Izmir later caused the British anxiety and, as a result, the "Ottoman government even appealed" to the British to transfer the prisoners.[128] The British continued to transfer prisoners to Malta, arguing that the trials in Istanbul were being "conducted in such a slow and lacklustre fashion that they didn't go much further than merely presenting a deceptive facade".[129] The attempt to establish a separate tribunal from scratch proved very difficult for the British. One of the most notable challenges they faced was that the Ottoman Tribunal refused to hand over

---

[121] *Ibid.*, p. 261.

[122] Charles Chernor Jalloh, "What Makes a Crime Against Humanity a Crime Against Humanity", in *American University International Law Review*, 2013, vol. 28, p. 5.

[123] Bobelian, 2009, p. 57, citing the British Prime Minister, David Lloyd George, see *supra* note 18.

[124] *Ibid.*

[125] *Crimes Against Humanity and Civilization*, 2004, p. 156, see supra note 21.

[126] The British had the Prisoner of War Section prepare a list of persons who mistreated British soldiers. See Akçam, 2006, p. 290, see *supra* note 16.

[127] Bilal Simsir, *Proceedings of Symposium on Armenians in the Ottoman Empire and Turkey (1912–1926)*, Bogazici University Publications, Istanbul, 1984, pp. 26–41.

[128] Akçam, 2006, p. 294, see *supra* note 16.

[129] *Ibid.*, p. 295.

evidence for prosecution in the Malta Tribunal. [130] A British High Commissioner explained that one reason for this may have been that since the "Peace Treaty had not yet come into force, no pressure [had] been put on the Turkish government or [its] officials". [131] Other reasons that were given by the British as to why evidence could not be found to try perpetrators included: [132]

1. Impossible to obtain from the central government any documents containing orders or instructions on this subject;

2. The Allied governments' hesitation in taking part in the trials of massacre suspects.

3. Officials in the Near East are completely indifferent when it comes to this issue.

4. A large part of the male Armenian population in the provinces and almost all of their intellectuals had been murdered.

5. Lack of public security means that people who could present evidence are afraid to come forward for fear of reprisals; the Allies' intentions in this respect are not trusted.

6. News is circulating that the Malta exiles will be released in the end.

The hopes for justice for the Armenians in Malta faded at the last when Winston Churchill, the British Secretary of State for War, decided in 1921 to exchange the prisoners of Malta for British officers that were held by the Ottoman Empire. [133] Further, to add salt to the fresh wound, the Treaty of Lausanne, penned at the Lausanne Peace Conference, "did ultimately proclaim a general amnesty for all political and military crimes committed between August 1, 1914 and November 20, 1922" which "effectively closed the book on the past and any chance of retribution". [134]

---

[130] Bobelian, 2009, p. 58, see *supra* note 18; and Akçam, 2006, p. 358, see *supra* note 16.

[131] Akçam, 2006, p. 358, see *supra* note 16.

[132] *Ibid.*, p. 359.

[133] Bobelian, 2009, p. 57, see *supra* note 18.

[134] Akçam, 2006, p. 366, see *supra* note 16.

12.3. Genocide No More? Armenia's Legacy

It is now imperative to discuss the legacy and contribution of the Armenian genocide to international criminal law and its history. The Tribunal, a major failure by today's standards, was a huge historical step for human rights and the recognition of the role of justice in post-war settings. Although it is not recognised as such, the Armenian genocide has become a cornerstone in international criminal law history because of the many contributions it has made. The trials from the Armenian genocide created a standard to hold high-level leaders accountable; they increased the range of prosecutable crimes; they improved the standards used in international courtrooms; and they inspired people to pursue justice when atrocities occur.

12.3.1. Accountability for Leadership

One of the biggest contributions arising from the Armenian genocide was the principle that perpetrators of international crimes should be held accountable. Indeed, the magnitude and severity of the crimes committed, which infringed upon human rights in the most extreme manner, clearly fell under the provisions of the Hague Conventions on the Laws and Customs of War.[135] Unfortunately, "international efforts to prevent the genocide wavered, and resulted in the gradual absence of international political and economic action to ensure that the perpetrators of the genocide would be brought to justice".[136]

At the end of the First World War, the Allied Powers began the process of ensuring that investigations and trials were held with regard to the fate of the Armenians. It is not disputed that political interference prevented the trials from running their course, and that more should have been done to prevent this. But one should take cognisance of the fact that this was the first time public trials against members of the ruling class were being held. [137] The members of the CUP who perpetrated the

---

[135] Kuyumjian, 2011, p. 251, see *supra* note 72.

[136] *Ibid.*, p. 260.

[137] There are differing interpretations of this. One is that the Treaty of Versailles, which is still largely followed today, means that head of states should be immune from prosecution. See Laura Barnett, "The International Criminal Court: History and Role", Background Paper, Parliament of Canada, 4 November 2008. Gregory Gordon argues that international criminal law may have started earlier than the twentieth century; see Gregory S. Gordon,

atrocities seemed to believe that even if they lost the war they had won their internal fight against the Armenian people.[138] They could not have predicted that the outside world would have shown any interest regarding their genocidal actions against the Armenians.

In the Treaty of Sèvres, the parties agreed that "the Turkish government undertakes to hand over [to] the Allied Powers the persons whose surrender may be required by the latter as being responsible for the massacres committed during the continuance of the state of war".[139] Subsequently, this pattern was replicated in the Nuremberg and Tokyo Tribunals and with the formation of *ad hoc* tribunals after the conflicts in the former Yugoslavia, Rwanda, Sierra Leone and other places. It is now an affirmative principle in international law that "the most serious crimes of concern to the international community as a whole must not go unpunished and that their effective prosecution must be ensured by taking measures at the national level and by enhancing international cooperation".[140] The need for accountability is replicated in the Genocide Convention which provides that "persons committing genocide [...] shall be punished, whether they are constitutionally responsible rulers, public officials or private individuals".[141]

It is important to note that through the Armenian trials the international community was for the first time jointly involved in the judicial management of the internal affairs of a nation.[142] The Treaty of Sèvres[143] was clear on the part of its mandate that Turkey bring forth

---

"The Trial of Peter Von Hagenbach: Reconciling History, Historiography, and International Criminal Law", Social Science Research Network, 16 February 2012.

[138] Gerard J. Libaridian, "The Ideology of the Young Turk Movement", in Gerard J. Libaridian (ed.), *A Crime of Silence: The Armenian Genocide*, Zed Books, London, 1985, p. 40.

[139] De Zayas, p. 86, citing Article 230 of the Treaty of Sèvres, see *supra* note 16,

[140] Preamble to the Rome Statute of the International Criminal Court.

[141] Convention on the Prevention and Punishment of the Crime of Genocide ('Genocide Convention'), Article 4, Adopted by Resolution 260 (III) A of the United Nations General Assembly, 9 December 1948.

[142] The nations that signed the treaty were: British Empire, France, Italy and Japan (the principal Allied Powers), Armenia, Belgium, Greece, The Hedjaz, Poland, Portugal, Romania, The Serb-Croat-Slovene State and Czecho-Slovakia on the one hand, and Turkey on the other hand.

[143] The Treaty of Peace between the Allied and Associated Powers and Turkey Signed at Sèvres ('Treaty of Sèvres'), 10 August 1920.

those who were culpable for the massacres.[144] As Aram Kuyumjian notes, "it was starting to become clear that the prevention of crimes of this magnitude called for universal responsibility of *erga omnes* obligations concerning the laws of 'humanity'".[145]

The interest of the international community was based on universal jurisdiction which generally protected the laws of war and the 'laws of humanity'.[146] As a result, the century's first international war crimes tribunal was born, but with questionable outcomes.[147] This was against a background of strong feelings against "internal interference" that "the state's right to be left alone automatically trumped any individual right to justice".[148] Interestingly, this need for a military tribunal was independent of any domestic criminal proceedings started by the Turkish government.[149]

The latter provision was echoed decades later when the International Criminal Tribunal for Rwanda ('ICTR') was formed to bring the perpetrators of the genocide in Rwanda to justice for their heinous acts. The domestic *Gacaca* (community court) trials[150] organised by the Rwandan government were not a bar to the continued prosecution of the perpetrators. Interestingly, the International Criminal Court ('ICC') Statute is clear that the mandate of the ICC "shall be complementary to national criminal jurisdictions".[151] The ICC will therefore find that a particular case is inadmissible and it will be unable to exercise its jurisdiction over it unless it can be shown that the national courts have

---

[144] Treaty of Sèvres, Article 226.

[145] Kuyumjian, 2011, p. 257, see *supra* note 72.

[146] Samantha Power, *A Problem from Hell: America and the Age of Genocide*, Basic Books, New York, 2002, p. 14.

[147] *Ibid.*

[148] *Ibid.*

[149] Treaty of Sèvres, Article 226.

[150] Maya Sosnov, "The Adjudication of Genocide: Gacaca and the Road to Reconciliation in Rwanda", in *Denver Journal of International Law and Policy*, 2008, vol. 36, no. 2, pp. 125–53.

[151] Rome Statute of the International Criminal Court ('ICC Statute'), Article 1. The preamble to the ICC Statute also states that "the International Criminal Court established under this Statute shall be complementary to national criminal jurisdictions" and that "it is the duty of every State to exercise its criminal jurisdiction over those responsible for international crimes".

proved to be either unwilling or unable to investigate or prosecute the crime that occurred.[152]

This principle of complementarity has been described as the cornerstone of the ICC.[153] History may explain the respective positions adopted by Armenia and Turkey with respect to the ICC's jurisdiction. Not surprisingly, during the discussions on the ICC Statute, the Armenian delegation was in favour of granting the ICC automatic jurisdiction over the crime of genocide.[154] They also favoured a strong and independent prosecutor who could initiate an investigation or prosecution based on their sources and independent of any referral by the Security Council or by any state party.[155] These positions, no doubt, were born out of their historical experiences. The Turkish representatives, on the other hand, emphasised the need for "assurances that the [...] Court would complement national courts and that the new regime would not call in question current law enforcement efforts.[156] They also opposed any *proprio motu* powers of the prosecutor[157] as this "risked submerging him with information concerning charges of a political, rather than a juridical nature".[158]

However, it is also important to note, conversely, that since the Turkish tribunals did not complete their work, many of the major perpetrators were left unscathed. Their failure to do so set the stage for subsequent historical developments in perpetrating gross atrocities, such as seen during the Second World War. The Allied Powers acted out of self-interest in their demand for accountability. However, when self-interest meant that some compromises needed to be made, the need for

---

[152] ICC Statute, Article 17(3).

[153] Mohamedel M. El Zeidy, *The Principle of Complementarity in International Criminal Law: Origin, Development and Practice*, Brill, Leiden, 2008.

[154] *Official Records*, vol. II, *Summary Records of the Plenary Meetings and of the Meetings of the Committee of the Whole*, United Nations Diplomatic Conference of Plenipotentiaries on the Establishment of an International Criminal Court Rome, A/CONF.183/13 (vol. II), 15 June 1998–17 July 1998, p. 78.

[155] *Ibid.*

[156] *Ibid.*, p. 106.

[157] *Ibid.*, p. 211.

[158] *Ibid.*, p. 124. See also pp. 311, 330.

accountability gradually gave way to "a self-imposed amnesia of World War I Allies".[159]

The declaration that members of the Turkish government would be held personally responsible for the massacres[160] remained just that: a mere declaration. For example, as noted previously, the Malta trials stopped by Churchill released Turkish prisoners in exchange for British prisoners. Also, the United States, which was not endangered by the Turkish horrors, was determined to maintain its neutrality in the war and refused to endorse this declaration by the Allies.[161] The Germans, on the other hand, wanted to retain the trust of its wartime ally and therefore chose to ignore the plight of the Armenians.[162] The Germans even provided a safe haven for the perpetrators of the genocide and bestowed national honours on some of them.[163] Other political considerations included Turkey's strategic position in the Middle East and the need to ensure Turkey's neutrality during the Second World War.[164]

The theme of non-accountability has been present through history, and the message has been clear that "redressing grievances against an abused people almost never by itself shapes foreign policy initiatives".[165] As a result, this later encouraged the emergence of the subsequent war criminals. The Nazi regime, for example, was emboldened by the lack of substantial justice towards the Armenians. Adolf Hitler was able to adopt some of the techniques that had been used against the Armenian people. He used the cover and threat of an international conflict in order to minimise international intervention and impose strict party discipline and secrecy, thereby espousing an ideology with racial and ethnic undertones,

---

[159] Khatchik Der Ghougassian, "The Armenian Genocide on the International Agenda: The Case for Diplomatic Engagement", Paper presented to the International Conference on "The Prototype Genocide of Modern Times, University of Sao Paul, Brazil, 22–24 April 2013, p. 229.

[160] Richard G. Hovannisian, *Armenia on the Road to Independence, 1918*, University of California Press, Los Angeles, 1967, p. 52.

[161] Power, 2002, p. 5, see *supra* note 146.

[162] Dadrian, 1996, p. xiv, see *supra* note 86.

[163] *Ibid.*, p. xv.

[164] Der Ghougassian, 2013, p. 229, see *supra* note 159.

[165] Richard Falk, "The Armenian Genocide", in *Resources for Teaching The Armenian Genocide*, The Armenian Genocide Resource Center of Northern California, p. 4.

among others.[166] When Hitler invaded Poland, he was bold enough to use the Armenians as an example of the disinterest in the world:

> Thus for the time being I have sent to the East only my "Death's Head Units" with the orders to kill without pity or mercy all men, women, and children of Polish race or language. Only in such a way will we win the vital space that we need. Who still talks nowadays about the Armenians?[167]

In the words of Archbishop Desmond Tutu:

> [I]t is possible that if the world had been conscious of the genocide that was committed by the Ottoman Turks against the Armenians, the first genocide of the twentieth century, then perhaps humanity might have been more alert to the warning signs that were being given before Hitler's madness was unleashed on an unbelieving world.[168]

Has anything changed with regards to the interplay of foreign policy and international criminal justice? The events in Syria[169] and Darfur[170] seem to indicate the contrary. We continue to live in a world where, despite mass atrocities, political considerations trump justice. It is not surprising, then, that the political motivation of the Allied Powers has been used to undermine the credibility of the outcome of the Armenian trials.

12.3.2. The Portfolio of Crimes

The term genocide received its definitional foundation from the events in Armenia. Raphael Lemkin, the individual who personally pushed for recognition of a separate offence of genocide, was emotionally disturbed by the events at the end of the Armenian massacre.[171] It did not make sense that the perpetrators of mass murder could not be tried under any

---

[166] Antony Beevor, *The Second World War,* Weidenfeld and Nicolson, 2012, p. 8

[167] "Armenian Genocide", United Human Rights Council, 2014.

[168] Archbishop Desmond M. Tutu, "Foreword", in Israel W. Charny (ed.), *Encyclopedia of Genocide*, vol. 1, ABL-CLIO, Santa Barbara, CA, 1999, pp. lvii–lviii.

[169] See International Federation for Human Rights, "China-Russia Disgraceful Veto in the Security Council Blocks ICC Referral of the Syria Situation", 22 May 2014.

[170] See Human Rights Watch, "UN Security Council: Address Inconsistency in ICC Referrals", 16 October 2012.

[171] Raphael Lemkin, "Genocide is a Crime Under International Law", in *American Journal of International Law*, 1947, vol. 41, no. 1, pp. 145–51.

law. He questioned this contradiction: "it is a crime [...] to kill a man, but it is not a crime for his oppressor to kill more than a million men? This is most inconsistent".[172] Determined to ensure that these events did not occur again without some mode of accountability, Lemkin went about the task of convincing states to recognise and punish the attempt to wipe out any national, ethnic or religious group as had happened to the Armenians. In his words:

> It seems inconsistent with our concepts of civilization that selling a drug to an individual is a matter of worldly concern, while gassing millions of human beings might be a problem of internal concern. It seems also inconsistent with our philosophy of life that abduction of one woman for prostitution is an international crime while sterilization of millions of women remains an internal affair of the state in question.[173]

Lemkin's painstaking efforts were rewarded when the crime of genocide was recognised in the 1948 Convention on the Prevention and Punishment of the Crime of Genocide ('Genocide Convention').[174] In the Genocide Convention, genocide is described as "any of the following acts committed with intent to destroy in whole or in part, a national, ethnic, racial or religious group as such: a) killing members of the group; b) causing serious bodily or mental harm to members of the group; c) deliberately inflicting on the group the conditions of life calculated to bring about its physical destruction in whole or in part; d) imposing measures intended to prevent births within the group; e) forcibly transferring children of the group to another group".[175] Apart from defining the crime of genocide, the Genocide Convention gave states the right to act in order to prevent, suppress, and punish the crime.[176] Further, the fact that the genocidal events occurred within a country's borders, as happened in the Ottoman Empire, did not by itself make the authorities less liable. As

---

[172] Power, 2002, p. 17, see *supra* note 146.

[173] *Ibid.*, p. 48.

[174] *Ibid.*, pp. 17–60.

[175] Genocide Convention, Article 2, see *supra* note 141.

[176] Genocide Convention, Article 6 provides that "persons charged with genocide or any of the other acts enumerated in Article 3 shall be tried by a competent tribunal of the State in the territory of which the act was committed, or by such international penal tribunal as may have jurisdiction with respect to those Contracting Parties which shall have accepted its jurisdiction".

noted by Samantha Power, "[s]tates would no longer have the legal right to be left alone".[177]

The Armenian genocide also made way for the emergence of 'crimes against humanity'. This concept was announced by the Public Declaration of the Allies on 24 May 1915, the Paris Peace Conference in 1919 and the Treaty of Sèvres of 10 August 1920.[178] The term was first used by the Allied victors who described that what happened to the Armenians was a clear case of crimes against humanity.[179] A statement by Britain, France and Russia noted:

> Such massacres have taken place from mid-April at Erzurum, Terdjan, Eghine, Bitlis, Moush, Sasoun, Zeytoun, and in all of Cilicia. The inhabitants of approximately a hundred villages in the vicinity of Van all have been killed and the Armenian quarter of Van besieged by Kurds. At the same time, the Ottoman government has acted ruthlessly against the defenceless Armenian population of Constantinople. In view of this new crime of Turkey against humanity and civilisation, the Allied Governments make known publicly to the Sublime Porte that they will hold all the members of the Turkish government as well as those officials who have participated in these massacres, personally responsible.[180]

In the subsequent Treaty of Sèvres, the object of the criminal trials was those "persons accused of having committed acts in violation of the laws and customs of war". The term of 'crimes against humanity', although used in a loose general sense rather than in a strict legal sense, slowly and surely gained currency with time. For example in the trial of Kemal, one of the principal suspects, the term 'crimes against humanity' was used several times by the prosecutor to give a description to the offences against the Armenians.[181]

Since the First World War the concept of crimes against humanity has evolved. The Commission on the Responsibility of the Authors of the War and on Enforcement of Penalties ('Commission on Responsibility')

---

[177] Power, 2002, p. 48, see *supra* note 146.

[178] Kuyumjian, 2011, p. 251, see *supra* note 72.

[179] Power, 2002, p. 5, see *supra* note 146.

[180] Hovannisian, 1967, p. 52, see *supra* 160.

[181] Dadrian, 1997, p. 34, see *supra* note 67.

was established during the Paris Peace Conference to investigate on "Violations on the Laws and Customs of War" [182] by the defeated countries after the First World War. The Commission on Responsibility identified the following war crimes: "systematic terror, murders and massacres, dishonoring of women, confiscation of private property, pillage, seizing of goods belonging to the communities, educational establishments, and charities; arbitrary destruction of public and private goods; deportation and forced labor; execution of civilians under false allegations of war crimes; and violations against civilians and military personnel".[183] Subsequently, the British government pursued prosecution for the deportations and massacres of the Armenian people based on the common law of war.[184] For its part, the ICC Statute describes crimes against humanity to include several acts[185] that are part of a "widespread or systematic attack directed against any civilian population, with knowledge of the attack".[186]

It is worth noting that although the Armenian massacres were not the first in history, they were the first time in modern history that a government intentionally and strategically turned against part of its population. While the initial theory was that the Armenians were being deported for their disloyalty to the state, it was later established that there were mass killings taking place under the watch of the government. While crimes against humanity are largely reported as used on the international

---

[182] Carnegie Endowment for International Peace, *Violations of the Laws and Customs of War: Report of the Majority and Dissenting Reports of the American and Japanese Members of the Commission on the Responsibility of the Authors of the War and on Enforcement of Penalties at the Conference of Paris*, Pamphlet No. 32, 1919, p. 23, reprinted in *American Journal of International Law*, 1920, vol. 122, nos. 1–2, pp. 95–154.

[183] Kuyumjian, 2011, p. 256, see *supra* note 72.

[184] William A. Schabas, *Genocide in International Law: The Crime of Crimes*, Cambridge University Press, Cambridge, 2000, p. 21.

[185] These acts include: murder; extermination; enslavement; deportation or forcible transfer of population; imprisonment or other severe deprivation of physical liberty in violation of fundamental rules of international law; torture; rape, sexual slavery, enforced prostitution, forced pregnancy, enforced sterilisation, or any other form of sexual violence of comparable gravity; persecution against any identifiable group or collectivity on political, racial, national, ethnic, cultural, religious, gender or other grounds; enforced disappearance of persons; the crime of apartheid; other inhumane acts of a similar character intentionally causing great suffering, or serious injury to body or to mental or physical health.

[186] ICC Statute, Article 7.

legal scene, nation states have also incorporated the term into national jurisprudence.[187]

12.4. Conclusion

Lemkin stated that "[i]n Turkey, more than 1,200,000 Armenians were put to death for no other reason than they were Christians. [...] Then one day, I read in the newspapers that all the Turkish criminals were released".[188] What have we learned from these events? Undoubtedly, the international community must "remain cohesive" and "unequivocally committed" to delivering justice after horrible atrocities happen.[189] The post-genocide events in Armenia prove that there is an acceptance in wanting to provide justice to victims. However, the events in Armenia also prove that justice gives way to politics. Nearly one hundred years later the international community continues to debate the facts surrounding the great crime that was perpetrated against the Armenians. As we have discussed in this chapter, the legacy of the Armenian genocide has had a significant impact on international criminal law, whether one recognises it or not. From the notion of holding leaders accountable to creating the parameters of genocide and crimes against humanity, Armenia is where international criminal law was born. As more evidence comes forward supporting the elements of genocide, and as more countries put politics aside to remember this atrocity in our historical memory, the contributions of Armenia to international criminal law will become further evident.

---

[187] Akçam, 2006, p. 222, see *supra* note 16.

[188] Raphael Lemkin, "Totally Unofficial Man", in Samuel Totten and Steven Leonard Jacobs (eds.), *Pioneers of Genocide Studies*, Transaction Publishers, New Jersey, 2002, p. 371.

[189] Dadrian, 1989, pp. 221, 227, see *supra* note 8.

PART 3

The Period Between the World Wars and Before Nuremberg and Tokyo

13

At the Crossroads of Law and Licence: Reflections on the Anomalous Origins of the Crime of Aggressive War[*]

Anatoly Levshin[**]

> – Yet when we came back, late, from the
>   hyacinth garden,
> Your arms full, and your hair wet, I could not
> Speak, and my eyes failed, I was neither
> Living nor dead, and I knew nothing,
> Looking into the heart of light, the silence.
>
> T.S. Eliot, *The Waste Land*

13.1. Introduction

When was the crime of aggressive war born? The Judgment of Nuremberg famously described aggressive war as a *malum in se*:

> War is essentially an evil thing. Its consequences are not confined to the belligerent States alone, but affect the whole world. To initiate a war of aggression, therefore, is not only an international crime; it is the supreme international crime differing from other war crimes in that it contains within itself the accumulated evil of whole.[1]

---

[*]   I would like to thank Jennifer Welsh for encouraging me to grapple seriously with the question at the heart of this chapter. Although that question received only a nominal mention in my graduate thesis, on which I commenced work under her supportive guidance, I now appreciate its pivotal importance to any attempt, however rudimentary, to explain the origins of the crime of aggressive war.

[**] **Anatoly Levshin** is a doctoral candidate in Political Science at Princeton University. He holds a B.A. (Honours) in Political Studies from Queen's University and an M.Phil. in International Relations from the University of Oxford. Among other academic prizes, he was awarded the Parker D. Handy Prize Fellowship in Public Affairs by Princeton University (2013–2014) and a doctoral fellowship from the Social Sciences and Humanities Research Council of Canada.

[1]   Yoram Dinstein, *War, Aggression and Self-Defence*, Cambridge University Press, Cambridge, 2011, p. 128.

However, to assert that the launching and prosecution of a war of aggression are essentially evil acts and that, therefore, they have always been criminal under international law, is to obscure the history of law with ahistorical normative valuations.[2] Stefan Glaser is guilty of this mistake when, in enquiring whether *jus ad bellum* had at all changed since the founding of the modern states system, he asserts: "We do not think so. In fact, from medieval canon lawyers, up to Grotius and Vattel, international law has strived to distinguish between cases where the use of force was legal and those where it was not".[3] However, the plain truth of the matter is that, as late as 1914, international law accorded sovereign states the licence to prosecute war in accordance with their national interests.[4] When, then, did the legal landscape of world politics change not simply from a permissive *jus ad bellum* to a *jus contra bellum* but to a *jus contra bellum* that recognised the launching of aggressive war as a criminal offence entailing individual accountability?

Two rival answers to this question permeate the scholarly literature: at the London Conference on Military Trials ('London Conference') in 1945 or at the Review Conference of the Rome Statute of the International Criminal Court ('Review Conference') in Kampala, 65 years later. In this chapter, I attempt to adjudicate between these competing views. This problem is more difficult than it may at first appear, however, for the opposition between these views conceals a troubling anomaly in the historical record. Both answers enjoy limited empirical corroboration,

---

[2]   This confusion is equally evident in Larry May, *Aggression and Crimes Against Peace*, Cambridge University Press, Cambridge, 2008 and Michael Walzer, *Just and Unjust Wars: A Moral Argument with Historical Illustrations*, Basic Books, New York, 2000.

[3]   Stefan Glaser, "The Charter of the Nuremberg Tribunal and New Principles of International Law", in Guénaël Mettraux (ed.), *Perspectives on the Nuremberg Trial*, Oxford University Press, Oxford, 2008, p. 67.

[4]   An excellent illustration of this fact can be glimpsed from a relevant provision in the US War Department Field Manual that was approved by the US Chief of Staff on 25 April 1914. The manual unequivocally pronounces that "the law of nations allows every sovereign Government to make war upon another sovereign State", US War Department, Office of the Chief of Staff, *Rules of Land Warfare*, Government Printing Office, Washington, DC, 1914, p. 25. For a general overview of the evolution of *jus ad bellum* in the modern states system, see Ian Brownlie, *International Law and the Use of Force by States*, Clarendon Press, Oxford, 1963; Dinstein, 2011, pp. 65–133, see *supra* note 1; Cornelis Pompe, *Aggressive War: an International Crime*, Martinus Nijhoff, The Hague, 1953; and Page Wilson, *Aggression, Crime and International Security: Moral, Political, and Legal Dimensions of International Relations*, Routledge, London, 2009.

---

but neither can satisfactorily account for those pieces of evidence upon which the other draws for primary support. Furthermore, because the two answers appear to be mutually exclusive, this fact of mixed empirical support also means that neither answer is true. How can this be? This anomaly has not yet received adequate attention in the scholarly literature, and it is the primary purpose of this chapter to explore it at length.

The chapter is divided into three core sections. The first section will outline the terms of the anomaly and examine the empirical evidence commonly adduced in support of the two rival positions. The second section will then propose one way of resolving the anomaly by showing that tracing the origins of the crime of aggressive war in a manner that is faithful to the seemingly incompatible aspects of the historical record requires us to move beyond our conventional assumptions about the development of international norms. I will argue that the crime of aggressive war was, indeed, born in 1945, but that it was not until 2010 that it finally became what, on these conventional assumptions, we could recognise as a fully realised norm. The third section will then explore, in a preliminary and suggestive manner, some of the possible causes responsible for putting the crime of aggressive war on such a heterodox path of development. It bears emphasis that causal explanation is not the primary goal of this chapter, and I will not seek to provide a definitive explanation of these unusual circumstances. My intention is merely to paint a brief historical sketch that may aid the reader in better grasping the anomaly and facilitate subsequent research on this question.

13.2. Conventional Views on the Origins of the Crime of Aggressive War

Two rival views on the origins of the crime of aggressive war prevail in the scholarly literature. The first view espouses what we may term the conventional narrative: namely, that the crime of aggressive war was born in the summer of 1945, and that the London Charter of the International Military Tribunal in Nuremberg ('London Charter') was the certificate of its birth. Yoram Dinstein articulates this view in his classic work *War, Aggression, and Self-Defence*: "the criminalisation of aggressive war in a treaty in force was attained only in the aftermath of World War II, upon the conclusion of the Charter of the International Military Tribunal annexed to an Agreement done in London in 1945".[5] Cornelis Pompe similarly honours the Agreement as "the first international penal charter",[6] while Hans Kelsen concurs that "the rules created by this Treaty and applied by the Nuremberg tribunal, but not created by it, represent certainly a new law, especially by establishing individual criminal responsibility for violations of rules of international law prohibiting resort to war".[7] This is the prevalent view in the fields of international history, political science and international criminal law.[8] It also embodies the aspiration of those observers of the Nuremberg Trials who saw in them an opportunity to deliver international relations from the perils of ruinous interstate rivalries and atavistic militarism into the security of enlightened supranationalism.[9]

Opposed to this narrative, we find the revisionist view that the London Charter and the Nuremberg Trials were nothing more than aberrant measures designed by the victorious powers to punish their defeated foes – certainly not harbingers of transformative and reciprocally binding legal principles. As Kirsten Sellars puts it, "[t]he experiment with crimes against peace proved to be an historical anomaly, born of the peculiar circumstances of the closing phase of the Second World War".[10] Gerry Simpson strikes a similar chord: "crimes against peace are controversial precisely because the use of force in international relations *remains a sovereign prerogative* that sovereigns are understandably unwilling to entirely disavow".[11] On this view, it was not until the Review Conference in Kampala, nearly 65 years later, that the international

---

[5] Dinstein, 2011, p. 126, see *supra* note 1.

[6] Pompe, 1953, p. 192, see *supra* note 4.

[7] Hans Kelsen, "Will the Judgment in the Nuremberg Trial Constitute a Precedent in International Law?", in Mettraux, 2008, p. 275, see *supra* note 3.

[8] This was the view of Ian Brownlie, of course; Brownlie, 1963, pp. 188–94, see *supra* note 4. An early critique of this view can be found in Georg Schwarzenberger, "The Judgment of Nuremberg", reproduced in Mettraux, 2008, p. 178, see *supra* note 3.

[9] Eugene C. Gerhart, *America's Advocate: Robert H. Jackson*, Bobbs-Merrill Company, New York, 1958, pp. 307–31, 455–68; Robert H. Jackson, "Nuremberg in Retrospect: Legal Answer to International Lawlessness", reproduced in Mettraux, 2008, pp. 354-71, see *supra* note 3; and Henry L. Stimson and McGeorge Bundy, *On Active Service in Peace and War*, Harper and Brothers, New York, 1948, pp. 584–91.

[10] Kirsten Sellars, *'Crimes against Peace' and International Law*, Cambridge University Press, New York, 2013, p. 259.

[11] Gerry J. Simpson, *Law, War and Crime: War Crimes Trials and the Reinvention of International Law*, Polity Press, Cambridge, 2007, p. 152 (emphasis added).

community transformed the launching of aggressive war from a merely unlawful act into a criminal act. As William A. Schabas, writing in 2005, put it, "it should seem obvious enough that ongoing work aimed at plugging the hole in the Rome Statute is to a large extent an exercise in the progressive development of international law, rather than in its codification, one of *lex feranda* rather than *lex lata*".[12] In recent years, the revisionist view has gained considerable attention in the study of international criminal law but has yet to percolate into related fields.

For the purposes of this chapter, the disagreement between these two points of view is far less interesting for its scholastic value than for an anomalous discrepancy in the historical record which it reveals. The conventional and revisionist narratives are formulated as incompatible alternatives and, therefore, must draw on incompatible pieces of evidence for empirical confirmation. The difficulty is that, on this particular matter, the historical record appears to point in two contradictory directions at once. Both narratives enjoy limited empirical corroboration, but neither can plausibly account for those pieces of evidence upon which the rival narrative draws for support. While the historical record corroborates the conventional narrative by allowing us to identify the London Charter as the instrument of criminalisation with reasonable confidence, it also undercuts that narrative by failing to reveal any meaningful antecedents or repercussions of criminalisation in that earlier historical period. However, if we accept this absence of observable implications as evidence against the conventional narrative and choose, instead, to trace the criminalisation to the Review Conference in Kampala, our position is similarly weakened by the existence of positive evidence which points to the summer of 1945 as the date of criminalisation. In the end, neither the conventional nor the revisionist narrative affords us an adequate grasp of the totality of the relevant portions of the historical record. Furthermore, because the two narratives claim exclusive validity and, therefore, cannot be true simultaneously, this fact of mixed empirical support necessarily means that neither narrative is true on its own terms. This is what we may call, for ease of reference, the paradox of the origins of the crime of aggressive war or, more simply still, the radical paradox.

---

[12] William A. Schabas, "Origins of the Criminalization of Aggression: How Crimes Against Peace Became the 'Supreme International Crime'", in Mauro Politi and Giuseppe Nesi (eds.), *The International Criminal Court and the Crime of Aggression*, Ashgate, Aldershot, 2004, p. 19.

Let us flesh out the terms of this paradox in greater length. Consider, first, the evidence in favour of the revisionist narrative. If we suppose, *ad arguendo*, that the London Charter was the instrument of criminalisation, then we should expect to find significant changes in the rhetoric and conduct of states consistent with that transformation in that historical period. Indeed, even slight changes in norms regulating recourse to war can produce reverberations reaching far beyond the domain of war. This is because, in relations among states, as among individuals bereft of effectual governance, the brooding possibility of war remains an ineradicable legacy of their anarchic condition.[13] For Joseph de Maistre, it was an axiom of history that "war is, in a certain sense, the habitual state of mankind, which is to say that human blood must flow without interruption somewhere or other on the globe, and that for every nation, peace is only a respite".[14] While the macabre implications of de Maistre's view can be disputed, his emphasis on the ubiquity of war remains, regrettably, beyond reproach. It is precisely due to this ubiquity that norms governing recourse to war as an instrument of political power are commonly thought to exert profound influence on the broad contours of the entire institutional edifice of the international society.[15] In any case, the criminalisation of aggressive war can hardly be dismissed as a minor transformation. Whether it occurred in 1945 or 2010, it not only reaffirmed that states no longer enjoyed an unlimited exercise of the right of war, that ultimate and jealously guarded prerogative of sovereign

---

[13] The classic statement of this point can be found in Thomas Hobbes, *Leviathan*, Cambridge University Press, Cambridge, 1991, pp. 86–90. Noel Malcolm's insightful *Aspects of Hobbes,* Clarendon Press, Oxford, 2004 offers a balanced interpretation of that passage. More recent restatements of Hobbes's original formulation can be found in Hans J. Morgenthau, *Scientific Man vs. Power Politics*, University of Chicago Press, Chicago, 1946, pp. 191–201 and Kenneth N. Waltz, *Theory of International Politics*, Waveland Press, Long Grove, IL, 2010, pp. 88–128.

[14] Joseph de Maistre, *Considerations on France*, Cambridge University Press, Cambridge, 1995, p. 23.

[15] Carl Schmitt operationalised this point in terms of the relationship between the underlying structure of the global *nomos* and the institution of war in that *nomos*; Carl Schmitt, *The Nomos of the Earth in the International Law of the* Jus Publicum Europaeum, Telos Press Publishing, New York, 2006, especially pp. 140–68 and 259–80. This is also a central theme in his later work *Theory of the Partisan: Intermediate Commentary on the Concept of the Political*, Telos Press Publishing, New York, 2007. For a statement of this point unburdened by strong metaphysical assumptions, consider instead Hedley Bull, *The Anarchical Society: A Study of Order in World Politics*, Palgrave Macmillan, London, 2002, pp. 178–93.

---

power, but, further, exposed rulers to the possibility of criminal punishment for violations of this prohibition.[16] However, searching for observable implications of such criminalisation on the assumption that it occurred in 1945 yields few meaningful findings. Three points merit notice in this regard.

First, the extraordinary selectivity displayed by the victorious powers in drafting the arraignment article, tailoring it to the wrongs of their defeated foes and, thus, exculpating their own inequities by the mere fact of its definitional narrowness, was already a telling indication that no meaningful effort would be undertaken subsequently to transform this legal innovation into a general rule of conduct.[17] It must not be forgotten that the San Francisco Conference on International Organisation, which concluded shortly before the signing of the London Charter, considered and quietly discarded the possibility of treating the launching of aggressive war as a criminal rather than merely an unlawful act.[18] In the course of negotiations in London, Robert Jackson, head of the US delegation, expended considerable effort to prove, against the opposition of his Soviet counterpart, General I.T. Nikitchenko, that the criminality of aggressive war ought to be construed as a general principle of conduct. He justly observed:

> I should think that our definition would sound pretty partial if we are defining an act as a crime only when it is carried out by the Axis powers. That is what I have in mind: If it is a good rule of conduct, it should bind us all, and if not, we should not invoke it at this trial. It sounds very partial to me, and I think we would get great criticism from it.[19]

---

[16] For a general discussion of the concept of criminalisation, see Nicola Lacey and Lucia Zedner, "Legal Constructions of Crime", in Mike Maguire, Rod Morgan and Robert Reiner (eds.), *The Oxford Handbook of Criminology*, Oxford University Press, Oxford, 2007, or Edwin H. Sutherland and Donald R. Cressey, *Principles of Criminology*, J.B. Lippincott Company, Chicago, 1955, pp. 8–13.

[17] For example, Simpson argues that "the conspiracy charges were one way in which this was done. The crime of aggression was reworked into a norm applicable to a state captured by a vicious cabal of conspirators intent on regional or global domination", Simpson, 2007, p. 149, see *supra* note 11.

[18] United Nations War Crimes Commission, *History of the United Nations War Crimes Commission and the Development of the Laws of War*, His Majesty's Stationery Office, London, 1948, pp. 185–87.

[19] Robert H. Jackson, *Report of Robert H. Jackson, United States Representative to the International Conference on Military Trials, London, 1945: A Documentary Record of*

It is a subtle irony that the final formulation of the arraignment clause, in its restrictive application to the European Axis Powers, as well as the rejection of the principle of the criminality of aggressive war at San Francisco altogether obscured this admonition, reaffirming, instead, that in world politics, "the standard of justice depends on the equality of power to compel".[20]

Second, war did not wither away in the wake of 1945, and state leaders have since shown little fear of criminal prosecution in commencing wars of aggression; nor, for that matter, have their enemies proved alacritous to threaten them with such prosecution.[21] The new norm remained very much confined to the margins of practical politics in the wake of the Second World War, exercising no measurable influence over the conduct of states and, until the end of the Cold War, subsisting largely in the writings of jurists and historians. As Jonathan Bush notes, "throughout the period, the potential applicability of the criminal law to interstate aggression plainly had no relevance in the outside world".[22] To be sure, civil activists undertook several attempts to hold political leaders accountable by drawing on the discourse of crimes against peace, of which the Russell-Sartre Tribunal on the intervention of the United States in the Vietnamese civil war is, perhaps, the most notable.[23] However, such attempts at discursive entrapment[24] proved few in number and, ultimately, ineffectual in their cumulative effect on the conduct of high

---

Negotiations of the Representatives of the United States of America, the Provisional Government of the French Republic, the United Kingdom of Great Britain and Northern Ireland, and the Union of Soviet Socialist Republics, Culminating in the Agreement and Charter of the International Military Tribunal, Division of Publications, US Department of State, Washington, DC, 1949, p. 336.

20 Thucydides, *History of the Peloponnesian War*, Penguin, New York, 1972, p. 402.

21 Jonathan A. Bush, "The Supreme Crime and Its Origins: The Lost Legislative History of the Crime of Aggressive War", in *Columbia Law Review*, 2002, vol. 102, no. 8, pp. 2387–95, especially p. 2392; Simpson, 2007, pp. 144–47, see *supra* note 11.

22 Bush, 2002, p. 2392, see *supra* note 21.

23 *Ibid.*, p. 2393.

24 For a general discussion of the concept of "discursive entrapment", see Bull, 2002, pp. 43–44, *supra* note 15; Andrew Hurrell, "Norms and Ethics in International Relations", in Walter Carlsnaes, Thomas Risse and Beth A. Simmons (eds.), *Handbook of International Relations*, Sage, London, 2002, p. 145; Marc Lynch, "Lie to Me: Sanctions on Iraq, Moral Argument and the International Politics of Hypocrisy", in Richard M. Price (ed.), *Moral Limit and Possibility in World Politics*, Cambridge University Press, Cambridge, 2008, pp. 169–76.

politics. In the capitals of the great powers, the scathing attitude to the very suggestion that their prerogative to wield the sword in defence of vital national interests could, even in principle, be subject to supranational oversight, was succinctly articulated by the US Secretary of State Dean Acheson: "law simply does not deal with such questions of ultimate power – power that comes close to the sources of sovereignty".[25] It is difficult to imagine a more truculent rebuke of the very concept of *jus contra bellum*.

Third, the criminalisation was preceded by a startling absence of domestic and international negotiations regarding the political desirability and costs of creating the new norm. Instead, the topic remained firmly within the purview of legal committees and conferences organised by the victorious powers to settle the narrow question of war crimes.[26] It is difficult to explain how such a radical norm could have developed without, at the very least, due calculations of its expected utility by the great powers. To be sure, norms can develop in the absence of deliberate planning, but it strains credulity to suppose that powerful states would have proved willing to relinquish their supreme prerogative to the haphazard whim of custom and unintended consequences. It is far more reasonable to conclude that the victorious powers admitted the criminality of aggressive war for the sole purpose of punishing defeated enemy leaders and officials but did not earnestly contemplate extending its applicability more broadly. The cumulative effect of these three observations is uncompromising. Supposing that aggressive war was criminalised in 1945 leads us to the seemingly inexorable conclusion that what was, arguably, one of the greatest transformative moments in the history of the modern states system appeared to have left few immediate impressions on the dynamics of that system.

The striking lack of observable implications of the criminalisation in that historical period certainly lends support to the revisionist narrative and may even incline us to the conclusion that aggressive war did not become a crime until 2010. This conclusion, though tempting, would be

---

[25] Elliott L. Meyrowitz, "What Does Law Have to Do with Nuclear Weapons?", in *Michigan State University-DCL Journal of International Law*, 2000, vol. 9, no. 1, p. 305.

[26] Sellars, 2013, pp. 47–112, see *supra* note 10; Arieh J. Kochavi, *Prelude to Nuremberg: Allied War Crimes Policy and the Question of Punishment*, University of North Carolina Press, Chapel Hill, 1998, especially pp. 201–29; Bradley F. Smith, *The Road to Nuremberg*, André Deutsch, London, 1981.

injudiciously precipitate, since considerable positive evidence exists confirming the London Charter as the instrument of criminalisation. To begin with, it was the London Charter that introduced the concept of crimes against peace into the lexicon of international law – not the Paris Peace Treaty of 1919, the Kellogg-Briand Pact of 1928, or the Kampala Amendment. Furthermore, the London Charter *is* widely acknowledged as the instrument of criminalisation in international practice. For example, we find this genetic attribution in Resolutions 95 and 177 of the General Assembly of the United Nations as well as in the national statutes and military codes of some of the great powers.[27] For example, the US Department of Defense revised its Field Manual on land warfare in 1956 to acknowledge the criminality of aggressive war.[28] Ian Brownlie argues that such widespread adherence indicates acceptance of "the Nuremberg Charter as a source of general international law".[29]

Perhaps the most convincing piece of evidence confirming the London Charter as the instrument of criminalisation can be found in longitudinal changes in patterns of public discourse. Before 1945, proposals to criminalise aggressive war were widely viewed as quixotic and impractical. The justificatory burden lay with proponents of criminalisation, and it was incumbent upon *them* to demonstrate the unacceptability of a permissive *jus ad bellum*. Consider, for example, the protracted exchange that took place between US Secretary of State Robert Lansing and Ferdinand Larnaude, the French jurist, both delegates to the Commission on the Responsibility of the Authors of the War and on Enforcement of Penalties ('the Commission'), over the course of the plenary sessions in the spring of 1919. Larnaude, adamant to punish the ex-Kaiser Wilhelm II for initiating the First World War, insisted that "the premeditated, carefully prepared commencement of hostilities" be

---

[27] For a general overview of these instruments, see Brownlie, 1963, pp. 188–94, *supra* note 4; Dinstein, 2011, pp. 129–30, *supra* note 1. For examples of bureaucratic enmeshment and legal internalisation of the criminality of aggressive war in national rules and laws, see Brownlie, 1963, pp. 187–88, *supra* note 4.

[28] Provision 498 of the Manual, under the heading "Crimes under International Law", reads: "Any person, whether a member of the armed forces or a civilian, who commits an act which constitutes a crime under international law is responsible therefor and liable to punishment. Such offenses in connection with war comprise: a. Crimes against peace [...]", US Department of the Army, *FM 27-10, Department of the Army Field Manual: The Law of Land Warfare*, Department of the Army, Washington, DC, 1956, p. 178.

[29] Brownlie, 1963, p. 191, see *supra* note 4.

recognised by the Commission as an international crime.[30] Lansing objected, remarking that while states had "no moral right" to wage "a wanton war",[31] existing law admitted *compétence de guerre* as an unrestricted sovereign prerogative: "*the essence of sovereignty* [is] *the absence of responsibility*".[32] When Larnaude contended that "the legality of a premeditated war should not be admitted",[33] Lansing sternly rebuked him, making liberal use of the established legal axiom:

> The Commission should not stagger at *the truth*. A new doctrine advocated by a very few men should not be permitted to change *the standing rule of the world* [...] [A] war of aggression ought to be declared to be a crime against international law but this had never been done and the paragraph should therefore stand as drafted.[34]

Larnaude eventually conceded that "the right of going to war was admitted",[35] but insisted that the article of arraignment be preserved to "emphasise the new sensibility of mankind" regarding the moral unacceptability of aggressive wars.[36] Lansing summarily dismissed his appeal: "the Commission should not let public opinion enter the question at all".[37] Established presumptions are difficult to overturn, and it is remarkable how easily Lansing was able to extinguish the force of Larnaude's proposal by exposing its inconsistency with accepted legal premises.[38]

This discursive situation remained almost unchanged until the final years of the Second World War. When, in 1944, the British Attorney General, Sir Donald Somervell, reasoned that the launching of aggressive war "is not a war crime or a crime in any legal sense", he was merely

---

30 FO 608/245, Document 3, p. 153, National Archives, UK ('TNA').

31 *Ibid.*, p. 189.

32 *Ibid.*, p. 191 (emphasis added).

33 *Ibid.*, p. 250.

34 *Ibid.* (emphasis added).

35 *Ibid.*

36 *Ibid.*, p. 239.

37 *Ibid.*

38 For a formal treatment of this point, see Neta C. Crawford, "*Homo Politicus* and Argument (Nearly) All the Way Down: Persuasion in Politics", in *Perspectives on Politics*, 2009, vol. 7, no. 1, pp. 118–19; Friedrich V. Kratochwil, *Rules, Norms, and Decisions: On the Conditions of Practical and Legal Reasoning in International Relations and Domestic Affairs*, Cambridge University Press, Cambridge, 1995, pp. 34–43.

expressing what was still, even at that late date, a common and uncontroversial view.[39] That view found an eloquent formulation in *War Criminals: Their Prosecution and Punishment*, a popular contemporaneous work composed by the Harvard criminologist Sheldon Glueck. Glueck expressly rejected the possibility of treating the launching of the war as a criminal act. The enumeration of penal charges proposed in the book, he noted,

> is not intended to include the "crime" of flagrantly violating solemn treaty obligations or conducting a war of aggression [...] [T]o prosecute Axis leaders for the crime of having initiated an unjust war, or having violated the "sanctity of treaties", would only drag a red herring across the trail and confuse the much clearer principle of liability for atrocities committed during the conduct of a war, be it a just or an unjust one.[40]

Even as late as 1944, Glueck's position accorded well with those of most other scholars and practitioners.

However, the justificatory burden shifted entirely onto the opponents of criminalisation in the wake of the London negotiations. As Bush puts it,

> It is notable how many mouths gave lip-service to the Nuremberg charge of aggressive war. Outside of Germany and Japan, the only public opposition to the criminality of aggressive war seemed to come from lawyers working for the clemency of convicted Germans [...] Everywhere else, there was only automatic endorsement of "Nuremberg" in general and the criminality of aggressive war in particular.[41]

The case of Glueck is particularly instructive in this regard. Having explicitly rejected the criminality of aggressive war in *War Criminals*, Glueck then reached the opposite conclusion in *The Nuremberg Trial and Aggressive War*, published only two years later:

> [D]uring the present century a widespread custom has developed among civilized States to enter into agreements expressive of their solemn conviction that unjustified war is

---

[39] Kochavi, 1998, p. 100, see *supra* note 26.

[40] Sheldon Glueck, *War Criminals: Their Prosecution and Punishment*, Alfred A. Knopf, New York, 1944, pp. 37–38.

[41] Bush, 2002, p. 2389, see *supra* note 21.

> so dangerous a threat to the survival of mankind and
> mankind's law that it must be branded and treated as
> criminal.[42]

Although the change in Glueck's position was, at least in part, an artefact of the work that he performed for the US prosecutorial team at Nuremberg, it was, nevertheless, representative of a broader and equally rapid transformation in public discourse. Jackson, in his reflections on the political impact of the Trials, neatly captured the magnitude of that change: "[no] one can hereafter deny or fail to know that the principles on which the Nazi leaders are adjudged to forfeit their lives constitute law – law with a sanction".[43] If the revisionist narrative were correct, we would not expect such an immense and rapid change in patterns of public discourse to coincide so neatly with the signing of the London Charter. After all, a mere manifest of victors' justice can hardly be expected to accomplish such a transformation.

When was the crime of aggressive war born then? Considerable evidence exists to support both the conventional and revisionist narratives, entangling extant attempts to date the crime's origins into the radical paradox. This is a crucial point which has not yet received adequate attention in the scholarly literature. Researchers investigating the criminalisation have proven content to overlook the anomalous inconsistencies in the historical record and provide evidence corroborating only their preferred narrative. It may even appear tempting to dismiss the radical paradox as a conceptual problem produced by absence of adequate empirical evidence rather than a genuine historical anomaly. Could we not resolve the paradox by procuring more data in support of one or the other narrative? I do not believe that we could, and it bears emphasis that this suggestion fundamentally misunderstands the character of our present difficulties. Even if it proves possible to accumulate a preponderance of evidence in support of one narrative as against the other, such an imbalance would not in the slightest diminish the strength of the paradox as long as some evidence remains to support the weaker narrative. Because the conventional and revisionist narratives are formulated in exclusive terms, neither can be accounted true so long

---

[42] Sheldon Glueck, *The Nuremberg Trial and Aggressive War*, Alfred A. Knopf, New York, 1946, p. 26.

[43] Kelsen, 2008, p. 274, see *supra* note 7.

as there remain anomalous facts in the historical record that cannot plausibly be subsumed within its chronological ambit.

The radical paradox results from this surprising fact that the historical record favours both the conventional and revisionist narrative, a fact that common sense stubbornly demurs to accept on grounds of their logical incompatibility. Common sense does not brook the possibility that the crime of aggressive war could have emerged multiple times in one century, unless we further suppose that the two births were separated by a temporary death – a possibility expressly contradicted by the evidence for the conventional narrative. Common sense demands singularity of origin. Unfortunately, history has not proven obliging in meeting this demand. It points us in two contradictory directions at once, directing our gaze first to London and then to Kampala, and, thus, frustrates our attempts to pinpoint the origins of the crime of aggressive war to a single temporal location. Confronted by the obduracy of empirical evidence, however, we are justified in enquiring whether it is not our common sense that is at fault on this point. After all, historical anomalies are not objective givens but merely discrepancies between empirical evidence and established theoretical expectations.

In the following section, I propose to outline a tentative solution to the radical paradox by framing it as a theoretical problem and demonstrating how unspoken theoretical assumptions undergirding the conventional and revisionist narratives are directly responsible for its production. We will begin by establishing the more general point that it is insensible to consider the emergence and evolution of norms in an abstract manner detached from prior theoretical considerations.

13.3. A Critical Analysis of Conventional Views and Theoretical Considerations

Tracing a norm's origins, development, acceptance or decay is an empirical exercise guided by the steady hand of theory.[44] For it is theory which delineates the ceaseless stream of political behaviour into these conceptual categories in the first place, specifying, for example, exactly when a norm can be said to have emerged, how a norm evolves, or what it

---

[44] This point is made indirectly in Adam R.C. Humphreys, "The Heuristic Application of Explanatory Theories in International Relations", in *European Journal of International Relations*, 2010, vol. 17, no. 2, pp. 259–65.

means for a norm to develop until it reaches the point of acceptance.[45] Consider, for example, the question of evolution. Drawing on the burgeoning literature on international norms, we can expect the evolutionary trajectory of most norms to follow one of two well-trodden paths.[46] Some are products of human design – they are sculpted by visionary entrepreneurs in response to the exigencies of social need or opportunities for personal advantage and, with the sustained assistance of powerful groups, they gradually penetrate and become assimilated into the very fabric of international conduct.[47] Others are products of human action undertaken in the service of custom rather than deliberate foresight. These latter norms evolve "more casually and more imperfectly", to borrow David Hume's incisive formulation,[48] as chance contributes its even share to their constitution.[49] Now, the notions at the heart of these complimentary heuristics – norm entrepreneurs, penetration and assimilation, and unintended consequences – are essentially theoretical categories. They empower us to venture beyond our immediate sensory environment to experience and apprehend a political universe rich in

---

[45] Kratochwil, 1995, pp. 25–8, see *supra* note 30; John Gerard Ruggie, *Constructing the World Polity: Essays on International Institutionalization*, Routledge, London, 1998, pp. 85–101; John R. Searle, *The Construction of Social Reality*, Penguin, New York, 1995.

[46] For a general discussion of norm development, see James G. March and Johan P. Olsen, *Rediscovering Institutions: The Organizational Basis of Politics*, Free Press, New York, 1989; Antje Wiener, *The Invisible Constitution of Politics: Contested Norms and International Encounters*, Cambridge University Press, Cambridge, 2008.

[47] For the classic statement of this view, Martha Finnemore and Kathryn Sikkink, "International Norm Dynamics and Political Change", in *International Organization*, 1998, vol. 52, no. 4, pp. 887–917. Illustrative applications of this view can be found in Martha Finnemore, *National Interests in International Society*, Cornell University Press, Ithaca, NY, 1996, pp. 34–127. The point on assimilation is absent from Finnemore's positivist formulation of the model, but it is required by the thesis of 'mutual constitution', which widely accepted by other constructivist scholars. For an informed discussion of this thesis, see Nicholas G. Onuf, *World of Our Making: Rules and Rule in Social Theory and International Relations*, Routledge, London, 1989.

[48] David Hume, *Essays, Moral, Political and Literary*, Liberty Fund, Indianapolis, 1985, p. 39.

[49] This view prevails especially in the tradition of enlightened conservatism, of which Hume, de Maistre and Edmund Burke are admirable exponents who require no introduction. A succinct statement of this view can be found in Friedrich Hayek, *Studies in Philosophy, Politics and Economics*, University of Chicago Press, Chicago, 1967, pp. 96–105.

---

intangibles, but they also limit us in our engagement with that universe to particular, often quite narrow, domains.[50]

The choice of theoretical framework for the analysis of a particular empirical problem ought to be governed by the pragmatic considerations of suitability and utility.[51] After all, theories that either tortuously twist evidence to make elementary sense of it, or purchase little explanatory power at the price of exorbitant simplifications, can hardly be considered appropriate. Instead, scholars should strive to attain a reflective equilibrium between the explanatory possibilities afforded by available evidence, on the one hand, and the explanatory focus of their chosen theoretical framework, on the other.[52] This point commands crucial importance, since even ostensibly purely descriptive statements about the evolution of international norms are laden with unspoken theoretical assumptions. Unconscious attachment to such assumptions, perhaps owing to unreflective deference to academic convention, can contribute to perilous distortions of the historical record whenever the pragmatic criteria of suitability and utility are violated.

Returning to the case of the criminalisation of aggressive war, it is precisely such attachment to what we may term the assumptions of non-monotonicity and bivalence that entangles extant accounts of the crime's origins into the radical paradox.[53] On the non-monotonic view, states are

---

[50] Norwood R. Hanson, *Patterns of Discovery: An Inquiry into the Conceptual Foundations of Science*, Cambridge University Press, Cambridge, 1961, pp. 271–84; Searle, 1995, pp. 1–58, see *supra* note 45.

[51] Norwood R. Hanson, *Perception and Discovery: An Introduction to Scientific Inquiry*, Freeman, Cooper and Co., San Francisco, 1970, p. 64.

[52] I borrow the concept of 'reflective equilibrium' from John Rawls, *A Theory of Justice*, Harvard University Press, Cambridge, MA, 1971, p. 20.

[53] These assumptions are implicit in mainstream models of norm development, such as Beth A. Simmons's functionalist theory of commitment, *Mobilizing for Human Rights: International Law in Domestic Politics*, Cambridge University Press, Cambridge, 2009, pp. 64–80; Margaret E. Keck and Kathryn Sikkink's theory of transnational advocacy networks *Activists beyond Borders: Advocacy Networks in International Politics*, Cornell University Press, Ithaca, NY, 1998, pp. 10–16; Wayne Sandholtz's model of norm cycles, "Dynamics of International Norm Change: Rules Against Wartime Plunder", in *European Journal of International Relations*, 2008, vol. 14, no. 1, pp. 101–12; or Alexander Wendt's thesis of international cultures, *Social Theory of International Politics*, Cambridge University Press, Cambridge, 1999, pp. 246–368. Richard M. Price's work on the chemical weapons taboo affords one notable exception to this trend, *The Chemical Weapons Taboo*, Cornell University Press, Ithaca, NY, 1997, especially p. 8.

---

assumed to be consistent in their normative commitments and, furthermore, they are assumed to maintain that consistency by summarily repudiating older norms clashing with their new commitments. Bivalence encourages scholars to think of the development of norms in terms of crisp thresholds of acceptance. On this second assumption, the existence of a norm at any given point in time is conceptualised as an elementary binary category – it is either accepted by the relevant political community or it is not. In effect, bivalence assumes that the development of a norm can be conceptualised as a unidimensional process in which a gestating norm must first accumulate sufficient support before it can reach a specified threshold and, thus, become an accepted norm. [54] The combination of non-monotonicity and bivalence restricts the range of admissible trajectories of a norm's development to cosmetic variations on the familiar scenario of rival norms succeeding each other in gradual temporal succession, of which at most one is recognised as accepted by the community at any one point in time. This scenario may well afford an appropriate heuristic for the study of some historical questions, but it is not uniformly applicable.[55]

---

[54] Bivalence is implicit in the Austinian view of law as command, a view that, to borrow the critique that John Stuart Mill targeted against historicism, "arrives at the annihilation of all moral distinctions except *success* and *not success*", Maurice Mandelbaum, *History, Man, and Reason: A Study in Nineteenth-Century Thought*, Johns Hopkins University Press, Baltimore, 1971, p. 137.

[55] I borrow this taxonomy from the study of formal logic, in which the term 'bivalence' denotes the metaphysical assumption that atomic propositions and well-formed formulae admit of two exclusive Boolean states, truth and falsehood. Bivalence is the cornerstone of classical logical systems, and its prevalence in the study of human reasoning is partly a reflection of its undeniable utility for the investigation of certain common empirical problems. However, reification of this assumption to the status of a metaphysical certainty can hamper our ability to reason about vague conceptual boundaries or dynamic systems that change in gradual increments. This point runs exactly parallel to our present discussion, and it may aid the reader in grasping the direction of my argument. The sorites paradox offers a useful example of an intuitively flawed syllogism whose invalidity is obscured by bivalence. For a general consideration of the paradox, see Merrie Bergmann, *An Introduction to Many-Valued and Fuzzy Logic: Semantics, Algebras, and Derivation Systems*, Cambridge University Press, Cambridge, 2008, pp. 1–7. Consider a finite heap of grains. Suppose that we remove one grain from the heap and observe that the heap is not appreciably diminished by this reduction. It is valid to conclude that a heap of grains is no less a heap for the loss of a single grain. However, this conclusion is no longer sustainable if we choose to iterate it recursively for as many times as there are grains in the heap, yielding the patently false conclusion that a heap is no less a heap for the loss of its final grain. As John Nolt puts it, "early in the sequence of inferences these premises lead to

Non-monotonicity excludes the possibility of what may be viewed as politically haphazard or schizophrenic behaviour in which a state, or, possibly, a group of states, upholds two or more seemingly inconsistent norms at the same time. For example, a state may simultaneously commit itself to inconsistent norms if its leadership finds it possible to assign different functions to those norms and, in thus insulating their mutually contradictory effects, extinguish much of the tension between them. Alternatively, an inconsistent normative posture may be the product of two or more national bureaucracies devising conflicting solutions for organising co-operation with foreign partners. Bivalence excludes the possibility that a norm can be realised only partially, that it may enjoy some, but not all, of the effects commonly associated with inveterate norms, and that, therefore, its progress cannot be assessed on a unidimensional scale with a crisp cut-off. For example, a norm may be favoured by vocal national constituencies that, although not sufficiently powerful to ensure its acceptance at the national level, can at least restrain their government from committing itself to the opposite normative principle. Or a norm may be entrenched in the bureaucratic procedures and legal codes of the very same states that refuse to endorse it publicly in international fora.[56] These examples are not intended to exhaust the range of complexity created by rejection of non-monotonicity and bivalence. They are meant only to convey the point that some meaningful historical scenarios are not captured, and, indeed, are distorted, by theoretical frameworks that rely on these assumptions.

---

conclusions that are either wholly true or approximately true. But as they are used to draw conclusion after conclusion, the conclusions become less and less true so that by the end of the sequence we arrive at a conclusion that is wholly false" (*Logics*, Wadsworth Publishing, Belmont, 1997, p. 421). In a certain sense, the paradox itself is entirely the product of a prior commitment to bivalence, which stipulates that every proposition is as true or false as any other and, so, occludes the possibility that consecutive applications of *modus ponens* can preserve truth only partially. Therefore, one way of solving the sorites paradox is to reject bivalence and allow for suitable gradations of truth. This strategy, implemented in infinite-valued logics, reconciles our intuitions and formal results by specifying that each recursive application of a sorites syllogism should diminish the truth of its conclusion by a corresponding margin. This solution is instructive as it reminds us that some conceptual problems are products not of objective givens but, rather, of the theoretical frameworks through which we perceive those givens.

[56] Andrew Hurrell denotes these possibilities 'bureaucratic enmeshment' and 'legal internalization', respectively, and they can be taken as evidence of a norm's acceptance in a given political society. Hurrell, 2002, pp. 145–46, see *supra* note 24.

In the case of the criminalisation of aggressive war, it is precisely non-monotonicity and bivalence that stymie our efforts to date the crime's origins by generating misleading theoretical expectations which are unwarranted by the empirical parameters of this particular historical problem. Upon relinquishing these assumptions, it is possible to acknowledge that, in a certain important sense, the crime *was* created in 1945. Witness its enmeshment in the bureaucratic procedures and legal codes of some states and the United Nations during the first decade of the Cold War, or the remarkable fact that almost no national political leader has openly contested the criminality of aggressive war since the Nuremberg Trials.[57] At the same time, however, it cannot be denied that the San Francisco Conference on International Organisation expressly refused to incorporate the principle of the criminality of aggressive war into the Charter of the United Nations and, instead, reaffirmed the weaker norm of the prohibition of aggressive war as the organising principle of the post-war world order. That fateful decision strongly shaped the subsequent impression that the doctrine of the criminality of aggressive war, enshrined in the Nuremberg Principles yet bereft of meaningful foundation in customary law, was, at best, an optional adjunct to the far more minimalist system of *jus contra bellum* developed in the Charter of the United Nations. It was only 65 years later that most states finally mustered the political will to commit themselves to the construction of a supranational infrastructure that, at last, institutionalised the formerly nebulous rule of criminality in a concrete political setting and on a reciprocal basis.

This is clearly a complex historical narrative that does not fit the conventional mould of non-monotonicity and bivalence. However, the proper conclusion to be drawn from this lack of fit is not that the crime of aggressive war was not born in 1945 but, rather, that our theoretical assumptions are inadequate for comprehending the unusual circumstances of its birth in their entirety. This conclusion effectively dissipates the historical anomaly at the heart of the radical paradox. By illuminating a developmental trajectory passing between the Scylla of non-monotonicity and the Charybdis of bivalence, it emancipates us from the imperative to consider the conventional and revisionist narratives as mutually exclusive possibilities. We are left at liberty to acknowledge that the crime of

---

[57] The exceptions are enumerated in Brownlie, 1963, p. 193, see *supra* note 4.

aggressive war was, indeed, born in 1945 and became a fully realised norm within the next decade, at least along the dimensions of bureaucratic and legal enmeshment. After all, it was the London Charter that introduced the criminality of aggressive war into the lexicon of international practice and established the precedent for subsequent engagements with the concept of crimes against peace. That first experiment was certainly imperfect, and we cannot overlook the pivotal role played by the realpolitik ingredients of cynicism, hypocrisy and egotism in making it possible. Nevertheless, it bears emphasis that such imperfections do not detract from the authenticity of the legal transformation ushered in by the London Charter. Of course, the new criminal rule had to await Kampala to become what, on a strictly non-monotonic and bivalent view, we may recognise as a fully realised norm. But this means only that, until that time, the crime of aggressive war endured a twilight existence. For those 65 years, it was, in the words of T.S. Elliot, "neither living nor dead" [58] – a victim of the political convenience of the victorious powers whose collusion in London effectively condemned it to straddle the line between political oblivion and fully fledged acceptance for decades.

13.4. In Defence of the Heterodox Developmental Trajectory of the Crime of Aggressive War

Throughout our discussion in the previous section, we have assumed that the heterodox developmental trajectory of the crime of aggressive war was, in part, the result of the political compromises reached in London. In this section, I should like to suggest some preliminary reasons in defence of this assumption. It may be objected that it would be more plausible to consider it an unintended consequence of contradictory bureaucratic choices made by the Allied Powers in the course of the Second World War. In the United States, for example, the tasks of punishing war criminals and designing the post-war international order were assigned to the Department of Defense and the Department of State, respectively. Working within this bifurcation, norm entrepreneurs favouring the criminalisation of aggressive war, such as, most notably, William C. Chanler, John J. McCloy, Edward Bernays, Henry Stimson and Robert

---

[58] This particular line is taken from the first part of T.S. Eliot, "The Waste Land", in *Selected Poems*, Faber and Faber, London, 2002, p. 42.

Jackson, were able to establish the principle of the criminality as a cornerstone of the American war crimes programme.[59] The Department of State adopted a different normative approach. Initial plans for the reconstruction of the international order after the war were proposed by the Informal Political Agenda Group, which consisted of Cordell Hull, then Secretary of State, Leo Pasvolsky, Isaiah Bowman, Sumner Welles, Norman Davis and Morton Taylor, in December, 1943. Hull, weary of the refusal of the Senate to ratify the Covenant of the League of Nations because it appeared to threaten its ability to exercise its constitutional prerogatives, was careful to maintain a minimalist position on the illegality of aggressive war. Predictably, the Informal Political Agenda Group did not consider the question of the criminality of aggressive war, nor was it added to the Department of State's programme at a later date.[60] Could we not conclude that this bureaucratic bifurcation is a sufficient explanation for the inconsistent posture assumed by the United States in promoting the criminalisation of aggressive war in London while quietly discarding that very same principle in San Francisco?

The logic of bureaucratic bifurcation certainly provides a partial explanation for the unusual circumstances of the birth of the crime of aggressive war, but we must keep in mind that those circumstances were also the direct consequence of strategic collusion by the victorious powers, especially the Soviet Union and the United States. After all, the conduct of negotiations in London was closely supervised by the highest executive authorities of the Allied Powers, and the question of whether the launching of aggressive war could be treated as an international crime was one of the most significant and enduring points of contention between the delegations.[61] The political significance of this question was simply too great – few remained blind to the fact that the outcome of the negotiations was bound to send shockwaves reaching far beyond the

---

[59]   Some of the most excellent sources on this topic are Bush, 2002, see *supra* note 22; Kochavi, 1998, see *supra* note 26; Smith, 1981, see *supra* note 26. See also Gary Jonathan Bass, *Stay the Hand of Vengeance: The Politics of War Crimes Tribunals*, Princeton University Press, Princeton, NJ, 2000, pp. 149–81.

[60]   Ruth B. Russell, *A History of The United Nations Charter: The Role of the United States, 1940–1945*, Brookings Institution, Washington, DC, 1958, especially pp. 220–24.

[61]   The question of the legal status of aggressive war was a central topic of discussion for at least seven of the 15 sessions for which transcripts are provided in Jackson's report (Documents XIII, XXII, XXXVII, XLII, XLIV, XLVII, and LI in Jackson, 1949, see *supra* note 19).

narrow issue of war crimes – for those leaders opposed to the criminalisation of aggressive war to blindly consign the outcome of the negotiations to the rhetorical skill of their representatives. As we shall see in a moment, this was especially true of Joseph Stalin, who personally monitored the negotiations and issued direct orders to Nikitchenko to reject any proposed formulation of the legal charges which could be construed as an endorsement of the criminality of aggressive war in general terms.

Indeed, throughout the negotiations, the Soviet delegation insisted on restricting the scope of the proposed charge to attempts at "aggression against or domination over other nations carried out by the European Axis in violation of the principles of international law and treaties".[62] This insistence faced vigorous opposition from Jackson, who, as we have already seen, refused to treat the criminality of aggressive war as anything other than a reciprocally binding principle enjoying general applicability: "If certain acts in violation of treatise are crimes, they are crimes whether the United States does them or whether Germany does them, and we are not prepared to lay down a rule of criminal conduct against others which we would not be willing to have invoked against ourselves".[63] But that is precisely what the Soviets opposed. They saw the London Conference as a vehicle for institutionalising a set of legal principles on the basis of which enemy leaders could be indicted, not as a forum for laying the normative foundations of the post-war international order.[64]

Bureaucratic bifurcation alone was not sufficient to allay the worry of the Soviet leadership that the London Conference would not be used to criminalise the launching of aggressive war through the back door. This point is lucidly conveyed in a confidential telegram sent by Vyacheslav Molotov, the Minister for Foreign Affairs of the Soviet Union, to Stalin on July 25, 1945. Broaching the matter of Jackson's position on the legal status of aggressive war, Molotov noted:

---

[62] As stated in "Redraft of Definitions of 'Crimes', Submitted by Soviet Delegation, July 23, 1945", reproduced as Document XLIII in Jackson, 1949, p. 327, see *supra* note 19.

[63] *Ibid.*, p. 330.

[64] For a general review of the Soviet position, see Sidney S. Alderman, "Negotiating on War Crimes Prosecutions, 1945", in Raymond Dennett and Joseph E. Johnson (eds.), *Negotiating with the Russians*, World Peace Foundation, New York, 1951, pp. 49–98 and George Ginsburgs, *Moscow's Road to Nuremberg: The Soviet Background to the Trial*, Martinus Nijhoff, The Hague, 1996.

> We believe that these unduly vague formulations make it possible to proscribe as international crimes military operations conducted in self-defence against aggression. As we know, in the course of the last war, our and Anglo-American troops invaded Germany, but that act cannot, from any reasonable point of view, be described as an international crime. *We believe that it would be possible to accept these formulations only on the condition that they are amended to specify expressly that they apply only to instances of fascist aggression.*[65]

That same day, Stalin received another confidential telegram on this matter from Andrey Vyshinsky, former Procurator General of the Soviet Union. Vyshinsky reported that, with respect to Jackson's insistence on treating the launching of aggressive war as an international crime, "we have given our delegation express orders to reject" his general formulations. Stalin's approval of Vyshinsky's order is recorded in the margins of the telegram, in pencil.[66]

It would be erroneous to conclude that this reluctance to endorse the criminality of aggressive war in general terms was driven solely by the cynical egotism of a totalitarian dictator who was himself responsible for authorising the Soviet invasions of Finland, Estonia, Latvia and Poland in 1939. In 1945 the sheer novelty and far-reaching implications of the criminalisation project, both in terms of implied sovereignty and uncertainty costs, meant that few policymakers, whether in the Soviet Union or elsewhere, were willing to consider it earnestly, even under the narrow rubric of war crimes. In this regard, it bears iteration that the intellectual ancestry of proposals to criminalise the launching of aggressive war is quite brief and sparse, dating merely to the first decades of the twentieth century.[67] After all, in the years before the First World War, international law did not restrict states in their ability to exercise the right of war, and this licentious permissibility left an indelible imprint on the institutional imaginations of contemporary thinkers and

---

[65] Cited in Natalya Lebedeva, *SSSR i Nurnbergskiy Process: Neizvestnye i Maloizvestnye Stranitsy Istorii*, Mezhdunarodnyi Fond "Demokratiya", Moscow, 2012, p. 211 (emphasis added, my translation).

[66] *Ibid.*, p. 210.

[67] Patrycja Grzebyk, *Criminal Responsibility for the Crime of Aggression*, Routledge, London, 2013, pp. 9–26, 79–97; Pompe, 1953, pp. 116–75, see *supra* note 4; Sellars, 2013, pp. 1–46, see *supra* note 10.

policymakers.[68] The criminalisation of aggressive war had only been attempted once before, in 1919, and, at that, in such a haphazard manner that the stillborn endeavour left the criminalisation project largely discredited as a hopelessly quixotic design.[69] A few telling examples drawn from the foreign policy circles in Britain and the United States may help to illustrate the point.

In 1944, in response to an enquiry by Sir Cecil Hurst, the British delegate to the United Nations War Crimes Commission ('UNWCC'), regarding whether the launching of aggressive war constituted an international crime, Frank Roberts of the Foreign Office wrote that the Allied Powers, in issuing the Moscow Declaration of 1943,

> had in mind the conduct of the arch-criminals in conducting and directing the war, and as these criminals will include those who planned and launched the war, *it would seem unnecessary* to enlarge the conception of "war crimes" in a way which at any rate *involves the probability of political and legal controversy.*[70]

Upon learning of Hurst's enquiry, Sir William Malkin, Roberts' superior, dismissed the whole matter as "a frightful waste of time" and a mere "outburst of dialectics".[71] On 18 August 1944 Sir Arnold McNair, in a memorandum for consideration by the UNWCC, similarly noted that "however desirable it may be *de lege feranda* to take steps which will enable Governments in future to punish the procuring [*sic*] of aggressive war as a criminal act – I do not consider that *de lege lata* a judge would hold that the effect of the [Kellogg-Briand] Pact was to make it a criminal act".[72] An identical conclusion was reached by the Office of the Judge

---

[68] In addition to the above sources and those enumerated in footnote 4, see Dinstein, 2011, pp. 75–81, *supra* note 1; Quincy Wright, "Changes in the Conception of War", in *American Journal of International Law*, 1924, vol. 18, no. 4, pp. 755–67.

[69] The definitive statement on this subject is James F. Willis, *Prologue to Nuremberg: Politics and Diplomacy of Punishing War Criminals of the First World War*, Greenwood Publishing, Westport, CT, 1982. For a more concise treatment, see Bass, 2000, pp. 58–105, *supra* note 59; M. Cherif Bassiouni, "World War I: 'The War to End All Wars' and the Birth of a Handicapped International Criminal Justice System", in *Denver Journal of International Law and Policy*, 2002, vol. 30, no. 3, pp. 244–91; Sellars, 2013, pp. 1–11, *supra* note 10.

[70] Document C15349, LCO 2/2976 (emphasis added) (TNA).

[71] Document C15349, FO 371/39007 (TNA).

[72] Document C43, p. 4, TS 26/69 (TNA).

Advocate General of the United States in a draft paper entitled "Is the Preparation and Launching of the Present War a War Crime?", published on 18 December 1944.[73] In sum, even as late as 1945, the institutional imaginations of most policymakers in the Allied states remained too heavily constrained by the operational presumptions of the permissive *jus ad bellum* which had existed before 1914, for them to contemplate, quite apart from prior strategic misgivings, that an international, or even supranational, criminal jurisdiction over matters of war and peace was at all possible.[74]

Returning to the negotiations in London, we can now assess the role that strategic co-ordination by the victorious powers played in putting the principle of the criminality of aggressive war on such a heterodox trajectory of development. Recall that the Soviet delegation did not oppose – indeed, it expressly endorsed – treating aggressive war as an international crime within the rubric of war crimes. It was Jackson's attempt to extend the new criminal rule beyond the confines of this rubric and transform it into a universal rule that occasioned the incessant objections of the Soviet delegation. The final formulation of the charges that we find in Article 6 of the London Charter clearly reflects the concerns and preferences of the Soviet delegation. Although it is not clear what prompted Jackson to acquiesce in such a compromise after days of obdurate disagreement, it is surely telling that his acquiescence followed immediately in the wake of Stalin's and President Harry Truman's negotiations in Potsdam, which concluded on 2 August 1945. Available records of their discussions contain only brief mentions of the London

---

[73] The paper is reproduced as Document 26 in Bradley F. Smith, *The American Road to Nuremberg: The Documentary Record 1944–1945*, Hoover Institution Press, Stanford, 1981, pp. 78–84.

[74] To be sure, the interwar period did witness a blossoming of theoretical contributions to the criminalisation project. Vespasian Pella, Robert Phillimore, Édouard Descamps, Nicolas Politis, Henri Donnedieu de Vabres, Megalos Caloyanni and Hugh Bellot were among the most distinguished jurists of the interwar period who developed the theoretical groundwork for the criminalisation project (although I know of no monograph treatment of these thinkers or of their contributions to the criminalisation project). A useful summary can be found in Grzebyk, 2013, pp. 82–85, see *supra* note 67. Curiously, Phillimore, Politis, de Vabres, Caloyanni and Bellot did not make any proposals to the League of Nations bearing on criminal law. Pella only consulted the League on the subjects of money laundering and harmonisation of domestic penal codes. It is reasonable to speculate that this lack of practical engagement contributed to the hesitancy of Allied policymakers in dealing with proposals for the criminalisation of aggressive war.

Conference.[75] However, in light of the fact that Stalin personally monitored the negotiations in London, it is not implausible to suppose that Truman offered him assurances that Jackson's position did not reflect a tacit commitment on the part of the United States to establishing the criminality of aggressive war as a general and reciprocally binding rule of conduct. It is possible that the two leaders agreed to endorse this new principle within the narrow rubric of war crimes on the supposition that doing so would not constitute a general endorsement of it, fully aware that the San Francisco Conference on International Organization had already rejected it.

13.5. Conclusion

We began this chapter by enquiring into the temporal origins of the crime of aggressive war and surveying two prevalent responses to this question. These responses, which we have termed the conventional and revisionist narratives of the crime's origins, are often formulated as incompatible alternatives. Throughout the chapter, my primary purpose has been to problematise this dichotomisation, to show that both narratives can contribute to our understanding of the crime's origins, and to expose the perils of formulating them in such starkly exclusive terms. The historical record provides limited empirical corroboration for both narratives. Thus, rigid attachment to the exclusivist view that only one of them can be true necessarily implies that neither is true. This is the essence of what we have termed the radical paradox, which, as I have sought to demonstrate, is not an immanent artefact of the historical record but, rather, of an incongruity between that record, on the one hand, and the assumptions of non-monotonicity and bivalence undergirding the exclusivist view of the two narratives, on the other. Rejecting these assumptions empowers us to strike a theoretical compromise that can faithfully accommodate what previously appeared to be glaring anomalies in the historical record. The consequent realisation that the crime of aggressive war was, indeed, born in 1945, but that it was not until 2010 that it finally became what, on these assumptions, we could recognise as a fully realised norm, effectively dissipates the radical paradox.

---

[75] A transcript of their discussion on war crimes can be found in *Foreign Relations of the United States, Diplomatic Papers: The Conference of Berlin (The Potsdam Conference) 1945*, vol. 2, US Government Printing Office, Washington, DC, 1960, pp. 525–57.

I would like to conclude this chapter with a word of encouragement to scholars who, whatever their field of study, find themselves saddled with theoretical conventions and inveterate assumptions that, in their opinion, distort reality more than they illuminate it. Theory is a servant of scientific enquiry, not its master. It is incumbent upon us to be bold and inventive in tailoring it to the circumstances of our problems and, in so doing, to resist the pressures of submitting to convention out of blind deference. In this chapter, I have defended the historical feasibility of a view of normative development that allows for schizophrenic normative commitments and multiple dimensions of acceptance, a view that contradicts mainstream models of normative development but is entirely warranted by the unusual parameters of my empirical problem. If this chapter succeeds in raising awareness of the explanatory potential afforded by pragmatism in the study of international norms as well as more broadly, it will have accomplished its purpose.

14

Before Nuremberg: Considering the Work of the United Nations War Crimes Commission of 1943–1948

Dan Plesch[*] and Shanti Sattler[**]

14.1. Introduction

It is a little-known fact that approximately 37,000 individuals were investigated and accused of committing war crimes as mid-level Axis officials during the Second World War, and that more than 2,000 criminal trials[1] were conducted following the conclusion of the war to try many of these individuals. These pre-trial investigations and the actual trials operated apart from those held by the International Military Tribunals ('IMT')[2] at Nuremberg and Tokyo. They were the effort of nations[3] that

---

[*] **Dan Plesch** is Director of the Centre for International Studies and Diplomacy, School of Oriental and African Studies, University of London, and directs the Centre's War Crimes Project. Previous academic appointments include Honorary Visiting Research Fellow at the Department of Peace Studies, Bradford University, Research Associate at Birkbeck College, University of London, and Senior Visiting Research Fellow at Keele University. Outside academia, he has acted as consultant and adviser to the British and US governments, the BBC, CNN, Sky News, Kroll Security International, Oxfam, the Foreign Policy Centre and Greenpeace. He was the independent adviser to the British government's Department of Constitutional Affairs on the implementation of the Freedom of Information Act. He is the author of *America, Hitler and the UN: How the Allies Won World War II and Forged a Peace* (2011).

[**] **Shanti Sattler** is Deputy Director of the War Crimes Project at the Centre for International Studies and Diplomacy, School of Oriental and African Studies, University of London. She holds an M.A. in International Studies and Diplomacy from SOAS and a B.A. in International Relations and Peace and Justice Studies (with Honors) from Tufts University, USA.

[1] United Nations War Crimes Commission, *History of the United Nations War Crimes Commission and the Development of the Laws of War*, His Majesty's Stationery Office, London, 1948 ("History of the UNWCC"), p. 518.

[2] The IMTs at Nuremberg and Tokyo were a series of criminal tribunals initiated and held by the Allied forces following the end of the Second World War. The investigations and trials focused on the conviction of high-level Nazi and Japanese war criminals.

[3] The nations that were states parties to the UNWCC were: Australia, Belgium, Britain, Canada, China, Czechoslovakia, Denmark, France, Greece, India, Luxembourg, the Netherlands, New Zealand, Norway, Poland, the US and Yugoslavia. South Africa was

conducted the proceedings in conjunction with an international war crimes commission. This commission was established by 17 Allied nations in October 1943 under the name the United Nations Commission for the Investigation of War Crimes. This name was soon changed to the United Nations War Crimes Commission ('UNWCC').[4]

The 17 Allied governments met at the British Foreign Office in London in October 1943 with a multilateral mission to create an entity that would quickly and effectively mobilise retributive justice efforts on an international scale. Each of the nations sent a representative, or in some cases two or three, who were generally legal professionals and political figures. The work of the UNWCC and its members has been unheeded and even forgotten in the historical and legal record of the Second World War era that focuses almost exclusively on the IMTs conducted at Nuremberg and Tokyo.

At the time of the first meeting of the 17 nations, the Second World War was well underway in Europe and parts of Asia. These countries, as affected states, were experiencing what they regarded as unprecedented atrocities being committed against military and civilian populations around the world by the Axis Powers. Consequently, their actions stemmed largely out of urgency to generate a response to the atrocities that was both legal and military in nature. To begin the effort, the government representatives initiated formal discussions on 20 October 1943 that focused on developing international criminal law to meet the needs of the unique circumstances. They also sought to advance standards and practices of how to bring justice to the international community.

The result was the creation of UNWCC[5] in reflection of the collaborative effort of the Allied nations. The formal work of the UNWCC maintained operation until March 1948. By the time it closed

---

only involved in setting up the UNWCC and did not create a national office, conduct investigations or host national trials. Denmark joined the UNWCC in July 1945.

[4] For discussion of the first meeting of the UNWCC, see History of the UNWCC, p. 112, *supra* note 1.

[5] This name reflected the names of a number of other civilian multinational organisations that were created in this period. For more background on the United Nations alliance, see Dan Plesch, *America, Hitler and the UN: How the Allies Won World War II and Forged A Peace*, I.B. Tauris, London, 2011; Egon Schwelb, "The United Nations War Crimes Commission", in *British Year Book of International Law*, 1946, vol. 23, pp. 363–64; and Arieh J. Kochavi, *Prelude to Nuremberg: Allied War Crimes Policy and the Question of Punishment*, University of North Carolina Press, Chapel Hill, 1998, pp. 27–62.

after nearly four and a half years, the men and women who served as Commissioners and their respective nations were directly responsible for making *prima facie* judgments on 36,000 cases brought to the UNWCC by different member states during that time. Many of the cases deemed substantial and worthy by the UNWCC went to trial led by the respective nations. By March 1943 the numerous investigations and *prima facie* judgments resulted in over 2,000 criminal trials[6] that were conducted around Europe and the Far East before national military civil courts and tribunals under the umbrella of the UNWCC.

In addition to conducting investigations and trials, the national representatives were tasked with debating and voting on pressing and controversial themes of international criminal and humanitarian law. Once agreed upon and adopted, the standards and concepts were put forth by the Commissioners to all member states as suggested advances of relevant law. In most cases, member states adopted the views of the UNWCC for use in their trials and national legal systems. Debates and publicised views of the UNWCC and its members also served as influential material for other international criminal justice efforts that concerned the Second World War, most specifically the London Charter of the International Military Tribunal in Nuremberg ('London Charter') that was initiated in 1945.

The critical work of the UNWCC in developing law and conducting investigations and trials between 1943 and 1948 represents a significant contribution to the development of multilateral collaboration, as well as customary international criminal law as defined by the elaboration of international legal standards and proceedings to combat impunity and promote justice in the wake of large-scale atrocities.[7]

Studying the work of the UNWCC exposes valuable contributions to addressing historical gaps concerning the familiar narrative of the Second World War and the response of the Allies to Axis crimes. It is also important to recognise the efforts of the UNWCC and the individual national representatives in the context of the current perception that there

---

[6]   History of the UNWCC, p. 518, see *supra* note 1.

[7]   We discuss the relationship of the UNWCC to customary international law in more detail in our article Dan Plesch and Shanti Sattler, "Changing the Paradigm of International Criminal Law: Considering the Work of the United Nations War Crimes Commission of 1943–1948", in *International Community Law Review*, 2013, vol. 15, pp. 203–23.

is a lack of international criminal legal practice for use as precedent. Central to this is the question following years of legal practice established by the International Criminal Tribunal for the former Yugoslavia ('ICTY') and the International Criminal Tribunal for Rwanda ('ICTR') about the existence of international criminal (customary) law. Research into the UNWCC and its work contributes to this debate, and ultimately the notion that this work contributes to customary international law.

In addition to debate over the existence of customary international law, anxiety surrounding the efficacy and value of the international justice initiatives currently in operation is prevalent. The United Nations *ad hoc* tribunals created for atrocities committed in Rwanda, Yugoslavia, Cambodia and Sierra Leone have all received extensive criticism. While the most common criticisms from the respective national communities as well as international governments and civil society focus on a variety of themes, questions of political meddling and neutrality, as well as prolonged duration of the investigations and proceedings and astronomical costs, are central to the discontent.[8]

This chapter serves to introduce the UNWCC, its structure and attendant national tribunals into the contemporary narrative about the historical origins of international criminal and humanitarian law. It is also an effort to prove that the work of the UNWCC and the individual participating nations provides a large and significant body of customary international criminal law that can and should be used in the practice and study of modern-day international law. We also argue that the UNWCC represents a rare yet successful attempt of state practice that clearly shows nations actively engaged in conflict seeking to address issues of justice prior to the reaching of comprehensive peace. We also show that the nations initiated their efforts to develop new principles of law to address the new atrocities of war prior to the start of the well-known proceedings that led to the London Charter.

To provide a comprehensive overview of the UNWCC and some of its notable members and support our core arguments, we rely on the

---

[8]   See, for example, Seeta Scully, "Judging the Successes and Failures of the Extraordinary Chambers of the Courts of Cambodia", in *Asian-Pacific Law & Policy Journal*, 2011, vol. 13, no. 1, pp. 300–53; Tom Perriello and Marieke Wierda, *The Special Court for Sierra Leone Under Scrutiny*, International Center for Transitional Justice, New York, 2006; Jon Silverman, "Ten Years, $900m, One Verdict: Does the ICC Cost Too Much?", in *BBC News*, 14 March 2012.

UNWCC's official history that was written and published by members in
1948,[9] and on the recently opened archives held at the UN Archives and
Records Management Section ('ARMS') in New York City, as well as
documents available through national archives of several member states
including the US, Britain and Australia. We acknowledge that there is still
more research and analysis to be done into the UNWCC and in particular
the accompanying national trials.

We start with an overview of the historical context and foundations
of the UNWCC, highlighting the major events and legal and political
agreements that supported its creation and shaped its legal character.
Following this, we focus on the defining characteristics of the UNWCC,
including the member nations as well as others that were involved, the
committee structure that formed the base of its operations and the sub-
commission located in the Far East. The second half of the chapter
explores the UNWCC's accomplishments as well as criticisms of its
work. We conclude with discussion of the UNWCC's legacy of its work
and points for future research and analysis.

14.2. The Origins and the Establishment of the UNWCC

After a year of discussions and deliberations, national representatives of
the 17 nations met for the first official meeting of the UNWCC on 26
October 1943, and immediately set out to discuss their work and mission
as the atrocities of the Second World War continued around Europe and
the Far East. The representatives were present with a team of official
recorders to represent the views and plans of their respective nations.
These individuals included Lord Atkin of Australia, the well-known
French architect of human rights law René Cassin, and representatives
from both China and India.

Among the first topics to be discussed at the initial meeting were
the grounds of what constituted an international crime in the specific
context of the world war and the responsibility of the UNWCC to develop
this concept.[10] One of the representatives from India, Sir Samuel

---

[9]   History of the UNWCC, see *supra* note 1. It was written by the members of the UNWCC
       and its Secretarial staff with the purpose of recording its work by future students and
       scholars of international law.

[10]   United Nations War Crimes Commission, Notes of Unofficial Preliminary Meeting Held at
       2:30 p.m. on the 25th October, 1943, at the Royal Courts of Justice, London ("Unofficial
       Preliminary Meeting") (http://www.legal-tools.org/en/go-to-database/record/ad8990/).

Runganadhan, initiated this conversation among the members by pointing to the need to define legal principles.[11] Supporting his urging, Atkin stated that Second World War offenders had "gone right outside the realm of law". He continued with the advice that the UNWCC should not make its list of war crimes "too minute".[12]

In addition to conversation about the development of international criminal law and the task at hand, the Chinese representative V.K. Wellington Koo recognised the need for specific attention to be paid to the Far East and suggested that a sub-commission be established alongside the primary London-based UNWCC that would be located in the Far East.[13]

Central to the discussions among these members of the UNWCC at their first meetings in 1943 were already established tenets of international law that they were able to rely upon as they pursued their goals through the establishment of solid legal foundation. The Hague Conventions of 1899 and 1907 were the primary agreements referenced by the Commissioners. The Hague Conventions represent the first collation of legal standards regarding actions in war in the modern era. Inspired by various conflicts, and most specifically the Lieber Code issued by Abraham Lincoln to the Union Forces in 1863 during the US Civil War, the two Hague Conventions further considered what behaviours should and should not be regarded as legal during wartime. The efforts of the member states served as some of the most substantial developments of international co-operation concerning the elaboration of war crimes and laws of war prior to the First and Second World Wars.

In response to the significant atrocities of the First World War, a group of experts in war crimes and legal prosecution from the US, Britain, France, Italy, Japan, Belgium, Greece, Poland, Romania and Yugoslavia established a Commission on the Responsibility of the Authors of War and on Enforcement of Penalties ('Commission on Responsibility') at the plenary session of the Paris Peace Conference in

---

[11] *Ibid.*

[12] The term 'war crimes' was used in a broad generic sense at this time rather than as one among several core international crimes in the usage of the twenty-first century.

[13] United Nations War Crimes Commission, Notes of a Second Unofficial Meeting Held on 2nd December, 1943, at 3:00 p.m. at the Royal Courts of Justice, London ("Second Unofficial Meeting") (http://www.legal-tools.org/en/go-to-database/record/3e7e05/); History of the UNWCC, p. 129, see *supra* note 1.

January 1919. The Commission on Responsibility was to address questions and needs concerning the powers responsible for the atrocities of the First World War and the pursuit of justice. The work of the Commission on Responsibility continued to develop the standards of the Hague Conventions to meet the specific context of the war. The efforts of the experts largely failed to achieve their general objective of dealing with the issues of prosecution for war crimes committed, as the Commission on Responsibility's recommendations were never followed. However, the Paris Peace Conference was successful in developing a further codification of 32 acts that it considered to be war crimes, and its legacy includes influencing the work of the UNWCC as well as the IMTs in Nuremberg and Tokyo.

Members of the UNWCC adopted many things from the Commission on Responsibility, not least its "Versailles List" of war crimes.[14] While some UNWCC representatives worried that the list of crimes was too long, ultimately it was this list that served as the basis for the legal precedent utilised by the UNWCC as it pursued investigations and prosecutions. There was a general agreement that the list was significant also because it was endorsed by both Italy and Japan, and that Germany had not opposed it.[15] Indeed, the Versailles List of war crimes served as inspiration for improving international efforts in this regard.[16] However, the UNWCC did not give a specific definition of a war crime, citing that to do so would have involved "limitation and exclusion".[17]

Despite the legal foundations established by the Hague Conventions, the Paris Peace Conference and specifically the Commission on Responsibility, the Second World War presented new challenges to international criminal law. In a report written for the UN

---

[14] For more information about the Commission on Responsibility and its relationship to the UNWCC, see Harry M. Rhea, "The Commission on the Responsibility of the Authors of War and on Enforcement of Penalties and Its Contribution to International Criminal Justice after World War II", in *Criminal Law Forum*, 2014, vol. 25, nos. 1–2, pp. 147–69.

[15] Second Unofficial Meeting, p. 2, see *supra* note 13.

[16] *Ibid.* United Nations War Crimes Commission, Notes of Third (Unofficial) Meeting Held on 4th January 1944 ("Third Unofficial Meeting") (http://www.legal-tools.org/doc/4cecd9/); United Nations War Crimes Commission and the United Nations Economic Social Council, Report: "Information Concerning Human Rights Arising from Trials of War Criminals" (E/CN.4/W.19), United Nations Economic and Social Council, 1948, pp. 8, 146–80 ("Information Concerning Human Rights").

[17] History of the UNWCC, p. 1, see *supra* note 1.

Human Rights Division published in 1948,[18] the UNWCC described the context of the time from the perspective of the Allied position and specifically the UNWCC members: "the Axis […] asserted the absolute responsibility of belligerents, who, it was asserted, were under no obligation to respect human rights, but were entitled to trample them underfoot wherever the military forces found them inconvenient for the waging of war". Regarding the legal implications of the Axis Powers, the report continued:

> This doctrine was repudiated as contrary not only to morality but to recognized international law which prescribed metes and bounds for the violation even in war of human rights. This latter doctrine involved also the further principle that there was individual responsibility for violations of human rights in war time, beyond the limits permitted by the law of war. The idea of individual responsibility, if it was to be conceived in terms of law involved a legal system and procedure, in order to decide the question of Individual criminality.[19]

Indeed, the UNWCC held in high regard the treaties and conventions established prior to the Second World War to guide the international community through pursuing justice in the wake of mass atrocity. Using these as a base, the UNWCC, in particular its Legal Committee, discussed and debated further definitions of war crimes and international crimes to address the complex context presented by the Second World War.

Aside from the international treaties and conventions, public statements that condemned enemy atrocities and detailed promises for retribution also influenced and fuelled the Allied states as they designed their collaboration. Strong public opinion and initiatives pushed by civil society accompanied the international statements and also supported the UNWCC as it determined its work and direction. One of the notable examples of such public influence was the London International Assembly.[20]

---

18 *Ibid.*, p. ii.

19 "Information Concerning Human Rights", p. ii, see *supra* note 16.

20 For more information about the London Assembly, see Kerstin von Lingen, "Setting the Path for the UNWCC: The Representation of European Exile Governments on the London International Assembly and the Commission for Penal Reconstruction and Development,

Several formal statements were issued by Allied nations starting in November 1940 when the Czech and Polish governments released a joint statement expressing concern for the unprecedented nature of Nazi atrocities being witnessed in their countries.[21] The Polish government released a second statement shortly after to inform the public about the Nazi attempt to eradicate Polish national identity.[22] The US President Franklin D. Roosevelt and the British Prime Minister Winston Churchill also released parallel statements nearly a year later, in October 1941, expressing their intention to seek retribution. Churchill used his statement to emphasise that atrocities were occurring "above all behind the German fronts in Russia". He added that retribution "[for] these crimes must henceforward take its place among the major purposes of the war".[23] Accompanying statements of other Allied nations, the Soviet Foreign Ministry issued notes on German atrocities to all nations with whom it had diplomatic relations in November 1941 and in 1942.[24]

This collection of statements from the Allied countries all carried forceful tones and strong intent to see judicial action. However, none mentioned legal process or specific plans.

The St James's Declaration ('Declaration') of January 1942 represented the first multilateral statement to directly declare the intention to bring Nazi perpetrators of atrocious acts against civilian populations to justice. Representatives of governments in exile, including Belgium, Czechoslovakia, Free France, Greece, Luxembourg, the Netherlands, Norway, Poland and Yugoslavia, joined together to issue the statement on Punishment for War Crimes at St James's Palace in London. China promptly responded with its pledge to subscribe to the principles put forth in the declaration.[25]

1941–1944", in *Criminal Law Forum*, 2014, vol. 25, nos. 1–2, pp. 45–76; History of the UNWCC, p. 441, see *supra* note 1.

[21] "Czechoslovakia and Poland", in *The Times*, 12 November 1940, p. 3.

[22] "German Crimes in Poland", in *The Times*, 20 December 1940, p. 3.

[23] M.E. Bathurst, "The United Nations War Crimes Commission", in *American Society of International Law*, 1945, vol. 39, pp. 565–68.

[24] Embassy of the USSR, *The Molotov Notes on German Atrocities*, His Majesty's Stationery Office, London, 1942; History of the UNWCC, pp. 87–108, see *supra* note 1.

[25] Trygve Lie, the Norwegian Foreign Minister and future first Secretary-General of the United Nations, was among the signatories.

The British Foreign Secretary, Anthony Eden, opened the meeting at St James's Palace and General Władysław Sikorski, Prime Minister of Poland, chaired. During the proceedings Eden explained that the practical purposes of the Declaration were to warn the enemy and offer a "glimmer of hope" to the peoples of occupied Europe. He stated bluntly that "the Declaration resolutely turns International Law in a new direction".[26] With the Declaration, the signatory states also brought attention to the issue of individual responsibility including command responsibility and collective (participatory) responsibility. Furthermore, the Declaration marked a formal statement of intent to the Axis Powers that they would face a judicial process. It stated:

> [...] whereas international solidarity is necessary in order to avoid the repression of these acts of violence simply by acts of vengeance on the part of the general public, and in order to satisfy the sense of justice of the civilised world [...] [the signatories] place among their principal war aims the punishment, through the channel of organised justice, of those guilty of or responsible for these crimes, whether they have ordered them, perpetrated them or participated in them.[27]

Despite the presence of Eden, Sikorski and the US Ambassador, none of these states endorsed the policies set forth in the Declaration in January. It was not until October 1942 that the "Big Three" Allied powers signed it. In response to the endorsements by the Big Three, the exiled governments began to lobby both Britain and the US for the creation of a UN commission to address war crimes.

The British government soon endorsed the creation of a United Nations Commission on Atrocities, whose function it would be to engage in fact-finding and produce reports. On 21 August 1942 Roosevelt issued a public declaration stating:

> The United Nations are going to win this war. When victory has been achieved, it is the purpose of the Government of the United States, as I know it is the purpose of each of the United Nations, to make appropriate use of the information

---

[26] United Nations Information Organisation, *Punishment for War Crimes: The Inter-Allied Declaration Signed at St James's Palace London on 13th January, 1942, and Relative Documents*, His Majesty's Stationery Office, London, 1942, p. 7.

[27] *Ibid.*

and evidence in respect to these barbaric crimes of the
invaders, in Europe and in Asia. It seems only fair that they
should have this warning that the time will come when they
shall have to stand in courts of law in the very countries
which they are now oppressing and answer for their acts.[28]

Both Britain and the US formally endorsed the creation of a United
Nations Commission for the Investigation of War Crimes in October
1942.[29] Negotiations on the terms of reference took a year until the
meeting in London on 20 October 1943 marked the start of the initiative,
under the new name, the UNWCC.

In further support of multilateral action against the Axis, the
British, Soviet and US foreign secretaries joined together at a meeting in
Moscow several days after the meeting that created the UNWCC.
Together, they produced a four-part Declaration of the Four Nations on
General Security ('the Moscow Declaration') of 30 October 1943 that
denounced Italy and the annexation of Austria by Germany. The final
section of the Moscow Declaration, entitled "Statement on Atrocities",
detailed the major three powers' general approach to war crimes.
Specifically, it announced the policy to investigate Axis war criminals
and put the accused perpetrators on trial in the nations where they had
committed their crimes. In the cases of crimes without clear geographical
reference, perpetrators would be tried based on joint decisions by the
Allied governments.[30] Roosevelt, Churchill and the Soviet leader Joseph
Stalin each signed the "Statement on Atrocities".

While the Soviet government was robust in its initial support for the
collaborative Allied response, as exemplified by the Moscow Declaration,
the Soviet Union did not go on to participate in the UNWCC for
numerous reasons. The British Lord Chancellor, Lord Simon, stated at the
opening of the first meeting of the UNWCC in October 1943 that the
Soviets were in agreement with its establishment, but that several points
of contention prevented them from joining at that time.[31] During the

---

[28]   Cordell Hull, *The Memoirs of Cordell Hull*, Hodder and Stoughton, London, 1948, p. 1184.

[29]   British Parliament, Commons Sitting of 17 December 1942, T.C. Hansard, London, series
5, vol. 385, 1942, cols. 2082–87.

[30]   Staff of the Committee on Foreign Relations and the Department of State, "The Moscow
Conference, October 13–30, 1943", in *A Decade of American Foreign Policy: Basic
Documents, 1941–49*, US Government Printing Office, Washington, 1950, DC, pp. 9–13.

[31]   History of the UNWCC, p. 113, see *supra* note 1.

planning for the work of the UNWCC, the Soviet Union openly stated its belief that it did not go far enough in investigating and punishing suspected war criminals. The Soviet Union specifically emphasised its discontent that the UNWCC did not make initial preparations to consider committing a war of aggression and crimes against humanity as war crimes. Moscow also strongly opposed the British refusal to accuse Rudolf Hess – the deputy Führer to Hitler who had parachuted into Britain on a diplomatic mission in 1941 – of war crimes.[32] The Soviet Union did go on to pursue its own war crimes trials independently.

14.3. Structure of the UNWCC

Seventeen core countries participated in the initiation of the work of the UNWCC in 1943. Australia, Belgium, Britain, Canada, China, Czechoslovakia, France, Greece, India, Luxembourg, the Netherlands, New Zealand, Norway, Poland, the US and Yugoslavia actively participated in the UNWCC from its first meeting or shortly thereafter. South Africa assisted in the efforts to set up the UNWCC and did not go on to conduct its own investigations or host national trials. Denmark joined the UNWCC in July 1945. At its eleventh meeting at the end of February 1944, a representative suggested that Brazil and Mexico might join the UNWCC based on respective experiences of suffering, but neither country pursued membership.[33]

Member countries granted the UNWCC three key specific duties:

1. To investigate and record the evidence of war crimes, identifying where possible the individuals responsible.
2. To report to the Governments concerned cases in which it appeared that adequate evidence might be expected to be forthcoming.
3. To make recommendations to member governments concerning questions of law and procedure as necessary for them to be able to fulfil their role of conducting trials.[34]

In order to carry out its duties effectively, the UNWCC assigned a chairman and organised itself into three committees that met on a weekly

---

[32] Kochavi, 1998, pp. 222–30, see *supra* note 5.
[33] United Nations War Crimes Commission, Minutes of Eleventh Meeting Held On 29th February 1944 (http://www.legal-tools.org/doc/099169/).
[34] History of the UNWCC, p. 3, see *supra* note 1.

basis. The first chairman was Sir Cecil Hurst of Britain, who was followed by one of Australia's representatives, Lord Wright of Durley, in January 1945. The three committees quickly began work. The first committee ('Committee I') was dedicated to facts and evidence. The second committee ('Committee II') handled matters of enforcement and the third committee ('Committee III') served as the forum for dialogue on legal affairs. The committee structure supported the UNWCC in effectively carrying out its specific tasks. It is important to recognise that the UNWCC did not play a role in apprehending or detaining any of the suspected war criminals nor did it directly participate in the prosecutions of the member governments' cases.

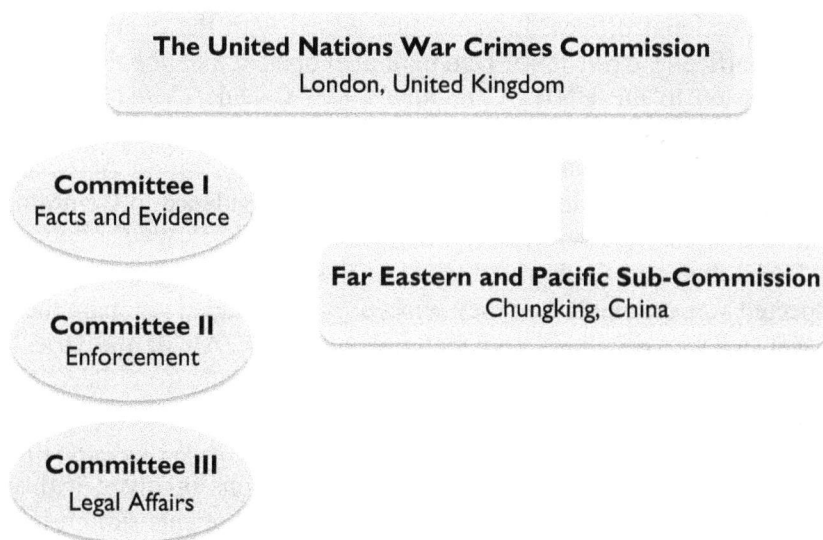

The United Nations War Crimes Commission
London, United Kingdom

Committee I
Facts and Evidence

Far Eastern and Pacific Sub-Commission
Chungking, China

Committee II
Enforcement

Committee III
Legal Affairs

Figure 1: The UNWCC Committee and Sub-Commission Structure

14.3.1. Committee I and the National Offices

Tasked with overseeing facts and evidence, Committee I collected evidence and information from the member states and evaluated charges on approximately 37,000 individuals who were suspected of being war criminals. Marcel de Baer from Belgium was appointed as the first chairman of Committee I upon its creation in 1944.

One of the first actions of Committee I was to propose that each member state designate national offices[35] which would serve to liaise between the UNWCC and its own national investigative and judicial bodies throughout the investigatory and trial processes. These offices were affiliated with the UNWCC but were formally official organs of their respective governments. In most cases, the national offices functioned under their respective ministries of justice.[36] The national offices worked throughout the duration of the operations of the UNWCC to co-ordinate investigations, collect evidence and prepare trials. When it was necessary, the national offices worked under the recommendations of the UNWCC to generate new legal structures to handle war crimes.[37]

Fifteen of the UNWCC member states joined the initial effort to establish national offices. Luxembourg joined with the opening of their national office in April 1945. Denmark also opened a national office after its admission to the UNWCC in June 1945. Canada closed its national office on May 28, 1946. Some of the national offices were transferred to their respective national capitals following the liberation of occupied countries, but their duties of reporting facts and evidence to Committee I continued through the national representatives to the UNWCC.[38]

Member states submitted cases to the UNWCC against alleged or suspected war criminals that they wished to be included amongst the lists of accused war criminals and material witnesses. All of the case files included details of the allegations as well as the evidence collected. The UNWCC recorded these cases and published all of the lists in their records. In addition to the documentation, the UNWCC, specifically Committee I, evaluated the evidence and allegations involved with each case in the presence of representatives of the governments submitting the

---

[35] *Ibid.*; United Nations War Crimes Commission, Minutes of Tenth Meeting Held On 22nd February 1944 ("Tenth Meeting") (http://www.legal-tools.org/doc/497f83/) and the accompanying "First Report of Committee I (Facts and Evidence) as Adopted by the Commission", C7 (1). A conference of all the national offices was held in London in May 1945. Also see United Nations War Crimes Commission, Minutes No. 60 Held On 10th May 1945 (http://www.legal-tools.org/en/doc/fed3f6/), Minutes No. 66 Held On 20th June 1945 (http://www.legal-tools.org/doc/455ef5/) and United Nations War Crimes Commission National Offices Conference held at The Royal Courts of Justice, London, 31 May–2 June 1945, minutes and documents.

[36] History of the UNWCC, p. 121, see *supra* note 1.

[37] The Netherlands laws for the trial of war criminals were enacted in 1943 and the French in 1944.

[38] History of the UNWCC, p. 121, see *supra* note 1.

---

charges and issued *prima facie* decisions on all of the cases that the national offices submitted to it following their investigation efforts. All decisions regarding the cases were made through an *ex parte* process.[39] The national offices were then tasked with either collecting further evidence in the cases where Committee I determined that insufficient proof existed or proceeded with trials with the cases approved by the UNWCC. All the national offices were encouraged to send summary trial reports to the UNWCC when prosecutions resulted. These were also recorded and published by Committee I in the wider UNWCC records.

While the national offices operated on a largely independent basis, they all reported about their investigations and progress directly to the main UNWCC headquarters in London. The UNWCC compiled lists of suspected war criminals based on the information coming from the national offices. Committee I worked to review the lists, starting in 1944 and concluding at the end of 1947 prior to the closing of the UNWCC. The main headquarters in London also convened a National Offices Conference in May and June 1945 to bring together the different representatives.[40] The conference served as a forum to discuss policy and practice of the different nations operating under the umbrella of the UNWCC concerning the pursuit and trial of war criminals. The papers produced from the conference included a number of municipal statutes for war crimes trials. As far as we are aware, the UNWCC conducted the only comparative analysis of the different national practices regarding war crimes policy to take place immediately following the Second World War. Some analysis of this comparative work is presented in a report that the UNWCC submitted to the UN in 1948.[41]

In addition to the national offices, some of the participating governments created war crimes commissions in their own countries. These commissions investigated alleged war crimes and also forwarded evidence and charges to the UNWCC in London. Yugoslavia was one of the first countries to do this, drafting regulations for a State Commission for Ascertaining the Crimes of the Occupying Forces in May 1944. In November 1944 the French Government instituted the *Service de recherche des crimes de guerre ennemis* in Paris.[42] Some European

---

[39] Some criticism of this is that it was based on hearsay evidence, a matter discussed by the UNWCC itself. See "Information Concerning Human Rights", *supra* note 16. We note that the colloquial sense of "hearsay" as gossip had been used to denigrate the work of the UNWCC as a whole. Also see the UN ARMS application package for the UNWCC.

governments-in-exile operating in London also worked to develop legislation for the creation of war crimes courts. For example, Belgium and the Netherlands both passed laws by August 1943 that created courts to try war crimes cases in their respective countries.[43]

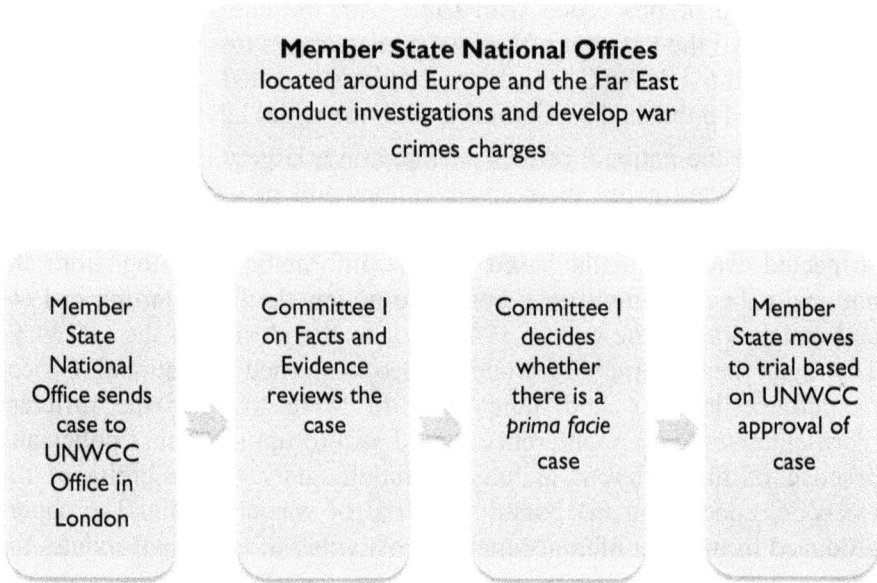

Member State National Offices
located around Europe and the Far East
conduct investigations and develop war
crimes charges

Member State National Office sends case to UNWCC Office in London	Committee I on Facts and Evidence reviews the case	Committee I decides whether there is a *prima facie* case	Member State moves to trial based on UNWCC approval of case

Figure 14: Core Process of UNWCC Investigation and Prosecution Operations

Supported by its committee structure, the UNWCC worked to assist the national offices in their investigations. It also investigated some cases on its own with the help of a small staff team in London that also liaised with governments through the national offices.[44]

---

40 Minutes and papers of the UNWCC National Offices Conference.
41 "Information Concerning Human Rights", pp. 125–45 and Appendix, see *supra* note 16.
42 History of the UNWCC, p. 123, see *supra* note 1.
43 E/CN.14-AM9 (1948) and Netherlands Extraordinary Penal Law Decree of 22 December 1943 (Statute Book D. 61) p. 130 and the Decrees of 22 December 1943 (Statute Book D. 62), p. 291.
44 UNWCC Internal Memo (18 Apr. 1945).

14.3.2. Committee II and the Military Tribunals

Committee II concerned enforcement, meaning all of the different measures that were considered necessary by the UNWCC to ensure the detection, apprehension, trial and punishment of people who were responsible for committing crimes in the Second World War. This committee supported all of the national offices and Committee I after it was initiated in the spring of 1944. It also worked closely with Committee III until it was eliminated and its duties were assumed by Committees I and III. The US Ambassador to Hungary, Herbert Pell,[45] led the efforts of Committee II to uphold the UNWCC's endorsement of a proposal for several enforcement mechanisms that surfaced early on in its work. The proposed mechanisms included a war crimes office in enemy territory[46] that contributed to the creation of the Central Registry of War Criminals and Security Suspects ('CROWCASS'), under the command of General Dwight D. Eisenhower, Supreme Commander of the Allied Expeditionary Force.[47] CROWCASS served to assist the UNWCC in tracing suspected war criminals. The plans also included a detailed proposal for mixed military tribunals under the major Allied commands. This was later adopted by many states.[48] In the case of Britain, these discussions within the UNWCC regarding how to bring accused war criminals to justice resulted in the issuing of the Royal Warrant and the creation of the British War Crimes Executive in July 1945.[49]

---

[45] For more information about Herbert Pell and his work at the UNWCC, see Graham Cox, "Seeking Justice for the Holocaust: Herbert C. Pell versus the US State Department", in *Criminal Law Forum*, 2014, vol. 25, nos. 1–2, pp. 77–110.

[46] United Nations War Crimes Commission, 21st mtg. at 3 (June 6, 1944) and the accompanying UNWCC Doc. C24 as well as United Nations War Crimes Commission, Minutes No. 22 Held On 13th June 1944 (http://www.legal-tools.org/doc/e28a9b/) and the accompanying UNWCC Doc. C30.

[47] United Nations War Crimes Commission, Minutes No. 32 Held On 19th September 1944 (http://www.legal-tools.org/doc/ea5649/). Also see UNWCC Doc. C 52(1) Recommendation in Favour of the Establishment by Supreme Military Commanders of Mixed Military Tribunals for the Trial of War Criminals.

[48] *Ibid.* The UNWCC approved the adoption of a proposal for a United Nations War Crimes Court (See the accompanying UNWCC Doc. C49, Doc. C50 and Doc. C58 Explanatory Memorandum).

[49] Memorandum from the Treasury Solicitors Office for the Attorney General, July 1945, pp. 1, 2, 4; The National Archives, UK ('TNA'), London, TS26, 897, pp. 27–33.

In its early years the UNWCC worked to assist some of the member states in designing and initiating the establishment of military tribunals. These tribunals served specifically to address complex situations that did not fit the realm of the national trials. One primary example reflected circumstances where the crimes investigated did not have specific geographic locations. Another example included crimes that were committed against Allied nationals in Germany and across parts of the Far East under various forms of colonial administration.[50] Military authorities (primarily from the US and Britain) aided their respective nations in both the investigations and also conducting the subsequent trials. This served in part so that trials could be conducted "without waiting for the initiative of any one Government on the matter".[51] Collectively, the participating Allied military authorities conducted a large number of trials across Europe and the Far East.[52] The commander-in-chief of the zone convened military trials and the judges were generally military officials. Most of the courts had a member with legal qualifications and in some cases the staff were assisted by lawyers representing the Judge Advocate General. There was no appeal option, but the commander-in-chief had the power to revise a case and sentence.[53]

The work and recommendations of Committee II directly influenced the creation and operation of the IMTs in Nuremberg and

---

[50] See the October 1945 *"Trial of Kapitänleutnant Heinz Eck and Four Others* accused of killing crewmembers of the Greek steamship *Peleus* in a British Military Court for the Trial of War Criminals" in United Nations War Crimes Commission, *Law Reports of Trials of War Criminals*, vol. 1, His Majesty's Stationery Office, London, 1947 ("Law Rerports").

[51] United Nations War Crimes Commission, Minutes No. 33 Held On 26th September 1944 (http://www.legal-tools.org/doc/c3c349/).

[52] The UNWCC's reliance on military authorities was in part due to its commitment to provide justice that was swift and effective. The meaning of this was debated among members throughout the existence of the UNWCC. The internal document "Recommendation in Favour of the Establishment by Supreme Military Commanders of Mixed Military Tribunals for the Trial of War Criminals" of 26 September 1944 declared that the strategy would be used in part "so that no criminals escape trial and punishment because of the inability to effect a speedy trial" (UNWCC Doc. C.52(1)). In hesitation, French representative André Gros addressed this idea in a written statement submitted at the UNWCC's thirty-first meeting on 12 September 1944. His first point stated, "Although the notion of swift justice is found in manuals of military law, 'justice' is something that does not admit of qualifying adjectives". Also see History of the UNWCC, p. 5, *supra* note 1.

[53] History of the UNWCC, p. 7, see *supra* note 1.

Tokyo as well as other international and inter-Allied tribunals that operated after the Second World War.[54]

14.3.3. Committee III

Committee III was created on 1 February 1944 and worked throughout the duration of the existence of the UNWCC to provide a forum for discussion and debate about concepts of international criminal law and develop recommendations for the member states. The active participation of key members of the exile governments greatly defined the work of Committee III, as it worked through complex legal questions from the member nations and ultimately produced decisions and recommendations to guide the practice of the national offices. Many of the questions focused on themes of jurisdiction, personal and collective responsibility, extradition, crimes against humanity, crimes against peace, the criminality of aggressive war, the protection of specific human rights and crimes committed by Axis governments against their own people. Committee III was not, however, empowered to make any decisions that were binding upon the UNWCC member governments. The work of Committee III is of particular interest in the study of state practice concerning the upholding of international criminal law under the focus themes.

When analysing the work of Committee III, it is important to acknowledge that some of the men who led the work of the committee had direct personal experience with Nazi crimes in their home countries, and that these experiences directly influenced their participation.[55]

14.3.4. The Far Eastern and Pacific Sub-Commission

At its founding meeting in 1943, Wellington Koo, the representative from China, suggested that a sub-commission be headquartered in the Far East to represent the UNWCC in the region and to conduct the work specifically related to crimes committed in the Far East. [56] The Far

---

[54] United Nations Archives, Predecessor Archives Group, "United Nations War Crimes Commission 1943–1949 Finding Aid", revised 1987, p. iii and History of the UNWCC, pp. 124, 454–57, see *supra* note 1.

[55] For more information about the representatives of the governments-in-exile to the UNWCC, see von Lingen, 2014, pp. 45–76, *supra* note 20.

[56] United Nations War Crimes Commission, Minutes No. 15 Held On 25th April 1944 (http://www.legal-tools.org/doc/14221b/); History of the UNWCC, p. 129, see *supra* note 1.

Eastern and Pacific Sub-Commission ('Sub-Commission') was created in June 1944 and its inaugural meeting held on 29 November 1944 in Chungking, then the capital of China. Wang Chung Hui was elected the first chairman. The Sub-Commission maintained its headquarters in Chungking until the Japanese surrendered, when it moved to Nanking.[57] It continued to operate through 1948 even after the London headquarters officially closed.[58] Approximately 90 per cent of the cases presented to the Sub-Commission came from the Chinese national office.[59] China went on to conduct war crimes tribunals in Nanking, Hangkow, Canton, Mukden, Taiyua, Peipine, Hsuchow, Tsinan, Shanghai and Formosa.[60] Eleven of the UNWCC member countries accepted the invitation to participation in the Sub-Commission.[61]

It is important to note that the participation of both China and India provided a substantial non-Western contribution to the work of the UNWCC overall. China took a leading role in the investigation and trial work conducted in the Far East through the Sub-Commission.[62] India, despite not being an independent state, had representation on the UNWCC and among the judges of some of the tribunals in the Far East.[63] India remained a member of the UNWCC after it gained independence in 1947.

14.3.5. General Operations and the Closing of the UNWCC

During its operations, Britain provided facilities for the UNWCC in London, first at the Royal Courts of Justice, and then at Church House from July 1945 to January 1946, and finally at Lansdowne House, Berkeley Square until its closure in 1948.[64] The administrative staff were both British and international. Additionally, all member states contributed

---

[57] History of the UNWCC, p. 13, see *supra* note 1.

[58] *Ibid.*, p. 129.

[59] *Ibid.*, p. 130.

[60] *Ibid.*, p. 516.

[61] The original countries included: Australia, Belgium, Britain, China, Czechoslovakia, France, India, Luxembourg, Netherlands, and the US. Poland was added subsequently. See *Ibid.*, p. 130.

[62] *Ibid.*

[63] Sir Samuel Runganadhan was India's first representative to the UNWCC, followed by Mr. Dutt.

[64] History of the UNWCC, p. 118, see *supra* note 1.

dues equally to provide all of the funding for the general operations including the salary of the chairman. The governments paid for the operations of their respective national offices and their national representatives to the UNWCC in London. [65] In 1944 the British Parliament passed a statute to outline the privileges, immunities and capacities of designated international organisations called the Diplomatic Privileges (Extension) Act. This applied to the UNWCC, and the specific immunities and privileges afforded to UNWCC members were further defined by an Order in Council, 1945 (S.R. & O., 1945, No. 1211).[66] Early in its work, it was decided that all members were entitled to vote on the proceedings of the UNWCC, and that the elected chairman was to place an additional vote in the case of a tie. All members were allowed to attend the meetings of any committee but only the committee's official members and the UNWCC's chairman could vote.[67]

National representatives began to discuss the closing of the UNWCC in the winter of 1947. The UNWCC ultimately concluded its work and closed its London headquarters in 1948. The national offices also began to cease operations at this time. While the exact reason for the abrupt closure of the UNWCC remains unclear, several scholars of the era argue that Britain and the US exerted strong pressure and influence in the matter of the closure[68] under their shared goal of rehabilitating Nazis into German society. [69] The UNWCC gives some insight into this in the introductory chapter of *History of the United Nations War Crimes Commission and the Development of the Laws of War* ('*History*'), when Lord Wright claimed "countries like the United States and Britain and the members of the British Commonwealth are now so overwhelmed by the crowd of problems consequent on the war, that they seem involuntarily to

---

[65] *Ibid.*, p. 116.

[66] *Ibid.*, p. 128.

[67] *Ibid.*, p. 120.

[68] We rely on Christopher Simpson's analysis of the closure of the UNWCC. He argues that the demise of the UNWCC was instigated by US officials in order to facilitate the rehabilitation of Nazis into the Western Zones of Germany. See Christopher Simpson, *The Splendid Blond Beast: Money, Law, and Genocide in the Twentieth Century*, Common Courage Press, Monroe, ME, 1995; Christopher Simpson, "Shutting Down the United Nations War Crimes Commission", in *Criminal Law Forum*, 2014, vol. 25, nos. 1–2, pp. pp. 133–46.

[69] Kerstin von Lingen, *Kesselring's Last Battle: War Crimes Trials and Cold War Politics, 1945–1960*, University Press of Kansas, Lawrence, 2009, pp. 72–75.

turn aside and forget war crimes".[70] Wright also said that he wrote personally to the US State Department requesting an extension for the US representative, Earl W. Kintner, specifically to allow him to conclude his task of documenting the work of the UNWCC in *History* and the Law Reports. Wright reported that the State Department "found themselves unable 'for budgetary reasons'".[71] Some of the nations resisted the closure, in particular the governments in exile.

Upon the closure of the London operations in 1948, the UNWCC gave its records that were deemed to be of historical value and importance to the United Nations. These archives included correspondence, meeting minutes from the general commission and the committees, trial summaries and charge files. Other documents deemed to not have historical value were destroyed. Most of the member states also gave documents from their work on the UNWCC to their respective national archives, including US, Britain and Australia, among others. The whereabouts of some documents remains unknown, including those documenting the work of several sub-committees and the first year and a half of Committee III's operations.

In the months leading up to the closure, the UNWCC Secretariat in London also prepared the UNWCC's official history and a 15-volume collection of national trials, *Law Reports of Trials of War Criminals*. They were both published by His Majesty's Stationery Office in London between late 1947 and 1949. While Wright led much of the drafting of *History*, Kintner played a key role in the editorship of the official history and wrote several important parts. He was aided by Elizabeth M. Goold-Adams (Belgium) and M. Cheyney, and also assisted by the Lieutenant Colonel H.H. Wade (Britain), Dr. J. Litawski (Poland), Dr. Radomir Živković (Yugoslavia), Dr. H. Mayr-Harting (Czechoslovakia) and G.A. Brand (Britain).[72] It is important to note that the reporting process was incomplete at the time that the UNWCC closed because many nations were not able to complete the processing and documentation of all of their respective trials in time for the reports and statistics to be included in the publications.

---

[70]   History of the UNWCC, p. 22, see *supra* note 1.

[71]   *Ibid.,* p. v.

[72]   *Ibid.*

In May 1948 the UNWCC also issued a report on the development of legal human rights standards both during and immediately following the Second World War. The report detailed the efforts of the different international criminal justice initiatives concerning human rights and also called for further research to be conducted into the war crimes trials at the end of the war by a range of academic disciplines.[73] This call for further research was also echoed in other UNWCC documentation. However, the UNWCC's intention to promote the study of its work and the accompanying national trials was largely futile. This was in large part because the entire UNWCC archive held by ARMS in New York was classified until 1987 when the rules of access were, in theory, loosened. But in practice the entire archive remained closed to public access until recently, with a few exceptions for select individuals approved through a lengthy vetting process.[74]

Following recent efforts,[75] all meeting minutes, correspondence and trial summary reports are available for public access through the International Criminal Court's ('ICC') Legal Tools Database.[76] Following a request from the US Government for a copy of the entire UNWCC archive,[77] it is now available in entirety to the public through the US Holocaust Memorial Museum.

---

[73] "Information Concerning Human Rights", p. vi, see *supra* note 16.

[74] In order to gain access to view the UNWCC archives at the United Nations Archives and Records Management Section, UN rules dictate that researchers must first write a letter to their national mission to the UN to explain their research and that it is "*bona fide*". The UN mission then must write a letter to the office of the UN Secretary-General who has the final approval. The US recently requested a copy of the entire UNWCC archive in partnership with the United States Holocaust Memorial Museum.

[75] The adjustment in the enforcement of the rules followed efforts of the War Crimes Project at the School of Oriental and African Studies, University of London to open the archives that started in the fall of 2011.

[76] See International Criminal Court (http://www.legal-tools.org/).

[77] In October 2013, in a speech at the Anti-Defamation League's National Commission Centennial Meeting, US Ambassador to the UN Samantha Power stated: "Remembrance is part of our agenda, too, which is why I am pleased to announce that the UN has agreed to make available to us a full copy of its War Crimes Commission Archives for transfer to Washington and the Holocaust Museum. This transfer will be of considerable benefit to scholars at a time when Holocaust denial is embraced by many who prefer diversionary fantasies to inconvenient facts. That general tendency – to ignore the hard lessons of the past – remains all too present in the world today. Even in the United States, according to the Justice Department, one hate crime is committed every hour". United States Mission to the United Nations, "Remarks by Ambassador Samantha Power, U.S. Permanent

14.4. The UNWCC's Role in the Development of International Criminal Law

The UNWCC's role in and contribution to the development of international criminal law can be summarised by the fact that it was the first multilateral initiative in the modern period to successfully conduct widespread investigations into crimes of war, and to provide structure and support to nations to prosecute suspected war criminals. This amounts to something remarkable.

It is important to recognise that though the duration of the UNWCC's operations was relatively short-lived, at less than five years, the operational period was longer than the IMTs in Nuremberg and Tokyo as well as other military tribunals of that era. The work of the UNWCC also amounts to a significant and substantial collection of state practice on issues related to international criminal law. Nations that conducted national military and/or municipal tribunals relied heavily on the UNWCC to provide approval for their investigations and charges against suspected war criminals before bringing cases to trial. It is also notable that state members accorded the UNWCC diplomatic status and contributed jointly to its operations, most significantly the operations of the Secretariat in London. Moreover, through the work of Committee III and the collaborative structure of the UNWCC, the national representatives adopted shared positions that were at times at odds with the policy of their national governments.

Viewed by the number of investigations and trials conducted, it is clear that the scale of the UNWCC's work is significantly greater than that of the IMTs as well as the *ad hoc* tribunals in existence today. Numbers aside, the work of the UNWCC also represents a rare example of constructive action and mobilisation for justice between nations and in times of active war. This action was a direct result of the urgency felt by the member countries, in particular the influence of the exiled governments in this regard. It was this urgency that prompted the Big Powers of the US and Britain in particular to heed to the proposals of the state members of the UNWCC to participate actively.[78] The practice of quick mobilisation of multilateral collaboration in support of national

---

Representative to the United Nations, At the Anti-Defamation League's National Commission Centennial Meeting, October 31, 2013", New York, 2013.

[78] Kochavi, 1998, p. 4, see *supra* note 5.

investigations stands in direct contrast to the international criminal law efforts initiated in the 1990s following the Cold War.

Another major contrast to the international criminal tribunals in operation today, as well as the ICC, is the UNWCC's success in facilitating trials that were quick and financially efficient. This was also a direct result of the overwhelming sense of urgency felt by many of the UNWCC member states during the period of operation. Indeed, during the initial discussions on designing the UNWCC structure and operations, Eden specifically noted the importance of trying and punishing suspects immediately after the war. He argued that this was in part to ensure rapid justice for the well-being of all survivors and victims of the crimes but also to prevent citizens from taking the law into their own hands. Eden and the UNWCC acted on the desire to avoid prolonged trials that would ultimately delay the process of restoring civil peace in Europe and the Far East.[79]

Viewed in the context of the current tribunals, the numbers that accompany the UNWCC's operations are startling. Some of the most complete records of the number of trials and people investigated are available in *History*. By the time it was published in 1948, the UNWCC reported that 36,529 individuals and units had been charged by the governments and included in the Committee I lists,[80] and that the UNWCC had received 8,178 cases from the member governments.[81] The official history also reported that 3,028 "war criminals and material witnesses" were included in the lists of the Sub-Commission.[82] Official reports and charge files also confirmed that governments that were not members of the UNWCC, such as Bulgaria, also submitted cases against individuals for review.

The UNWCC also reported in *History* on the approximately 2,000 associated trials that took place around Europe and the Far East between late 1945 and March 1948, specifically stating that the trials involved approximately 25,000 individuals. More than one defendant was involved in many of the UNWCC-supported trials. *History* also detailed the verdicts and outcomes of the trials. It documented that 24,000 "minor"

---

[79] *Ibid.*, p. 30.
[80] History of the UNWCC, p. 509, see *supra* note 1.
[81] *Ibid.*, p. 508.
[82] *Ibid.*, p. 514.

criminals received death sentences or imprisonment,[83] and that 5,193 individuals were acquitted. It is also important to note that 148 cases were "not accepted"[84] by Committee I due to insufficient evidence presented to justify a prosecution of the persons or units charged.[85] In most of the cases, Committee I asked the national offices to present more evidence for further consideration instead of dropping the case immediately. This was pursued in some instances.

14.5. Key Structural Aspects of the UNWCC

The analysis of the UNWCC's structure and work provides significant insight into the practice of different key states in the international arena as well as the development of modern international criminal law. Here we examine two specific themes: the relationship between the UNWCC and the national trials; and a comparison of the cost and time structures between the UNWCC and the current tribunals.

14.5.1. The Relationship between the UNWCC and the National Trials

As we have described it throughout this chapter, the UNWCC was an international body formed and run by its member governments. *History* states that its character as an international organisation and intergovernmental agency "has never been doubted".[86] However, the relationship between the UNWCC and the member nations and their national trials is not clear in modern scholarship and often misunderstood. While the actual UNWCC is regularly overlooked in legal and historical writings about the Second World War period, some of the trials conducted by the different nations have received substantial attention. However, these trials are often not recognised to be part of the large effort of the UNWCC. Here we outline the relationship between the UNWCC and the nations in more detail and highlight some of the commonly referenced trials.

---

83   *Ibid.*, p. 518.
84   *Ibid.*
85   *Ibid.*, p. 531.
86   *Ibid.*, p. 127.

The UNWCC outlined this relationship fairly thoroughly in the introductory chapter of *History*. The authors detail the preparatory work completed by the UNWCC members to be ready to conduct legitimate trials following the end of the war, stating clearly that the work conducted in 1944 and 1945 was of prime importance even though the ideas and plans that were elaborated by the UNWCC at that time were not yet published. It was during this time that representatives were determining the structure of the UNWCC and communicating ideas with their respective nations. Ultimately, "the plan of this great machinery for the enforcement of law was sufficiently ready when the time came".[87]

As we have noted, the structure and practice that was agreed upon during the preparatory period of 1944–1945 was that the UNWCC would operate as a Secretariat and umbrella agency in London, with the national offices operating to address investigatory and prosecution needs in the areas directly affected by conflict around Europe and the Far East. There was extensive communication between the national offices and the UNWCC, directed by the representatives for all of the nations that were based in London. A central part of this communication and the relationship between the UNWCC and the national offices was the work of Committee I. Committee I supported all of the national and military efforts through its role in examining evidence and each case in its entirety. The national and military officers acted directly on the basis of the recommendations and decisions of Committee I. The committee contributed significantly to each trial conducted and to the examination of the actions and guilt of each of the 36,800 individuals recorded in the lists. The UNWCC also facilitated the national process of amending and adapting national laws to suit the international scale of the crimes.

To further assist the national offices in the work, the UNWCC convened a National Office Conference in May 1945. This Conference was generally regarded as being useful and ultimately a success. The staff of the national offices worked on the difficult tasks of tracing and detecting criminals. Some teams of national investigatory staff were located in headquarters in the key zones but travelled as was necessary to carry out their work and collect information.

The many military trials that took place in cases involving for example complex geographic locations, groups of victims that represented

---

[87] *Ibid.*, p. 4.

multiple nationalities and crimes committed inside Germany and occupied territories were also supported directly by the UNWCC through the members of the nations representing each of the militaries.

With the process for prosecutions well outlined in advance and supported by thorough investigations, the UNWCC member nations and some militaries began trials in 1945. The US and Britain led the effort with the conducting of the Hadamar, *Peleus* and Belsen trials. These trials covered topics ranging from the murder of hundreds of people by drugs in a medical institution (Hadamar), the murder of the survivors of a torpedoed ship (*Peleus*) and murder and abuse of thousands of people in a concentration camp, including by poisonous gas (Belsen).

The Hadamar trial (*United States v. Alfons Klein et al.*) took place on 8–15 October 1945 in Wiesbaden, Germany to address crimes of the euthanasia facility found in western Germany. The accused individuals were staff members of a medical facility in Hadamar who were suspected of taking part in intentional killing of thousands of individuals by injection of poisonous drugs.[88] A commission of US military officials was granted the power to conduct the trial. The suspected war criminals pleaded a defence of superior orders, and were all found guilty. Three were sentenced to death by hanging, one to life imprisonment and the remaining three to imprisonment of 35, 30 and 20 years. The Hadamar trial is commonly referenced as the instigator of precedent regarding the practice of euthanasia and crimes against humanity. While the trial is discussed in various scholarly accounts that focused on the Second World War, including by the United States Holocaust Memorial Museum, it is rarely, if ever, connected to the UNWCC.[89]

The *Peleus* trial ("Trial of Kapitänleutnant Heinz Eck and Four Others for the Killing of Members of the Crew of the Greek Steamship Peleus, Sunk on the High Seas") was conducted by a British Military Court in Hamburg on 17–20 October 1945. The trial examined the killing of survivors of a sunken Allied ship on the night of 13/14 March 1944 in the Atlantic Ocean. Firing and throwing grenades, the crew of the German submarine sunk the Greek steamship and proceeded to attempt to kill the surviving members of the crew. Five crew members who survived the attack were called as witnesses. The court acknowledged the complexity

---

[88] "Law Reports", 1947, p. 46, see *supra* note 50.

[89] *Ibid.*, pp. 46–51.

of the matters facing them in the context of international law established at that time, considering in particular the location of the crime and the aggression against defenceless individuals. All of the accused were found guilty.[90] This trial is also referenced for its focus on the defence of superior orders, which signifies a lawful command and law of complex geographic locations. It is generally credited to the British military without reference to the UNWCC for its influence in the legal recommendations that influenced the case.

While not often immediately evident, this system of the UNWCC and the nations operating through their national offices, and in some cases their militaries, supported approximately 2,000 trials. Ultimately between late 1945 and March 1948, approximately 1,000 cases were tried in Europe involving the sentencing of approximately 2,700 individuals identified to be "minor" or mid-level criminals. A comparable number of individuals were tried during this same time period in the Far East.[91] Many of these trials involved a small number of mid-level defendants and did not receive much attention. However, some have been cited extensively in legal and historical writings, but often without reference to the UNWCC.

The number of cases tried by the nations working under the umbrella of the UNWCC and supported by the foundational work conducted through multilateral co-operation between 1943 and 1945 was unprecedented at the time and remains so today in terms of both numbers and also geographic scope and diversity of the crimes addressed. The lack of documentation of the connection between the UNWCC and these national military trials creates an incomplete picture of international justice in the wake of the Second World War, and also restricts the continued study of the UNWCC and this unique but effective system. This is likely due to various reasons, not least the difficulties faced by the national offices and thus the UNWCC in documenting their investigation efforts during the war and trials after the end of the war. As the documentation from the UNWCC and the national trials becomes more available, it is likely that the connection between each of the trials and the UNWCC will be better articulated. The model deserves further study and analysis.

---

[90] *Ibid.*, pp. 1–21.
[91] History of the UNWCC, p. 4, see *supra* note 1.

14.5.2. Trial Duration and Operational Costs

A ubiquitous criticism of the *ad hoc* tribunals currently in operation, as well as the ICC, is the prolonged duration of their respective investigations and trial proceedings as well as the astronomical costs associated with their operations. Here we explore the trial lengths and operational costs of the UNWCC and offer points of comparison with the contemporary context.

14.5.2.1. Investigation and Trial Duration

The difference between the UNWCC and current war crimes trials in the duration of the proceedings is stark. A key feature of the UNWCC was that it completed its tasks swiftly. *History* states: "It was widely felt that justice should not be delayed"[92] as "delay will mean escape of the guilty".[93] By 1948, when the UNWCC ceased operations, 8,178 cases had been examined, as a result of the thousands of investigations conducted by the national offices.[94] Following preparatory work and the submission of charge files to the UNWCC and their subsequent approval, most UNWCC-supported trials lasted between four and five days,[95] while other cases that were more complex lasted three to six weeks.[96]

This is in direct contrast to the current trials that take many years. For example, Bosnian Serb Army officer Vidoje Blagojević was convicted by the ICTY in May 2007 after a trial lasting 17 months on charges of direct involvement in the Srebrenica massacre.[97] Senior-level officials Milomir Stakić and Goran Jelisić were found guilty of crimes against humanity and other serious violations of international humanitarian law after trials lasting approximately one year.[98] At the ICTR in Arusha, Jean-Paul Akayesu was found guilty of genocide and

---

[92] *Ibid.*, p. 4.

[93] *Ibid.*, p. 109.

[94] *Ibid.*, p. 484.

[95] See the *Peleus* Trial that lasted from 17–20 October 1945; "Law Reports", *supra* note 50.

[96] *Ibid.* See for example the Belsen Trials that lasted for a total of 54 days in court.

[97] International Criminal Tribunal for the former Yugoslavia, *The Prosecutor v. Blagojević and Jokić*, Judgment, 9 May 2007, IT-02-60-A (http://www.legal-tools.org/doc/7483f2/).

[98] International Criminal Tribunal for the former Yugoslavia, *The Prosecutor v. "Brecko" Goran Jelisić*, 19 October 1999, IT-95-10-T (http://www.legal-tools.org/en/go-to-database/record/7483f2/).

crimes against humanity after a two-year trial.[99] Following a trial at the Special Court for Sierra Leone ('SCSL') lasting nearly four years, the Revolutionary United Front senior officer and commander Issa Sesay was found guilty of crimes against humanity and other serious violations of international humanitarian law.[100] On 26 July 2010, 17 months after his trial at the Extraordinary Chambers in the Courts of Cambodia ('ECCC') began, the former Khmer Rouge leader, Kaing Guek Eav (alias Duch), was found guilty of crimes against humanity and grave breaches of the Geneva Conventions of 1949. [101] Prolonged lengths of trials and proceedings have significant implications for high operating costs for the tribunals as well.

14.5.2.2. Operational Costs

Wright frequently stated that the UNWCC was the least expensive international commission known in history. If that were in fact the case in the 1940s, it is very likely that his statement remains true today. The UNWCC reported its annual expenditures as follows: 10 October 1943– 31 March 1944 (£730), 1 April 1944–31 March 1945 (£4,238), 1 April 1945–31 March 1946 (£12,462), 1 April 1946–31 March 1947 (£15,137), and 1 April 1947–31 March 1948 (£15,388).[102] Adjusted for inflation, these totals amount respectively to: £28,215, £163,806, £469,014, £552,561 and £524,975, totalling £1,738,573[103] (US$2,927,510) in 2014 values.

In contrast, the former Assistant Prosecutor at the ECCC, Stuart Ford, estimates that the international community will have spent approximately US$6.3 billion on the international courts[104] in operation

---

[99] The International Criminal Tribunal for Rwanda, *The Prosecutor v. Jean-Paul Akayesui*, 2 September 1998, 96-4-T (http://www.legal-tools.org/en/go-to-database/record/b8d7bd/).

[100] The Special Court for Sierra Leone, *The Prosecutor v. Sesay, Kallon and Gbao (RUF case)* (Case 15), 2 March 2009, SCSL-04-15 (http://www.legal-tools.org/doc/7f05b7/).

[101] The Extraordinary Chambers in the Courts of Cambodia, *The Prosecutor v. Guek Eav Kaing, alias 'Duch'* (Case 001) 26 July 2010, 001/18-07-2007 (http://www.legal-tools.org/doc/dbdb62/).

[102] History of the UNWCC, p. 134, see *supra* note 1.

[103] Historical inflation rates were calculated through the online tool at This is Money.

[104] Under the term "international courts", Ford includes the ICC, ICTY, the SCSL and the ECCC.

---

since 1993 by the time most of them close in 2015.[105] By the end of 2010 the international community had already spent more than $4.7 billion.[106] Ford also estimates that the ICTY will be the most expensive international criminal tribunal, spending approximately US$2.3 billion during its lifetime, followed by the ICTR at US$1.75 billion, the ECCC at US$338 million and the SCSL at US$275 million. He claims that the ICC will spend an estimated $1.6 billion by 2015.[107] If broken down by dollars per verdict, the figures of the current international criminal courts and tribunals are staggering, and raise the question of how much justice is worth.[108] The ICTY recognises that its budget is not small, but states:

> [T]he expense of bringing to justice those most responsible for war crimes and helping strengthen the rule of law in the former Yugoslavia pales in comparison to the cost of the crimes. The lives lost, the communities devastated, the private property ransacked and the cultural monuments and buildings destroyed, as well as the peace-keeping efforts by the international community are incomparably more expensive.[109]

The structure and operations of the UNWCC, and their total cost in today's figures, suggest that it is possible to achieve justice without prolonged proceedings and the astronomical costs that accompany them. This subject requires further research and analysis as well as assessment in the contemporary context.

14.6. Criticisms of the UNWCC and its Legacy

As with present-day international criminal justice initiatives, the UNWCC was and continues to be subject to theoretical, practical and socially-based scrutiny of its work and also its legacy. In this section we review key criticisms of the UNWCC that surfaced during its years of operation and continue to mark it since its closure. We also review the primary legacies

---

[105] Stuart Ford, "How Leadership in International Criminal Law is Shifting from the U.S. to Europe and Asia: An Analysis of Spending on and Contributions to International Criminal Courts", in *Saint Louis University Law Journal*, 2011, vol. 55, p. 956.

[106] *Ibid.*, p. 960.

[107] *Ibid.*, pp. 960–61.

[108] Dan Plesch and Shanti Sattler, "70 Years of Evolution in Prosecuting War Crimes", in Irwin Arieff (ed.), *A Global Agenda: Issues Before the United Nations 2011–2012*, United Nations Association of the USA, New York, 2011; Silverman, 2012, see *supra* note 8.

[109] ICTY Official Website, "The Cost of Justice".

of the UNWCC both in an independent sense and also in the context of the contemporary field of international criminal law.

14.6.1. Criticisms of the UNWCC

Perhaps the most common criticism of the UNWCC was based on the fact that it was limited in power and scope. This frustrated some members of the public and civil society at a time when there were widespread demands for significant action from governments.[110] Specific concerns around this issue focused on the fact that the UNWCC was not a comprehensive system of law and order in that it could not act directly to apprehend suspects and execute trials to bring them to justice. A subsequent criticism was that of inconsistencies between the practices of each member nation. This was also a reflection of the different economic and political capacities of each country in the final years of the war and its immediate aftermath. There has also been criticism of the nature of the legal processes employed by the different countries as they operated under the umbrella of the UNWCC. Questions have arisen about the general lack of appeal options for people convicted in the trials as well as quick pace of the investigative and judicial processes.

Along with the IMTs, the UNWCC is also criticised as exemplifying victors' justice. However, this should be examined in context. If there had been no victory for the Allies then no trials would have been conducted and thus no justice would have been achieved. Events show that all of the states concerned with fighting impunity for the crimes of the Second World War focused political and economic capital on this issue from the St James's Declaration onwards. Collectively, the Allies rejected mob rule and formally warned the enemy they would be placed on trial. The efforts of countries to participate in the design and operation of the UNWCC show that they chose to subject their national prosecutions to international approval, and based this process on constructed standards of evidence and recommendations derived from multilateral dialogue that decided what was and was not an international crime. The fact that the UNWCC rejected some proposed prosecutions due to insufficient evidence also suggests an attempt to conduct a fair

---

[110] History of the UNWCC, pp. 3–4, see *supra* note 1 for the UNWCC's response to this specific criticism.

process, as does its record of acquitting a significant number of defendants.

When assessing the effectiveness of the UNWCC to bring about fair investigations and justice for war crimes it is important to consider the context under which the nations were operating. Their efforts were marked by a sense of urgency to act both boldly and quickly. Politically, the context was marked not only by the war itself but also the early dynamics of what eventually became the Cold War. A clear indication of this was the Soviet Union's refusal to join the UNWCC and its establishment of an independent entity to investigate and prosecute suspected war criminals. The power politics of the US and British governments clearly grew in intensity and scope throughout the life of the UNWCC, creating difficulties for its operation which ultimately contributed to its closure.[111]

Other criticisms related to the multilateral nature of the UNWCC's work as well as the complexity of conducting interventions in times of serious conflict. For example, one criticism was a lack of transparency in its work and the limited access granted to the media to cover the proceedings. This was directly linked to security issues concerning the timing and scale of its work.

The hasty and premature closure of the UNWCC was also a source of discontent for critics and supporters alike. The closure exposed the political influences of the larger powers and generated confusion and criticism at the time and also into the future. The closure affected the documentation of the UNWCC's work severely, most notably as it led to incomplete recording of statistics about both the national and military trials conducted in Europe and the Far East as well as the number of people involved in investigations as suspects, witnesses and victims.

14.6.2. The Legacy of the UNWCC

The overarching legacy of the UNWCC is its success in instigating pivotal theoretical development of international criminal law and accompanying practical action. While largely overlooked by modern legal proceedings, the work of the UNWCC offers a valuable legacy of expansive legal precedent on a range of issues of international criminal

---

[111] Cox, 2014, pp. 77–110, see *supra* note 45; Simpson, 2014, pp. 133–46, see *supra* note 68.

and humanitarian law. A part of this legacy is its unique focus on holding mid-level criminals to justice as opposed to the current practice of focusing on the leaders of mass atrocities and those most responsible. Another key part of this legacy is the sheer number of trials conducted through efforts supported by the UNWCC.

The success of the UNWCC in following through with action is especially important when compared with the largely unsuccessful efforts by some of the same nations to initiate international criminal justice efforts following the First World War. The UNWCC, along with the IMTs at Nuremberg and Tokyo, deserves credit for the fact that trials and punishment are common practice in international criminal law 70 years later. It is also important to recognise that the standard of working to afford a fair trial to suspected war criminals is also strived for today.

Another inheritance of the UNWCC is found in the example it set for effective multilateral collaboration and action. Its work serves as evidence that nations of varying size and power came together under a common goal through regular dialogue and action on various issues of shared interest.

Importantly, another key bequest of the UNWCC was its direct influence on the development of the Nuremberg Charter in the summer of 1945 and subsequently the proceedings at Nuremberg and Tokyo. The support given to the IMTs provided by the UNWCC is, however, rarely acknowledged in the modern literature concerning this period. Meeting minutes of Committee III confirm this support as they provide details on several visits by Justice Robert Jackson to the UNWCC in London, and quote him thanking the UNWCC for its work and citing specific issues debated by the UNWCC and subsequent decisions on legal matters that he planned to adopt at Nuremberg.[112]

Several of the UNWCC's actions related to the advancement of women and nations representing the Global South are also notable legacies of its work. More research is needed into both of these topics, but it is clear that there were several instances of women serving as active representatives of their governments in both general sessions and committee meetings. Reports, documents and photographs show that

---

[112] For more information about the UNWCC's contribution to the Nuremberg trials, see "Developments in the Concept and Procedure of Trying War Criminals", History of the UNWCC, 1948, pp. 435–76, see *supra* note 1.

women represented the governments of Belgium, France and Norway at different times towards the end of the UNWCC's operations.[113] Meeting minutes also reveal that China and India were active participants in all aspects of the UNWCC's operations. Both held consistent representation in the general sessions as well as the committees, and provided substantial contributions in discussions and decision-making. China obviously directed most of the investigation and trials efforts by the UNWCC in the Far East through its leadership of the Sub-Commission.[114] India also had representation on the UNWCC from the beginning of its operations and remained active even after it gained independence in 1947, despite not being an independent state for most of the duration of the UNWCC. Indian judges also participated in some of the tribunals in the Far East.

14.7. Conclusion

It is important to consider the work of the UNWCC and its contribution to the origins and development of international criminal law. It instigated monumental advances through the dedicated work of the member states both during and after the Second World War. Further research into the work of the UNWCC is necessary to continue to determine its legacy and contribution to the historical origins of international criminal and humanitarian law and its relevance to contemporary legal proceedings and international criminal justice initiatives.

The UNWCC itself also heeded the call for further investigation and consideration of its legacy. In *History*, the UNWCC declares: "Now at the conclusion of this cataclysmic struggle there has been occasion for the growth of immensely far reaching new principles and rules of war. But their true meaning and importance [of the UNWCC's work] will involve much thought and research".[115] It is time to introduce that work and the work of each of its member states into the historical and contemporary narratives around international criminal and humanitarian law. Such research would inevitably reveal new precedents related to the

---

[113] See Committee on Facts and Evidence ('Committee I'), Minutes No. 67 Held on 19th July 1946 (http://www.legal-tools.org/doc/ac4703/). France's Claude Capiomont and Norway's Miss Raag are listed as "Members of the Commission, not members of Committee I, and Representatives of the National Offices".

[114] History of the UNWCC, p. 130, see *supra* note 1.

[115] *Ibid.*, p. i.

work of the UNWCC and the state practice of the member nations, as well as important knowledge that could be relevant to contemporary proceedings and processes in the complex investigation and prosecution of war crimes.

15

Defining Crimes Against Humanity: The Contribution of the United Nations War Crimes Commission to International Criminal Law, 1944–1947

Kerstin von Lingen[*]

15.1. Introduction

Until the Second World War, legal theory provided that war crime trials could involve only atrocities which had been committed in a state's own territory or against its own nationals.[1] However, many crimes perpetrated by the Axis Powers in the Second World War were of a novel nature, either attacking minorities of their own state or annexing territories without even declaring war at all. As these crimes did not fall within the hitherto accepted notion of war crimes, the call for a new definition of war crimes was already being discussed during wartime, and the need to form an internationally accepted standard in dealing with mass atrocities was advocated. One result of the political impact of these debates was the foundation of the United Nations War Crimes Commission ('UNWCC') in 1943, which assumed its duties in early 1944.[2] It formed an

[*] **Kerstin von Lingen** is Independent Research Group leader and Postdoctoral Researcher/Lecturer in History at Heidelberg University within the Cluster of Excellence "Asia and Europe in a Global Context". The group is entitled "Transcultural Justice: Legal Flows and the Emergence of International Justice within the East Asian War Crimes Trials, 1946–1954". She is the author of *Kesselring's Last Battle: War Crimes Trials and Cold War Politics, 1945–1960*, University of Kansas Press, Lawrence, 2009, and the editor of the volume *Kriegserfahrung und nationale Identität in Europa nach 1945* [Memory of War and National Identity in Europe after 1945], Schoeningh, Paderborn, 2009. Her most recent book, *Allen Dulles, the OSS and Nazi War Criminals: The Dynamics of Selective Prosecution*, Cambridge University Press, Cambridge, 2013, examines Nazi war criminals' protection through Allied intelligence services.

[1] Arieh J. Kochavi, "Britain and the Establishment of the United Nations War Crimes Commission", in *English Historical Review*, 1992, vol. 107, no. 423, p. 325.

[2] For an overview of the UNWCC, see Dan Plesch, *America, Hitler and the UN: How the Allies Won World War II and Forged a Peace*, I.B. Tauris, London, 2011; and Dan Plesch and Shanti Sattler, "A New Paradigm of Customary International Criminal Law: The UN

internationally accepted advisory body and was concerned with formulating a minimum standard in dealing with mass atrocities while the war still raged. It brought together legal scholars from different countries, among them most prominently from the European exile governments, and furthered discussions about justice for war crimes.

When assessing the concepts that emerged from these debates, the notion of 'crimes against humanity' – as laid down within the London Charter for the International Military Tribunal at Nuremberg in 1945 – is one of the results of debates within the UNWCC and its predecessors that still has significance today.[3] The concept of crimes against humanity confirmed that "citizens are under protection of international law even when they are victimized by their own compatriots".[4] As a legal tool, it is among the most known and has acquired "enormous resonance in the legal and moral imaginations of the post-World War II world".[5]

It is less known that the term 'crimes against humanity' was not an invention of the tribunal at Nuremberg,[6] but it was likely to have been already defined in various legal commissions during the war years in Britain. This chapter argues how the UNWCC's Legal Committee, based in London and chaired by the Czech representative Bohuslav Ečer (1893–1954) and with Egon Schwelb (1899–1979) as its influential secretary, played a key role in codifying this concept and thus broadened international criminal law in general. The first appearance of the term in the Charter for the Nuremberg Tribunal ('Nuremberg Charter'), set up during the London Conference in the summer of 1945, seemed to follow in large part the recommendations of the legal circles around the UNWCC, although it is not completely possible to prove the link between Justice Robert Jackson advocating the term during the conference,[7] and the

---

War Crimes Commission of 1943–1948 and Its Associated Courts and Tribunals", in *Criminal Law Forum*, 2014, vol. 25, nos. 1–2, pp. 17–43.

3   For an overview on the history of the term, see Geoffrey Robertson, *Crimes Against Humanity: The Struggle for Global Justice*, Allen Lane, New York, 1999.

4   Beth Van Schaack, "The Definition of Crimes Against Humanity: Resolving the Incoherence", in *Columbia Journal of Transnational Law*, 1998/99, vol. 37, p. 791.

5   David Luban, "A Theory of Crimes Against Humanity", in *Yale Journal of International Law*, 2004, vol. 29, no. 85, p. 86.

6   *Ibid.*, p. 86, where Luban points out that "no record exists of how the term crimes against humanity came to be chosen by the framers of the Nuremberg Charter", see *supra* note 5.

7   Robert Jackson, in his report to the government as well as in the conference session of 2 August 1945, is cited: "I may say that the term was suggested to me by an eminent scholar

earlier works of both the London International Assembly ('LIA') and the
UNWCC, as no written record exists. It is very feasible that Hersch
Lauterpacht could be the missing link,[8] as he convened with Jackson
before the London Conference and proposed the term.[9] However, this
chapter argues that by suggesting the term to a powerful conference
member, to whom the lawyers from smaller European exile communities
had no access, Lauterpacht might have summed up the ongoing debates
he had had with his colleagues in various legal circles over the previous
three years, where he was a member together with Ečer and Schwelb.
This argument is further bolstered by the fact that Lauterpacht, in his
earlier memorandum on the "Punishment of War Crimes" given to the
LIA in 1942, had not mentioned the term 'crimes against humanity' at
all.[10]

The time was ripe to finally codify the concept, which had been
debated for many years already, "because it was feared that under the
traditional formulation of war crimes, many of the acts of the Nazis would
go unpunished".[11] It attempted to address such diverse crimes as the
persecution of political opponents, including Communists and Social
Democrats within Germany, the persecution of German Jews, and the
crimes committed against occupied civilians like the Czechs during the
so-called Sudetenland crisis in 1938. Further, the concept was equally

---

[8]   of international law", in Robert H. Jackson, *Report of Robert H. Jackson United States
Representative to the International Conference on Military Trials*, London, 1945, part
LIX, Minutes of Conference Session of 2 August 1945, p. 416.

[8]   Maarti Koskenniemi, *The Gentle Civilizer of Nations: The Rise and Fall of International
Law 1870–1960*, Cambridge University Press, Cambridge, 2001, draws on Lauterpacht's
decisive role within the British prosecution, for which he drafted the opening and closing
speeches. See the chapter "Lauterpacht: The Victorian tradition in international law", pp.
388–89.

[9]   William Schabas strongly underlines the fact that an eminent academic, whom he
identifies as Lauterpacht, had suggested the term to Jackson. See William Schabas,
Unimaginable Atrocities: Justice, Politics and Rights at the War Crimes Tribunals, Oxford
University Press, Oxford, 2012, p. 51; this claim is underscored by Elihu Lauterpacht, *The
Life of Hersch Lauterpacht*, Cambridge University Press, Cambridge, 2010, p. 272.

[10]   National Archives UK, LCO 2/ 2973, Papers of the Cambridge Commission, Committee
of Crimes against International Public Order, Memorandum of H. Lauterpacht on
'Punishment of War Crimes', 52 pages, n.d. but probably July 1942.

[11]   Van Schaack, 1998/99, p. 789, see *supra* note 4. M. Cherif Bassiouni also observes that
the term 'crimes against humanity' was the "product of exigent historical circumstances";
see M. Cherif Bassiouni, "'Crimes Against Humanity': The Need for a Specialized
Convention", in *Columbia Journal of Transnational Law*, 1994, vol. 31, no. 3, p. 472.

applicable for crimes committed against Chinese nationals by Japanese troops in Manchuria in 1932. All these were crimes committed by a state against its own citizens, on its own territory, prior to an official state of war. In short, statutory definitions of crimes against humanity underline "that they criminalize atrocities and severe persecutions inflicted on civilian populations as part of an organized plan by a state or a state-like organization".[12] While the war still raged, the Allies, after the discovery of countless atrocities by the Axis Powers, found themselves under tremendous public pressure to speedily hold those responsible for the atrocities to account. Thus they desired a joint international tribunal to set a new legal precedent, in order to constitute a "building block for the evolution and development of international criminal law".[13] To cite William Schabas, what was new in Nuremberg was "a genuine and determined attempt to hold individuals criminally accountable for such behaviour", meaning, "atrocities [which] went beyond the sovereign authority of states", even "if it had not previously been codified in a formal sense".[14]

However, during the trials of the Nuremberg era, the concept of crimes against humanity did not manifest itself in the full meaning as it has today. Rather, it became bound to the conventional concept of war crimes at the time. The term appeared first in UNWCC meetings in 1944 and was coined to address criminal responsibility of the Nazi leaders for internal atrocities, mainly against German Jews, but – for the sake of legal expediency and in order to avoid criticism of retroactive law – it had then been associated with one of the other two criminal concepts, as war crimes and crimes against peace.[15] This formed a nexus between crimes against humanity and international armed conflict, which was initially not intended, but seen during the Nuremberg era as the only way to make it judiciable and to incorporate it into national jurisdictions. As Schabas observes, this "restrictive terminology requiring a nexus with armed conflict continues to haunt the international prosecution of human rights atrocities, many of which are actually committed during peacetime".[16]

---

[12] Luban, 2004, p. 91, see *supra* note 5.

[13] Bassiouni, 1994, p. 472, see *supra* note 11.

[14] Schabas, 2012, p. 53, see *supra* note 9.

[15] William Schabas, *An Introduction to the International Criminal Court*, Cambridge University Press, Cambridge, 2011, p. 42.

[16] *Ibid.*

The Charter, which set the frame for the International Military
Tribunal ('IMT') at Nuremberg, was set up at a conference in London
during the summer of 1945. It gave a first definition of the term in Article
6(c), stating that crimes against humanity should address prohibited acts
committed against a civilian population. [17] It responded thus to the
"horrific novelty of the twentieth century: politically organized
persecution and slaughter of people under one's own political control".[18]
Thus, for the first time protection by means of international criminal law
was extended to civilians of the same state as the perpetrators, pushing
aside the dictates of national law shielding perpetrators from accounting
for their individual criminal responsibility.[19] At the International Military
Tribunals at Nuremberg and Tokyo,[20] as well as in the following war
crimes trials, crimes against humanity were a highly contested concept.
This mirrored the earlier scepticism of the UNWCC lawyers who feared
not only the criticism of retroactive law but also the problem of
sovereignty, which was touched on by enabling the prosecution of crimes
against any population, including a non-national population. But together
with the other term coined at the London Conference in 1945, 'crimes
against peace', crimes against humanity also reflected an emerging rule of
customary international law.[21]

Today, crimes against humanity has found its place in international
criminal law, namely in the Statute of the International Criminal Court
('ICC'), and developed into "a precise, if not entirely unequivocal legal
term in national and international penal law".[22] The main features of
crimes against humanity, as laid down in the ICC Statute in Article 7, are
still the same as discussed in the UNWCC: these crimes are punishable,
no matter whether they occurred in war or in peace, and a country is
entitled to prosecute these crimes if members of its own national as well
as "any civilian population" are concerned. In short, the concept goes
beyond national jurisdiction and enables prosecution of atrocities which

---

[17] Van Schaack, 1998/99, p. 789, see *supra* note 4.

[18] Luban, 2004, p. 94, see *supra* note 5.

[19] Bassiouni, 1994, p. 465, see *supra* note 11.

[20] In the Charter for the Tokyo trial, it is Article 5(c), see Bassiouni, 1994, p. 459, *supra* note 11.

[21] Bassiouni, 1994, p. 461, see *supra* note 11.

[22] Michael Geyer, "Crimes Against Humanity", in Gordon Martel (ed.), *The Encyclopedia of War*, Wiley Online Library, Blackwell, 2012.

may have occurred (or started) before an official outbreak of war. The concept of crimes against humanity thus represents an important legal tool in the Nuremberg era, especially with regard to Holocaust-related crimes in Europe. It is an important landmark and a changing point in legal thinking.

The debate about the concept of crimes against humanity is most interesting, as demonstrated in the discussion here. It reflects the development of international criminal law during the war years and the significant contribution European exiled lawyers made to it. By analysing the memoranda and meeting transcripts of the UNWCC and its predecessors, it becomes clear, even at first glance, that the term stood at the centre of the UNWCC debates: the term 'crimes against humanity' turned up in the headlines in 29 meetings, and the notions of the two concepts together – crimes against humanity and crimes against peace – were discussed in 72 meetings. It is therefore crucial to take a closer look at these debates in order to understand the provenance of the term.

15.2. Predecessors of a Concept: The Idea of Civilised Warfare

The idea of civilised warfare started as a kind of by-product to the foundation of the International Red Cross in 1863. Its core aim was to relieve wounded or imprisoned soldiers as well as civilians from the horrors of war. Important in this regard were the two Peace Conferences at The Hague (1899 and 1907), where a Convention on the Laws and Customs of Warfare was agreed. To fill the gap with regard to the legality of certain acts or actors of violence, which had not yet been codified,[23] Fyodor F. Martens (Friedrich von Martens), the foremost Russian international lawyer of the Tsarist period, suggested the following preamble (which later became known as the Martens Clause):

> Until a more complete code of the laws of war is issued, the
> High Contracting Parties think it right to declare that in cases
> not included in the Regulations adopted by them,
> populations and belligerents remain under the protection and
> empire of the principles of international law, as they result
> from the usages established between civilized nations, from

---

[23] *Ibid.*

the laws of humanity, and the requirements of the public conscience.[24]

This was the first attempt to codify the notion "that international law encompassed transcendental humanitarian principles that existed beyond conventional law".[25] However, there had been ongoing debates since the mid-nineteenth century[26] to enforce what we would today term human rights standards, with Britain holding an influential position due of its consideration of imperial responsibility.[27]

The Hague Convention did not aim at giving a complete code of the rules of warfare, as it left this preamble open to amendments.[28] Sheldon Glueck interpreted the Martens Clause as "a precautionary statement".[29] It was thus debatable in legal circles whether the preamble itself constituted a law.[30] It was after all purposely placed "within a document which dealt with war crimes in the narrowest and technical sense", which no doubt gives the preamble authority as a legal guideline.[31] Although the clause had been intended as a diplomatic solution to the 'deadlock' of the Hague Peace Conferences – until a more complete set of laws of armed conflict could be decided upon – in order to affirm "that the community of nations was not to assume that the law was silent on matters that were not

---

[24] Rupert Ticehurst, "The Martens Clause and the Laws of Armed Conflict", in *International Review of the Red Cross*, 1997, vol. 37, no. 317, p. 125.

[25] Van Schaack, 1998/99, p. 796, see *supra* note 4.

[26] Schabas, 2012, p. 52, see *supra* note 9; Robertson, 1999, pp. 17–22, see *supra* note 3.

[27] Michelle Tusan, "'Crimes Against Humanity': Human Rights, the British Empire, and the Origins of the Response to the Armenian Genocide", in *American Historical Review*, 2014, vol. 119, no. 1, p. 47.

[28] Bohuslav Ečer, "Scope of the Retributive Action of the United Nations According to Their Official Declaration: The Problem of 'War Crimes' in Connection with the Second World War", UNWCC III/4(a), 27 April 1944, at p. 3 (https://www.legal-tools.org/doc/6335bd/). Ečer underlined that "[i]t would mean that acts which are not expressively forbidden by the Hague Regulations are legitimate".

[29] *Ibid.* Reference is made to a report by Sheldon Glueck of Harvard to the LIA meetings, December 1943, p. 7.

[30] *Ibid.* Ečer emphasised that "Lord Cave in his article 'War Crimes and their punishment' designated the laws of humanity and the requirements of the public conscience of the Preamble as *lex non scripta*, i.e. as law, and says expressly that this law is to be extracted", and concluded that the preamble was a part of international law.

[31] Schwelb in his report "Material for the Preparation of a Definition of 'Crimes against Humanity'", compiled by Egon Schwelb, III/33, 1946, at p. 1 (https://www.legal-tools.org/doc/c52df5/).

codified in treaty form", it was elevated to the rank of a legal notion by repetition: in the Hague Convention of 1907, the Geneva Convention of 1929 on the Sick and Wounded,[32] as well as the Geneva Conventions of 1949.[33] The Martens Clause reflects nineteenth-century humanitarian thinking and the interest in crimes of general international concern, such as piracy and slave trade. As Geyer notes, the concept is a "longstanding feature of the western legal tradition", and he concludes that "[t]he notion of a set of crimes against all has prevailed, even as the idea of a 'standard of civilization' has receded".[34] Bassiouni, in the wake of the Yugoslav wars, emphasises that the idea of humanity not only emerged out of the history of the long and bloody twentieth century, but had for centuries been shared "within laws and writings throughout Western, Judeo-Christian, Islamic and other civilizations", which expressed the values and beliefs "that life, liberty, physical integrity and personal dignity are the fundamental rights of humanity".[35] However, the central point was the translation of nineteenth-century humanitarianism − often rooted in "strident evangelicalism and moralizing liberalism" − into "twentieth-century modes of representation".[36]

Tusan makes the point that Britain's perceived double role as a "defender of oppressed Christian peoples" on the one hand and a "tolerant global empire made up of many faiths" on the other had come under pressure during the First World War, and thus "influenced thinking about an international justice at the moment when the world's attention first turned to the Armenian massacres".[37] The first diplomatic document to use the term 'crimes of humanity' was a joint Allied declaration of May 1915, which accused the Ottoman Empire "of crimes against humanity and civilization" with regard to atrocities against the Armenians.[38] There

---

[32] Bassiouni, 1994, p. 461, see *supra* note 11.

[33] Emily Crawford, "The Modern Relevance of the Martens Clause", in *ISIL Yearbook of International Humanitarian and Refugee Law*, vol. 6, Sydney Law School Research Paper No. 11/27, 2006, pp. 1–18. See also Fabian Klose, "The Colonial Testing Ground: The International Committee of the Red Cross and the Violent End of Empire", in *Humanity*, 2011, vol. 2, no. 1, p. 108.

[34] Van Schaack, 1998/99, p. 796, see *supra* note 4; Geyer, 2012, see *supra* note 22.

[35] Bassiouni, 1994, p. 488, see *supra* note 11.

[36] Tusan, 2014, p. 50, see *supra* note 27.

[37] *Ibid.*, pp. 51–52.

[38] Schabas, 2011, p. 41, see *supra* note 15; Geyer, 2012, see *supra* note 22.

had been some controversy around the term "civilization", which the Russians wanted to replace with "Christianity".[39] However, when the war was over, the perceived need to amend international law vanished under the demands of *Realpolitik*.

In 1919, during the Paris Peace Conference, a group of experts from 15 Allied states convened in a Commission on the Responsibility of the Authors of War and on Enforcement of Penalties ('the Paris Commission') and provided some recommendations. In its report, the Commission stated that "in spite of the explicit regulations, of established customs and the clear dictates of humanity, Germany and her Allies have piled outrage upon outrage".[40] It further observed that the defendants were "guilty of offences against the laws and customs of war, or the laws of humanity" and therefore "liable to criminal prosecution".[41] Schwelb observed that this constituted for the first time a juxtaposition of offences against the laws and customs of war corresponding to the later Articles 6(b) and 6(c) of the Nuremberg Charter.[42]

Under the heading of "Offences against the laws of humanity", the Paris Commission compiled a long list of atrocities committed during the First World War (which later became known as 'the Versailles list').[43] Although the Versailles list represents a first step in coining a legal definition of a minimum standard in warfare, there was considerable resistance to using the term 'crimes against humanity' in the Commission's report from one of the major powers. [44] The US representative Robert Lansing feared a "confusion of moral precepts and legal writ", and saw a "lack of legal precedence" and "subjective definition of the dictates of humanity".[45] Although Lansing confirmed that the First World War had shown a new class of crimes, which he termed "wanton acts which cause needless suffering" and "perpetrated without adequate military reason", he underlined that the prosecution of

---

[39] Geyer, 2012, see *supra* note 22.

[40] Schwelb, 1946, p. 2, see *supra* note 31.

[41] *Ibid.*

[42] *Ibid.*

[43] Van Schaack, 1998/99, p. 796, see *supra* note 4; Geyer, 2012, see *supra* note 22.

[44] Bassiouni, 1994, p. 458, see *supra* note 11.

[45] Geyer, 2012, see *supra* note 22.

such "crimes against civilization" must follow principles of legality rather than general principles of humanity.[46] He stated:

> The laws and principles of humanity vary with the individual, which, if for no other reason, should exclude them from consideration in a court of justice, especially one charged with the administration of criminal law.[47]

As a consequence, the term 'crimes against humanity' was not mentioned in the relevant provisions.[48] But Article 227 of the Versailles Peace Treaty underlined that Kaiser Wilhelm II should be brought before an international court, "for a supreme offence against international morality and the sanctity of treaties". However, this did not take effect as the emperor had sought asylum in the Netherlands.[49] Schwelb observed that this article can nevertheless be seen as a predecessor to the later Article 6(a) of the Nuremberg Charter (charge for crimes against peace), if one understands that crimes against peace are not "merely contraventions of a moral code, but violations of legal provisions".[50]

With Articles 228 to 230, the Versailles Peace Treaty laid the ground for the establishment of the first war crimes tribunal to try German war criminals.[51] These trials were held in Leipzig in the early 1920s and resulted in only a handful of convictions, thus constituting a grave setback for the idea of international criminal justice. Nevertheless, the trials at least emphasised the existence of war crimes under international criminal law.[52]

With regard to the Armenian cause, it was agreed in the Peace Treaty of Sèvres to form an Allied Court to punish Turkish atrocities (without mentioning – on request of the US delegation – the terms 'crimes against humanity' or 'laws of humanity' at all), but it never came into force.[53] Instead, several trials were held between 1919 and 1922 under the Ottoman government, acting under British pressure, which resulted in the

---

[46] *Ibid.*

[47] Van Schaack, 1998/99, p. 797, see *supra* note 4.

[48] *Ibid.* See also Schwelb, 1946, p. 2, see *supra* note 31.

[49] Schwelb, 1946, p. 1, see *supra* note 31.

[50] *Ibid.*, p. 2.

[51] William Schabas, "International Justice for International Crimes: An Idea Whose Time Has Come", in *European Review*, 2006, vol. 14, no. 4, p. 421.

[52] Schabas, 2011, p. 52, see *supra* note 15.

[53] Van Schaack, 1998/99, p. 797, see *supra* note 4.

execution of three minor officials for 'crimes against humanity'.[54] In short, the idea of an Allied high court to prosecute war crimes, discussed during the 1919 Paris Peace Conference negotiations, failed with regard to both German and Ottoman defendants. Bassiouni emphasises that the leading powers thus allowed the period after the First World War to become a "bypassed occasion to establish definitive law".[55]

15.3. Debates Within the UNWCC About 'Crimes Against Humanity'

The unprecedented Nazi war of aggression and occupation of half of Europe after the breakout of war in September 1939 formed the basis for growing concerns among the governments of nine states forced into exile,[56] and the call was made to set up new norms and to establish guidelines for trials after the end of the conflict.[57] In particular, the Czech and Polish exiled government representatives, echoed by their Belgian and Dutch counterparts, hoped that by establishing rigorous legal guidelines, the Nazis could be deterred from committing further crimes. In analysing the scholars' contributions to meetings and memoranda, it becomes clear that although they had to act according to the expectations of their respective governments in exile, they acted in the first place as legal scholars deeply marked by personal experience of forced exile, in the sober attempt to find a viable solution to bring criminals to trial, and thus answered the political demands of their officials.[58]

In London in the early 1940s, legal circles consisting of exiled lawyers of smaller Allied nations had already started debating how to approach crimes committed in the ongoing war. It was an epistemic

---

[54] Tusan, 2014, p. 65, see *supra* note 27.

[55] Bassiouni, 1994, p. 466, see *supra* note 11.

[56] The nine countries were: Belgium, Czechoslovakia, France, Greece, the Netherlands, Luxembourg, Norway, Poland and Yugoslavia.

[57] Arieh J. Kochavi, *Prelude to Nuremberg: Allied War Crimes Policy and the Question of Punishment*, University of North Carolina Press, Chapel Hill, 1998, p. 3; Kirsten Sellars, *'Crimes against Peace' and International Law*, Cambridge University Press, Cambridge, 2013, p. 60. The term 'war of aggression' was new, to distinguish the Nazi war from the earlier concept of *bellum iustum*, the just war, which is a war of defence only.

[58] Kerstin von Lingen, "Setting the Path for the UNWCC: The Representation of European Exile Governments on the London International Assembly and the Commission for Penal Reconstruction and Development, 1941–1944", in *Criminal Law Forum*, 2014, vol. 25, pp. 45–76.

community of lawyers, which can be understood as agents of a new supranational policy.[59] Most of them were already prominent lawyers in their home countries but forced into exile by Nazi politics.[60] Since they first convened in 1941, two forerunners, the International Commission for Penal Reconstruction and Development, emanating from the faculty of law at the University of Cambridge ('Cambridge Commission'), and the LIA – the contents of which overlapped with the debates later pursued by the UNWCC (with many members being present in all three bodies) – advocated new ideas of post-war justice. Thus the work of the UNWCC can be seen as the institutional result of very lively theoretical discussions in semi-official circles, which had been ongoing for some time and involved different groups of experts, lobbyists, exiled politicians and scholars. The circles in which these lawyers acted were, however, backed by politicians and lobbyists (who also took part in the meetings), fighting for recognition of their causes among British and US governmental officials,[61] thus giving the work of these two committees at least a semi-official if not governmental (at least from their exiled governments' perspective) character. Although these predecessors of the UNWCC were powerless to affect outcomes,[62] they were crucial to the war crimes debate, and they helped to coin important concepts.

Two of the most active advocates of international criminal law in London were the Czech representatives Bohuslav Ečer (1893–1954) and Egon Schwelb (1899–1979). Schwelb was later nicknamed "Mr. Human Rights",[63] as he was appointed deputy director of the Human Rights

---

[59] *Ibid.*, p. 46.

[60] The list of positions is impressive: when checking the files of the International Commission of Penal Reconstruction and Development, of 16 members coming from exile countries, five were former ministers of justice, five were high court judges, two were law professors, the others their assistants; see National Archives UK, LCO 2/2973, Papers of the International Commission for Penal Reconstruction and Development, member list.

[61] For an overview on British policy towards the central European governments in exile, see Detlef Brandes, *Großbritannien und seine Osteuropäischen Alliierten: Die Regierungen Polens, der Tschechoslowakei und Jugoslawiens im Londoner Exil vom Kriegsausbruch bis zur Konferenz von Teheran*, Oldenbourg, Munich, 1988; Peter Heumos, *Die Emigration aus der Tschechoslowakei nach Westeuropa und dem Nahen Osten, 1938–1945*, Oldenbourg, Munich, 1989, pp. 28–54.

[62] Kochavi, 1998, p. 23, with a special reference on the Czech position, see *supra* note 57.

[63] Apparently, he earned the nickname from a conference introduction in 1970, where he was presented under this heading, see Foreword to the article Egon Schwelb, "The Teaching of

Division of the UN in 1947. Both can be perceived as transnational legal actors who were highly interested in formalising how war crimes committed in Europe during the Second World War – and beyond – should be handled. As this discussion will show, legal scholars like Ečer and Schwelb contributed to the eventual coining of the term 'crimes against humanity' during their years in exile.

When Allied lawyers met in 1943 and 1944 to prepare a viable war crimes prosecution after the armistice, their first concern was to agree on the notion that a community of nations, often called the "united nations",[64] was *entitled* to "intervene juridically against crimes committed against any civilian population, before and during the war, and whether it was irrelevant whether or not such crimes were committed in violation of the domestic law of the country where perpetrated".[65] This was especially important in that civilian populations would be "protected against violations of international criminal law also in cases where the alleged crimes have been committed against their own subjects".[66]

The debate in the predecessor organisations broadened the academic understanding of what constitutes a war crime. Until 1939, legal theory maintained that war crimes must be dealt with in military courts, or in civilian courts applying the laws of war – a line the British Foreign Office still adhered to during the 1940s – and could only involve cases which had been committed within a state's own territory or against its nationals.[67] Many scholars considered it "legally unsound to hold the Nazis responsible for crimes committed against Germans within the borders of Germany".[68] However, the unprecedented record of crimes committed by Nazi forces against both the civilian populations of occupied countries and some of their own nationals made it necessary to

---

the International Aspects of Human Rights", in *American Journal of International Law*, 1971, vol. 65, no. 4, pp. 242–46.

[64] The term 'United Nations' was the formal name for 'the Allies' following the "Declaration by United Nations" of 1 January 1942. See *Yearbook of the United Nations 1946–47*, Department of Public Relations, United Nations, New York; Plesch, 2011, see *supra* note 2.

[65] Egon Schwelb, "Crimes Against Humanity", in *British Year Book of International Law*, 1946, vol. 178, no. 23, p. 179.

[66] *Ibid.*

[67] Kochavi, 1992, p. 325, see *supra* note 1.

[68] Schabas, 2011, p. 42, see *supra* note 15.

extend the definition of war crimes from a strict sense to a larger context, which was initially termed "war crimes and analogous offences".[69] For this reason, defining the term 'war crimes' proved crucial.

War crimes, as observed by the Belgian Judge Marcel de Baer in a meeting of the LIA in 1942, could include offences against national laws, and were therefore punishable by national courts, or – in a wider sense – war crimes could be seen as "offences against the *ius gentium*, or against international agreements (such as The Hague and Geneva Conventions) or unwritten internationally recognised ethical rules, and for some of these offences no sanctions have hitherto been designed".[70] The need to formulate a new legal category to fit these needs, which later became known as crimes against humanity, was already mirrored in the second definition. In its report of 28 September 1943, de Baer suggested that "at the earliest possible moment, a protocol should be agreed between the Governments of the United Nations, defining what acts should be punishable as war crimes, and setting up machinery for the prosecution and punishment of such crimes, to take effect immediately after the armistice".[71] This task was taken on by the UNWCC.

As an organisation the UNWCC was composed of three committees, of which the Legal Committee in London seems to have provided the most important inputs towards the development of contemporary international law.[72] The Facts and Evidence Committee (Committee I), chaired by de Baer, was to establish whether the submitted evidence was legally sufficient to open a case. The Committee on Means and Methods of Enforcement (Committee II) would recommend the adoption of methods and machinery, while the Legal Committee (Committee III), chaired by the Czech representative Ečer and his secretary Schwelb, carried out advisory functions within the UNWCC. In this regard, the Legal Committee spearheaded the legal debate as "it was active in the

---

[69] Schwelb, 1946, p. 185, see *supra* note 65.

[70] National Archives UK, TS 26/873, London International Assembly, Reports on Punishment of War Crimes; proposal of M. de Baer "Suggestions for the scope of work for the commission, provisional plan of work", April 1942.

[71] United Nations War Crimes Commission, *History of the United Nations War Crimes Commission and the Development of the Laws of War*, His Majesty's Stationery Office, London, 1948, p. 99.

[72] On structure and core process of UNWCC, see Plesch and Sattler, 2014, p. 28, *supra* note 2.

clarification of legal issues, the gradual elimination of uncertainties in the spheres of the laws of war and the promotion of rules, many of which were to become part of contemporary penal law".[73]

In 1944 the UNWCC, especially its Legal Committee, was concerned with finding a viable solution to bring atrocities that were not connected to military action to trial – especially crimes against political opponents, occupied civilians or European Jews. The UNWCC chairman, Sir Cecil Hurst, underlined in a letter to the British foreign secretary Anthony Eden in May 1944 that the UNWCC was struggling with a definition of war crimes and had come to the conclusion that a number of crimes fell outside of the hitherto accepted definitions, as they had been committed on racial, religious or political grounds in enemy territories.[74] The Lord Chancellor, Viscount Simon, replied on 23 August 1944, emphasising that the task of the UNWCC was limited to observing and advising, which did not include the coining of new law. "This would open a very wide field", Simon stated, and warned the UNWCC that it should not concern itself with these "serious difficulties" unless a position of the British government was adopted.[75] This exchange of letters was the result of ongoing debates – following a notion of the US representative Herbert Pell in March 1944 – referring to the use of the new term 'crimes against humanity' with regard to Jewish victims and internal reports submitted by Ečer in the spring 1944.[76]

Ečer had submitted a proposal to the UNWCC on 27 April 1944, dealing with the problem of aggressive war and advocating the use of the term 'crimes against humanity' in an international criminal court.

---

[73] United Nations War Crimes Commission, p. 169, see *supra* note 71.

[74] Schwelb, 1946, p. 3, see *supra* note 31.

[75] *Ibid.*

[76] Pell's UNWCC note of 18 March 1944 runs: "It is clearly understood that the words 'crimes against humanity' refer, among others, to crimes committed against stateless persons or against any person because of their race and religion; such crimes are judiciable by the United Nations or their agencies as a war crime" (https://www.legal-tools.org/doc/2aa8b6/). Pell had used the term already in February in a private letter to his friend, President Franklin D. Roosevelt, where he seems to connect even Roosevelt himself to coining the term: "What are we to do about the Jews in Germany ... the offences against them certainly seem to be described in your phrase 'crimes against humanity'". Herbert C. Pell, Letter to the President, February 16, 1944. Roosevelt, FD 1936–45, General Correspondence, Papers of Herbert Claiborne Pell, FDR Library. I am grateful to my colleague Graham Cox, Texas, for pointing this out to me.

However, the British UNWCC representative Arnold McNair, as chairman of a four-person sub-committee dealing with questions of *ius ad bellum* and *ius in bello*, rejected this proposal as too far-reaching, pointing out that the existing laws had to be respected, and the issue went back for debate.[77] McNair – following his earlier criticism when he was the chair of the Cambridge Commission – was especially against Ečer's idea of holding heads of states accountable and applying what McNair saw as retroactive law. Ečer, in return, felt it was unacceptable that those who had broken the law so many times should go unpunished simply because established national codes were not sufficient to deal with them. He held the position that the expansive nature of the Second World War had created a new situation – with war crimes incomparable to earlier conflicts – to which new legal responses had to be formulated. He stressed that the Nazis "had stepped outside international intercourse and exempted themselves from the protection afforded belligerents by humanitarian law".[78] Ečer wrote that "[p]reparation and launching of the present war must be punished as a crime against peace", and "if there are gaps in law, it is our duty to fill them".[79]

In a memorandum submitted to the UNWCC in May 1944, entitled "Scope of the Retributive action of the United Nations according to their official Declarations – The Problem of War Crimes in connection with the second World War", Ečer amended his earlier report, following a two-fold argumentation. First, he underlined that it was not a transgression of competencies of the UNWCC when it suggested further handling of the war crimes problem including broadening the whole concept; and second, he advocated the use of the term 'crimes against humanity' by drawing on its prior use in international criminal law.[80] He agreed with the views of Hurst who stated that the scope of the UNWCC had to be enlarged "when new facts and especially cases submitted by the governments demonstrated that it would be desirable to recommend to the Allied governments a wider and larger conception of war crimes".[81] In assessing

---

[77] Sellars, 2013, pp. 58–64, see *supra* note 57.

[78] *Ibid.*, p. 61.

[79] National Archives UK, FO 371/39005, UNWCC, Minutes of 36th meeting, 17 October 1944 (https://www.legal-tools.org/doc/3d0ae8); see also Sellars, 2013, p. 63, see *supra* note 57, on the connection with the Russian legal scholar Aron Trainin.

[80] Ečer, 1944, p. 5, see *supra* note 28.

[81] *Ibid.*, p. 2.

the historical record of Nazi crimes, Ečer stated that the UNWCC had received several accounts on the planned nature of Nazi warfare especially in Eastern Europe, where not only Jews but also members of the Soviet intelligence services, burgomasters, controllers of commerce, engineers and officers were slaughtered by Schutzstaffel ('SS') troops without prior trials.[82] The Polish government had emphasised in these reports that a considerable number of crimes committed in occupied Poland had not even "a remote connection with military necessity", and proposed the new term 'crimes against humanity' to cover these offences. The French delegation, together with the Polish scholars, also raised the question of collective responsibility to address certain formations such as the Gestapo or SS which were involved in these new crimes on a regular basis. Ečer suggested that since political leaders of the Allies had referred to justice being delivered on several occasions, it was important to "adapt the task of the Commission to the Allied declarations and to the public opinion which is relying on these declarations".[83]

By debating the Martens Clause and the Versailles achievements, Ečer underlined that the Preamble of the Hague Convention – the Martens Clause – was of immense value for the work of the UNWCC, as the Martens Clause referred to the term 'humanity'.[84] He also questioned the tendency of UNWCC documents to speak of the Nazis as a "gangster regime" or a "pathological system" (at the suggestion of Glueck), as these terms "involved an element of irresponsibility which I would avoid, [as I] wished to underline the criminal responsibility of the Nazi rulers".[85] After debating the various legal achievements, referring to debates within the Cambridge Commission and the LIA, citing also the (unratified) Geneva Protocol for the Pacific Settlement of Disputes of 1924 and the report of Lauterpacht before the Cambridge Commission, Ečer asked in conclusion:

> The question is, shall we go back? Is the standard of 1924 in this question too advanced in the light of the experience of 1939/1944? Should we be more reactionary than the League of Nations in 1924 and in 1937? Or in other words, shall we go backwards when social change requires progress?[86]

---

[82] *Ibid.*

[83] *Ibid.*, p. 3.

[84] *Ibid.*, p. 4.

[85] *Ibid.*, p. 5.

[86] *Ibid.*, p. 7.

He made the point that, in his view, crimes against humanity were the most important concept of all, as they had been committed "as the real cause of all the other crimes, as the source of the war, the *malum in se*".[87]

Ečer recalled in his memoirs his deep personal commitment: "The atmosphere was charged with high voltage, being – in my opinion – at stake the whole point of this war in the assessment of international law; our work absolutely must result in the victory of justice over the dark forces of evil and the fact that those who started the war shall face deserved punishment".[88] It seems that his initiative focused heavily on Holocaust crimes, which until then had been dealt with among the bulk of Nazi occupation crimes, an act that minimised their uniqueness. Ečer was therefore seen as a friend of the Jewish cause.[89] But the UNWCC, in its meeting of 10 October 1944, took a different stand. Ečer maintained his minority opinion, questioning whether the foundation and enactment of the present war represented crimes that fell within the jurisdiction of the UNWCC.

The British government was still reluctant to respond to the new term. In a debate in the House of Commons on 4 October 1944, referring to the killings of political prisoners at the Buchenwald concentration camp, Eden stated that "[c]rimes committed by Germans against Germans, however reprehensible, are in a different category from war crimes and cannot be dealt with under the same procedure".[90] This notion was reaffirmed in a debate on 31 January 1945.[91] There was still some way to go to include the concept crimes against humanity in international law. The time came when the war was over and the first international tribunal was set up.

---

[87]   *Ibid.*

[88]   Bohuslav Ečer, Jak jsem je stíhal, ed. by Edwarda Cenka, Naše vojsko, Prague, 1946, p. 162 (my translation).

[89]   Apparently, Herbert Pell made this comment in a message to his government, when Ečer threatened to resign from the UNWCC in September 1944. See Jan Lanicek, *Czechs, Slovaks and the Jews, 1938–1948: Beyond Idealization and Condemnation*, Palgrave Macmillan, New York, 2013, p. 99.

[90]   Schwelb, 1946, p. 5, see *supra* note 31.

[91]   *Ibid.*

15.4. 'Crimes Against Humanity' in Court: The Nuremberg Era

The International Military Tribunal at Nuremberg, 1945–1946 ('Nuremberg Tribunal') followed the statute drawn up at the London Conference in the summer of 1945. The statute set up the structure and basis for the prosecution of the major war criminals, [92] and its main achievement consisted in formulating the first legal definition of 'crimes against humanity'. [93] Article 6(c) of the Nuremberg Charter defined crimes against humanity as

> a distinct set of crimes, namely murder, extermination, enslavement, deportation, and other inhumane acts committed against any civilian population, before or during the war, or persecutions on political, racial and religious grounds in execution of or in connection with any crime within the jurisdiction of the tribunal, whether or not in violation of the domestic law of the country where perpetrated. [94]

The last part of the definition was decisive in so far as it established the supremacy of international law over municipal law. [95]

Article 6(c) of the Nuremberg Charter found its equivalent in Article 5(c) of the Tokyo Charter, and both Charters were clearly connected through defining 'crimes against humanity', 'aggression' and 'war crimes'. [96] Article 6(c) of the Charter reflected the desire of the Allies not to be restricted "to bringing to justice those who had committed war crimes in the narrower sense ... but that also such atrocities should be investigated, tried and punished as have been committed on axis territory, against persons of axis nationality". [97] The Nuremberg Tribunal could now, simply by using the new tool, also address "acts committed by Nazi

---

[92] Bassiouni, 1994, p. 4, see *supra* note 11.

[93] Wolfgang Form underlines the similar wording of the definition to crimes against humanity in both the UNWCC and the London Charter as proof. See Wolfgang Form, "Strategies for 'Genocide Trials' after World War II: How the Allied Powers Deal with the Phenomenon of Genocide in Occupied Germany", in Christoph Safferling and Eckart Conze (eds.), *The Genocide Convention 60 Years after its Adoption*, Asser, The Hague, 2010, p. 77.

[94] Nuremberg Charter, Article 6(c). See Geyer, 2012, see *supra* note 22.

[95] Van Schaack, 1998/99, p. 791, see *supra* note 4.

[96] Bassiouni, 1994, p. 463, see *supra* note 11.

[97] Schwelb, 1946, p. 183, see *supra* note 65.

---

perpetrators against German victims, who were thus of the same nationality as their oppressors, or against citizens of a state allied with Germany".[98]

According to David Luban, five features can be distinguished that characterise the laws of crimes against humanity in all its subsequent embodiments:[99] crimes against humanity are typically committed against fellow nationals; they are international crimes; they are committed by politically organised groups acting under the colour of 'policy'; they consist of the most severe acts of violence and persecution; and they are inflicted on victims "based on their membership in a population rather than on individual characteristics". [100] As Luban notes: "The distinguishing feature of the crime against humanity is not the actor's genocidal intent, but the organized, policy-based decision to commit the offences".[101]

However, the meaning of the term has met with considerable scepticism and has been "plagued by incoherence" even since this formulation.[102] Schwelb tried to set the path very clearly in his "Report on the Meaning of 'Crimes against Humanity'", which he submitted to the UNWCC in March 1946. He stated that crimes against humanity had (a) been committed by defendants from the Axis states or their allies, could (b) be committed by individuals as well as by members of an organisation, and were (c) distinguished into "crimes of the murder-type" and "persecution".[103] In this regard, it was irrelevant whether a crime of the "murder-type" had been committed before or during the war. "Persecutions", Schwelb argued, had to be committed on political, racial or religious grounds and in connection with any crime within the jurisdiction of the tribunal (crimes against peace, war crimes, or even crimes against humanity of the murder type).[104] Hence, the crimes would not only be committed on a personal level but also be connected to the

---

[98] Van Schaack, 1998/99, p. 790, see *supra* note 4.

[99] Luban, 2004, pp. 93, 108, see *supra* note 5.

[100] *Ibid.*, pp. 103, 108.

[101] *Ibid.*, p. 98.

[102] Van Schaack, 1998/99, p. 792, *supra* note 4; Diane F. Orentlicher, "Settling Accounts: The Duty to Prosecute Human Rights Violations of a Prior Regime", in *Yale Law Journal*, 1991, vol. 100, no. 8, p. 2585.

[103] Schwelb, 1946, p. 6, see *supra* note 31.

[104] *Ibid.*, p. 7.

above-mentioned crimes. For example, "by enacting legislation which orders or permits crimes against humanity", the charge could be met.[105]

Schwelb even formulated a "distinction between crimes against humanity and ordinary common law", pointing out "that 'inhumane' common crimes become crimes against humanity, if, by their purpose or magnitude, they become the concern of Foreign Powers and, consequently, the concern of International Law".[106] He also rejected the notion that crimes against humanity were connected to violation of domestic laws and stated, in the view of possible defence strategies:

> Compliance with municipal law is no defence to a charge for a crime against humanity. It is submitted that it is the only one application of the general rule permeating the modern law of war crimes that superior order is no defence, when the order is illegal.[107]

Schwelb thereby underlined that the Nuremberg Charter laid down explicitly the supremacy of international law over municipal law.

In this regard, the Nuremberg Charter not only "broadened the jurisdictional scope of a pre-existing category of crimes" but also represented "an expansion of international law beyond clear prior precedent",[108] and this "jurisdictional extension of normative proscription to a different context, irrespective of the diversity of citizenship, posed a fundamental question". It should be observed that there was considerable preoccupation as to the point of whether this constituted new law or was based on legal precedents. Only when the Nuremberg trials were concluded did it become apparent that the term had made "judiciable what had been general principles".[109] In 1946 the UN General Assembly stated its opinion, that the crimes against humanity as defined by the Nuremberg Charter and the judgments of the Nuremberg Tribunal were crimes according to international law.[110] This UN resolution was reaffirmed in 1950[111] and worked into the Draft Code of Offences against the Peace and

---

[105] *Ibid.*, p. 14.

[106] *Ibid.*, p. 10.

[107] *Ibid.*, p. 8.

[108] Bassiouni, 1994, p. 466, see *supra* note 11.

[109] Geyer, 2012, see *supra* note 22.

[110] *Ibid.*

[111] The International Law Commission had in 1950 reaffirmed the Nuremberg Principles. See Bassiouni, 1994, p. 464, see *supra* note 11.

Security of Mankind of 1954, which was, however, left incomplete by the International Law Commission of the UN due to Cold War constraints following the Korean War.[112]

The judges at the Nuremberg Tribunal were nevertheless quite cautious in applying the new concept and treated it for the most part as a subsidiary crime connected to other war crimes.[113] The fact that crimes against humanity were only addressed as a subsidiary charge alongside conventional war crimes, or crimes against peace, has become known as the 'war nexus'.[114] The war nexus allowed the Allied legal staff to "condemn specific inhumane acts of Nazi perpetrators committed within Germany without threatening the entire doctrine of state sovereignty".[115] The French judge Henri Donnedieu de Vabres expressed his criticism of the concept, when he stated, looking back at the Nuremberg Tribunal:

> The theory of crimes against humanity is dangerous; dangerous for the people by the absence of precise definition; dangerous for the States because it offers a pretext to intervention by a State, in the internal affairs of weaker states.[116]

By contrast, Justice Jackson underlined that it was not the concept of sovereignty which was at stake here, but a duty of free people to call for justice for the victims of Nazi barbarism. He made the war nexus connection of crimes against humanity very clear:

> It has become a general principle of foreign policy of our government from time immemorial that the internal affairs of another government are not ordinarily our business; that is to say, the way Germany treats its inhabitants ... is not our affair any more than it is the affair of some other government to interpose itself in our problems. The reason that this program of extermination of Jews and destruction of

---

[112] Geyer, 2012, see *supra* note 22. For the end of the work of the Law Commission see M. Cherif Bassiouni, *Crimes Against Humanity in International Criminal Law*, Kluwer Law International, The Hague, 1999.

[113] Schwelb, 1946, *supra* note 31; Geyer, 2012, see *supra* note 22.

[114] Van Schaack, 1998/99, p. 791, see *supra* note 4.

[115] *Ibid.*

[116] Cited in Joseph Y. Dautricourt, "Crime Against Humanity: European Views on Its Conception and Its future", in *Journal of Criminal Law and Criminology*, 1949, vol. 40, no. 2, pp. 170–75. The original can be found in *Revue de droit pénal et de criminologie*, 1946/47, p. 813.

the rights of minorities becomes an international concern is
this: it was a part of a plan for making an illegal war. Unless
we have a war connection as a basis for reaching them, I
would think we have no basis for dealing with atrocities.
They were a part of the preparation for war or for the
conduct for the war insofar as they occurred inside of
Germany, and that makes them our concern.[117]

The French jurist André Gros objected to the war nexus, noting that
there was no need to tie the prosecution of atrocities to acts of aggression.
He feared that it would be very difficult for prosecutors to prove
persecutions in pursuit of aggression, as "even the Nazi plan against the
Jews [shows] no apparent aggression against other nations".[118] In contrast,
the British prosecutor David Maxwell Fyfe underlined that he saw no
difficulties in linking anti-Jewish measures to a general plan of
aggression.[119] The British prosecutor Hartley Shawcross agreed with the
US stand and pointed to the practical use of the war nexus, when he
observed in his summation that "the crime against the Jews, insofar as it is
a crime against humanity and not a war crime as well, is one which we
indict because of its close association with the crime against the peace".[120]

Only with Control Council Law No. 10 ('CCL 10'), released by the
Allies in occupied Germany in 1946, was the link between the state of
war and crimes against humanity dropped.[121] Alone within the British
Zone of Occupation in Germany, courts applying CCL 10 held around
150 trials "exclusively involving crimes against humanity, committed
between 1933 and the end of the war", which addressed crimes against
German or stateless victims; many of them were Jewish.[122]

However, the courts treated the concept of crimes against humanity
with caution and rejected especially Ečer's initial idea of punishing
crimes that occurred prior to the state of war. Also Schwelb had explicitly

---

[117] Jackson Report, cited in Van Schaack, 1998/99, p. 799, see *supra* note 4.

[118] *Ibid.*, p. 800.

[119] *Ibid.*

[120] *Ibid.* See also *The Trial of the Major War Criminals, Proceedings of the International
Military Tribunal sitting at Nuremberg. Concluding Speeches by the Prosecution*, vol. 19,
IMT, Nuremberg, 1947, p. 471.

[121] Bassiouni, 1994, p. 464, see *supra* note 11; Schwelb report on the definition of crimes
against humanity, 22 March 1946, p. 8 (https://www.legal-tools.org/doc/c52df5/); see also
Geyer, 2012, *supra* note 22.

[122] Form, 2010, p. 80, see *supra* note 93.

underlined in his report that two groups of crimes – crimes within Germany before and during the war, and crimes in occupied (and therefore temporary Axis territory states) during the war – fell outside the notions of war crimes and had to be addressed otherwise, something that was even admitted by Jackson in his introductory speech at Nuremberg.[123] The US prosecutor agreed, with regard to the extermination of Jews, that although usually how a government treats its own inhabitants is thought to be of no concern to other governments, the mistreatment of the Jews had passed "in magnitude and savagery any limits of what is tolerable by modern civilization", and therefore other nations "by silence, would take a consenting part in these crimes". [124] The Nuremberg Tribunal was nevertheless reluctant, and its judgment stressed that

> [t]he tribunal therefore cannot make a general declaration that the acts before 1939 were crimes against humanity within the meaning of the charter, but from the beginning of the war in 1939, war crimes were committed on a vast scale, which were also crimes against humanity.[125]

The result was that all crimes committed, for example in Poland or Czechoslovakia/Sudentenland, prior to the outbreak of the war in September 1939 could not be indicted, due to the lack of a war nexus, as "it has not been satisfactorily proven that they were done in execution of, or in connection with any such crime".[126]

With regard to the Charter of the International Military Tribunal for the Far East at Tokyo ('Tokyo Tribunal'), which was modelled after the Nuremberg Charter, crimes against humanity were also included, although the sentence "persecution on religious grounds" was omitted.[127] However, persecutions on political or racial grounds still remained punishable under crimes against humanity at the Tokyo Tribunal. The term was also debated at the UNWCC Far Eastern and Pacific Sub-Commission in Chungking, China. The Sub-Commission agreed not to address crimes against Taiwanese as crimes against humanity. This was

---

[123] Schwelb, 1946, p. 11, see *supra* note 31.

[124] *Ibid.*, p. 12.

[125] *The Trial of the Major War Criminals, Proceedings of the International Military Tribunal sitting at Nuremberg. Judgment*, vol. 1, IMT, Nuremberg, 1947, p. 254; also cited in Van Schaack, 1998/99, p. 804, see *supra* note 4.

[126] *Ibid.*

[127] Schwelb, 1946, p. 9, see *supra* note 31.

logical since the Taiwanese people had been part of the Japanese empire during the war, and they were thus occupied civilians with Japanese citizenship.[128] When looking into the trial records of not only the Tokyo Tribunal but also the national war crimes courts set up in East Asia, whether in the former European colonies or China, it is apparent that the courts were reluctant to use the concept of crimes against humanity. Ongoing scholarship underlines the fact that in the Dutch trials held in the Netherlands East Indies (Indonesia) and French trials in Indochina, there was no mention of the term at all.[129] Lisette Schouten notes with regard to the trials held in the East Indies:

> [I]n contrast to their home country, the Netherlands for the Dutch Indies government decided not to include 'crimes against humanity' in their definition of war crimes. It regarded 'crimes against humanity' primarily as a provision to punish crimes against own nationals and did not want to 'engage' with the crimes Japanese had committed against Japanese. Furthermore they were convinced, unlike in the homeland, that adjudication of the crimes committed in the Indies could take place without an inclusion of 'crimes against humanity'. However, it could well be that this decision was made to prevent Dutch and KNIL [Koninklijk Nederlands Indisch Leger, Royal Netherlands East Indies Army] soldiers being accused of this particular offence during the re-occupation of the Indies.[130]

As the archival record of Chinese trials is not yet complete, it can only be established from a sample of 240 sentences that China used the concept at least once, when it came to the trial of Takashi Sakai, who was

---

[128] United Nations War Crimes Commission, Minutes of the Thirty-sixth Meeting of the Far-Eastern and Pacific Sub-commission of the United Nations War Crimes Commission, 14 January 1947 (http://www.legal-tools.org/en/go-to-database/record/dc1e12/).

[129] See the chapters by Lisette Schouten, "'From Tokyo to the United Nations': B.V.A. Röling, International Criminal Jurisdiction and the Debate on Establishing an International Criminal Court, 1949–1957", *HOICL*, vol. 2, pp. 177–212; and Ann-Sophie Schoepfel-Aboukrat, "War Court as a Form of State Building: The French Prosecution of Japanese War Crimes at the Saigon and Tokyo Trials", *HOICL*, vol. 2, pp. 119–41.

[130] Lisette Schouten, "Post-war Justice in the Dutch East Indies, 1946–1949", in Kirsten Sellars (ed.), *Trials for International Crimes in Asia: The Evolution of Principles of Liability*, forthcoming 2014.

tried for the crime of aggression as well as for crimes against humanity committed at Nanking.[131] The tribunal specified that Sakai was guilty of

> [i]nciting or permitting his subordinates to murder prisoners of war, wounded soldiers; nurses and doctors of the Red Cross and other non-combatants, and to commit acts of rape, plunder, deportation, torture and destruction of property, he had violated the Hague Convention concerning the Laws and Customs of War on Land and the Geneva Convention of 1929. These offences are war crimes and crimes against humanity.[132]

In this regard, it is also clear that in the Far East the war nexus prevailed. The verdict against Sakai (who was found guilty and sentenced to be shot) emphasised that he had been convicted for inciting his troops to atrocities. Since he pleaded innocent, as he did not have knowledge of these crimes, he was also found guilty of failing to ensure the discipline of his troops. The sentence stated: "[a]ll the evidence goes to show that the defendant knew of the atrocities committed by his subordinates and deliberately let loose savagery upon civilians and prisoners of war". The "principle that a commander is responsible for the discipline of his subordinates, and that consequently he may be held responsible for their criminal acts if he neglects to undertake appropriate measures or knowingly tolerates the perpetration of offences on their part", was a rule generally accepted by nations and their courts of law in the sphere of the laws and customs of war.[133] The trial against Sakai therefore stands in line with the jurisprudence created with regard to this rule after the Second World War. The most famous instance in Asia was the Tomoyuki Yamashita case, and in the European theatre of war the Wilhelm von Leeb, Erich von Manstein and Albert Kesselring cases.[134]

---

[131] See the chapter by Anja Bihler, "Late Republican China and the Development of International Criminal Law: China's Role in the United Nations War Crimes Commission in London and Chongqing", *HOICL*, vol. 1, pp. 507–40. See also Chinese War Crimes Military Tribunal of the Ministry of Defence, Nanking, "Law Report of Trials of War Criminals", case 83 of Takashi Sakai, His Majesty's Stationery Office, London, 1949, vol. 14, p. 2.

[132] *Ibid.*, p. 7.

[133] *Ibid.*

[134] See Kerstin von Lingen, *Kesselring's Last Battle: War Crimes Trials and Cold War Politics, 1945–1960*, University Press of Kansas, Lawrence, 2009.

After the Nuremberg trials, Schwelb laid down his legal conclusions for the UNWCC from the debates he had witnessed, strongly advocating the idea of crimes against humanity.[135] In an essay Schwelb underlined that the terms war crimes and crimes against humanity may often overlap.[136] However, the concept of crimes against humanity does allow for crimes committed before a military conflict to be brought to justice, but poses some difficulty for labelling crimes inflicted on civilians by their rightful governments. As a concept, crimes against humanity suggest that universally binding ethical and moral principles exist and they are shared by most countries in the world. Schwelb also emphasised, in the view of the later trials, that there was "no defence that the act alleged to be a crime was lawful under the domestic law of the country where it was perpetrated".[137] He argued that "[a] crime against humanity is an offence against certain general principles of law which, in certain circumstances, become the concern of international community, namely, if it has repercussions reaching across international frontiers, or if it passes 'in magnitude or savagery any limits of what is tolerable by modern civilization'".[138]

Schwelb was reluctant to accept that a crime's connection with a war was a deciding factor for the Nuremberg Tribunal to try the crime. He concluded in the following terms:

> The Crime Against Humanity, as defined in the London Charter, is not, therefore, the cornerstone of a system of international criminal law equally applicable in times of war and of peace, protecting the human rights of the inhabitants of all countries of all civilian population against anybody, including their own states and governments.

Rather, crimes against humanity were "a kind of by-product of the war, applicable only in times of war" and designed "to cover cases not covered by norms of the traditional laws and customs of war".[139] The Nuremberg Charter, which implemented the term crimes against humanity for the first

---

[135] Egon Schwelb, Report on the Bearing of the Nuremberg Judgment on the Interpretation of the Term "Crimes against Humanity", 26 October 1946 (https://www.legal-tools.org/doc/4edb22/).

[136] Schwelb, 1946, p. 189, see *supra* note 65.

[137] *Ibid.*, p. 193.

[138] *Ibid.*, p. 195.

[139] *Ibid.*, p. 206.

time, would, in Schwelb's understanding, serve to "make sure that inhumane acts violating the principles of the laws of all civilized nations committed in connection with war should not go unpunished".[140]

15.5. Conclusion

The notion of 'crimes against humanity' and the delineation of the charge into its constituent elements took place towards the end of the Second World War, with European exiled lawyers at the Cambridge Commission, the LIA, the UNWCC and other academic circles contributing to it, though attempts to define the term had already been made during the First World War.

As we have seen, the concept of crimes against humanity as laid down in the Nuremberg Charter in Article 6(c) had several components: it defined offences against any civilian populations, consisted always of numerous incidents of the same nature, was perpetrated on the basis of higher orders or state policy, and distinguished between crimes of the murder type and crimes of persecution, the latter if perpetrated on political and racial (in Europe, also religious) grounds.[141] The crimes were "characteristically committed against fellow nationals, or others in occupied territories under the perpetrator's control"; state sovereignty provided no shield from culpability, and the crimes were committed by organised groups.[142] For the sake of avoiding the criticism of applying retroactive law, the new principle became bound to other charges during the Nuremberg trials, namely conventional war crimes, thus connecting it to a state of aggression. This so-called war nexus proved a burden to international criminal law and later significantly limited the use of crimes against humanity in violent acts that occurred during, for example, the Cold War and wars of decolonisation,[143] the crimes of military dictatorships in Latin America or apartheid crimes in South Africa.[144] By

---

[140] *Ibid.*

[141] Schwelb, 1946, p. 13, see *supra* note 31.

[142] Luban, 2004, p. 117, see *supra* note 5.

[143] Fabian Klose, *Human Rights in the Shadow of Colonial Violence: The Wars of Independence in Kenya and Algeria*, University of Pennsylvania Press, Philadelphia, 2013; see also Klose, 2011, *supra* note 33.

[144] Van Schaack, 1998/99, p. 793, see *supra* note 4. It could perhaps have been circumvented by codifying "the classic international law doctrine of humanitarian intervention", as Van Schaack suggests on p. 847. Humanitarian intervention is defined as "the intervention by

this token, an "unconditional application of sovereignty has the potential to result in impunity for gross human rights violation committed within the boundaries of a state".[145]

It took a while until the concept found its way into national jurisdictions.[146] After the formation of the United Nations Organisation in San Francisco in 1945, several commissions were set up to continue the work of both the UNWCC and other predecessors, especially in framing what would later become the ICC in 2002. The concept of crimes against humanity had first fully been realised at the Eichmann trial in Jerusalem in 1961 (and thus became inextricably linked with Holocaust crimes). The concept gained its wider meaning in the 1990s, as an effect of the jurisprudence of the International Criminal Tribunals for the former Yugoslavia and for Rwanda.[147] Two factors contributed to this outcome: the end of the Cold War and the emergence of a powerful human rights movement, which began "to develop a victim-oriented discourse that required states to ensure that perpetrators of atrocities were brought to justice".[148]

However, it was only half a century after the Nuremberg trials, with the adoption of the ICC Statute in 1998 and foundation of the ICC, that crimes against humanity became the subject of a comprehensive, multilateral convention. [149] Only the ICC Statute offers a consensus definition of crimes against humanity, and thus marks "the welcome culmination of a slow but steady process of erosion of the significance of state sovereignty in the process of international law formation".[150] The

---

one state into the territorial integrity of another state in order to protect individuals who are the victims of abuses by fellow citizens that the state is unwilling or unable to protect". If the drafters of the IMT Charter would not have been so focused on the principle of sovereignty, but more on the protection of individuals, then the "doctrine of humanitarian intervention suggests that the existence of a widespread or systematic attack against a civilian population provides the hook on which international jurisdiction can hang".

[145] *Ibid.*, p. 846.

[146] On the use of "crimes against humanity as a universal principle at the ICC", see Kerstin von Lingen, "'Crimes Against Humanity': Einer umstrittene Universalie im Völkerrecht im 20. Jahrhunderts", in *Zeithistorische Forschungen/Studies in Contemporary History*, 2011, vol. 8, no. 3.

[147] Geyer, 2012, see *supra* note 22; Robertson, 1999, pp. 446–501, see *supra* note 3.

[148] Schabas, 2011, p. 422, see *supra* note 15.

[149] Van Schaack, 1998/99, p. 792, see *supra* note 4.

[150] *Ibid.*, p. 850.

long journey from debates within the UNWCC, which was an advisory body that could not establish international law, to the Charters of the Nuremberg and Tokyo Tribunals, which indeed established international law, reflects the permanent tension between the ideas of justice and practical political considerations.

The evolving definition of crimes against humanity since the Nuremberg Tribunal shows that the principles guiding the contemporary codification of international criminal law were shifting. Although they were previously drafted to protect state sovereignty, the new principles have become more concerned with "condemning injurious conduct and guaranteeing the accountability of individuals who subject others, including their compatriots, to inhumane acts".[151] In this regard, Article 6(c) reflects the tension in international law between state sovereignty and human rights as an overarching goal of the international system.[152] In looking back to the achievements of the London Charter,[153] Ečer was quite confident that international law would help to protect peace in future generations. He wrote:

> As far as crimes against humanity are concerned, I see the importance of this particular provision of the Charter and the verdict also in the fact that certain human rights, namely the right to freedom of thought and religious beliefs and the right to pledge allegiance to nation and race, are placed under the protection of the international community and become articles protected under international law. I believe this has special significance for beyond the [Nuremberg] trial. The Charter itself will not protect elementary human rights all over the world, as it is primarily concerned with German crimes, but the Charter indisputably marked the start of the development of international law towards international protection of elementary human rights.[154]

---

[151] *Ibid.*, p. 795.

[152] *Ibid.*, p. 846.

[153] Ečer was not present at the negotiations, as all the smaller countries, which had been so important in drafting the war crimes policy, had been excluded from the conference. See William Schabas, "The United Nations War Crimes Commission's Proposal for an International Criminal Court", in *Criminal Law Forum*, 2014, vol. 25, p. 186.

[154] Ečer in his memoirs entitled *Jak jsem je stíhal* [How I prosecuted], Prague, 1946, cited by Eduard Stehlik, "Bohuslav Ečer and the Prosecution of War Crimes", in *European*

Schwelb, after observing the Nuremberg trials followed by the setting up of the Tokyo Tribunal and municipal courts in different European countries, was very eager for a law concerning crimes against humanity to be embedded in national laws, "namely, the principle that the protection of a minimum standard of human rights should be guaranteed anywhere, at any time and against anybody".[155] Schwelb set an agenda for the later UN resolutions when he concluded that legal norm-setting was not enough, if political implementation was missing. As he observed in 1946, "[t]he task of making the protection of human rights general, permanent and effective still lies ahead".[156]

By this token, the criminalisation of 'crimes against humanity' was "intended not only to punish World War II perpetrators, but to deter future human depredations and to enhance the prospects of world peace".[157] The use of crimes against humanity in the tribunals of the 1990s is thus, in the view of Bassiouni, above all "a reaffirmation of the world community's condemnation of such acts, irrespective of the outcome".[158] Or, as Luban puts it, the term is significant because "understanding the twin meanings of 'humanity' means something universal and immensely important". Recognising its worth is "the least we owe the dead".[159]

Conscience and Communism, Proceedings of the International Conference, Prague, 2–3 June 2008, p. 59.

[155] Schwelb, 1946, p. 225, see *supra* note 65.

[156] *Ibid.*, p. 226.

[157] Bassiouni, 1994, p. 493, see *supra* note 11.

[158] *Ibid.*, p. 494.

[159] Luban, 2004, see *supra* note 5, p. 161.

16

Late Republican China and the Development of International Criminal Law: China's Role in the United Nations War Crimes Commission in London and Chungking

Anja Bihler[*]

> Dealing with inconceivable as well as
> expected atrocities the dedicated men and
> women of the UNWCC performed admirably.
> History should judge their effort kindly.[1]

16.1. Introduction

During the height of the Second World War, the Allied Nations set up an organisation to deal with the problem of war criminals. The United Nations War Crimes Commission ('UNWCC') consisted of a main commission in London and later the Far Eastern and Pacific Sub-Commission ('the Sub-Commission') in Chungking, China.[2] The members of the UNWCC were delegates who had been selected by the Allied governments, and their main task was to review and classify evidence of wartime atrocities and draw up a list of war crimes suspects.[3]

Until recently the UNWCC has attracted rather scant scholarly attention and was often dismissed as having been of little importance. The

---

* **Anja Bihler** is currently a Ph.D. candidate in Chinese Studies under university scholarship at Heidelberg University, Germany. She holds a Magister Artium in Chinese Studies, Economics and Law from Ludwig-Maximilians-University ('LMU'), Munich, Germany. In 2012 she was a member of the Jessup Moot Court Team representing the LMU Institute for International Law. She is pursuing her Ph.D. within the Transcultural Justice research group of the Cluster of Excellence "Asia and Europe in a Global Context" at Heidelberg University.
1 George J. Lankevich (ed.), *United States Archives, New York: United Nations War Crimes Commission*, Garland Publishing, New York, 1990, p. ix.
2 Chungking is the old romanisation for the Chinese city of Chongqing.
3 The governments were supposed to set up a so-called National Office, an organ that would collect and submit evidence of war crimes committed in the respective country to the UNWCC.

---

main reason for this was the perceived failure of the UNWCC to assert any direct influence on the most important post-war trials in Nuremberg and Tokyo. Only now, when most of the materials documenting the work of the UNWCC have become more easily accessible, is there a renewed interest in this topic. The wealth of information now allows for a far more detailed and careful assessment of the efforts that were made in the UNWCC. A number of recent publications have already shown that historical research on the UNWCC gives us a better understanding of its contribution to the development of international criminal law. The legal discussions that took place between the representatives of the member countries have proven to be especially helpful for clarifying the evolution of several important concepts in the history of international criminal law.

This chapter seeks to contribute to the ongoing effort of re-evaluating the contributions of the UNWCC by focusing on the role of one of the participating nations: the Republic of China ('China').[4] This allows not only for a more nuanced and detailed understanding of the work of the UNWCC but also an opportunity to explore non-European contributions to the development of international criminal law. This chapter does not intend to make any contribution to the theoretical discussion on Eurocentrism in international law, but merely seeks to emphasise the international quality of the UNWCC.[5] To revisit the legal discussions that took place in the UNWCC gives us a more complete picture of the legal opinions prevalent at the time, including those of scholars from smaller and less influential countries.

The chapter is divided into four main sections. Parts one and two consist of a historical introduction to China's participation in the UNWCC in London and in the Sub-Commission in Chungking. Part three focuses on the legal discussions that were held in the main UNWCC and its Legal Committee and it sheds light on China's position on several issues of international law. The fourth and final part discusses the series of war crimes trials reports that were issued by the UNWCC and their continuing importance for modern international criminal law.

---

[4] In this chapter the term Republic of China is used to refer to the Chinese nation between 1912 and 1949.

[5] For an overview see for instance Martti Koskenniemi, "Histories of International Law: Dealing with Eurocentrism", in *Rechtsgeschichte*, 2011, vol. 19, pp. 152–77.

16.2. China and the UNWCC in London

China was just one of several nations[6] that decided to join the UNWCC, but was the only member that had an additional panel set up in its own territory. This first part illustrates the role China played in the process of setting up the UNWCC, from the initial stage when the idea was developed until the time when the first meetings were convened.

16.2.1. Developing the Idea of a War Crimes Commission

In the 1940s news about atrocities being committed by the Germans continued to arrive in London, where not only the British but also a number of politicians belonging to the exile governments had gathered.[7] While powerless to directly stop the atrocities, they seemed to have the faint hope that public condemnation of these acts as war crimes could potentially prevent further outrages. The memory of the failure to hold perpetrators of war crimes responsible after the Great War[8] was still fresh in the minds of many and it impressed on them the need to work towards a common strategy amongst all the Allies. Both the US President Franklin D. Roosevelt and the British Prime Minister Winston Churchill had previously made statements condemning wartime atrocities, but those statements had been vague and had not entailed any concrete measures. With the US still being a neutral country at the time Roosevelt condemned the German killing of hostages[9], Churchill had declared that

---

[6]   Countries with representatives when regular meetings began in 1944: Australia, Belgium, Britain, China, Czechoslovakia, France, Greece, India, Luxembourg, Netherlands, Norway, Poland, United States, Yugoslavia; additional countries that had participated at the constituent meeting of the UNWCC on 20 October 1943: Canada, New Zealand, Union of South Africa.

[7]   For an overview see Martin Conway, "Legacies of Exile: The Exile Governments in London During the Second World War and the Politics of Post-War Europe", in Martin Conway and José Gotovitch (eds.), *Europe in Exile: European Exile Communities in Britain 1940–45*, Berghahn Books, Oxford, 2001, pp. 255–74.

[8]   "According to traditional interpretations, this attempt at trying German war criminals proved abortive to the point that, in the Allied discussions during the Second World War, 'the fiasco of the Leipzig trials' was regarded as an ideal example of how *not* to proceed"; see Jürgen Matthäus, "The Lessons of Leipzig: Punishing German War Criminals after the First World War", in Patricia Heberer and Jürgen Matthäus (eds.), *Atrocities on Trial: Historical Perspectives on the Politics of Prosecuting War Crimes,* University of Nebraska Press, Lincoln, 2008, p. 3.

[9]   "Franklin D. Roosevelt On the execution of hostages by the Nazis", *Department of State Bulletin,* 25 October 1941.

"[r]etribution for these crimes must henceforth take its place among the major purposes of the war".[10]

In an effort to nudge forward more concrete actions, nine of the smaller Allied nations issued a joint declaration, the so-called St James's Declaration ('the Declaration'), on 13 January 1942 in which they condemned German action as contrary to international law.[11] Article 3 of the Declaration stated that the signatories "place amongst their principal war aims the punishment, through the channel of organized justice, of those guilty and responsible for these crimes, whether they have ordered them, perpetrated them, or in any way participated in them".[12]

Although China was not a signatory to the Declaration, the Chinese government had sent an observer and later confirmed in writing that they subscribed to the principles of the Declaration and "intended, when the time comes, to apply the same principles to the Japanese occupying authorities in China".[13] After this first initiative more concrete steps towards the fulfilment of the St James's goals were taken later that year by the bigger powers. During a House of Lords debate on 7 October 1942, the Lord Chancellor Lord Simon spoke for the British government and expressed the need to set up a commission to deal with the question of war criminals "without further delay".[14] The same day Roosevelt equally issued a statement in support of the British suggestion declaring that the US government was "prepared to cooperate with the British and other Governments in establishing a United Nations Commission for the Investigation of War Crimes". "It was not the intention of the

---

[10] Arieh J. Kochavi, *Prelude to Nuremberg: Allied War Crimes Policy and the Question of Punishment,* University of North Carolina Press, Chapel Hill, 1998, p. 15.

[11] Signatory nations: Belgium, Czechoslovakia, the Free French National Committee, Greece, Luxembourg, the Netherlands, Norway, Poland, Yugoslavia; Present as observers: Britain, the US, the USSR, China and India.

[12] Full text of the Declaration reprinted in "The Inter-Allied Conference, January 13 1942", in *Bulletin of International News,* 1942, vol. 19, no. 2, pp. 50–53.

[13] Telegram, The Ambassador to the Polish Government in Exile (Biddle) to the Secretary of State, 14 January 1942, in United States Department of State, *Foreign Relations of the United States Diplomatic Papers, 1942 General; the British Commonwealth; the Far East,* ("Foreign Relations of the United States 1942"), US Government Printing Office, Washington, DC, 1942, p. 45.

[14] United Nations War Crimes Commission, *History of the United Nations War Crimes Commission and the Development of the Laws of War* ("History of the UNWCC"), His Majesty's Stationery Office, London, 1948, pp. 109–10.

government", the statement continued, "to resort to mass reprisals but to mete out just and sure punishment".[15] The British had informed the European Allies about the statements in advance but had not found the time to "obtain the views of the Soviet and Chinese governments".[16]

This shows that China was not yet involved in the process when the idea for a war crimes commission was still being developed and discussed. The initial initiative was a product of the hope and determination of the smaller allies to engage the big powers in a dialogue about war crimes and the punishment of war criminals. The focus was clearly on German crimes committed in the European theatre of war; Japanese atrocities in Asia did not seem to have played a decisive role.

16.2.2. China's Role in Setting Up the UNWCC

Even though the British had pledged to set up a commission without further delay, it took another year before the inaugurating meeting of the UNWCC was finally held on 20 October 1943. The long delay between the initial announcement and the actual setting up of the UNWCC reflected not only the rather low priority the governments had accorded to the project but also the slow process of communication, especially with the Soviet Union and China.[17] The one-year interval, however, had still not been enough to come to an agreement with the Soviet Union over the number of delegates it would be entitled to send. Consequently, no Soviet delegate attended this first or any of the following meetings of the UNWCC. The lack of support from the Soviet Union seriously weakened its influence.

China, on the other hand, was given a rather prominent role in the process of setting up the UNWCC. A reason for this is revealed in an internal memorandum of the British Foreign Office from December 1942. The author of the memorandum voiced his opinion that "the Chinese are very touchy about being treated as one of the four major Allies and [...] I think it would save subsequent ill feeling and trouble if they were now

---

[15] "President Franklin D. Roosevelt's Statement of War Crimes", White House News Release, 7 October 1942.

[16] Telegram, The Ambassador in the United Kingdom (Winant) to the Secretary of State, 6 October 1942, in Foreign Relations of the United States 1942, p. 60, see *supra* note 13.

[17] Kochavi, 1998, p. 27, see *supra* note 10.

included in the preliminary consultations".[18] This point of view was apparently adopted or shared by the Foreign Office. When they subsequently sent a memorandum inquiring about China's position on the UNWCC, the Foreign Office expressed the desire to "concert our general line of action with United States, Soviet, Chinese governments",[19] thereby granting China an equal standing with the other major powers.

China, probably pleased with the demeanour of the British, eventually answered that the Chinese government agreed with the British suggestions and had only minor amendments to make with regard to the details of the working of the UNWCC.[20] Interestingly enough, the Chinese Executive Yuan (executive branch of government) had already issued the decision that China would join the UNWCC on 15 June 1943, but had instructed the Ministry of Foreign Affairs and the Judicial Administration Bureau to wait until a favourable answer from the US had been received before sending a reply to London.[21]

British deference to the Chinese and Chinese attention to the US were a reflection of the special political constellation of the three countries at that time. The discussion about setting up a war crimes commission took place in a period during which the US was willing to support China as an emerging great power and to grant China the political status accordingly.[22] Chiang Kai-shek, Chairman of the National Government, was well aware of the fact that China was the weakest of the four allies,[23] but was still enraged when Churchill spoke about the "big three"

---

[18] Internal Memorandum, 11 December 1942, FO 371/34363, National Archives, UK ("TNA"), cited in Wenwei Lai, "Forgiven and Forgotten: The Republic of China in the United War Crimes Commission", in *Columbia Journal of Asian Law,* 2012, vol. 25, no. 2, p. 310.

[19] Confidential memorandum, UK Foreign Office to the Chinese Embassy in London, March 1943, Guoshiguan File 020-010117 0051-0057.

[20] Message to the Chinese Embassy in London, date unclear, Guoshiguan File 020-010117-0020-0094.

[21] Decision Executive Yuan, 68th meeting, 15 June 1943, Guoshiguan file 014-000001-444-0932.

[22] John W. Garver, "China's Wartime Diplomacy", in James C. Hsiung and Steven I. Levine (eds.), *China's Bitter Victory: The War with Japan, 1937–1945,* M.E. Sharpe, Armonk, NY, 1992, p. 24.

[23] Rana Mitter, *China's War with Japan, 1937–1945: The Struggle for Survival,* Allen Lane, London, 2013, p. 300.

instead of the "big four".[24] Churchill, on the other hand, thought that it was "affectation on the part of the US to pretend that China is a power in any way comparable to the other three".[25] So it seems safe to assume that the special status accorded to China was more an attempt to please the US than any real reflection of the political importance China possessed at the time.

China, on the other hand, did claim a special status for itself in the UNWCC based on the argument that China was the country that had suffered the most and the longest at the hands of the enemy.[26] This again was closely related to the different perceptions of China's role in China and in the West. The Chinese thought of their country as the "first and most consistent foe of axis aggression", but when it came to the Western Allies China was "a battered nation on its knees waiting for the American and British to save it from certain destruction at the hands of the Japanese".[27]

In the words of the later Chinese delegate to the UNWCC, China had decided to join the UNWCC for reasons of international solidarity.[28] This explanation aptly reflected China's newly developing self-understanding as a major power at the time. China was eager to be represented in the UNWCC even though it was, especially in the beginning, a distinctly European affair. With the exception of India and Australia, which were still participating as British Dominions, the Republic of China was the only country representing the Asia-Pacific region.

16.2.3. China's Representatives in the UNWCC

V.K. Wellington Koo, as an eminent diplomat and acting ambassador to Britain, suggested that the Chinese government should wait for the US to appoint a delegate first and only then select its own representative who

---

[24]   *Ibid.*, p. 301.

[25]   *Ibid.*

[26]   History of the UNWCC, p. 114, see *supra* note 14.

[27]   Mitter, 2013, p. 244, see *supra* note 23.

[28]   United Nations War Crimes Commission, Minutes of Eighteenth Meeting Held on 16 May 1944 ("Minutes No. 18") (http://www.legal-tools.org/doc/f2acc0/).

would need to match the US representative in terms of rank.[29] "If Washington should merely send a technical man, we might appoint Dr. Y.L. Liang, a good lawyer well versed in international law", Koo argued. "If the US should appoint an ambassador other than the American ambassador in London as its representative, we might appoint [...] ambassador Wunsz King".[30] The government's final decision was to appoint Wellington Koo himself with Liang Yunli as the second representative and Wunsz King as his substitute.[31]

Members of the UNWCC were first of all representatives of the sending governments and supposed to act in the best interest of their countries. Many of the members of the UNWCC, however, were legal scholars with more or less strongly held professional opinions. In addition, the question of war crimes and war criminals was for many a personal and often emotional topic. In some cases this led to situations of conflict between the national representatives and the national governments.[32] In contrast, the Chinese members of the delegation dutifully reported the matters discussed back to Chungking and only acted on instruction. On several occasions, however, they were forced to voice their personal opinions because the communication between London and Chungking was unsatisfactorily slow and instructions often did not arrive in time for the meetings of the UNWCC.[33] It is thus interesting to take a closer look at these representatives in order to understand parts of their personal backgrounds and motivations.

In selecting the Chinese ambassador to Britain as its representative, the Chinese government made an obvious and safe choice but at the same time they had also selected a person only moderately popular in the British diplomatic circle. When Koo was originally appointed ambassador

---

[29] V.K. Wellington Koo [顾维钧], *Gu Weijun huiyilu* [顾维钧回忆录], Zhonghua shuju, Beijing, 1997, p. 603.

[30] Lai, 2012, p. 312, see *supra* note 18.

[31] The names are rendered in the form in which they appear in the UNWCC documents. The Chinese names are as follows: Dr. Koo: Gu Weijun [顾维钧], Dr. Liang: Liang Yunli [梁鋆立], Dr. King: Jin Wensi [金问泗].

[32] Kochavi, 1998, p. 92, see *supra* note 10.

[33] United Nations War Crimes Commission, Minutes of Sixty-Ninth Meetings Held on July 11th, 1945 ("Minutes No. 69") (http://www.legal-tools.org/doc/4bb57e/). For instance the minutes of the fifth meeting of the Far Eastern and Pacific Sub-Commission on 15 March 1945 only reached the members of the main UNWCC in London on 11 June 1945.

---

in 1941 the initial reaction in the British Foreign Office was decidedly negative, and Britain even suggested the Chinese might want to reconsider their decision. Some in the Foreign Office intensely disliked him, describing him as one of Britain's bitterest enemies from the 1920s.[34] His anti-British and pro-American attitude was well known. He had even allowed himself to make a rather undiplomatic comment in an early book published in 1912 that may serve to illustrate the point. When discussing British merchants in Canton who had resisted the application of Chinese law to themselves, Koo offered the following explanation:

> The disrespect toward the territorial laws, predicable of foreigners in China generally, was so aggravated, in the case of the British at Canton, by the characteristic Anglo-Saxon pride and faith in the superiority of their own race and in the supremacy of their own institutions that they could not see how any of their countrymen could have committed a crime in China.[35]

The US delegate Herbert Pell, on the other hand, had been Koo's friend since their time as classmates at Columbia University. Pell called Koo "one of the most intelligent men Columbia ever graduated", while Koo admitted that it was his friend Pell "who helped China most in the UNWCC".[36] Even as a student at Columbia Koo had been concerned with questions of international law and graduated with a thesis on the legal status of aliens in China.[37] Later he became the Chinese representative to many important international conferences and continued to use international law as the preferred tool to improve China's international standing.[38]

Liang Yunli was probably the most proficient in the topic of war crimes and the most specialised in questions of international law. Before attending the meetings of the UNWCC he had already been involved in the London International Assembly ('LIA'), a predecessor organisation of

---

[34] Stephen G. Craft, *V.K. Wellington Koo and the Emergence of Modern China*, University Press of Kentucky, Lexington, 2004, p. 140.

[35] Wellington Koo, *The Status of Aliens in China*, Columbia University, New York, 1912, p. 80.

[36] Lai, 2012, p. 313, see *supra* note 18.

[37] Jonathan Clements, *Wellington Koo: China – Makers of the Modern World*, Haus Publishing, London, 2008, p. 31.

[38] Craft, 2004, p. 20, see *supra* note 34.

the UNWCC, working on questions of international criminal law. He had received law degrees both from China and the US, and had served in several legal and political positions in China before being sent to London to join the Chinese embassy. He became a member of the UNWCC's Legal Committee and even asked for his name to be substituted for that of Koo on the official lists, insisting that he had been elected in his own right and not as a substitute for the Chinese main delegate.[39] In 1946 he transferred as a member to the newly established United Nations in New York and went on to become the Director of the Division of Development and Codification of International Law.

Wunsz King, like Koo, was a graduate of Columbia University and their career paths had crossed early on. They had both been part of the Chinese delegation to the 1919 Peace Conference, King as the secretary to the delegation, Koo as the leading delegate.[40] He had spent time working for the Chinese Ministry of Foreign Affairs and at the League of Nations before becoming ambassador to the Netherlands in 1941. After his transfer to London he was the ambassador to the Netherlands and Belgium; later he also became the ambassador to Czechoslovakia, Poland and Norway.[41] In the memoirs of his diplomatic work King described his work for the UNWCC in just two short sentences, merely recalling that he had been asked to temporarily act as the substitute for Koo who was attending the Dumbarton Oaks Conference.[42] But this was clearly a task he did not attach too much importance to; it faded into the background as compared to other more pressing issues he had attended to as an ambassador.

The representatives China selected, including the representatives who attended the National Office Conference at the Royal Courts of Justice, were without exception well qualified for the work of the UNWCC. This becomes glaringly obvious if contrasted with the background of, for instance, the US representative Pell, who possessed no legal qualification but was a Harvard University friend of Roosevelt.[43]

---

[39] United Nations War Crimes Commission, Minutes of Eighty-Sixth Meeting Held on November 14th, 1945 ("Minutes No. 86") (http://www.legal-tools.org/doc/0ad815/).

[40] Clements, 2008, p. 73, see *supra* note 37.

[41] Jin Wensi [金问泗], *Waijiao gongzuo de huiyi* [外交工作的回忆], Chuanji wenxue chubanshe, Taibei, 1968, p. 90.

[42] *Ibid.*, p. 102.

[43] Kochavi, 1998, pp. 51–52, see *supra* note 10.

The qualification of the Chinese team, however, is probably more accurately described as a reflection of the high quality of Chinese diplomats generally at the time and should not be understood as a sign that the Chinese government attached special importance to the UNWCC. In fact the attendance record of Koo and Liang was far from complete because they were also frequently chosen to attend other important international conferences, such as the Dumbarton Oaks[44] and the San Francisco conferences.[45] This resulted in quite a number of meetings of the Legal Committee without any Chinese representative at all.

16.2.4. Determining the UNWCC's Competencies

Soon the core question of what the competencies of the UNWCC should be was discussed. During the preliminary meeting on 20 October 1943, Simon had already stated the British position that the UNWCC had essentially two purposes: first, to investigate and record evidence of war crimes; and second, to report cases in which sufficient evidence was available.[46] The British seemed especially wary of the UNWCC having too much influence and they sought to restrict it to the function of collecting evidence. When negotiating the setting up of the UNWCC, the Foreign Office had already been worried that it would "develop its own momentum" which might result in unwanted suggestions to the governments.[47] It soon became clear, however, that even if the UNWCC were just to discharge the duty of classifying offences it would still occasionally need to discuss questions of law. Britain thus suggested that a separate body, the so-called Technical Committee, should be established to deal with all questions of law. This idea did not find the support of the majority of the UNWCC and Bohuslav Ečer, the Czech delegate, was especially vocal in his objection. He argued that the UNWCC, as a body "composed of highly qualified lawyers and experts, and presided over by one of the most distinguished international lawyers and experienced international judge, should not be confined solely to this work for which a body of well-trained officials would be sufficient". [48] The Chinese

---

44 Koo, 1997, p. 630, see *supra* note 29.

45 *Ibid.*, p. 618.

46 History of the UNWCC, p. 113, see *supra* note 14.

47 Kochavi, 1998, p. 28, see *supra* note 10.

48 *Ibid.*, p. 93.

delegate agreed on the point that the Technical Committee was superfluous.[49]

16.3. China and the Sub-Commission in Chungking

The UNWCC consisted of both a main commission situated in London and a Sub-Commission situated in China's wartime capital Chungking.[50]

16.3.1. China's Role in Setting Up the Sub-Commission

The British had, from the beginning, suggested that the UNWCC might sit in different panels in addition to the headquarters. In a memorandum enquiring about the Chinese position on joining, the Foreign Office had suggested that "if London were accepted as the headquarters, his Majesty's government would propose that panels of the commission should, if the governments concerned so desire, be established in Washington, Moscow, Chungking".[51] The Foreign Office was apparently aware of the fact that the Chinese government attached great importance to Japanese war crimes being examined in Chungking, and thought to secure general acceptance for this proposition that they considered to be a "concession"[52] and an "attempt to please China".[53]

The Chinese government had, indeed, from the early stages of the consultations expressed their determination to have a panel set up in China. As soon as the main commission in London had successfully been established the Chinese representative Koo started lobbying for this cause. During an ambassador's lunch in April 1944, especially organised for this purpose, Koo tried to impress on his fellow diplomats that "the creation of a Far Eastern panel or branch of the war crimes commission had been contemplated from the outset" and that the Chinese government "was

---

[49] Telegram Ambassador in the United Kingdom (Winant) to the Secretary of State, January 27 1944, United States Department of State, *Foreign Relations of the United States Diplomatic Papers, 1944* ("Foreign Relations of the United States 1944"), vol. 1, US Government Printing Office, Washington, DC, 1944, p. 1274.

[50] After the end of the war the Sub-Commission transferred to the new Chinese capital Nanjing.

[51] Confidential Memorandum, UK Foreign Office to the Chinese Embassy in London, March 1943, Guoshiguan File 020-010117 0051-0057.

[52] Lai, 2012, p. 311, see *supra* note 18.

[53] Kochavi, 1998, pp. 51–52, see *supra* note 10.

anxious to have the branch created, as it had a very large number of cases of war crimes to submit".[54] A special committee on the establishment of a Sub-Commission was set up and Koo was duly elected as the Chairman. Again he stated that "a large number of Chinese cases were ready for examination and his government accordingly thought the Far Eastern panel of the commission which had been contemplated from the outset might now be brought into being". [55] Koo was also able to make use of the private connection with Pell who supported him in his endeavour.[56] When the question turned to the competencies the new panel had Pell argued that the panel should take the form of a Sub-Commission rather than a committee and enjoy the greatest degree of independence possible; a suggestion that was finally accepted by the UNWCC.[57] The efforts that were made to have a separate panel set up for the Far East shows that China was not content with playing a role in Europe but wanted a leading position in Asia instead. The idea was to turn Chungking into the centre for the prosecution of war criminals in Asia, just as London was in Europe.

16.3.2. The Sub-Commission and its Representatives

The foreign delegates to the Sub-Commission were mostly the diplomatic representatives to China at the time. [58] As was the case with the headquarters in London, the Chinese government selected highly qualified persons to attend to the work of the Sub-Commission. Wang Chung-Hui,[59] whose name had also been included in the discussion on who should become the Chinese delegate to London,[60] was elected as the Chairman of the Sub-Commission. He was the secretary general of the Supreme National Defence Council, and could look back on an illustrious career in law and politics, having served as the Minister of Foreign

---

54   Summary of Discussion, 13 April 1944, Guoshiguan file 020-010117-0051-0058.

55   Committee on the Establishment of a Far Eastern and Pacific Sub-Commission, Meeting 1, 4 May 1944, Guoshiguan File 010117-0051-0063.

56   Lai, 2012, p. 313, see *supra* note 18.

57   *Ibid.*, p. 314.

58   For a complete list of delegates of the Sub-Commission see History of the UNWCC, p. 130, *supra* note 14.

59   Wang Chung-hui: Wang Chonghui [王宠惠].

60   "If Dr. C.H Wang could represent us it would be ideal", Dr. T.V. Soong to Dr. K.C. Wu, 16 April 1943, Guoshiguan File 020-010117-0020-0126.

Affairs, Minister of Justice and judge at the Permanent Court of International Justice.[61] He commanded respect among lawyers as well as diplomats and had a reputation for being one of the foremost legal scholars in China.[62] He, too, was absent for a long period of time representing China at international conferences [63] before he finally resigned from the Sub-Commission in July 1946,[64] arguing that his numerous other responsibilities did not allow him to adequately fulfil his role as Chairman. P.C. Chang, the counsellor of the Executive Yuan, served the Sub-Commission as secretary general until he was appointed the new Chinese general counsel in New York in February 1946.[65]

16.3.3. The Sub-Commission's Competencies

The inaugural meeting of the Sub-Commission was held in Chungking on 29 November 1944[66] and it was off to a rather slow start. Despite many previous assurances to the contrary, the Chinese National Office was not able to supply the Sub-Commission with sufficient cases to examine. The Sub-Commission turned out to be the type of institution the British had initially imagined for London: almost exclusively concerned with reviewing evidence and compiling name lists of war crimes suspects. Legal questions were referred back to London for decision.[67] Judging from the available documents, it seems as if the Sub-Commission did not produce any draft legislation or memoranda or even the general recommendations on how to deal with Japanese war criminals. All in all

---

61 For an overview over life dates and career see Duan Caihua [段彩华], "Wang Chonghui xiansheng dashi nianbiao" [王宠惠先生大事年表], in Humenzhen renminzhengfu (ed.), *Wang Chonghui yu zhonghua minguo* [王宠惠与中华民国], Guangdong renmin chubanshe, Guangzhou shi, 2007, p. 390.

62 Liu Baodong [刘宝东], "Faxuejia Wang Chonghui: shengping zhushu sixiang" [法学家王宠惠:生平著述思想], in Humenzhen renminzhengfu, 2007, p. 100, see *supra* note 61.

63 He attended the San Francisco Conference in 1945.

64 His successor was Dr. Liu Chieh, the Vice Minister of Foreign Affairs.

65 Report of the British Embassy in Chungking, 21 February 1946, TNA, FO 371/57567.

66 Report of the Far Eastern and Pacific Sub-commission of the United Nations War Crimes Commission, Guoshiguan File 020-010117-0054-0035.

67 Question of deliberate bombardments being referred back to the main commission, Sub-Commission. United Nations War Crimes Commission, Minutes of the Thirty-Fifth Meeting of the Far Eastern and Pacific Sub-Commission of the United Nations War Crimes of Commission, 10 a.m. Tuesday, December 10th, 1946, Ministry of Foreign Affairs ("Minutes No. 35" (http://www.legal-tools.org/doc/234ffd/).

---

the connection between the UNWCC in London and the Sub-Commission was rather weak and communication between the groups was slow and cumbersome. Even Liang stated that the Chinese embassy in London had no more information available to them than those contained in the minutes which the Sub-Commission routinely sent to headquarters.[68]

16.3.4. The Sub-Commission's Work and Foreign Critique

What began as a prestige project soon turned into a source of embarrassment for the Chinese government. After they had put enormous efforts into setting up their own panel, the work of the Sub-Commission remained unsatisfactory. So unsatisfactory, indeed, that the foreign delegates soon started reporting back to their governments in very unfavourable terms.

Initially there was a period of delay because the Chinese National Office had failed to submit cases on the standard forms used by the UNWCC. [69] The National Office, however, continued to elicit dissatisfaction when the cases they eventually submitted were not readily forthcoming, low in number and of insufficient quality. George Atcheson, the US delegate to the Sub-Commission, spoke of the "apparent inability of the present Chinese National Office to present cases appropriately prepared and investigated". [70] The delegates first chose the most diplomatic avenue of addressing the issue during the regular meetings of the Sub-Commission. During the fifth meeting in March 1945, for instance, the Australian delegate, Keith Officer, voiced his dissatisfaction over the fact that since its inception the Sub-Commission had not handled a single case. Other members agreed and the Secretary General was urged

---

[68] The United States Commissioner, United Nations War Crimes Commission (Hodgson) to the Secretary of State, 6 August 1945; United States Department of State, *Foreign Relations of the United States: Diplomatic Papers, 1945, in The British Commonwealth, The Far East* ("Foreign Relations of the United States 1945"), vol. 6, US Government Printing Office, Washington, DC, 1945, p. 904.

[69] United Nations War Crimes Commission, Minutes of the Fourth Meeting of the Far Eastern and Pacific Sub-Commission of the United Nations War Crimes Commission, 4 p.m. Friday, February 23rd, 1945, at 305 Chung San Road, Chungking ("Minutes No. 4") (http://www.legal-tools.org/doc/d8a3e5/).

[70] Memorandum, George Atcheson, 3 April 1945, cited in Lai, 2012, pp. 330–31, see *supra* note 18.

to "expedite (the) work (of the National Office) so as to ensure a steady flow of cases to the Sub-commission for examination".[71]

When no improvement was achieved the delegates started to think about ways to exert external pressure on the Chinese government. The British ambassador Seymour called on the chargé d'affaires of the US embassy and "express[ed] his concern over the lack of progress being made by the Chinese national office [...] due to the failure by the Chinese government to take the necessary action to make this office effective". When reporting back to the department of state the chargé mentioned that he was "of the opinion that the situation may have to be taken up with the Generalissimo[72] and direct instructions [might have to be] issued by him in order to make Chinese participation really effective".[73]

It seems that the work of the Chinese National Office was unsatisfactory due to a combination of factors. In part it was the unwillingness of the Chinese government and in part the inability to carry out the required work to an appropriate standard. It might seem surprising to suggest lack of commitment to the work of the Sub-Commission after the Chinese government had so vehemently insisted on a Sub-commission to be set up. But the time between the lobbying process in London and the complaints in Chungking had seen a change in the Chinese policy towards the prosecution of war criminals. While there had been genuine interest in prosecuting war criminals during the final years of the war, the issue of war crimes was no longer a priority for the Chinese government after the war had come to a close.[74] On the other hand, the Chinese National Office was also plagued by practical difficulties in their attempt to submit *prima facie* cases to the Sub-Commission. China had already started collecting evidence of Japanese atrocities a few years earlier, but a lot of the material that was initially collected lacked detailed information on the war

---

[71] Far Eastern and Pacific Sub-Commission, Minutes of the Fifth Meeting of the Far Eastern and Pacific Sub-Commission of the United Nations for Crimes Commission, 4 p.m. Friday, March 16th, 1945, at 305 Chung San Road, Chungking ("Minutes No. 5") (http://www.legal-tools.org/doc/3494b3/).

[72] "Generalissimo" was another term used to refer to Chiang Kai-shek.

[73] The Chargé in China (Briggs) to the Secretary of State, 20 April 1945, in Foreign Relations of the United States 1945, 1945, pp. 96–97, see *supra* note 68.

[74] Zuo Shuangwen [左双文] "Guomin zhengfu yu chengchu riben zhanfan jige wenti de zai kaocha" [国民政府与惩处日本战犯几个问题的再考察], *Shehui kexue yanjiu* [社会科学研究], 2012, no. 6, p. 150.

crimes suspects required for criminal prosecutions.[75] In 1944 the Chinese government had already set up a new structure charged with a more systematic collection of evidence,[76] the Chinese Commission for War Crimes Investigation ('Chinese Commission').[77] But the quality and number of cases that the Chinese Commission had been able to prepare for the Sub-Commission was insufficient still and led to the massive complaints from the foreign representatives.

The representatives' strategy to exert pressure was eventually effective and the Chinese government finally had no choice but to react to the criticism. "On June 7th 1945, the Chinese Ministry of Foreign Affairs notified the Sub-Commission by letter that the Chinese National Office had been abolished and its work of investigating war crimes had been entrusted to the Ministry of Justice and translation work to the Ministry of Foreign Affairs. Hope [was expressed] that soon there would be a steady flow of cases to the Sub-Commission for examination".[78] What the government did to address the criticism was to set up yet another commission on how to deal with war criminals,[79] which started work on 6 December 1945[80] and consisted of six different government bodies working together.[81]

In addition to the reorganisation of the National Office, the Chairman Wang Chung-Hui had also left the Sub-Commission, leading to a situation where the "work of the Sub-Commission [...] [was] almost

---

[75] Toshiya Ikō [伊香俊哉], "Zhongguo guomin zhengfu dui riben zhanfan de chuzhi fangzhen" [中国国民政府对日本战犯的处置方针], translated by Lu Peng [芦鹏], in *Nanjing datushashi yanjiu* [南京大屠杀史研究], 2012, no. 4, p. 91.

[76] *Ibid.*, p. 92.

[77] Official Chinese name: Diren zuixing diaocha weiyuanhui [敌人罪行调查委员会]. Guo Biqiang [郭必强] and Jiang Liangqin [姜良芹] (eds.), *Nanjing datusha shiliaoji* [南京大屠杀史料集], vol. 19, *Rijun zuixing diaocha weiyuanhui diaocha tongji* [日军罪行调查委员会调查统计], Jiangsu renmin chubanshe, Nanjing, 2006, p. 70. Minutes of the 5th Meeting of the Chinese Commission for War Crimes Investigation, 29 July 1944.

[78] Far Eastern and Pacific Sub-Commission, Minutes of the Sixth Meeting of the Far Eastern and Pacific Sub-Commission of the United Nations War Crimes Commission, 4 p.m. Friday, June 8th, 1945, at 305 Chung San Road, Chungking ("Minutes No. 6") (http://www.legal-tools.org/doc/941c34/).

[79] 战犯处理委员会 [Commission on War Criminals].

[80] Ikō, 2012, p. 91, see *supra* note 75.

[81] Zuo, 2012, p. 150, see *supra* note 74.

suspended".[82] After the reorganisation of the Chinese National Office it was "functioning more efficiently"[83] but the only nation willing to file cases with the Sub-Commission now was China itself.[84] With regard to the Sub-Commission, China had become a victim of its own ambitions. After having invited all the foreign delegates to participate in the Sub-Commission in Chungking, they were in an excellent position to supervise and comment on the Sub-Commission's progress and to witness the sudden change in the war crimes policy of the Chinese government.

All of this led the Chairman of the UNWCC in London, Lord Wright, to conclude later that the UNWCC "had not been of first rate importance in the Far East" and that "affairs in the Far East had better be left to the Far East unless some particular connection arose".[85] Given all the negative reactions and practical difficulties the Sub-Commission faced it is not surprising that there was the desire to wind it up at an early date. Stating that it considered its task already completed, the Sub-Commission informed the delegates in London of their request, arousing suspicion amongst some of them. Two delegates remarked that from the minutes of the Sub-Commission it was clear that "very big numbers of complaints were still under investigation" and thus found it hard to reconcile this with the Sub-Commission's own statement.[86] After some discussion, however, a resolution was passed to wind up the Sub-Commission by 31 March 1947.[87]

16.4. China and the Legal Discussion in the UNWCC

After the idea of a Technical Committee had been abandoned discussions on questions of law became an important and, from today's perspective, especially interesting part of the UNWCC's work. Because of their

---

[82] Chang Pingshuen to Wang Huacheng, 18 June 1945, Guoshiguan File no. 020-010117-0052-0167.

[83] Telegram, The Ambassador in China (Hurley) to the Secretary of State, 28 July 1945, in Foreign Relations of the United States 1945, p. 901, see *supra* note 68.

[84] Telegram, The American Ambassador in China (Hurley) to the Secretary of State, 9 September 1945, in *Ibid.*, p. 924

[85] United Nations War Crimes Commission, Minutes of the Hundred and Thirty-First Meeting Held on 29 October 1947 ("Minutes No. 131") (http://www.legal-tools.org/doc/574109/).

[86] United Nations War Crimes Commission, Minutes of Meeting Held on Wednesday, 12th March 1947, at 3 p.m. ("Minutes No. 124") (http://www.legal-tools.org/doc/981934/).

[87] *Ibid.*

continued relevance for modern-day international criminal law only discussions pertaining to war crimes, crimes against humanity and aggression will be taken into consideration for the purpose of this chapter. Before turning to the questions of the law proper it might be helpful to keep in mind one caveat: when speaking about 'war crimes' many delegates used the term interchangeably to mean either war crimes in the strict sense or a general term encompassing a variety of crimes including crimes against humanity and aggression. In addition, the term was used to denote the legal concept of war crimes as well as a concept to delineate the jurisdiction of the UNWCC. At times there also seemed to have been a fair amount of confusion among the delegates themselves about these different levels of discussion. An additional difficulty in trying to follow the legal discussions presents the fact that, on suggestion of the US delegate Pell, debates in the UNWCC were not recorded.[88] This means that a big part of the discussion that took place can only be reconstructed indirectly, relying on private documentation or correspondence between the delegates and the national governments.

16.4.1. War Crimes

With the official name being the "United Nations War Crimes Commission"[89] it is not surprising that Cecil Hurst, then Chairman, chose to raise the question of what constitutes a war crime during the first meeting of the UNWCC. Ečer felt that the term "War Crime was a conception of the past and [that] it had been surpassed by the method of total war". He suggested "Axis crimes" as a novel term that would include not only crimes as defined by international law but also as a concept wider in scope. Unsurprisingly other delegates were not prepared to go so far. Lord Atkin, who represented Australia, however, equally felt that the offenders had gone "right outside the realms of law" and he stressed that "it was important to free oneself from legalistic notions, whereby crimes could only be punished if they fell within the definition of war crimes". The Chinese delegate, Koo, said "that the Commission

---

88 Kochavi, 1998, p. 95, see *supra* note 10.

89 The name United Nations War Crimes Commission was a suggestion by the Americans to find a more legal-sounding name for what the British had initially called the Commission for the Investigation of War Atrocities.

must approach its task from a practical point of view" and that "all war crimes should be punished according to the conscience of humanity".[90]

After the initial euphoria had been replaced by an atmosphere of pragmatism, the UNWCC decided to follow a more conventional path. "It decided to proceed upon the footing that international law regards as a war crime any offence against the laws and customs of war [...] The Commission further decided however that it would be convenient for the purposes of its own work to adopt the list of war crimes prepared by the Responsibilities Commission of the Paris Peace Conference 1919 [the 'Commission on Responsibilities'] so that the National Offices might know the various headings under which war crimes can be grouped".[91] An additional factor in this decision was that both Italy and Japan had been involved in the drafting process for the list while Germany had at least never openly objected to it.[92] The UNWCC treated the document as an open list that could be amended if circumstances so demanded.[93] To China, the list soon acquired additional meaning and importance because it was heavily relied upon during the drafting of the War Crimes Trials Regulations in 1946.[94] Article 3 of these Regulations, containing a definition of acts that would be considered a war crime, was basically a reproduction of the list drawn up by the Commission on Responsibilities. The only noticeable difference being that in the Chinese legislation the individual items appeared in a different order and that a number of additional items were added to the original list.

The discussion about the definition of the term war crime is an example of how the work of the UNWCC influenced the Chinese interpretation and usage of an international legal instrument. The UNWCC seemed to have fostered the mutual exchange of ideas among

---

[90] United Nations War Crimes Commission, Notes of Unofficial Preliminary Meeting Held at 2:30 p.m. on the 25th October 1943, at the Royal Courts of Justice, London ("Unofficial Preliminary Meeting") (http://www.legal-tools.org/doc/ad8990/).

[91] UNWCC Progress Report, Adopted by the Commission on 19 September 1944, Guoshiguan File 020-010117-0021-0035.

[92] Commission on the Responsibility of the Authors of the War and on Enforcement of Penalties, *Violation of the Laws and Customs of War: Reports of Majority and Dissenting Reports of American and Japanese Members of the Commission of Responsibilities, Conference of Paris 1919,* Clarendon Press, Oxford, 1919, p. 80.

[93] Guoshiguan File no. 020-010117-0053-0010.

[94] War Crimes Trials Regulations [战争罪犯审判条例], 24 October 1946.

the delegates and across national borders; it also facilitated the introduction of new thinking on international law.

16.4.2. Crimes Against Humanity

The realities of the war presented the delegates with atrocities that failed to fit into the established categories of war crimes. Two factors were especially problematic: the period of time during which an atrocity was committed and the status of the victims. Some crimes had been committed before the start of the actual war and some of the victims were enemy nationals suffering under the hands of their own rightful governments. Classical legal doctrine, however, only considered a crime to be a war crime if it was committed against enemy nationals during the time of hostilities.

The question of the time frame had been a very important concern for the Chinese from the very beginning and Koo had already stated during the very first meeting of the UNWCC that his government "reserved the right [...] to raise the question of the period of time which [will be] investigated".[95] China's main concern was to extend the jurisdiction of the UNWCC to all acts committed after 18 September 1931, the date of the so-called Mukden incident that marked the beginning of the Japanese invasion in Manchuria.[96] The British, however, seemed worried that if the Chinese suggestion was accepted the Czechs might then demand investigations into the Sudetenland Crisis in March 1939 which might raise uncomfortable questions for Britain, which had supported the annexation in the Munich agreement of 1938.[97] In the end, the question of the time period proved to be only a minor problem for the UNWCC, and both the main body as well as the Sub-Commission decided to deal with cases that had occurred before the official start of the war.

A far bigger issue was whether the UNWCC should restrict itself to cases where the victims were Allied nationals. This question was especially pressing because of the German atrocities committed against the German Jewish community and other German citizens. In one of the

---

[95] History of the UNWCC, p. 114, see *supra* note 14.

[96] Telegram, Ministry of Foreign Affairs to the Chinese embassy in London, undated, Guoshiguan File 020-010117-0020-0094.

[97] Kochavi, 1998, p. 55, see *supra* note 10.

first meetings of the Legal Committee, Pell drew attention to these circumstances. Some delegates, especially the British, Greek and Norwegian, were of the opinion that crimes committed by Germans against their own nationals could not be included in the term war crimes "however compelling the need to punish them" might be.

A different position was represented by the US, and strongly supported by Czechoslovakia and the Netherlands.[98] The Czech delegate prepared a report on this matter, arguing that these offences should not be considered an internal matter of the affected countries.[99] After some further study the Legal Committee submitted a report coming to the conclusion that the UNWCC would need to bring its "methods and principles [...] into line with the principles expressed in the Allied declarations"[100] and suggested to define 'crimes against humanity' as "crimes committed against any person without regard to nationality, stateless persons included, because of race, nationality, religious or political belief, irrespective of where they have been committed".[101] In 1944 Liang argued for China, however, that he preferred a strict definition of war crimes which would exclude atrocities committed by a government against its own citizens.[102] Other delegates were also unsure whether their governments would support such a progressive policy. The Chairman of the UNWCC finally decided to address a letter to the British government asking if they desired that the UNWCC restricted itself to crimes committed against Allied nationals. The failure of the British government to respond to the UNWCC's letter in a timely manner turned into an *éclat*. It became obvious how sensitive the issue had become when Ečer withdrew from all committees and threatened to leave the UNWCC over the dispute. Pell reported back to Washington that he feared the issue would enrage the Jewish community and would "arouse [them] into hostility".[103] The British government, however, answered that they were

---

[98]   History of the UNWCC, p. 174, see *supra* note 14.

[99]   *Ibid.*, p. 175.

[100] *Ibid.*, p. 176.

[101] *Ibid.*

[102] Lai, 2012, p. 319, see *supra* note 18.

[103] The American delegate at the United Nations War Crimes Commission (Pell) to the Secretary of State, 27 September 1944, in Foreign Relations of the United States 1944, p. 1367, see *supra* note 49.

of the opinion that the UNWCC should only deal with crimes committed against Allied victims.[104]

In the end the UNWCC never took a definite stand on this question until the drafting of the Nuremberg Charter.[105] Only in January 1946, after it was clear that the International Military Tribunal would not only prosecute for war crimes in the strict sense but also for crimes against humanity and aggression, did a new round of discussions regarding the definition of war crimes and especially the limits of the jurisdiction of the UNWCC begin.

The Chairman felt strongly that the authority of the UNWCC should extend to all war crimes in the widest sense. Liang felt unable to contribute to the discussion because he had not received instructions from Chungking in time.[106] When the discussion resumed at the next meeting he felt compelled to speak on his own responsibility and stated that he was of the opinion that "crimes against peace and against humanity should be put on the same footing as War Crimes in the limited sense, and that the Commission's jurisdiction included them".[107] Because he had still received no instructions from his government he had to abstain from voting.[108] I have not been able to find material that would explain why the Chinese government failed to send any instructions on this question. But it seems reasonable to suggest that they did indeed support Liang's opinion on this point, because the concept of crimes against humanity was eventually included in the Chinese War Crimes Trials Regulations.[109]

It is interesting to note, however, that the Sub-Commission in Chungking followed a different course on this question and decided that Japanese crimes against Japanese citizens would not be included in the work of the Sub-Commission.[110] As a result, atrocities committed against

---

[104] History of the UNWCC, p. 176, see *supra* note 14.

[105] *Ibid.*

[106] United Nations War Crimes Commission, Minutes of Ninety-Second Meeting Held on 3rd, January 1946 ("Minutes No. 92") (http://www.legal-tools.org/doc/f786cd/).

[107] United Nations War Crimes Commission, Minutes of Ninety-Third Meeting Held on January 30th, 1946 ("Minutes No. 93") (http://www.legal-tools.org/doc/78e610/).

[108] Countries also abstaining: the US, Canada, New Zealand, Norway, France.

[109] War Crimes Trials Regulations [战争罪犯审判条例], 24 October 1946.

[110] Far Eastern and Pacific Sub-Commission, Minutes of the Thirty-Sixth Meeting of the Far Eastern and Pacific Sub-Commission of the United Nations War Crimes Commission, 10

those from Korea and Taiwan, who still had Japanese citizenship during the war, were also excluded.

16.4.3. War of Aggression

Whether or not waging an aggressive war should be considered a crime under international law and whether it should be included in the term 'war crimes' and fall under the jurisdiction of the UNWCC was, according to the Chairman "[b]y far the most important issue of substantive law to be studied by the Commission and its Legal Committee".[111]

In March 1944 the Czech representative argued in the Legal Committee that the paramount crime of the Axis leaders was the starting of the war. The Legal Committee at first agreed and included the idea in a draft resolution on the "Scope of the Retributive Action of the United Nations".[112] They advocated the view that waging a war of aggression should be treated as a war crime and fall under the jurisdiction of the UNWCC. The representatives, however, were unsure whether their respective governments would support such an interpretation.[113] A special Sub-Committee was entrusted with the task of studying the question further. [114] The British representative came to the conclusion that "aggressive war however reprehensible did not represent a crime in international law".[115] The majority of the Sub-Committee and the Legal Committee agreed and reports were handed to the main UNWCC for discussion. [116] Ečer's minority report only found support among the delegates from Australia, China, New Zealand, Poland and Yugoslavia.[117]

Both Koo and Liang were absent from London when this important topic was discussed and King represented the Chinese interests in the

---

a.m. Tuesday, January 14th, 1947, Ministry of Foreign Affairs ("Minutes No. 36") (http://www.legal-tools.org/doc/dc1e12/).

[111] Jonathan A. Bush, "'The Supreme Crime' and Its Origins: The Lost Legislative History of the Crime of Aggressive War", in *Columbia Law Review*, 2002, vol. 102, no. 8, p. 2348.

[112] History of the UNWCC, p. 180, see *supra* note 14.

[113] *Ibid.*, p. 181.

[114] The Sub-Committee consisted of the British, Czechoslovak, Dutch and US representatives.

[115] History of the UNWCC, p. 181, see *supra* note 14.

[116] *Ibid.*, p. 182.

[117] *Ibid.*, p. 183.

UNWCC. He reacted to the British suggestion that aggression, *de lege lata*, was not a crime under international law in the following manner:

> With all his admiration for Professor McNair's legal opinion, and for the opinion so ably expressed [...] he was inclined to think that [...] while sound in theory, was too narrow and legalistic and lagged far behind the movement of the enlightened public opinion which regarded those acts as illegal, and considered that the political and military leaders responsible should be tried and punished. Was it not, he asked, within the competence of this Commission to bring this matter to the attention of the Governments so that the question might be settled on the political level? Perhaps, in due course, another attempt would be made to codify International Law, and some ruling might then be given to the effect that acts for the preparation and launching of wars of aggression was illegal, and that their authors should be punished.[118]

Koo later stated in a message to the Chinese Ministry of Foreign Affairs that Hurst tried to draft a formula that would be acceptable to all parties and tried to avoid the need to actually vote in the full UNWCC. Koo said that Hurst and he agreed that there was "no difference of opinion expressed before the commission on fundamental question whether such acts should be punished as criminal [...] Difference of opinion was on how they should be punished whether on political level or by judicial process".[119] The majority of delegates, however, thought the question was a critical one and preferred to wait for instructions from their governments.[120] As a result no final report or recommendation was adopted on this issue in the end.[121]

Probably not a pure coincidence, it was the representatives from Czechoslovakia and China who fought for criminal responsibility to be

---

[118] United Nations War Crimes Commission, Minutes of Thirty-Fifth Meeting Held on October 10th, 1944, Report on Whether Preparation and Launching a War Can Be Considered a War Crime, ("Minutes No. 35") (http://www.legal-tools.org/doc/daeb97/).

[119] Telegram, Chinese Embassy in London to the Chinese Ministry of Foreign Affairs, 26 December 1944, Guoshiguan File 020-010117-0052-0033.

[120] The American Representative in the United Nations War Crimes Commission to the Secretary of State, 2 November 1944, in Foreign Relations of the United States 1944, p. 1391, see *supra* note 49.

[121] History of the UNWCC, p. 185, see *supra* note 14.

attached to aggression. Both countries had lost parts of their territory to Germany and Japan before the actual war and under the eyes of the world community. As one of the signatories of the Munich Agreement in 1938 that had granted Germany the annexation of the Sudetenland, Britain had understandably little enthusiasm to have the topic discussed.[122] China had lost Manchuria to the Japanese in 1931 and spent considerable time and energy in trying to convince the international community and the League of Nations to acknowledge this as an act of aggression. Koo had been the Chinese delegate representing China's interest before the League of Nations in 1931 in the Manchuria conflict and in 1937 over further Japanese aggression. Both times he had been only moderately successful. The Lytton Report in 1932 had not contained an outright condemnation of Japan but recognised the special nature of Japanese rights in Manchuria instead.[123] In August 1937 Koo at least achieved a condemnation of Japanese aerial bombing of Chinese cities and saw the League of Nations reject the Japanese claim that it was acting in self-defence but again no concrete measures followed.[124]

The UNWCC was thus another forum for China to raise the question of Japanese aggression in China one more time. If the UNWCC were willing to adopt aggression as a war crime falling under its jurisdiction, there was a chance that several Japanese would be listed as war crime suspects for participation in a war of aggression. This would in turn help to establish that Japan had been guilty of aggressive behaviour towards China since 1931.

16.4.4. Putting the Discussion into Perspective

While the foregoing account focuses on the legal discussions in the UNWCC, it is important to remember that they did not take place in isolation but formed just one part of a longer and ongoing discourse on war crimes. Several organisations in Europe and the US had already started discussing similar questions of international law before the UNWCC as an official body took up the topic. This fact is especially noteworthy as some of the members of the UNWCC had also been

---

[122] Kochavi, 1998, p. 55, see *supra* note 10.

[123] Thomas W. Burkman, *Japan and the League of Nations: Empire and World Order, 1914–1938*, University of Hawaii Press, Honolulu, 2008, p. 170.

[124] *Ibid.*

members of those predecessor organisations. Unlike in the UNWCC, where the delegates had to represent the sending governments, the predecessor organisations had allowed them to participate in their private capacity and form their personal and professional opinions on questions of the prosecution of war criminals.

The International Commission for Penal Reconstruction and Development, for instance, was a semi-official group made up of members of the Law Faculty at the University of Cambridge and important scholars of international and criminal law.[125] As early as 1941 at least some of the members of this commission had come to the opinion that under the Kellogg-Briand Pact the initiation of a war might be considered a crime.[126] This is interesting to note, since the majority of the members of the UNWCC later found it impossible to agree with such a statement.

Another close connection existed between the UNWCC and the London International Assembly ('LIA') that had a number of members who consequently went on to become representatives in the UNWCC.[127] Even though the LIA was not an official body, its members were chosen by the national governments and in turn it made recommendations to the respective governments.[128] The LIA members had also concerned themselves with the questions of war crimes, crimes against humanity and aggression and had issued a recommendation that stated the following:

> Moreover, [...] the commission recommended that those responsible for the crime of war i.e. unprovoked aggression should be branded as criminals and adequately punished. In respect of the extermination of Jews it was recommended that punishment should be imposed not only when the victims were allied Jews but even when the crimes had been

---

[125] History of the UNWCC, p. 95, see *supra* note 14. Members listed: M. Aulie (Norway), Dr. Benes (Czechoslovakia), M. Bodson (Luxembourg), Prof. Cassin (France), M. de Baer (Belgium), Dr. de Moor (Netherlands), Dr. Glaser (Poland), M. Kaeckenbeck (Belgium), M. Stavropoulos (Greece), Dr. Vlajic (Yugoslavia).

[126] Bush, 2002, p. 2341, see *supra* note 112.

[127] De Baer (Belgium), Liang (China), Ečer (Czechoslovakia), Stavropoulos (Greece), de Moor (Netherlands), Bodson (Luxembourg) and Colban (Norway).

[128] Historical Survey of the Question of International Criminal Jurisdiction: Memorandum submitted by the Secretary General, United Nations General Assembly, International Law Commission, 1949, A/CN.4/7/Rev.1, p. 18.

committed against stateless Jews or any other Jews in Germany or elsewhere.[129]

It is tempting to speculate about the reasons the LIA delegates apparently had no difficulties in declaring crimes against humanity and aggression as criminal under international law. One explanation might be that they were acting in their private capacity and were able to express their personal opinions as legal experts without the need to take their governments' policy into considerations.

This short introduction is of course by no means a systematic or comprehensive account of the legal discussion that took place during the war. But it is already sufficient to suggest that there were individual legal scholars that had come to the conclusion that waging a war of aggression or atrocities committed by a state against its own nationals should entail criminal responsibility. The UNWCC, however, had a far more conservative approach, choosing to rely on the list of war crimes that had already been drawn up in 1919 and refusing to accept the more progressive ideas of a crime of aggression and crimes against humanity. Only when the London Conference created a new legal reality with the Nuremberg Charter was the UNWCC willing to change its course. China had supported the more conservative majority on the question of non-Allied victims but had been a supporter of the idea to criminalise the waging of an aggressive war.

16.5. UNWCC and the War Crimes Trials Reports

Another important task that was carried out by the UNWCC was the collection and publication of a series of war crimes trials reports covering the national proceedings against war criminals in the member countries. The UNWCC published 15 volumes of transcripts of war crimes trials plus accompanying material such as the translations of national legislation and commentary prepared by the staff of the UNWCC between 1947 and 1949.[130] The UNWCC took the task of reporting on war crimes very

---

[129] London International Assembly, *The Punishment of War Criminals: Recommendations of the London International Assembly*, London, 1944, p. 7.
[130] All the volumes are now available online.

seriously and started in 1945 to put pressure on the governments, including the Chinese, to report war crimes trials to the UNWCC.[131]

In the foreword to the first volume published in 1947, Wright, as Chairman of the UNWCC, expressed aptly what he considered to be the importance of this undertaking:

> I cannot sufficiently emphasize what I regard as the great importance of these reports from the point of view of the future development of International Law as applied to war crimes. [...] these reports will show, for the practitioner or the student, the particular problems which have arisen and how in practice they have been dealt with and also show to the historian of the laws of war the practice of courts in applying those laws to particular cases. These reports are of the highest value and will prevent what would otherwise happen, namely the want of a correct record of the most significant cases which have been tried.[132]

And as Wright had predicted, the reports turned into an important, if not the most important, source on post-war class B and C war crimes trials. Until today these volumes continue to play an important role because they offer English translations of material that would otherwise be inaccessible to many. In order to illustrate its importance, it suffices to point out that modern *ad hoc* courts have made use of these cases reported by the UNWCC.[133] In many countries access to the trial records has also been restricted or at the very least requires the interested person to look for the material in historical archives.

Because of the strong reliance on the reports issued by the UNWCC, and the lack of access to alternative or additional material, it becomes essential to remember that the cases published were of course a very small selection of the overall number of cases available and a deliberate selection as such. According to the UNWCC, "the trials selected for reporting, however, are those which are thought to be of the

---

[131] Letter, Lord Wright to Wellington Koo, 20 December 1945, Guoshiguan File 020-010117-0041-0044.

[132] United Nations War Crimes Commission, *Law Reports of Trials of War Criminals*, vol. 1, His Majesty's Stationery Office, London, 1947, p. x.

[133] For an example of International Criminal Tribunal for Yugoslavia usage of post-Second World War cases see: Michael P. Scharf, *Customary International Law in Times of Fundamental Change: Recognizing Grotian Moments*, Cambridge University Press, Cambridge, 2013, pp. 75–76.

greatest interest legally and in which important points of municipal and international law arose and were settled".[134]

The reader cannot help but to notice an imbalance in the numbers of cases that were published for each country. Out of the 89 cases selected for publication more than half were trials held by the US and the British courts.[135] One explanation for this can be found in the number of cases that each country submitted to the UNWCC. The US had submitted by far the highest number of cases followed by Britain, France and Australia.[136] No trial records at all were received from Denmark, Belgium, Czechoslovakia or Yugoslavia.[137] China, somewhat curiously, decided to send just a single report, that of the case of Takashi Sakai, that was printed in the fourteenth volume of the reports.

Archive material suggests that several important decisions made by Chinese tribunals were being translated into English for submission to the UNWCC in 1948.[138] It is unclear why only one report was sent in the end. It is probably sensible to assume the reason to be time constraints or a change in policy which had prevented more cases reaching London. This one case is of special importance because it is until today the only judgment that is readily available in an English translation. The majority of the original Chinese judgments are still not openly accessible, with the exception of a select few that were reproduced in Chinese newspaper articles in the 1940s.

So an interesting question to ask is surely why did the Chinese government decide to select this particular case? I have been unable to find material directly explaining why this case was selected over others but the special circumstances of the trial does offer a plausible explanation. Takashi Sakai was tried before the War Crimes Military

---

[134] Text on the inside of the front cover of United Nations War Crimes Commission, *Law Reports of Trials of War Criminals*, vol. 15, His Majesty's Stationery Office, London, 1949 ("Law Reports of Trials of War Criminals").

[135] 28 American Cases, 27 British Cases.

[136] Number of Cases reported to the UNWCC (number of cases published): United States 809 (28), Britain 524 (27), Australia 256 (5), France 254 (11), the Netherlands 30 (7), Poland 24 (4), Norway 9 (5), Canada 4 (1), China 1 (1). Law Reports of Trials of War Criminals, vol. 15, p. xvi, see *supra* note 134.

[137] Law Reports of Trials of War Criminals, p. 203, see *supra* note 134.

[138] Chinese Ministry of Defence to the Ministry of Foreign Affairs, 8 May 1948, Guoshiguan File 020-010117-0054-0092.

Tribunal of the Ministry of National Defence in Nanking in August 1946 for crimes against peace, war crimes and crimes against humanity. In addition to atrocities committed on the mainland, he was also indicted for his participation in the invasion of Hong Kong. As the "Conqueror of Hong Kong"[139] his case received enormous attention both from the Chinese as well as from the British side. The British authorities in Hong Kong initially tried to obtain permission to interrogate Sakai in Nanking[140] and have him handed over for trial in a British court in Hong Kong. When these requests met with resistance from the Chinese side the British relented but still insisted that at least a report on the trial should be sent to them because both British and Canadian soldiers had been victims in the case.[141] Under these circumstances one trial report could conveniently be used to satisfy demands from different sides as well as to placate public opinion. In addition, the *Shen Bao*, one of the major Shanghai-based newspapers at the time, had already published several articles on the trial of Sakai, including a full reprint of the judgment over a series of three articles.[142] It thus seems reasonable to assume that it was not an accidental decision to choose the case of Sakai for publication in the trial reports; on the contrary, this was a case meant and prepared for publication.

However, the effect that the Chinese were eventually able to achieve by selecting the Sakai case was far from ideal. Especially the legal content and argumentation of the case provoked harsh criticism by the UNWCC and especially from Wright. In his foreword to the volume that contained the decision, the Chairman of the UNWCC stated his opinion that the Chinese court had misinterpreted an important legal concept. He criticised the usage and interpretation of the concept of aggression as employed by the judges and came to the conclusion that this case should not be considered a suitable precedent in international law. He explained that:

---

[139] Suzannah Linton, "Rediscovering the War Crimes Trials in Hong Kong, 1946–48", in *Melbourne Journal of International Law*, 2012, vol. 13, no. 2, p. 340.

[140] T.W. Kwok Hong Kong to the Chinese Ministry of Foreign Affairs, 4 May 1945, Guoshiguan File 020-010117-0033-0019.

[141] Headquarters Land Forces Hong Kong to Dr. Wang Shih Chieh (Minister of Foreign Affairs), 20 June 1946, Guoshiguan File 020-010117-0033-0026.

[142] *Shen Bao* [申报] (Shanghai edition), 31 August 1946 / 4 September 1946 / 5 September 1946.

> the main current of thought and decisions on crimes against peace which have been given since the end of the war has been that such crimes can only be committed as a matter of legal principle by accused individuals who may be described as acting on the policy-making level. In this particular case, however, it is difficult to see that the accused came within that category. I do not think that this decision can be relied on as substantially affecting the general current of authority on this matter.[143]

The fact that the Chinese judgments were, with that one exception, not reported in the war crimes trials reports make the Chinese cases practically inaccessible for a wider English-speaking audience. Even until recently, the original judgments in Chinese were also not readily available to the general public. So it is not surprising to see the Chinese post-war trials being described as an "obscure" topic even in recent literature.[144] This leads to a situation where judgments of Chinese military tribunals have been completely ignored in the research on international criminal law. The war crimes trials reports now have the unfortunate effect of perpetuating the negative assessment of the Chinese trials and the Chinese interpretation of international law in general based on the analysis of just a single case. I do not want to suggest that these cases should be used as precedents, nor do I even suggest that they have fulfilled basic requirements that might make them suitable for legal research. Whether these cases can still be of value for present-day international criminal law is a question that can only be answered after more careful and detailed study of the Chinese trials and a better understanding of the historical circumstances in which they took place.

16.6. Conclusion

> The commission has suffered much reproach and depreciation. But it has kept its course. It has at least held aloft the banner of international justice. It has been a rallying centre for those who had that justice at heart. It would have

---

[143] Law Reports of Trials of War Criminals, vol. 14, pp. x–xi.

[144] Roger S. Clark, "The Crime of Aggression: From the Trial of Takashi Sakai, August 1946, to the Kampala Review Conference on the ICC in 2010", in Kevin J. Heller and Gerry J. Simpson (eds.), *The Hidden Histories of War Crimes Trials*, Oxford University Press, Oxford, 2013, p. 390.

been a sad day for the future of mankind if justice were not
vindicated. I feel that justice will be vindicated this time.[145]

After studying the UNWCC and its work for some time it is hard to not
agree with the above quotation from Wright, who was speaking at a
conference in the summer of 1945. While the UNWCC might not have
been immediately influential on the big international tribunals held after
the war, it was definitely a "rallying centre" for a number of very
dedicated individuals attempting to use international law to achieve what
they considered justice for the victims of the war. With the memory of the
"fiasco of Leipzig" still present, and the reality of new and unimaginable
atrocities committed during the war, the members of the UNWCC
steadfastly advocated the use of law to vindicate justice and worked in a
dedicated fashion towards this goal over a time span of several years. This
in itself should suffice to guarantee acknowledgment of their tireless
efforts. In addition, the work of the UNWCC proves to be a fascinating
opportunity to study the discourse on questions of international law and
international criminal law during and immediately after the Second World
War.

The UNWCC counted some of the most eminent legal scholars
among its members and was a forum where differing and diverse opinions
could be voiced and discussed. Today, this allows us to reconstruct a
more complete picture of the legal opinions held at the time because the
UNWCC gave especially the smaller Allied countries the opportunity to
argue their positions. It is especially interesting to see that China was
actively involved in the work of the UNWCC as a country with
comparatively little experience in the realm of international law. The US
and Britain had only relinquished their extraterritorial rights in China in
early 1943 and the Chinese municipal justice system was still regarded
with much suspicion in the Western world.[146] This scepticism towards the
Chinese, or what was more generally perceived as the "oriental legal
system", was also present among the members of the UNWCC.[147] During

---

[145] Lord Wright speaking at the opening session of the National Offices Conference, "Justice
Will be Vindicated", in *The Times*, 1 June 1945, p. 2.

[146] Dong Wang, *China's Unequal Treaties: Narrating National History,* Lexington Books,
Lanham, 2005, p. 93.

[147] Report of Commission II (later Commission I) On The Trial of War Criminals: Question 1
– Will Adequate Punishment of All War Criminals Be Procurable by the Application of
the Penal Code of Each Nation Concerned, May 1942, TNA, TS 26/873.

his time as a member of LIA, Marcel de Baer, later the Belgian delegate to the UNWCC, for instance, stated the following opinion when reviewing national criminal legislations and whether they could be used to try war criminals:

> Japanese or Chinese Law: I have endeavored in vain to obtain some precision about these criminal laws, but with due respect for our honoured Ally, and due admiration for the way in which they are fighting our common foe, even the Chinese law does not seem to coincide with Occidental ideas on this subject [...] Conclusion: With the exception of quislings and traitors I suggest it is not desirable that war criminals should be dealt with according to municipal law.[148]

While the municipal legal system was often still seen as deficient, China had a number of well-respected experts in the realm of international law. Given the ongoing discussion on the Eurocentric nature of international law, the study of the UNWCC offers a unique chance to understand more about the contribution of China as a non-Western nation to the development of international criminal law during this critically important period.

---

[148] *Ibid.* On The Trial of War Criminals: Question 2 – Concerning the Criminals in Respect of Whom the Municipal Law Provides Means of Punishment, Is It Desirable That Any or All of Them Should Be Dealt with According to That Law?

17

Founding Nuremberg: Innovation and Orthodoxy at the 1945 London Conference

Kirsten Sellars[*]

No document better conveys the roughness and expediency of the negotiations leading up to the tribunal at Nuremberg than the transcript of the four-power London Conference, held from 26 June to 2 August 1945. Their success was by no means assured: the Americans repeatedly threatened to walk out, the British fretted over German counter-charges, the French objected to crimes against peace, and the Soviets refused anything other than *ad hoc* charges. This was history in the making, and its making was an unedifying business.

The negotiations started smoothly enough, and the chief American prosecutor, Robert Jackson, thought he would have the conference wrapped up within a week.[1] This initial optimism soon gave way to frustration, and then to outright pessimism. On 4 July he cabled Secretary of State James Byrnes: "Negotiations [...] progressing slowly due difficulty Russian understanding our system of law and our difficulty comprehending theirs."[2] On 25 July he complained to Telford Taylor: "We have a great deal of trouble with some of our friends, who are very hard to understand. I think we are going to get an agreement, but some days I think not."[3] On 1 August, the day before the end of the conference, he told Samuel Rosenman that he had given up hope of reaching a consensus.[4] Throughout, he repeatedly threatened to abandon the negotiations, either

---

[*] **Kirsten Sellars** is a Research Fellow at the Centre for Asian Legal Studies at the National University of Singapore's Faculty of Law. She focuses on Asian perspectives on public international law, with a particular interest in uses of force, international criminal law and law of the sea. This chapter is excerpted from her book, *'Crimes against Peace' and International Law*, Cambridge University Press, Cambridge, 2013. Her next book, the edited volume, *Trials for International Crimes in Asia*, will be published by Cambridge University Press in 2015.

[1] B.F. Smith, *Reaching Judgment at Nuremberg*, André Deutsch, London, 1977, p. 48.

[2] Jackson to Byrnes, 4 July 1945: Box 110, Jackson Papers, Library of Congress ("LoC").

[3] Tele-conference, 25 July 1945: Box 110, Jackson Papers, LoC.

[4] John W. Wheeler-Bennett and Anthony Nicholls, *The Semblance of Peace: The Political Settlement After the Second World War*, Macmillan, London, 1972, p. 401.

by leaving the trial to be run by the Europeans or proceeding with an American-run trial.[5] These were not idle threats, and had they been carried out, the effect would have been profound, given that the United States held almost all the potential defendants and much of the incriminating evidence.

In the event Jackson stayed and the negotiations continued, with wrangles over the prosecution of organisations, the scope of the court's Charter, and the location of the proposed tribunal. Delegates also tried to get to grips with the differences between each other's criminal justice systems vis-à-vis the respective roles of judges and prosecutors, the tendering of evidence and the rights of defendants. The trial plan that emerged was based on a modified common law model that embodied concepts unfamiliar to the civil law delegates: they reportedly "boggled" at the idea of calling defendants as witnesses,[6] and were shocked that the defence would not have prior knowledge of the whole case against their clients.[7] Some practices were never satisfactorily explained, leading the Soviet delegate to enquire on the final day: "What is meant in the English by 'cross examination'?"[8]

17.1. The Question of Individual Responsibility

The radical premise of the proposed tribunal was that individuals could be held personally responsible for crimes of war under international law – an idea that represented a significant departure from previous practice. "Of course," Jackson wrote, "this principle of individual responsibility is a negation of the old and tenacious doctrine of absolute and uncontrolled sovereignty of the state and of immunity for all who act under its orders. The implications of individual accountability for violation of International Law are far-reaching and many old concepts may be shaken thereby."[9] Yet the Americans did not arrive in London with a fully formed proposal for the incorporation of individual responsibility into the Charter. Early drafts

---

[5] London Conference, *Report of Robert H. Jackson, United States Representative, to the International Conference on International Trials*, Department of State, Washington DC, 1949 ("London Conference"), pp. 213, 343, 370. This was not just brinkmanship, as Jackson threatened the same in private correspondence with Byrnes and McCloy (Smith, 1977, pp. 53–54, see *supra* note 1).

[6] London Conference, 1949, p. 190.

[7] *Ibid.*, p. 319.

[8] *Ibid.*, p. 403.

of the section setting out the crimes under the Tribunal's jurisdiction (later Article 6) made no specific reference to individual responsibility. Because it was not spelt out that responsibility for those violations rested with individuals, the door was left open for the judges to debate whether individuals or states (the latter being the traditional subject of international law) could be held to account for them.

In Washington, Hans Kelsen, who was then advising the Treaty Section of the Judge Advocate General's Department, considered this question in an untitled and hitherto overlooked memo, which was then passed to Jackson in London. Kelsen broached the subject of how to create new law, and in particular how to posit the innovative concept of individual responsibility under international law. He argued that it was important to "establish certain guarantees", [10] and drafted a paragraph emphasising that individuals would be held personally responsible for the enumerated crimes:

> *Persons* who, acting in the service of any state (of one of the Axis powers) or on their own initiative, have performed acts by which any rule of general or particular international law forbidding the use of force, or any rule concerning warfare, or the generally accepted rules of humanity have been violated, as well as persons who have been members of voluntary organizations whose criminal character has been established by the court, *may be held individually responsible* for these acts or for membership in such organizations *and brought to trial and punishment* before the court.[11]

Kelsen's point was taken. Jackson thereafter insisted that the Charter specify that *individuals* were responsible for the enumerated crimes, saying:

> We must declare that [the accused] are answerable personally, and I am frank to say that international law is indefinite and weak in our support on that, as it has stood over the recent years [...T]he Tribunal might very

---

9   R.H. Jackson, "Foreword", E.W. Kintner (ed.), *Trial of Alfons Klein, Adolf Wahlmann, Heinrich Ruoff, Karl Willig, Adolf Merkle, Irmgard Huber, and Philipp Blum: The Hadamar Trial*, William Hodge, London, 1949, pp. xv–xvi.

10   Kelsen, untitled, *c.* July 1945: Box 104, Jackson Papers, LoC.

11   *Ibid.* (emphases added).

> reasonably say, that no personal responsibility resulted if we failed to say it when we are making an agreement between the four powers which fulfils in a sense the function of legislation.[12]

He was absolutely adamant that the judges should not be given the option "to adjudge that, while these persons had committed the acts we charge, these acts were not crimes against international law and therefore to acquit them".[13]

The principle was duly declared. Article 6, which set out the various crimes on the Tribunal's roster, stated: "The following acts, or any of them, are crimes coming within the jurisdiction of the Tribunal for which there shall be individual responsibility.[14] The commanding "shall" made it clear that the Charter was binding on the Tribunal, and that if a person had committed the designated crimes, he could not be deemed *not* personally responsible. At the same time, Article 7 denied the accused the traditional sovereign immunity defence – a defence which pierced the membrane of sovereignty and provided for individual responsibility under international law.

17.2. The Problem of Aggression

Of all the crimes, the major sticking point at the conference was the formulation of the crime of aggression. There were serious disagreements over both its remit and its definition, for, as British delegate David Maxwell Fyfe stated early on, there were "different schools of thought as to whether that is an existing offence against international law [... and] whether we are breaking new ground".[15] All parties agreed that Germany had violated treaties and agreements; the dissension arose over the idea that such actions were *crimes*, not delicts, for which *individuals*, not states, were liable. It was thus the issues of criminality – and hence individual liability – of aggression, that generated the most controversy.

Jackson maintained that aggression was the heart of the case – "the crime which comprehends all lesser crimes"[16] – and he did so for several

---

[12] London Conference, p. 331, see *supra* note 5.

[13] *Ibid.*, p. 330.

[14] *Ibid.*, p. 423.

[15] *Ibid.*, p. 98.

[16] *Ibid.*, p. 51.

reasons. The charge had two overwhelming advantages: it provided a conceptual framework for the interpretation of events that occurred preparatory to and during the Second World War; and it enabled the prosecution to target the highest-level civilian and military planners of the war. In addition, the charge addressed a specifically American – or more precisely, Democratic Party – political problem. Isolationism had been a major political force in the United States before the war, and it was widely expected that it would revive after the war's end. The laying of charges of aggression against the Germans provided a justification for the United States' abandonment of neutrality in 1940–1941, thereby retrospectively exonerating the Roosevelt Administration, and, connected to that, countering the anticipated resurgence of isolationist sentiment against Truman's post-war shouldering of responsibilities in Germany and elsewhere. In short, the charge of crimes against peace was harnessed to the United States' internationalist cause.

There was little chance of the other conference delegates overlooking this point, because Jackson repeatedly drew their attention to it. He explained that most Americans were three thousand miles from the scene of the war, and had not suffered German depredations first hand.[17] They were consequently less motivated by their immediate experiences of atrocities than by the broader consideration of world order. "The thing that led us to take sides in this war is that we regarded Germany's resort to war as illegal from its outset, as an illegitimate attack on the international peace and order," he said.[18] It was mainly on the basis of German *aggression* that the United States justified, prior to its entry into the war, "its lend-lease and other policies of support for the anti-Nazi cause".[19] This was why Jackson was irritated that the Allied beneficiaries of lend-lease were not now willing to wholly support the view that aggression was a crime. He felt that he and others had embarked upon a contentious domestic policy in Washington to assist the Allies, and that they in return should help him to vindicate this policy. He said:

> [T]he justification was made by the Secretary of State [Cordell Hull], by the Secretary of War, Mr. Stimson, by myself as Attorney General, that this war was illegal from

---

[17] *Ibid.*, p. 126.

[18] *Ibid.*, pp. 383–84.

[19] *Ibid.*, p. 127.

the outset and hence we were not doing an illegal thing in extending aid to peoples who were unjustly and unlawfully attacked [...] We want this group of [Allied] nations to stand up and say, as we have said to our people, as President Roosevelt said to the people [...] that launching a war of aggression is a crime and that no political or economic situation can justify it. If that is wrong, then we have been wrong in a good many things in the policy of the United States which helped the countries under attack before we entered the war.[20]

Jackson's argument that the Allies should mount aggression charges to satisfy American public opinion and justify the policies of Roosevelt's Administration must have struck the other delegates as deeply, even shockingly, parochial. But his points were not entirely misdirected, for he was perfectly well aware that the Allies had an equally strong interest in perpetuating American internationalism, from which they all gained in terms of enhanced global status, financial support or military security. They certainly had no wish to see the United States withdraw once again into isolation as it had after the previous war, leaving Europe in a state of near destitution.

17.3. The Issue of Retroactivity

Just before the opening of the negotiations, the American delegates, who were determined to set the terms of the debate, distributed a trial plan that proposed the following categories of crime:

1) That at some time prior to 1 September 1939 the defendants entered into a common plan or enterprise aimed at the establishment of complete German domination of Europe and eventually the world [...]

2) That on or about 1 September 1939, and at various times thereafter, the defendants launched illegal wars of aggression [...]

4) That before and after the launching of such illegal wars [...] the defendants instigated, committed or took a consenting part in atrocities and other crimes.[21]

---

[20] *Ibid.*, p. 384.

[21] *Ibid.*, pp. 64–65.

The formula proposed a logical sequence of criminality, from conspiracy to aggression to war crimes and "other crimes" (later entitled "crimes against humanity"). It also presented the launching of wars of aggression as a discrete crime, distinct from war crimes and "other crimes". Yet as British conference secretary R.A. Clyde observed, it was plain from the outset that there was dissent from the other delegations.[22] At first they tried to postpone the discussion of crimes, by delegating the matter to a drafting committee somewhat earlier than was warranted. But after inconclusive debates there, the question was sent back to the full conference, where it had to be faced.[23]

It was at this point, nearly four weeks into the negotiations, that André Gros made a stand against the American construction of the charge of aggression. His main objection to the American proposal was that it held the German leaders personally responsible for actions that were not considered criminal when they had taken place. His point was that when they had launched their invasions, war was considered to be unlawful but not criminal: "If we declare war a criminal act of individuals, we are going farther than the actual law."[24] He predicted that the defence would raise Robert Lansing and James Brown Scott's objections to charging the former Kaiser in 1919[25] (though he omitted to mention that at the same time, Clemenceau had supported the idea of trying Wilhelm II). And he pointed out that the League of Nations had concluded on several occasions that an aggressor state was required to repair the damage that it had caused, but had not proposed criminal sanctions: "We think it will turn out that nobody can say that launching a war of aggression is an international crime – you are actually inventing the sanction."[26] A few days later he denounced the aggression charge as "ex post facto legislation".[27]

It was this fateful phrase, ex post facto, that would dog future discussion of crimes against peace. None of the delegates doubted for a moment that Germany had embarked on unlawful wars under the terms of

---

[22]   Clyde to Scott Fox, 28 July 1945, 3, National Archives, UK ('TNA'), FO 371/51031.

[23]   Ibid.

[24]   London Conference, p. 295, see supra note 5.

[25]   Ibid., p. 297.

[26]   Ibid., p. 295.

[27]   Ibid., p. 335.

the Kellogg-Briand Pact – Gros made this point himself later during the negotiations.[28] But were these wars criminal? The delegates were all perfectly well aware that the interwar years were characterised by an absence of *opinio juris* or state practice to support this contention. So, to get around this problem, Gros proposed a "bottom up" rather than "top down" plan for trying the German leaders. He argued that the Germans had first broken treaties, and then "annexed populations, run concentration camps, and violated international law by criminal acts against people, [...] acts which in fact are criminal in all legislation".[29] Thus, he reasoned, "we start from the bottom, say that there have been indisputable crimes and go up the line of responsibility to the instigator of the war".[30] There was therefore an important difference between French and American conceptions: Gros regarded a war of aggression as a catalyst for other crimes, whereas Jackson regarded a war of aggression as a crime *per se*.[31]

Whichever way the charges happened to be laid, Gros's main concern was that the Charter should not depart from existing law. "My difficulty is that this charter is not made to declare new international law," he said, "it is made to punish war criminals and the basis must be a safe one."[32] To this end, he submitted on 19 July a draft on crimes stating:

> The Tribunal will have jurisdiction to try any person who has [...] directed the preparation and conduct of:
>
> i) the policy of aggression against, and of domination over, other nations, [...] in breach of treaties and in violation of international law;
>
> ii) the policy of atrocities and persecutions against civilian populations;
>
> iii) the war, launched and waged contrary to the laws and customs of international law;[33]

---

[28]   *Ibid.*, p. 385.

[29]   *Ibid.*, p. 297. This comment suggests that Gros had no difficulty with the equally newly minted crimes against humanity charge because its constituent elements were already prohibited under national jurisdictions.

[30]   *Ibid.*, p. 296.

[31]   R.H. Jackson, "Some Problems in Developing an International Legal System", in *Temple Law Quarterly*, 1948, vol. 22, p. 154.

[32]   London Conference, p. 297, see *supra* note 5.

[33]   *Ibid.*, p. 293.

This proposal was cautious on both the crime of aggression and on individual responsibility. First, it avoided the taint of retroactivity because it did not declare aggression to be a crime under international law. It merely stated that the charge was for a "policy of aggression [...] in breach of treaties and in violation of international law" – a formulation that did not go beyond the law as it stood at the time. Second, it sidestepped the unprecedented nature of an international trial of individuals by stating that the Tribunal "will have the jurisdiction" to try those who had directed the preparation and conduct of aggressive wars. In other words, by simply creating a jurisdiction rather than dictating the crimes, it passed to the judges the responsibility for deciding whether aggression was a crime, and if so, who should be held accountable.[34]

Gros's proposal forced Jackson onto the defensive. He restated his belief that aggression was the pre-eminent problem: "[O]ur view," he said, "is that this isn't merely a case of showing that these Nazi Hitlerite people failed to be gentlemen in war; it is a matter of their having designed an illegal attack on the international peace."[35] He also insisted that American opinion had moved on since 1919, as indicated by the Roosevelt Administration's move away from neutrality.[36] Unfortunately for Jackson, though, international law had not followed where those policies had led, and this was precisely the conundrum raised by Gros. According to R.A. Clyde, the Americans then agreed to accept the French proposals as a basis of discussion – despite their very different approaches to the problem – but eventually Jackson called a halt.[37] Clyde recalled that "all he had to say was that he was not prepared to depart from Article 6 in its original form: and the meeting stranded".[38] Although Clyde does not elaborate further, it is reasonable to conclude that the French gave way in order to avoid scuttling the conference.

---

[34] R.A. Clyde wrote: "[T]he French attach great importance to their draft because it avoided declaring, as a matter of international law, that to launch a war of aggression, or, for the matter of that, to make a breach of a treaty, was a matter for which the Head of the State that did it, could, in his own person, be hanged" (Clyde to Scott Fox, 28 July 1945, p. 4, TNA, FO 371/51031).

[35] London Conference, p. 299, see *supra* note 5.

[36] *Ibid.*

[37] Clyde to Scott Fox, 28 July 1945, p. 5, TNA, FO 371/51031.

[38] *Ibid.*

17.4. Excising the Causes of War

When discussing the problem of aggression, the delegations were agreed on one thing: they did not want the Tribunal to address the causes of the Second World War. The Europeans had no wish to embroil their prosecution teams in debates about appeasement of or collaboration with the Nazi regime in the 1930s, which would cast their nations' foreign policies in an unfavourable light. Jackson, meanwhile, had no wish to defend the European Allies' actions, which would play into the hands of those in the United States who wanted to revive isolationist debates about entanglements in discreditable Old World affairs.[39]

There was certainly plenty of scope for debate about the causes of the war. A memo drafted by the State Department in summer 1945 anticipated some of the arguments that the defence might raise:

> English support of German 'equality' in arms.
>
> English sanction of German acquisition of areas occupied by 'racial' Germans (Runciman Report, in particular).
>
> French and possibly English consent to German 'free hand' in the East (Bonnet-Ribbentrop Accord of December, 1938).
>
> Colonel Beck's refusal to negotiate the Danzig issue.
>
> Beck's declaration that 'anschluss' of Danzig with Germany would be cause of war.
>
> Polish atrocities against Germans in Poland, 1938–39.
>
> Mobilization of Poland in August 1939.
>
> Alleged British-French plans to invade Norway.
>
> Alleged 'encirclement' of Germany.
>
> Defence against bolshevism.
>
> War is no crime.
>
> Imperialism of British.
>
> Dollar Diplomacy of Americans.
>
> Russian Aggression against Finland.[40]

---

[39] London Conference, p. 380, see *supra* note 5.

[40] "Assistance to Mr Justice Jackson in Preparation of Case", *c.* July–August 1945 (with hand-written annotation: "From State Dept"), 7: Box 1: RG238, US Counsel for the Prosecution, Wheeler correspondence, National Archives and Records Administration, Maryland ('NARA').

Anticipating the difficulties, Telford Taylor advised his American colleagues against allowing such discussions into the courtroom. "It is important that the trial *not* become an inquiry into the *causes* of the war," he wrote, adding:

> It can not be established that Hitlerism was the sole cause of the war, and there should be no effort to do this [...] The question of causation is important and will be discussed for many years, but it has no place in this trial, which must rather stick rigorously to the doctrine that the planning and launching of aggressive war is illegal.[41]

So how might a ban on debate about the causes of the war be introduced without appearing to restrict the rights of the defendants and without raising suspicions about Allied motives? This was a tricky matter, not least because it obviously went against what was needed: a thorough airing of the issues that had contributed to tensions in Europe, so as to enable the court to determine whether the ensuing actions were aggressive.

As it turned out, a solution was close to hand. Early in the negotiations, the Soviet delegate Iona Nikitchenko asked, "Don't you think it reasonable that provisions must be made to stop all attempts to use the trial for propaganda?"[42] Jackson replied affirmatively, but stressed the importance of "skilful" drafting of a provision to avoid the suggestion that "the nations conducting this trial are afraid of something[43] From this exchange onwards, it became apparent that any discussion of the causes of the war (which was desirable from a legal point of view) could be recast as Nazi propaganda (which obviously was not). Two days later, the British delegates returned to this question. The draft under consideration stated that the Tribunal should "disallow action by defendants which will cause unreasonable delay or the introduction of irrelevant issues or evidence".[44] The British stiffened this formula by stating that the Tribunal should "take strict measures to prevent any action which will cause

---

41   Taylor, "An Approach to the Preparation of the Prosecution of Axis Criminality", 2 June 1945, 2: Box 7, RG238, US Counsel for the Prosecution, Washington, correspondence 1945–46, NARA (original emphases).

42   Jackson Report, p. 84, see *supra* note 5.

43   *Ibid.*

44   *Ibid.*, p. 59.

unreasonable delay and rule out any irrelevant issues including attempts to introduce irrelevant political propaganda".[45]

Jackson was not happy with this amendment. He pointed out that such a forthright reference to propaganda would make it appear as if the Allies were trying to exclude inconvenient lines of enquiry. He thought that American critics would ask who had inserted this phrase, and predicted that those unfriendly to Britain would say, "I told you so" and those unfriendly to Russia would say, "I knew it all the time".[46] At this point, another American delegate, William J. Donovan, suggested replacing the words "including attempts to introduce irrelevant political propaganda" with "of whatever kind or nature"[47] – a broader formulation that covered practically any contingency. The upshot of this was that no overt prohibition on propaganda appeared in the Charter. The delegates went along with the American decision to tackle the problem by less direct but more effective means. Article 18 opens with the following clauses:

> The Tribunal shall
>
> (a) confine the Trial strictly to an expeditious hearing of the issues raised by the charges,
>
> (b) take strict measures to prevent any action which will cause unreasonable delay, and rule out irrelevant issues and statements of any kind whatsoever,[48]

This article, read in conjunction with Articles 1 and 6 stating that the Tribunal was convened to try "major war criminals of the European Axis", indicated that criticism of Allied actions during the proceedings would not be acceptable. But in case the point was missed, Jackson used his opening speech at Nuremberg to instruct the judges and warn the defence about the limits imposed by the Charter. Debates about the causes of the war would cause unwarranted delay, he argued, and were anyway irrelevant to the charge of crimes against peace and the conspiracy to commit them. No political, military, economic or other considerations may serve as justification for aggression, so there would be no need to

---

[45] *Ibid.*, p. 88.

[46] *Ibid.*, p. 102.

[47] *Ibid.*

[48] *Ibid.*, p. 426.

consider Germany's reasons for going to war. He continued, by way of disclaimer:

> It is important to the duration and scope of this Trial that we bear in mind the difference between our charge that this war was one of aggression and a position that Germany had no grievances. We are not inquiring into the conditions which contributed to causing this war. They are for history to unravel. It is no part of our task to vindicate the European *status quo* as of 1933, or as of any other date. The United States does not desire to enter into discussion of the complicated pre-war currents of European politics, and it hopes this trial will not be protracted by their consideration. The remote causations avowed are too insincere and inconsistent, too complicated and doctrinaire to be the subject of profitable inquiry in this trial.[49]

On the whole, the Tribunal accepted this instruction. It restricted the submission of evidence about Allied activities, and largely acceded to the time frame set out by the Indictment on crimes against peace – from 1 September 1939 (the initiation of war against Poland) to 11 December 1941 (the declaration of war against the United States). Consequently, material related to antecedents was frequently excluded: when, for example, the defence repeatedly tried to present evidence suggesting that the terms of the Treaty of Versailles were unjust or imposed under duress, the Tribunal ruled that further references to it would be inadmissible.[50] As a result, the defence could not really challenge the aggression charge on grounds of, say, provocation or condonation, because they could not refer consistently to events before the war. They had no option but to fight on the only ground allowed, namely that the charge was a retroactive enactment.

17.5. The Debate About Definition

In Jackson's view, another way to foreclose debates about the political and economic causes of the Second World War would be to incorporate within the Nuremberg Charter a *definition* of aggression focusing

---

[49] International Military Tribunal, *Trial of the Major War Criminals before the International Military Tribunal*, The Blue Series, 42 vols., vol. 2, IMT, Nuremberg, 1947–49, p. 149.
[50] *Ibid.*, vol. 10, p. 90.

narrowly upon the physical act of attack.[51] He warned that without such a definition,

> Germany will undoubtedly contend, if we don't put this in, that this wasn't a war of aggression although it looked like it. They will say that in reality they were defending against encirclement or other remote menaces. Then you are in the whole political argument of who was doing what to whom in Europe before 1939.[52]

Jackson's main aim for summoning up a definition was therefore to protect the prosecuting powers from counter-charges[53] (he expressed no interest whatsoever in the other purpose of definition, which is to articulate the elements of a crime for the purposes of clarity). In the meantime, his advisors scoured the international record for a ready-made definition of aggressive war, and duly produced the Soviets' 1933 Convention for the Definition of Aggression,[54] which set out examples such as declaration of war; armed invasion; attack on a nation's territory, vessels or aircraft; naval blockade; and support for armed bands.

The delegates of the Soviet Union, France and (less openly) Britain[55] were all absolutely opposed to defining aggression – indeed, Jackson recalled that the disagreements over this "threatened at times to break up the Conference".[56] Nikitchenko, perhaps contrary to expectation, ignored Jackson's summoning of the Soviet treaty, and instead made his

---

[51] London Conference, p. 302, see *supra* note 5. Sidney Kaplan of the Judge Advocate General's Treaty Project advised Jackson: "Unless the protocol defines aggression, or unless the Tribunal will accept some limiting definition by way of construction, there is a risk that the trial will become one of 'war guilt' or at least that difficult and complicated issues relating to the defendants' excuses and justifications will be relevant, e.g., frontier incidents, etc." (Kaplan to Jackson, "Present Status of and Immediate Prospects for JAG Treaty Project", 3 July 1945: Box 108, Jackson Papers, LoC).

[52] London Conference, p. 302, see *supra* note 5.

[53] *Ibid.*, pp. 273, 302, 305–6.

[54] *Ibid.*, pp. 273–74. The treaty referred to was signed by Afghanistan, Estonia, Latvia, Persia, Poland, Romania, Turkey and the Soviet Union on 3 July 1933.

[55] Maxwell Fyfe initially appeared to support the idea of definition, but withdrew when Jackson came under fire from the Soviets and French. It is possible that he had strayed from the Foreign Office brief on this issue; Patrick Dean noted that at the conference Maxwell Fyfe "gave way on two points which were of vital importance to the Foreign Office", only one of which was later retrieved with "a great effort" (Dean, 10 August 1945, TNA, FO 371/51033).

[56] Jackson, "Some Problems", 1948, p. 153, see *supra* note 31.

---

case by reference to the UN Charter, which had been signed a few weeks earlier. "We looked through the Charter," he said, "and observed that, while aggression is mentioned several times, it is not defined anywhere [...] Apparently, when people speak about 'aggression', they know what that means, but, when they come to define it, they come up against difficulties which it has not been possible to overcome up to the present time."[57] He added that the London negotiators were in any case not in a position to draft a definition because it "would really be up to the United Nations or the security organization which has already been established to go into questions of that sort". [58] Gros took up Nikitchenko's theme, arguing that a definition of aggression would anticipate decisions arrived at by the United Nations, and that if the latter's interpretation differed from the Tribunal's, "we would be in difficulty".[59] (This was the first post-war outing of an argument that is still being used by powerful states today.)

The Soviet and French response was understandable. Both countries had a huge stake in the preservation of their newly acquired Security Council prerogatives. Mindful of Article 39 of the UN Charter, which invests the Security Council with the power to determine the existence of, and make recommendations on, "any threat to the peace, breach of the peace, or *act of aggression*",[60] they had no wish to create a competing source of authority, which might be used to undermine the Big Five's freedom of action. When warning of a potential jurisdictional conflict between the International Military Tribunal and the UN Security Council over aggression, Nikitchenko and Gros were expressing the plain and unvarnished fear that the London Conference would take away privileges won at the San Francisco Conference. This is why Nikitchenko, who was prepared to compromise on many issues raised at the London Conference so long as the proposed tribunal dealt solely with the Germans, was not prepared to compromise on this one.

Jackson countered that the judges would require a definition that would enable them to avoid the minefield of extenuating circumstances

---

57 London Conference, p. 328, see *supra* note 5.
58 *Ibid.*, p. 303.
59 *Ibid.*, p. 304.
60 Charter of the United Nations, *Documents of the United Nations Conference on International Organization*, United Nations Information Organizations, New York, 1945–55, vol. 15, p. 343.

thrown up by the German defence. Without this, he was sure that a common law judge would say to a defendant, "You may prove your claim",[61] opening the door to arguments about provocation, threats and economic strangulation.[62] So, he said, the delegates had a choice: "We either have to define it now, in which case it will end argument at the trial, or define it at the trial, in which case it will be the subject of an argument in which the Germans will participate."[63] Jackson was outnumbered, and no definition appeared.

17.6. More Limits on Aggression

The Americans were not the only delegates to propose restrictions to the charge of aggression. The French and Soviets both drafted proposals explicitly limiting the aggression charge to the European Axis powers, and the British voted in support of these. On 19 July the French submitted a draft referring to "the policy of aggression against, and of domination over, other nations, carried out by the European Axis powers in breach of treaties and in violation of international law".[64] Four days later, the Soviet delegates proposed a similar formula: "Aggression against or domination over other nations carried out by the European Axis in violation of the principles of international law and treaties."[65] The crimes against peace charge was thus conceived as an *ad hoc* charge. As Erich Hula noted the following year, "[T]he Nuremberg rule on crimes against peace [...] is not so much what any law is meant to be, that is, a general rule to be generally applied, but rather what was called in Jacobin France *une loi de circonstance*. In other words, the Nuremberg rule on crimes against peace aims exclusively at a definite group of purposely selected men."[66]

Robert Jackson was uneasy with this particular selective approach, and when the Soviets produced their formula, he baulked. In his view, the charge of aggression should be presented as being universally applicable to all nations, even if it happened to be applied only in the context of an *ad hoc* trial. He said:

---

[61] London Conference, p. 306, see *supra* note 5.

[62] *Ibid.*, p. 305.

[63] *Ibid.*, p. 302.

[64] *Ibid.*, p. 293.

[65] *Ibid.*, p. 327.

[66] E. Hula, "Punishment for War Crimes", in *Social Research*, 1946, vol. 13, p. 17.

> If certain acts in violation of treaties are crimes, they are crimes whether the United States does them or whether Germany does them, and we are not prepared to lay down a rule of criminal conduct against others which we would not be willing to have invoked against us. Therefore, we think the clause 'carried out by the European Axis' so qualifies the statement that it deprives it of all standing and fairness as a juridical principle.[67]

The Soviets and the French did not budge. Even Maxwell Fyfe, who usually supported the American position, questioned Jackson's approach: "no one in the future could say we were discriminating in limiting this definition to Axis aggression", he argued, because the whole trial was already so limited.[68] (He added, in an unusually open acknowledgment of states' interests, that the point "seems one on which we are governed by limitations from our governments".)[69] Their concern was that the aggression charge might prove to be a double-edged sword, for had not Britain and France declared war on Germany, and had not the Soviets invaded Finland and Poland? All in all, Nikitchenko insisted, a general condemnation "would not be agreeable".[70]

This debate between Jackson and the European delegates was replicated elsewhere in the conference. Sidney Alderman, the chairman of the drafting committee, recalled how the Soviets held out against a general application of the crime there too. One obvious sticking point, Alderman noted, was the fact that "our allies, the Russians, had invaded Poland at the same time that Hitler invaded the country".[71] The Soviets contended that they had not waged aggressive war but "merely came in the back door, peacefully, and to protect their own interests and boundaries at the same time that Hitler waged aggressive war through the front door".[72] Even so, they were "very sensitive as to any properly generalized definition of the launching and waging of aggressive war".[73]

---

[67] London Conference, 1949, p. 330, see *supra* note 5.

[68] *Ibid.*, p. 336.

[69] *Ibid.*

[70] *Ibid.*, p. 387.

[71] Alderman draft chapter, "The London Negotiations for War Crimes Prosecutions", 41: Box 112, Jackson Papers, LoC.

[72] *Ibid.*

[73] *Ibid.*

For example, a subcommittee draft, produced on 11 July, with text still to be agreed inside square brackets, read as follows:

> (c) [Invasion or threat of invasion of or] initiation of war against other countries in breach of treaties, agreements or assurances between nations or otherwise in violation of International Law.[74]

It was interesting, Alderman observed, that the bracketed phrase, "invasion or threat of invasion of or", had been reserved by the Soviet delegate, "obviously since it could hardly be argued that Russia had not *invaded* Poland, even if it could be argued that Russia had not launched or waged aggressive war against Poland".[75]

A compromise was reached because the Europeans knew that the Tribunal's jurisdiction would in any case be restricted to the German leadership, and because Jackson suggested adding a reference to the Axis powers to the preamble of Article 6, which he said would remove the immediate problem but nonetheless "keep the idea of a limitation".[76] The first clause of the preamble was duly modified to read as follows:

> *Article 6.* The Tribunal established by the Agreement referred to in Article 1 hereof for the trial and punishment of the major war criminals of the European Axis countries shall have the power to try and punish persons who, acting in the interests of the European Axis countries, whether as individuals or as members of organizations, committed any of the following crimes.[77]

This passage referred to the "European Axis" twice, as well as citing Article 1, which declared that the Tribunal was established "for the just and prompt trial and punishment of the major war criminals of the European Axis".[78]

One way or another all the negotiating teams sought to restrict the scope and content of the charge of crimes against peace: the French and Soviets proposed limiting its application to the European Axis powers alone, while the Americans proposed drafting a narrow definition to

---

[74] *Ibid.*, p. 42.

[75] *Ibid.* (emphasis added).

[76] London Conference, p. 361, see *supra* note 6.

[77] *Ibid.*, p. 423.

[78] *Ibid.*, p. 422.

forestall the defence. Although none succeeded entirely, they accepted this state of affairs only because both the charges and the Tribunal itself were *ad hoc*.

17.7. The "Common Plan or Conspiracy" Proposal

In its final form, Article 6(a) stated that "major war criminals of the European Axis countries" were being tried for certain crimes, first among them:

> (a) *Crimes against Peace*: namely, planning, preparation, initiation or waging of a war of aggression, or a war in violation of international treaties, agreements or assurances, or participation in a common plan or conspiracy for the accomplishment of any of the foregoing;[79]

This formula contained within it three elements: engaging in a war of aggression; engaging in a war in violation of international treaties; and participating in "common plan or conspiracy" for the accomplishment of the others.[80] It is the third and final element, "common plan or conspiracy", that we shall now consider.

When constructing the general trial plan, the Americans conceived of conspiracy as playing a dual role, both as a substantive crime punishable in its own right, and as a method of establishing liability for other substantive crimes. Both approaches appear in Article 6. In the aforementioned crimes against peace paragraph, "common plan or conspiracy" is treated as a substantive crime, alongside "planning, preparation, initiation or waging of a war of aggression" and "planning, preparation, initiation or waging of [...] a war in violation of international treaties, agreements or assurances".

Another reference to "common plan or conspiracy" appears in the final paragraph of Article 6, beneath the paragraphs setting out crimes against peace, war crimes and crimes against humanity. This reads, in its entirety: "Leaders, organizers, instigators and accomplices participating in the formulation or execution of a common plan or conspiracy to commit any of the foregoing crimes are responsible for all acts performed by any

---

[79] *Ibid.*, p. 423.

[80] A war might be both a war of aggression and a war in violation of treaties, but the Americans insisted that aggression was a stand-alone crime irrespective of whether treaties had been violated; *ibid.*, pp. 380, 387.

persons in execution of such plan."[81] Here, "common plan or conspiracy" is proposed as a method for establishing liability for the commission of the previously cited crimes, including crimes against peace.

The Americans had initially conceived the "common plan or conspiracy" theory in autumn 1944 because, as its creator Murray Bernays had argued, it enabled them to reach those senior figures otherwise beyond the law, such as the SS bureaucrats responsible for the organisation of the exterminations,[82] and leading civilian financiers and bankers, such as Hjalmar Schacht.[83] There were other motives too. By the beginning of the London Conference, the Americans still feared that they might not uncover sufficient evidence to convict some of the most obvious candidates, and saw the charge as potentially easing the burden of establishing individual guilt. As Jackson explained to his fellow delegates, the charge was useful because "a common plan or understanding to accomplish an illegal end by any means, or to accomplish any end by illegal means, renders everyone who participated liable for the acts of every other".[84] Later at the Conference, Maxwell Fyfe pressed Jackson to say more on the subject, asking: "Mr. Justice Jackson, just to clarify the discussion, could your point be fairly put this way: that you want the entering into the plan to be made a substantive crime?"[85] Jackson replied: "Yes. The knowing incitement and planning is as criminal as the execution."[86] This approach later assumed its concrete form as Count 1 of the Indictment.

This idea of holding the German leaders to account for "common plan or conspiracy" was accepted by all delegates without a great deal of discussion, despite some claims in the later literature that the civil law delegates opposed it.[87] The American and Soviet delegates in particular

---

[81]   *Ibid.*, p. 423.

[82]   *Ibid.*, pp. 138–39.

[83]   *Ibid.*, p. 254.

[84]   *Ibid.*, p. 129.

[85]   *Ibid.*, p. 376.

[86]   *Ibid.*

[87]   Bradley Smith wrote that when the charge was suggested, the Soviets and French delegates "seemed unable to grasp all the implications of the concept; when they finally did grasp it, they were genuinely shocked" (Smith, 1977, p. 51, see *supra* note 1). Smith's comment was repeated in Arieh J. Kochavi, *Prelude to Nuremberg: Allied War Crimes Policy and the Question of Punishment*, University of North Carolina Press, Chapel Hill, 1998, p. 225, and Stanislaw Pomorski, "Conspiracy and Criminal Organizations", in G. Ginsburgs and

were strong advocates of such doctrines – which, although arising from very different legal traditions and practices, served not dissimilar purposes. (The umbrella term "common plan or conspiracy" was coined in deference to the distinctions between common law and civil law.[88]) At the conference, Nikitchenko, who, as a former judge at Soviet purge trials was already well versed in the uses of complicity, explained to his colleagues that "we should not, of course, confine ourselves to persons who have actually committed the crimes but should also especially reach those who have organized or conspired them".[89] André Gros, who also hailed from the civil law jurisdiction, was likewise favourably disposed towards the doctrine, stating that: "There has been an organized banditry in Europe for many years [...] and we want to show that those crimes have been executed by a common plan."[90] The British delegates, who were perhaps most familiar with the potential uses of the conspiracy doctrine, expressed no strong views, although they sought legal guidance on its applicability at Nuremberg. Anthony Eden wrote to Winston Churchill: "This, I am advised, is sound in law, though it is a new departure to apply it in the international sphere."[91]

17.8. A New Legal Regime

At the end of the Second World War, the Allies sought peace, security and the consolidation of their spheres of influence. This aim was reflected in their respective efforts to criminalise disruptions of the *status quo* detrimental to their own interests. Many jurists – from Hersch

---

V.N. Kudriavtsev (eds.), *The Nuremberg Trial and International Law*, Martinus Nijhoff, Dordrecht, 1990, pp. 218–19. Others claim that Jackson had to compel his fellow delegates to accept the conspiracy charge, such as Judith N. Shklar, *Legalism: Law, Morals, and Political Trials*, Harvard University Press, Cambridge, MA, 1964, p. 239, fn. 78; and Jeffrey D. Hockett, "Justice Robert H. Jackson, the Supreme Court, and the Nuremberg Trial", in *Supreme Court Review*, 1990, vol. 257, p. 269. These claims are not borne out by the transcript.

[88] London Conference, p. 387, see *supra* note 6.

[89] *Ibid.*, p. 298.

[90] *Ibid.*, p. 382. Pierre Renouvin, the French delegate to the negotiations over the Indictment, did, however, raise the tactical concern that the prosecution would be compelled to examine the causes of the war in the course of proving conspiracy. "Minutes of Meeting of Committee Four", 10 September 1945, 4: War crimes file, K. Lincoln papers, Harry S. Truman Presidential Museum and Library.

[91] Eden to Prime Minister, 17 July 1945, p. 2, TNA, PREM 4/100/12.

Lauterpacht in Cambridge, to Andrei Vishinsky and Aron Trainin in Moscow, to Bohuslav Ečer and Robert Wright in London, to Henry Stimson and William Chanler in Washington – shaped the concept of crimes against peace. Robert Jackson's great achievement was to put aggression at the centre of the case against the German leaders as the principal substantive crime. This was a victory for the Americans, who believed that the Germans' worst crime had been to launch wars that had drawn the Allies into a ruinous global conflict. If, in the process, they could consolidate an internationalist consensus at home, and bring about "containment by integration" of powerful allies abroad,[92] then so much the better. But before Jackson had departed for the London Conference, he had sounded a note of caution about the high expectations associated with tribunals, noting that: "Courts try cases, but cases also try courts."[93] The Nuremberg court would soon be put to this test.

---

[92] J.L. Gaddis, *Strategies of Containment: A Critical Appraisal of Postwar American National Security Policy*, Oxford University Press, Oxford, 1982, p. 9.

[93] R.H. Jackson, "The Rule of Law Among Nations", in *American Bar Association Journal*, 1945, vol. 31, p. 292.

PART 4

Interdisciplinary Analysis of Nuremberg's Record and Legacy

18

The Nuremberg Legacy in the Historical Development of International Criminal Law

David S. Koller[*]

The International Military Tribunal at Nuremberg ('Nuremberg Tribunal' or 'Nürnberg Tribunal') and the subsequent trials carried out by the Allied occupying powers after the Second World War (collectively with the Nuremberg Tribunal, 'the Nuremberg trials' or 'the Nürnberg trials') are often asserted to have played a key role in the development of international criminal law. In academic publications, speeches and conferences, the Nuremberg Tribunal or trials are frequently linked directly to the establishment of more recent institutions, in particular the International Criminal Tribunal for the former Yugoslavia ('ICTY') and the International Criminal Court ('ICC').[1] To a large extent, reference to Nuremberg has been used as a rhetorical device, to convey a sense of origin and of movement or progressive development of international law from Nuremberg to The Hague, typically with the aim of enjoining the reader, listener or participant to support this progressive development.[2]

---

[*]   **David Koller** is Legal Officer, United Nations (Department of Management). He was previously a legal officer at the Appeals Chamber of the International Criminal Court. He holds a J.D. from the New York University School of Law (*cum laude*) and was awarded the Dean's Scholarship. Since 2004 he is a member of the Bar of the State of New York. He has published in the areas of public international law and international criminal law. The views expressed herein are those of the author and do not necessarily reflect the view of the United Nations.

[1]   See, for example, Claire Nielsen, "From Nuremberg to The Hague: The Civilizing Mission of International Criminal Law", in *Auckland University Law Review*, 2008, vol. 14, p. 81; Richard Goldstone, "Historical Evolution – From Nuremberg to the International Criminal Court", in *Penn State International Law Review*, 2007, vol. 25, p. 763; Claus Kress, "Versailles–Nuremberg–The Hague: Germany and International Criminal Law", in *The International Lawyer*, 2006, vol. 40, no. 1, p. 15; Patricia Wald, "Running the Trial of the Century: The Nuremberg Legacy", in *Cardozo Law Review*, 2006, vol. 27, no. 4, p. 1559; Benjamin Ferencz, "From Nuremberg to The Hague: A Personal Account", in Mark Lattimer and Philippe Sands (eds.), *Justice for Crimes Against Humanity*, Hart Publishing, Oxford, 2004, p. 31; Theodor Meron, "From Nuremberg to The Hague", in *Military Law Review*, 1995, vol. 149, p. 107.

[2]   David S. Koller, "… and New York and The Hague and Tokyo and Geneva and Nuremberg and…: The Geographies of International Law", in *European Journal of International Law*, 2012, vol. 23, no. 1, pp. 99–105.

The actual link between the Nuremberg trials and their supposed successors is often glossed over, and historical accuracy may be sacrificed for heuristic purposes.[3] This chapter examines this frequently hidden history in an effort to understand the impact of the Nuremberg trials on the subsequent development of international criminal courts and tribunals.

The starting point is David Kennedy's proposal "that we see international legal history as a terrain on which to read the development of ideas about identity, geography, and entitlement".[4] The primary objective is not to ascertain whether or to what extent more recent developments faithfully reflected or departed from the law and practice of the Nuremberg trials, but rather to understand *how* and *why* the Nuremberg trials and their legacy may have shaped legal discourse and the outcome of legal discussions from the establishment of the Nuremberg Tribunal in 1945 until the present. This chapter examines the role that reference to the Nuremberg trials and the International Military Tribunal for the Far East ('Tokyo Tribunal') played in political and legal debates along the way to the establishment of the ICC, namely: 1) efforts in the late 1940s and early 1950s to codify and to further develop the Nuremberg legacy through the United Nations General Assembly and its International Law Commission ('ILC'); 2) revitalised efforts after the end of the Cold War by the ILC to establish a Code of Offences against the Peace and Security of Mankind ('Code of Offences') and to consider the question of an international criminal jurisdiction; 3) the establishment of *ad hoc* mechanisms such as the ICTY and the International Criminal Tribunal for Rwanda ('ICTR'); and 4) the Ad Hoc Committee, Preparatory Committee and Rome Conference negotiations leading to the adoption of the ICC Statute on 17 July 1998.

18.1. Creation of the "Nuremberg Legacy", 1945–1954

In some ways, the creation of the Nuremberg legacy preceded even the opening, let alone the conclusion of, the Nuremberg trials. Participants in the establishment and conduct of the Nuremberg Tribunal and trials were consciously aware that the importance of their actions would extend well beyond their own time. They viewed the trials, and their roles in the trials,

---

[3]   *Ibid.*, p. 104, fn. 34.
[4]   David Kennedy, "The Disciplines of International Law and Policy", in *Leiden Journal of International Law*, 1990, vol. 12, no. 1, p. 101.

not only as creating new precedents in international law but also as paving the way for the establishment of a permanent international criminal court and ushering in a new era of international peace. In the preface to his report to the United States ('US') President Harry S. Truman on the conference to establish the Nuremberg Tribunal, the American Chief Prosecutor at Nuremberg, Robert H. Jackson, summarised a view held by many of Nuremberg's protagonists as follows:

> The principles of the [Nuremberg Tribunal's] charter, no less than its wide acceptance, establish its significance as a step in the evolution of a law-governed society of nations. The charter is something of a landmark, both as a substantive code defining crimes against the international community and also as an instrument establishing a procedure for prosecution and trial of such crimes before an international court [...] The codification of these principles and their adoption by so many nations would seem to close the chapter on that era when all wars were regarded as legally permissible even though morally reprehensible. It ushers international law into a new era where it is in accord with the common sense of mankind that a war of deliberate and unprovoked attack deserves universal condemnation and its authors condign penalties.[5]

Underlying the fundamental debates over the form, jurisdiction and procedure of the Nuremberg Tribunal were larger debates about whether the international community's response to mass atrocities should be determined by power politics or by the rule of law,[6] and the process of creating the Nuremberg Tribunal was closely interwoven with the establishment of the United Nations ('UN') and a new post-war order. It should come as no surprise then that, in the wake of the Nuremberg Tribunal, international lawyers and other policymakers who had fought to ensure that high-ranking German officials were subjected to judicial

---

[5] Robert Jackson, *Report of Robert H. Jackson, United States Representative to the International Conference on Military Trials: London, 1945*, US Department of State, Pub. 3080, Washington, DC, 1949. See also John J. Parker, "The Nuremberg Trial", in *Journal of the American Judicature Society*, 1946, vol. 30, pp. 109–15; Telford Taylor, *The Anatomy of the Nuremberg Trials: A Personal Memoir*, Little, Brown and Co., New York, 1993, p. 226; Ferencz, 2004, see *supra* note 1.

[6] See David S. Koller, "The Faith of the International Criminal Lawyer", in *New York University Journal of International Law and Politics*, 2008, vol. 40, no. 4, p. 1019.

punishment sought to consolidate and to enshrine the gains they had achieved in a new legal document or documents.

The impetus to codify the gains in international law represented by the Nuremberg Tribunal came to a large extent from the US which had been the key proponent of the judicial approach adopted at Nuremberg – in contrast to the British and Soviets who initially favoured summary executions, either without trials or with mere show trials.[7] On 9 November 1946 Francis Biddle, the American judge on the Nuremberg Tribunal, submitted his report on the Nuremberg Tribunal to Truman.[8] In describing the accomplishments of the Nuremberg Tribunal, he stated: "But of greater importance for a world that longs for peace is this: the Judgment has formulated, judicially for the first time, the proposition that aggressive war is criminal, and will be so treated".[9] Looking to the future, Biddle declared:

> The conclusions of Nürnberg may be ephemeral or may be significant. That depends on whether we now take the next step. It is not enough to set one great precedent that brands as criminal aggressive wars between nations. Clearer definition is needed. That this accepted law was not spelled out in legislation did not preclude its existence or prevent its application, as we pointed out in some detail in the Judgment. But now that it has been so clearly recognized and largely accepted, the time has come to make its scope and incidence more precise [...] In short, I suggest that the time has now come to set about drafting a code of international criminal law.[10]

Biddle proposed to entrust the task of drawing up this code to the UN, and he noted that the US had already placed the issue on the agenda of the UN General Assembly.[11] In his response on 12 November 1946 Truman concurred with Biddle's assessments on the significance of the Nuremberg Tribunal in prohibiting aggressive war and in contributing to

---

[7] *Ibid.*

[8] US Department of State Bulletin, 1946, vol. 15, pp. 954–57.

[9] *Ibid.*, p. 956.

[10] *Ibid.*

[11] *Ibid.*

peace, on the value of an international criminal code and on the UN taking up this undertaking.[12]

A few days later, the US proposed a draft resolution to the Sixth (Legal) Committee of the UN General Assembly ('Sixth Committee').[13] This draft resolution would have "reaffirm[ed] the principles of international law recognized by the Charter of the Nürnberg Tribunal and the judgment of the Tribunal" and would have "direct[ed] the [General] Assembly Committee on the Codification of International Law [...] to treat as a matter of primary importance the formulation of the principles of the Charter of the Nürnberg Tribunal and of the Tribunal's judgment in the context of a general codification of offences against the peace and security of mankind or in an International Criminal Code".[14] Following Soviet objections, the draft resolution was amended to direct the Committee to develop *plans for* the formulation of such principles and not to formulate the principles themselves.[15] China proposed including a reference to the Tokyo Tribunal, and this reference was included in the preamble but not the operative paragraphs of the resolution.[16] On 11 December 1946 the General Assembly adopted Resolution 95 (I) which affirmed the principles of international law recognised in the Charter and Judgment of the Nuremberg Tribunal and directed the Committee on the Progressive Development of International Law and its Codification ('Committee of Seventeen', named after its number of members), established in Resolution 94 (I), to "treat as a matter of primary importance plans for the formulation, in the context of a general codification of offences against the peace and security of mankind, or of an International Criminal Code, of the principles recognized in the Charter of the Nuremberg Tribunal and in the Tribunal's judgment.".

The newly established Committee of Seventeen recommended that the task of formulating the principles should be entrusted to the ILC

---

[12] *Ibid.*, p. 954.
[13] Resolution Relating to the Codification of the Principles of International Law Recognized by the Charter of the Nürnberg Tribunal, UN Doc. A/C.6/69, 15 November 1946.
[14] *Ibid.*
[15] The Charter and Judgment of the Nürnberg Tribunal: History and Analysis, UN Doc. A/CN.4/5, 1946, p. 13.
[16] *Ibid.*

which the Committee of Seventeen proposed be set up.[17] The Committee of Seventeen recommended that the ILC would draft both a convention setting out the Nuremberg principles and a broader detailed draft plan of general codification of offences against the peace and security of mankind.[18] In the context of the Committee's discussions, the French representative Henri Donnedieu de Vabres, formerly the French judge at the Nuremberg Tribunal, proposed also the establishment of an international judicial body with jurisdiction over such offences.[19] The majority of the Committee agreed to draw the attention of the General Assembly to the potential need for an international judicial authority to enforce any such code but did not go so far as to call for its establishment.[20] At the same time, several delegations took the view that even considering the question of an international judicial authority exceeded the Committee's mandate.[21]

At its second session in November 1947 the General Assembly established the ILC[22] and entrusted it with formulating the principles of international law recognised in the Charter and Judgment of the Nuremberg Trial and preparing a draft code of offences against the peace and security of mankind, within which the Nuremberg principles would sit.[23] A year later, on 9 December 1948, the General Assembly adopted the Convention on the Prevention and Punishment of the Crime of Genocide ('Genocide Convention') and invited the ILC in that context "to study the desirability and possibility of establishing an international judicial organ for the trial of persons charged with genocide or other crimes over which jurisdiction will be conferred upon that organ by international conventions".[24] Thus, the three aspects foreseen to comprise

---

[17] Plans for the Formulation of the Principles of the Nuremberg Charter and Judgment: Report of the Committee on the Progressive Development of International Law and its Codification, UN Doc. A/332, 21 July 1947 ("Plans for the Formulation of Principles"), para. 2.

[18] *Ibid.*

[19] Draft Texts Relating to the Charter and Judgment of the Nuremberg Tribunal, Memorandum by the Delegate for France, UN Doc. A/AC/10/34, 27 May 1947.

[20] Plans for the Formulation of Principles, para. 3, see *supra* note 17.

[21] *Ibid.*

[22] United Nations General Assembly, Resolution 174 (II), 17 November 1947.

[23] United Nations General Assembly, Resolution 177 (II), 17 November 1947.

[24] United Nations General Assembly, Resolution 260 (III), 9 December 1948.

the Nuremberg legacy – the Nuremberg Principles, Code of Offences proposed by the Americans and the judicial body proposed by the French – were all handed over to the ILC, albeit to proceed along separate tracks.

18.1.1. The Nuremberg Principles

Much of the consideration of the ILC over its first two sessions was devoted to methodological questions concerning the nature and scope of its work. The ILC considered that the General Assembly had already affirmed the principles of Nuremberg in its resolutions and that its role was not to ascertain whether there were in fact such principles or to ascertain their legal status "but merely to formulate them".[25] Extensive discussion was devoted in particular to the question of whether the ILC should seek to identify general principles of international law underpinning the Charter and Judgment of the Nuremberg Tribunal or whether it should restrict itself to formulating the principles as they were set out in the Charter and the Judgment. Some, such as Georges Scelle, advocated an ambitious approach, urging the ILC not only to formulate the general principles of international law underpinning the Judgment,[26] but also to "lay down the general principles of an international penal code".[27] In this respect, Scelle echoed the initial ambition of Biddle, Truman, Donnedieu de Vabres and other key protagonists who had contributed to the establishment of the Nuremberg Tribunal and pushed for the further development of the law on this basis. Others such as Manley O. Hudson and Vladimir Koretsky, the American and Soviet experts respectively, took a much narrower view, arguing that the Nuremberg Tribunal's jurisdiction was limited to trying persons acting in the interests of Germany or other Axis Powers and questioning whether it was possible to identify general principles of international criminal responsibility and liability.[28] Their views recalled the Soviet view of the Nuremberg Tribunal which saw it as an exercise of state power by the victors of the war as their sovereign right.

---

[25] Report of the International Law Commission on the Work of its First Session, UN Doc. A/CN.4/13 and Corr. 1–3, 12 April 1949, para. 26.

[26] *Ibid.*, para. 27.

[27] Summary Record of the Twenty-sixth Meeting, UN Doc. A/CN.4/SR.26, 24 May 1949, para. 34.

[28] *Ibid.*, paras. 2–3, 79–80.

Underlying the two views were competing perspectives not only of the basis of the Nuremberg Tribunal's legitimacy but also of how the international order should be organised.[29] Scelle's view reflected the idea of an international order in which disputes were to be resolved on the basis of appeal to the rule of law, where states placed their faith in neutral independent arbiters and where individuals could be held directly responsible under international law. This view was most strongly integrated with foreign policy in the US in comparison to other states, and it reached a pinnacle worldwide right at the end of the Second World War with the establishment of the Nuremberg Tribunal with strong American backing. [30] Koretsky's position reflected a view, quickly gaining increasing traction with the onset of the Cold War, of a world order governed by the balance of power between two superpowers, wherein law was cognisant of and operated within the context of political concerns.[31] In joining Koretsky in questioning the broader significance of the Nuremberg Tribunal, and in seeking to ensure that the law accommodated the concerns of political and military leaders, [32] Hudson's position reflected a significant change in the American approach with the onset of the Cold War.[33] Ultimately, the ILC members took a middle ground, rejecting Scelle's ambitious call but at the same time emphasising that the Nuremberg Tribunal acted on the basis of international law and applied a more general principle of individual criminal responsibility under international law.[34] Given the divergent views among its members, the ILC opted not to pass judgment on the consistency of the Nuremberg Principles with international law or on how such principles should be applied in the future.

---

[29] See *supra* note 5 and sources cited therein; see also Summary Record of the Twenty-ninth Meeting, UN Doc. A/CN.4/SR.29, 27 May 1949, paras. 22–27.

[30] Mark Mazower, *Governing the World: The History of an Idea, 1815 to the Present*, Penguin, London, 2012, chap. 3; see also Koller, 2008, pp. 1046–49, *supra* note 6.

[31] Mazower, 2012, chap. 8, see *supra* note 30. This differing view was reflected for instance in Koretsky's insistence (not shared by others) that members of the ILC were appointed as government representatives and not as independent experts (to the extent that he boycotted the ILC meetings in 1950 in objection to the presence of the Chinese expert who had been nominated by the Kuomintang government).

[32] Summary Record of the Twenty-seventh Meeting, 25 May 1949, UN Doc. A/CN.4/SR.27, para. 18.

[33] Mazower, 2012, chap. 8, see *supra* note 30.

[34] Summary Record of the Twenty-sixth Meeting, 1949, paras. 1–47, see *supra* note 27.

Regarding the content of the principles, the ILC quickly decided that it should focus on principles contained in Section II ("Jurisdiction and General Principles") of the Nuremberg Charter and, in particular, on Articles 6, 7 and 8 therein. These articles pertained to the subject matter jurisdiction of the Nuremberg Tribunal and principles of individual criminal responsibility, including the principles that neither an individual's official position nor the fact that he or she may have acted under superior orders would relieve a defendant from criminal responsibility, although acting pursuant to orders may mitigate punishment "if justice so requires".[35] A proposal to also take into account the Tokyo Tribunal was rebuffed by the Special Rapporteur appointed by the ILC, the Greek professor Jean Spiropoulos, on the basis that the ILC was fully occupied considering just the Nuremberg Tribunal; little further attention was given to the Tokyo Tribunal.[36]

Most of the ensuing discussion focused on refining the language used in the Nuremberg Charter. While several of the debates concerned important points of legal principle – in particular with respect to whether acting pursuant to superior orders could serve as a defence or serve to mitigate punishment and, if so, under what conditions – the debates did not depart significantly from the Charter. An extensive discussion took place with respect to the jurisdiction of the Charter. Some members argued that the crimes defined in the Nuremberg Charter and applied in the Judgment were too restrictive, in particular that international law did not require crimes against humanity to be committed in connection with the war.[37] A smaller number argued that the Charter's definitions may have been too broad, raising the perspective of military officials fearful of being held liable under the definition of crimes against peace.[38] Ultimately, given the lack of agreement, the ILC decided to restrict itself to adopting, essentially verbatim, the definitions set out in the Nuremberg Charter.

---

[35] Summary Record of the Seventeenth Meeting, UN Doc. A/CN.4/SR.17, 9 May 1949, para. 37.

[36] *Ibid.*, para. 25.

[37] See, for example, Summary Record of the Twenty-eighth Meeting, UN Doc. A/CN.4/SR.28, 26 May 1949, para. 26; Summary Record of the Twenty-seventh Meeting, 1949, paras. 75–76, see *supra* note 32.

[38] See, for example, Summary Record of the Twenty-seventh Meeting, 1949, paras. 18, 33, 38, *supra* note 32.

The one issue which was not initially included in the draft principles but which was subsequently added in the discussions of the ILC was to recognise the rights of defendants to a fair trial. A minority view, expressed most forcefully by the Soviet expert and reminiscent of the Soviet approach to the Nuremberg Tribunal generally,[39] contended that the purpose of the Nuremberg Tribunal was to impose punishment and that "[i]t was not logical, therefore that concern for the protection of the accused should appear in the formulation of [the] principles".[40] However, the majority contended that guaranteeing the rights of the defence was an important issue of substantive law which needed to be included.[41]

In 1950 the ILC adopted and presented to the General Assembly seven principles, based largely on Articles 6 to 8 of the Nuremberg Charter.[42] These principles (annexed to this chapter) provided that: 1) individuals may be held criminally responsible under international law; 2) such responsibility is not relieved by the lack of domestic penalties; 3) official position does not relieve from responsibility; 4) acting pursuant to superior orders does not relieve responsibility (provided a moral choice was possible); 5) individuals charged have the right to a fair trial; 6) crimes against peace, war crimes and crimes against humanity are punishable as crimes under international law; and 7) complicity in the commission of these crimes is also a crime.

18.1.2. The Draft Code of Offences Against the Peace and Security of Mankind

The issue of a draft Code of Offences was taken up by the ILC at its first session in 1949. Whereas the ILC saw its role in relation to the Nuremberg Principles as formulating principles already established and adopted by the General Assembly, this task was seen to fall more clearly within the ILC's role of advancing the progressive development of

---

[39] See Koller, 2008, fn. 74 and sources cited therein, see *supra* note 6.

[40] Summary Record of the Twenty-eighth Meeting, 1949, para. 78, see *supra* note 37.

[41] See Summary Record of the Seventeenth Meeting, 1949, paras. 38–48, see *supra* note 35.

[42] "Principles of International Law Recognized in the Charter of the Nürnberg Tribunal and in the Judgment of the Tribunal", in *Yearbook of the International Law Commission*, 1950, vol. 2, para. 97.

international law.[43] In this task, the ILC was not bound by the Nuremberg Principles but was free to go beyond the Charter and Judgment of the Nuremberg Tribunal.[44] As stated in a memorandum by the Secretary General, prepared by Professor Vespasian V. Pella, President of the International Association of Penal Law, to assist the ILC in its task:

> C'est l'esprit et non pas la lettre de Nuremberg qui compte dans cette oeuvre. Le jugement de Nuremberg doit, indépendamment de sa valeur juridique, politique et philosophique, devenir générateur d'institutions nouvelles. Il doit constituer non seulement la consécration de certains principes de droit international déjà confirmés par l'Assemblée générale des Nations Unies et que la Commission a été chargée de formuler, mais également une première étape dans la voie qui mène à la protection, par le droit pénal, de la paix et de la sécurité de l'humanité.[45]

A similar view was urged upon the ILC by Bert Röling, the Netherlands representative in the General Assembly's Sixth (Legal) Committee and dissenting judge at the Tokyo Tribunal who took the view that the ILC could depart from the Nuremberg Charter, noting that the Tokyo Tribunal and national courts had diverged from Nuremberg.[46]

In the ILC, the Soviet representative, Koretsky, took the view that drafting a code of crimes was a matter for national governments, outside the ILC's competence.[47] However, Spiropoulos, the ILC rapporteur on the Nuremberg Principles and on this topic, took the view, ultimately adopted by the ILC, that a distinction should be drawn between crimes such as piracy, drug trafficking or slavery which concerned primarily conflicts of jurisdiction and which could be dealt with by national courts[48] and a category of "international crimes" threatening the peace and security of

---

[43] Summary Record of the Thirtieth Meeting, UN Doc. A/CN.4/SR.30, 31 May 1949, paras. 27–29.

[44] Summary Record of the Fifty-fourth Meeting, UN Doc. A/CN.4/SR.54, 26 June 1950, paras. 44–73.

[45] Memorandum Concerning a Draft Code of Offences Against the Peace and Security of Mankind, UN Doc. A/CN.4/39, 24 November 1950, para. 18.

[46] *Ibid.*, para. 13 (citing UN Doc. A/C.6/SR.160).

[47] Summary Record of the Thirtieth Meeting, 1949, para. 33, see *supra* note 43.

[48] Draft Code of Offences Against the Peace and Security of Mankind: Report by J. Spiropoulos, Special Rapporteur, UN Doc. A/CN.4/25, 26 April 1950 ("Spiropoulos Report: Draft Code of Offences").

mankind which began to be recognised with the Treaty of Versailles and which were given effect by the Nuremberg and Tokyo Tribunals.[49] As described by the ILC in its report to the General Assembly at its third session, the logic behind focusing on these offences was:

> that the meaning of this term ["offences against the peace and security of mankind"] should be limited to offences which contain a political element and which endanger or disturb the maintenance of international peace and security.[50]

Spiropoulos reluctantly included war crimes in his report to the ILC on the following basis:

> This crime is comprised in article 6 (b) of the Nürnberg Charter. In reality it does not affect the peace and security of mankind and, consequently, from a purely theoretical point of view, it should have no place in the draft code. Nevertheless, as we have seen, it figures among the crimes enumerated in the Nürnberg Charter. It is only on account of this connexion that we suggest its inclusion in the draft code.[51]

In 1951 the ILC presented a first draft Code of Offences to the General Assembly.[52] The draft mirrored to a large extent the Nuremberg Principles. It contained five articles covering: 1) individual criminal responsibility for the offences under international law; 2) the definition of offences; 3) the lack of Head of State immunity; 4) the unavailability of superior orders as a defence; and 5) the punishment of offences. The offences listed under Article 2 concerned primarily acts of aggression, the threat or use of force by one state against another, incursion of a state's territory, fomenting of civil strife, undertaking or encouraging terrorist activities, violations of treaties intended to maintain peace and security and acts such as annexation. Acts of genocide were included on the basis of the recently adopted Genocide Convention.[53] Inhuman acts, or crimes

---

[49]   See Memorandum Concerning Draft Code, 1950, para. 8, see supra note 45; Spiropoulos Report: Draft Code of Offences, paras. 57 ff., see *supra* note 48.

[50]   Report of the International Law Commission on its Third Session, 16 May to 27 July: Official Records of the General Assembly, Sixth Session, Supplement No. 9, UN Doc. A/CN.4/48 and Corr. 1 and 2, 1951 ("Report on Third Session"), para 58 (a).

[51]   Spiropoulos Report: Draft Code of Offences, para. 67, see *supra* note 48.

[52]   Report on Third Session, 1951, paras. 54 ff., see *supra* note 50.

[53]   *Ibid.*, para. 59, article 2 (9).

against humanity, and war crimes were included on the basis of their inclusion in the Nuremberg Charter, albeit with small modifications from their definition in the Nuremberg Charter.[54] In particular, whereas the Nuremberg Charter limited jurisdiction over crimes against humanity to offences committed in connection with crimes against peace or war crimes, the Code of Offences provided for jurisdiction if the crime was committed in connection with any other offence therein.[55] The ILC did not go so far however as adopting the approach suggested by Hsu Shuhsi, the Chinese expert, who suggested eliminating the nexus altogether.[56] Conspiracy was also included on the basis of the Nuremberg Charter, while attempt and incitement were included on the basis of the Genocide Convention.[57] The ILC presented a revised draft Code of Offences to the General Assembly in 1954, whereupon the General Assembly decided to postpone further consideration of the Code of Offences pending the work of a Special Committee set up to deal with the difficult issue of defining aggression.[58]

18.1.3. Question of an International Criminal Jurisdiction

The ILC also took up the question of an international criminal jurisdiction at its first session and immediately found itself split, with two different perspectives on the desirability and feasibility of establishing an international criminal jurisdiction. Exceptionally, the ILC mandated two Special Rapporteurs to prepare working papers on the question.[59] In his report, the Panamanian diplomat Ricardo Alfaro traced the history of efforts to establish an international judicial body with criminal jurisdiction, and he situated the agreement to establish the Nuremberg Tribunal within this history as the moment when "[o]fficial action passed from mere desiderata or plans to actual deeds".[60] He further elaborated:

---

[54] *Ibid.*, article 2 (10).

[55] *Ibid.*

[56] See Summary Record of the Two-hundred and Sixty-ninth Meeting, UN Doc. A/CN.4/SR.269, 16 July 1954, para. 17.

[57] Report on Third Session, 1951, para. 59, see *supra* note 50.

[58] United Nations General Assembly, Resolution 897 (IX), 14 December 1954.

[59] Report on First Session, 1949, para. 34, see *supra* note 25.

[60] Question of an International Criminal Jurisdiction: Report by Ricardo J. Alfaro, Special Rapporteur, UN Doc. A/CN.4/15, 3 March 1950 ("Alfaro Report: International Criminal Jurisdiction"), para 37.

> That it is possible to establish an international criminal organ of penal justice is demonstrated by actual experience. A judicial organ of that type was created by the Geneva Convention of 1937 for the trial of persons responsible for acts of international terrorism. Two International Military Tribunals were set up by multilateral agreements, one in Nürnberg in 1945, the other in Tokyo in 1946. These two tribunals did actually function and fulfil their mission. Seven different drafts for statutes of an international judicial organ have been formulated, plus the charters of Nürnberg and Tokyo, and their texts show that the constitution of an international court is possible and feasible, despite the many differences existing among them.[61]

The other rapporteur, the Swedish lawyer Emil Sandström, took a much more pessimistic view of the desirability and feasibility of an international criminal jurisdiction and a much more limited view of the significance of the Nuremberg Tribunal. According to Sandström:

> The Nürnberg trial has been pointed out as an example, and at the same time the desire to create a permanent international criminal jurisdiction has its origin, to a large extent, in certain criticisms of that trial, which might be met by the establishment of a permanent jurisdiction. Such a permanent jurisdiction would eliminate the impression that the judgement is a victor's vengeance. In this respect one must keep in mind that the Nürnberg trial was the result of an extraordinarily complete defeat and a complete agreement between the victors on the questions involved in the trial. The victors were also able to exercise sovereignty in the defeated countries.[62]

Both Alfaro and Sandström recognised similar limitations in the Nuremberg Tribunal, but they drew different conclusions. For Alfaro, a permanent body – established on a firm legal basis, with specialised judges chosen without distinction as to nationality, and offences defined in a statute or treaty – would overcome the criticisms of the Nuremberg Tribunal.[63] In Alfaro's view, the Nuremberg Principles, the draft Code of

---

[61]   *Ibid.*, para. 128.

[62]   Question of an International Criminal Jurisdiction: Report by Emil Sandström, Special Rapporteur, UN Doc. A/CN.4/20, 30 March 1950 ("Sandström Report: International Criminal Jurisdiction, 1950"), para. 38.

[63]   Alfaro Report: International Criminal Jurisdiction, para. 40, see *supra* note 60.

Offences and the question of an international criminal jurisdiction were "inseparable and mutually complementary".[64] For Sandström, there was no guarantee that the same weaknesses would not befall a permanent international criminal court, and he recommended instead the creation of a special chamber of the International Court of Justice if needed.[65]

The ILC sided with Alfaro and recommended to the General Assembly that setting up an international criminal judicial organ was both desirable and feasible.[66] Upon receiving the report of the ILC, the General Assembly set up a committee of Member States to prepare concrete proposals.[67] The committee prepared a draft statute,[68] and the General Assembly reappointed the committee to consider comments of states and review the draft statute.[69] However, in 1954 the General Assembly decided to postpone further consideration pending consideration of the Special Committee on the question of defining aggression.[70]

18.1.4. Conclusion on the Establishment of the Nuremberg Legacy

For many involved in the United Nations in the late 1940s and early 1950s, the Nuremberg Tribunal was, in the words of the ILC member Roberto Cordova, a "landmark in history".[71] It was not the beginning of efforts to establish an international criminal code or international criminal court as previous efforts were consistently acknowledged, but it was significant as the moment where these efforts "passed from mere desiderata or plans to actual deeds".[72] In this view, Nuremberg was a step towards a world order based on the rule of law, and the lawyer's role in legal history was to contribute to the progressive development of this order. At the same time, a competing view persisted, reflecting another

---

[64] *Ibid.*, para. 51.

[65] Sandström Report: International Criminal Jurisdiction, 1950, paras. 38–40, see *supra* note 62.

[66] Report of the International Law Commission on its Second Session, 5 June to 29 July 1950, UN Doc. A/1316, 1950, para. 140.

[67] United Nations General Assembly, Resolution 489 (V), 12 December 1950.

[68] Draft Statute for an International Criminal Court, UN Doc. A/AC.48/4, 5 September 1951, annex I.

[69] United Nations General Assembly, Resolution 687 (VII), 5 December 1952.

[70] United Nations General Assembly, Resolution 898 (IX), 14 December 1954.

[71] Summary Record of the 45th Meeting, UN Doc. A/CN.4/SR.45, 13 June 1950, para. 47.

[72] Alfaro Report: International Criminal Jurisdiction, para. 37, see *supra* note 60.

---

school of thought equally embedded in the experience of Nuremberg. Under this school of thought, the maintenance of peace and security was the domain, if not the responsibility, of a select group of states and the lawyer was careful to heed the views of the military and political elite. Unable to bridge a compromise between these fundamentally opposing views, the ILC adopted the Nuremberg Principles, and set to draft a Code of Offences and to consider the establishment of an international judicial body to enforce this code, without addressing either the extent of the obligation to punish crimes under international law or many of the fundamental criticisms of the selectivity of the first instances of international criminal justice – criticisms which had been voiced most loudly by Judge Radhabinod Pal in his dissenting opinion at the Tokyo Tribunal. The net effect was to affirm the right of states to pursue international criminal justice but to leave open the question of their obligation to do so, a legacy which continues to be seen in international criminal justice today. The role of the Nuremberg Tribunal in these debates was primarily to demonstrate the possibility (but also the weaknesses) of a judicially based order. The actual content of the Nuremberg trials was less discussed, but it did have a significant impact, for example in the inclusion of war crimes and crimes against humanity in the draft Code of Offences.

The Tokyo Tribunal was largely absent from the debates for reasons which are not entirely clear. The Nuremberg Tribunal had been established first and had concluded its trial by the time the General Assembly took up its task, but the General Assembly did not object to China's suggestion to include also reference to the Tokyo Tribunal in its resolution calling for the codification of the Nuremberg Principles. Part of the explanation for the focus on Nuremberg may be due to the individuals involved – such as Biddle, Truman and Donnedieu de Vabres – all of whom had played key roles in the establishment of the Nuremberg Tribunal and were instrumental in moving the ILC to act (whereas suggestions to consider the Tokyo Tribunal came from, *inter alia*, China and the Tokyo Tribunal Judge Röling). However, it may also reflect a Eurocentric focus within the UN prior to the large-scale decolonisation that would soon follow, as well as a differing approach in the treatment of certain high-ranking Japanese and German officials, highlighted most notably by the lack of trial for the Japanese Emperor. Had the General Assembly and the ILC given greater consideration to the Tokyo Tribunal, they would also have been forced to confront not only the more vocal criticisms of the Tokyo Tribunal by some of its judges but also the potentially deeper challenge of a Tribunal whose structure – promulgated unilaterally by the Supreme Commander of the Allied Forces and comprising judges from 12 States – was at odds with the privileged position accorded to the selected great powers in the formation and conduct of the Nuremberg Tribunal, and mirrored by the veto accorded to the permanent members of the Security Council.

18.2. The Nuremberg Legacy Reawakened: ILC Debates, 1986–1996

In the years that followed the decision of the General Assembly to postpone consideration of the draft Code of Offences and the question of an international criminal jurisdiction, there was little concrete progress in further developing the Nuremberg legacy. The hopes of Biddle, Truman, Donnedieu de Vabres, Alfaro and others of a permanent judicial body with criminal jurisdiction over international crimes remained just that.

In the late 1970s and into the early 1980s, following the adoption by the General Assembly of Resolution 3314 (XXIX) on the definition of aggression, a renewed push to take up the draft Code of Offences came from a mix of Eastern Bloc states and members of the Non-Aligned Movement ('NAM').[73] Both groups agreed on the need to develop the Code of Offences, drawing attention to issues such as Israel's bombing of Lebanon, the threat of nuclear war and apartheid in South Africa.[74] Frequent references were made to the Nuremberg Tribunal and Principles.[75] However, only the NAM states (joined by some Western states that were sceptical of the need for developing the Code of Offences) were in favour also of establishing an international court, while Eastern Bloc countries preferred to punish such offences via national courts.[76] On 10 December 1981 the General Assembly invited the ILC to

---

[73] Analytical Paper Prepared Pursuant to the Request Contained in Paragraph 256 of the Report of the Commission on the Work of its Thirty-fourth Session, UN Doc. A/CN.4/365, 23 March 1983, paras. 8–47.

[74] *Ibid.*, paras. 23–31.

[75] *Ibid.*, paras. 9–14, 40–49.

[76] *Ibid.*, paras. 126–39.

resume its work and to review the draft Code of Offences, but it made no mention of the question of an international criminal jurisdiction.[77]

18.2.1. Draft Code of Offences/Crimes against the Peace and Security of Mankind

From the beginning, the ILC adopted a more distanced and critical view of the Nuremberg Tribunal than it had in the 1940s and 1950s. The Special Rapporteur appointed by the ILC, the former Senegalese Foreign Minister Doudou Thiam, noted in his first report:

> The Nürnberg system is undoubtedly an important precedent, to which we shall revert. But its incidental and contingent features and the ad hoc character of the tribunal which it instituted are matters for regret. The criticisms levelled at the Nürnberg system are too well known to require much discussion here. It has been blamed for violating the principle *nullum crimen sine lege, nulla poena sine lege*, since the acts were made crimes and the penalties were established after the event. It has been criticized for placing the vanquished under the jurisdiction of the victors and for setting up ad hoc jurisdictions, whereas the protection of those brought to trial and the rights of the defence required that the offences and the penalties should have been established beforehand.[78]

Yet, the Nuremberg Tribunal served as an important precedent for the ILC's work, and reference was made throughout the ensuing debates to the Nuremberg Tribunal and the Nuremberg trials. Often this took the form of trying to refine precise language, looking at how difficult issues had been resolved in the case law. For example, in 1986 the Special Rapporteur made extensive reference to the jurisprudence not only of the Nuremberg trials but also the Tokyo Tribunal and the judgment of the Supreme Court of the United States in the Yamashita case in asserting that international law recognised a broad concept of complicity.[79] It

---

[77] United Nations General Assembly, Resolution 36/106, UN Doc. A/RES/36/106, 10 December 1981.

[78] First Report on the Draft Code of Offences Against the Peace and Security of Mankind, UN Doc. A/CN.4/364, 18 March 1983.

[79] Report of the International Law Commission on the Work of its Thirty-eighth Session, 5 May to 11 July 1986, UN Doc. A/41/10, 1986, paras. 118 ff.

should be noted, however, that other members of the ILC drew differing conclusions from the jurisprudence. As stated in the ILC's report:

> some members of the Commission took the view that the concepts of complicity and conspiracy in the broad sense should apply to crimes against peace and possibly to crimes against humanity [...] Other members of the Commission expressed serious misgivings with respect to the idea of collective responsibility, even if it were restricted only to crimes against peace, such as aggression.[80]

Similarly extended – and inconclusive – discussions took place with respect to the defence of superior orders,[81] the principle of command responsibility[82] and the scope of criminal responsibility for planning or preparing of aggression.[83] Relevant precedents from the Nuremberg or other trials were cited extensively in the commentaries attached to draft articles proposed and adopted by the ILC.[84] However, the fact that something was addressed one way by the Nuremberg or Tokyo Tribunal or in subsequent trials was not in itself outcome determinative or seen as binding by members of the ILC.

Frequently, the Charters of the Nuremberg and Tokyo Tribunals served as a starting point for discussions and as checklists against which to evaluate proposals. The most significant use of such reference was in the context of the crime of aggression. While some ILC members were not in favour of including aggression either within the Code of Offences or within the jurisdiction of an international court being considered, others considered it a step backwards to not include the crime which had been considered at Nuremberg as the supreme crime.[85] Furthermore, the commentary to the draft Code of Offences adopted in 1996 noted that

---

80 *Ibid.*, paras. 126–27.

81 *Ibid.*, paras. 155–68; Report of the International Law Commission on the Work Of Its Thirty-ninth Session, 4 May to 17 July 1987, UN Doc. A/42/10, 1987, para. 51.

82 Report of the International Law Commission on the Work of its Fortieth Session, 9 May to 29 July 1988, UN Doc. A/43/10, 1988.

83 *Ibid.*, paras. 224–28.

84 *Ibid.*, Commentary to draft articles on superior responsibility and lack of official position immunity.

85 Report of the International Law Commission on the Work of its Forty-sixth Session, 2 May to 22 July 1994, UN Doc. A/49/10, 1994, pp. 38–39; Report of the International Law Commission on the Work of its Forty-seventh Session, 2 May to 21 July 1995, UN Doc. A/50/10, 1995, para. 63.

"[t]he Charter and the Judgment of the Nürnberg Tribunal are the main sources of authority with regard to individual criminal responsibility for acts of aggression".[86] Similarly, the terminology of 'war crimes' and 'crimes against humanity' used in the Nuremberg and Tokyo Charters was maintained even though it had been surpassed respectively by the language of 'armed conflict' reflected in the Geneva Conventions[87] and, at least arguably, eclipsed by the new language of 'human rights violations'.[88] In other areas, reference to precedent was used where such precedent was seen as an illustration of a good idea even though it was not a legal requirement. For instance the recognition of the Nuremberg Tribunal of the evolving customary law of war was used as an argument in favour of having a non-exhaustive, illustrative list of war crimes.[89]

The ILC members did not see themselves as bound to the language of the Nuremberg and Tokyo Tribunals if they saw good reason to depart. This was in particular the case when it came to expanding the scope of potential criminal liability or when reliance could be placed on subsequent legal developments. Thus, the draft Code of Offences adopted by the ILC in 1996 omitted the requirement found in the Nuremberg Charter of a nexus between crimes against humanity and other crimes,[90] and it extended the application of conspiracy to war crimes and crimes against humanity as well as instituting a new provision on "responsibility for attempt".[91] The definitions of both crimes against humanity and war crimes were updated in light of intervening developments such as the Genocide and Geneva Conventions.

18.2.2. Draft Statute for an International Criminal Court

From the very beginning of its renewed consideration of the draft Code of Offences, the ILC on its own initiative took up the question of whether it

---

[86] Report of the International Law Commission on the Work of its Forty-eighth Session, 6 May to 26 July 1996, "Draft Code of Crimes against the Peace and Security of Mankind", UN Doc. A/51/10, 1996, commentary to Article 16, para. 5.

[87] Report of the International Law Commission on the Work of its Forty-first Session, 2 May to 21 July 1989, UN Doc. A/44/10, 1989, paras. 104–5.

[88] Report on the Forty-seventh Session, 1995, para. 88, see *supra* note 85.

[89] Report on the Forty-first Session, 1989, paras. 114–19, see *supra* note 87.

[90] Report on the Forty-seventh Session, 1995, see *supra* note 85.

[91] Report of the International Law Commission on the Work of its Forty-second Session, 1 May to 20 July 1990, UN Doc. A/45/10, 1990, paras. 43, 59.

---

should restrict itself to developing only a Code of Offences in the narrow sense or whether it should also consider how such a Code would be implemented.[92] As before, differing views were expressed with some in favour of establishing an international criminal court and others preferring that the Code of Offences be enforced by national courts.[93] On 4 December 1989 the UN General Assembly adopted Resolution 44/39, in which it asked the ILC to again take up the question of an international criminal court. The competing views of world order were again aired in the ILC. While some members came out in favour of establishing a permanent international criminal jurisdiction modelled on the Nuremberg Tribunal, others – like Sandström 40 years previous – depicted Nuremberg and Tokyo as the products of a unique setting and a set of circumstances existing at that time. According to the ILC report, "In the view of these members, this was an area in which law and politics were particularly intermingled, and politics seemed to be clearly showing that the mechanism proposed was unrealistic".[94] This divide was replicated particularly in debates about whether there should be a permanent independent court or recourse to *ad hoc* courts established by the Security Council,[95] and in debates regarding the respective roles of the Security Council and the proposed court, if it were to be established, in making determinations with respect to aggression.[96]

In 1994 the ILC adopted a draft Statute for an International Criminal Court, together with commentaries to the articles therein.[97] The same tension found earlier in the Nuremberg Tribunal and in the preparation of the initial draft Code of Offences was manifested again:

> As regards the question of whether the Commission should be more ambitious or more cautious in its approach, the members who favoured the former approach felt that the present draft was not sufficiently international or universal in

---

[92] First Report on the Draft Code of Offences, para. 4, see *supra* note 78.

[93] Report on the Thirty-ninth Session, 1987, para. 35, see *supra* note 81.

[94] Report of the International Law Commission on the Work of its Forty-fourth Session, 4 May to 24 July 1992, UN Doc. A/47/10, 1992, para. 31.

[95] Report of the International Law Commission on the Work of its Forty-fifth Session, 3 May to 23 July 1993, UN Doc. A/48/10, 1993, paras. 55–59.

[96] Report of the International Law Commission on the Work of its Forty-third Session, 29 April to 19 July 1991, UN Doc. A/46/10, 1991, paras. 141–165.

[97] Report on the Forty-sixth Session, 1994, see *supra* note 85.

its conception of the court, that it gave too much prominence to inter-State relations rather than a direct relationship between the individual and the international community, that its reliance on the traditional treaty approach might delay the establishment of the court, and that a more cautious approach would not sufficiently take into account the need for new mechanisms to address the recurring problem of ethnic violence in internal as well as international armed conflicts. Those who favoured the latter approach expressed the view that an instrument providing for an international criminal jurisdiction must take into account current international realities, including the need to ensure coordination with the existing system of national jurisdiction and international cooperation, that the establishment and effectiveness of the court required the broad acceptance of the statute by States which might require limiting its scope, that the political aspects of the topic required a realistic approach in which those were left to the decision of States, and that the preparation of the draft statute was, anyway, an unprecedented exercise in creative legislation for the Commission, one that needed to be tempered by a strong sense of practicality.[98]

The ILC draft contained five crimes: three of which (crimes against humanity, war crimes and aggression) were directly rooted in Nuremberg; the other two were genocide and a provision for incorporating additional treaty crimes. Concerning the crime of aggression, the ILC made a reference to the Nuremberg Tribunal and to the 1974 General Assembly definition, and it stated that despite the difficulties in defining aggression, "[i]t would thus seem retrogressive to exclude individual criminal responsibility for aggression (in particular, acts directly associated with the waging of a war of aggression) 50 years after Nürnberg".[99] However, in the commentary, the ILC attributed its decision to include the other crimes primarily to the fact that they had been included in the Statute of the ICTY which had been adopted in the intervening years.[100] Before continuing on with the consideration of the establishment of the ICC, it is useful to revert to consider the establishment of the ICTY and the ICTR.

---

[98] *Ibid.*, para. 48.

[99] *Ibid.*, p. 39.

[100] *Ibid.*, p. 38.

18.3. Establishment of the ICTY and ICTR, 1993–1994

Few references to the Nuremberg trials, or indeed to judicial precedents generally, are to be found in the history of debates around the establishment of the ICTY and the ICTR. This may be attributable to the fact that the Statutes of these bodies were drafted relatively quickly with a focus on responding to immediate and particular needs. These Statutes were adopted by the Security Council in 1993 and 1994, respectively, in the exercise of its mandate to maintain and to restore international peace and security without the extensive, detailed debate on fine points of law that was taking place concurrently in the ILC.

In the case of the ICTY, the Commission of Experts – initially established to examine and to consider whether war crimes had been committed – made reference in its interim report to the Nuremberg Principles to support its assertion that acting pursuant to superior orders did not relieve responsibility.[101] A French proposal for the establishment of a tribunal which would inform the Statute drafted by the Secretary General relied on the Nuremberg and Tokyo Tribunals to assert that there should be no defence of acting pursuant to superior orders, that leaders and other officials should not be immune from responsibility, and that the tribunal should focus on the major offenders.[102] The draft also sought to address certain criticisms of the Nuremberg and Tokyo Tribunals. It asserted that the subsequent development of customary international law would immunise the tribunal from claims that it applied the law retroactively and that an impartial international tribunal would avoid criticisms of being "victor's justice".[103] In one specific and explicit departure from Nuremberg and Tokyo, the French draft proposed that the right to initiate proceedings for review of judgment based on new facts should not be limited to the prosecution as had been the case with Nuremberg.[104] Slovenia responded to the French proposal, relying on the Nuremberg Tribunal precedent, to argue that the jurisdiction of any

---

[101] Interim Report of the Commission of Experts Established Pursuant to Security Council Resolution 780 (1992), annexed to Letter dated 9 February 1993 from the Secretary General Addressed to the Security Council, S/25274, 10 February 1993, para. 54.

[102] Letter dated 10 February 1993 from the Permanent Representative of France to the United Nations Addressed to the Secretary-General, UN Doc. S/25266, 1993.

[103] *Ibid.*

[104] *Ibid.*

tribunal should be dated back to the beginning of the conflict and not to the date of Croatia's and Slovenia's recognised independence as proposed by the French.[105] Several other states also made proposals, but largely without referring to Nuremberg or Tokyo. In his report to the Security Council transmitting the draft Statute for the ICTY, which was adopted by the Security Council, the Secretary General did not engage in extensive commentary, but he did note that the inclusion of violations of the laws and customs of war and of crimes against humanity was based on the Nuremberg Tribunal's Charter and Judgment.[106]

In the case of the ICTR, the Commission of Experts went into greater details in its interim report on the definition of crimes and on individual criminal responsibility than had its counterpart for the ICTY, an effort necessitated by the fact that the situation in Rwanda concerned a situation of non-international armed conflict where there was less certainty as to the applicable law.[107] The Commission of Experts considered that, even as set out in the Nuremberg Charter and as applied by the Nuremberg Tribunal, the concept of crimes against humanity applied equally to acts perpetrated against civilians of the perpetrators' nationality.[108] The Commission of Experts attributed the requirement of a nexus between crimes against humanity and the war, as stated in the Nuremberg Charter, to the specific purposes for which the Tribunal had been set up, and it considered that this did not reflect a general requirement of international law.[109] The Commission of Experts further traced the development of law since 1945, including the adoption of the Genocide Convention and the International Convention on the Suppression and the Punishment of the Crime of Apartheid, which it took to have broadened the scope of crimes against humanity beyond that set out in the Nuremberg Charter, rendering these crimes applicable also to the situation in Rwanda where there was no international armed

---

[105] Letter dated 20 April 1993 from the Permanent Representative of Slovenia to the United Nations Addressed to the Secretary-General, UN Doc. S/25652, 1993.

[106] Report of the Secretary-General Pursuant to Paragraph 2 of Security Council Resolution 808 (1993), UN Doc. S/25704), 3 May 1994.

[107] Letter dated 1 October 1994 from the Secretary-General Addressed to the President of the Security Council, UN Doc. S/1994/1125, 4 October 1994, annex.

[108] *Ibid.*, para. 115.

[109] *Ibid.*, paras. 114–15.

conflict.[110] Thus, the Commission of Experts partly relied on but also distinguished the Nuremberg trials. In addition, the Commission of Experts relied on the Nuremberg trials for general principles of individual criminal responsibility including superior responsibility, the lack of immunity based on official position and the lack of exculpatory defence of superior orders.[111]

In adopting the Statutes of the ICTY and the ICTR, several Security Council members made explicit reference to the Nuremberg Tribunal and portrayed these new *ad hoc* mechanisms as reiterations of, if not improvements on, the key accomplishments of Nuremberg.[112] A number of states, in the Security Council and outside, attributed "broader significance" to the ICTY and ICTR as the resumption or advancement of the process of establishing an international criminal court which had begun at Nuremberg.[113]

18.4. Establishment of the ICC, 1994–1998

Following the adoption of the draft Statute for an international criminal court by the ILC in 1994, further discussions on the basis of the draft Statute took place in the Ad Hoc Committee, the Preparatory Committee and finally the Diplomatic Conference of Plenipotentiaries on the Establishment of an International Criminal Court ('Rome Conference') which met in Rome in the summer of 1998 and adopted the Rome Statute of the International Criminal Court ('ICC Statute') on 17 July 1998 (as well as several informal gatherings). Unlike the ILC negotiations which were among independent experts (albeit nominated and elected by member states and receiving inputs from states), from the beginning of

---

[110] *Ibid.*, para. 116.

[111] *Ibid.*, paras. 129–31.

[112] Provisional Verbatim Records of the 3175th Meeting Held on 22 February 1993, UN Doc. S/PV. 3175, 22 February 1993 (statements of Albright [United States] and Arria [Venezuela] in relation to the ICTY); Provisional Verbatim Records of the 3453rd Meeting Held on 8 November 1994, UN Doc. S/PV.3454, 8 November 1994 (statements of Keating [New Zealand] and Kovanda [Czech Republic] in relation to the ICTR).

[113] See, for example, Statement of Kovanda, UN Doc. S/PV.3453, *supra* note 112; General Assembly Official Records, 50th Session: 22nd Plenary Meeting, UN Doc. A/50/PV.22, 6 October 1995 (statement of Liechtenstein); General Assembly Official Records, 50th Session: 7th Plenary Meeting, UN Doc. A/50/PV.7, 26 September 1995 (statement of Netherlands).

the Ad Hoc Committee, negotiations of the ICC Statute took place among states, with all states formally able to participate on an equal footing.

Whereas the ILC discussions had initially begun with the Charter and the Judgment of the Nuremberg Tribunal, by the time the ILC was finalising its draft ICC Statute, a number of additional precedents – including both conventions such as the Geneva Conventions and the Additional Protocols and new institutions such as the ICTY and ICTR – were available. Discussions in the Ad Hoc Committee started generally from the ILC draft, but reference was made to the Nuremberg trials and to other similar precedents at a number of points in the process. Reference to the Nuremberg Tribunal was particularly important among those states advocating for inclusion in the ICC Statute of the crime of aggression which was not found in the Statutes of the ICTY and ICTR.[114] These states did not rely alone on the Nuremberg Charter but also on General Assembly Resolution 3314 (XXIX), independent expert bodies as well as the ongoing work of the ILC on the draft Code of Offences/Crimes which itself relied heavily on Nuremberg.[115] As in the ILC process, these states argued that to not include aggression would be "a retrogressive step" in relation to the Nuremberg Tribunal.[116] In a familiar refrain, other states argued that the crime of aggression was essentially a political issue and that the Nuremberg Tribunal took place in a situation of unique circumstance where the political powers had already characterised the war as one of aggression.[117] They did not criticise the Nuremberg Tribunal or seek to minimise its significance, but they either characterised it

---

[114] Report of the Ad Hoc Committee on the Establishment of an International Criminal Court, UN Doc. A/50/22 (Supp.), 7 September 1995, para. 63 ("Report of the Ad Hoc Committee") (http://www.legal-tools.org/en/doc/b50da8/).

[115] *Ibid.*

[116] *Ibid.*; see also Report of the Preparatory Committee on the Establishment of an International Criminal Court, vol. 2, UN Doc. A/51/22 (Supp.), 14 September 1996 ("Report of the Preparatory Committee") (http://www.legal-tools.org/doc/03b284/).

[117] Report of the Ad Hoc Committee, para. 64, see *supra* note 114; Summary of the Proceedings of the Preparatory Committee During the Period 25 March–12 April 1996, UN Doc. A/AC.249/1, 8 May 1996, para. 31 ("Summary of the Proceedings of the Preparatory Committee") (http://www.legal-tools.org/en/doc/d7aad5/); Report of the Preparatory Committee, para 71, see *supra* note 116.

differently[118] or argued that there was a need for more certainty on the definition before including it in the draft statute.[119]

In the context of war crimes and crimes against humanity, states also made reference to the Charters of the Nuremberg and Tokyo Tribunals as sources of precedent along with the Statutes of the ICTY and the ICTR.[120] Where the ICTY and ICTR Statutes had expanded the scope of criminal liability (e.g. by loosening or removing the requirement of a nexus between crimes against humanity and aggression), states sought to distinguish the Nuremberg Tribunal, either by characterising it as having been superseded by subsequent developments[121] or by interpreting the Nuremberg Charter as including requirements which were more restrictive than required by international law at the time.[122] Once again, the Nuremberg and Tokyo Tribunals were used in support of the argument that official position should not relieve liability.[123] The Nuremberg Tribunal was also cited in the Preparatory Committee and at the Rome Conference by states seeking to provide for corporate criminal responsibility[124] and *in absentia* trials.[125] However, as in other areas where there was substantive disagreement, other states sought to

---

[118] See, for example, Comments Received Pursuant to Paragraph 4 of General Assembly Resolution 49/53 on the Establishment of an International Criminal Court: Report of the Secretary-General, UN Doc. A/AC.244/1/Add.2, 1 April 1995, para. 18 (http://www.legal-tools.org/en/doc/866fdd/).

[119] Ad Hoc Committee on the Establishment of an International Criminal Court: Summary of Observations Made by the Representative of the United Kingdom of Great Britain and Northern Ireland on 3, 4, 5, 6 and 7 April 1995, 8 April 1995 (http://www.legal-tools.org/en/doc/664ac1/).

[120] Report of the Ad Hoc Committee, paras. 76–79, see *supra* note 114; Summary of the Proceedings of the Preparatory Committee, paras. 39–48, see *supra* note 117.

[121] *Ibid.*, paras. 76–79.

[122] United States Delegation, Crimes Against Humanity: Lack of a Requirement for a Nexus to Armed Conflict, ICC Preparatory Works, 25 March 1996 (http://www.legal-tools.org/en/doc/1163fc/).

[123] Report of the Preparatory Committee, para 193, see *supra* note 116; Summary of the Proceedings of the Preparatory Committee, para. 90, see *supra* note 117.

[124] Report of the Preparatory Committee, para. 194, see *supra* note 116; Summary of the Proceedings of the Preparatory Committee, para. 91, see *supra* note 117; Summary Record of the First Meeting of the Committee of the Whole, A/CONF.183/1/SR.1, 16 June 1998 ("Summary Record of the First Meeting 1998"), paras. 32–33.

[125] Proposals Made by the Delegation of The Netherlands: Articles 5, 27, 37, 38, 44, 44 a, 44 b, 48, ICC Preparatory Works, 13 August 1996 (http://www.legal-tools.org/en/doc/3e6d09/).

---

distinguish or to offer differing interpretations of the Nuremberg Charter.[126]

As the prospect of establishing the ICC became closer to a reality, the Nuremberg Tribunal took on a new role in statements at the Rome Conference. From the opening of the conference by the temporary President, representatives of several states and non-governmental organisations – including the Committee of Former Nuremberg Prosecutors who physically represented the Nuremberg Tribunal at the Rome Conference – drew on and made reference to the Nuremberg and Tokyo Tribunals in urging their fellow participants to seize the moment and to adopt the Statute of the ICC.[127] As stated by former Nuremberg Prosecutor Benjamin Ferencz, in his address to the Rome Conference:

> Ever since the Nuremberg judgement, wars of aggression had undeniably been not a national right but an international crime. The Charter of the United Nations prescribed that only the Security Council could determine when aggression by a State had occurred, but it made no provision for criminal trials. No criminal statute could expand or diminish the Council's vested power. Only an independent court could decide whether an individual was innocent or guilty, and excluding aggression from international judicial scrutiny was to grant immunity to those responsible for it.[128]

Similar remarks were made by a number of delegations who drew a line from the Nuremberg and Tokyo tribunals through the *ad hoc* mechanisms to the establishment of the ICC.[129] For his part, the French Minister of Foreign Affairs, Hubert Védrine, drew a connection back not only to the Nuremberg and Tokyo Tribunals, but to the preceding views expressed by those such as Donnedieu de Vabres. Like Alfaro some 50 years previously, he depicted Nuremberg as a key moment in the progress towards the establishment of the ICC. In his words:

---

[126] NGO Coalition on the ICC, "Netherlands, Italy, Francophone Africa Line up Behind French Push for Trials in Absentia", in *On the Record*, OTR ICC, vol. 1, no. 10 (Part 1), 30 June 1998 (http://www.legal-tools.org/uploads/tx_ltpdb/doc32599.pdf); Summary Record of the First Meeting 1998, paras. 38, 57, see *supra* note 124.

[127] See, for example, Summary Record of the First Plenary Meeting, *supra* note 124, para. 6.

[128] Summary Record of the Third Plenary Meeting, A/CONF.183/SR.3, 16 June 1998, para. 120.

[129] See, for example, Summary Record of the Seventh Plenary Meeting, A/CONF.183/SR.7, 18 June 1998, para. 35.

> In France 75 years ago, when many of the atrocities that were to mar the 20th century had yet to be committed, Henri Donnedieu de Vabres, an eminent legal expert and future judge at the Nuremberg Tribunal, proposed the creation of an International Criminal Court designed to combat the impunity of very large-scale criminals. Many others thought along similar lines. The Nuremberg and Tokyo Tribunals, in the particular climate of the immediate post-war years, put some flesh on the bones of this idea. It cropped up again in the 1948 Genocide Convention but went no further at that time. All of us here know how the stalemate of the Cold War halted all progress for almost forty-five years. But all of us are also aware how, from the ending of the stand-off in the early Nineties, this pressing need began to be felt again in the world's conscience. Two ad hoc tribunals were then created, one in 1993 for Yugoslavia, the other in 1994 for Rwanda. The delegations gathered in Rome today for almost five weeks have met with the firm intention of bringing the process to completion, culminating in the creation of a Court that is effective and hence universal, that is designed to last and that meets the requirements of justice.[130]

The role of the Nuremberg Tribunal in debates had thus come full circle. As in the original proposals of Donnedieu de Vabres, Jackson, Biddle and others, reference to Nuremberg was used not only to guide technical discussions but also to motivate, to inspire and to compel others to act towards establishing a permanent international criminal court. While these statements were partially directed at other participants, they were frequently intended also for domestic consumption.[131] In such

---

[130] Statement by Mr. Hubert Vedrine, Minister of Foreign Affairs of the French Republic, 17 June 1998 (http://www.legal-tools.org/uploads/tx_ltpdb/doc40693.pdf); see also Discours de S.E. M. Luc Frieden, Ministre de la Justice du Grand-Duché de Luxembourg, 18 June 1998 (http://www.legal-tools.org/uploads/tx_ltpdb/doc40692.pdf); Statement by H.E. Mr M.V. Raditapole Alternate Leader of the Delegation of the Kingdom of Lesotho to the United Nations Diplomatic Conference of Plenipotentiaries on the Establishment of an International Criminal Court, 15 June–17 June 1998 (http://www.legal-tools.org/uploads/tx_ltpdb/doc27827.pdf); UN Secretary-General Declares Overriding Interest of International Criminal Court Conference must be that of Victims and World Community as a Whole, 16 June 1998 (http://www.legal-tools.org/en/doc/a7b2c1/); Statement by the Honorable Bill Richardson United States Ambassador to the United Nations at the United Nations Plenipotentiaries Conference on the Establishment of an International Criminal Court, 18 June 1998 (http://www.legal-tools.org/doc/c2766e/).

[131] See, for instance, the various statements put out by the American Bar Association.

circumstances, reference to Nuremberg and to its legacy served as a shorthand for certain shared values and ideals.

18.5. Conclusion

Reference to the Nuremberg Tribunal and trials played a number of different roles in the process leading to the establishment of the ICC. Participants in, and proponents of, the Nuremberg Tribunal and trials used the opportunity to push not only for the codification of the principles of the Charter and Judgment of the Nuremberg Tribunal but also to promote the further development of an international order wherein the interests of states would be subordinated to the independent application of the rule of law and where individuals would be held directly accountable under international law. At the same time, equally embedded in the legacy of Nuremberg was and remains an understanding of the Nuremberg Tribunal as the product of agreement among four Great Powers as well as a commitment to ensuring that the legal order remains grounded in the reality of international politics. Similar competing views were manifested from the deepest structural issues to the finest technical points, wherein reference to the Nuremberg Tribunal and trials was frequently used to buttress arguments but was rarely determinative of the outcome. The enduring legacy of Nuremberg is not one but multiple. While the Nuremberg Principles and subsequent developments capture a common core of agreement, they also leave open the possibility of a wide range of perspectives. In such circumstances, persuasive appeal to the legacy of Nuremberg presupposes a certain shared understanding of the Nuremberg Tribunal's significance which may not be always universally shared in the same way. As the development of international criminal law progresses, we should be mindful to consider the extent to which our understanding of the Nuremberg legacy is commonly shared, and to consider the implications of placing such particular emphasis on this Tribunal and its trials in comparison to other less well-recognised developments (such as the Tokyo Tribunal). While appeal to the legacy of Nuremberg has proven effective in building support for the international criminal law project in certain States with strong historical attachment to Nuremberg, would not similar attention to the Tokyo Tribunal or to various domestic trials serve a similar purpose elsewhere?

Annex: The Nuremberg Principles

Principle I

Any person who commits an act which constitutes a crime under international law is responsible therefor and liable to punishment.

Principle II

The fact that internal law does not impose a penalty for an act which constitutes a crime under international law does not relieve the person who committed the act from responsibility under international law.

Principle III

The fact that a person who committed an act which constitutes a crime under international law acted as Head of State or responsible Government official does not relieve him from responsibility under international law.

Principle IV

The fact that a person acted pursuant to order of his Government or of a superior does not relieve him from responsibility under international law, provided a moral choice was in fact possible to him.

Principle V

Any person charged with a crime under international law has the right to a fair trial on the facts and law.

Principle VI

The crimes hereinafter set out are punishable as crimes under; international law:

a. **Crimes against peace:**

    i. Planning, preparation, initiation or waging of a war of aggression or a war in violation of international treaties, agreements or assurances;

    ii. Participation in a common plan or conspiracy for the accomplishment of any of the acts mentioned under (i).

b. **War crimes:**

Violations of the laws or customs of war which include, but are not limited to, murder, ill-treatment or deportation to slave-labor or for any other purpose of civilian population of or in occupied territory, murder or ill-treatment of prisoners of war, of persons on the seas, killing of hostages, plunder of public or private property, wanton destruction of cities, towns, or villages, or devastation not justified by military necessity.

c. **Crimes against humanity:**

Murder, extermination, enslavement, deportation and other inhuman acts done against any civilian population, or persecutions on political, racial or religious grounds, when such acts are done or such persecutions are carried on in execution of or in connection with any crime against peace or any war crime.

Principle VII

Complicity in the commission of a crime against peace, a war crime, or a crime against humanity as set forth in Principles VI is a crime under international law.

19

Doubts about *Nullum Crimen* and Superior Orders: Language Discrepancies in the Nuremberg Judgment and their Significance

Guido Acquaviva[*]

19.1. Introduction

Over the past decades, the Judgment ('Nuremberg Judgment') issued by the International Military Tribunal ('IMT') in Nuremberg relating to the Second World War actions of the German major war criminals has been analysed by not only legal professionals but also historians, sociologists and other scholars.

In contrast to the practice of contemporary international criminal tribunals, the Nuremberg Judgment was issued in three official, and equally authoritative, languages: English, French and Russian.[1] Unsurprisingly, a few significant discrepancies have been noted between portions of the English and French versions.[2] For instance, in the seminal book on

---

[*] **Guido Acquaviva** works as Senior Legal Officer in Chambers at the Special Tribunal for Lebanon ('STL'). Prior to his appointment at the STL, he worked for six years as Legal Officer at the International Criminal Tribunal for the former Yugoslavia ('ICTY'). He also served for one year as a Legal Officer in the Office of the ICTY President. His education includes an LL.M. in International and Comparative Law from Tulane Law School (Fulbright Scholar) and a Ph.D. in International Relations from the University of Padova. He is a member of the faculty of the LL.M. in International Criminal Law and Crime Prevention (University of Turin and UNICRI) and a lecturer at the Geneva Academy of International Humanitarian Law and Human Rights. He also serves as a co-chair of the Editorial Committee of the *Journal of International Criminal Justice*.

[1] Charter of the International Military Tribunal, Article 25, 8 August 1945 ("Nuremberg Charter") (http://www.legal-tools.org/doc/64ffdd/). In fact, although the Nuremberg Charter states that "[a]ll official documents shall be produced, and all court proceedings conducted, in English, French and Russian, and in the language of the Defendant", German was considered essential only to enable participation, and ultimately a "fair trial", for the accused *during* the proceedings, but not at the moment of the final judgment.

[2] The texts referred to in this chapter are: International Military Tribunal, *The Trial of German Major War Criminals: Proceedings of the International Military Tribunal Sitting at Nuremberg, Germany*, Judgment, part 22 (22 August 1946 to 1 October 1946), 1 October 1946, ("Nuremberg Judgment") (English) (http://www.legal-tools.org/doc/45f18e/); IMT, *Procès des grands criminels de guerre devant le Tribunal*

superior orders written by Yoram Dinstein in 1965, discrepancies relating to the IMT's findings on the defence of superior orders between the English and French versions were identified and explained.[3] Years later, Antonio Cassese also remarked – and elaborated upon – differences between those two same languages in relation to the applicability of the *nullum crimen* principle to the trial.[4]

While these discrepancies could, in theory, have been caused by mere translation mistakes, a more careful analysis seems to suggest a different explanation: they appear to be rooted in how the Judges understood the problems presented to them and betray the solutions offered by each of the Judges in light of their language, training and legal background. Discrepancies were therefore either intentional or due to lack of mutual understanding among the Judges.[5] Moreover, the impact of these language discrepancies might not have been limited to the text of the Nuremberg Judgment itself. Rather, it is possible that any difference in the various language versions went on to influence the legal discourse on crimes against humanity and other key concepts, affecting scholars and practitioners in different ways – essentially, depending on which language they were using and relying upon. Thus, for instance, French scholars (reading the French text on the import of *nullum crimen* at Nuremberg) came to different conclusions as to the meaning of the principle of legality in international criminal proceedings than their English-speaking colleagues.

This chapter aims at carrying this research onwards, focusing on two major discrepancies (on *nullum crimen* and on superior orders) among the English, French and Russian versions of the Nuremberg Judgment and assessing how they have influenced subsequent scholars,

---

   Militaire International – texte official en langue française, Nuremberg, 1947 (French); N.S. Lebedeva and V.V. Ishchenko (eds.), *Nurnbergskii Prozess: Uroki Istorii* [*The Nuremberg Process: Lessons of History*], Juridicheskaja Literatura, Moscow, 1996, p. 561 ff. (Russian).

3   Yoram Dinstein, *The Defence of 'Obedience to Superior Orders' in International Law*, A.W. Sijthoff, Leiden, 1965, p. 149.

4   Antonio Cassese, *International Criminal Law*, Oxford University Press, Oxford, 2008, pp. 105–6.

5   See Guido Acquaviva, "At the Origins of Crimes against Humanity – Clues to a Proper Understanding of the *Nullum Crimen* Principle in the Nuremberg Judgment", in *Journal of International Criminal Justice*, 2011, vol. 9, no. 4, pp. 881–903, where the matter is sketched in a preliminary fashion.

lawmakers and judges that have dealt with those issues. This analysis is placed within a contemporary trend of scholarly interest that attempts to shed some light on the language – and ultimately cultural – differences among legal practitioners when pleading and ruling in international trials.[6] In the first part, the discrepancies in relation to these two areas of the law – areas that have been much debated and discussed to date – are identified. Their likely origin is then explored. On the basis of this analysis, the discussion then attempts to shed some light on the consequences of these different language versions on the academic and judicial discourse following Nuremberg. In practice, I will try to assess if and how after 1947 these different texts have had an impact not just on the academic discussions about the Nuremberg experience but also on the domestic and international jurisprudence related to war crimes and crimes against humanity.[7] The final section will then draw some tentative conclusions on the consequences, if any, that the language discrepancies at Nuremberg had on subsequent legal discourse and case law.

19.2. Language Discrepancies at Nuremberg and their (Likely) Origin

As mentioned above, two important discrepancies have been noted by scholars in the three equally authoritative versions of the Nuremberg Judgment, one relating to the issue of *nullum crimen sine lege* (the principle of legality) and the other relating to the wording of the defence of superior orders. It is first necessary to set out these different texts side by side to fully appreciate their import, so as to then attempt to surmise the reasons, if any, behind these differences.

---

[6] Recently, Michael Bohlander, "Language, Intellectual Culture, Legal Traditions, and International Criminal Justice", in *Journal of International Criminal Justice*, 2014, forthcoming. For interesting reflections on the diffusion, translation and transnational exchanges of cultural legal norms and (procedural) practices in international non-criminal matters, see also Benjamin Brake and Peter J. Katzenstein, "Lost in Translation? Nonstate Actors and the Transnational Movement of Procedural Law", in *International Organization*, 2013, vol. 67, pp. 725–57.

[7] These two themes (scholarly discussions and case law) are treated together because, as will be seen, it is hard to conceptually distinguish them: from Henri Donnedieu de Vabres to Antonio Cassese and Theodor Meron, often scholars who had written on these topics have later become judges deciding international criminal cases, and then again commented upon other judges' decisions on the same topic. More generally, the relatively limited amount of jurisprudence in the field of international crimes appears to force international tribunals to heavily rely on academic discussions on the most complex topics.

19.2.1. Language Discrepancies in the Three Versions

19.2.1.1. *Nullum Crimen*

The first (set of) differences relates to the issue of the applicability of the principle of legality,[8] articulated in the Universal Declaration of Human Rights in the following terms:

> No one shall be held guilty of any penal offence on account of any act or omission which did not constitute a penal offence, under national or international law, at the time when it was committed.[9]

With reference to international law, it is today considered axiomatic that "[a] person may be held guilty of an act or an omission that was not punishable by the applicable national law at the time the offence was committed so long as this was punishable under international treaty law or customary law at the time the offence was committed".[10]

The principle of legality featured prominently during the Nuremberg trial, due to the novelty of at least two sets of charges against the accused: crimes against peace and crimes against humanity. While most of the theoretical discussion on *nullum crimen* in the Nuremberg Judgment (as well as in subsequent trials related to the crimes committed by the Axis Powers in Europe) relates to the controversial concept of

---

[8] The Latin expression "*nullum crimen sine lege*" was formulated by the German scholar Paul Johann Anselm Ritter von Feuerbach. See P.J.A. von Feuerbach, *Lehrbuch des gemeinen in Deutschland gültigen peinlichen Rechts*, Hayer, Giessen, 1832, pp. 12–19, translated and reprinted in English as "The Foundations of Criminal Law and the *Nullum Crimen* Principle", in *Journal of International Criminal Justice*, 2007, vol. 5, pp. 1005–8. See also Stefan Glaser, "Les pouvoirs de juge en droit international penal", in Oscar A. Germann (ed.), *Stellung und Aufgabe des Richters im modernen Strafrecht: mélanges Oscar Adolf Germann*, Stämpfli, Bern, 1959, pp. 77–78.

[9] Universal Declaration of Human Rights, Article 11(2), 10 December 1948. The principle has been reiterated at both international and domestic levels and is now considered to be part and parcel of the fundamental principles of a fair trial that must be recognised in all judicial systems.

[10] Manfred Nowak, *U.N. Covenant on Civil and Political Rights: CCPR Commentary*, 2nd ed., N.P. Engel, Strasbourg, p. 281. For the judicial application of this principle, see European Court of Human Rights, *Kolk and Kislyiy v. Estonia (Admissibility)*, Application Nos. 23052/04, 24018/04, Judgment, 17 January 2006; Supreme Court of Canada, *R v. Finta*, (1994) 1 SCR 701, Judgment, 24 March 1994, pp. 781–84 (per La Forest J.); High Court of Australia, *Polyukhovich v. Commonwealth* (1991) 172 CLR 501, Judgment, 14 August 1992, pp. 572–76 (per Brennan J.).

---

crimes against peace, it was also germane to the charges of crimes against humanity. This is because despite the fact that most of the accused were cumulatively charged – and ultimately convicted – for war crimes and crimes against humanity in relation to the same acts, two accused (Julius Streicher and Baldur von Schirach) were only convicted for crimes against humanity. While for the other accused, therefore, crimes against humanity could in theory be construed as a variation of the conviction for war crimes, the sentences for those two individuals had to account in a very concrete way for the uniqueness of crimes against humanity as a separate category of crimes spelled out for the first time only in the Nuremberg Charter. The relevant sections of the Nuremberg Judgment read as follows:

English	French	Russian
[...] the maxim *nullum crimen sine lege* is not a limitation of sovereignty, but is in general a principle of justice [...] On this view of the case alone, it would appear that the maxim has no application to the present facts.[11]	[...] la maxime: *Nullum crimen sine lege* ne limite pas la souveraineté des États; elle ne formule qu'une règle généralement suivie [...][12]	Принцип 'нуллум кримен сине леге...' не означает ограничения суверенности, а лишь является общим принципом правосудия. [...] Если рассматривать этот вопрос только в свете настоящего дела то можно сделать вывод что это принцип при данных обстоятельствах неприменим.[13]
Streicher's incitement to murder and extermination at the time when Jews in	Le fait que Streicher poussait au meurtre et à l'extermination, à	Подстрекательства Штрейхера к убийству и уничтожению в то время

---

[11] Nuremberg Judgment, p. 444, see *supra* note 2.

[12] This French text can be rendered into English as: "*Nullum crimen sine lege* does not limit States' sovereignty: it merely formulates a generally followed rule". As mentioned above, the second portion of the statement appearing in English (and Russian) is simply excised from the French text.

[13] This Russian text can be rendered into English as: "The principle '*nullum crimen sine lege*' does not mean a limitation of sovereignty, but only constitutes a general principle of justice. If we consider this question only in light of the current case, then we can draw the conclusion that the principle is not applicable given the circumstances".

| the East were being killed under the most horrible conditions clearly constitutes persecution on political and racial grounds in connection with War Crimes, as defined in the Charter, and constitutes a crime against humanity.[14] | l'époque même où, dans l'Est, les Juifs étaient massacrés dans les conditions les plus horribles, réalise 'la persécution pour des motifs politiques et raciaux' prévue parmi les crimes de guerre définis par le Statut, et constitue également un crime contre l'Humanité.[15] | когда евреи на Востоке умерщвлялись самым ужасным образом, несомненно, являются преследованием по политическим и расовым мотивам в связи с совершением военных преступлений, как они определены Уставом, и являются, таким образом преступлением против человечности.[16] |

There is no doubt, looking at the above table, that the three versions of the two passages in question diverge in some, often significant, respects. In particular, the French version of the passage on the principle of legality, instead of speaking of a "principle of justice", insists on the fact that *nullum crimen* is a rule ("*règle*") that does not limit the sovereignty of states (the words "rule" and "states" do not appear in the English or Russian texts). Moreover, and more importantly, the French text does not have any reference to the principle of legality as being inapplicable to proceedings before the IMT.

If one reads only the English text, it would seem that the *nullum crimen* maxim is merely a general principle not binding on the Judges, probably in light of the recognition that the Nuremberg Charter provided the boundaries of the IMT's jurisdiction. This understanding would allow the Judges to convict the defendants for crimes against humanity

---

[14] Nuremberg Judgment, p. 502, see *supra* note 2.

[15] This French text can be rendered into English as: "The fact that Streicher incited to murder and extermination, at the time when Jews in the East were being massacred under the most horrible conditions, constitutes the 'persecution on political or racial grounds' provided for among the war crimes defined in the Statute, and also constitutes a crime against humanity".

[16] This Russian text can be rendered into English as: "Streicher's incitements to murder and extermination at a time when Jews in the East were being killed in a most horrible way, undoubtedly constitute persecution on political and racial grounds in connection with the commission of war crimes, as defined in the Charter, and thus constitute crimes against humanity".

regardless of their established guilt for the corresponding war crimes, by balancing the "principle" of *nullum crimen* with the "principle" that punishing heinous conduct such as massive extermination and persecutions cannot be deemed unjust.[17] In other words, on the basis of these texts, *nullum crimen* is merely a principle of justice. Not being a clear and binding rule, it allows a court the possibility of weighing other competing principles, assessing in particular whether it would be more just to leave this type of crime unpunished or, instead, punish them on the basis of (retroactive) law. The English and Russian versions hint at this dichotomy, and reach the unambiguous conclusion that the *nullum crimen* principle should actually not be applied at Nuremberg.

If one reads the French text, however, the conclusion is utterly different: the *nullum crimen* maxim appears to rise to the level of a fully-fledged "rule", binding the IMT regardless of the dictates of the Nuremberg Charter (which would at most establish the jurisdiction of the IMT, not the applicable law). The conclusion is inexorable, in such (French) perspective, that Streicher could only be convicted of crimes against humanity if his deeds also at the same time ("*également*") amounted to war crimes, firmly established in customary law at the time of their commission.

The Russian text has two main interesting features. First, it is different from both the English and the French in that it considers *nullum crimen* as a general principle of justice. The English and French texts refer instead to *nullum crimen* being, respectively, "in general a principle of justice" or "*une régle généralment suivie*". Second, and more importantly, the Russian version appears to be the most precise of the three in keeping crimes against humanity distinct from war crimes, when it states that Streicher's actions "constitute persecution on political and racial grounds in connection with *the commission of* war crimes, as defined in the Charter" (in order to establish the jurisdictional requirements of Article 6(c)). It then proceeds to conclude that these crimes "thus [or 'in this way'] constitute crimes against humanity" (making the factual finding required on the basis of the charges). Overall, this text supports the English version that does not require a finding of

---

[17] This is the understanding of Streicher's conviction in Egon Schwelb, "Crimes Against Humanity", in *British Year Book of International Law*, 1946, vol. 23, pp. 206–7.

guilt for war crimes before establishing guilt for crimes against humanity, thus maintaining a clearer distinction between the two categories.

In conclusion, despite their differences, the English and Russian versions appear to consider Streicher's individual criminal responsibility for crimes against humanity as a legitimate outcome, in view of the circumstance that the principle of legality was deemed a mere principle inapplicable in the instant case, probably due to the enormity of the crimes in question. The French version, on the other hand, does not explain how a conviction could actually be entered against Streicher for persecution, except in so far as it suggests that the criminalisation of the conduct in question complied with *nullum crimen* because persecution also amounted to a war crime.

19.2.1.2. Superior Orders

Another complex legal issue with which the Nuremberg Judges had to contend was the allegation by defence counsel, and by several accused themselves, that the acts committed should not be imputed to the accused, because they were merely following orders from above. As the IMT itself stated,

> [t]he procedure within the Party was governed in the most absolute way by the "leadership principle" (*Führerprinzip*). According to the principle, each Führer has the right to govern, administer, or decree subject to no control of any kind and at his complete discretion, subject only to the orders he received from above. This principle applied in the first instance to Hitler himself as the leader of the Party, and in a lesser degree to all other Party officials. All, members of the Party swore an oath of "eternal allegiance" to the Leader.[18]

As the Allied had suspected during the war, defendants could easily evoke this defence to excuse their behaviour in a "legal" way, simply by referring to this legal principle to shift the responsibility, as it were, "upwards", and ultimately to Hitler himself. To such a contention, the Nuremberg Charter (at Article 8) already provided an answer: "The fact that the defendant acted pursuant to order[s] of his Government or of a

---

[18] Nuremberg Judgment, p. 414, see *supra* note 2.

superior shall not free him from responsibility, but may be considered in mitigation of punishment".

The Nuremberg test (enshrined in Article 8 of the Nuremberg Charter) has generally been considered as enshrining a rule of absolute liability, i.e. the principle according to which superior orders ought *never* to provide an excuse for the commission of international crimes.[19] Paola Gaeta, in her seminal article on the defence of superior orders in customary law and in the Rome Statute of the International Criminal Court ('ICC Statute'), contended that a close scrutiny of national legislation and case law shows how the customary rule on superior orders upholds the absolute liability approach as enshrined in the Nuremberg Charter.[20] Other scholars instead suggest that a limited defence of superior orders would actually tally with the case law related to, as well as with the rationale of, military duties and obligations imposed on soldiers.[21]

Be that as it may, Article 8 is undoubtedly adamant in rejecting superior orders as a defence. In theory, then, the plea of superior orders was completely rejected in the Nuremberg Charter – there was no room for an assessment of the *mens rea* of the accused in the context of such plea.[22] This was due to Soviet insistence on the wording, due to the fact that, i) no crime should be excused, and ii) that the major war criminals would not be akin to low-level privates with no knowledge about the illegality of the instructions received.[23]

This did not of course stop the accused at Nuremberg from arguing the point, as feared, in an attempt to ascribe the responsibility to the even higher echelons of the German political and military leadership and, ultimately, to Hitler himself. Moreover, and in the face of the plain language of the Nuremberg Charter, the defendants argued that the reference to "orders" should actually be interpreted as meaning "manifestly illegal orders", which was clearly supported by the text of the

---

[19] Dinstein, 1965, p. xviii, see *supra* note 3.

[20] Paola Gaeta, "The Defence of Superior Orders: the Statute of the International Criminal Court versus Customary International Law", in *European Journal of International Law*, 1999, vol. 10, p. 172.

[21] Alexander Zahar, "Superior Orders", in Antonio Cassese (ed.), *The Oxford Companion to International Criminal Justice*, Oxford University Press, Oxford, 2009, p. 525.

[22] Dinstein, 1965, pp. 117–18, see *supra* note 3.

[23] *Ibid.*, fn. 403.

Article. It should be noted that all of the Nuremberg prosecutors, including the French ones, had asserted that the drafters of the Nuremberg Charter had already considered whether the orders need to be manifestly illegal and whether the high level of the accused allowed them to claim that they had no knowledge of the illegality, and had decided *a priori* that both questions would be answered in the negative.[24] This attempt in turn prompted the IMT to categorically state:

> The provisions of this Article [8] are in conformity with the law of all nations. That a soldier was ordered to kill or torture in violation of the international law of war has never been recognised as a defence to such acts of brutality, though, as the Charter here provides, the order may be urged in mitigation of the punishment.[25]

Had the IMT limited itself to this remark, much confusion could have been avoided. Instead, the Judges resolved to add:

English	French	Russian
The true test, which is found in varying degrees in the criminal law of most nations, is not the existence of the order, but whether moral choice was in fact possible.	Le vrai critérium de la responsabilité pénale, celui qu'on trouve, sous une forme ou sous une autre, dans le droit criminel de la plupart des pays, n'est nullement en rapport avec l'ordre reçu. Il réside dans la liberté morale, dans la faculté de choisir, chez l'auteur de l'acte reproché.[26]	Подлинным критерием в этом отношении, который содержится в той или иной степени в формулировках в уголовном праве большинства государств, является не факт наличия приказа, а вопрос о том, был ли практически возможен моральный выбор.[27]

---

24 *Ibid.*, p. 133.

25 Nuremberg Judgment, p. 447, see *supra* note 2.

26 This French text can be rendered into English as: "The true criterion of criminal responsibility, which is found in one form or another, in the criminal law of most countries, does not relate to the order received. It lies in the moral freedom, in the ability to choose, by the author of the act alleged".

The English and Russian versions of this passage appear short and clearer than the French one, which may at first sight appear more complex. The French actually uses two expressions (moral freedom and the ability/possibility – "*faculté*" – to choose), where one single phrase (pointing to "moral choice") characterises the other two texts. At a close inspection, however, the French version may actually better explain the reasoning of the Judges than the English one, especially if one adopts the Russian text as an interpretative tool. The context appears important.

The portion of the Judgment immediately preceding the passage discussed here points to the legal notion that if a soldier is ordered (for instance) to kill in violation of the international law of war, he is not allowed to plead the order as a defence, but (as the Charter provides in Article 8), the order may be urged in mitigation of the punishment. The English text talks about a "test"; however, it then does not continue with what common law judges, lawyers or scholars would expect, i.e. the enunciation of a clear test, a standard with prongs to follow so as to properly assess the impact of orders on mitigation.

The passage in question instead talks about a criterion (in English, a test), but then moves on to discuss a *different* matter – not mitigation, but rather instances where punishment should be avoided completely. According to the French and Russian versions, however, it is more evident that, after the discussion on superior orders, the Judges are moving to discuss a different topic: the foundation of individual criminal responsibility (which is not explicitly referenced in the English text). This of course must always be found in personal fault, so as to avoid any instance of objective liability unrelated to personal guilt. It should be noted in this respect that the Russian version adds an important dimension: that the choice must have been concretely possible in the circumstances of the specific case, and that therefore no general and abstract "test" can be devised and applied in this respect.

Thus, the Judgment – when read in French and Russian – makes it clear that superior orders are never a defence *per se*. However, it adds the remark that the individual ordered to carry out the crime must be found to

---

27 This Russian text can be rendered into English as: "The true criterion in this respect which occurs to some extent in formulations in criminal law of most countries, is not the fact of whether the order existed, but the question of whether a moral choice was practically possible".

have had sufficient freedom to choose between various possible courses of action in order to be convicted. Failing this, his *mens rea* would be lacking, and the accused must be deemed as not guilty. In other words, lack of punishment in these cases would not flow from the order received *per se*, but rather due to the perpetrator's lack of *mens rea* in the specific circumstances of the case, if a separate finding is made that the perpetrator indeed lacked the ability to freely choose to act. The English text, by not explaining what the test is supposed to be applied to, generates some confusion.

The French text (which helpfully uses two complementary expressions ("moral freedom" and "ability to choose") is thus clearer in showing that there are two different topics discussed in these two important passages of the Nuremberg Judgment: mitigation (when the superior order was given), on the one side, and lack of responsibility (where – regardless of any superior order – the *mens rea* of the accused was lacking), on the other.[28] The two passages have no relationship one with the other ("*[l]e vrai critérium de la responsabilité pénale* [...] *n'est nullement en rapport avec l'ordre reçu*"), so that even if there was an order from the top, this would not mean automatic criminal liability for the subordinates – they could still plead that, even if they complied with an order, they lacked the necessary moral freedom and therefore did not have the *mens rea*.[29]

If one were to read the English text on its own, the two areas of the law (mitigation and lack of responsibility) would appear much less distant, so that confusion might be created as to the effect of one plea on the other. In a sense, it is unfortunate that the Judges chose to make such an important remark on the *mens rea* requirement immediately after the discussion on the plea of superior orders, because this has hitherto generated some confusion.

Dinstein, pointing to the French and English discrepancies, developed his theory of *mens rea*, according to which "the fact of obedience to orders constitutes not a defence *per se* but only a factual

---

[28] This passage is indeed often used in French academic writings to discuss the "principle of individual responsibility" at Nuremberg. See, for instance, Jacques Verhaegen, *Le droit international pénal de Nuremberg: acquis et régressions*, Bruylant, Brussels, 2003, pp. 45–46.

[29] Dinstein, 1965, p. 150, see *supra* note 3.

---

element that may be taken into account in conjunction with the other circumstances of the given case within the compass of a defence based on lack of *mens rea*, that is, mistake of law or fact or compulsion".[30]

19.2.2. Suggestions on the Reasons for Discrepancies in the Nuremberg Judgment

Historians seem to agree that the first version of the Judgment was drafted in English by Judge Norman Birkett,[31] while the English-speaking Judges' aides had actually been working on several legal questions even prior to the close of the proceedings.[32] This draft was then translated into French and Russian under tight security measures.[33] A Russian scholar indeed suggests that the Soviet Judge Iona Nikitchenko "approved" the structure and the form of the draft Judgment, which had been worked upon by Birkett.[34]

In any event, if the (English) draft was translated into French and Russian and was used by the interpreters at the various sessions as the basis for Judges' deliberations, it would seem that it was Judge Birkett who had more influence in the drafting of the crimes against humanity sections of the Nuremberg Judgment. Considering the similarity of the English and the Russian texts (read and understood by six out of eight Judges) as opposed to the French one (translated by the language staff, redrafted by one of the two French Judges, or a combination of the two), it would thus appear unlikely that the Judges during deliberations ever discussed the nuances of the French text.

There is therefore some basis to suggest that the French Judges – and Henri Donnedieu de Vabres in particular – tried hard to ensure that

---

[30] *Ibid.*, p. 88.

[31] Bradley F. Smith, *Reaching Judgment at Nuremberg*, Basic Books, New York, 1977, p. 119.

[32] Telford Taylor, *The Anatomy of the Nuremberg Trials: A Personal Memoir*, Knopf, New York, 1993, p. 549, referring to Biddle's notes.

[33] Smith, 1977, p. 144, see *supra* note 31. See also Joseph E. Persico, *Nuremberg: Infamy on Trial*, Penguin, New York, 1994, p. 390: in order to prevent leaks of information, the translators were sequestered in a former military barracks, pages were apparently provided to typists in random order and the defendants' sentences were left blank until the last minute.

[34] Natalia S. Lebedeva, "SSSR i Niurnbergskij prozess", in *Mezhdonarodnaja zhizn*, 1996, vol. 9, p. 110.

the *nullum crimen* principle was consecrated as a fully-fledged rule directly applicable by the IMT vis-à-vis the defendants. Thus, the principle of legality made its way into the French text of the Judgment as a *rule* of international law trumping even the letter of the Nuremberg Charter. This in turn did allow for crimes against humanity convictions alone, but only as long as the facts showed a connection with crimes against peace and war crimes. On the contrary, English-speaking and Soviet Judges instead found themselves agreeing – perhaps somewhat oddly – that the *nullum crimen* (a mere principle, to be balanced out with other principles, such as what we would call today "the fight against impunity") could cede way to higher considerations of justice in the extreme circumstances dictated by the Nuremberg trial.

In relation to superior orders, the language differences are definitively less marked – there is certainly no sentence "forgotten" in the French version as was the case for the discussion on the principle of legality. In this instance, instead, the French text assists in explaining more clearly that the topics discussed in the relevant paragraphs are actually two, rather than one: the Judges started off by considering the plea of superior orders, and categorically stated – as the Charter mandated them to do – that superior orders is not a defence *per se*. Then, however, they moved on to elaborate on the fact that the issue, especially for high-level defendants such as those being tried at Nuremberg by the IMT, is not so much whether superior orders negate individual criminal responsibility, but rather that the necessary *mens rea* must be in any case established in the concrete circumstances of the case. It is conceivable that an individual who has received orders from his superiors finds himself in the circumstances of not being able to exercise his freedom of choice. The origins of this discrepancy are more difficult to ascertain than in the case of the *nullum crimen* passages. It could be surmised that the same conceptual clarity and intellectual preoccupations that had led the French Judges to excise a sentence from the portion related to the rule of strict legality, might have prompted them to add conceptual clarity to the issue of *mens rea*, especially since this passage is also inserted into the section of the Judgment dealing with "The Law of the Charter", i.e. the general part, but more as an "appendix" to the issue of superior orders, where the plea of the accused most closely resembled a defence related to lack of intent.

19.3. The Import of the Nuremberg Language Discrepancies in Subsequent Legal Discourse and Case Law

The first step in analysing the impact (if any) of the language discrepancies identified above is of course that of assessing whether scholars, in their reflections on Nuremberg, and on the evolutions from the IMT judgment, have adverted to such differences and have taken them into account when developing their own attempts at clarifying the import of the Judgment and its significance for future reflections on international criminal justice.

19.3.1. *Nullum Crimen*

19.3.1.1. Academic Writings

Even today, while no doubt is expressed that the principle of legality is a fundamental rule applicable both in domestic criminal prosecutions and in international ones,[35] its applicability *to the IMT proceedings* is still questioned, just like it was in 1946. English-language literature has carefully attempted to find a balance between defending the wording of the Nuremberg Judgment for what it meant at the time and raising doubts as to its continued significance today[36] for, as one author put it, trying "to

---

[35] Theodor Meron, "International Law in the Age of Human Rights: General Course on Public International Law", in *Recueil des cours*, 2003, vol. 301, pp. 121–32; Susan Lamb, "*Nullum Crimen, Nulla Poena Sine Lege* in International Criminal Law", in Antonio Cassese, Paola Gaeta and John R.W.D. Jones (eds.), *The Rome Statute of the International Criminal Court: A Commentary*, Oxford University Press, Oxford, 2002, pp. 735–55. As to how the Nuremberg Judgment has been read in this type of scholarship, see *inter alia*: Stefan Glaser, "Les pouvoirs du juge en droit international pénal", in *Revue pénale Suisse*, 1959, vol. 75, pp. 86–92; Beth Van Schaak, "*Crimen Sine Lege*: Judicial Lawmaking at the Intersection of Law and Morals", in *Georgetown Law Journal*, 2008, vol. 97, p. 140; Leena Grover, "A Call to Arms: Fundamental Dilemmas Confronting the Interpretation of Crimes in the Rome Statute of the International Criminal Court", in *European Journal of International Law*, 2010, vol. 21, p. 551.

[36] Antonio Cassese, "*Nullum Crimen Sine Lege*", in Antonio Cassese (ed.), *The Oxford Companion to International Criminal Justice*, Oxford University Press, Oxford, 2009, pp. 438–41; Gerhard Werle, *Principles of International Criminal Law*, 2nd ed., Asser Press, The Hague, 2009, pp. 36–39; Matthew Lippman, "Crimes against Humanity", in *Boston College Third World Law Journal*, 1996, vol. 17, pp. 190–91 (on *nullum crimen* in general) and p. 194 (on Streicher's conviction); Georg Schwarzenberger, *International Law, vol. 2: The Law of Armed Conflict*, Stevens & Sons, London, 1968, pp. 23–27 (who emphasises that the foundation of the Nuremberg decisions on crimes against humanity was the existing prohibitions in civilised nations). See also Hans Waldock, "General

---

defend the apparent retroactivity of the Nuremberg prosecution of crimes against humanity".[37]

In general, Soviet legal scholarship after the Second World War considered the interaction between "general human morality" and "international law" as the basis for the prohibition of crimes against humanity (amongst other *delicta juris gentium*) at the international level.[38] No issue of *nullum crimen* is usually raised in this respect.[39] Decades later, Soviet scholarship – even if recognising that crimes against humanity and aggression could theoretically pose a *nullum crimen* issue – tenaciously continued challenging allegations of unfairness in this respect regarding the Nuremberg episode.[40] In this sense, from the 1940s onwards the portion of the Nuremberg Judgment relating to the principle of legality had a very clear and transparent reading by Soviet and Russian scholarship, which at most stated that the Nuremberg Charter (and Judgment) played a significant role in the fight against crimes against humanity, by setting out clearly the elements of the crimes involved[41] – but never questioned the appropriateness of convicting certain defendants

---

Course on Public International Law", in *Recueil des cours*, 1962, vol. 106, p. 221 (according to whom the criminality under international law of crimes against humanity was still equivocal at the time). A rare example of official criticism of the Nuremberg Judgment on this basis occurred during the negotiations for the Genocide Convention, when the representative for Peru attacked the trial as an "improvisation" which disregarded the *nullum crimen* "rule". See UN Doc. A/C.6/SR.109, cited in William A. Schabas, *Genocide in International Law*, Cambridge University Press, Cambridge, 2000, p. 79.

[37] William A. Schabas, "Retroactive Application of the Genocide Convention", in *University of St. Thomas Journal of Law and Public Policy*, 2010, vol. 4, no. 2, p. 50; see previously also, James Popple, "The Right to Protection from Retroactive Criminal Law", in *Criminal Law Journal*, 1989, vol. 13, no. 4, pp. 251–62.

[38] Grigory Ivanovic Tunkin, *Law and Force in the International System*, Progress Publishers, Moscow, 1985, pp. 148–49.

[39] Aleksandr Michajlovic Larin, "Nuremberg Trial: the Law against War and Fascism", originally published in Russian in 1995 and reprinted in Guénaël Mettraux (ed.), *Perspectives on the Nuremberg Trial*, Oxford University Press, Oxford, 2008, p. 553. See also M. Gus, "Niurnbergskij prozess", in *Mirovoe chosianstvo i mirovaja politika*, 1946, nos. 10–11, p. 54, making the clear link between aggression and war with Nazi policies.

[40] See, for instance, Natalja S. Lebedeva, *Podgotovka Niurnbergskogo Prozessa*, Nauka, Moscow, 1975, pp. 130–32, 138–40. More recently, N.A. Zelinskaja and I.V. Dremina-Volok, "Prinzipy 'nullum crimen sine lege' i 'ex post facto' v mezhdunarodnom ugolovnom prave", in G.I. Bogush and Elena Nikolaeva Trikoz (eds.), *Mezhdunarodnoe ugolovnoe pravosudie: Sovremennie problemy*, IPPP, Moscow, 2009, pp. 124–26.

[41] Among all, see Aron Naumovic Trainin, *Isbrannyie trudy*, Moscow, especially p. 894.

---

for these charges. [42] At most, very recent scholarship recognises the Nuremberg precedent as an exception to the principle of *nullum crimen* justified by special heightened social danger for all of the international community of the crimes committed. [43]

It is mainly the French Judge Donnedieu de Vabres and scholars evidently relying on the French version of the Nuremberg Judgment who point out that Streicher's conviction could only be entered because his acts *also* amounted to war crimes, in line with the Judge's understanding of the Charter's provisions [44] and, maybe more importantly, of fundamental human rights. [45] According to Donnedieu de Vabres himself, the approach taken in the Nuremberg Judgment allowed the judges to remain in keeping with the spirit and the letter of the principle of *nullum crimen, nulla poena sine lege*.

> In accordance with Article 6 of the Statute, the tribunal did not exclude the notion of "crimes against humanity"; but it is instructive to explain the effort it made to minimize its consequences [...] As for the wartime period, the Tribunal gathered "war crimes" and "crimes against humanity" under the same heading for most of the accused, thus side-stepping a problematic distinction and, practically merging, the crimes against humanity into the "war crimes" category. [46]

---

[42] See recently Aleksandra Jurevna Skuratova, *Mezhdunarodnije prestuplenija: sovremennije problemi kvalifikazii*, Moscow, 2012, pp. 87–91.

[43] N. N. Kadirova, "Problema opredelenija prinzipov mezhdunarodnogo ugolovnogo prava", in *Vestnik Cheliabinskogo gosudarstvennogo universiteta*, 2012, no. 27, p. 70

[44] Henri Donnedieu de Vabres, "Le procès de Nuremberg devant les principes modernes du droit pénal international", in *Recueil des cours*, 1947, vol. 70, p. 520 and 526, fn. 1; see also P. de Lapradelle, "Le procès des grands criminels de guerre et le développement du droit international", in *Nouvelle Revue de droit international privé*, 1947, cited by Donnedieu de Vabres in various passages of his course before the Hague Academy.

[45] The French Declaration of the Rights of Men and of the Citizens of 1789 provides that: "A person shall only be punished by virtue of a law established and promulgated before the offence". The Declaration of the Rights of Men and of the Citizens of 1793 later elaborated that: "No one ought to be tried and punished except after having been heard or legally summoned, and except in virtue of a law promulgated prior to the offence. The law which would punish offences committed before it existed would be a tyranny: the retroactive effect given to the law would be a crime".

[46] Henri Donnedieu de Vabres, "The Nuremberg Trial and the Modern Principles of International Criminal Law", in Guénaël Mettraux (ed.), *Perspectives on the Nuremberg Trial*, Oxford University Press, Oxford, 2008, p. 241.

Some scholars working in French did indeed accept the conclusion that crimes against humanity did not pose problems of *nullum crimen* at Nuremberg because such crimes were effectively already criminalised in domestic jurisdictions[47] or constituted war crimes.[48] Others have been more guarded in their conclusions, denying any issue with the principle of legality at Nuremberg and simply noting the connection between crimes against humanity and crimes against peace, rather than war crimes, as a way to establish the IMT's jurisdiction.[49] One of the most coherent and careful proponents of the strict principle of legality in contemporary criminal law, Stefan Glaser, specifically considered the *nullum crimen* rule, and its corollary of the prohibition of retroactive punishment, applicable to international criminal law as a fundamental concept to prevent injustice; he, however, did not proceed to analyse with any attention the text of the Nuremberg Judgment relating to crimes against humanity and thus did not notice any conceptual inconsistency in the conviction for crimes against humanity by the IMT.[50] Even authors writing *in English* on Nuremberg and its impact on French jurisprudence related to crimes against humanity and genocide do not specifically note the language discrepancies potentially leading to (or stemming from) different understandings of the principle of legality.[51]

One interesting exception in this respect is that of Jacqueline Rochette writing in 1956, who (though not quoting the Nuremberg Judgment on this issue) stated that the *nullum crimen* clause simply "formulates a generally followed rule and is not applicable to the facts

---

[47]   Jacques Bernard Herzog, "Les principes juridiques de la répression des crimes de guerre", in *Revue pénale Suisse*, 1946, p. 277 ff.

[48]   François Bedarida (ed.), *Touvier, Vichy et le crime contre l'humanité – Le dossier de l'accusation*, Seuil, Paris, 1997, p. 28; see also historian Annette Wieviorka, *1961: Le process Eichmann*, Editions Complexe, Brussels, 1989, p. 139, when referring to the Nuremberg precedent.

[49]   Jacques Descheemaeker, *Le Tribunal Militaire International des grands criminels de guerre*, Pedone, Paris, 1947, pp. 20–27, 35, 79–80 ; see also Jean Graven, "Les crimes contre l'humanité", in *Recueil des cours*, 1950, vol. 76, pp. 466–67, who regrets that the IMT was not more courageous in establishing crimes against humanity as crimes *per se* rather than in connection with war crimes and crimes against peace.

[50]   Glaser, 1959, p. 86 ff,. see *supra* note 35.

[51]   Caroline Fournet, *Genocide and Crimes against Humanity: Misconceptions and Confusion in French Law and Practice*, Hart Publishing, Oxford, 2013.

---

contested" against the defendants at Nuremberg.[52] In this case, a French author appears to have relied not on the French text – which, as discussed, does not contain the sentence according to which the principle of legality is inapplicable to the present case – but rather on the English one. The alternative explanation is that she construed (rightly, as evidenced by the English and Russian versions of the Judgment) the French text as implicitly discarding the *nullum crimen* "rule" because it was inapplicable in the context of the IMT. In any event, the author then proceeds to link the criminalisation of crimes against humanity to the war of aggression, undoubtedly (in her view) criminalised by 1939, following the wording of the Nuremberg Charter.

In any event, the assumption that war crimes and crimes against humanity form one whole in the Nuremberg Judgment due to a perceived lack of "independence" of the latter category is still at the heart of most discussions on the topic in French legal literature.[53] Unsurprisingly, French legal scholarship on international crimes continued to hold the same view after the Nuremberg Judgment.[54]

19.3.1.2. Case Law

The Nuremberg Judgment's pronouncements on the issue of retroactive application of the law of crimes against humanity have at times been quoted in international and domestic case law, but their significance has generally been limited. It is interesting to note that the International Criminal Tribunal for the former Yugoslavia ('ICTY') Appeals Chamber

---

[52] Jacqueline Rochette, *L'individu devant le droit international*, Éditions Montchrestien, Paris, 1956, pp. 135 and 139.

[53] See, for instance, E. Zoller, "La définition des crimes contre l'humanité", in *Journal de droit international*, 1993, vol. 120, pp. 554–55 (citing only the French version of Streicher's conviction passage and referring to Donnedieu de Vabres's misgivings); Hisakazu Fujita, "Le crime contre l'humanité dans les procès de Nuremberg et de Tokyo", in *Kobe University Law Review*, 2000, vol. 34, pp. 5–8 (citing Donnedieu de Vabres's position on the matter that *"crimes contre l'humanité sont confondus avec les crimes de guerre"*); Sévane Garibian, "Souveraineté et légalité en droit pénal international: le concept de crime contre l'humanité dans le discours des juges à Nuremberg", in Marc Henzelin and Robert Roth (eds.), *Le droit pénal à l'épreuve de l'internationalisation*, Georg, Geneva, 2001, pp. 29 ff., especially pp. 44–45 (discussing various cultural influences, but only referring to the French version of the Judgment); J.-M. Varaut, *Le procès de Nuremberg: Le glaive dans la balance*, Perrin, Paris, 1992, pp. 376–79.

[54] See, for instance, Stefan Glaser, *Infraction international, ses éléments constitutifs et ses aspects juridiques*, Librairie générale de droit et de jurisprudence, Paris, 1957, pp. 50–51.

in *Milutinović et al.* quoted the IMT when the latter declared *nullum crimen* simply as a "principle of justice", and proceeded to interpret that expression as follows:

> [A] criminal conviction can only be based on a norm which existed at the time of the acts or omission with which the accused is charged were committed. The tribunal must further be satisfied that the criminal liability in question as sufficiently foreseeable and that the law providing for such liability must be sufficiently accessible at the relevant time for it to warrant a criminal conviction [...][55]

Thus, it could be said that – despite criticisms as to its application in concrete cases (such as joint criminal enterprise ['JCE'] or inhumane acts) – the ICTY has actually stated that the "principle" of legality, as it was in Nuremberg a hard and fast "rule", should be followed under all circumstances. Nonetheless, for the purpose of the present analysis, it must be recognised that the ICTY and the other contemporary international criminal courts and tribunals have never relied on the wording of the Nuremberg Judgment to deny an accused's defence that a crime (or a mode of liability) was being applied retroactively. Thus, the language discrepancies in the Nuremberg Judgment have not played any role in international criminal jurisprudence and, in general, in domestic ones.[56]

A few domestic cases dealing with crimes against humanity however appear to quote the relevant portions of the Nuremberg Judgment, and deserve at least a cursory analysis. In *Attorney General of the Government of Israel v. Eichmann*, the issue of *nullum crimen* was raised by the defendant. The situation had clearly changed from Nuremberg: the Israeli Judges were applying domestic – and not international – law; moreover, the advances of human rights law during the 1940s and 1950s could be said to have created a customary rule of international law (rather than a mere principle) against retroactive

---

[55] ICTY Appeals Chamber, *Prosecutor v. Milutinović et al.*, Case No. IT-99-37-AR72, Decision on Dragoljub Ojdanić's Motion Challenging Jurisdiction – Joint Criminal Enterprise, 21 May 2003, para. 37.

[56] See, for instance, French Cour de Cassation, *France v. Paul Touvier*, Case No. 92-82409, Judgment, 27 November 1992, where the Nuremberg Charter is often cited for the definition of crimes against humanity, but not the Nuremberg Judgment. A cultural bias against citing precedents, even when they may clarify the letter of a general international instrument criminalising certain conduct, may explain this.

punishment. Nonetheless, the two courts deciding on the case dismissed any plea related to *nullum crimen*, simply referring to the maxim as being "in general a principle of justice"[57] and even stating that *nullum crimen* had yet to become a rule of customary international law.[58] Clearly, the quoted passages from Nuremberg are from the English version, and therefore they fully rely on the common understanding of what the law was in 1945 (but possibly not in 1962!).

In *R. v. Finta*,[59] the Supreme Court of Canada quoted, without acknowledging it, the Nuremberg precedent to accept retroactive application of criminal law, by defining *nullum crimen* a mere "principle of justice". When discussing the principle of legality, the judgment explicitly says:

> The impugned sections do not violate ss. 7 and 11(g) of the [Canadian Charter of Rights and Freedoms] because of any allegedly retrospective character. The rules created by the Charter of the International Military Tribunal and applied by the Nuremberg Trial represented "a new law". The rule against retroactive legislation is a principle of justice. A retroactive law providing individual punishment for acts which were illegal though not criminal at the time they were committed, however, is an exception to the rule against ex post facto laws. Individual criminal responsibility represents certainly a higher degree of justice than collective responsibility. Since the internationally illegal acts for which individual criminal responsibility has been established were also morally the most objectionable and the persons who committed them were certainly aware of their immoral character, the retroactivity of the law applied to them cannot

---

[57] District Court of Jerusalem, *Attorney General of the Government of Israel v. Eichmann*, Judgment, 11 December 1961, para. 27.

[58] Israeli Supreme Court, *Attorney General of the Government of Israel v. Eichmann*, Judgment, 29 May 1962, para. 8. See also the passage stating that "[...] one may indeed agree that the sense of justice generally recoils from punishing a person for an act committed by him for which at the date of its commission he could not have known – since it had not been yet prohibited by law – that he would become criminally liable. But this value judgment cannot be extended to the odious crimes attributed to the appellant, all the more so when dealing with the range and magnitude of their commission as described in the judgment. In such a case the above-mentioned maxim [not *rule*] loses its moral value and is deprived of its ethical foundation".

[59] *R. v. Finta*, see *supra* note 10.

be considered as incompatible with justice. Justice required the punishment of those committing such acts in spite of the fact that under positive law they were not punishable at the time they were performed. It follows that it was appropriate that the acts were made punishable with retroactive force.[60]

Similar references to Nuremberg abound in the Judgment. Even in this case, however, where English-speaking Judges sat side by side with French-speaking Judges, there is no mention of the language discrepancies in Nuremberg.

19.3.2. Superior Orders

In relation to the issue of superior orders, the language differences proved particularly interesting and important for Dinstein (who however did not appear to look at the Russian version). The comparison between the English and the French texts indeed allowed Dinstein to clarify the optimal meaning of the clause, reconciling the hard rule enshrined in Article 8 of the Nuremberg Charter with the remark on the *mens rea*. The Russian text also clearly supports his *mens rea* theory: actually, in light of Dinstein's own findings as to the Soviet insistence on the hard rule on strict liability regardless of superior orders (the fact that the Russian text tallies with the French one and actually clarifies that the findings of fact in the concrete circumstances of the case) could exonerate accused persons from responsibility, and make the significance of his interpretation of this passage of the Nuremberg Judgment all the more interesting.[61] At times, it was suggested – as hinted above – that Nuremberg did not modify the customary standard, but simply applied it to extreme circumstances, i.e. to cases where – due to the high-level positions of the defendants at Nuremberg – superior orders would never negate the knowledge that the conduct in question was unlawful – but it was just that, an *a priori* application of the general principle to high-level defendants.[62]

---

[60]   *Ibid.* (per Gonthier, Cory and Major JJ.).

[61]   See also Robert Cryer, *Prosecuting International Crimes*, Cambridge University Press, Cambridge, 2005, pp. 294–95, who supports Dinstein's interpretation of the superior order passage in the Nuremberg Judgment (though only referring to the English version).

[62]   See, for example, Hilaire McCoubrey, "From Nuremberg to Rome: Restoring the Defence of Superior Orders", in *International and Comparative Law Quarterly*, 2001, vol. 50, p. 390.

Some scholars show the understanding that superior orders – even if it should not be considered a defence in and of itself – can work as evidence of an overall lack of choice, and therefore *mens rea*, by the subordinate.[63] It is noteworthy in this respect that the Charter of the International Military Tribunal for the Far East ('Tokyo Charter') added an oft-forgotten clause, according to which "the fact that an accused acted pursuant to order [...] shall, *of itself*, be sufficient to free such person from responsibility" (emphasis added). This clarification points to the fact that superior order would not function as a defence *per se*, but could contribute to a defence of duress or other element negating the *mens rea*.

Legal scholars working in French make the distinction on the basis of the (French version of the) text of the Nuremberg Judgment – thus clearly drawing a conceptual difference between the mitigating circumstances and even acquittals based on the lack of subjective element (intent, *mens rea*) from the concept of superior orders as a possible full defence.[64] In France, in relation to the plea of superior orders, even much later than the Nuremberg Trial, there was a candid recognition that "[t]he line between constraint [duress] and *libre arbitre* was also a tenuous one".[65]

Russian scholars who devoted some attention to the issue of *nullum crimen* do not as a whole discuss the Nuremberg Tribunal's findings on superior orders, and it is therefore hard to establish whether legal discourse – and case law – in Russian has been shaped by the language used by the IMT. But there is nothing that suggests that scholars and commentators other than Dinstein actually relied on the different language versions to reach their results or plead for a specific interpretation.[66]

---

[63] See, for example, Gaeta, 1999, for instance at p. 178 ("[i]f he *elects* to obey, he takes the risk of being punished, along with his superior, for committing a criminal act", emphasis added), *supra* note 20; but also Alexander Sack, "War Criminals and the Defence of Superior Order in International Law", in *Lawyers Guild Review*, 1945, vol. 5, p. 15 (even before the Nuremberg Judgment).

[64] Rochette, 1956, p. 135, see *supra* note 52.

[65] Frédéric Mégret, "The Bordeaux Trial, Prosecuting the Oradour-sur-Glane Massacre", in Kevin Heller and Gerry Simpson (eds.), *The Hidden Histories of War Crimes Trials*, Oxford University Press, Oxford, 2013, pp. 153–54.

[66] This is true even for those who just analyse the Nuremberg precedents in order to interpret domestic criminal law provisions; see, for instance, Eric David, "L'excuse de l'ordre superieur et l'état de necessité", in *Revue Belge de droit international*, 1978–1979, vol. 14, pp. 65 ff.

Similarly, no judgment by international or domestic criminal tribunals adverts to the language discrepancy in this case. It is maybe interesting to note that the *Kaing Guek Eav (Duch)* Appeal Judgment of the Extraordinary Chambers in the Courts of Cambodia ('ECCC') – possibly the most culturally 'French' of the international and internationalised jurisdictions – distinguishes superior orders from duress and lack of intent,[67] but again without referring to the language of Nuremberg.

Once again, the *Finta* case in Canada could have provided some hints to the different language versions, due to the presence on the bench of French-speaking as well as of English-speaking judges. At page 835, the Judgment does cite the French version of the Nuremberg Judgment relating to superior orders, including the portion which states that the true criterion for individual criminal responsibility resides in *"la liberté morale, dans la faculté de choisir, chez l'auteur de l'acte reproché"*.[68] However, the discussion in *Finta* does not substantially benefit from this quote, since the language differences are not even used to explicitly support Dinstein's interpretation of the rule in question.

19.4. Conclusions: The Consequences of Language Discrepancies in Subsequent Legal Discourse and Case Law

Having briefly discussed the reactions of scholars and courts of law to the two sets of language discrepancies identified in the Nuremberg Judgment, discrepancies that have been often ignored and have therefore clearly had a minimal impact, it is now apposite to draw some preliminary conclusions.

From the above analysis – which of course has not parsed all domestic cases dealing with crimes against humanity or superior orders – it would seem that courts and academics appear overall unaware of the fact that the Nuremberg Judgment was written in three equally authoritative texts. Therefore, it is extremely rare to come across discussions relying on the inevitable discrepancies that tend to appear – for the reasons discussed above – when a complex legal document such as the one under consideration here is authoritative in different versions.

---

[67] ECCC Supreme Court, Case File/Dossier No. 001/18-07-2007-ECCC/SC, Judgment, 3 February 2012, for instance at paras. 62 and 364–365.

[68] *R. v. Finta*, see *supra* note 10.

As *Eichmann* and *Finta* show, the discrepancies in relation to the *nullum crimen* issue – though noted by scholars like Cassese – have been generally overlooked by the case law and had no discernible impact on the reasoning or on the result of those decisions. For Israel, reliance on the English text in *Eichmann* supported better, than the French text, the prosecution's attempts at convicting the accused not just for war crimes, but for genocide as well.

In relation to superior orders, Dinstein's work in the 1960s showed that working on language discrepancies could actually assist in coming to terms with an obscure passage of the Nuremberg Judgment. However, there is no evidence that this exercise was used to support later findings of responsibility by courts, except maybe implicitly when citing Dinstein's own work (and without acknowledging the different languages' significance to his theory).[69]

A final remark remains to be made. While the language discrepancies in relation to superior orders – minor as they were – are not explicitly referred to in legal papers and case law, it might still be that their significance and deeper meaning have had an effect on the international arena. What could be surmised from the situation is the following. The issue of superior orders was added as a topic to be included in the future Statute of the ICC from the very early stages.[70] There is certainly no proof that, when discussing the draft Statute of the ICC, the delegates were aware of the different language versions at Nuremberg. What remains likely is, on the contrary, that each delegate had prepared the discussions on superior orders on the basis of briefings in his own language, which might have included the relevant portions of the Nuremberg Judgment, in English, in French or in Russian (or in other translations based on one of these languages).

As is well-known, the various drafts evolved from provisions such as "A person who commits a crime pursuant to an order of a government official or a superior is individually responsible; however, it is a defense that the accused was acting pursuant to orders which he or she did not know, and a person of ordinary sense and understanding would not have

---

[69] See, in particular, ICTY Appeals Chamber, *Prosecutor v. Dražen Erdemović*, Case No. IT-96-22, Separate and Dissenting Opinion of Judge Stephen, 7 October 1997, paras. 59–60.

[70] See, for instance, "Preparatory Committee on International Criminal Court Concludes First Session", 13 April 1996, (http://www.legal-tools.org/doc/f861fe/).

known, were unlawful".[71] It is possible that during these negotiations, the French-speaking delegates, or at least those who had an education in the sources of international criminal law, focused on their own cultural and legal background, in turn shaped by the language in which they might have read Nuremberg. This would have assisted the French-speaking delegates in clarifying the distinction between rejecting superior order as a defence and, on the other hand, recognising the centrality of the *mens rea* in assigning guilt, and therefore criminal responsibility.

What I am suggesting here – without any strong empirical evidence, however – is that the variety of language and legal cultures express a richness, something that the international criminal legal system can benefit from, for instance because it allows a better understanding. The issue of superior orders, and the careful analysis carried out by Dinstein on that issue, for instance, show that reading together the English, French and Russian versions (all authoritative!) of the Nuremberg Judgment could actually facilitate a better understanding of what probably was in the minds of the Judges, thus providing a better interpretative tool for today's application (or non-application) of those principles. While contemporary international criminal judgments are published in only one authoritative language, the cultural and legal influences underpinning the words and expressions chosen by the Judges likely require a deeper understanding of their origin and application in each specific circumstance.

---

[71] United States Delegation, "Redraft of ILC Article 20 on ICC Jurisdiction with Proposed Elements", 23 March 1996, (http://www.legal-tools.org/doc/efc778/); but see also the rolling text circulated in Rome on 16 June 1998 (http://www.legal-tools.org/doc/ca7cae/).

20

Promoting International Criminal Law:
The Nuremberg Trial Film Project and US
Information Policy after the Second World War

Axel Fischer[*]

20.1. Introduction

From 1943 onwards – by implementing the United Nations War Crimes
Commission ('UNWCC') and issuing the Declaration of the Four Nations
on General Security ('Moscow Declaration') – the will to deal juridically
with the Nazi crimes was put into action by the Allies of the Second
World War. The prospect of the punishment of the major European Axis
war criminals by an International Military Tribunal ('IMT')[1] confronted
the United States ('US') not only with the consolidation of legal and
diplomatic questions but also a realisation of the need for an *acceptance*
of such dealings with mass crimes. US officials recognised more far-
reaching perspectives in the internationally co-ordinated prosecution and
punishment of war crimes as part of a new post-war world than the
immediate punishment of some 20 accused persons. They saw the
possibility of creating a system of stability and peace by banning
aggressive warfare and by establishing a lawful and constitutional method
of dealing with state, mass and war crimes. The US authorities therefore
decided to disseminate the forward-looking idea of international criminal
law that was to be implemented by the IMT. Gordon Dean, the public
relations officer of the Office of the US Chief of Counsel for the
Prosecution of Axis Criminality ('OCCPAC'), put it this way: "to tell the

---

[*] **Axel Fischer** specialises in media and literary studies, after being employed in the fields
of marketing, public relations and culture management. He became a Research Fellow at
the universities of Wuppertal und Marburg, Germany. As a member of the International
Research and Documentation Centre for War Crimes Trials ('ICWC') at the University of
Marburg he has been engaged for the last four years with the film footage produced on the
occasion of the International Military Tribunal ('IMT') in Nuremberg. Since February
2012 he has been responsible for the research project "The US American Film Project on
the Nuremberg Trials: A Contribution to the Political Culture of Post-War Germany".

[1] The IMT, actually situated in Berlin, was in session in the Palace of Justice in Nuremberg
from 14 November 1945 to 1 October 1946.

---

story of why we are trying the major war criminals rather than shooting them without trial".[2]

For that purpose, an information campaign was launched, using all available mass media and addressing different target groups. The campaign paid special attention to the German public, which was – given the framework of the occupation – an audience that could be reached via an information policy of maximum control. In addition, both American and international audiences were considered important and, with regards to these target groups, US officials wanted to gain as much control as possible. Various US military agencies therefore were involved in film-making for the IMT, leading to the production and distribution of a total of four films and more than 20 issues of a newsreel covering the trial. This chapter focuses on this use of film for the dissemination and visual design of the IMT. It highlights the specific approach of the US as a key actor at Nuremberg in relation to the film campaign and draws out some conclusions on long-term effects of the films within debates on legal politics in Germany after 1990, when international criminal law underwent a revival.

20.2. The Output of the US Film Project for the IMT

There were two main purposes for the production of films: convincing the IMT and convincing the public. For the first purpose two films – *Nazi Concentration and Prison Camps*, 60 minutes, 29 November 1945 and *The Nazi Plan*, 195 minutes, 11 December 1945[3] – were produced, later put forward in evidence (and screened in the courtroom) by the US prosecution team. For the second purpose two further films, one short – *That Justice Be Done*, 11 minutes, 18 October 1945 – and another long documentary film – *Nürnberg und seine Lehre* (*Nuremberg: Its Lessons for Today*) 75 minutes, November 1948[4] – and 24 newsreel issues – *Welt*

---

2   Memorandum, 30 July 1945, RG238, entry PI-21 51/26, folder Motion Picture, National Archives and Records Administration, Maryland ('NARA').

3   The dates are the day of the first release.

4   *Nuremberg: Its Lesson for Today* is the title that was first used for an English version of the film that was never released for a US audience at the time. The film was only screened for the Army television in the 1950s. The title also served as the label during the work on the film. The title was later used for a restored version of the film in 2009.

im Film [*World in Film*], 7 September 1945–22 December 1946[5] – were produced, as well as a total of about 32 hours of footage of the proceedings in Courtroom 600 in the Palace of Justice in Nuremberg.[6]

During the IMT, film and photographic evidence was presented. This was conceived not only to convince the IMT but also to have a mass impact on a worldwide audience. The impressions from the films would be carried into the world through the public and especially via the representatives of the world's press present in the courtroom. This can be concluded from the fact that the Office of Strategic Services ('OSS') clearly paid special attention to the ability of the courtroom design to create an impressive presentation of the evidence when planning its rebuilding.[7] These photographic and film exhibits have become icons of Nazi crimes and National Socialist German society. The OSS was charged with the task of providing photographic evidence – both stills and films – for the IMT. The OSS did so, among other ways, by producing two films. The films represent an innovative approach to the medium and the evidence gathered of Nazi war crimes, either by compiling meaningful extracts of Nazi newsreels, as in *The Nazi Plan*, or of atrocity material shot on the occasion of the liberation of concentration camps and other crime scenes, as in *Nazi Concentration and Prison Camps*. The latter film was screened at the IMT on 29 November 1945 as Exhibit 2430-PS[8] and the former on 11 December 1945 as Exhibit 3054-PS[9].

---

[5]   *Welt im Film*, nos. 17, 24, 26, 27, 29, 30, 31, 36, 38, 40, 41, 43, 44, 45, 46, 49, 50, 51, 58, 60, 63, 67, 71 and 82.

[6]   This footage also served the newsreel reporting of American and international newsreel companies, both governmental and commercial. It was passed on to them, on demand. As this coverage was not produced by official US agencies it is not focused on in the discussion here.

[7]   See RG226, entry NM54-85, boxes 39 and 42, especially Schwurgerichtssaal–Erweiterung, 16 August 1945; RG226, entry NM54-85/39, folder 648, letter, 12 June 1945; RG226, entry NM54-85 /42, folder "Plan of Court Room" (NARA).

[8]   International Military Tribunal, *Trial of the Major War Criminals before the International Military Tribunal*, IMT, Nuremberg, 1947 (*"Trial of Major War Criminals"*), pp. 431–434. See also Nuremberg Military Tribunal, *The International Military Tribunal in Session at Nuremberg, Germany*, Judgment, 1 October 1946 ("Judgment") (http://www.legal-tools.org/en/go-to-database/record/45f18e/).

[9]   *Trial of the Major War Criminals* pp. 400–1, see *supra* note 8. For the scripts of both films see RG238, entry PI-21 51/26, folder Photographic Evidence, Document No. 3054-PS and Document No. 2430-PS (NARA).

The other group of films, produced mainly for publicity purposes, addressed the world, US and German audiences. The specific interest in targeting these groups, and the diverse nature of the films, was based on the US foreign and occupation policy. The first film to promote the IMT was *That Justice Be Done*. This film basically idealises American self-understanding and establishes a connection between the IMT and American founding myths. A key argument promotes the notion that fair trials corresponded with the ideas of the Founding Fathers and the US Constitution. The IMT was presented as a manifestation of the spirit of the US and its higher morality. The film is – especially in the early part – based on a montage that establishes very quickly a meaningful contrast between Nazism and America's founding myths, on the one hand, and a connection between US history and the need for fair trials, on the other. Due to army red tape the film was only finished two months later than planned. From a contemporary perspective, this little film offers a very valuable insight into how the US authorities wanted their actions, with respect to the punishment of war crimes after the Second World War, to be understood.

A total of about 39 hours of film produced in connection with the trial survives today. This includes about 32 hours of uncut footage shot in the Palace of Justice in Nuremberg that amounts to the biggest single collection of audio-visual material from the IMT. Shot by US Army camera teams, the footage was provided for government and commercial newsreel companies worldwide as well as the production of *Nürnberg und seine Lehre*. (Some of the material was also passed to the Soviets and used in the production of *Sud Narodov* [*The Tribunal of the Peoples*, screened as *The Judgment of the People* in the US], a film that was released in 1946 and summed up the trial from the Soviet perspective.)

The film campaign addressed the German public in particular. Thus, the American–British occupation newsreel *World in Film* comprises 24 reports covering the trial from the Fall of Berlin in 1945 onwards. The newsreel was screened in the American and British zones of occupation, areas covered by the current *Länder* of Schleswig-Holstein, Niedersachsen, Hessen, Bayern, a part of Baden-Württemberg, Hamburg, Bremen and a part of Berlin. Twenty-two of the reports were produced out of the footage shot in Nuremberg, while two were from preliminary events. From the footage of the courtroom and from that collected for the evidence films, a new film was produced and released only in November

1948, *Nürnberg und seine Lehre*, a 75-minute documentary that summarises the whole trial by keeping as close as possible to its actual chronology. Both the newsreel reports and the documentary were, above all, the responsibility of the Office of Military Government, United States ('OMGUS') and the War Department. In 2009 Sandra Schulberg, the daughter of Stuart Schulberg, who directed *Nürnberg und seine Lehre*, released a restored English version of the film, *Nuremberg: Its Lesson for Today*, also known as The Schulberg/Waletzky Restoration.[10]

20.3. Background of the Film Campaign

The IMT film project must be understood as part of larger developments under President Franklin D. Roosevelt's administration. This was the strikingly professional and intensive use of the mass media. In this way, the administration succeeded in attracting young film-makers who willingly contributed to Roosevelt's policy. One institution that arose from this commitment was the US Film Service, which was tasked to propagate measures taken by the government to the general population – especially measures that were taken in connection with the New Deal reform policy in the 1930s. The service was run by documentary film-maker Pare Lorentz, later often called "FDR's film-maker".[11] Established by Roosevelt himself in 1938 within the framework of the National Emergency Council, the organisation was to be closed in 1940 when US Congress cancelled its budget as the Republicans feared that the governing Democrats could abuse it for party politics. Despite its brief existence, the US Film Service was nevertheless the blueprint for the authorities that were later responsible for the production of film propaganda during the war, above all the Office of War Information (formerly the Office of Facts and Figures) and the Field Photographic Branch of the OSS. With the establishment of these organisations, any common criticism was overcome and the US emerged as a major actor

---

[10] For further details see http://www.nurembergfilm.org/.

[11] Lorentz must be considered one of the most influential film-makers in US film history. See William Alexander, *Film on the Left: American Documentary Film from 1931 to 1942*, Princeton University Press, Princeton, NJ, 1981; Robert L. Snyder, *Pare Lorentz and the Documentary Film*, University of Nevada Press, Reno, 1994.

within the media sector.[12] These experiences significantly influenced official US post-war information and occupation policy.

The whole IMT film campaign, however, was not the idea of propaganda specialists. It was a major concern of US Chief Prosecutor, Robert H. Jackson, who arranged the whole campaign on 8 June 1945 and determined its parameters:[13]

    a)   To collect, evaluate, integrate and present all photographic evidence of war crimes, with such assistance from other Departments and agencies of the Government as may be required;

    b)   To make a one-reel short within the next 45 days, according to the plan approved by Justice Jackson;

    c)   To prepare for the filming of the international trial;

    d)   To prepare a documentary film, following the trial, concerning the entire prosecution;

    e)   To film the interrogation of certain prominent Nazis, per the Justice's directions; and

    f)   Such other photographic projects as the Justice may approve.[14]

While being integrated into the American war crimes programme in December 1944, the OSS launched the so-called war crimes project which also contributed to the IMT.[15] Its influence was not limited to the

---

[12]   For concerns in connection with the US state as a media actor, see Henry P. Pilgert, *Press, Radio and Film in West Germany, 1945–1953,* Historical Division, Office of the Executive Secretary, Office of the US High Commissioner for Germany, 1953, p. 2.

[13]   Another example of the extent to which lawyers involved in the punishment of war criminals were open to "progressive" public relations ideas in connection with their duties see the correspondence between Michael Musmanno, presiding judge in the Einsatzgruppen case and OMGUS officials. Musmanno articulates his intention to make a film in which he wanted to prove that Hitler was killed in the last days of the war. His film would prevent the forming of a legend. The idea was rejected for formal reasons. See RG260/AG48/35/5, Bundesarchiv Koblenz ("BAK"). Musmanno later published the story in a book: Michael Angelo Musmanno, *Ten Days to Die*, Doubleday, Garden City, NY, 1950, translated as *In 10 Tagen kommt der Tod,* Droemersche Verlagsanstalt, 1950. Only five years later *Ten Days to Die* was filmed by Georg Wilhelm Pabst as *Der letzte Akt* after Erich Maria Remarque had adapted the novel for the screen.

[14]   Memorandum, 12 June 1945, RG226, entry UD 90/12, folder "126" (NARA).

[15]   Memorandum, 12 April 1945, RG238 PI-21 51/26, folder Memoranda (NARA).

allocation of administrative and legal personnel,[16] the investigation of facts or the criminal history of Nazi Germany, as it also extended to the public relations policy and the preparation of the visual presentation of evidence. The OSS operated a Field Photographic Branch, run by the Hollywood director John Ford, and a Representation Branch, headed by the architect Daniel Kiley, who would later become responsible for the rebuilding of the courtroom in Nuremberg. Both branches had gained experience in visual design, film-making and political communication. The OSS's intensive support in the preparation phase of the trial was surely an important factor in enhancing the filming of the IMT.

Faced with a new foreign policy, the task of occupying Germany, and the need not only to bring the war to an end militarily but also to be seen to act with justice, the US authorities developed a multiple strategy that had an impact on film production in connection both with war crimes and the war crimes trials. All these films were differing expressions of a radically innovative way to use the film medium as an integral component in prosecuting and punishing war crimes as well as – if possible – preventing similar crimes in the future. In particular, they attempted to integrate the audio-visual representation of war crimes and war crimes trials in an educational programme. The judicial coming-to-terms with the war crimes committed was integrated into a broader, holistic programme to change and reorganise the political, economic and social life of post-war Germany. The public opinion surveys and a number of reports compiled by the Intelligence Branch of the OMGUS from demographic research conducted in the American zone offer insights into the methods of integrating the war crimes trials into the re-education of Germans.[17] These reflected the educational potential attached to the IMT, understood as a vehicle to teach the truth about the overthrown regime and therefore

---

[16] For a list of personnel allocated to the IMT staff and its recruitment inside the OSS see RG226, entry 146A/9, folder War Crimes Personnel; RG226, entry NM54-1/13, folder War Crimes Personnel; RG226, entry UD 90/15, folder 196A and 202 (NARA).

[17] For contemporary literature on re-education see US Department of State, Division of Research for Europe, *The Progress of Reeducation in Germany*, Department of State, Division of Research for Europe, Office of Intelligence Research, 1947. For the latest research see Katharina Gerund and Heike Paul (eds.), *Die amerikanische Reeducation-Politik nach 1945: Interdisziplinäre Perspektiven auf America's Germany*, Transcript-Verlag, 2014. On US film propaganda in Germany see Cora Sol Goldstein, *Capturing the German Eye: American Visual Propaganda in Occupied Germany*, University of Chicago Press, Chicago, 2009.

chosen to support the democratic process.[18] Fair and constitutional trials as an instrument to avenge crimes that cost the lives of millions must have been considered unprecedented as well as progressive at that time. This dealing with mass crimes should be explained to the public in occupied Germany, the world and at home in the US. For the German viewers, the trial would point out the personal guilt of the accused, the criminal character of National Socialism, and portray its crimes as well as demonstrate the superiority of Western democracy. By teaching the idea of constitutional rights, the IMT would thus serve as a lesson in democracy.

20.4. US Film Policy for the IMT

20.4.1. General Considerations

From an early draft paper – issued by the US prosecution authority and prepared by the press relations officer of OCCPAC and former press spokesman of the Attorney General, Gordon Dean – we learn about the scope and the aims of a desirable information policy in connection with the IMT:

> The good to come from the trial of the major European Axis war criminals by the IMT will depend almost entirely on the character of the educational campaign which is conducted before, during and after the trials. In fact, if such a campaign fails it would be better that there be no trials.[19]

In the 15 pages that followed, Dean developed requirements for an educational campaign that focused the understanding of the world on what will be done, why it will be done and that what will be done will be right. The paper can be understood as a statement of principles for a future information strategy for the IMT, especially the specific position of the US within the international system, as it was a major topic and should

---

[18] Anna J. Merritt and Richard L. Merritt (eds.), *Public Opinion in Occupied Germany: The OMGUS Surveys, 1945–1949*, University of Illinois Press, Urbana, 1970; Richard L. Merritt, *Democracy Imposed: U.S. Occupation Policy and the German Public, 1945–1949*, Yale University Press, New Haven, 1995, pp. 70–83. For the surveys see *Merritt Collection on Public Opinion in Germany,* Photographic Services, University of Illinois Library, 1980, microfilm, Reel 1–9.

[19] Memorandum by Gordon Dean, 30 May 1945, RG238, entry PI-21 51/26, folder Memoranda, p. 1 (NARA).

be made clear to the world. Dean's paper listed the characteristics that would make the campaign a success. The world must understand a) that the trial came as fast as possible, b) that the proceedings were public, dignified and fair, c) that those guilty were convicted, and d) that the Nazi conspiracy – the crimes and the system behind it – were revealed and portrayed by the trial. The major problems, according to Dean, were the position of the IMT within a diverse system of the prosecution of war crimes worldwide and the need for constant control of the dissemination of the IMT during and after its existence.

An outstanding characteristic in connection with the IMT was the strategy of the prosecution team as well as that of the film-makers to prove the crimes whenever possible with documents produced by or out of the mouths of the accused when testifying. Dean therefore suggested that the written, audio or audio-visual recording of statements would be "of terrific propaganda value"[20] and – already at that early date – the production of an official film of the proceedings for historical purposes as well as for the worldwide audio-visual dissemination of the trial. (From minutes that recorded decisions taken by the IMT in "closed sessions" at the end of September and beginning of October 1946, we also learn that a number of documents produced during the trial were chosen to be archived for historical reasons.[21]) As all the film material would be produced by US Army or OSS camera teams in a courtroom redesigned exclusively by the Americans, there would be at least a *de facto* monopoly on the moving images of the trial – although of course other national or commercial newsreel- and film-makers were free to process further, cut or comment on the film sequences, as they pleased. The foreign policy of the US increasingly tended towards intervention and engagement abroad. Therefore, the American authorities were anxious to

---

20 *Ibid.*, p. 10.

21 The Tribunal stated that a number of documents would be archived and even edited. The printing of 10,000 English, 5,000 French, 5,000 Russian and 5,000 German versions of the trial record; a copy of a corrected transcript of the shorthand notes; an uncorrected copy; the electronic (audio) recording of the trial; four copies of the Indictment; the originals of the rules of the procedure; the minutes of the closed sessions of the Tribunal; and a lot of original documents introduced into the trial, visual aids, affidavits, films, etc. were to be archived by the General Secretary of the IMT and then passed to the Permanent Court of International Justice at The Hague. See Minutes of 29 September and 1 October 1946, "Minutes of Closed Sessions of the IMT", International Research and Documentation Center for War Crimes Trials, University of Marburg, Germany.

make clear to the world the specific standpoint of the US and its unique contributions to the trial.

The facts investigated and proven by the trial were only one aspect of the intended representation. A second, as we have seen, was the standpoint as well as the unique contributions of the US. And a third was *how* the facts, revealed by the trial, were found. The *fairness* of the trial, especially the procedure of the taking of evidence, was a major concern of the attempts to propagate the IMT. From the beginning it was clear to those responsible in the various US authorities that the IMT should serve as an important event to promote values such as justice, constitutionality and democracy. In order to serve the ambitious aims connected with the plans to prosecute war crimes in an international tribunal, the various communication efforts of the US government and Army were designed to underline and support exactly these specific points of interest. The US took the lead in an internationally co-ordinated system to prosecute war crimes and to organise a new order for wider parts of the world after the Second World War. The US also recognised the feasibility of establishing a foreign policy and an international trade policy that would give it a dominant role in the world.[22] But in accordance with that role, the US would be dependent on a worldwide acceptance of its positions. It must be understood in this context that the IMT was earmarked by the OMGUS and the State Department as *the* ideal opportunity to demonstrate the will of the US to resume responsibility for the declared worldwide democratic and economic progress. The US was considered *the* prototype of a democratic, constitutional and prosperous polity. In addition to establishing a working international criminal law, a strong signal would also be sent to potential perpetrators worldwide – a signal that would potentially affect the future stability of world politics.

---

[22] This chapter does not have the space to develop this point further. Nonetheless, from the records of OMGUS we learn that it was desirable not only to screen US films favoured for re-education purposes but also to open the German market for the US film industry. See Letter, 28 July 1947, RG260/AG 47/32/1, BAK; Cable, 18 December 1947, RG260/AG 47/32/1, BAK. Another strategy was to produce films in Germany for the world market. The idea behind this was to keep the costs for the films low as production in Germany was only one-third the cost compared to the US. The films would thus have an advantage in the world market where they also could drive out Soviet-controlled films. See Letter 21 July 1947, RG260/AG 47/31/7, BAK. OMGUS also tried to place *Nürnberg und seine Lehre* at the Venice Film Festival. See Cable, 8 July 1948, RG260/AG 48/35/4, BAK. So both propaganda *and* economic aspects should complement each other in the international market.

But the IMT also served as a means of communication within the US itself. After the burdens of the war, and that of the occupation which it had to carry, the American people should see the trial as something positive and productive that would demonstrate that "it was worth it": "upon them [the film-makers] will also rest the responsibility for producing an historic record that will stand as a permanent justification of our democracy as well as serve as a deterrent to the conquered peoples for all time".[23]

The educational programme to propagate the IMT took place in a period in which the US rose to the status of *the* dominant power in the world. But taking on this role necessarily meant giving it substance. And this substance would also be dependent on the credibility the US gained among the world's nations. The IMT was chosen to demonstrate this – by word, sound and image.

20.4.2. The Visual Design of the IMT

The more it became clear that it would be desirable to photograph and film the IMT proceedings, so the visual design of the trial gained increasing importance. As already noted, the physical site was exclusively planned and prepared by US authorities and Army.[24] During the preparations for the trial it was a major concern to create an appropriate place for the event. For the coverage during the course of the trial it was a priority to create a favourable impression by the dissemination. This was the reason that the Representation Branch of OSS undertook considerable efforts to redesign the courtroom in all its "historicist"[25] pomp. In order to create the impression that lawyers would argue factually, objectively and

---

[23] A Note on the Film Record of the War Criminal Trials, undated, RG226, entry UD90/12, folder 126 (NARA). The paper was issued as a first manual for the filming of war crimes trials, most probably in early summer 1945.

[24] Documented especially in the records of the OSS: RG226, entry NM-54 85/39, folders Nürnberg Court House, 648 and 660; and RG226, entry NM-54 85/42, folders 689 and Plan of Court Room (NARA).

[25] "Historicist" in this context refers to an epoch in German architecture that is characterised by the recourse to styles from former epochs such as Romanesque, Gothic or Renaissance during the late nineteenth and early twentieth centuries. This style fell during the period of the ascent of German nationalism. The Palace of Justice in Nuremberg was erected from 1909 to 1916 in a neo-Renaissance style, a style preferred for public buildings and especially court buildings at that time.

"free from passion"[26] in a sober atmosphere, the courtroom needed a new design. "The cases must be clearly presented, expeditiously handled, and well reported to the world at large".[27] Aesthetic as well as technical requirements had to be considered:

> Work has nevertheless already been started on preliminary plans for the layout and fixtures required. They include chart changers, display panels, projection equipment, public address and intercommunication systems, lighting, and camera and sound recording installations.[28]

The interior design was revised, the furniture was exchanged for that with a plain design and lifts were installed. The courtroom was enlarged to be big enough to admit all the military and administrative staff, the press representatives and the public – more than 300 or sometimes even 400 people attended the busiest hearings of the IMT. A good impression of the courtroom before the rebuilding is available in photographs taken by the OSS. These pictures show dark and lavishly decorated furniture, chandeliers hanging low into the room, a dark panelled ceiling and historic paintings on the walls.[29] All the changes, the installation of the technical equipment and the new aesthetic of the courtroom served the intended effects of the photo-realist reproduction and the reporting of the whole. The ceiling was turned into a gigantic illumination, cabins were constructed that were connected with the courtroom by Plexiglas windows through which one could film and take still pictures without disturbing the proceedings. An amplification system was installed not only to enable the translation process of the multilingual proceedings but also to allow the recording of sound. And in addition, the layout of the courtroom was changed to fit the presentation of evidence (witnesses as well as charts, visual aids and films[30]) and to serve the audio-visual staging. The positions of the judges' bench and that of the prosecution were changed. In order to promote the visualisation of the opposition of

---

26. A term used by the narrator in *That Justice Be Done* (0:05:27). See also Final Script, 28 September 1945, RG226, entry UD 90/12, folder *That Justice Be Done*, p. 6 (NARA).

27. Presentation Branch Work on War Crimes Project, 14 June 1945, RG226, NM-54 85/42, folder 689, p. 4 (NARA).

28. *Ibid.*

29. Photographs, RG226, entry NM54-85/39, folder 653 (NARA).

30. With the exception of Britain all prosecution teams presented films that served as evidences.

the Tribunal and the defendants, both parties would face each other, positioned on either side of the courtroom. The prosecution teams were placed in front of the press and visitors, facing the witness stand and the display panel positioned on the front side where the judges' bench used to be. The redesign offered a good view for the visitors and the press of the witness stand and the display panel – adopting the prosecution's perspective. These results seem to contradict initial ideas that were talked about at the end of May and beginning of June 1945:

> If the trials are to be held abroad, are they likely to be held in actual courtrooms of the country selected? If in an enemy country, will there be some psychological and political advantage in reproducing as closely as possible the courtroom arrangements customary to that country?[31]

Despite all changes the courtroom underwent, parts of the old design were retained. That was perhaps in order to offer a visual connection for the German spectators and viewers. Curiously enough, ornaments that initially adorned the courtroom when it was built in the early twentieth century were later used as visual effects structuring the narration in *Nürnberg und seine Lehre*. These three ornaments were neo-baroque cartouches: one with the Ten Commandments and Justitia's scales; another depicting Eve offering an apple to Adam; and on the third, an hourglass with wings. These cartouches might have served the purpose of reminding the Germans as well as others in the audience that there must have been a sense for law and justice in an earlier time in Germany.

20.4.3. Principles of Filming the IMT

Besides the deliberations concerning the techniques to be used by the media and the fitting out of the courtroom, a first draft for the filming was prepared,[32] highlighting key aspects of the audio-visual representation of the trial. These aspects concerned the specifics of the representation of war crimes trials in general and the one in Nuremberg in particular. These principles were elaborated when it became clear that the US would be in

---

[31] The Courtroom of the International Tribunal, undated, RG226, entry NM54-85/42, folder Plan of Court Room (NARA).

[32] A Note on the Film Record of the War Crimes Trials, undated, RG226, entry UD 90/12, folder 126 (NARA).

the position to decide on and prepare the physical site of the trial. These guidelines touched on the following:

- the homogeneity of the "narration" in the coverage of a probably long-lasting trial;
- the staging of certain "standard" situations that would arise repeatedly, resulting from the rules of procedure;
- the coherence of filming and sound recording examinations of witnesses, especially in regard to the anticipated confusion resulting from the "Babylonian" multilingualism of the trial (e.g. when a German-speaking witness is being examined by an English-speaking prosecutor);
- the impression of the defence and the prosecution and the likely clashes of both parties evoked in the film representation – whereby the impression of "impartiality of the proceedings"[33] must be assured;
- the transportation of the importance and singularity of the event among others by pointing out the attention that would be paid by the international press;
- the dramatic staging of the verdict and the sentencing.[34]

It was the intention to transform the act of jurisprudence into a regular film narration, a narration that would not only make clear to the viewers what was happening at the IMT but also dramatise and shape the course of events, create a specific impression and provide a lesson. The different participants were assigned specific roles in the drama. The staging aimed at creating a uniform and coherent impression. And the presentation of the trial should carry its historic meaning and provide a sense of "greatness" to the event. Thus the film project was supposed to go beyond just showing the punishment of some 20 war criminals. With respect to the idea of producing a "historic record" and with regards to how the final films were designed in terms of content, we can conclude that the IMT was a vehicle to create a particular image of Nazi Germany and National Socialism as a whole that would serve the short- and medium-term aims connected with the pacification and reorganisation of Germany. And indeed, the moving images from the films – the boycott of

---

[33] *Ibid.*

[34] The sentencing then was *not* filmed but only sound recorded.

Jewish shops, Hitler's speeches, the corpses piled up in the concentration camps – have become, down the years, emblematic of the whole criminal history of Nazi Germany and icons of the war and the systematic extermination of millions of human beings.

20.5. The Films

Different aspects were dealt with variously through the formal, dramaturgical and narrative composition of the films. Specific issues of representation were adapted to different formats – newsreels, short and long documentary films. The representation of the history of National Socialism, the history of the war, the crimes, the course of the trial itself, and the impression of a constitutional as well as appropriate handling of the case all posed different challenges to the film-makers. And, in turn, each was tackled differently, in terms of form as well as content. The following section provides a cursory overview of how the formal conditions were used by the film-makers and how some major areas of content were adapted into the film narration of the trial.

20.5.1. The Short Format

The 10-minute short *That Justice Be Done* is very concisely composed out of material that is clearly differently connoted: atrocity shots; confiscated German newsreel, including shots of leading Nazis; views of American national monuments as well as government buildings; and animation. The format of the short itself suggests a brief and pointedly visual argumentation. *That Justice Be Done* above all aims at emotional persuasion rather than at intellectual discourse or legal reasoning. This can be highlighted in one of the first scenes of the film. Here the script offers insights into the editing method, the film's formal structure and also the obvious intentions of its producers. In one of the early versions of the script, the film was to have started with "[t]he most horrifying shot available of corpses with Germans reacting [...] Still another shot – more personal this time – a man carrying the broken body of a little girl [...] Series of shots of people crying at burials".[35] The actual film did not start with these sequences, but the intention was accomplished in a different way with the following sequence: "[t]he most hysterical and vicious

---

[35] Nazis on Trial, undated, RG226, entry UD 90/12, folder *That Justice Be Done*, p. 1 (NARA).

[shots of Hitler] that can be found in our library"[36] alternately combined with mass shots of his followers. This evokes a sense of the personal guilt of Hitler but also the fact that the German masses are shown cheering their leader when he says: "If I, Adolf Hitler, can send the flower of the German nation into the hell of war without the smallest pity for spilling precious German blood, then surely I have the right to remove millions of an inferior race that breeds like vermin".[37] In respect to this statement the atrocity shots are then sarcastically commented on with "And this is one promise Der Führer kept".[38] Before this, the first sequence of the film has already shown the Jefferson Memorial and quoted the main author of the US Constitution with words concerning the fight against tyranny. This operation – opening the film with a low camera shot surrounding the Jefferson statue, mass shots and close-ups of Hitler in the Berlin Sportpalast combined with atrocity shots [0:00:44–0:02:30] – briefly and expressively points out essential issues of the film and attracts the viewer's attention quite effectively. The film's editing combines images of significant expressiveness – charged with different meanings – with plain and strong words. This results in a clear level of comprehension and the evocation of strong feelings. The argumentation developed in *That Justice Be Done* is prompt. This characteristic is very beneficial for a film that, due to formal conditions, has no space for lengthy argumentation.

20.5.2. The Epic Format

The most epic film produced in connection with the IMT is surely the "evidence film" *The Nazi Plan* (introduced as evidence 3054-PS at the trial). Using confiscated German newsreel material, it recounts the rise to power of the Nazis, their criminal plans and the implementation of these plans, including the course of the war, for more than three hours. Indeed, the history of National Socialist Germany over a period of more than 12 years requires such an epic depiction. The film, expounding Nazi plans step by step and systematically, consists of four parts, with 83 scenes: I. The Rise of the NSDAP, 1931–1933; II. Acquiring Totalitarian Control of

---

36 Final Script, 28 Sept 1945, RG226, entry UD 90/12, folder *That Justice Be Done* ("Final Script"), p. 2 (NARA).

37 *Ibid.* The English translation is spoken in the film by a narrator who imitates a German accent.

38 *Ibid.*, p. 3.

Germany, 1933–1935; III. Preparation for Wars of Aggression, 1936–1939; and IV. Wars of Aggression, 1939–1944.[39] Epic elements also can be detected in the two other long documentaries. *Nazi Concentration and Prison Camps* is compiled out of footage shot by the Allies on the occasion of the detection of concentration, prison, work and extermination camps, mass graves and other crime scenes where victims of the Nazis were imprisoned, tortured, killed and made to disappear. In the course of about an hour these places are listed and marked by corresponding inserts. The film emphasises the extent of the total as well as the personal suffering, by showing piles of corpses, the mass of the imprisoned and individuals with their specific suffering. In this way, the lists of places as well as the use of maps refer to the spatial (and also moral) scale on which the Nazis accomplished their deeds. Each camp on the list is portrayed with significant impressions: for example, shots of dead prisoners on the electric fences, partially burned; prisoners with signs of extreme weakness and wasting; specific infrastructure for the extermination processes like a gas chamber in Dachau or the well-known gate of Buchenwald. In long shots the dimensions of each camp are shown and the number of victims suggested. In medium shots and close-ups the film creates a certain intimacy and identification with single victims – and also dead ones.

Nürnberg und seine Lehre, summarising the course of the IMT and its outcome, is characterised by an even more distinct epic form. The film especially emphasises the four counts of the Indictment (each taking approximately 10 minutes), while also portraying prominent crimes and war criminals. Besides taking into account at least the most important issues raised by the trial, the IMT, which lasted almost a year, also requires a narration that presents the duration of the trial appropriately. Therefore the film is designed with visual marks such as architectural ornaments and fade-to-blacks not only to structure the narration but also to create an impression of the time passing as the trial proceeds. Remarkably, the film also consists of flashbacks, for example, when a witness is testifying about an event that then is visually and narratively reconstructed by a collage of confiscated footage complete with commentaries that were prepared later. So the film presents some clues of

---

[39] Document No. 3054-PS, undated, RG238, entry PI-21 51/26, folder Photographic Evidence (NARA).

the size and sheer scale of the IMT itself and of the crimes it was dealing with.

20.5.3. Serialism

Far from being epic, the newsreel coverage tends towards a different direction, thereby performing a different function. Serialism provides an important contribution to the intended impact of the trial in Germany – especially with regards to the re-education concept. The joint American–British newsreel *Welt im Film*,[40] presented over 43 weeks, must be considered a supplement to the daily and much more up-to-date[41] reporting in the newspapers and on radio. Nevertheless, the newsreel format offered a valuable contribution in creating a certain familiarity with the trial, its protagonists and the crimes tried – the accused, in all probability, did not need any further popularisation. Serialism stressed the efforts made by the legal and other personnel to keep the trial running. It was this serialism of the newsreel that corresponded to serial elements of the trial, as with the fact that (standard) situations like examinations, the tendering and furnishing of documents, and so on returned repeatedly. Whereas the examinations were staged like single, outstanding events,[42] the constant taking of documentary evidence was generally depicted by showing rooms filled with desks covered in papers. Further, the constant newsreel coverage offered the possibility of creating a recognition value – visual, linguistic and musical significance suitable to setting the trial apart from other news stories. The newsreel-makers used the same music, the same very plain font for titles, and the titles referred to the serial character of the event.[43] This enabled the creation of a visualisation of the

---

[40] Nineteen out of 43 issues covered the trial during its course; another three issues addressed a preliminary meeting of the IMT in Berlin, the preparation of the trial site and summarise the trial for the end-of-year review.

[41] As only a limited number of cinemas were working and only a very limited number of copies of the newsreel were available, issues often were screened with a considerable delay.

[42] *Welt im Film*, No. 41, *Paulus als Zeuge*; *Welt im Film*, No. 45, *Göring im Kreuzverhör*; *Welt im Film*, No. 51, *Schacht im Kreuzverhör*, *Welt im Film*, No. 58, *Papen und Speer sagen aus: Anklagen und Enthüllungen*; and *Welt im Film*, No. 60, *Hitlers Chauffeur sagt aus*.

[43] *Welt im Film*, No. 30, *Zweiter Bildbericht aus dem Gerichtssaal*; *Welt im Film*, No. 36, *Neues vom Nürnberger Prozess*; and *Welt im Film*, No. 44, *Nürnberg: Die Verteidigung*, etc.

---

constancy with which the trial was pushed forward. And it pointed out the sobriety with which the Allies fulfilled their obligations. It also served to demonstrate the constant existence of constitutionality and the maintenance of public order. By highlighting certain events in the course of the trial – marked as "uncovering" or "sensation" – it was furthermore possible to provide moments of suspense for the viewers.

By using these different formats the American military film-makers adapted audio-visual representation to the various structural characteristics of the trial and to differing communication situations and communication modes. The different topics related to the trial were also predominantly handled in different ways by the various films.

20.5.4. The History of National Socialism

The historical evolution of National Socialism and National Socialist Germany is portrayed in *The Nazi Plan*. The preparations for war – the unlawful rearmament of the German Army, the violation of international treaties, the fraudulent propaganda and diplomacy of Nazi Germany – and finally the outbreak and the different phases of the war are systematically depicted. This depiction does not use film produced after the events but that produced by the Nazis themselves. The credits read:

> 4. This motion picture was made in Berlin, Germany,
> from August to November, 1945. The sources of the
> film are as follows:
>
> a) Universum-Film A.G. (UFA)
>   i) UfA Ton-Woche
>   ii) DeuligtonWoche
>   iii) Die Deutsche Wochenschau
>   iv) UFA Auslandswochenschau
> b) Fox Tönende Wochenschau A.G.
> c) Paramount News (Germany)
> d) UFA Film Kunst
> e) Tobis Filmkunst
> f) Reichsministerium für Volksaufklarung und
>   Propaganda

g) Reichspropagandaleitung (RPL)[44]

The very carefully chosen and edited extracts, culled from the enormous amount of confiscated German newsreel material and films such as *Triumph des Willens* (*Triumph of the Will*), were gathered, collated and then itemised according to its content by the OSS. A compendium produced by the OSS in preparation for the trial provides information of the intentions relating to this kind of evidence:

> For the first time in the history of legal procedure and jurisdiction, it has become possible to present in sound and picture the significant events of an historical period.
>
> In the case of the present war crimes trial, the International Court is in the position to found its examination of the responsibility and guilt of the Nazi leaders, their accomplices and organized followers on the basis of factual evidence presented in the form of documentary photographs and original speeches.
>
> Newsreels, made on the spot, are presented in chronological order, revealing how the Nazis have prepared, started and prolonged the second World War.[45]

The compendium then lists – day by day – newsreel sources with relevant content. On this basis the OSS cited the material and then organised it with respect to the various categories relevant for the intended prosecution. Categories were divided into sub-categories, and so the producers were therefore able to specify and encode the film material very precisely. For example "100 [first level of categorisation] Measures taken within Germany [...] 140 [2nd level of categorisation] Violence against organizations: 141 Churches 142 Trade-Unions [3rd level of categorisation]".[46] So this complex, systematically compiled film – a stock of nearly four hours of images – portrays the history of National Socialism in a way that it was seen, assessed and considered favourably for the immediate objectives of the prosecution but most probably also for long-term purposes, such as historiography. The four parts of the film are

---

[44] Document No. 3054-PS, undated, RG238, entry PI-21 51/26, folder Photographic Evidence (NARA).

[45] Newsreel from 1933 to 1944 Showing How Nazis Prepared, Started and Prolonged the Second World War, undated, RG226, entry A1 99/138, folder 922 (NARA).

[46] Preliminary Code for Classification of War Crimes, undated, RG226, entry NM-54 85/39, folder 1363 (NARA).

especially tailored to the conspiracy and the aggressive warfare theses, from a contemporary point of view, presenting the whole range of the systematic extermination of Sinti and Roma, Polish, Czech and Soviet citizens as well as Jews. As one of two films used in evidence, *The Nazi Plan* must be understood in addition to the other one that provides dramatic footage usually presented in connection with the extermination processes, albeit portraying the "collapse" of the extermination programme caused by the progress of the Allies. In contrast to *The Nazi Plan*, *That Justice Be Done* only touches on the criminal history by showing an enacted scene with a uniformed arm sweeping away the Versailles Treaty and the Kellogg-Briand Pact – a not very elaborate but nevertheless quite effective and prompt way of communication.

As an important part of the trial, especially in connection with count one of the Indictment ("common plan or conspiracy") put forward by the US prosecution team, *Nürnberg und seine Lehre* also focuses on the historic development of National Socialism. Specific chapters of German history – now designated as crimes by the IMT – were chosen especially to illustrate the US prosecution team's "narration" of the rise to power, the planning and implementing of the crimes in the context of the "Nazi conspiracy" idea. For that purpose, footage originally compiled for the production of the two evidence films was used. The briefer presentation and the extended knowledge *after* the trial also caused a more precise and convincing choice of the confiscated footage. As a result, *Nürnberg und seine Lehre* has provided images that have been used in numerous other films over the past 60 years to depict the early years of National Socialist Germany.

20.5.5. The Crimes

Iconographic images of the Nazi crimes also came from film and photographic records that were made during the liberation of the Nazi camps. These records were originally meant to serve as photographic and film evidence for the unthinkable conditions the Allied armies were confronted with as they entered enemy territory. This stock was also assessed and systemised in a sophisticated way by the OSS to serve the prosecution's purposes at the IMT. Overviews of the available material were prepared,[47] descriptions of single sequences written, capturing dates, location information and origins.[48] For their use as evidence, the moving images compiled for *Nazi Concentration and Prison Camps* were completed with affidavits confirming that the film does not contain special effects or was not later manipulated or retouched.[49] So the conditions in the camps, as consequences of the various crimes committed beforehand, are documented and depicted with very dramatic images, undoubtedly considered at the time as unimpeachable sources. Like the atrocity pictures screened by all the Allies in their respective zones of occupation,[50] the photographic evidence was given credit for convincingly proving Nazi crimes. For that purpose, the US and the other Allied occupation authorities also published illustrated leaflets, with a wide circulation, to spread the truth about the concentration camps being liberated at the time.[51] A very narrow selection of these horrifying images is also contained in *That Justice Be Done*. The film brings to mind again the reason for the trial and deepens the marked differences between the perpetrators and their judges. In *Nürnberg und seine Lehre* the atrocity shots make the crimes immediate in order to re-narrate the prosecution's case, by providing both the visual evidence for the justification of the prosecution as well as the validity of the charges. The first part of the film is a kind of an epilogue portraying the miserable conditions in post-war Europe and the suffering of the people – especially in Germany. In this way, a certain similarity between the images of the victims of Nazism (atrocity shots) and the suffering of post-war German society living in ruins can be ascertained. These emblematic images of suffering human beings correspond in a certain way. So, curiously enough, the images of the crimes and the images of the victims of such crimes could offer potential for the German viewers to also identify themselves as victims of

---

47 Camera Notes from which Nazi Concentration Picture was Made Shown at Nuremberg as Evidence, undated, RG226, entry A1 90/44, folder 700 (NARA).

48 Detailed descriptions of footage in RG226, entry UD 90/12, folders 125, 127 (NARA).

49 Document No. 2430-PS, undated, RG238, entry PI-21 51/26, folder Photographic Evidence (NARA).

50 The US side, for example, screened Hanus Burger's *Todesmühlen* (*Death Mills*), an approximately 25-minute-long documentary compiled from footage shot on the occasion of the detection of crime scenes, exhumations of mass graves and forced visits of German civilians to these crime scenes.

51 The US authorities published the leaflet *KZ. Bildbericht aus fünf Konzentrationslagern*, not otherwise specified.

National Socialism. This had two potential outcomes: to distance the German audience from their belief in the Nazi ideology, on the one hand, and to create solidarity with the victims, on the other.

In the newsreel coverage, the crimes in respect to their victims only appear in abstract verbalism. The defendants might serve as substitutes for the crimes. But seeing all the film output as *one* campaign, consisting of elements complementing each other, I would argue that the newsreel coverage is clearly designed to present the crimes themselves prominently. [52] In addition, the presentation on the radio, and in newspapers, pamphlets and so on must be considered.

20.5.6. The Fairness of the IMT

Through the systematic ordering of approximately 32 hours of footage shot in Courtroom 600,[53] we know that from more than 400 sequences,[54] 95 consist of examinations of witnesses by the defence; another 60 sequences show examinations by the prosecution. Including cross-examinations, the ratio of defence to prosecution is not less than 111 to 130 – nearly balanced.[55] The creation of the impression of a fair trial was a major topic in the representation of the trial. And film documents of the proceedings in the courtroom suggested themselves as a suitable category of film material for pointing out the fairness of the conduct of the trial. In this footage, we can see the example of the presiding judge responding to the needs of the defence or the possibilities of the defence acting freely. As the newsreel coverage was exclusively edited from these film records made in the courtroom it is not surprising that, in this format, the defence is portrayed extensively. But the behaviour of the defence, in contrast to

---

[52] Two phases of the public relations strategy of the US authorities to deal with the Nazi crimes can be detected. The first phase was dominated by the representation of the crimes (for example, atrocity pictures); the second phase focused on the trials (IMT, Dachau Trials, Spruchkammerverfahren). With the time lag of nearly two years between the end of the trial and the premiere of *Nürnberg und seine Lehre* the film no longer fell into that scheme.

[53] The uncut footage shot on the occasion of the IMT and other war crimes trials, as well as events in connection with the occupations after the Second World War by the US Army Signal Corps, are archived at RG111 ADC (NARA).

[54] As a "sequence" we designate the smallest content-based unit of film that could be isolated from the 32 hours of film by synchronising it with the trial record.

[55] The work is collated and stored in a database that can be accessed at the ICWC, University of Marburg.

the very firm position of the prosecution, also emphasises the gravity and notoriety of the accusations. Regularly, the defence counsels were not able to challenge the position of the prosecution or its witnesses. In *Nürnberg und seine Lehre* the largest part is devoted to the prosecution case that takes up about 45 minutes out of the 75 minutes of the whole film. As already mentioned, this part is compiled from footage from the two evidence films. Images from the courtroom itself mainly serve as hooks for recounting the story of the accused's crimes. In contrast, the case for the defence is portrayed exclusively by such film material, with the narration accentuating the extent to which the defence acts in favour of its clients. Although *That Justice Be Done* is relatively short, fairness is an important aspect of the justification of the intention to try the major war criminals. Indeed, fairness, understood as an essential element of a constitutional trial, attains *the* most prominent position in the film's discourse. As we have already shown, the film starts with a statement of Jefferson and thus already points in that direction. When it comes to the crimes and the places where they were committed, the film arrives at its central motif and by doing this reflects a crucial aspect of the public impact of the trial:

> How can we rectify these crimes? We may arrest the sadist in charge in Buchenwald – but we cannot torture him to death as he tortured his victims. We may accuse the physician who used medicine not as an instrument of life, but as an instrument of death – but we cannot inject him with deadly germs as he injected his patients [...] Why? The answer of law-abiding nations is found in the words of the historic Moscow Declaration [...] Public trial, equality before the law, the right of defendants to prepare their own defence – a trial so orderly, so thorough, so free from passion [...][56]

The film then shows significant visual representations of the US as a democratic and constitutional polity, such as a monument of George Washington or the Supreme Court. As the crimes were considered sufficiently documented and proven ("People are now pretty well convinced that the atrocities took place and that they were wholesale"[57]), it had become an urgent concern to categorise the upcoming trial of the

---

[56] Final script, pp. 4–5, see *supra* note 36.
[57] Motion Picture Concerning War Crimes, 14 June 1945, RG238, entry PI-21 51/26, folder Gordon Dean (NARA).

major war criminals in the context of the legal and constitutional tradition of the US. So fairness served as a means of self-assurance (*That Justice Be Done*) as well as a criterion for the presumably sceptical German viewers to judge the trial positively (*Welt im Film, Nürnberg und seine Lehre*). From the public opinion surveys conducted by the Intelligence Branch of the OMGUS we learn that the question of whether the trial was seen as fair or not was considered as most important.[58]

20.5.7. Self-Presentation

As we have seen, the presentation of the US prosecuting war crimes was very closely tied to the creation of an aura of *fairness*. This intended effect, of course, was dependent on the modality in which the trial was conducted – a fact that increased the significance of the procedural rules. In order to create the desired external visibility of the IMT, common law procedural rules were favoured by the OSS and other agencies involved in the preparations for the trial. When taking a close look at footage that was shot during the IMT proceedings, it becomes clear that it was exactly this structure given by the procedural rules, similar to those of the common law, which had an impact on the filming routine of the camera teams. And having this in mind, the specific way in which the courtroom was rebuilt becomes even more plausible: it was redesigned, among other ways, by rearranging the positions of the several parties involved in the trial. The evidence – represented by visual aids, charts, films and witnesses – was placed in front of the press and visitors (also a favoured camera position); the judges' bench and the defence bench were placed on opposing sides of the room so that these two parties would face each other. The defence and the prosecution occupied a rostrum placed in the middle of the courtroom in relation to the witness stand. This configuration served the dynamics of the filming, especially when shooting testimonies. And this configuration – emphasising and visualising the idea of a fair trial – becomes abundantly clear in the newsreel coverage and in *Nürnberg und seine Lehre*, films produced exclusively for the German audience, an audience that was supposed to develop increasing sympathy for the US occupation power.

---

[58] Merritt and Merritt, 1970; Merritt, 1995; Merritt Collection on Public Opinion in Germany, 1980, see *supra* note 18.

Produced for an American audience, the US standpoint emphasised in *That Justice Be Done* tends more to a draft of a self-image. Also understood as a fight against intolerance, racism and oppression, their engagement in the prosecution of war crimes also had a more precarious aspect: the daily racism in US society was not only limited to the American South. (Just some years earlier, when being drawn into the Second World War, race riots broke out that cost the lives of black workers in Mobile, Detroit and other cities.) In that respect, the film offers a positive prospect for the US itself, initiated by its resumption of responsibility thousands of miles across the Atlantic.

Besides the procedural rules through which the US became visible as a key actor, another unique contribution was count one of the Indictment before the IMT: "the common plan or conspiracy".[59] It was not only that count one was presented by the US team, it was also a very complicated one – initiated, prepared and developed in particular by the US. And it was part of the film representation produced by the US authorities right from the beginning and detectable in nearly all the film output with the exception of *Nazi Concentration and Prison Camps*. *That Justice Be Done* only gives a clue about this idea of explaining, interpreting and prosecuting the Nazi crimes. In the images, we see prominent Nazis together and talking to each other and, completed by a commentary, this could be construed as conspiring. *The Nazi Plan* is more or less exclusively devoted to the portrayal of the conspiracy by classifying single events of National Socialist history into a conspiracy schema. In *Nürnberg und seine Lehre*, there are visual representations of prominent Nazis that are seen as making "intrigue" and the corresponding commentary also emphasises the conspiratorial aspect. Extracts from *The Nazi Plan* are used when re-narrating the rise to power of the Nazis and the implementation of their war plans. The summary made and the conclusions drawn in *Nürnberg und seine Lehre* also emphasise the conspiracy idea when dealing with parts of the trial that were not devoted to count one of the Indictment. The most obvious manifestation are those parts of the film in which the aggressive warfare of Nazi Germany is portrayed by the systematic violation of one treaty after another, on one hand, and by giving future opponents a false sense of security by means of a mendacious diplomacy, on the other. By pointing out the systematic

---

[59] *Trial of the Major War Criminals*, p. 29, see *supra* note 8.

approach *and* by showing the fraudulent habits of the Nazi elite, all dimensions of the "conspiracy" were fully captured by the film narration.

The newsreel coverage that represents the American contribution must be seen in connection with the conditions provided by the format. That is to say, an IMT report was framed by other news items in a *Welt im Film* newsreel. The efforts undertaken by the US authorities to organise public life, to improve supplies to the population and to drive forward the reconstruction of the country were set in an obvious connection to the trial. In addition, the filming routine emphasised the American presence by showing US military police behind the defendants, the American prosecution team and judges, as well as the US flag, all very favourably situated for the cameras. So beyond being the subject of a single report, the US was omnipresent in the images – a result of the opportunity the US authorities had to design, configure and furnish the courtroom in a favourable manner. A further result of these measures was the suppression of the visibility of the Soviet presence to a considerable extent.

20.6. Outlook

The contribution of films produced about war crimes and war crimes trials to the memory and historiography of Nazism, war, extermination, and the juridical reckoning with this complex, has long been emphasised by scholars.[60] The special interest of these studies often lies in the status of audio-visual representations in the field of memory.[61] But an analysis

---

[60] Two current studies are Ulrike Weckel, "Disappointed Hopes for Spontaneous Mass Conversions: German Responses to Allied Atrocity Film Screenings, 1945–46", in *Bulletin of the German Historical Institute*, 2012, no. 51, pp. 39–53; James Gow, Milena Michalski and Rachel Karr, "Pictures of Peace and Justice from Nuremberg to the Holocaust: *Nuremberg: Its Lesson for Today*, *Memory of the Camps*, and *Majdanek: Cemetery of Europe* – Missing Films, Memory Gaps and the Impact beyond the Courtroom of Visual Material in War Crimes Prosecution", in *The Journal of the Historical Association*, 2013, vol. 98, pp. 548–66.

[61] For the theoretical concepts see Harald Welzer (ed.), *Das soziale Gedächtnis. Geschichte, Erinnerung, Tradierung*, Hamburger Edition, Hamburg, 2001; Alexander Jackob, "Jenseits der Zeugenschaft: zur Kritik kollektiver Bilder nach 'Holocaust'", in *Augenblick. Marburger und Mainzer Hefte zur Medienwissenschaft*, 2004, vol. 36, pp. 10–25. Often these studies explicitly or implicitly refer to the idea of "collective memory" developed by Maurice Halbwachs. See Maurice Halbwachs, *La mémoire collective: Ouvrage posthume*, Presses Universitaires de France, Paris, 1950; Maurice Halbwachs, *Les cadres sociaux de la mémoire,* Presses Universitaires de France, Paris, 1952.

of dynamics that such films developed in socio-political processes still remains under-researched.

The films pose challenges that emerge as a result of their history and the role they take on in political processes in the present-day. The output of the IMT film campaign can be reproduced in the US National Archive as well as used without any copyright restrictions – and film-makers have done so many times. The number of films produced by using material from the films considered here far exceeds the originals. The images produced between 1945 and 1948 are today much more present in the cinema and especially on television, as well as on the internet, than ever before. Documentary and feature films, television reports and video features have been significant in creating images of the Nuremberg Trial and in representing it at a time when Germany was dealing with the collapse of the Soviet bloc, the fall of the Berlin Wall, the war in Yugoslavia and the revitalisation of international criminal law more generally.

> The reunification of Germany marked the beginnings of a positive approach to the Nuremberg legacy: the new generation of judges, politicians and academics was increasingly sympathetic to international criminal justice, and adopted the Nuremberg precedent by dealing with crimes committed in the East during the Cold War.[62]

Now on the "winning side" of history, official German legal politics increasingly expanded on two fonts: internally and externally. These were the juridical dealing with the German Democratic Republic's past and the efforts undertaken by what is euphemistically called the international community to create bodies for the administration and enforcement of international criminal law. Incidentally, this corresponded with German efforts to gain more influence in the United Nations. From the early 1990s onwards, German film-makers like Bengt von zur Mühlen and Heinrich Breloer, popular journalists like Guido Knopp and numerous other television programme makers have produced scores of films compiled from the archived materials, in addition to dramatising them. These films were – intentionally or not – means of representing the debates on legal politics in Germany. The question in this context is: How did these films

---

[62] Christoph Burchard, "The Nuremberg Trial and its Impact on Germany", in *Journal of International Criminal Justice*, 2006, vol. 4, no. 4, p. 800.

impact on this situation? To conclude this chapter, I give some indications for answering this question – though in no way meant to be systematic or even exhaustive.

It is fundamental to find out the viewpoints inherent in these images. First, essentially only 25 hours of the proceedings were filmed, a radical reduction from the 218 days that the IMT sat.[63] What was filmed is a very small selection, which is far from being representative. Testimonies were chosen over lengthy deliberations and persistent negotiations concerning the continuation of the proceedings (approximately two and a half hours). The Soviet Union is extremely underrepresented, especially when compared with the US. An American prosecutor is seen in 89 sequences; Jackson in another 58; the US Judge Francis Biddle is shown in 50; and his colleague John Parker in another 32 sequences. Soviet judges and prosecutors only appear in a total of 67 sequences of the uncut footage from of the courtroom. The outcome of the trial – the Judgment and sentencing, only two of the 218 days – takes up about two and a half hours of footage.[64] It is also important to bear in mind that the shooting of the trial took place on a specially prepared and designed stage,[65] shot routinely by specialists. The two evidence films also represent a strict selection, one that was made to impress the court and the world audience – hardly systematic and also far from being representative. All the images from the IMT that come down to us provide all the significant characteristics of a narrative, aesthetic and dramatic prefiguration. These films nevertheless constitute the corpus of moving images that document the IMT complex.

This corpus of moving images has already gained considerable status within the field of audio-visual mass communication, especially in Germany where these images, with the undeniable potential for becoming icons, have been screened countless times.[66] They have accumulated meaning through which they assume the possibility of representing the

---

[63] The fact that approximately 35 hours of film exist is due to the fact that sometimes the same situation was shot with two cameras from different angles, or shots were taken outside the courtroom.

[64] All figures are results of our analysis, see *supra* note 54.

[65] Staging of Trials. The Courtroom of the International Tribunal, 12 June 1945, RG226, entry NM-54 85/42, folder Plan of Court Room (NARA).

[66] Cornelia Brink, *Ikonen der Vernichtung: Öffentlicher Gebrauch von Fotografien aus nationalsozialistischen Konzentrationslagern nach 1945*, Akademie Verlag, Berlin, 1998.

complex of National Socialism, war and extermination as a *pars pro toto*. These images therefore potentially effectively shape communication processes as their mere presence activates associations and narratives that are retrievable for most recipients. This significance harbours a number of perils, as the associations and narratives may affect the prefiguration of the perception, offer a misleading virtual orientation, and create the effect of apathy and insensitivity. These iconographic images can accelerate communication processes, on one hand, yet these processes also run the risk of being restrained by a pervasive connotation, on the other. Film-makers like Marcel Ophüls, Claude Lanzmann and Romuald Karmakar have responded to this and avoided using footage from these sources.

The IMT was transformed into a *narration* consisting of epic as well as of pointedly short stylistic elements. War crimes, war criminals and their punishment were caught by visually impressive shots and montages providing iconographic portrays and shock effects. The trial was trimmed and shaped to meet the demands for *storytelling* and to convince *visually*. These (audio) visual fragments suggest themselves for repeated presentation. But arbitrarily re-using these film fragments also means a blurring of their original context. And this may cause an intensifying of their inherent characteristics. When these film fragments are presented again, this happens in connection with a "story" told. The historical moving images serve as *illustrations* and as moments of *authentication* for film ideas developed decades after the events took place, under the dynamics of a movement to revive international criminal law in Germany – in a totally different socio-political and historical locus. The retrospective use of the images in this specific locus necessarily affects certain perspectives on the historical event. As Christoph Burchard puts it, the reference to the IMT was used to enforce international criminal law that developed after the fall of the Berlin Wall. Therefore there is a tendency to construe the IMT as the starting point of a positive and consequently logical development, provisionally culminating in the establishment of the International Criminal Court in The Hague and the implementation of international criminal law in German national law, both in 2002. In the context of this perspective, the footage offers a functional utility for the narration of the success story of international criminal law in association with German history.

The films represent the final victory over National Socialism – not by weapons but by reason. This victory in Germany is often interpreted as the re-birth of Germany as a democratic polity. Therefore these images also suggest themselves to be used for the drafting of a self-image consisting of the success story of the democratic development of West Germany. Taking the perspective inherent in the moving pictures offers one way of assuming a position from which the majority of contemporary German society is able to stage itself as the winner over its own criminal past. In addition, these images provide arguments for the official German position in disputes concerning the supranational establishment and enforcement of international criminal law. The images further bear the potential of being used *against* their original producers by emphasising the alleged moral failure of nations that do not ratify the ICC Statute – in contrast to those who "have learned their lessons from history". This predetermination by using the Nuremberg example often seems to obstruct a self-critical appraisal of Germany's history as well as with its position in the field of international criminal law.

These are just some indications that suggest the potential inherent in historic film material which deserves to be studied systematically. This requires a very precise analysis of the quantitative appearance of the IMT footage – also in relation to political agenda setting – as well as a close qualitative study of the singular way the footage has been used in recent history.

INDEX

A

A Tale of Two Cities, 112
Abdülhamid II, Sultan, 381
Acheson, Dean, 417
Acquaviva, Guido, xxxix, 11, 15, 597, 598
Adachi, Hatazō, 70
aiding and abetting, 41, 48, 54–55, 59, 326, 337–38
Akayesu
  case, 29, 31, 77–80, 82
  Trial Chamber, 77, 82
Akira, Hirota, 70–71
Alderman, Sidney, 430, 557–58
Alfaro, Ricardo, 577, 578, 579, 581, 592
Ali, Mehmet, 280
Allied Commission on the Responsibility of the Authors of the War and on Enforcement of Penalties, 362
Allied Expeditionary Force, 453
Allied occupation
  of Germany, 26
Allied Powers, 3, 13, 156, 160, 171, 175–76, 188–89, 191, 193, 214, 216–18, 221–22, 226–27, 235–36, 249–50, 253–54, 256, 259–60, 290, 308–9, 315, 333, 341, 345, 349, 351, 362, 370, 377, 385–86, 397–98, 400, 402, 428–29, 432, 493
Alsace, 347, 353
Altstötter, Josef, 26, 291
American, vii, xvii, 15, 19, 25, 27, 32, 42–44, 65, 68–69, 74–75, 83, 88, 138, 142, 147, 171, 176–83, 185–89, 193, 195–96, 202–5, 211, 217, 219, 223, 225–28, 235, 240, 247–48, 251, 253–54, 262–67, 269, 301, 303–4, 307, 339, 344, 350–51, 361–62, 364, 366–67, 371, 373–74, 384, 395, 402, 405, 429, 431–33, 445, 447, 481, 487, 513–15, 524, 526, 528, 531, 536, 541, 545–49, 551–52, 557, 560, 562, 567–68,
571–72, 593, 623–29, 631, 633, 637, 640–41, 648–49, 651
American
  Civil War, 240
American Nuremberg Trial Film Project, 15
Amin, Idi, 139
Amnesty regulations, 316
Amtsgruppe A, 58, 59
Ankara, 192, 387
Ankara Province, 387
Aquinas, Thomas, 150, 237
armed conflicts, xxv, 97, 99–100, 113, 586
Armenian, viii, xxxvi, 14, 174, 178–79, 183, 191, 193, 261, 264, 274–75, 277–78, 287, 291, 296, 379–88, 390–94, 396–98, 400–2, 404–6, 481, 482, 484
Armenian
  Christians, 291
  massacres, viii, 178, 191, 275, 287, 386, 405, 482
Armenian Reform Agreement, 174
Armenian Revolutionary Federation, 288
Armenians
  deportation of, 292, 382
Art of War, The, 101–2
Asia, viii, xxvii, 3, 8, 16–17, 24, 26, 148, 165, 193, 195, 438, 447, 468, 475, 499, 500, 507, 511, 513, 519, 541
Asian
  governments, 12
Asquith, H.H., 221, 360, 364
Atatürk, Mustafa Kemal, 192, 287, 386
Atkin, Lord James, 441–42, 525
Auschwitz, 28
Australia, 17, 26, 70, 151, 171, 289, 295, 437, 441, 448–49, 456, 458, 509, 513, 525, 530, 536, 600
Australian
  war crimes programme, 70
  war crimes trials, 25
Austria, 210, 213, 227, 239, 242, 264, 383, 390, 447

O

P

FICHL PUBLICATION SERIES

OTHER VOLUMES IN THE
FICHL PUBLICATION SERIES

Morten Bergsmo, Mads Harlem and Nobuo Hayashi (editors):
Importing Core International Crimes into National Law
Torkel Opsahl Academic EPublisher
Oslo, 2010
FICHL Publication Series No. 1 (Second Edition, 2010)
ISBN 978-82-93081-00-5

Nobuo Hayashi (editor):
National Military Manuals on the Law of Armed Conflict
Torkel Opsahl Academic EPublisher
Oslo, 2010
FICHL Publication Series No. 2 (Second Edition, 2010)
ISBN 978-82-93081-02-9

Morten Bergsmo, Kjetil Helvig, Ilia Utmelidze and Gorana Žagovec:
The Backlog of Core International Crimes Case Files in Bosnia and Herzegovina
Torkel Opsahl Academic EPublisher
Oslo, 2010
FICHL Publication Series No. 3 (Second Edition, 2010)
ISBN 978-82-93081-04-3

Morten Bergsmo (editor):
Criteria for Prioritizing and Selecting Core International Crimes Cases
Torkel Opsahl Academic EPublisher
Oslo, 2010
FICHL Publication Series No. 4 (Second Edition, 2010)
ISBN 978-82-93081-06-7

Morten Bergsmo and Pablo Kalmanovitz (editors):
Law in Peace Negotiations
Torkel Opsahl Academic EPublisher
Oslo, 2010
FICHL Publication Series No. 5 (Second Edition, 2010)
ISBN 978-82-93081-08-1

Morten Bergsmo, César Rodríguez Garavito, Pablo Kalmanovitz and Maria Paula Saffon (editors):
Distributive Justice in Transitions
Torkel Opsahl Academic EPublisher
Oslo, 2010
FICHL Publication Series No. 6 (2010)
ISBN 978-82-93081-12-8

Morten Bergsmo (editor):
Complementarity and the Exercise of Universal Jurisdiction for Core International Crimes
Torkel Opsahl Academic EPublisher
Oslo, 2010
FICHL Publication Series No. 7 (2010)
ISBN 978-82-93081-14-2

Morten Bergsmo (editor):
Active Complementarity: Legal Information Transfer
Torkel Opsahl Academic EPublisher
Oslo, 2011
FICHL Publication Series No. 8 (2011)
ISBN 978-82-93081-55-5 (PDF)
ISBN 978-82-93081-56-2 (print)

Sam Muller, Stavros Zouridis, Morly Frishman and Laura Kistemaker (editors):
The Law of the Future and the Future of Law
Torkel Opsahl Academic EPublisher
Oslo, 2010
FICHL Publication Series No. 11 (2011)
ISBN 978-82-93081-27-2

Morten Bergsmo, Alf Butenschøn Skre and Elisabeth J. Wood (editors):
Understanding and Proving International Sex Crimes
Torkel Opsahl Academic EPublisher
Beijing, 2012
FICHL Publication Series No. 12 (2012)
ISBN 978-82-93081-29-6

Morten Bergsmo (editor):
Thematic Prosecution of International Sex Crimes
Torkel Opsahl Academic EPublisher
Beijing, 2012
FICHL Publication Series No. 13 (2012)
ISBN 978-82-93081-31-9

Terje Einarsen:
The Concept of Universal Crimes in International Law
Torkel Opsahl Academic EPublisher
Oslo, 2012
FICHL Publication Series No. 14 (2012)
ISBN 978-82-93081-33-3

莫滕·伯格斯默 凌岩 （主编）:
国家主权与国际刑法
Torkel Opsahl Academic EPublisher
Beijing, 2012
FICHL Publication Series No. 15 (2012)
ISBN 978-82-93081-58-6

Morten Bergsmo and LING Yan (editors):
State Sovereignty and International Criminal Law
Torkel Opsahl Academic EPublisher
Beijing, 2012
FICHL Publication Series No. 15 (2012)
ISBN 978-82-93081-35-7

Morten Bergsmo and CHEAH Wui Ling (editors):
Old Evidence and Core International Crimes
Torkel Opsahl Academic EPublisher
Beijing, 2012
FICHL Publication Series No. 16 (2012)
ISBN 978-82-93081-60-9

YI Ping:
戦争と平和の間——発足期日本国際法学における「正しい戦争」
の観念とその帰結
Torkel Opsahl Academic EPublisher
Beijing, 2013
FICHL Publication Series No. 17 (2013)
ISBN 978-82-93081-66-1

Morten Bergsmo (editor):
Quality Control in Fact-Finding
Torkel Opsahl Academic EPublisher
Florence, 2013
FICHL Publication Series No. 19 (2013)
ISBN 978-82-93081-78-4

All volumes are freely available online at http://www.fichl.org/publication-series/. Printed copies may be ordered from distributors indicated at http://www.fichl.org/torkel-opsahl-academic-epublisher/distribution/, including from http://www.amazon.co.uk/. For reviews of earlier books in this Series in academic journals, please see http://www.fichl.org/torkel-opsahl-academic-epublisher/reviews-of-toaep-books/.

www.ingramcontent.com/pod-product-compliance
Lightning Source LLC
Chambersburg PA
CBHW050529190326
41458CB00045B/6766/J